# GOOD

IRE

# THE
# GOOD HOTEL GUIDE 2011

## GREAT BRITAIN & IRELAND

Editors:

Desmond Balmer
and Adam Raphael

Editor in chief:

Caroline Raphael

Founding editor:

Hilary Rubinstein

THE GOOD HOTEL GUIDE LTD

www.goodhotelguide.com

The Good Hotel Guide Ltd

This edition first published in 2010 by
The Good Hotel Guide Ltd
1 3 5 7 9 10 8 6 4 2
Copyright © 2010 Adam and Caroline Raphael
Maps © 2010 David Perrott

Contributing editors:
Bill Bennett
Nicola Davies
Aileen Reid

Production: Hugh Allan
Managing editor: Alison Wormleighton
Designer: Lizzy Laczynska
Text editor: Daphne Trotter
Consultant: Caroline Blake
Researcher: Sophie MacLean
Computer consultant: Derek French

Website design by Nalim Lakhi, 1506 Ltd, London

NEATH PORT TALBOT
LIBRARIES

2300019315 4

| HJ | POR REF | 26-Oct-2010 |
| 914.106 | | £20.00 |

A CIP catalogue record for this book may be found in the British Library.

ISBN 978 0 9549404 5 4

Printed and bound in Spain by Graphy Cems

MIX
Paper from
responsible sources
FSC® C007507
www.fsc.org

*'A good hotel is where the guest comes first'*

Hilary Rubinstein,
founding editor of the *Good Hotel Guide*

# CONTENTS

## ABOUT THE *GOOD HOTEL GUIDE*

The *Good Hotel Guide* is the leading independent guide to hotels in Great Britain and Ireland. It is written for the reader seeking impartial advice on finding a good place to stay. Hotels cannot buy their entry as they do in most rival guides. No money changes hands, and the editors and inspectors do not accept free hospitality on their anonymous visits to hotels.

Readers play a crucial role by reporting on existing entries as well as recommending new discoveries. Unlike reader-review websites, which are open to abuse from unscrupulous hoteliers and guests with a grudge, these reports are carefully filtered. The *Guide*'s editors make a balanced judgment based on the reports, backed where necessary by an anonymous inspection.

The selected hotels are as independent as we are. Most are small, family owned and family run. They are places of character, where the owners and their staff spend time looking after their guests rather than reporting to an area manager. We look for a warm welcome, with flexible service. Diversity is the key to the selection: simple B&Bs are listed alongside grand country houses and city hotels.

Our website works in tandem with the printed *Guide*. It carries the entries for many, but not all, of our selected hotels. Unlike the printed *Guide*, hotels pay a small fee for inclusion on the website. The website is easy to search and carries many tempting special offers from *Guide* hotels. It also has a small selection of good hotels in mainland Europe.

# INTRODUCTION

The 34th edition of the *Good Hotel Guide* marks a giant leap forward into the visual age. We have made radical changes, introducing full colour, and photographs of our selected hotels. These changes have been made possible by the success of the *Guide*'s website and the launch of an iPhone application in June 2010.

The revenues from the website and the app help subsidise the printed edition, which remains at the heart of what we do, because it is the guarantee of the *Guide*'s independence. Hotels do not pay to be included. The editors select the entries entirely on merit, making unbiased judgments based on reports from inspectors and readers. The website and the app are attracting a new, often younger, audience. The casual reader still expects free access to the website, which is why we ask the selected hotels to pay a small fee towards development and maintenance costs. If they choose not to pay, their hotel remains listed, but without the detail and photographs published in the print edition.

These are turbulent times in publishing. As we went to press, Rupert Murdoch placed his newspaper websites behind a pay wall, saying that this is the only way quality journalism can flourish. The *Guide*'s iPhone app, which can be downloaded for just £2.99, points the way forward and will help us provide the honest and unbiased content that hotel guests have the right to expect. We hope you enjoy our new look.

*Desmond Balmer and Adam Raphael*
July 2010

# HOW TO USE THE *GOOD HOTEL GUIDE*

We have two categories of hotel in the *Guide*: there are 450 main entries which we believe to be the best of their type in Great Britain and Ireland; in addition, we list 400 hotels on a Shortlist, which identifies possible new main entries (as yet untested) alongside suggested accommodation in towns and cities where we have a limited selection of main entries.

A full page is devoted to each main entry, giving our considered judgment based on anonymous inspections and reader reports. There are full colour photographs and an easy-to-read information panel.

The Shortlist, at the back of the book, carries an abbreviated description of each hotel, with the essential information. There are no photographs in the Shortlist: many of these hotels have chosen to be included on our website where pictures are carried.

## HOW TO FIND A GOOD HOTEL

The main entries and the hotels in the Shortlist are listed alphabetically (by country) under the name of the town and village.

The maps, at the back of the book, can be used to find a hotel. Each hotel's location is marked: a small house indicates a main entry, a triangle a Shortlist one. We give the map number and grid reference at the top of each entry.

There are two indexes: one lists hotels alphabetically by name, the other lists hotels by county.

*Editor's Choice* is for readers looking for ideas: we suggest hotels to match your mood or interests, perhaps romance or sport, for a family or for gourmets. We highlight hotels in a wide range of categories, giving a short profile and a cross-reference to the main entry.

## HOW TO READ AN ENTRY

**INFORMATION PANELS** We give the number of bedrooms without detailing the type of room (the distinction between a single room and a small double for single use, a standard or a superior double, a junior or a senior suite varies widely between hotels). We give the geographical location, but not detailed driving directions. As with room types, these are best discussed with the hotel when booking; directions are usually found on a hotel's website.

**PRICES** We give each place's estimated prices for 2011, or the 2010 prices, which applied when the *Guide* went to press. The figures indicate the range of price per person from off-season to high season. A set meal can be no-choice or table d'hôte. The 'full alc' price is the cost per person of a three-course meal with a half bottle of wine; 'alc' indicates the price excluding wine. These figures cannot be guaranteed. *You should always check prices when booking.*

**SYMBOLS** The label 'New' at the top of an entry identifies a hotel making its first appearance in the *Guide*, or one returning after an absence. We say 'Unsuitable for &' when a hotel tells us that it cannot accommodate wheelchair-users. We do not have the resources to inspect such facilities or to assess the even more complicated matter of facilities for the partially disabled. It is best to discuss such details directly with the hotel.

NAMES We give the names of the readers who have nominated or endorsed a hotel in brackets at the end of each entry. We do not name inspectors, correspondents who ask to remain anonymous, or those who have written critical reports.

FACILITIES We give an outline of the facilities offered by each hotel. We suggest that you check in advance if specific items (tea-making equipment, trouser press, sheets and blankets instead of a duvet, etc) are important to you.

CHANGES We try to ensure that the details we provide are correct, but inevitably they are subject to change. Small places sometimes close at short notice off-season. Some change hands after we have gone to press.

VOUCHERS Hotels which join our voucher scheme have agreed to give readers a discount of 25% off their normal bed-and-breakfast rate for one night only. These hotels are identified at the base of the information panel. You will be expected to pay the full price for other meals and all other services. *You should request a voucher reservation at the time of booking.* A hotel may refuse to accept it at busy times. The six vouchers in the centre of the book are valid until the publication of the next edition of the *Guide*.

# FREQUENTLY ASKED QUESTIONS

## HOW DO YOU CHOOSE A GOOD HOTEL?

The hotels we like are relaxed, unstuffy and personally run. There is no overriding standard (we like diversity), though you will find that most hotels in the *Guide* are family owned and family run. We do not inspect hotels with a checklist or a set of boxes to tick. We seek less tangible signs of excellence: a sense of character; the warmth of the welcome; a flexible attitude to guest requests. Most of all, we look for places where the needs of the guest come first.

## WHAT ARE YOUR LIKES AND DISLIKES?

*We like*

* Flexible times for breakfast (our favourite question: 'What time would suit you?').
* A choice between blankets and sheets and a duvet (offered when booking).
* Fresh milk with the tea tray in the room (in a flask or a fridge).
* Good bedside lighting (some of us like reading in bed).
* Proper hangers in the wardrobe (we are not all thieves).

*We dislike*

* Stuffy dress codes (does anyone wear a tie on holiday?).
* Bossy notices in the bedroom (why treat everyone as a potential worst guest?).
* Intrusive background music.
* Hidden service charges (or nudging for a gratuity on the credit card handset).
* Little packs of butter and jam, and packaged juices at breakfast (we're here for a treat).

## HOW DO YOU HEAR ABOUT NEW HOTELS?

We keep our ear to the ground for new ideas, planned new hotels and changes of ownership. Our readers and inspectors tell us of discoveries they have made. When we think that a place looks promising, we send inspectors to stay overnight. They pay their way and do not declare their connection with the *Guide*. This gives us a unique view of a hotel through the eyes of the guest. We cannot be swayed by freebies or sanctimonious service.

## WHY DO YOU INCLUDE SO MANY B&BS?

B&Bs offer excellent value for money. You may not find the full range of services in a B&B, but the better ones give many four- and five-star hotels a run for their money. Many readers prefer the friendliness of a small B&B to the anonymity of a larger chain hotel. Expect the bedrooms in a B&B listed in the *Guide* to be well equipped, with thoughtful extras. We think breakfast is as important a meal as dinner, and you can be sure of a good start to the day at a B&B listed in the *Guide*.

## WHY DO YOU DROP HOTELS FROM ONE YEAR TO THE NEXT?

Readers are quick to tell us if they think standards have slipped at a hotel. If the evidence is overwhelming, we drop the hotel from the *Guide* or perhaps downgrade it to the Shortlist. If the reports are mixed, and it is a place that we have previously liked, we send an inspector. When a hotel is sold, we look for reports since the new owners took over. If these aren't forthcoming, we put the hotel on the Shortlist, or omit it, until more evidence has been gathered.

## WHY DO YOU ASK FOR 'MORE REPORTS, PLEASE'?

We ask for more reports when we have not heard about a hotel for at least two years. Sometimes, readers stay at a favourite hotel on which they have reported before, but do not write to tell us that standards are being maintained. 'More reports, please' is a polite reminder to our army of readers that we require an update. If we don't receive a report after three years, we send an inspector or put the hotel on our Shortlist.

## WHAT IS TO STOP A HOTELIER FROM WRITING HIS OWN REPORT?

We log on our database every report we receive, recording the name and address of the sender. We ignore anonymous reports. It is possible that an unscrupulous hotelier might write under an assumed name. This would fall into another category which we treat with caution: a single report from an unknown correspondent. We are always pleased to receive reports from new readers, and we particularly value those newcomers who send us reports on two or more hotels. We stay on our guard when a new reporter comments on one hotel only. We sometimes receive a batch of collusive letters (usually encouraged by the hotelier) with effusive praise. These are easy to spot. A new trend is a single critical report, often from a reader with a grudge who also posts the complaint on review websites. We treat these with equal caution, sometimes asking for the hotelier's side of the story.

## WHAT SHOULD I TELL YOU IN A REPORT?

How you enjoyed your stay. We welcome reports of any length. Of course, we are delighted when a reader takes the trouble to describe a hotel at length, reporting on the welcome, the decor, the facilities and the food. But even a short report can tell us a great deal, especially when it is about the people (the owners, the staff, the other guests). Sometimes an anecdote can light up a description. A recent favourite was about a hotelier who was asked whether breakfast could be taken in the room. 'Breakfast in bed is almost compulsory,' he replied. That brief story tells much about the attitude to the guest (and suggests a sense of humour).

## HOW SHOULD I SEND YOU A REPORT?

You can email us at editor@goodhotel guide.com. Or you can write to us at the address given on the report forms at the back of the *Guide* (though it is not vital that you use these forms).

## I AM A HOTELIER: HOW DO I GET MY HOTEL INTO THE *GUIDE*?

Write to us (or email) and tell us about your hotel and its ethos, and why it would belong in the *Guide*. We are always looking for discoveries. We might send inspectors, but we won't tell you they are coming.

# CÉSARS 2011

We give our *César* awards to the ten best hotels of the year. Named after César Ritz, the most celebrated of hoteliers, these are the Oscars of hotel-keeping, the accolade hoteliers most want to win. The winners vary greatly in size and style; what they have in common is how well they look after their guests.

### ❦ LONDON HOTEL OF THE YEAR
**NUMBER SIXTEEN**
Tim and Kit Kemp have created a special place at their white stucco 19th-century town house. No detail has been overlooked in the beautifully conceived bedrooms. The welcome is warm, from a well-trained staff. The library and the lush garden are good places to relax.

### ❦ DEVON HOTEL OF THE YEAR
**WHITEHOUSE, CHILLINGTON**
A peaceful rear garden is one of the surprises at this Georgian house in a South Hams village. The owners, Tamara Costin, Matthew Hall and Ally Wray, who have given it a flamboyant 21st-century interior, look after their guests in friendly, informal style.

### ❦ RESTAURANT-WITH-ROOMS OF THE YEAR
**RESTAURANT 36 ON THE QUAY, EMSWORTH**
Everything is done with understated elegance at Ramon and Karen Farthing's restaurant-with-rooms overlooking the harbour of an attractive fishing village. She is a welcoming hostess, directing the well-paced service in the beautifully laid dining room. His first-class cooking perfectly contrasts textures and flavours.

### ❦ FARM GUEST HOUSE OF THE YEAR
**THISTLEYHAUGH FARM, LONGHORSLEY**
The Nelless family welcome visitors with warmth to their old farmhouse in a remote corner of Northumberland. The charming Enid Nelless presides with her daughters-in-law, Zoë and Janice. The bedrooms are thoughtfully equipped; guests are encouraged to enjoy the splendid public rooms. The communal dinner is much enjoyed.

### ❦ FAMILY HOTEL OF THE YEAR
**SWINTON PARK, MASHAM**
At their family home, a Grade II* listed Gothic castle, Mark and Felicity Cunliffe-Lister create a relaxed and unfussy atmosphere in which children are made to feel welcome. There are lots of corners for guests to sit in, and a multitude of activities for all ages. Dinner is innovative.

### ❧ CITY HOTEL OF THE YEAR
**OLD BANK, OXFORD**

Jeremy Mogford's stylish conversion of three stone buildings in the centre of Oxford is discreet, luxurious and well run. The best bedrooms have views of the dreaming spires; even smaller rooms lack nothing. Service is prompt in the buzzing *Quod* restaurant, a favourite Oxford meeting place.

### ❧ B&B OF THE YEAR
**MILLGATE HOUSE, RICHMOND**

Austin Lynch and Tim Culkin have furnished their early Georgian stone house with imagination, filling the charming public rooms with delightful objects. They are engaging hosts who look after guests with care. There are thoughtful extras in the bedrooms. The gardens are cleverly planted and well maintained.

### ❧ SCOTTISH HOTEL OF THE YEAR
**KILLIECRANKIE HOUSE, KILLIECRANKIE**

The welcome is warm and sincere at Henrietta Fergusson's white dower house in enchanting gardens at the entrance to the Pass of Killiecrankie. She is a thoughtful hostess, creating an immediate feel-good factor. The young staff are courteous. Mark Easton's modern British cooking is exceptional.

### ❧ WELSH COUNTRY HOTEL OF THE YEAR
**TŶ MAWR, BRECHFA**

At their 16th-century farmhouse in a tranquil setting on the edge of the Brechfa forest, Annabel Viney and Stephen Thomas do the simple things well. They are welcoming hosts, encouraging visitors to feel at home. His flavourful cooking brings the best out of fine local produce.

### ❧ IRISH HERITAGE HOUSE OF THE YEAR
**MOUNT VERNON, NEW QUAY**

Mark Helmore and Ally Raftery's renovated 18th-century villa, on Flaggy Shore where the Burren meets the sea, is a find. They have furnished the house beautifully, filling it with interesting objects. Guests are welcomed in warm house-party fashion. Dinner is delicious.

# REPORT OF THE YEAR COMPETITION

Readers' contributions are the lifeblood of the *Good Hotel Guide*: we cannot afford to make an annual inspection of every hotel in the *Guide*. Everyone who writes to us is a potential winner of the Report of the Year competition. Each year a dozen correspondents are singled out for the helpfulness and generosity of their reports. They win a copy of the *Guide*, and an invitation to our annual launch party in October. The following generous readers are winners this year.

GILL ALLEN of London
DR RICHARD BARRETT of Salisbury
JILL AND MIKE BENNETT of St Albans
JENNY BUCKLEY of Bognor Regis
SARAH GODDARD of Dublin
IAN MALONE of Ferndown
LYNN MASON of Rothbury
FRANK G MILLEN of Northolt
FIONA MITCHELL-ROSE of Edinburgh
PETER AND KAY ROGERS of Hereford
MARY WILMER of Cambridge
KEN AND PRISCILLA WINSLOW
    of Lydiard Millicent, Swindon

# JOIN THE *GOOD HOTEL GUIDE* READERS' CLUB

Send us a review of your favourite hotel.
As a member of the club, you will be entitled to:
  1. A pre-publication discount offer
  2. Personal advice on hotels
  3. Advice if you are in dispute with a hotel

The writers of the 12 best reviews will each win a free copy of the *Guide* and an invitation to our launch party.

**Send your review via:**
our website: www.goodhotelguide.com
or email: editor@goodhotelguide.com
or fax: 020-7602 4182
or write to:

*Good Hotel Guide*
Freepost PAM 2931, London W11 4BR (no stamp is needed in the UK)

or, from outside the UK:

*Good Hotel Guide*
50 Addison Avenue, London W11 4QP England

# EDITOR'S CHOICE

A visit to a hotel should be a special occasion. This section will help you find a good hotel that matches your mood, whether for romance or for sport, or perhaps to entertain the children. Turn to the full entry for the bigger picture.

## DISCOVERIES
There are 150 new hotels in the *Guide* this year. Here are some of the most interesting finds

### DEAN STREET TOWNHOUSE
LONDON

In Soho, this Grade II Georgian building has been transformed into the latest offshoot of Nick Jones's *Soho House*. It has a contemporary, informal vibe although the lobby feels more like that of a London club than a boutique hotel. The bedrooms have a more modern look, with a large bed, a soft seagrass carpet; generous extras in the ultra-modern bathroom. The adjoining restaurant has the feel of a Parisian brasserie (the dishes are English).
*Read more, page 57.*

### AUSTWICK HALL
AUSTWICK

'Excellent hosts', Michael Pearson and Eric Culley have 'lovingly' brought back to life this handsome old manor house on a wooded hillside on the edge of a pretty village. They have furnished the interesting interiors in a 'clever mix of old and new'. The bedrooms have antiques, polished old floorboards. Mr Pearson serves an 'enjoyable' dinner menu; breakfast is 'very good'.
*Read more, page 83.*

### COLLINGWOOD ARMS
CORNHILL ON TWEED

'A real find,' said a *Guide* hotelier who came across John Cook's Grade II listed Georgian posting inn in a small village in 'magnificent countryside' near Flodden Field. Local craftsmen worked 'inside and out' to renovate the building. The staff are 'extremely friendly'. The 'comfortable' bedrooms have antique furnishings; 'many extras' in the period bathrooms. Derek Weekley serves 'well-cooked' dishes on a short menu.
*Read more, page 146.*

### THE BANK HOUSE
KING'S LYNN

On the quayside in the 'rich historic centre' of King's Lynn, this Grade II listed Georgian merchant's house has been renovated by Jeannette and Anthony Goodrich, who own the *Rose & Crown*, Snettisham. Stuart Deuchars, who worked at *St John's*, London ('the cooking shows the influence'), serves a brasserie menu in three dining areas.
*Read more, page 196.*

## THE VOBSTER INN
LOWER VOBSTER

In a 'lovely, quiet' village near Frome, this old inn has been renovated by Rafael and Peta Davila, 'hard-working, charming and attentive' hosts. They have 'seamlessly merged the old and new' in the rustic bar and dining room. The bedrooms have a 'cool modern look'; bathrooms are well equipped. Mr Davila cooks 'very good' contemporary dishes.
*Read more, page 216.*

## TREVALSA COURT
MEVAGISSEY

On a cliff on the edge of a Cornish village, John and Susan Gladwin's small hotel was built as an Arts and Crafts holiday home in 1937. The house has mullioned windows, a sweeping staircase and wood-panelled dining room. 'Everything is fresh and contemporary.' Most of the bedrooms face the sea. Colin Grigg's cooking is 'above average'.
*Read more, page 232.*

## CHERRY TREES
STRATFORD-UPON-AVON

Gill and Phil Leonard's modern house is a 'revelation', said a *Guide* inspector who has been seeking 'a decent B&B in the town for 25 years'. It is 'perfectly situated', south of the River Avon near a footbridge to the theatre. There are many 'thoughtful touches' in the three bedrooms: all are on the ground floor; two have direct access to the private garden.
*Read more, page 303.*

## TIGH AN DOCHAIS
BROADFORD

'On an island with a multitude of grim B&Bs, this place shines out.' On Broadford Bay on the Isle of Skye, Neil Hope and Lesley Unwin's striking contemporary house has uninterrupted sea, island and mountain views. The guest lounge and dining room have full-length picture windows. There is solid oak flooring throughout; contemporary art. The bedrooms, on the ground floor, are well furnished.
*Read more, page 350.*

## BLAR NA LEISG AT DRUMBEG HOUSE
DRUMBEG

'Something special is going on here: a rare combination of supremely comfortable accommodation and top-notch food in a heart-stoppingly beautiful place.' *Guide* inspectors loved Anne and Eddie Strachan's small restaurant-with-rooms, a renovated laird's house by a loch on the Assynt peninsula. They have decorated with flair. She is the 'gifted' cook; he runs front-of-house 'with courtesy and grace'. The 'wonderful' breakfast is served at a time to suit guests.
*Read more, page 358.*

## MOUNT VERNON
NEW QUAY

On Flaggy Shore where the Burren meets the sea, this 18th-century villa was the summer home of Lady Gregory, writer and patron of the arts. It is run as a 'private country house' by Mark Helmore and Ally Raftery. The bedrooms are beautifully furnished, bathrooms are smart and modern. They serve a 'faultless' dinner at a communal table. The couple advise guests on exploration of the Burren.
*Read more, page 497.*

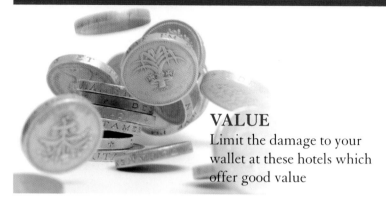

# VALUE

Limit the damage to your wallet at these hotels which offer good value

## ABBEY HOUSE
### ABBOTSBURY

Run as a guest house by the 'very professional' Jonathan and Maureen Cooke, this 15th-century building has lawns sloping down to a millpond; beyond is an ancient tithe barn. There are flagstone floors, panelled doors, original windows; lots of chintz and knick-knacks in the cosy lounge and cottagey bedrooms. B&B £35–£50 per person. Evening meals for house parties only.
*Read more: page 72.*

## THE OLD STORE
### HALNAKER

Once the village store and bakery, Patrick and Heather Birchenough's Grade II listed Georgian building has long been liked for the warmth of the welcome and the 'excellent value'. There are beamed ceilings, a small lounge. Some bedrooms look across fields to Chichester cathedral. Breakfast has free-range eggs, local sausages. There is a pub across the road for evening meals. B&B £35–£65 per person (higher during Goodwood events).
*Read more: page 176.*

## CHARLES COTTON HOTEL
### HARTINGTON

'A bargain for the Peak District', this stone-built 17th-century coaching inn in an attractive village has 'a happy buzz'. The food is 'excellent and imaginative', the service first class. There are original beams, white-painted walls, pine furnishings in the bedrooms; bunk beds in family rooms. Breakfast is as good as dinner. B&B £45–£55 per person, dinner £25.
*Read more: page 180.*

## DALEGARTH HOUSE
### KESWICK

Bruce and Pauline Jackson create an 'intimate and informal atmosphere' at their white-fronted traditional Edwardian guest house a 'stone's throw' from Derwentwater. It is 'one of the best bargains around'. The bedrooms, traditionally decorated, spotlessly clean, have flowers from the garden. Meals, taken in a red-carpeted, chandelier-lit dining room, are 'a tasty treat'. D,B&B £62–£70 per person.
*Read more: page 195.*

## MOLESWORTH MANOR
### LITTLE PETHERICK

In a tiny village near Padstow, Jessica and Geoff French run their 17th-century former rectory as a B&B. They provide complimentary tea for arriving guests. There is 'plenty of sitting room and bedroom space'. Children are encouraged to play in the 'attractive' gardens. The 'superb' breakfast has fresh fruit salads and compotes, freshly baked muffins and a daily special, as well as full English. B&B £35–£55 per person.
*Read more: page 209.*

## THE MISTLEY THORN
### MISTLEY

'Welcoming, with good food; exceptional value.' Sherri Singleton and David McKay run their restaurant-with-rooms in a yellow-painted 18th-century coaching inn in a small village on the Stour estuary. Sherri Singleton and Chris Pritchard have a *Michelin* Bib Gourmand for their menus, which specialise in seafood. The bedrooms are decorated in taupe and cream; some face the estuary. D,B&B £60–£77.50 per person.
*Read more: page 235.*

## THE BLACK SWAN
### RAVENSTONEDALE

'Likeable and friendly', Alan and Louise Dinnes have restored this once run-down Victorian pub into a hub of village life. They have incorporated a village shop in a downstairs room. Real ales are served in the bar. An extensive menu of 'generous portions of straightforward food', much of it sourced locally, is served in two dining rooms. Bedrooms are well equipped; two have direct outdoor access. B&B £37.50–£62.50 per person, dinner £26.
*Read more: page 273.*

## BEALACH HOUSE
### DUROR

Surrounded by woods and mountains (much wildlife), Jim and Hilary McFadyen's 'handsome, well-maintained' building is the only dwelling in 'stunning' Salachan Glen. Visitors are greeted on first-name terms and given complimentary tea with 'delicious' cake by a log fire. A complimentary glass or two of wine is offered at dinner (her cooking is 'superb'). B&B £40–£55 per person, dinner £28.
*Read more: page 360.*

## CRAIGATIN HOUSE AND COURTYARD
### PITLOCHRY

Martin and Andrea Anderson are 'charming' hosts at their 'warm and inviting' house in wooded grounds close to the town centre. 'Very good value.' The house is well appointed, spotless. Breakfast has a buffet of porridge with whisky, compote of apricots, fresh fruit salad. Cooked dishes include 'a divine omelette Arnold Bennett'. B&B £39–£52.50 per person.
*Read more: page 392.*

## THE HAND AT LLANARMON
### LLANARMON DYFFRYN CEIRIOG

The prices are 'very reasonable' at Martin and Gaynor De Luchi's 'unpretentious' old drovers' inn in a village at the head of a pretty valley. Bedrooms are 'comfortable, clean, with ample hot water'; housekeeping is 'immaculate'. In the large restaurant, 'straightforward, hearty' food is enjoyed. D,B&B £60–£87.50 per person.
*Read more: page 431.*

# GREEN
Enjoy a guilt-free stay at these places which take active measures to protect the environment

**ONE ALDWYCH**
LONDON
The environmental policy at Gordon Campbell Gray's ultra-modern hotel touches every department. The fitting of waterless urinals has saved 130,000 litres of water a year; daylight sensor switches have reduced energy consumption (a system that will pay for itself). An elected environmental officer manages the policies and communicates them to the staff.
*Read more: page 64.*

**PASKINS TOWN HOUSE**
BRIGHTON
Susan and Roger Marlowe hold a Green Business Tourism Gold Award at their quirky B&B in a conservation area near the sea. Towels are washed with soap nut shells (leading to less chemical waste); low-energy light bulbs are in their eighth year of service; soap and shampoo are synthetic-free, animal-free. Breakfast has organic local ingredients; Fairtrade tea and coffee.
*Read more: page 121.*

**TIMBERSTONE**
CLEE STANTON
In deep countryside in the hills above Ludlow, Alex Read and Tracey Baylis have renovated and extended their charming house. A ground heat pump supplies heat and hot water (supplemented by a wood-burning stove). All vegetable waste is composted in the garden, and everything possible is recycled. She cooks organic ingredients, and Fairtrade tea and coffee are used for dinner and breakfast.
*Read more: page 141.*

**OVERWATER HALL**
IREBY
Owners Stephen Bore and Adrian and Angela Hyde are 'committed to being considerate, not only to their guests and staff, but also towards the environment' at their castellated Grade II listed Georgian mansion. They avoid products imported by aircraft, and food items packaged in polystyrene or plastic. A biomass boiler that burns environmentally friendly fuel has been installed.
*Read more: page 194.*

**AUGILL CASTLE**
KIRKBY STEPHEN
'From recycling to investing in new technology, nothing is overlooked,' say Simon and Wendy Bennett, who run their Victorian fantasy-Gothic castle in

informal style. The kitchen has modern energy-saving equipment; heating stoves use fuel from managed local woods and compressed sawdust bricks from a nearby sawmill. They will 'gladly ferry guests to and from the nearest public transport'.
*Read more: page 197.*

### SWINTON PARK
MASHAM

Mark and Felicity Cunliffe-Lister are committed to cutting food miles and reducing carbon emissions at their family-friendly Gothic castle. Their four-acre restored walled garden has 60 varieties of fruit, herbs and vegetables to supply the kitchen and cookery school. They installed a carbon-neutral woodchip boiler and an eco-friendly laundry. Water in the bedrooms is provided in reusable bottles.
*Read more: page 226.*

### THE SCARLET
MAWGAN PORTH

Sisters Emma Stratton, Deborah Wakefield and Rebecca Whittington built their design hotel to 'the highest eco standards'. It has a natural ventilation system rather than air conditioning. Heating comes from a biomass boiler; solar panels warm the chlorine-free indoor swimming pool. Unused guest soaps are reused as stain removers in the laundry. 'Even the candle wax is sent back to the local firm to be used again.'
*Read more: page 229.*

### STRATTONS
SWAFFHAM

'From day one, our guiding principle has been to source and prepare the fabulous seasonal produce on our doorstep,' say Vanessa and Les Scott, who bought their Palladian-style villa in 1990. They have been pioneers in raising environmental standards, following a policy that covers practical things (recycling, etc) and broader issues (a discount of 10 per cent on the B&B rate is given to visitors who arrive by public transport).
*Read more: page 307.*

### THE LOVAT
FORT AUGUSTUS

Guests are encouraged to calculate their carbon footprint when travelling to Caroline Gregory's eco-friendly former railway hotel on the southern shore of Loch Ness. Visitors travelling by public transport are given a discount (as are those cycling or walking). A biomass woodchip burner provides heating and hot water; eco-friendly cleaning products are used, so are energy-saving lamps.
*Read more: page 366.*

### Y GOEDEN EIRIN
DOLYDD

John Rowlands, who runs this small guest house near Caernarfon with his wife Eluned, encourages respect for 'the cultural as well as the natural environment'. The bilingual couple share their culture with guests by filling the house with contemporary Welsh art and books (many written by Dr Rowlands). They follow recycling and composting policies, serve local organic food and Fairtrade tea and coffee, and have installed solar panels. Guests arriving by train are met at Bangor. Public transport is recommended for day trips to interesting places.
*Read more: page 425.*

# FAMILY

All too rare in Britain, these are places where parents can relax knowing that their children are welcomed

## THE BLAKENEY HOTEL
### BLAKENEY

'Perfect' for families, Michael Stannard's traditional hotel faces the tidal estuary and salt marshes. During school holidays children stay free if sharing an adult's room. There is much to occupy young people: children's channels on digital TV, an indoor swimming pool, a games room with table tennis, pool and darts, board games. Good beaches nearby.
*Read more: page 103.*

## THE TROUT AT TADPOLE BRIDGE
### BUCKLAND MARSH

Parents themselves, Gareth and Helen Pugh have made their old Cotswold pub 'as child-friendly as possible'. It stands in a large garden that slopes down to the Thames. A small electric punt is available for visitors, or you can hire a larger boat at a nearby yard. There are games and toys, plenty of space in the garden. The children's menus are 'decent (no nuggets)'.
*Read more: page 128.*

## THE EVESHAM HOTEL
### EVESHAM

Children are 'genuinely welcomed' at John and Sue Jenkinson's quirky, informal hotel. Young guests are charged according to age and amount of food eaten. They have play areas (with swings, trampoline, slides, etc) in the grounds. There's an indoor swimming pool and a games room. Everyone loves the themed bedrooms (Alice in Wonderland, a family suite, among the beams, Safari, etc).
*Read more: page 165.*

## MOONFLEET MANOR
### FLEET

Part of von Essen's Luxury Family Hotels group, this sprawling Georgian manor house is in large grounds above the Fleet lagoon. The very young can be left in the Four Bears' Den, which is Ofsted-registered. Their older siblings have the run of a large indoor play area, which has a trampoline, table tennis, soft tennis, table football, computer games, etc. There are play areas, swings and slides in the large grounds. Children sharing their parents' room stay free.
*Read more: page 168.*

## AUGILL CASTLE
### KIRKBY STEPHEN

Simon and Wendy Bennett run their Victorian Gothic folly in informal house-party style. Their children welcome visiting young as 'special friends'. There's plenty to attract children in the grounds: a playground, a fort in the forest, a tree house. In the evenings, younger guests have fun with films and popcorn, while adults enjoy a quiet drink in the bar. Many of the bedrooms are big enough for a family. *Read more: page 197.*

## SWINTON PARK
### MASHAM

'You could tell that it is run by people who have children,' said a parent visiting Mark and Felicity Cunliffe-Lister's family home, a creeper-clad 17th-century castle. Young visitors have a 'great playroom' with ping-pong, billiards, toys. Family activity days include treasure hunts, pony rides, feeding the ducks. There are 'half-term heaven' packages and children's cookery courses. *Read more: page 226.*

## BEDRUTHAN STEPS HOTEL
### MAWGAN PORTH

There is much for children to do at this large, purpose-built family hotel in a village above a golden, sandy beach in north Cornwall. It has an indoor play area, an Ofsted-registered nursery, a soft play and ball pool for toddlers, a junior assault course and a teenagers' room. A family dining option has special menus for adults and children. *Read more: page 228.*

## CALCOT MANOR
### TETBURY

'We don't just accept children, we love having them here,' says Richard Ball, managing director of this Cotswold hotel. Suites have a bedroom for parents and a sitting room with a bunk bed or sofa bed for the young. Older children have an unsupervised play area; there's a playzone for their younger siblings; for the youngest an Ofsted-registered crèche. Adults enjoy the spa (where special times are allocated for children). *Read more: page 313.*

## TREFEDDIAN HOTEL
### ABERDYFI

There are reduced rates for children at the Cave family's traditional hotel above a golden beach on Cardigan Bay. Young visitors have playrooms and a playground, their own supper menu. Baby-monitoring is available. There is an indoor swimming pool; in the large grounds are tennis and a pitch-and-putt course. *Read more: page 411.*

## PORTH TOCYN HOTEL
### ABERSOCH

Parents can relax in the pretty gardens while their children enjoy the many activities at the Fletcher-Brewer family's hotel on the Lleyn peninsula. Children have a dedicated area with a cosy 'snug' (TV and DVDs) and a games room with table tennis. High chairs, cots and baby-listening devices are available. Excellent beaches close by. *Read more: page 412.*

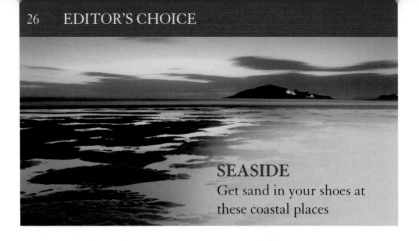

## SEASIDE
Get sand in your shoes at these coastal places

### BURGH ISLAND HOTEL
BIGBURY-ON-SEA

The period atmosphere has been meticulously maintained at this Art Deco hotel on a private tidal island in sandy Bigbury Bay. Guests are driven across the sand when the tide is out; at high tide, the island is reached by a specially built sea tractor. There is a natural swimming pool in the rocks; one of the suites is on stilts above a private beach.
*Read more: page 100.*

### HELL BAY HOTEL
BRYHER

On the western side of this small island reached only by boat, this contemporary hotel stands above a fine sandy beach. In the unlikely event that this is crowded, guests can walk to other good beaches on the island. Accommodation is mainly in suites, decorated in appropriate seaside colours (each has a terrace or a balcony); huge seascapes are hung in the restaurant.
*Read more: page 126.*

### BEDRUTHAN STEPS HOTEL
MAWGAN PORTH

This large, purpose-built hotel on a cliffside in a seaside village stands above a golden, sandy beach with rock pools for young explorers. Atlantic breakers make this surfing territory and there are many good beaches nearby. There is much other than the beach for children to do: play areas, indoor and outdoor swimming pools, children's clubs, and 'water fun sessions'.
*Read more: page 228.*

### DRIFTWOOD HOTEL
PORTSCATHO

Steep steps in the grounds of this contemporary hotel on the Roseland peninsula lead through woodland to a private beach. The modern interiors (colours are white with shades of blue; driftwood tables and lamps) reflect the setting. Almost all the bedrooms have superb views of the sea. There is good walking in both directions along the Cornish Coast Path.
*Read more: page 270.*

### SOAR MILL COVE HOTEL
SOAR MILL COVE

Surrounded by National Trust land, this single-storey stone and slate hotel stands above a beautiful beach, framed by cliffs. It is popular with families: children are warmly welcomed with small swimming pools, a play area, activity packs. Sea-facing rooms have a patio which catches the afternoon sun. *Castaways*, a coffee bar in the grounds, is for muddy paws and younger guests. *Read more: page 299.*

### DUNVALANREE IN CARRADALE
CARRADALE

Sea tours can be arranged at Alan and Alyson Milstead's small hotel/restaurant above a sandy beach in a fishing village. There are 'breathtaking' views across Kilbrannan Sound to the Isle of Arran. Local seafood is a highlight of Mrs Milstead's cooking. A ground-floor room, which has French doors leading on to a patio with a table and chairs, has immediate access to the shore. *Read more: page 352.*

### THE COLONSAY
COLONSAY

'You can bask on a splendid golden beach' (there are a dozen to choose from) on this eight-mile-long Hebridean island, which is connected with the neighbouring island of Oransay at low tide by a strip of sand. Grey seals, otters, dolphins, even whales can be spotted. This unpretentious hotel is owned by a group headed by the laird and his wife, Alex and Jane Howard. Bedrooms are simply furnished, 'comfortable, spotless'. *Read more: page 354.*

### CEOL NA MARA
TARBERT

The Isle of Harris is noted for its broad, long and glistening white sandy beaches, which can be explored from John and Marlene Mitchell's B&B. The Gaelic name of their renovated stone house above a rocky tidal loch translates as 'music of the sea'. 'Friendly and hard-working' hosts, they earn 'full marks for everything'. There are lovely views from all the windows. *Read more: page 402.*

### THE DRUIDSTONE
BROADHAVEN

Families like this 'family holiday centre' for its relaxed, informal welcome for children. The setting is wonderful: on a cliff-top above a huge sandy beach (safe for swimming). Regulars like the 'rough around the edges' feel. Surfing, sailing, windsurfing and canoeing are all available on the beach or nearby. Children have high tea around a big kitchen table. It is recommended for travellers looking for character rather than perfection. 'Definitely more shabby chic than high end luxury (a good thing).' *Read more: page 417.*

### THE WHITE HOUSE
HERM

On the approach by boat, visitors to this tiny car-free island see a long stretch of sand that unfolds into three beaches – Bear's, Fisherman's and Harbour. Over the hill is Shell Beach, rich in colour from tiny shells. The island's only hotel, redecorated this year, has no TVs, bedroom clocks or telephones as 'they don't seem appropriate'. The only obtrusive sounds on the car-free island are the occasional tractor or a piping oystercatcher at night. *Read more: page 457.*

## COUNTRY HOUSE
Elegance, luxury and plenty of pampering can be counted on at these rural retreats

### BARNSLEY HOUSE
BARNSLEY

In a Cotswold village, this beautiful William and Mary house has been sensitively refreshed by the owners of nearby *Calcot Manor*. The public areas have wide wooden floorboards, cream colours, stone walls. Mirrors on window shutters in the dining room draw the gardens (created by the late Rosemary Verey) into the house. The bedrooms have state-of-the-art technology, great comfort. The young staff show a well-judged blend of friendliness and formality.
*Read more: page 86.*

### FARLAM HALL
BRAMPTON

Approached up a sweeping drive, this manorial house stands in an 'immaculate' landscaped garden with a large ornamental lake. It has been run in hands-on style by the Quinion family for 35 years. It is liked for the 'sense of humour' that runs alongside old-fashioned service. Public rooms are ornate, with patterned wallpaper, open fires; bedrooms are traditionally furnished. Barry Quinion cooks 'delicious' country house meals.
*Read more: page 115.*

### GIDLEIGH PARK
CHAGFORD

The North River Teign runs through the extensive grounds of this luxurious hotel in lovely rural surroundings. There are formal gardens, marked walks, a croquet lawn. Executive chef Michael Caines has two *Michelin* stars for his classic French menus. Supremely comfortable beds, and welcoming touches (fresh fruit, mineral water and a decanter of Madeira or port) are in the bedrooms.
*Read more: page 134.*

### SUMMER LODGE
EVERSHOT

In large grounds in an old Dorset village, this country house was built as a retreat for the Earls of Ilchester, and enlarged by Thomas Hardy. Public rooms have gilt mirrors, brass fenders, swags. Fine fabrics, patterns, heavy drapes are in the bedrooms. Chef Steven Titman serves a seasonal menu of modern dishes with French influences.
*Read more: page 164.*

### COMBE HOUSE
GITTISHAM

Ken and Ruth Hunt's Grade I listed Elizabethan manor house stands in a

vast estate of woodland, meadows and pastures. They preside in an informal manner, creating a 'warm feeling'. Public rooms have oak panelling, antiques, fresh flowers, 18th-century portraits. The gardens supply 40 per cent of the produce for chef Hadleigh Barrett's modern cooking.
*Read more, page 171*

## HAMBLETON HALL
HAMBLETON

On a peninsula jutting into Rutland Water (an 'intoxicating' setting), Tim and Stefa Hart's Victorian mansion is liked for its 'old-world charm'. The interiors are classic: fine fabrics, antiques, open fires, sumptuous sofas and cushions. The spacious bedrooms have floral fabrics; the best overlook Rutland Water. Aaron Patterson has a *Michelin* star for his seasonal cooking. 'The food was divine: everything was cooked and presented to perfection.'
*Read more: page 177.*

## LIME WOOD
LYNDHURST

In large grounds in the New Forest, this Regency manor house has been given a £30 million make-over and reopened as a 'relaxed' country house hotel. The lounges have been styled 'with flair and humour', with antiques and quirky, oversized modern furniture. The bedrooms are in the main house and three new buildings in the grounds.
*Read more, page 220*

## HOTEL ENDSLEIGH
MILTON ABBOT

Olga Polizzi has created a modern, comfortable country house hotel with her imaginative restoration of this luxurious Regency shooting and fishing lodge. The house has original panelling, contemporary paintings, many artefacts; candles provide much of the lighting at night. It stands in well-maintained gardens (many rare trees) on an estate running down to the River Tamar.
*Read more: page 234.*

## GILPIN HOTEL AND LAKE HOUSE
WINDERMERE

The Cunliffe family run their Edwardian country house in informal style. It is 'never stuffy'; the attention to detail is commended. The hands-on family create a 'warm' atmosphere. It stands in extensive grounds, with terrace, pond, waterfall, croquet lawn and llama paddock, within the Lake District national park. The bedrooms are made up twice a day. Chef Russell Plowman is 'passionate about using local and organic ingredients'.
*Read more: page 331.*

## GLENAPP CASTLE
BALLANTRAE

'Luxury is standard' at Graham and Fay Cowan's restored 19th-century Scottish baronial castle. There are fine paintings, Middle Eastern rugs, intricate plasterwork and an oak-panelled entrance and staircase. The chef, Adam Stokes, serves 'imaginative' dishes. Spacious bedrooms have an open fire, and views of the gardens or over the Irish Sea to Ailsa Craig. The large wooded grounds have a lake, a walled garden and a Victorian glasshouse.
*Read more: page 346.*

## CITY CHIC
At these contemporary city hotels expect cutting-edge style and high-tech fittings

### ONE ALDWYCH
LONDON

Even the smaller bedrooms are stylish at Gordon Campbell Gray's ultra-modern conversion of the Edwardian offices of the *Morning Post*. The thoughtfully designed rooms have all the latest technology. The double-height lobby, dominated by the giant statue of an oarsman, has extravagant flower arrangements. The service, by the smartly dressed young staff, is often praised.
*Read more: page 64.*

### THE ROCKWELL
LONDON

Two Victorian terrace houses on the Cromwell Road have been given a clean, modern look by Michael Squire and Tony Bartlett. The competent young staff create an informal vibe. The spacious lobby has bold patterned wallpaper, an open fire. The bedrooms have bright colours, bespoke light oak furnishings; bathrooms are smart and well equipped. Contemporary dishes are served in a restaurant overlooking a courtyard garden.
*Read more: page 66.*

### THE ZETTER
LONDON

A glass door opens on to a white-walled lobby with a pink Murano glass chandelier at this converted 19th-century warehouse in Clerkenwell. Bedrooms are decorated in vintage-modern style; bright splashes of colour on a neutral background. All have state-of-the-art entertainment and technology. The restaurant, which overlooks St John's Square, has re-opened after renovation as *Bistrot Bruno Loubet* (run by the eponymous French chef).
*Read more: page 69.*

### DRAKES
BRIGHTON

The bedrooms in Andy Shearer's modern conversion of two 19th-century town houses have an extravagant modern decor ('with a touch of decadence', says the brochure). They have hand-made beds, contemporary ceiling mouldings, natural wood; colours are cream and brown. Front rooms have a freestanding bath with a view of the sea.
*Read more: page 119.*

## HOTEL DU VIN BRIGHTON
BRIGHTON

Between The Lanes and the seafront, this collection of Gothic revival and mock-Tudor buildings houses the Brighton branch of this chain of contemporary hotels. Original features were highlighted in the conversion: a carved wooden staircase with gargoyles; a double-height hall, which houses the bar. The bedrooms are modern and well equipped; the big bathrooms have a retro look.
*Read more: page 120.*

## HOTEL DU VIN BRISTOL
BRISTOL

An old industrial building (Grade II listed) has been imaginatively converted into a striking contemporary hotel close to the centre of town. A glass canopy entrance leads to spacious public areas and a sweeping steel and oak staircase. There are huge beds in the stylish bedrooms; bathrooms have state-of-the-art fittings. The brasserie restaurant is liked for its buzz.
*Read more: page 122.*

## HOPE STREET HOTEL
LIVERPOOL

On a Georgian street linking the two cathedrals, two adjacent buildings (one in the style of an Italian palazzo) have been given a striking modern interior. Original iron beams and exposed brickwork have been retained. The bedrooms have a solid wood floor, cherry wood furniture; suites have a sophisticated entertainment system. There are leather sofas and pop music in the bar; dramatic floor-to-ceiling glass sculptures in the restaurant where chef Paul Askew serves modern dishes.
*Read more: page 210.*

## HART'S HOTEL
NOTTINGHAM

Tim Hart's purpose-built hotel, in a quiet cul-de-sac on the site of the city's medieval castle, has striking lines, curved buttresses, lots of glass. There is art on the walls, brightly coloured seating, a vast window in the lobby. The bedrooms, decorated in masculine colours, have good-quality furnishings, well-planned lighting. Light meals, and wine and champagne by the glass, are served in the bar; excellent food in the associated *Hart's* restaurant.
*Read more: page 252.*

## MALMAISON
OXFORD

The sheer drama of this unusual conversion of Oxford's Victorian castle jail attracts attention. There are metal walkways, cell doors with spy holes (reversed for today's guests). Bedrooms in the A-wing atrium are created from three cells (two for the sleeping area, one for the bathroom). The governor's old house has a mini-cinema; mezzanine rooms with four-poster beds. Bistro meals are served in the underground brasserie.
*Read more: page 257.*

## OLD BANK
OXFORD

On the High, opposite All Souls, Jeremy Mogford's elegant conversion of three buildings (one a former bank) is filled with his collection of modern art. The well-appointed bedrooms are modern, relaxing; many overlook the dreaming spires. The old banking hall houses *Quod*, a lively bar/restaurant, popular with town and gown.
*Read more: page 258.*

# ROMANCE

In the mood for love? These hotels have rooms ripe for romance

### THE PORTOBELLO
LONDON

Favoured by A-list celebrities, this Bohemian little hotel in Notting Hill has quirky themed bedrooms. Share the oversized bath in a Japanese water garden basement suite; this room has a private shell grotto terrace. The Round Room is dominated by a huge circular bed; it has a large freestanding Edwardian bathing machine, a Moroccan lantern and muslin curtains.
*Read more: page 65.*

### BARNSLEY HOUSE
BARNSLEY

In a quiet Cotswold village, this William and Mary house was the home of Rosemary Verey, who created its celebrated garden. It is now a country house hotel. Stay in the cottage suite which adjoins the potager; it has a private terrace; a wood-burning stove in the lounge; a roll-top bath and separate shower in the bathroom. Dinner is 'exceptional', in the panelled restaurant which faces the garden.
*Read more: page 86.*

### LINTHWAITE HOUSE
BOWNESS-ON-WINDERMERE

Overlooking Lake Windermere, this creeper-covered, white and stone house has a loft suite where guests can sleep under the stars. It has a sliding glass panel in the ceiling that opens up to allow stargazing: a telescope is provided. The panel closes automatically if there is rain. The suite, with its own entrance, has an open-plan design; the highlight in the bathroom is a huge freestanding Italian bath.
*Read more: page 112.*

### DRAKES
BRIGHTON

'We had the ridiculous pleasure of taking a bath while overlooking the sea.' Try one of the sea-facing bedrooms at this seafront boutique hotel, close to The Lanes and the Pavilion. These have a freestanding bath by the window. All rooms have an extravagant modern decor, bordering on decadent. 'A great candidate for a romantic weekend.'
*Read more: page 119.*

## HELL BAY HOTEL
### BRYHER

The next stop is America at this contemporary hotel on an isolated west-facing bay on the smallest of the inhabited Scilly islands (no made-up roads, few inhabitants). You can walk straight to the beach from the terrace of a ground-floor suite. The rooms, each of which has a sitting area, are decorated in appropriate seaside colours. Cornish artworks hang in the spacious lounge. *Read more: page 126.*

## LE MANOIR AUX QUAT'SAISONS
### GREAT MILTON

'A really superb hotel for the special occasion', Raymond Blanc's luxury domain stands in gardens of 'stunning beauty' in a pretty Oxfordshire village. M. Blanc, who believes in the power of romance, has worked with leading interior designers to create some interesting suites. Blanc de Blanc, with a private garden, is layered in shades of white. Even standard rooms have a luxurious bathroom. *Read more: page 173.*

## LAVENHAM PRIORY
### LAVENHAM

'It was like being a lord of the manor.' Step back centuries at Tim and Gilli Pitt's beautiful half-timbered house, originally a priory, later an Elizabethan merchant's house. The 13th-century Great Hall has a beamed ceiling, huge inglenook fireplace. The five bed chambers, reached by an oak Jacobean staircase, are spacious; unusual beds (four-poster, polonaise, or sleigh), creaking floorboards. *Read more: page 203.*

## THE OLD RAILWAY STATION
### PETWORTH

'The quaintness of the location and buildings adds a special charm.' This is a B&B with a difference, a Grade II* listed Victorian railway station, with adjacent four Pullman carriages. The biggest bedrooms are in the former station building; the most romantic are in converted Pullman railway cars. They have a comfortable bed, and a surprising amount of furniture. *Read more: page 265.*

## ARDANAISEIG
### KILCHRENAN

Recently voted Scotland's most romantic hotel, this baronial mansion stands in beautiful gardens on remote Loch Awe. Stay in the old boathouse on the shore of the loch. It has been converted into a suite; double-height windows open on to a deck above the water. The bedroom, on a mezzanine level, has uninterrupted views across the water. *Read more: page 377.*

## INIS MEÁIN RESTAURANT AND SUITES
### INIS MEÁIN

The 'middle island' is the quietest of the Aran islands off the Galway coast. Islander Ruairí de Blacam built his restaurant-with-rooms to blend with the craggy surroundings. Three simple suites have a well-stocked fridge, books about the island; 'wonderful views'. Guests can borrow bicycles to explore the island with a packed lunch. The cooking is 'superb'. *Read more: page 486.*

# GOURMET

Savour the pleasures of the table at these hotels and restaurants-with-rooms without having to drive home after dinner

## THE MARQUIS AT ALKHAM
ALKHAM

On a slope at the southern end of the Kent Downs, this white-painted 200-year-old inn has an inviting contemporary interior (exposed brickwork, wide-beamed oak flooring, modern fabrics). Head chef Charles Lakin has a rising *Michelin* star for his seasonal, locally sourced menus with dishes like crown of spring chicken, pot roast leg, sarladaise potatoes, Madeira jus.
*Read more, page 74.*

## BLAGDON MANOR
ASHWATER

In rolling north Devon countryside, Steve and Liz Morey run their 17th-century manor house (Grade II listed) as a restaurant-with-rooms. The atmosphere is unstuffy; 'Liz Morey has a sixth sense, knowing what guests would like before they do.' His food is 'manna from heaven', with dishes like parsley panna cotta, ham hock and lentil salad; poached Cornish turbot, wilted spinach and tiger prawns, crab and coconut milk.
*Read more: page 82.*

## LITTLE BARWICK HOUSE
BARWICK

In lovely countryside near the Somerset/Devon border, Tim and Emma Ford's restaurant-with-rooms, in a 19th-century dower house, is 'as good as ever'. He has the 'deftest of touches' in the kitchen, using local ingredients for his modern dishes, perhaps warm terrine of lemon sole and salmon lobster sauce; roasted wild roe deer, braised red cabbage, rösti.
*Read more: page 87.*

## READ'S
FAVERSHAM

David Pitchford has a *Michelin* star at his restaurant-with-rooms in an elegant Georgian manor house. He runs it with his wife, Rona, who directs the unfussy service. He uses vegetables and herbs from the walled gardens for his 'excellent' modern dishes, eg, terrine of confit chicken and root vegetables; English pork chop, chicken and black pudding mousse, caramelised Cox's apples.
*Read more: page 167.*

## THE STAR INN
HAROME

In a pretty Yorkshire village, this 14th-century thatched longhouse is now a

*Michelin*-starred restaurant-with-rooms. Andrew Pern cooks 'superb' modern dishes reflecting his northern roots, eg, terrine of ham knuckle, spiced pineapple pickle; North Sea fish pie, melted Montgomery Cheddar and herb topping. *Read more: page 179.*

### MR UNDERHILL'S
LUDLOW

In gardens by the River Teme below Ludlow Castle, Christopher and Judy Bradley's popular restaurant-with-rooms is 'run to high standards'. 'Sheer perfection: it is hard to believe he is self taught.' He has a *Michelin* star for his eight-course set menu, which 'kicks off' with three tiny dishes (perhaps sorrel velouté; a cone of marinated salmon; duck liver custard); 'venison with elderberries and black pudding crumb is a favourite; top-drawer desserts'. *Read more: page 217.*

### MORSTON HALL
MORSTON

Tracy and Galton Blackiston run their Jacobean flint-and-brick mansion on the north Norfolk coast as a restaurant-with-rooms (*Michelin* star). She is front-of-house, he the chef, working with Samantha Wegg. There is no choice on the four-course dinner menu, which might include braised neck of lamb, haricot beans; roasted loin of veal, potato gnocchi, braised onions, tomato fondue and Buccaneers sauce. *Read more: page 239.*

### THE THREE CHIMNEYS
DUNVEGAN

Food lovers have been making the pilgrimage for 25 years to Eddie and Shirley Spear's acclaimed restaurant-with-rooms in a remote setting by Loch Dunvegan in north-west Skye. She is patronne/director; Michael Smith is the acclaimed chef, using local meat and fish in dishes like Skye lochs fruits de mer; saddle of wild rabbit, Ayrshire bacon, pearl barley, nettles, juniper sauce. *Read more: page 359.*

### PLAS BODEGROES
PWLLHELI

Chris and Gunna Chown run their restaurant-with-rooms in a white Georgian manor house in wooded grounds on the Lleyn peninsula. She is the warm, professional front-of-house; he is passionate about local ingredients for his classic cooking. Pre-starters are served in the bar. In the L-shaped dining room, 'broccoli soup was delicious; the tender lamb had masses of flavour; I was even tempted by the light cinnamon shortbread with rhubarb and apple'. *Read more: page 448.*

### THE CROWN AT WHITEBROOK
WHITEBROOK

At this former 17th-century drovers' inn in a village near Monmouth, James Sommerin has a *Michelin* star for his 'original, flavoursome' dishes based on local ingredients. His inspiration is the cooking of his mother and grandmother. The 'comfortably small portions leave room for the little extras served between courses and the delicious bread'. Try Welsh venison loin, spiced carrot, coffee, sorrel and wild mushroom. *Read more: page 454.*

## GASTROPUBS

Interesting cooking and a lively atmosphere can be expected at these old inns and pubs

### THE VICTORIA
LONDON

Near Richmond Park, this pub with a neighbourhood feel is run by celebrity chef Paul Merrett. In the daytime, young mothers drop in for coffee; in the evening locals gather at the bar. In the conservatory restaurant, he serves a frequently changing menu of modern British dishes, perhaps stinging nettle broth, poached egg; rose veal escalope, organic veal sausage, garlic and aubergine aïoli.
*Read more: page 68.*

### THE HORSE AND GROOM
BOURTON-ON-THE-HILL

At the top of the hill in a Cotswold village, this Georgian coaching inn is run in personal style by brothers Tom and Will (the chef) Greenstock. There are ancient beams, wooden floors and tables, sisal matting. Vegetables from the garden, and local ingredients, cooked 'with passion', are on a blackboard menu, perhaps fried haloumi, pea, broad bean and chicory salad, chilli and mint dressing; spiced lamb, aubergine cannelloni.
*Read more: page 109.*

### THE TROUT AT TADPOLE BRIDGE
BUCKLAND MARSH

Lawns run down to the River Thames at Gareth and Helen Pugh's old stone pub by a narrow bridge. The bar (popular with locals) and eating areas have stone walls, original fireplaces. Helen Pugh is in charge of front-of-house; chef Pascal Clavaud serves a seasonal menu with blackboard specials, eg, breast of guineafowl, beetroot purée, Tatin of wild mushrooms, duck foie gras.
*Read more: page 128.*

### THE SUN INN
DEDHAM

Piers Baker's yellow-painted old coaching inn has established a following for the quality of the Italian cooking. In the open-plan dining room, the chef, Ugo Simonelli, serves a daily-changing menu using local and seasonal ingredients. Typical dishes: spaghettini with squid and ink; chicken roasted with peppers, tomatoes, garlic, onion and thyme. 'Worth seeking out by any serious food lover.'
*Read more: page 157.*

## THE ANGEL INN
HETTON

In the Yorkshire Dales, Juliet Watkins's old drovers' inn was one of the first pubs to take food seriously. Bruce Elsworth, the chef/director, serves an Anglo-French bar menu with daily blackboard specials, and a carte in the restaurant (dishes like seared halibut, rösti, cauliflower purée, scallops and lobster sauce).
*Read more: page 186.*

## THE LORD POULETT ARMS
HINTON ST GEORGE

Owners Stephen Hill and Michelle Paynton have restored their 17th-century inn in a pretty Somerset village in a modern idiom: bare flag and wooden floors, open fires, oak tables, antique chairs. Chef Gary Coughlan serves a seasonal menu, using fruit and vegetables from local allotment holders, eg, artichoke purée, crème fraîche; venison loin, parsnip purée, roasted root vegetables, red cabbage.
*Read more: page 187.*

## THE GURNARD'S HEAD
ZENNOR

In as isolated position on the north Cornish coast near Land's End, Charles and Edmund Inkin's restored pub/restaurant is a 'wonderfully relaxing and enjoyable place'. Local farmers deliver vegetables and herbs for chef Bruce Rennie's modern menus with dishes like oyster rissole; sole, white beans, pearl onions, spinach.
*Read more: page 339.*

## KILBERRY INN
KILBERRY

In a 'magical' position on the Kintyre peninsula, David Wilson and Clare Johnson's unpretentious old inn is much liked. Clare Johnson, assisted by Tom Holloway and John McNulty, has a *Michelin* Bib Gourmand for modern cooking on a short, seasonal menu. Try smoked haddock and watercress tart; roasted mini-leg of lamb, petits pois à la française.
*Read more: page 376.*

## THE FELIN FACH GRIFFIN
FELIN FACH

Between the Brecon Beacons and the Black Mountains, this old inn is run as a dining pub by brothers Charles and Edmund Inkin. Chef Simon Potter has simplified the food, focusing on local suppliers and the inn's organic kitchen garden. His short supper menu might include tartare of locally smoked salmon; wild halibut, young summer vegetables, lemon butter.
*Read more: page 426.*

## THE BELL AT SKENFRITH
SKENFRITH

Janet and William Hutchings's white-painted 17th-century coaching inn is by an old stone bridge in a village in the Welsh Marches. The chef, Rupert Taylor, who has worked at *Fifteen* and *The Fat Duck*, 'takes his inspiration from the inn's organic kitchen garden and local produce' for his modern dishes, perhaps sirloin of Brecon beef, miniature cottage pie, horseradish mash, braised savoy cabbage.
*Read more: page 450.*

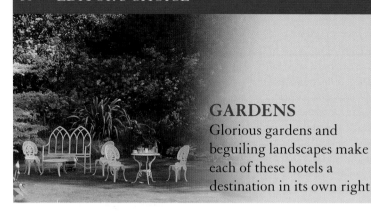

# GARDENS
Glorious gardens and beguiling landscapes make each of these hotels a destination in its own right

**BARNSLEY HOUSE**
BARNSLEY

The Cotswold home of the late Rosemary Verey, acclaimed garden designer and author, is now run as a luxury hotel. The gardens remain true to her creation of layered (sometimes self-seeding) planting that creates colour and interest in every season. Her bold approach is reflected in a mix of features, including a laburnum walk, a temple with a pool, a potager and a knot garden.
*Read more: page 86.*

**LINDETH FELL**
BOWNESS-ON-WINDERMERE

Diana Kennedy's Edwardian house stands in lovely grounds overlooking Lake Windermere. The gardens were laid out by Thomas Mawson (a renowned Windermere landscape gardener), who filled them with rhododendrons, azaleas and specimen trees. When at its best, in spring and early summer, it is open to the public. A small lake is a haunt for wildlife. Lawns are laid for bowls and croquet.
*Read more: page 111.*

**HOB GREEN**
MARKINGTON

With wide views across a valley, this traditional 18th-century hotel owned by the Hutchinson family has award-winning gardens in 800-acre grounds. Walkways and paths lead through extensive herbaceous borders to feature lawns. The garden has a rockery, a pergola; a large greenhouse, and a walled kitchen garden. Beyond are woodlands and a farm.
*Read more: page 224.*

**MEUDON**
MAWNAN SMITH

At the head of a wooded valley leading to a private beach, the Pilgrim family's traditional hotel has a fine example of a Cornish 'hanging garden'. It was designed by Robert Were Fox, who planted specimens from early RHS expeditions to the Yangtze and the Himalayas. Giant Australian tree ferns were brought as ballast by packet ships to Falmouth, and thrown overboard in the bay. There are many rare shrubs, plants and trees.
*Read more: page 231.*

## HOTEL ENDSLEIGH
MILTON ABBOT

Humphry Repton was commissioned by the Duchess of Bedford to design the gardens for this shooting and fishing lodge in an extensive wooded estate running down to the River Tamar. It is now run by Olga Polizzi as a luxury hotel. Repton created forested walks, wild meadows, a rose and jasmine walkway. There are rare and grand trees, a parterre beside the veranda, and a shell-covered summer house.
*Read more: page 234.*

## MILLGATE HOUSE
RICHMOND

Just off the town's cobbled square, this Georgian house has an award-winning sheltered walled garden renowned for its clever planting. Owners Austin Lynch and Tim Culkin open it to the public from April to October. Guests can enjoy the garden in all seasons. Meandering paths lead through luxuriant planting; two of the three bedrooms overlook the garden and beyond to the River Swale and the Cleveland hills.
*Read more: page 275.*

## STONE HOUSE
RUSHLAKE GREEN

Visitors to Jane and Peter Dunn's 15th-century house (with 18th-century modifications) are encouraged to explore the huge grounds. They have an ornamental lake, gazebos, a rose garden, a 100-foot herbaceous border, a walled herb, vegetable and fruit garden. In warm weather, guests can sit in the summer house, and visit the greenhouses.
*Read more: page 282.*

## RAMPSBECK
WATERMILLOCK

On the shore of Lake Ullswater, this elegant 18th-century house stands in extensive parkland and gardens. The formal gardens are divided by yew hedges; stone steps give access to different levels. The flower beds on the Dial Lawn are informally planted in pastel shades. The rose garden has 12 geometric beds under-planted with cottage garden plants.
*Read more: page 324.*

## BODYSGALLEN HALL AND SPA
LLANDUDNO

'Beautifully situated' in parkland and gardens with views of Snowdonia and Conwy, this Grade I listed 17th-century mansion is now owned by the National Trust. A rare parterre of box hedges is filled with sweet-scented herbs; there's a walled rose garden; interesting trees including medlar and mulberry; a rockery with a cascade.
*Read more: page 434.*

## CASHEL HOUSE
CASHEL BAY

In a sheltered bay on the Connemara coast, the McEvilly family's 19th-century manor house has rambling gardens, which are 'full of surprises'. Kay McEvilly runs the house and takes a keen interest in the gardens which were planted by a previous owner, Jim O'Mara, a parliamentarian and keen botanist. There are exotic flowing shrubs, camellias, rare magnolias, woodland walks. Mrs McEvilly delights in sharing the gardens with guests.
*Read more: page 471.*

## FISHING
No need to cast around for the best beats; these hotels all have private access to rivers and lakes

### THE ARUNDELL ARMS
LIFTON

Adam Fox-Edwards has taken over the running of this sporting hotel from his mother, Anne Voss-Bark, whose passion for fishing inspired it for half a century. It has 20 miles of water on the Tamar and six of its tributaries. The sea trout pools on the River Lyd beats were given a facelift this year. Fishing courses are run for all levels, tackle is sold and maps are provided.
*Read more: page 208.*

### HOTEL ENDSLEIGH
MILTON ABBOT

Built as a shooting and fishing lodge by the Duchess of Bedford, Olga Polizzi's luxurious hotel is a member of the Endsleigh fishing club. It has seven rods on eight miles of the River Tamar (some of the best salmon and sea trout fishing in England). The club's ghillie is available to assist guests.
*Read more: page 234.*

### THE INN AT WHITEWELL
WHITEWELL

Charles Bowman's quirky 300-year-old inn stands high above the River Hodder in the Forest of Bowland. The inn has seven miles of river with 14 pools and 'lots of interesting runs'. There are four rods on the Hodder for trout, sea trout and salmon in season. The inn is filled with family antiques, old paintings, oriental rugs. There is plenty of room to relax in the public areas.
*Read more: page 327.*

### TOMDOUN HOTEL
INVERGARRY

Ghillie Peter Thomas can supply tackle as well as local knowledge at this simple sporting hotel off a single-track drovers' road to Skye. Fishermen have access to 25,000 acres of water on the Upper Garry and six hill lochs where they can fish from a boat or on the bank. A three-day course for beginners covers both loch and river fishing. *Tomdoun* is 'an interesting, quirky place in a stunning setting'. Facilities are limited (no TV, telephone, etc, in the bedrooms).
*Read more: page 373.*

### ARDANAISEIG
KILCHRENAN

Owned by Bennie Gray, this stone baronial mansion stands in a beautiful garden on Loch Awe, noted for its wild brown trout. Boats are available for

fishing on the loch where perch and pike abound (also rouge rainbow trout escapees from fish farms). There is a small trout lochan for fly-casting.
*Read more: page 377.*

## GLIFFAES
CRICKHOWELL

This smart sporting hotel stands in wooded grounds on a broad sweep of the Usk, one of the best brown trout rivers in England and Wales. It has two private stretches on the river, one immediately below the hotel. The Usk's spawning grounds have been revitalised by a European-funded programme. Three-day fly-fishing courses are held for beginners. Visitors like the 'homely feel, nothing formal or starchy'. The best bedrooms have a river view and balcony.
*Read more: page 422.*

## TYNYCORNEL
TALYLLYN

On the shore of 222-acre Lake Talyllyn (which it owns), this white-fronted inn has been a fishing hostelry since 1800. The lake is famed for its natural brown trout fisheries. It is at the head of Afon Dysynni, a river famed for its sea trout. Tuition, tackle and picnic lunches are available. There is a drying room and freezer facilities. Fishing stories aplenty can be heard in the bar. 'It deserves its place in the *Guide* for the location alone.'
*Read more: page 452.*

## BALLYVOLANE HOUSE
CASTLELYONS

Justin and Jenny Green have four beats on a 24-mile stretch of the Blackwater, the finest salmon fishing river in

Ireland. These are available at all times in season. When conditions on the river are impossible, there is fly-fishing for rainbow trout on three lakes in the grounds. The Greens run their Georgian home on house-party lines.
*Read more: page 473.*

## NEWPORT HOUSE
NEWPORT

Thelma and Kieran Thompson hold the fishing rights to eight miles of the River Newport and also have fishing on Lough Beltra West, one of the few fisheries in Ireland where salmon can be fished from a boat. 'All our fish are wild; we do not stock or ranch the system,' they say. Their Georgian mansion is liked for the unstuffy atmosphere.
*Read more: page 498.*

## CURRAREVAGH HOUSE
OUGHTERARD

In a glorious setting of lake, lawns and woodland, the Hodgson family combine friendliness with professionalism at their early Victorian manor house. The fishing on Lough Corrib, an important wild brown trout lake, is a major draw. The family have their own boats and ghillies on the lake, which also has pike, perch and a small run of salmon from May to July. Visitors like the 'easy charm, the welcoming atmosphere, and the beauty of the setting'. Many of the bedrooms have views of the lough.
*Read more: page 499.*

# WALKING
Your boots are meant for walking at these hotels which cater for the serious and the casual walker alike

## BIGGIN HALL
BIGGIN-BY-HARTINGTON

High in the Peak District, this small hotel is popular with walkers for its 'simple, unfussy' style. Footpaths lead in all directions over beautiful countryside; disused railway tracks nearby provide flat walking. The 17th-century house has antiques, attractive public rooms. Bedrooms in a barn conversion have a porch.
*Read more: page 102.*

## SEATOLLER HOUSE
BORROWDALE

Away from the main tourist areas, this unpretentious guest house is at the head of the beautiful Borrowdale valley. Walkers and climbers have enjoyed the camaraderie and good value for more than a century. It is free of 'modern intrusions' like television and radio. Dinner is taken with 'a degree of do-it-yourself conviviality' at two oak tables. There is non-stop coffee (which can be taken out in a flask) and an honesty bar.
*Read more: page 106.*

## UNDERLEIGH HOUSE
HOPE

'Generous' hosts Philip and Vivienne Taylor provide maps and packed lunches for walkers at their barn and cottage conversion in the Hope valley in the Peak District national park. All bedrooms have fine views over the garden and surrounding countryside. The Thornhill Suite has direct access from outside via a stone staircase, an adjoining lounge. 'Our waterproofs were taken away to be dried.' Good walking starts at the door.
*Read more: page 189.*

## OVERWATER HALL
IREBY

In a quieter part of the northern Lake District, this castellated Georgian mansion stands in large grounds beside Overwater Tarn, close to Bassenthwaite Lake. There is good walking (and climbing) in every direction. Lovers of wildlife will enjoy sighting red squirrels in the grounds. Ordnance Survey maps are made available to guests.
*Read more: page 194.*

## LASTINGHAM GRANGE
LASTINGHAM

In large grounds on the edge of the North Yorkshire Moors national park, this traditional hotel is run by Bertie Wood, helped by his mother, Jane, and brother, Tom. There is excellent walking in the moors and dales. Guided walks are available: perhaps a llama trek on the moors, or a dawn safari through forest and woodland, returning in time for breakfast.
*Read more: page 201.*

## HEDDON'S GATE HOTEL
MARTINHOE

On the steep slopes of the heavily wooded Heddon valley, this former Victorian hunting lodge is a walker's paradise. Superb walks begin at the door, or you can venture out to explore Exmoor. Return in time for an 'excellent' afternoon tea (complimentary). The traditional hotel is 'comfortable and quiet' (no mobile phone signal; poor TV reception): the old-fashioned decor is 'not for modernists'.
*Read more: page 225.*

## HAZEL BANK
ROSTHWAITE

There is immediate access from the grounds to many well-known peaks from this Lakeland grey stone house in a wooded Borrowdale location. The owners, Rob van der Palen and Anton Renac (the chef), are 'friendly and relaxed'. There are pleasant walks along the River Derwent, up the Langstrath or over to Watendlath. The cooking is much admired. Packed lunches are available.
*Read more: page 280.*

## HOWTOWN HOTEL
ULLSWATER

Popular with walkers (a car-free holiday is possible), this unsophisticated hotel on the quiet eastern shore of Lake Ullswater is run in relaxed style by Jacquie Baldry and her son, David. Walkers can ask for a substantial picnic before heading out along the shores of the lake, or on to the wooded hillside. There is no phone, television or radio in the simple bedrooms, most of which have lake views.
*Read more: page 316.*

## DEESIDE HOTEL
BALLATER

In the delightful mountainous countryside of the Cairngorm national park, this Victorian house is run as a 'home from home' by Gordon Waddell (the chef) and Penella Price ('unfailingly pleasant'). They promise 'great walks for all ages and of varying degrees of exertion': three start from the back gate. Drying facilities and packed lunches are available.
*Read more: page 347.*

## PEN-Y-GWRYD HOTEL
NANT GWYNANT

An institution among the climbing and walking fraternity, this old inn is run by brothers Rupert and Nicolas Pullee, who have taken on day-to-day responsibility from their parents. It was the training base for the 1953 Everest expedition. Any child under 13 who climbs Snowdon is inducted in the Snowdon Club. Substantial packed lunches.
*Read more: page 440.*

## GOLF
At these places golfers can enjoy some of the best courses on these islands

**THE MOUNT**
BIDEFORD
Andrew and Heather Laugharne can arrange discounts for their guests at the Royal North Devon course at Westward Ho. The fast greens at the course, the oldest links in England, are at their most testing when the wind blows. The second green, shaped like a small upturned saucer, is especially hard to hold. The Laugharnes' handsome Georgian house stands in part-walled gardens close to the town centre.
*Read more: page 99.*

**TREGLOS HOTEL**
CONSTANTINE BAY
At Jim and Rose Barlow's traditional hotel on the north Cornwall coast, guests are given special rates to the family's Merlin Golf and Country Club nearby. This hilltop heathland course is particularly good for beginners, who can sign up for tuition. Other excellent courses are within easy driving distance.
*Read more: page 145.*

**BUDOCK VEAN**
MAWNAN SMITH
PGA professional David Short offers three-day golf schools and a free winter workshop at the attractive nine-hole parkland course in the grounds of Martin and Amanda Barlow's traditional hotel. He organises competition weeks played over four local courses. Hotel guests also qualify for reduced green fees at several nearby clubs.
*Read more: page 230.*

**THE CLEEVE HOUSE**
MORTEHOE
Golfers can choose between the challenges of links or parkland courses at this small, unpretentious hotel in a village above Woolacombe. For a full day's golf, play the two championship links courses (East and West) at nearby Saunton; parkland courses include Ilfracombe, a relatively short but testing layout with spectacular views over the Bristol Channel.
*Read more: page 240.*

**GILPIN HOTEL AND LAKE HOUSE**
WINDERMERE
The entrance to Windermere golf club is almost opposite this Edwardian country house hotel. Golfing breaks with tuition are offered at the undulating

course, described as 'Gleneagles in miniature'. It may appear short, but it is challenging, with narrow fairways, natural water hazards and blind second shots into greens.
*Read more: page 331.*

## GLENAPP CASTLE
BALLANTRAE

Some of Scotland's best links courses are within easy reach of this 19th-century baronial castle (now a luxury hotel) in South Ayrshire. They include Turnberry, a regular venue for the Open championship. Tee times can be arranged here and at Royal Troon, another historic Open venue. Guests have access to the private course at nearby Caley Palace.
*Read more: page 346.*

## 2 QUAIL
DORNOCH

Enthusiastic golfers, Michael and Kerensa Carr run their Victorian stone house in this seaside town as a licensed B&B. They no longer have a restaurant, as Mr Carr has taken the position of executive chef at the historic Royal Dornoch championship golf course. Visiting golfers can sample his style of cooking after a round on these famous links which have been played since 1616. The former Open champion Tom Watson is among the leading golfers who like to play the course.
*Read more: page 357.*

## THE DOWER HOUSE
MUIR OF ORD

Robyn and Mena Aitchison are friendly hosts at their gabled cottage-orné in a large garden bordered by two rivers.

He is a keen golfer and can advise guests on the 25 courses within an hour's drive. Try the championship links at Nairn, which has hosted the Walker Cup: you can see the Moray Firth from every hole, and it is possible to strike the ball into the sea on the first seven.
*Read more: page 386.*

## TREFEDDIAN HOTEL
ABERDYFI

Guests at this large, traditional Edwardian hotel are given concessionary rates at Aberdyfi links course, which lies below the hotel on the dunes of Cardigan Bay. The toughest test is the 12th, a par-3 to an elevated green with the sea to the right, and a steep bank to the left that kicks away anything other than the correct shot. Younger players can limber up on the pitch-and-putt course in the grounds.
*Read more: page 411.*

## STELLA MARIS
BALLYCASTLE

Golf memorabilia and photographs are on the walls of this converted 19th-century coastguard station in north Mayo. Each of the bedrooms is named after a golf course. Terence McSweeney, who runs it with his wife, Frances Kelly, is a sports writer and works for the US PGA in Florida during the winter. He can guide golfers to the world-class links at Enniscrone and Carne and, further afield, Rosses Point and Westport. A 100-foot conservatory along the front of the building has uninterrupted views across the bay.
*Read more: page 464.*

## DOGS

No need to leave your best friend behind when visiting these hotels where dogs command special treatment

### THE REGENT
AMBLESIDE

Dog owners can come and go as they please from courtyard rooms at Christine Hewitt's hotel opposite a slipway on Lake Windermere. 'We are a family of dog lovers and we welcome dogs,' she says. 'We can prepare food for dogs the same as their owners; special requests and diets are no problem.' Visiting dogs can run 'tail-waggingly free' on Borrans Park and Bird House Meadow, a short stroll from the door.
*Read more: page 76.*

### BLAGDON MANOR
ASHWATER

*Blagdon* loves dogs,' say Liz and Steve Morey at their 17th-century manor house in rolling north Devon countryside. The resident chocolate Labradors, Nutmeg, Cassia and Mace, 'look forward to meeting new friends'. Canine visitors are given a fleece blanket, towel, dog bowl and treats 'to make sure their stay is as comfortable as yours'. Good walking in 17 acres of open fields leading from the garden.
*Read more: page 82.*

### COMBE HOUSE
GITTISHAM

A thatched cottage in the grounds of Ken and Ruth Hunt's Grade I listed Elizabethan manor house is recommended for guests with 'doggy friends'. The cottage has a walled garden where pets can safely play. Visiting dogs are given a 'welcome pack'. There is excellent walking on the large estate of woodland and pastures.
*Read more: page 171.*

### OVERWATER HALL
IREBY

'Well-behaved' dogs are 'genuinely welcomed, on or off the leash' at this castellated Georgian mansion in an isolated part of the northern Lake District. Pets are allowed in the bedrooms and one of the lounges (but no sitting on chairs). They can enjoy (unleashed) the 18-acre grounds, including a woodland boardwalk. A dog-sitting service is offered for 'those rainy days when you want to visit an art gallery'.
*Read more: page 194.*

## PEN-Y-DYFFRYN
### OSWESTRY

This country hotel is popular with dog owners, whose pets stay free of charge. Four bedrooms in a coach house, each with a private patio, open on to the gardens, which are safe from passing traffic. The former Georgian rectory is on the last hill in Shropshire, close to the Welsh border. There is good walking from the door, including the circular Offa's Dyke Path.
*Read more: page 256.*

## THE BOAR'S HEAD
### RIPLEY

Dogs are allowed in two courtyard rooms at Sir Thomas and Lady Ingilby's 'elegant but not stuffy' old inn in a model village on their castle estate. These rooms may be smallish, but a 'turn-down Bonio is placed in each dog's basket, and water bowls are provided'. Owners must be 'well trained'. The inn is a combination of pub and country hotel. The management is 'cheerful, enlightened and inspirational'.
*Read more: page 276.*

## PLUMBER MANOR
### STURMINSTER NEWTON

Visitors bringing their pet can stay in a courtyard bedroom at this 17th-century manor house. These rooms have direct access to the well-kept gardens and the car park. 'Dogs will love it here,' say the Prideaux-Brune family owners, who have two resident black Labradors. Visiting dogs are not allowed in the main house.
*Read more: page 306.*

## THE BONHAM
### EDINBURGH

'The demand for pooch-friendly hotels' is recognised at this town house hotel in a quiet square near the West End. A 'doggy dreams' package includes a welcome toy and treat, a dog bed and advice from the concierge on walks and grooming parlours. Chefs will prepare a 'luxury' bowl of meat, vegetables and gravy for an 'in-room meal'.
*Read more: page 362.*

## KILCAMB LODGE
### STRONTIAN

The outdoor life of the Highlands 'simply has to be shared with your best pal', say Sally and David Fox, whose old stone lodge is on the shore of Loch Sunart. Towels are provided for drying pets after swimming from the hotel's own beach. The gardens are 'perfect for exercising your dog': there are no flower beds or ornamental gardens 'to worry about'. Visitors may find some doggy treats in the bedroom. Six rooms have loch views; three face the gardens.
*Read more: page 401.*

## RATHMULLAN HOUSE
### RATHMULLAN

A superior doggy room in a courtyard extension with a patio door leading to the garden is provided at the Wheeler family's handsome white mansion. Dogs have a 'room within a room', with a bed and toys, and a doormat decorated with patterns of paws. They also have an outdoor area to run around in; pooper-scoopers are provided for owners whose canines prefer to roam on a two-mile sandy beach.
*Read more: page 501.*

# TENNIS AND SWIMMING

Each of these hotels has a tennis court (T) and/or a swimming pool (S)

**LONDON**
**One Aldwych** (S)

**ENGLAND**
**Regent,**
  Ambleside (S)
**Hartwell House,**
  Aylesbury (T,S)
**Bath Priory,**
  Bath (S)
**West Coates,**
  Berwick-upon-Tweed (S)
**Burgh Island,**
  Bigbury-on-Sea (T,S)
**Blakeney,**
  Blakeney (S)
**Frogg Manor,**
  Broxton (T)
**Hell Bay,**
  Bryer (S)
**Brockencote Hall,**
  Chaddesley Corbett (T)
**Gidleigh Park,**
  Chagford (T)
**Tor Cottage,**
  Chillaton (S)
**Treglos,**
  Constantine Bay (S)
**Corse Lawn House,**
  Corse Lawn (T,S)
**Rectory,**
  Crudwell (S)

**Old Whyly,**
  East Hoathly (T,S)
**Summer Lodge,**
  Evershot (T,S)
**Evesham,**
  Evesham (S)
**Moonfleet Manor,**
  Fleet (T,S)
**Stock Hill House,**
  Gillingham (T)
**Hambleton Hall,**
  Hambleton (T,S)
**Pheasant,**
  Harome (S)
**Feversham Arms,**
  Helmsley (S)
**Esseborne Manor,**
  Hurstbourne Tarrant (T)
**Ilsington Country House,**
  Ilsington (S)
**Augill Castle,**
  Kirkby Stephen (T)
**Feathers,**
  Ledbury (S)
**Bedruthan Steps,**
  Mawgan Porth (T,S)
**Scarlet,**
  Mawgan Porth (T)
**Budock Vean,**
  Mawnan Smith (T,S)
**TerraVina,**
  Netley Marsh (S)

Hotel Penzance,
  Penzance (S)
Ennys,
  St Hilary (T,S)
Star Castle,
  St Mary's (T,S)
Tides Reach,
  Salcombe (S)
Soar Mill Cove,
  Soar Mill Cove (T,S)
Plumber Manor,
  Sturminster Newton (T)
Launceston Farm,
  Tarrant Launceston (S)
Calcot Manor,
  Tetbury (T,S)
Nare,
  Veryan-in-Roseland (T,S)
Gilpin Hotel and Lake House,
  Windermere (S)
Watersmeet,
  Woolacombe (S)
Middlethorpe Hall,
  York (S)

**SCOTLAND**
Glenapp Castle,
  Ballantrae (T)
Kinloch House,
  Blairgowrie (S)
Greshornish House,
  Edinbane (T)
Isle of Eriska,
  Eriska (T,S)
Eaglescairnie Mains,
  Gifford (T)
Ardanaiseig,
  Kilchrenan (T)
New Lanark Mill,
  Lanark (S)
Kirroughtree House,
  Newton Stewart (T)
Skirling House,
  Skirling (T)

**WALES**
Trefeddian,
  Aberdyfi (T,S)
Porth Tocyn Hotel,
  Abersoch (T,S)
Sychnant Pass Country House,
  Conwy (S)
Glangrwyney Court,
  Crickhowell (T)
Gliffaes,
  Crickhowell (T)
Bodysgallen Hall and Spa,
  Llandudno (T,S)
St Tudno,
  Llandudno (S)
Lake,
  Llangammarch Wells (T,S)
Portmeirion Hotel,
  Portmeirion (S)

**CHANNEL ISLANDS**
White House,
  Herm (T,S)
Atlantic,
  St Brelade (T,S)
Longueville Manor,
  St Saviour (T,S)

**IRELAND**
Cashel House,
  Cashel Bay (T)
Marlfield House,
  Gorey (T)
Shelburne Lodge,
  Kenmare (T)
Rosleague Manor,
  Letterfrack (T)
Currarevagh House,
  Oughterard (T)
Rathmullan House,
  Rathmullan (T,S)
Coopershill,
  Riverstown (T)
Ballymaloe House,
  Shanagarry (T,S)

# DISABLED FACILITIES

Each of these hotels has at least one bedroom equipped for a visitor in a wheelchair. You should telephone to discuss individual requirements

**LONDON**
**Goring**
**Montague on the Gardens**
**One Aldwych**
**Zetter**

**ENGLAND**
**Wentworth,**
  Aldeburgh
**Rothay Manor,**
  Ambleside
**Hartwell House,**
  Aylesbury
**Bath Priory,**
  Bath
**Leathes Head,**
  Borrowdale
**Millstream,**
  Bosham
**White Horse,**
  Brancaster Staithe
**Frogg Manor,**
  Broxton
**Hell Bay,**
  Bryher
**Blackmore Farm,**
  Cannington
**Brockencote Hall,**
  Chaddesley Corbett

**Gidleigh Park,**
  Chagford
**Beech House & Olive Branch,**
  Clipsham
**Treglos,**
  Constantine Bay
**Hipping Hall,**
  Cowan Bridge
**Clow Beck House,**
  Croft-on-Tees
**Coach House at Crookham,**
  Crookham
**Dart Marina,**
  Dartmouth
**Fallen Angel,**
  Durham
**Summer Lodge,**
  Evershot
**Evesham,**
  Evesham
**Angel Inn,**
  Hetton
**Byfords,**
  Holt
**Salthouse Harbour,**
  Ipswich
**Hope Street,**
  Liverpool

**Lime Wood,**
  Lyndhurst
**Cottage in the Wood,**
  Malvern Wells
**Swinton Park,**
  Masham
**Bedruthan Steps,**
  Mawgan Porth
**Scarlet,**
  Mawgan Porth
**Meudon,**
  Mawnan Smith
**Manor House,**
  Moreton-in-Marsh
**Redesdale Arms,**
  Moreton-in-Marsh
**Cleeve House,**
  Mortehoe
**TerraVina,**
  Netley Marsh
**Jesmond Dene House,**
  Newcastle upon Tyne
**Three Choirs Vineyards,**
  Newent
**Beechwood,**
  North Walsham
**Hart's,**
  Nottingham
**Grange at Oborne,**
  Oborne

Malmaison,
  Oxford
Old Bank,
  Oxford
Old Parsonage,
  Oxford
Seafood Restaurant,
  Padstow
Elephant,
  Pangbourne
Penzance,
  Penzance
Old Railway Station,
  Petworth
Black Swan,
  Ravenstonedale
Bourgoyne,
  Reeth
St Michael's Manor,
  St Albans
Seaview,
  Seaview
Rose & Crown,
  Snettisham
Titchwell Manor,
  Titchwell
Nare,
  Veryan-in-Roseland
Watersmeet,
  Woolacombe
Old Vicarage,
  Worfield
Dean Court,
  York
Middlethorpe Hall,
  York

SCOTLAND
Boath House,
  Auldearn
Dunvalanree in Carradale,
  Carradale

Three Chimneys and
  House Over-By,
  Dunvegan
Bonham,
  Edinburgh
Lovat,
  Fort Augustus
Lynnfield,
  Kirkwall
New Lanark Mill,
  Lanark
Langass Lodge,
  Locheport
Craigatin House,
  Pitlochry
Viewfield House,
  Portree
Skirling House,
  Skirling
Torridon,
  Torridon

WALES
Harbourmaster,
  Aberaeron
Ye Olde Bulls Head,
  Beaumaris
Hand at Llanarmon,
  Llanarmon Dyffryn
  Ceiriog
Bodysgallen Hall & Spa,
  Llandudno
Lake,
  Llangammarch Wells
Hafod Elwy Hall,
  Pentrefoelas
Portmeirion,
  Portmeirion

CHANNEL ISLANDS
Braye Beach,
  Braye

IRELAND
Mustard Seed at Echo
  Lodge,
  Ballingarry
Stella Maris,
  Ballycastle
Seaview House,
  Ballylickey
Quay House,
  Clifden
Rayanne House,
  Holywood
Sheedy's,
  Lisdoonvarna
Rathmullan House,
  Rathmullan
Barberstown Castle,
  Straffan

# LONDON

London has more than its share of faceless corporate hotels. If you know where to look, you can still find places of character reflecting the vision of hands-on owners. *Number Sixteen*, part of Tim and Kit Kemp's personally run Firmdale group, is our London hotel of the year for the attention to detail and the outstanding service.

# LONDON

## THE ARCH

**NEW**

In a residential street near Marble Arch, seven elegant Georgian town houses have been converted into a designer hotel. Owned by AB Hotels, it is managed by Beccy Gunn. Regular *Guide* reporters, 'tempted by an opening rate', in early 2010 were impressed: 'The warm welcome included a greeting by the manager. The attractive public rooms are decorated with humour: quirky sculptures, unusual works of art; background music (groan!) except in the beautiful library.' Each bedroom is done in one of ten colour schemes. 'The decor in our room was eclectic, confusing; furniture of conflicting designs; the dots on the wool throw clashed with the stripes of the cushions. The lighting was good, and storage was carefully thought out; a well-stocked bathroom. My husband was impressed by the high-tech features; I was more impressed by the coffee machine and the fresh milk in the fridge.' Breakfast has 'an imaginative hot menu, excellent coffee, an impressive range of cereals, fruits, etc; delicious jams in little Kilner jars'. The restaurant, *HUNter 486*, has a British menu (eg, fish pie) plus some fancier fare. (*Wendy Ashworth*)

50 Great Cumberland Place
London W1H 7FD

T: 020-7724 4700
F: 020-7724 4744
E: info@thearchlondon.com
W: www.thearchlondon.com

BEDROOMS: 82, 2 suitable for &.
OPEN: all year.
FACILITIES: lobby, lounge, library, restaurant.
BACKGROUND MUSIC: in public areas.
LOCATION: near Marble Arch, underground Marble Arch.
CHILDREN: all ages welcomed.
DOGS: allowed, assistance dogs only in public areas.
CREDIT CARDS: all major cards.
PRICES: [2010] room (*excluding VAT*) £180–£350, breakfast £10–£18.95, set meals £16.50–£19.50, full alc £50, weekend rates (including breakfast), Christmas/New Year packages.

# LONDON

## THE CAPITAL

*❦César award in 2008*

'We were very happy with our visit,' says a trusted correspondent returning this year to David Levin's discreet hotel in a side street near Harrods. A liveried footman ushers guests into a small entrance hall with an open fire. 'Reception staff and the concierge were exceeding helpful.' Mr Levin has been joined this year by his daughter, Kate, as manager. The bedrooms are luxurious: 'We had a very nice junior suite, with well-made reproduction antique furniture and comfortable chairs. It was tasteful, with elegant marble fittings in the bathroom.' Jerome Ponchelle has taken over as chef in the restaurant, cooking 'outstanding' dishes in 'classic British and French style with robust flavours', eg, roast fillet of lamb 'Grand-Mère', lemon thyme sauce, gratin dauphinoise. Dinner in the less formal brasserie was 'enjoyed very much'. At lunchtime from Friday to Sunday a silver trolley service with seasonal dishes has been reintroduced. A 'good' breakfast buffet has fruit salad, yogurts, cereals and fruit juices. Mr Levin also owns *The Levin*, next door (see entry). (*Wolfgang Stroebe*)

22–24 Basil Street
London SW3 1AT

T: 020-7589 5171
F: 020-7225 0011
E: reservations@capitalhotel.co.uk
W: www.capitalhotel.co.uk

BEDROOMS: 49.
OPEN: all year.
FACILITIES: lift, sitting room, bar, restaurant, brasserie/bar next door, 2 private dining rooms, only restaurant suitable for &.
BACKGROUND MUSIC: none.
LOCATION: central, underground Knightsbridge, private car park (£6 an hour, £30 a day).
CHILDREN: all ages welcomed.
DOGS: small dogs allowed.
CREDIT CARDS: all major cards.
PRICES: [2010] room £230–£455, breakfast £16–£19.50, set dinner £70 (*plus 12½ % discretionary service charge*), various packages – see website.

# LONDON

## CHURCH STREET HOTEL

'A lovely, unusual place to stay', José and Mel Raido's idiosyncratic hotel is on the corner of a busy ('far from glamorous') street near Camberwell Green in south London. The Greek/Spanish brothers have decorated in flamboyant style, with bright reds, ochres, dramatic blues and greens in the bedrooms, kitsch ornaments and paintings in the twisting corridors. They have 'created the feel of a Spanish or Cuban casita', said inspectors. The simply furnished bedrooms have 'good bedding' on metal-framed beds; 'nice details' include a hand-written note of welcome, a jar of hot sauce; the bathrooms have colourful tiles. Eight of the smaller rooms have shared bathrooms. Some walls are thin, and noise may be heard. The Havana lounge, with an honesty bar, has a high ceiling, colonial fans and oak blinds. The new restaurant, *Angels and Gypsies*, serves tapas dishes (eg, calamari Romana style; lavender- and rosemary-rubbed lamb cutlets with garlic aïoli). Breakfast in the *Havana* room is a help-yourself affair with organic breads and cereals, pastries, freshly squeezed juices and free-range eggs.

29–33 Camberwell Church Street
London SE5 8TR

T: 020-7703 5984
F: 020-7358-4110
E: info@churchstreethotel.com
W: www.churchstreethotel.com

BEDROOMS: 28.
OPEN: all year.
FACILITIES: lounge/breakfast room, unsuitable for &.
BACKGROUND MUSIC: relaxed in public areas.
LOCATION: Camberwell Green, underground Oval.
CHILDREN: all ages welcomed.
DOGS: not allowed.
CREDIT CARDS: Amex, MasterCard, Visa.
PRICES: B&B £50–£70 per person, weekend deals, Christmas/New Year packages.

**25% DISCOUNT VOUCHERS**

# LONDON

Map 2:D4

## DEAN STREET TOWNHOUSE NEW

Once owned by the Novello family, this Grade II Georgian building has been transformed into the latest offshoot of Nick Jones's *Soho House*; all-comers are welcomed, though club members get preferential rates. 'The style is surprisingly traditional,' say inspectors in 2010. 'The lobby is more London club than boutique hotel; light wooden panelling, reclaimed oak floors, armchairs in discreet corners.' The 'broom cupboard' is the smallest room: others come in four sizes (and prices): tiny, small, medium, bigger. The tiny room, 'dominated by an enormous bed', is 'best for people on the move'. A small room 'was bigger than it sounds, with considerable character; a folksy feel (sage-patterned wallpaper, soft seagrass carpet). A very comfortable bed; generous extras in an immaculate bathroom. The only weakness was a lack of storage (a brass rack with five hangers).' Tables must be booked in advance for the dining room which has 'the buzz of a Parisian brasserie'. The dishes are English: 'Highlights were a light smoked haddock mousse with a buttery sauce; cod with mussels, a shellfish and chervil sauce.' An à la carte breakfast was 'superb'.

69–71 Dean Street
London W1D 3SE

T: 020-7434 1775
E: info@deanstreettownhouse.com
W: www.deanstreettownhouse.com

BEDROOMS: 39.
OPEN: all year.
FACILITIES: lifts, lobby, dining room, private dining room.
BACKGROUND MUSIC: in dining room.
LOCATION: Soho, underground Piccadilly Circus.
CHILDREN: all ages welcomed.
DOGS: only guide dogs allowed.
CREDIT CARDS: Amex, MasterCard, Visa.
PRICES: [2010] room £90–£270, alc breakfast £12–£15, full alc £40.

# LONDON

Map 2:D4

## DURRANTS

❧ *César award in 2010*

'Long may it continue in a world of corporate sameness and excessive trendiness.' Praise in 2010 for the Miller family's traditional hotel, a conversion of four Georgian houses just north of Oxford Street. Ian McIntosh is the manager; 'smiles abound' among his staff. 'The bar is a lovely place to come to after a day out and around.' Another comment: '*Durrants* will always endear itself to those with a weak spot for faded English style. It does keep up to date with the important things: the beds are good quality with plump pillows, silky bedlinen; bathrooms are modern and work; proper keys.' The bedrooms vary greatly in style and size. 'We were enchanted with our large room, full of light; a great bathroom overlooking the mews at the back.' Front rooms might get some traffic noise. Generous portions of international dishes are served in the restaurant (eg, grilled fillet of beef with truffle mash). The 'good' breakfast is served at table; 'no buffet with guests jostling one another over the muesli'. (*Mary Wilmer, Laura Gordon, Ralph Kenber*)

26–32 George Street
London W1H 5BJ

**T:** 020-7935 8131
**F:** 020-7487 3510
**E:** enquiries@durrantshotel.co.uk
**W:** www.durrantshotel.co.uk

**BEDROOMS:** 92, 7 on ground floor.
**OPEN:** all year, restaurant closed 25 Dec evening.
**FACILITIES:** lifts, ramp, bar, restaurant, lounge, 5 function rooms.
**BACKGROUND MUSIC:** none.
**LOCATION:** off Oxford Street, underground Bond Street, Baker Street.
**CHILDREN:** all ages welcomed.
**DOGS:** only guide dogs allowed.
**CREDIT CARDS:** Amex, MasterCard, Visa.
**PRICES:** [2010] room £125– £425, breakfast £13.50–£17, full alc £50 (*excluding 'optional' 12½ % service charge*), weekend offers.

# LONDON

Map 2:D4

## THE GORING

♀ *César award in 1994*

Jeremy Goring is the fourth generation of his family to run this traditional hotel, which celebrated its centenary in 2010. It is close to Buckingham Palace (famously, royal visitors have been said to prefer the comforts of the hotel, the first in the world to have private bathrooms). It is liked by *Guide* readers for the 'good old-fashioned ambience', the 'welcoming family feel'. 'Worth every pound, professional in all respects,' is a typical comment. The managing director, David Morgan-Hewitt, has been at the *Goring* for 20 years; many of the staff are long-serving. The bedrooms, individually designed, capture 'the residential atmosphere of an English country house'. Some have a private terrace, many face the garden. The dining room, which has glass chandeliers by Swarovski, was designed by David Linley. Chef Derek Quelch serves traditional British dishes, eg, glazed Scottish lobster omelette; boiled Lincolnshire ham knuckle, creamed potatoes, mustard sauce. Breakfast has a 'mind-boggling selection of fruits'. Children are welcomed with a story library, an activity book and a gift bag. (*BP, DC*)

Beeston Place
Grosvenor Gardens
London SW1W 0JW

T: 020-7396 9000
F: 020-7834 4393
E: reception@thegoring.com
W: www.thegoring.com

BEDROOMS: 71, 2 suitable for &.
OPEN: all year.
FACILITIES: lift, ramps, lounge bar, terrace room, restaurant, function facilities, civil wedding licence.
BACKGROUND MUSIC: none.
LOCATION: near Victoria Station, garage, mews parking, underground Victoria.
CHILDREN: all ages welcomed.
DOGS: not allowed.
CREDIT CARDS: all major cards.
PRICES: [2010] room (*excluding VAT*) £199–£345, breakfast £23, set dinner £47.50, Christmas/New Year packages.

# LONDON

Map 2:D4

## HAZLITT'S

❦ *César award in 2002*

'You rarely see or hear other guests; it feels more like a private club than a hotel.' Peter McKay's stylish B&B hotel spreads over two 'beautifully adapted' historic buildings in Soho. An inspector enjoyed the 'discretion': no signage over the door. The 'welcoming foyer' has soft colours, fresh flowers, gilt-framed pictures. Reception is low-key but friendly ('always a greeting'). The bedrooms are traditionally furnished; panelled walls, mellow old furniture, sloping floorboards; some rooms are 'opulent and quirky'. Eight are in a 'seamless' extension, a conversion of a house to the side and back (with a lift). A small newer room was 'furnished with style, panelled walls, a 17th-century carved oak bed head, superb bedlinen and mattress, well-thought-out storage and fittings'. The Duke of Monmouth suite, on two storeys, has a roof garden with retractable glass roof. Breakfast ('simple and good') is delivered to the room: 'We had a lovely bowl of fresh berries, freshly squeezed orange and grapefruit juice, a bacon panini.' An oak-panelled library has an honesty bar. A room-service menu is available from 11 am to 10.30 pm.

6 Frith Street
London W1D 3JA

T: 020-7434 1771
F: 020-7439 1524
E: reservations@hazlitts.co.uk
W: www.hazlittshotel.com

BEDROOMS: 30, 2 on ground floor.
OPEN: all year.
FACILITIES: lift, sitting room, unsuitable for &.
BACKGROUND MUSIC: none.
LOCATION: Soho (front windows triple glazed, rear rooms quietest), NCP nearby, underground Tottenham Court Road, Leicester Square.
CHILDREN: all ages welcomed.
DOGS: not allowed.
CREDIT CARDS: all major cards.
PRICES: room (excluding VAT) £175–£750, breakfast £10.95, special breaks.

# LONDON

Map 2:D4

## THE LEVIN

On a quiet Knightsbridge street, this intimate hotel, named after its owner, David Levin, is next door to its grander sister, *The Capital* (see entry). Harald Duttine is the manager. 'Expensive, but it can't be faulted for service, room (especially the bed), facilities and location,' was an inspector's conclusion. A reader thought it 'a lovely place to stay'. The 'elegant' lobby has a wooden parquet floor, pistachio-coloured walls, comfortable settees and chairs (and books to borrow). A small old-fashioned lift leads to the 'well-equipped' bedrooms. 'Our room had a small hallway with a large wardrobe; a curved sofa by the bay window, modern silk/satin fabrics, dark wood furniture; a supremely comfortable bed. Everything you need in the well-lit bathroom.' Continental breakfast, included in the room rate, is available between 7.30 and 11.30 am in the basement brasserie, *Le Metro*, which is open to the public. It has a simple all-day menu with dishes like fishcakes with lime crème fraîche; sausages and mash with red onion gravy. Some wines come from David Levin's organic vineyard in the Loire valley. (*T and MH, and others*)

28 Basil Street
London SW3 1AS

T: 020-7589 6286
F: 020-7823 7826
E: reservations@thelevinhotel.co.uk
W: www.thelevinhotel.co.uk

**BEDROOMS:** 12.
**OPEN:** all year, restaurant closed Sun night and 24–26 Dec, 1 Jan.
**FACILITIES:** lobby, library, honesty bar, bar/brasserie (*Le Metro*), access to nearby health club/spa, unsuitable for &.
**BACKGROUND MUSIC:** none.
**LOCATION:** central, underground Knightsbridge (Harrods exit), private car park (£30 a night).
**CHILDREN:** all ages welcomed, under-12s must be accompanied by an adult, cot £30 per night.
**DOGS:** not allowed.
**CREDIT CARDS:** all major cards.
**PRICES:** [2010] B&B (*excluding VAT and 5% 'discretionary' service charge*) £122.50–£142.50 per person, full alc £25, seasonal offers, Christmas/New Year packages.

# LONDON

Map 2:D4

## THE MONTAGUE ON THE GARDENS  `NEW`

'Every time you go in, someone will say "hello" and ask if they can help; it's the sort of place that redeems your faith in London.' A report this year earns a full *Guide* entry for this Georgian town house near the British Museum. Part of the Red Carnation group, it is managed by Dirk Crokaert. 'The staff are commendably friendly, efficient; unlike some hotels, they don't speak like trained robots.' The public rooms are ornate; the lounge has bright red walls, crystal chandeliers, antique side tables; a pianist plays in the evening in the 'cosy' bar. The themed bedrooms are 'outrageously over the top; we always look forward to finding out what room we'll have; will it be Zebra, Safari, Madame de Pompadour? Whichever style, the rooms are comfortable, with many extra touches that are unusual in this middling price range: robes, slippers, an ironing board. If it isn't there, they will bring it instantly and cheerfully.' Martin Halls serves modern British dishes in the 'good' *Blue Doors* bistro; alfresco meals are taken on a terrace. (*Mary Wilmer*)

15 Montague Street
London WC1B 5BJ

T: 020-7637 1001
F: 020-7637 2516
E: infomt@rchmail.com
W: www.montaguehotel.com

BEDROOMS: 100, 1 suitable for &.
OPEN: all year.
FACILITIES: lobby, lounge, 2 conservatories, civil wedding licence, terrace.
BACKGROUND MUSIC: in public areas.
LOCATION: Bloomsbury, underground Russell Square.
CHILDREN: all ages welcomed.
DOGS: allowed.
CREDIT CARDS: all major cards.
PRICES: [2010] room (*excluding VAT*) £135–£355, breakfast £16.50, set meals £24.50, full alc £65, website offers, Christmas/New Year packages.

# LONDON

Map 2:D4

## NUMBER SIXTEEN  NEW

*César award: London hotel of the year*

On a quiet tree-lined street, this white stucco 19th-century townhouse belongs to Tim and Kit Kemp's small group of six London hotels; Anja Groetsch was appointed manager in 2010. 'It is a special place,' says an inspector. 'The welcome was warm; the staff were exceptional; well groomed, helpful.' Mrs Kemp designed the bedrooms in classic English style. 'Our charming small room was beautifully conceived: a pristine, pale grey carpet, red curtains, cream roller blinds. It was thoughtfully equipped: automatic lighting in the good-sized wardrobe, a full-length mirror, a clothes brush; superb bedlinen on a supremely comfortable bed; good reading lights. Glass doors opened on to a narrow balcony facing the street; it was quiet at night.' Downstairs is a drawing room, a 'comfortable library with a well-stocked honesty bar', and a conservatory that opens on to a 'lush, tree-filled garden'. No restaurant: a 24-hour room service menu of light meals is available. Breakfast has 'first-class coffee, a good display of juices, fruit, yogurts, cereals, pastries'.

16 Sumner Place
London SW7 3EG

T: 020-7589 5232
F: 020-7584 8615
E: sixteen@firmdale.com
W: www.firmdalehotels.com

BEDROOMS: 42, 5 on ground floor.
OPEN: all year.
FACILITIES: drawing room, library, conservatory, civil wedding licence, garden.
BACKGROUND MUSIC: none.
LOCATION: Kensington, underground South Kensington.
CHILDREN: all ages welcomed.
DOGS: not allowed.
CREDIT CARDS: all major cards.
PRICES: [2010] room £120–£280, breakfast £18.50, special offers, Christmas/New Year packages.

# LONDON

Map 2:D4

## ONE ALDWYCH

❦ *César award in 2005*

'The beautifully dressed staff are wonderfully pleasant,' says a visitor this year to Gordon Campbell Gray's ultra-modern conversion of the Edwardian offices of the *Morning Post*. 'The staff, rather than the posh fixtures and fittings, justify the considerable cost of staying.' Stefan Soennichsen is the manager. The interesting building, 'shaped like a wedge of cheese within a triangle of traffic-ridden London', has a dramatic double-height lobby dominated by a giant statue of an oarsman, extravagant flower arrangements. The bedrooms vary considerably in size: 'Our room was small for the price but immaculate, in cool shades of ice blue to grey/green and pale cream. Beds are top of the range; the noisy eco-toilets take some getting used to.' All rooms are triple glazed against traffic noise. There are two restaurants: the 'relaxed' *Indigo*, on a balcony ('excellent and not bad value'), and the more formal *Axis*, on the lower ground floor. 'Breakfast, expensive but delicious, was efficiently served at table by charming young waiters.' *Dukes Hotel*, St James, is under the same ownership (see Shortlist). (*Mary Wilmer*)

1 Aldwych
London WC2B 4RH

T: 020-7300 1000
F: 020-7300 1001
E: reservations@onealdwych.com
W: www.onealdwych.co.uk

BEDROOMS: 105, 6 suitable for &.
OPEN: all year.
FACILITIES: lifts, 2 bars (live DJ Sat evening), 2 restaurants, function facilities, screening room, health club (18-metre swimming pool, spa, sauna, gym), civil wedding licence.
BACKGROUND MUSIC: in lobby bar.
LOCATION: Strand (windows triple glazed), valet parking, underground Covent Garden, Charing Cross, Waterloo.
CHILDREN: all ages welcomed.
DOGS: only guide dogs allowed.
CREDIT CARDS: all major cards.
PRICES: [2010] room/suite (*excluding VAT*) £225–£1,295, breakfast £15–£23, pre- and post-theatre menu (*Indigo* and *Axis*) £16.75–£19.75, full alc (*Axis*) £40, promotional offers, New Year package.

# LONDON

## THE PORTOBELLO

An early example of shabby chic, this Bohemian little hotel on a residential street in Notting Hill has long been popular with celebrities from the world of music, fashion and the theatre. It is owned by Tim and Cathy Herring with partner Johnny Ekperigin, who manages it with Hanna Turner. The entrance hall and ground-floor drawing room are filled with gilt mirrors, military pictures and potted palms. The decor in the corridors might seem faded, but visitors like the 'sense of character: nothing anonymous here'. It is best to review the bedroom descriptions on the website and discuss them when booking. Some cabin rooms have a very small bathroom. 'Special' rooms are recommended. A third-floor room had 'a supremely comfortable four-poster bed, sofa, good storage, a tiny balcony; a splendid bathroom'. The Round Room has a large freestanding Edwardian bathing machine, a round bed. Continental breakfast, included in the room rate, can be taken in the bedroom or the drawing room. Snacks and light meals are available at any time. *The Portobello*'s residents get a discount at *Julie's*, the owners' nearby restaurant.

22 Stanley Gardens
London W11 2NG

T: 020-7727 2777
F: 020-7792 9641
E: info@portobellohotel.com
w: www.portobellohotel.com

BEDROOMS: 21.
OPEN: all year, except 24–29 Dec.
FACILITIES: lift, small bar, foyer/lounge, access to nearby health club, unsuitable for &.
BACKGROUND MUSIC: none.
LOCATION: Notting Hill, meter parking, underground Notting Hill Gate.
CHILDREN: all ages welcomed.
DOGS: not in public rooms.
CREDIT CARDS: Amex, MasterCard, Visa.
PRICES: B&B (continental) £140–£175 per person, full alc £40, New Year package.

# LONDON

Map 2:D4

## THE ROCKWELL

With a 'clean modern look and an informal vibe', this contemporary hotel has been created from two Victorian terrace houses on Cromwell Road. 'The staff are friendly and competent,' says a visitor this year. Inspectors agreed: 'We arrived early to a warm welcome; the receptionist could not have been more helpful, finding information for us on her computer.' The spacious lounge/lobby has a high ceiling, bold patterned wallpaper, an open fire, big sofas. The bedrooms vary in size: 'Our large garden room was decorated in bright colours; light oak furnishings with a wardrobe and dressing table with mirror; chairs at the end of the bed. The well-lit bathroom had under-floor heating, a large powerful shower. Doors opened on to a small patio below the courtyard garden.' Breakfast, in a room facing the garden, has a buffet of cereals, cut citrus fruit, freshly squeezed orange juice, salamis, hams and cheese; a range of cooked dishes. Light meals (eg, fishcakes with mango chilli sauce, stuffed chicken with spinach, tomato and pine nuts) are available. A half-board package is 'very reasonable'. (*John Colfryn, and others*)

181 Cromwell Road
London SW5 0SF

T: 020-7244 2000
F: 020-7244 2001
E: enquiries@therockwell.com
W: www.therockwell.com

BEDROOMS: 40, some on ground floor.
OPEN: all year.
FACILITIES: lift, ramps, lobby, lounge, bar, restaurant, conference room, garden.
BACKGROUND MUSIC: in lobby and library area.
LOCATION: 1 mile W of West End, opposite Cromwell Hospital, underground Earls Court.
CHILDREN: all ages welcomed.
DOGS: not allowed.
CREDIT CARDS: Amex, MasterCard, Visa.
PRICES: room £120–£180, breakfast £9.50–£12.50, full alc £28, website offers, Christmas/New Year packages.

# LONDON

## TWENTY NEVERN SQUARE

Liked for its reasonable prices and relative tranquillity for a central London hotel, this converted red brick town house is owned by the Mayflower group. Close to Earls Court, it is opposite an attractive Victorian garden square. Bedrooms are exotically furnished: the best face the square. The Ottoman Suite has a turquoise and gold king-size bed, a crystal chandelier, a roll-top bath and an open fireplace; a private balcony overlooks the gardens. The Scheherazade Suite has Persian silks and oriental furnishings; the Sleigh Double has a mahogany sleigh bed and silk-draped canopy. The four smaller rooms on the third and fourth floor, with a more subtle colour scheme, are 'clean, well equipped, comfortable'. All have free Wi-Fi, CD-player, widescreen TV. Guests can enjoy complimentary afternoon tea served in a small lounge with armchairs. The conservatory-style *Café Twenty* is where pre-theatre drinks and the 'generous' continental breakfast are taken. This is included in the room price; cooked costs extra (except on some packages). A 'South African-style' barbecue can be held for parties and special occasions. More reports, please.

20 Nevern Square
London SW5 9PD

T: 020-7565 9555
F: 020-7565 9444
E: hotel@twentynevernsquare.co.uk
W: www.twentynevernsquare.co.uk

BEDROOMS: 20.
OPEN: all year.
FACILITIES: lounge, restaurant, small garden, unsuitable for &.
BACKGROUND MUSIC: in public rooms.
LOCATION: central, underground Earls Court.
CHILDREN: all ages welcomed.
DOGS: not allowed.
CREDIT CARDS: Amex, MasterCard, Visa.
PRICES: B&B £39.50–£89 per person, cooked breakfast £9, special offers.

# LONDON

## THE VICTORIA

Close to Richmond Park (and 25 minutes from Waterloo by train), this refurbished pub-with-rooms is owned by celebrity chef Paul Merrett and his business partner, Greg Bellamy. Inspectors liked the 'neighbourhood feel, good atmosphere, and good value for London'. In the daytime 'mums drop in for a coffee, locals come for an evening drink'. The simple bedrooms (some are small) are in a separate building, connected by a covered walkway. 'Ours had a medium-sized bed with a duvet; a little dress rack with hanging shelves; a small, efficient shower room. It was quiet at night; some noise from trains and aircraft in the morning.' Paul Merrett's frequently changing modern British menu has 'good bistro-style' dishes (eg, slow-baked pork shoulder, aubergine purée, Provençal jus. It is served in a conservatory restaurant (dark wood floors, leather seating) and, in warm weather, on a large, pretty terrace. Children are positively encouraged and can play on a slide and climbing frame in the garden. Breakfast has 'good orange juice, delicious chunky marmalade, DIY toast from good bread'.

10 West Temple Sheen
London SW14 7RT

T: 020-8876 4238
F: 020-8878 3464
E: bookings@thevictoria.net
W: www.thevictoria.net

BEDROOMS: 7, 3 on ground floor.
OPEN: all year.
FACILITIES: bar, restaurant, garden, unsuitable for &.
BACKGROUND MUSIC: in bar and restaurant.
LOCATION: Mortlake (5 mins' walk) to Waterloo/Clapham Jct, car park.
CHILDREN: all ages welcomed.
DOGS: allowed in bar and garden.
CREDIT CARDS: MasterCard, Visa.
PRICES: [2010] B&B (continental) £57.50–£105 per person (higher in Wimbledon weeks), cooked breakfast £6.50, full alc £36, tailor-made breaks, Christmas/New Year packages.

**25% DISCOUNT VOUCHERS**

# LONDON

Map 2:D4

## THE ZETTER

In fashionable Clerkenwell, this Victorian warehouse (later the headquarters of Zetters football pools) has been converted into a 'romantic yet anonymous' contemporary hotel by restaurateurs Mark Sainsbury and Michael Benyan. In 2010 the crescent-shaped restaurant, which overlooks St John's Square, was renovated and re-opened as *Bistrot Bruno Loubet*: the French chef can be seen in an open kitchen preparing dishes like lyonnaise salad, Beaujolais dressing; confit lamb shoulder, white beans and preserved lemon. 'Excellent cooking,' said a visitor in 2010. There is a brunch menu on Sunday and, in summer, alfresco drinking and dining on the square. Bedrooms, which vary considerably in size, are decorated in 'vintage-modern style'; bright splashes of colour on a neutral background. All have state-of-the-art entertainment and technology. Vending machines in the corridors dispense champagne, soft drinks, deodorants. A green ethos is followed; drinking water is pumped from a well below the building; guests can hire bicycles; air conditioning switches off when a window is opened. Breakfast, which costs extra, has a wide choice of cooked dishes.

86–88 Clerkenwell Road
London EC1M 5RJ

T: 020-7324 4444
F: 020-7324 4456
E: info@thezetter.com
W: www.thezetter.com

BEDROOMS: 59, 1 suitable for &.
OPEN: all year.
FACILITIES: 2 lifts, ramps, cocktail bar/lounge, restaurant, 2 function/meeting rooms, civil wedding licence.
BACKGROUND MUSIC: eclectic mix ('not loud').
LOCATION: Clerkenwell, by St John's Sq, NCP garage 5 mins' walk, underground Farringdon.
CHILDREN: all ages welcomed.
DOGS: only guide dogs allowed.
CREDIT CARDS: Amex, MasterCard, Visa.
PRICES: room £180–£423, breakfast from £12.50, full alc £40, New Year package.

# ENGLAND

There is a hotel for every taste, and every budget, in our wide range of interesting places to stay in England. Country house hotels are listed alongside modest B&Bs; modern dining pubs stand alongside good-value guest houses. The common factor is the warmth of the welcome and the sense of caring for the guest.

# ABBOTSBURY Dorset

Map 1:D6

## ABBEY HOUSE

On the site of an 11th-century abbey, this 15th-century building has lawns sloping down to a millpond; beyond is a huge tithe barn, said to be the oldest in England. Run as a guest house by the 'very professional' Jonathan and Maureen Cooke, it is loved by *Guide* readers for the 'kindness, friendliness' and good value. 'No detail has been missed,' writes a visitor returning in 2010. There are flagstone floors, panelled doors, original windows; plenty of books in the 'cosy' lounge; a traditional decor of chintz and knick-knacks. The 'excellent' breakfast, taken in a room (thought to have been the Abbey infirmary) with a beamed ceiling and large fireplace, has freshly squeezed fruit juices, home-made muesli, cereals, porridge and a wide choice of cooked dishes. Bedrooms vary in size: one, inside the main roof gable, has a separate sitting room; four of the five have facilities en suite. Light lunches and cream teas are served in summer in the garden. Evening meals are available for house parties; a comprehensive list of local eating places is provided. (*Suzanne Lyons, CH*)

Church Street
Abbotsbury DT3 4JJ

T: 01305-871330
F: 01305-871088
E: info@theabbeyhouse.co.uk
W: www.theabbeyhouse.co.uk

BEDROOMS: 5.
OPEN: all year, tea room open for lunches Apr–Sept, dinners for house parties only.
FACILITIES: reception, lounge, breakfast/tea room, 1½-acre garden (stage for opera), sea 15 mins' walk, unsuitable for &.
BACKGROUND MUSIC: classical, sometimes.
LOCATION: village centre.
CHILDREN: not under 12.
DOGS: not allowed.
CREDIT CARDS: none.
PRICES: B&B £35–£50 per person, 1-night bookings sometimes refused bank holiday Sat.

# ALDEBURGH Suffolk

Map 2:C6

## THE WENTWORTH

'Relaxed and well run', this traditional seaside hotel has been owned by the Pritt family for 90 years. Michael Pritt, the grandson of the founder, is 'much in evidence; he runs a tight ship', says a visitor this year. 'Unchanged; comfortable without being smart,' is another comment in 2010. Visitors ('many, like us, of a certain age') are pleased to 'see the same familiar faces among the staff from year to year'. The bedrooms, which vary in size, are 'of a high standard and very comfortable'. Rooms with a sea view have binoculars. *Darfield House*, opposite, has large rooms and a garden, but no sea view. Mr Pritt says that in response to a visitor comment, he has renewed many of the mattresses this year; a power shower is being installed in every bedroom. One of the lounges has a log fire; another 'sumptuous' sofas. Tim Keeble, appointed chef in late 2009, has established a new kitchen garden; he embraces a 'grow it, cook it, eat it' ethos for his menus which might include duck salad, home-made piccalilli; pan-fried haddock, spinach mash, pea velouté. (*Helen Anthony, Bryan Blaxall, Helen Peston*)

Wentworth Road
Aldeburgh IP15 5BD

T: 01728-452312
F: 01728-454343
E: stay@
   wentworth-aldeburgh.co.uk
W: www.wentworth-aldeburgh.com

BEDROOMS: 35, 7 in *Darfield House* opposite, 5 on ground floor, 1 suitable for &.
OPEN: all year.
FACILITIES: ramps, 2 lounges, bar, restaurant, private dining room, conference room, 2 terrace gardens, shingle beach 200 yds.
BACKGROUND MUSIC: none.
LOCATION: seafront, 5 mins' walk from centre, car park, train Saxmundham 8 miles.
CHILDREN: all ages welcomed.
DOGS: not allowed in restaurant.
CREDIT CARDS: all major cards.
PRICES: B&B £64–£121 per person, D,B&B £70–£132, set menus £22–£24, weekend/midweek breaks, Christmas/New Year packages, 1-night bookings refused Sat.

**25% DISCOUNT VOUCHERS**

## ALKHAM Kent

Map 2:D5

# THE MARQUIS AT ALKHAM

Strikingly lit at night, this white-painted 200-year-old inn is 'perched on a slope' at the southern end of the Kent Downs. Only ten minutes from the Channel Tunnel, it is 'the perfect stop-over en route to France'. The interior is contemporary ('immediately inviting', said an inspector): wide-beam oak flooring, modern fabrics, dark wood tables and exposed brickwork, pale grey walls with half-panelling; a small seating area has dark leather sofas. The 'delightful' and 'stylishly decorated' bedrooms have pocket-sprung mattresses, cotton bedding, and fresh milk in a Thermos for tea. The De Pamier Suite has a large bedroom and a separate sitting room (sofa bed, desk chair), a deep bath and views across the valley. Head chef Charles Lakin was awarded a rising *Michelin* star in 2010 for his seasonal, locally sourced menus. Main courses might include saddle of Godmersham rabbit, black pudding stuffing, vintage cider sauce. A 'lovely' breakfast buffet has croissants and home-made jam in miniature Kilner jars; 'beautifully presented' cooked choices include Whitstable kippers.

Alkham Valley Road
Alkham CT15 7DF

T: 01304-873410
F: 01304-873418
E: info@themarquisatalkham.co.uk
W: www.themarquisatalkham.co.uk

BEDROOMS: 8, 3 in cottages 3 mins' drive away.
OPEN: all year, restaurant closed Sun evening/Mon lunch (bar snacks).
FACILITIES: bar, lounge, dining room, civil wedding licence, small garden, unsuitable for &.
BACKGROUND MUSIC: 'instrumental' in public areas.
LOCATION: 4 miles W of Dover.
CHILDREN: all ages welcomed.
DOGS: allowed in cottages.
CREDIT CARDS: Amex, MasterCard, Visa.
PRICES: [2010] B&B £47.50–£107.50 per person, D,B&B £69.50–£174.50, set meals £19.50–£24.95, full alc £55, special breaks, Christmas/New Year packages.

**25% DISCOUNT VOUCHERS**

# ALSTON Cumbria

## LOVELADY SHIELD

'The welcome is warm, the rooms, while not deluxe, are pleasant and the dining room is a good place to be.' Much praise comes this year for Peter and Marie Haynes's country hotel, secluded in mature gardens on the banks of the River Nent. Another comment: 'As good as ever; eager but relaxed service. The owner and the staff take time to talk to guests.' The white-fronted building stands on the site of a 13th-century convent. The public rooms and bedrooms are furnished in country house style: 'No sign of trendy "designer bleak".' The 'comfortable' bedrooms vary in size; the largest has a separate sitting area; some are small. In the smart restaurant, where 'standards of dress are maintained', the long-serving chef, Barrie Garton, serves an 'excellent' daily-changing menu. 'Outstanding dishes: sublime Swiss cheese and potato soup; excellent partridge and wild boar; delicious chocolate tart with lemon meringue ice cream.' There is no muzak, and 'no noise other than the stream running through the grounds; bliss'. Good walking from the door. (*Graham Fisher, David Fisher, and others*)

Lovelady Lane
nr Alston CA9 3LX

T: 01434-381203
F: 01434-381515
E: enquiries@lovelady.co.uk
W: www.lovelady.co.uk

BEDROOMS: 12.
OPEN: all year.
FACILITIES: 2 lounges, bar, restaurant, conference facilities, civil wedding licence, 2-acre grounds (river, fishing, croquet, woodland walks), unsuitable for &.
BACKGROUND MUSIC: none.
LOCATION: 2 miles N of Alston on A689.
CHILDREN: all ages welcomed.
DOGS: not allowed in public rooms.
CREDIT CARDS: Amex, MasterCard, Visa.
PRICES: B&B £80–£150 per person, D,B&B £100–£170, set dinner £46.50, special breaks, Christmas/ New Year packages.

**25% DISCOUNT VOUCHERS**

# AMBLESIDE Cumbria

## THE REGENT

Opposite a slipway and pier on Lake Windermere, Christine Hewitt's white-fronted hotel is managed by her son, Andrew. Serious flooding in the area in November 2009 damaged two ground-floor suites. These were reopened within three months after renovation in contemporary style. 'A true family-run hotel,' says a returning visitor in 2010. 'Although it has been modernised, the staff retain their old-fashioned courtesy.' Bedrooms vary considerably in size and shape. Garden rooms, which are on the first floor, have a spa bath, king-size bed, a large sitting area and a private terrace looking over the garden. The Sail Loft Room has a private wooden terrace with a lake view. Smaller rooms are 'comfortable and well equipped'. All rooms have TV, CD-player, tea- and coffee-making facilities, a PlayStation. The cooking of the chef, John Mathers, served in a split-level restaurant, is praised by readers. His daily-changing menu might include Morecambe Bay potted shrimps, spicy couscous; haddock, courgette ribbons, capers, pesto dressing. Breakfast, served until midday, is 'varied and innovative'. A single-room supplement is no longer charged on special breaks. (*Simon Rodway, and others*)

Waterhead Bay
Ambleside LA22 0ES

T: 015394-32254
F: 015394-31474
E: info@regentlakes.co.uk
W: www.regentlakes.co.uk

BEDROOMS: 30, 10 in courtyard, 5 in garden, 7 on ground floor.
OPEN: all year, except Christmas.
FACILITIES: ramp, lounge, sun lounge, bar, restaurant, small indoor swimming pool, courtyard, ¼-acre garden, on Lake Windermere.
BACKGROUND MUSIC: classical/jazz in public rooms.
LOCATION: on A591, S of centre, at Waterhead Bay.
CHILDREN: all ages welcomed.
DOGS: not allowed in public rooms.
CREDIT CARDS: MasterCard, Visa.
PRICES: [2010] B&B £49.50–£77.50 per person, D,B&B £87.50–£92.50, full alc £44, New Year package, 1-night bookings refused Sat.

**25% DISCOUNT VOUCHERS**

# AMBLESIDE Cumbria

Map 4: inset C2

## ROTHAY MANOR

♚ *César award in 1992*

In a 'delightful' setting, a short walk from the head of Lake Windermere, this traditional hotel has been owned by the Nixon family for more than 40 years. 'They are excellent hosts,' say visitors in 2010. Nigel Nixon is 'much in evidence'; the manager, Peter Sinclair, 'fits in well with the family tradition'. Children are welcomed. 'It may look like a hotel for the more mature,' says a visitor this year. 'But it is a family hotel: our children were welcomed into the lounges and were allowed to eat their high teas at dinner time, so felt very grown up.' The public rooms are 'light, comfortable'. In the dining room, Jane Binns's cooking is 'simple but always artistically presented': 'We particularly enjoyed the fish main courses, such as lemon sole with salmon mousse.' The bedrooms are 'comfortable, well furnished and decorated'. Some rooms have a balcony: 'I greatly enjoyed watching people toiling up Wansfell Pike.' Breakfast 'provides everything you could ask for': freshly squeezed orange juice, freshly baked croissants, a Cumberland platter. (*Dorothy Brining, Brenda and Bob Halstead, Margaret H Box*)

Rothay Bridge
Ambleside LA22 0EH

T: 015394-33605
F: 015394-33607
E: hotel@rothaymanor.co.uk
W: www.rothaymanor.co.uk

BEDROOMS: 19, 2 in annexe, 2 suitable for &.
OPEN: all year except 3–27 Jan.
FACILITIES: ramp, 2 lounges, bar, 2 dining rooms, meeting/conference facilities, 1-acre garden (croquet), free access to local leisure centre.
BACKGROUND MUSIC: none.
LOCATION: ¼ mile SW of Ambleside.
CHILDREN: all ages welcomed.
DOGS: not allowed.
CREDIT CARDS: all major cards.
PRICES: [2010] B&B £70–£150 per person, D,B&B £97.50–£190, set dinner £59.50, special breaks (antiques, bridge, Scrabble, walking, etc), Christmas/New Year packages, 1-night bookings refused Sat.

# AMPLEFORTH North Yorkshire

Map 4:D4

## SHALLOWDALE HOUSE

*César award in 2005*

'Everything first class; our fifth visit; we enjoyed our stay as much as ever.' 'There is nothing you can fault.' More enthusiastic reports this year for this architect-designed 1960s house on the southern edge of the North York Moors. The owners, Phillip Gill and Anton van der Horst, are 'kind and hospitable'; their 'knowledge of the district is very helpful'. Guests are greeted at their car and helped with their luggage; tea and home-made cakes are 'quickly produced' in a downstairs drawing room with lovely views. The three bedrooms also have the views: two are en suite, one has a private bathroom across the corridor. 'Our large room and bathroom had everything, including binoculars and torches by the bed.' A four-course no-choice meal is served by arrangement (preferences discussed in advance). The style is 'domestic/eclectic': dishes like slow-roasted Ryedale lamb, aubergine and tomato compote. Breakfast includes Cumbrian dry-cured bacon and home-made preserves. The house is conveniently situated for Castle Howard and Rievaulx Abbey. (*John and Christine Moore, Richard Creed*)

West End, Ampleforth
nr York, YO62 4DY

T: 01439-788325
F: 01439-788885
E: stay@shallowdalehouse.co.uk
W: www.shallowdalehouse.co.uk

BEDROOMS: 3.
OPEN: all year except Christmas/New Year, occasionally at other times.
FACILITIES: drawing room, sitting room, dining room, 2½-acre grounds, unsuitable for ♿.
BACKGROUND MUSIC: none.
LOCATION: edge of village.
CHILDREN: not under 12.
DOGS: not allowed.
CREDIT CARDS: MasterCard, Visa.
PRICES: [2010] B&B £47.50–£58.75 per person, set dinner £35, 1-night bookings occasionally refused weekends.

# ARLINGHAM Gloucestershire

Map 3:D5

## THE OLD PASSAGE  `NEW`

In an 'appealing' rural position on the banks of
the River Severn, this restaurant-with-rooms is
'well managed' by owner Sally Pearce, and 'on an
upswing', says an inspector in 2010. The green,
white-shuttered building stands alone amid fields
on an oxbow bend of the river upstream from
Slimbridge nature reserve. There is a small sun
lounge by the entrance and an ante-room where
breakfast is taken. In the dining areas ('light, airy,
well kept'), Mark Redwood's menus specialise in
seafood: 'We enjoyed memorable Fowey mussels;
pan-fried gurnard showed real finesse, especially
the brown shrimp and hazelnut risotto; service
was prompt but unforced. The English house
wine, from nearby Three Choirs, was reasonably
priced.' Each of the three bedrooms is named
after a fish: 'Tuna was smallish, pretty, tastefully
unfussy, with contemporary low-key furnishings;
leather chairs by a window; a bright, pleasing
bathroom.' A 'light' breakfast, included in the
room price, has porridge, boiled eggs with toast
soldiers, fruit, muesli, toast and preserves ('all
expertly prepared and served'). Alternatives,
which cost extra, include hot smoked salmon
with poached egg, oysters and Bloody Mary.

Passage Road
Arlingham GL2 7JR

T: 01452-740547
E: oldpassage@ukonline.co.uk
W: www.theoldpassage.com

BEDROOMS: 3.
OPEN: all year except Christmas,
restaurant closed Sun night/Mon.
FACILITIES: sitting room, restaurant,
1½-acre garden, only restaurant
suitable for &.
BACKGROUND MUSIC: in restaurant.
LOCATION: ¼ mile W of Arlingham.
CHILDREN: all ages welcomed.
DOGS: allowed by arrangement, not
in public rooms.
CREDIT CARDS: Amex, MasterCard,
Visa.
PRICES: [2010] B&B £40–£65 per
person, D,B&B (midweek) £60, full
alc £40–£60.

`25% DISCOUNT VOUCHERS`

# ARUNDEL West Sussex

Map 2:E3

## ARUNDEL HOUSE

'Extremely good in every way,' says a regular
*Guide* correspondent this year, praising Luke
Hackman and Billy Lewis-Bowker's Grade II
listed 19th-century merchant's house, which they
run as a restaurant-with-rooms. Mr Hackman is
the chef serving 'excellent' modern British dishes,
perhaps crab cake, celeriac remoulade, sweet chilli
jam; flash-fried rabbit, mushroom stuffed apple
and potato cake. The restaurant is in two rooms
on either side of the entrance. Background music
is played 'at all times', they say, 'but you should
never hear the same track twice'. Mr Lewis-Bowker
is the general manager; his wife, Emma, designed
the contemporary bedrooms, which have writing
desk, flat-screen TV, complimentary Wi-Fi,
drench shower, bathrobes in the bathroom. Tea-
and coffee-making facilities are not provided ('to
keep clutter to a minimum'); hot drinks are
delivered to the room free of charge when the
restaurant is open. Breakfast (served from 8 to 10
am) is also praised; it has own-recipe granola,
home-made bread, a 'lovely seasonal fruit platter',
warm croissants and pastries; extensive cooked
choices. Vouchers are provided for a nearby safe
car park. (*Anthony Meakin*)

11 High Street
Arundel BN18 9AD

T: 01903-882136
W: www.arundelhouseonline.com

BEDROOMS: 5.
OPEN: all year except 24–31 Dec,
restaurant closed Sun/Mon.
FACILITIES: restaurant, unsuitable
for &.
BACKGROUND MUSIC: swing/jazz in
restaurant.
LOCATION: town centre.
CHILDREN: not under 16.
DOGS: not allowed.
CREDIT CARDS: Amex, MasterCard,
Visa.
PRICES: [2010] B&B £40–£80 per
person, full alc £44.

**25% DISCOUNT VOUCHERS**

# ARUNDEL West Sussex

Map 2:E3

## THE TOWN HOUSE

In a commanding position at the top of Arundel's steep High Street, this restaurant-with-rooms, owned by Lee Williams (the chef) and his wife, Katie, is liked by readers (and an inspector) for the quality of the cooking. 'Excellent food; friendly, accommodating staff,' says a visitor in 2010. Upstairs in the Grade II listed Regency building, the bedrooms have many period features, including 19th-century moulded plaster panels. One room is reached by a flight of steps which seem to lead to a blank wall (it originally provided access to the house next door). Two have a four-poster bed, one has a balcony; these rooms (criticised in last year's *Guide*) have been given new oak and leather furniture this year. Rooms at the front may experience some traffic noise. In the dining room, which has a carved and gilded 16th-century Florentine ceiling, Mr Williams's 'fine dining' menu might include grilled supreme of guineafowl, confit leg, braised lentils and bacon. Bread is home baked, and breakfast is continental or full English. No lounge or grounds, so 'best for a short stay'. (*M Crosby, and others*)

65 High Street
Arundel BN18 9AJ

T: 01903-883847
E: enquiries@thetownhouse.co.uk
W: www.thetownhouse.co.uk

BEDROOMS: 4.
OPEN: all year except 25/26 Dec, 2 weeks Feb, 2 weeks Oct, restaurant closed Sun/Mon.
FACILITIES: restaurant, unsuitable for &.
BACKGROUND MUSIC: in restaurant.
LOCATION: top end of High Street.
CHILDREN: all ages welcomed.
DOGS: not allowed.
CREDIT CARDS: Diners, MasterCard, Visa.
PRICES: [2010] B&B £42.50–£60 per person, D,B&B (midweek) £60–£75, set dinner £22–£27.50, 1-night bookings refused weekends in high season.

**25% DISCOUNT VOUCHERS**

## ASHWATER Devon

Map 1:C3

### BLAGDON MANOR

🏆 *César award in 2006*

'Unstuffy, with high levels of service and superb food.' Praise from trusted reporters in 2010 for Steve and Liz Morey's 17th-century manor house (Grade II listed) in rolling north Devon countryside. The Moreys tell us they have chosen to operate as a restaurant-with-rooms, opening from Wednesday to Sunday. His cooking continues to be much admired: 'Steve's food is manna from heaven. We particularly liked the cabbage-wrapped duck confit,' is a typical comment. The 'welcoming' hosts have a 'no-problem attitude' to any dietary requirements. 'Liz Morey has a sixth sense, knowing what guests would like before they do,' says a returning visitor. There is a 'surprisingly wide choice of relaxing public rooms' with fresh flowers, original features (heavy oak beams, slate flagstones). The 'nicely furnished' bedrooms are all different. 'Our standard room had double aspect views of the grounds, freestanding bath and good toiletries.' Breakfasts are 'delicious'. The owners have three chocolate Labradors, and guests' dogs 'are positively welcomed'. (*Bill and Patsy Bennett, GC*)

Ashwater EX21 5DF

T: 01409-211224
F: 01409-211634
E: stay@blagdon.com
W: www.blagdon.com

BEDROOMS: 7.
OPEN: all year Wed–Sun, except Jan.
FACILITIES: ramps, lounge, library, snug, bar, conservatory, restaurant, private dining room, 20-acre grounds (3-acre gardens, croquet, giant chess, gazebo, pond), unsuitable for &.
BACKGROUND MUSIC: none.
LOCATION: 8 miles NE of Launceston.
CHILDREN: not under 12.
DOGS: not allowed in restaurant, conservatory.
CREDIT CARDS: MasterCard, Visa.
PRICES: [2010] B&B £67.50–£97.50 per person, set lunch £17–£20, dinner £33–£38, midweek winter breaks, 1-night bookings refused Christmas.

**25% DISCOUNT VOUCHERS**

# AUSTWICK North Yorkshire

Map 4:D3

## AUSTWICK HALL `NEW`

On a wooded hillside on the edge of a pretty village, this handsome old manor house has been 'lovingly brought back to life' by Michael Pearson and Eric Culley. They are 'excellent hosts', say inspectors. 'We knew we would have an enjoyable stay when, as we arrived in rain, Michael came down the steps with a huge umbrella.' The interesting interiors have 'a clever mix of old and new'. The 'huge' entrance hall is dominated by a rosewood table; it has plenty of seating, magazines and books, 'lots of local information'. The 'relaxing' lounge has sofas and armchairs, bookcases, a wood-burning stove. 'We were brought excellent coffee and home-made biscuits without charge.' A 'splendid' central staircase curves out to two open landings. 'Our huge bedroom was well lit; the old floorboards and bed frame were polished; a marble fireplace, antique wardrobe, a writing desk.' Mr Pearson serves a short dinner menu (likes and dislikes discussed): 'We enjoyed orange and carrot soup; tasty salmon fillet with prawn sauce; a huge bowl of vegetables; everything simple, with good portions and ingredients. Breakfast was very good.'

Townhead Lane
Austwick LA2 8BS

T: 01524-251794
E: austwickhall@austwick.org
W: www.austwickhall.co.uk

BEDROOMS: 5.
OPEN: all year except 3–31 Jan.
FACILITIES: hall, sitting room, drawing room, dining room, civil wedding licence, 13-acre gardens, unsuitable for &.
BACKGROUND MUSIC: none.
LOCATION: edge of village.
CHILDREN: not under 16.
DOGS: not allowed.
CREDIT CARDS: MasterCard, Visa.
PRICES: [2010] B&B £62.50–£160 per person, D,B&B £30 added, set dinner (Sat) £30, full alc £43, Christmas/New Year packages, 1-night bookings refused weekends.

# AUSTWICK North Yorkshire

Map 4:D3

## THE TRADDOCK

'The graciousness of this house is revealed once you are inside the walled, gravelled front court,' says a regular *Guide* reporter visiting the Reynolds family's Georgian country house in the Yorkshire Dales. 'Paul Reynolds and his staff were consistently courteous, cheerful, helpful.' There are antiques, log fires, many original features in the public rooms. The bedrooms, individually designed, have portraits in gilt frames, brocade curtains with swags. 'My small room was clean and comfortable, with recessed ceiling lighting; a modern shower, good toiletries.' In the dining room, the chef is John Pratt. The service at dinner 'was prompt, but never rushed; delicious canapés preceded a meal that was always a pleasure, with gradual changes on the menu during the week. The rib-eye steak and local lamb were particularly fine, served perfectly medium rare. Wine, from a respectable list, was good value.' Breakfast has a wide 'and lavish' choice. A visitor leaving early had 'a wonderful honey and banana smoothie and freshly brewed coffee'. The small garden 'is an attractive place to sit in the sun'. (*Robert Gower, E and DG Stevens*)

Austwick, via Lancaster
LA2 8BY

T: 01524-251224
F: 01524-251796
E: info@austwicktraddock.co.uk
W: www.thetraddock.co.uk

BEDROOMS: 12, 1 on ground floor.
OPEN: all year.
FACILITIES: 3 lounges, 2 dining areas, function facilities, 1-acre grounds (sun deck), only public rooms accessible to &.
BACKGROUND MUSIC: 'if needed' in lounge and dining rooms.
LOCATION: 4 miles NW of Settle, train Settle, bus.
CHILDREN: all ages welcomed.
DOGS: allowed in public rooms on lead.
CREDIT CARDS: MasterCard, Visa.
PRICES: [2010] B&B £45–£90 per person, D,B&B £75–£120, full alc £52, Christmas/New Year packages, 1-night bookings refused weekends in season.

**25% DISCOUNT VOUCHERS**

# AYLESBURY Buckinghamshire

Map 2:C3

## HARTWELL HOUSE

❦ *César award in 1997*

'Good food and service, and pleasingly quiet grounds.' Praise this year from regular correspondents for this luxury hotel, in a magnificent stately home in extensive parkland. Owned by the National Trust (who receive all profits), it is managed by Richard Broyd's Historic House Hotels (see also *Middlethorpe Hall*, York, *Bodysgallen Hall*, Llandudno, Wales). The long-serving director/general manager, Jonathan Thompson, leads a 'friendly' staff. The mansion has Jacobean and Georgian features with decorative ceilings and panelling, fine paintings and antique furniture in the four elegant drawing rooms. Bedrooms have a flat-screen TV and Wi-Fi; some have air conditioning. 'We were upgraded on arrival to a very good room at the front.' Sixteen rooms (some split-level) are in a 'sensitively' converted stable block. In the candlelit dining room, the chef, Daniel Richardson, deploys ingredients from sustainable sources for his menus, eg, roast Aylesbury duck breast and confit leg, parsnip and crème fraîche gratin. The dress code in the evening is smart casual. (*Anne and Denis Tate, and others*)

Oxford Road
nr Aylesbury HP17 8NR

T: 01296-747444
F: 01296-747450
E: info@hartwell-house.com
W: www.hartwell-house.com

BEDROOMS: 46, 16 in stable block, some on ground floor, 2 suitable for ♿.
OPEN: all year.
FACILITIES: lift, ramps, 4 drawing rooms, bar, 3 dining rooms, pianist in vestibule Fri/Sat evening, conference facilities, civil wedding licence, spa (swimming pool, 8 by 16 metres), 90-acre grounds (tennis).
BACKGROUND MUSIC: none.
LOCATION: 2 miles W of Aylesbury.
CHILDREN: not under 4.
DOGS: allowed in some rooms.
CREDIT CARDS: Amex, MasterCard, Visa.
PRICES: [2010] B&B £100–£325 per person, D,B&B from £130, set dinner from £29.95, full alc £46, special breaks, Christmas/New Year packages.

**25% DISCOUNT VOUCHERS**

# BARNSLEY Gloucestershire

## BARNSLEY HOUSE    **NEW**

In a village near Cirencester, this beautiful William and Mary house was the home of Rosemary Verey, who created its celebrated garden. After her death, it was turned into a contemporary hotel. It was bought in 2009 by the owners of *Calcot Manor*, Tetbury (see entry). They have refurbished throughout 'with great sensitivity', says an inspector. The manager is Michele Mella. 'The young staff are charm itself, showing a well-judged blend of formality and friendliness; the welcome is warm, the atmosphere relaxed.' The public areas have wide wooden floorboards, cream colours and part stone walls, 'a huge vase of asparagus fern and cow parsley'. In the panelled restaurant, mirrors on the shutters reflect the light from the garden. The chef is Graham Grafton. 'The food was exceptional: we enjoyed gazpacho with crab and courgettes; tender lamb with pea and bean fricassée; portions were measured, the service well paced.' A junior suite was newly decorated: 'Moss-green walls, deep pile cream carpet, lots of light; a view of the garden from a secret porthole window.' The gardens 'retain the self-seeded informality established by Rosemary Verey'.

Barnsley, nr Cirencester GL7 5EE

T: 01285-740000
F: 01285-740925
E: info@barnsleyhouse.com
W: www.barnsleyhouse.com

BEDROOMS: 18, 7 in stable yard, 1 in cottage, 11 on ground floor.
OPEN: all year.
FACILITIES: lounge, bar, restaurant, cinema, meeting room, civil wedding licence, terrace, 11-acre garden (spa with heated outdoor hydrotherapy pool), unsuitable for &.
BACKGROUND MUSIC: eclectic in restaurant.
LOCATION: 5 miles NE of Cirencester.
CHILDREN: all ages welcomed.
DOGS: allowed in stable yard rooms, not in grounds.
CREDIT CARDS: Amex, MasterCard, Visa.
PRICES: [2010] B&B £137.50–£162.50 per person, D,B&B (Sun-Thurs) £162.50, set dinner £42.50, full alc £60, special breaks, Christmas/New Year packages, 1-night bookings occasionally refused Sat.

# BARWICK Somerset

## LITTLE BARWICK HOUSE

❦ *César award in 2002*

'As good as ever.' 'How it should be done.' Tim and Emma Ford's restaurant-with-rooms in an early 19th-century dower house in lovely countryside remains ever popular with readers. The welcome is friendly, efficient. 'Within minutes of arriving we were seated with tea and fruitcake in front of the drawing room fire.' Emma Ford is the 'calm, smiling' front-of-house; her husband 'has the deftest of touches' in the kitchen: his modern cooking, based on local ingredients, 'is the yardstick we judge other chefs by'. A couple of dishes change daily on his menu (perhaps Cornish scallops, crispy bacon, white truffle oil; breast of maize-fed guineafowl, mushroom risotto). 'We'll long remember the Grand Marnier crème brûlée.' Wines by the glass are 'generous and good'. The attention to detail in the bedrooms is liked: fresh flowers; a choice between duvet and blankets and sheets; a flask of fresh milk. 'Although no room is large, they are comfortably furnished and decorated.' (*Bryan Blaxall, R and J Barrett, Tim Messenger*)

Barwick, nr Yeovil BA22 9TD

T: 01935-423902
F: 01935-420908
E: reservations@barwick7.fsnet.co.uk
W: www.littlebarwickhouse.co.uk

BEDROOMS: 6.
OPEN: all year except Christmas, 2 weeks Jan, restaurant closed Sun evenings, midday on Mon and Tues.
FACILITIES: ramp, 2 lounges, restaurant, conservatory, 3½-acre garden (terrace, paddock), unsuitable for &.
BACKGROUND MUSIC: none.
LOCATION: ¾ mile outside Yeovil.
CHILDREN: not under 5.
DOGS: not allowed in public rooms.
CREDIT CARDS: MasterCard, Visa.
PRICES: [2010] B&B £69–£77 per person, D,B&B £85–£120, set dinner £39.95, 2-night breaks, 1-night bookings sometimes refused.

# BASLOW Derbyshire

Map 3:A6

## THE CAVENDISH

*César award in 2002*

'Highly recommended; welcoming staff, exceptional rooms, excellent food.' New praise comes this year for this traditional country hotel run for the Chatsworth estate by Eric Marsh. He is 'present from 8 am to 8 pm, dispensing easy charm, often helping with luggage,' says a fan (and trusted reporter). One visitor, who found the service 'old-fashioned', complained of parsimony ('cooked breakfast charged by the item'). Refurbishment continues: this year, the *Garden Room* and lounge areas have been refreshed 'to stunning effect'. The chef is now Wayne Rogers, who provides fine dining in the *Gallery* restaurant (dishes like Bolsover smoked haddock tortellini, grilled black pudding). The less formal *Garden Room* has an all-day menu. All bedrooms overlook the Chatsworth estate. 'Well-proportioned' superior rooms have 'thick carpeting, high ceilings: well-cared-for antiques sit alongside modern touches, such as a large television'. 'Cloud-like duvets' and fluffy towels all suggest 'maximum comfort'. There are jugs of fresh milk in a 'well-stocked' mini-fridge. (*Alan Melville, Padi Howard, and others*)

Church Lane
Baslow DE45 1SP

T: 01246-582311
F: 01246-582312
E: info@cavendish-hotel.net
W: www.cavendish-hotel.net

BEDROOMS: 24, 2 on ground floor.
OPEN: all year.
FACILITIES: lounge, bar, 2 restaurants, 2 meeting rooms, ½-acre grounds (putting), river fishing nearby.
BACKGROUND MUSIC: classical in *Gallery*.
LOCATION: on A619, in Chatsworth grounds.
CHILDREN: all ages welcomed.
DOGS: not allowed.
CREDIT CARDS: all major cards.
PRICES: [2010] room £128–£215, breakfast £18.50, set meals £30.25–£48.55 (5% '*service levy*' *added to all accounts*), midweek breaks, 1-night bookings sometimes refused.

**25% DISCOUNT VOUCHERS**

## BASLOW Derbyshire

### FISCHER'S BASLOW HALL

ℚ *César award in 1998*

'Staff are friendly, knowledgeable and attentive' at Max and Susan Fischer's restaurant-with-rooms, a Grade II listed manor house near the Chatsworth estate. A 'cheerful soul', he is the hands-on owner/chef; she is front-of-house in the 'formal but friendly' restaurant. Mr Fischer and Rupert Rowley, the head chef, have a *Michelin* star for their modern European cooking (dishes like loin of rare-breed pork, apple and cider sauce, celeriac, deep-fried langoustine). 'Substitute dishes were not a problem when we took the tasting menu,' says a visitor this year. 'We stayed in a beautiful room in the main part of the house. Our spacious bathroom had a Victorian bath with a rainfall showerhead above. The fittings were traditional, but modern and efficient; the only disappointment was that things that are free in most hotels (Wi-Fi, early morning tea, cooked breakfast) cost extra.' The 'bakery' breakfast has 'a good choice' of fresh fruit, cereals, yogurt, pastries and bread. (*Ken Winslow, and others*)

Calver Road
Baslow DE45 1RR

T: 01246-583259
F: 01246-583818
E: reservations@
   fischers-baslowhall.co.uk
W: www.fischers-baslowhall.co.uk

BEDROOMS: 11, 5 in *Garden House*.
OPEN: all year except 25/26 and 31 Dec, restaurant closed to non-residents Sun night/Mon lunch.
FACILITIES: lounge/bar, breakfast room, 3 dining rooms, function facilities, civil wedding licence, 5-acre grounds, unsuitable for &.
BACKGROUND MUSIC: none.
LOCATION: edge of village.
CHILDREN: not under 12 in restaurant after 7 pm.
DOGS: not allowed.
CREDIT CARDS: MasterCard, Visa.
PRICES: [2010] B&B £75–£110 per person, English breakfast from £6, set dinner £42–£68, 1-night bookings refused for superior rooms at weekends in season.

# BASSENTHWAITE LAKE Cumbria

Map 4: inset C2

## THE PHEASANT

The 19th-century huntsman John Peel was a regular visitor at this L-shaped inn between the lakes and fells of the northern Lake District. Owned by the trustees of the Inglewood estate, it is managed by Matthew Wylie. 'He and his wife are excellent hosts; the ambience, service and food remain consistently high,' say returning visitors this year. There is no background music in the lounges (polished parquet floors, fresh flowers and log fires) or the bar (old oak settles). The bedrooms vary in size. Larger rooms have a sitting area and extras (CD-player, iPod/iPhone dock). Dogs are allowed in two garden rooms in an adjacent lodge. All rooms now have a flask of fresh milk; guests can choose between blankets and sheets or duvets. Bryn Evans was appointed executive chef in June 2010 to oversee new dining arrangements. A fine-dining room overlooking the fells has been created. Bistro-style dishes (steak and chips, pasta, etc) are now served in the original dining room. (*Robert Cooper, Carolyn Unger*)

Bassenthwaite Lake
nr Cockermouth CA13 9YE

T: 017687-76234
F: 017687-76002
E: info@the-pheasant.co.uk
W: www.the-pheasant.co.uk

BEDROOMS: 15, 2 on ground floor in lodge.
OPEN: all year except 25 Dec.
FACILITIES: 3 lounges, bar, dining room, 10-acre grounds, lake 200 yds (fishing), unsuitable for &.
BACKGROUND MUSIC: none.
LOCATION: 5 miles E of Cockermouth, ¼ mile off A66 to Keswick.
CHILDREN: not under 8.
DOGS: allowed in lodge bedrooms and public rooms.
CREDIT CARDS: MasterCard, Visa.
PRICES: [2010] B&B £85–£105 per person, D,B&B £115–£135, set dinner £35–£39.95, midweek breaks, New Year package, 1-night bookings refused Sat.

**25% DISCOUNT VOUCHERS**

# BATH Somerset

Map 2:D1

## APSLEY HOUSE

The Duke of Wellington built this elegant house in 1830 for his mistress. Furnished with fine antiques and paintings, it is now run as a guest house ('with the feel of a hotel', say visitors) by the owners, Nicholas and Claire Potts, and their managers, the 'smart, friendly' Duncan and Anél Neville. This year four more bathrooms have been upgraded, the house has been painted and new gravel laid on the drive. The Wellington Room (the most expensive) has a king-size bed, a slipper bath. Visitors like the up-to-date magazines in the rooms, the toiletries in large bottles, the water on the bedside table. A ground-floor four-poster room, with a walk-in shower, is suitable for visitors with limited mobility. Families can stay in a converted coach house in the garden. There's an honesty bar in the lounge. Breakfast, served in a dining room with floor-to-ceiling windows, has fresh fruit, marmalade in a jar, an extensive cooked selection. A light supper is available by arrangement during the week in the quieter months. It is a 20-minute walk to the city centre. (*T and NC*)

141 Newbridge Hill
Bath BA1 3PT

T: 01225-336966
F: 01225-425462
E: info@apsley-house.co.uk
W: www.apsley-house.co.uk

BEDROOMS: 11, 1 on ground floor, 1 self-contained apartment.
OPEN: all year except 24/25/26 Dec.
FACILITIES: drawing room, bar, dining room, ¼-acre garden.
BACKGROUND MUSIC: Classic FM in dining room.
LOCATION: 1¼ miles W of city centre.
CHILDREN: all ages welcomed (under-2s free).
DOGS: only guide dogs allowed.
CREDIT CARDS: Amex, MasterCard, Visa.
PRICES: [2010] B&B £30–£85 per person, 1-night bookings refused Sat and bank holidays.

**25% DISCOUNT VOUCHERS**

# BATH Somerset

Map 2:D1

## THE BATH PRIORY

On the outskirts of the city, Andrew and
Christina Brownsword's luxury hotel, a listed
mansion in 'well-kept' grounds, has 'the feel of
a country house'. Sue Williams is the manager;
Michael Caines, who holds two *Michelin* stars
at the sister hotel, *Gidleigh Park*, Chagford (see
entry), is the executive chef. 'Excellent,
comfortable; exceptional cooking,' says a visitor
in 2010. Inspectors agreed: 'We were warmly
greeted, well looked after.' The 'elegant' drawing
room and lounge have belle époque chandeliers
and mirrors, fine paintings, flowers. In the 'more
intimate' dining room, the service of the modern
dishes is precise: 'A delectable pumpkin velouté
as a pre-starter; standout dishes were Aylesbury
duck's egg with wild garlic and chanterelle;
perfect pollack with sauerkraut.' Children are
welcomed: four family suites have been added
in an adjacent building. The best bedrooms
overlook the gardens. A smaller room, at the
front, was 'attractive: cream panelled walls, a
gentle floral theme, sofas and chairs, plenty of
storage; a spacious smart bathroom'. Guests have
access to a small spa. The city centre is 20
minutes' walk away. (*WK Wood, and others*)

Weston Road, Bath BA1 2XT

T: 01225-331922
F: 01225-448276
E: mail@thebathpriory.co.uk
W: www.thebathpriory.co.uk

BEDROOMS: 31, 3 on ground floor,
4 family suites in adjacent building,
1 suitable for &.
OPEN: all year.
FACILITIES: ramps, lounge bar, library,
drawing room, 2 dining rooms,
private dining rooms, wine room,
conference facilities, civil wedding
licence, spa (heated indoor pool), 4-
acre grounds (heated outdoor pool).
BACKGROUND MUSIC: none.
LOCATION: 1½ miles W of centre.
CHILDREN: no under-8s in restaurant
at night.
DOGS: allowed in 3 bedrooms, not in
public rooms.
CREDIT CARDS: Amex, MasterCard,
Visa.
PRICES: [2010] B&B £92.50–£297.50
per person, set dinner £65–£90, full alc
£75, special breaks, Christmas/New
Year packages, 1-night bookings
refused weekends.

# BATH Somerset

## NUMBER 30

Within easy walking distance of the city's historic centre, David and Caroline Greenwood's B&B was enjoyed again this year. 'They were very hospitable,' say visitors, 'providing us with good care and dining recommendations.' Another comment: 'The effort made to meet individual needs is impressive: it included matching our preference for the way porridge is made.' The light and airy Victorian house is decorated in pastel colours throughout. Bedrooms, mainly blue and white, are well equipped: 'Ours had a CD-player, flat-screen TV and a large, comfortable double bed; good water pressure in the bathroom.' Three rooms have facilities en suite; the fourth has an adjacent private bathroom. One room has been designed 'with allergy sufferers in mind', say the owners. Free Wi-Fi is available. Breakfast was 'thoroughly well prepared with high-quality ingredients'; fresh fruit, fruit compote, leaf tea, home-made muesli, smoked salmon and scrambled eggs, organic toast and a 'very good' full English. There is a range of vegetarian options. Help is given with luggage. Car parking, 'highly prized' in this busy city, is available by arrangement. (*Shreepal Gosrani, and others*)

30 Crescent Gardens
Bath BA1 2NB

T/F: 01225-337393
E:  numberthirty@talktalk.net
W:  www.numberthirty.com

BEDROOMS: 4.
OPEN: all year except Christmas/New Year.
FACILITIES: dining room, patio garden, unsuitable for &.
BACKGROUND MUSIC: none.
LOCATION: 5 mins' walk from centre, parking.
CHILDREN: not under 12.
DOGS: not allowed.
CREDIT CARDS: MasterCard, Visa.
PRICES: B&B £47.50–£72.50 per person, 1-night bookings refused weekends.

# BATH Somerset

Map 2:D1

## THE QUEENSBERRY

A conversion of four 18th-century town houses, Laurence and Helen Beere's boutique hotel is in a 'beautifully proportioned' residential street, ten minutes' walk from the city centre. 'A warm welcome and very comfortable accommodation,' says a visitor this year. 'The decor, though minimalist, contrasts with the architectural elegance of the street.' (Another guest thought it 'gloomy'.) The lounges have been redecorated this year, and a contemporary bar area has been created. The 'slick' valet parking is much appreciated; the 'helpful staff' are praised in 2010. Bedrooms are individually styled and decorated. 'Ours, in the attic, was bright, but a little cluttered with unrelated furniture.' Another was 'very spacious, as was the bathroom, well equipped and comfortable'. In the split-level basement restaurant, chef Nick Brodie serves a 'superb' modern menu (eg, grey mullet with skate cheeks, Bombay potato, onion bhaji). The background music was 'raucous at dinner, more conducive to digestion at breakfast'. The 'very good' breakfast can be served in the restaurant or in one of the four 'delightful' small terraced gardens. (*Sir Patrick Cormack, Dr Alec Frank, Roger Viner*)

4–7 Russel Street
Bath BA1 2QF

T: 01225-447928
F: 01225-446065
E: reservations@
   thequeensberry.co.uk
W: www.thequeensberry.co.uk

BEDROOMS: 29, some on ground floor.
OPEN: all year, restaurant closed Mon lunch.
FACILITIES: lift, 2 drawing rooms, bar, restaurant, meeting room, 4 linked courtyard gardens, unsuitable for &.
BACKGROUND MUSIC: in restaurant and bar.
LOCATION: near Assembly Rooms.
CHILDREN: all ages welcomed.
DOGS: not allowed.
CREDIT CARDS: MasterCard, Visa.
PRICES: [2010] B&B £77.50–£232.50 per person, D,B&B £99–£257.50, full alc £46, 1-night bookings sometimes refused Sat.

# BATH Somerset

Map 2:D1

## TASBURGH HOUSE

Backed by gardens and a meadow park that run down to the Kennet and Avon canal, this red brick Victorian house is a few minutes by taxi or bus from the city centre. The 'hands-on' owner, Sue Keeling, runs it with her daughter, Antonia. The bedrooms (each named after an English author) vary in size: John Keats can accommodate three people, Percy Shelley five. Two are on the ground floor; a family suite is on the second floor. Six bathrooms have been upgraded this year and the public areas (where music plays all day) have been redecorated. Antonia Keeling, whose background is in catering, cooks simple suppers from Monday to Thursday, on a short menu served in a pretty conservatory with a chandelier (perhaps beef in red wine; vegetarian Wellington). Restaurant lists are also available for Bath. The continental breakfast has home-made muesli, bread from a local bakery; guests can squeeze their own oranges; cooked dishes cost extra. In good weather you can walk along the canal, past fields with sheep. Hen parties and functions are catered for. More reports, please.

Warminster Road
Bath BA2 6SH

T: 01225-425096
F: 01225-463842
E: hotel@bathtasburgh.co.uk
W: www.bathtasburgh.co.uk

BEDROOMS: 12, 2 on ground floor.
OPEN: 14 Jan–21 Dec.
FACILITIES: drawing room, dining room, conservatory, terrace, 7-acre grounds (canal walks, mooring), unsuitable for ♿.
BACKGROUND MUSIC: throughout the day.
LOCATION: on A36 to Warminster, ½ mile E of centre.
CHILDREN: all ages welcomed.
DOGS: only guide dogs allowed.
CREDIT CARDS: Diners, MasterCard, Visa.
PRICES: [2010] B&B (continental breakfast) £55–£95 per person, set dinner (Mon–Thurs) £27.50, special breaks, 1-night bookings refused Sat.

## BEAMINSTER Dorset

Map 1:C6

### BRIDGE HOUSE

'Standards remain consistently high.' Praise in 2010 from visitors of 20 years' standing for Mark and Joanna Donovan's 'pleasant, relaxing' hotel, a former priest's house by a bridge in this pretty market town. A family this year were impressed by 'the unfailingly cheerful staff'. Dating back to the 13th century, the building has old beams, mullioned windows, inglenook fireplaces, thick stone walls. The Donovans, who have a young son, welcome children, who can share a family suite with their parents in the coach house. A small ground-floor room was 'cosy, with a large bed, excellent bedlinen; bathrobes and good toiletries in the immaculate bathroom. Our only niggle was an occasional lack of hot water.' The quietest rooms face a walled garden. Stephen Pielesz is head chef for the brasserie and the oak-beamed dining room with conservatory extension. 'Our meals were delicious, with fresh local ingredients, and home-made bread, preserves and ice creams.' Summer meals can be taken in the garden. (*Mrs VG Bates, and others*)

3 Prout Bridge
Beaminster DT8 3AY

T: 01308-862200
F: 01308-863700
E: enquiries@bridge-house.co.uk
W: www.bridge-house.co.uk

BEDROOMS: 13, 4 in coach house, 4 on ground floor.
OPEN: all year.
FACILITIES: hall/reception, lounge, bar, conservatory, brasserie, restaurant, civil wedding licence, ¼-acre walled garden, al fresco dining.
BACKGROUND MUSIC: light jazz and classical.
LOCATION: 100 yards from centre.
CHILDREN: all ages welcomed.
DOGS: allowed in coach house, in bar except during food service.
CREDIT CARDS: Amex, MasterCard, Visa.
PRICES: [2010] B&B £58–£103 per person, D,B&B £83–£130, full alc £30 (brasserie)–£50 (restaurant), special breaks, Christmas/New Year packages, 1-night bookings refused weekends and bank holidays.

**25% DISCOUNT VOUCHERS**

# BEAULIEU Hampshire

Map 2:E2

## MONTAGU ARMS

Recommended by a visitor this year for 'good food and a warm welcome', this much-extended 18th-century building stands in beautiful gardens in the New Forest national park. Managed by Philip Archer, the brick-faced, wisteria-clad building is traditionally decorated with oak panelling, chintz armchairs and sofas, a log fire in the lounge. The 'well-furnished' bedrooms vary greatly: some overlook Beaulieu Palace, others the garden; some suites have a four-poster bed. Early morning tea or coffee can be delivered to the room. In the *Terrace* restaurant (smart dress code, no trainers or denim), the chef, Matthew Tomkinson, has a *Michelin* star for his 'refined' cooking (dishes like Cornish sea bass, smoked bacon, sweet shallots, red chicory). There is an informal bar/brasserie, *Monty's*, which serves traditional fare (sirloin steak, Caesar salad, a Sunday roast). Children under eight have supper here. Afternoon teas are 'lavish'. Breakfasts, which have a wide choice of home-made pastries and well-cooked hot dishes, are 'excellent'. Guests may use a health club at *Careys Manor*, a sister hotel six miles across the forest. (*EJT Palmer*)

Palace Lane
Beaulieu SO42 7ZL

T: 01590-612324
F: 01590-612188
E: reservations@
   montaguarmshotel.co.uk
W: www.montaguarmshotel.co.uk

BEDROOMS: 22.
OPEN: all year, *Terrace* restaurant occasionally closed Mon.
FACILITIES: lounge, conservatory, bar/brasserie, restaurant, civil wedding licence, garden, access to nearby spa, only public rooms suitable for &.
BACKGROUND MUSIC: none.
LOCATION: village centre.
CHILDREN: all ages welcomed (under-3s stay free).
DOGS: not allowed.
CREDIT CARDS: Amex, MasterCard, Visa.
PRICES: [2010] B&B £89–£169 per person, D,B&B £129–£209, full alc £65, special breaks, Christmas/New Year packages, 1-night bookings refused Sat in season.

**25% DISCOUNT VOUCHERS**

# BERWICK-UPON-TWEED Northumberland    Map 4:A3

## WEST COATES

In mature gardens a short walk from the centre of an interesting border town, this 19th-century merchant's house is the family home of Karen Brown. It is 'warmly' recommended by a reader for the 'welcome and comfort'. Bedrooms are 'beautifully' furnished, and have 'everything one could want': books and magazines, a flask of chilled water and 'home-made cake on the hospitality tray each day'. One room has antique furniture and a spacious dressing room/bathroom; there is a freestanding roll-top bath in two bathrooms. 'An accomplished cook', Mrs Brown serves a no-choice three-course dinner menu using local and seasonal produce, perhaps a seafood platter (half a lobster, crab claws, langoustines); Borders beef, Marsala and mushrooms. Breakfast, taken at a communal table in the kitchen, is substantial and includes a choice of cereals, muesli, fruit compote; smoked haddock with poached egg, full English; home-made bread and preserves. There is a pool house with a heated swimming pool and hot tub. Mrs Brown runs a cookery school. (*JTR*)

30 Castle Terrace
Berwick-upon-Tweed TD15 1NZ

T/F: 01289-309666
E:   karenbrownwestcoates@
     yahoo.com
W:  www.westcoates.co.uk

BEDROOMS: 3.
OPEN: all year except 3 weeks Christmas/New Year.
FACILITIES: sitting/dining room, 2½-acre garden, 12-metre indoor swimming pool, hot tub, croquet, unsuitable for &.
BACKGROUND MUSIC: 'varied'.
LOCATION: 10 mins' walk from centre.
CHILDREN: not allowed.
DOGS: not allowed.
CREDIT CARDS: MasterCard, Visa.
PRICES: B&B £45–£60 per person, D,B&B £80–£95, full alc £35, special breaks, 1-night bookings refused weekends.

# BIDEFORD Devon

Map 1:C4

## THE MOUNT

'A super B&B', this handsome Georgian house is close to the town centre and the quay with its medieval bridge. The owners, Andrew and Heather Laugharne, are 'pleasant and friendly', says a visitor in 2010. The house is in a part-walled garden with large and handsome trees, and 'ample car parking'. The lounge has an open fire, grand piano and well-stocked library; in the dining room are Venetian pictures and antique furniture. Striking colours abound; red walls highlight the white-painted, winding staircase. Local produce is used for breakfast, 'delicious, good and well cooked'. The bedrooms 'vary widely in style: traditional to modern, restful to flamboyant. One pleasing room had a huge bed, excellent storage.' 'The beds, bedding and towels are of the highest quality.' The house has a licence to sell drinks: the Laugharnes promise 'a good selection of wines and spirits'. 'Good walking on the Devon Coast Path; the Tarka Trail with 31 miles of traffic-free cycling passes close to the house.' *Yeoldon House*, Northam (see entry), is recommended for dinner. (*A Roy, Sarah and Tom Mann*)

Northdown Road
Bideford EX39 3LP

T: 01237-473748
F: 01271-373813
E: andrew@themountbideford.co.uk
W: www.themountbideford.co.uk

BEDROOMS: 8, some family, 1 on ground floor.
OPEN: all year, except Christmas.
FACILITIES: ramp, lounge, breakfast room, ⅓-acre garden.
BACKGROUND MUSIC: none.
LOCATION: town centre.
CHILDREN: all ages welcomed.
DOGS: not allowed.
CREDIT CARDS: Amex, MasterCard, Visa.
PRICES: B&B £32–£40 per person, 1-night bookings may be refused.

# BIGBURY-ON-SEA Devon

## BURGH ISLAND HOTEL

'Wonderfully romantic', this large white Art
Deco building stands like a ship on a private
tidal island in Bigbury Bay. The owners, Tony
Orchard and Deborah Clark, have renovated
throughout. 'The period atmosphere has been
meticulously maintained, down to the last
teapot and door knob,' say inspectors in 2010.
'You have to like the 1930s music played in
the beautiful public rooms.' The dining room
is candlelit in the evening, when black tie is
encouraged but not demanded. 'The atmosphere
is relaxed, you can dine when you like. We were
looked after by a charming Slovenian brother
and sister.' The chef, Conor Heneghan, serves
modern dishes on a seasonal menu (eg, peppered
duckling breast, chestnut lentils, beetroot purée):
'Dinner was good; bream and lemon tart were
tasty.' Bedrooms vary hugely: the Mermaid Suite
has a separate lounge, views over the natural
rock swimming pool. 'Our simple, small room,
decorated in brown, had a sofa; a sea outlook
from a balcony with chairs.' Breakfast has 'leaf
tea, excellent bread, no packages'. At high tide,
guests are transported by sea tractor.

Burgh Island
Bigbury-on-Sea TQ7 4BG

T: 01548-810514
F: 01548-810243
E: reception@burghisland.com
W: www.burghisland.com

BEDROOMS: 25, 1 suite in beach house,
apartment above Pilchard Inn.
OPEN: all year, restaurant closed Sun
evening.
FACILITIES: lift, sun lounge, Palm
Court bar, dining room, ballroom,
children's games room, spa, civil
wedding licence, 12-acre grounds on
27-acre island (30-metre natural sea
swimming pool, tennis).
BACKGROUND MUSIC: in public areas.
LOCATION: 5 miles S of Modbury,
private garages on mainland.
CHILDREN: not under 5, no under-12s
at dinner.
DOGS: not allowed.
CREDIT CARDS: MasterCard, Visa.
PRICES: [2010] D,B&B £192.50–£300
per person, set dinner £57, full alc £75,
special events, Christmas/New Year
packages, 1-night bookings
sometimes refused weekends.

# BIGBURY-ON-SEA Devon

Map 1:D4

## THE HENLEY

♀*César award in 2003*

'One of our favourites: relaxed, low-key, unfussy; good food.' 'Everything is as good as ever; we can't wait to go back.' Praise comes again this year for this Edwardian beach house on a cliff above the Avon estuary. The owners, Martyn Scarterfield and Petra Lampe, have a small daughter, Marika Anne; 'her addition is very welcome,' say returning visitors. The public rooms have Lloyd Loom chairs, magazines and binoculars. 'Everyone meets for pre-dinner drinks, while Petra recites the menu in her inimitable way.' Her husband's 'wonderful' cooking 'never disappoints'. The short menu 'may not change much but we don't mind; we enjoyed a fantastic rack of lamb. Sometimes when they are busy, you can wait between courses. This is not a place to be in a rush; everything is freshly prepared.' The simple bedrooms, recently upgraded, 'are pleasant with good bathroom and sea views; housekeeping is good'. Breakfast, 'served when you like', is 'tasty'. The cliff path has been closed for repair. (*Jane and Stephen Savery, Jenny Morgan, Colin and Jennifer Beales*)

Folly Hill
Bigbury-on-Sea TQ7 4AR

T/F: 01548-810240
E:   thehenleyhotel@btconnect.com
W:  www.thehenleyhotel.co.uk

BEDROOMS: 5.
OPEN: Mar–Oct.
FACILITIES: 2 lounges, bar, conservatory dining room, small garden (steps to beach, golf, sailing, fishing), Coast Path nearby, unsuitable for &.
BACKGROUND MUSIC: jazz, classical in the evenings in lounge, dining room.
LOCATION: 5 miles S of Modbury.
CHILDREN: not under 12.
DOGS: not allowed in public rooms.
CREDIT CARDS: Amex, MasterCard, Visa.
PRICES: [2010] B&B £56.50–£68 per person, D,B&B (3 nights min.) £79–£102, set dinner £34, 1-night bookings refused weekends.

# BIGGIN-BY-HARTINGTON Derbyshire     Map 3:B6

## BIGGIN HALL

'A wonderful base for a walking visit to the Derbyshire Dales', James Moffett's Grade II* listed 17th-century building, with stone walls, antiques and mullioned windows, is run in relaxed house-party style. Steven Williams is the manager. The simple bedrooms are spacious; eight are in the main house (including the oak-beamed master suite which has a four-poster), others are in the courtyard, the 'bothy' and the lodge. 'Our room may have been approaching its make-over date, but it was delightfully warm, with plenty of space.' The lounge, with its massive stone fireplace (dated 1672), is a gathering place for guests before dinner, which is served at 7 pm in the beamed dining room. The chef, Mark Wilton, uses local produce for his traditional dishes, eg, honey-roasted ham, creamy Dijon sauce; Bakewell tart with custard. 'Excellent, without being flamboyant or pretentious.' Breakfast, served between 8 and 9 am, is a hot and cold buffet (kippers are available on request). 'A variety of circular, scenic walks starts from the front door.' Winter breaks are 'excellent value'. (*Bob and Deborah Steel, and others*)

Biggin-by-Hartington
Buxton SK17

T: 01298-84451
E: enquiries@bigginhall.co.uk
W: www.bigginhall.co.uk

BEDROOMS: 20, 12 in annexes, some on ground floor.
OPEN: all year.
FACILITIES: sitting room, library, dining room, meeting room, civil wedding licence, 8-acre grounds (croquet), River Dove 1½ miles, unsuitable for &.
BACKGROUND MUSIC: classical.
LOCATION: 8 miles N of Ashbourne.
CHILDREN: not under 12.
DOGS: allowed in some bedrooms, not in public rooms.
CREDIT CARDS: MasterCard, Visa.
PRICES: [2010] B&B £39–£68 per person, D,B&B £53–£82, set dinner £19.50, Christmas/New Year packages, 1-night bookings sometimes refused.

**25% DISCOUNT VOUCHERS**

# BLAKENEY Norfolk

Map 2:A5

## THE BLAKENEY HOTEL

'A most appealing place', this 'unpretentious but comfortable' hotel is on the quayside of a tidal estuary; 'a few steps and you are among the crabbers and boats'. Owned by Michael Stannard, it is managed by Ann Thornalley: 'The whole crew, from kitchens to front-of-house, provides unflappable service,' says a returning visitor in 2010. Another guest says: 'One of the charms of the building is its irregularity. This means the rooms vary greatly, and it is worth discussing your choice when you book.' A garden room 'was a trifle old-fashioned, but comfortable; housekeeping was immaculate'. Visitors returning to their favourite room were 'delighted to find it stylishly redecorated'. 'It was clean, smart, with a new bathroom; a lovely estuary view.' The restaurant is 'pleasingly consistent; main courses are fairly traditional but have fresh local produce and nicely cooked vegetables'. 'Mr Stannard appeared at dinner every night.' Light meals are served in the bar and on the terrace. 'This is the perfect family hotel; the children particularly appreciated the swimming pool.' (*David Nicholls, Mary Wilmer, Sir John Hall*)

Blakeney
nr Holt NR25 7NE

T: 01263-740797
F: 01263-740795
E: reception@blakeney-hotel.co.uk
W: www.blakeney-hotel.co.uk

BEDROOMS: 63, 16 in *Granary* annexe opposite, some on ground floor.
OPEN: all year.
FACILITIES: lift, ramps, lounge, sun lounge, bar, restaurant, function facilities, indoor heated swimming pool (12 by 5 metres), steam room, sauna, spa bath, mini-gym, games room, ¼-acre garden.
BACKGROUND MUSIC: none.
LOCATION: on quay.
CHILDREN: all ages welcomed.
DOGS: allowed in some bedrooms, not in public rooms.
CREDIT CARDS: all major cards.
PRICES: [2010] B&B £74–£135 per person, D,B&B £86–£147, set dinner £27.50, full alc £56, activity breaks, Christmas/New Year packages, 1-night bookings sometimes refused Fri/Sat, bank holidays.

# BLOCKLEY Gloucestershire

Map 3:D6

## LOWER BROOK HOUSE **NEW**

'A good place, full of character', this converted mill (Grade II listed), is in a Cotswold village noted for its silk production. It is run as a 'welcoming and homely' small hotel by owners Julian and Anna Ebbutt. An inspector was 'enchanted by candles lit in the window' as she arrived. Downstairs, there is a small dining room, and two sitting areas, decorated 'in bold colours; a medley of personal objects, antique and modern, displayed to advantage'. The bedrooms are small: 'A lot of thought has been put into the well-being of guests; our room was decorated in plain, modern style; a king-size bed filled much of the space; everything was spotless; a Thermos of cold milk with the coffee-making facilities was a nice touch; the bathroom was well equipped.' Mrs Ebbutt cooks 'plain, homely, British' dishes: 'Julian serves the meals competently; everything on a hot plate; chicken with wild mushrooms, onions, and stuffing soaked in Marsala was delicious; scrumptious sticky toffee pudding. Breakfast was very good indeed; a small buffet with freshly pressed orange juice, good toast, heavenly preserves; cooked dishes were copious.'

Lower Street
Blockley GL56 9DS

T: 01386 700286
F: 01386-701400
E: info@lowerbrookhouse.com
W: www.lowerbrookhouse.com

BEDROOMS: 6.
OPEN: all year except Christmas, restaurant closed Sun night.
FACILITIES: lounge, restaurant, 1-acre garden, unsuitable for &.
BACKGROUND MUSIC: in restaurant at night.
LOCATION: centre of village.
CHILDREN: not under 10.
DOGS: not allowed.
CREDIT CARDS: Amex, MasterCard, Visa.
PRICES: [2010] B&B £40–£92.50 per person, full alc £34, special offers, New Year package, 1-night bookings sometimes refused Sat.

**25% DISCOUNT VOUCHERS**

# BORROWDALE Cumbria

Map 4: inset C2

## THE LEATHES HEAD HOTEL

'The ideal small hotel with friendly hands-on owner/managers.' Roy and Janice Smith's gabled Edwardian house, on an elevated site with views across the Borrowdale valley, is 'thoroughly recommended' this year. Returning visitors welcomed the 'improvements they have introduced modern TVs; a flask of fresh milk and iced water in the bedrooms'. 'There is excellent access for the slightly disabled; and pretty good, too, if you are in a wheelchair,' said one guest. 'We had a large downstairs room, very comfortable and clean.' The double-aspect rooms, recommended by readers, have been upgraded for 2010, with queen-size bed and renovated bathroom. There are three lounge areas; one has oak panels, armchairs, pictures in wooden frames; a sunroom has wicker chairs and excellent views. There are books (including walking guides) and games. The long-serving chef, David Jackson, serves modern English dishes (eg, sesame and lemongrass fishcakes; roast loin of pork, sage and a cider jus) on a daily-changing four-course menu. 'The meals were varied, well cooked and served on hot plates. Most enjoyable.' 'Good value.' (*Michael and Betty Hill, Derek Ward*)

Borrowdale
Keswick CA12 5UY

T: 017687-77247
F: 017687-77363
E: enq@leatheshead.co.uk
W: www.leatheshead.co.uk

BEDROOMS: 12, 3 on ground floor, 1 suitable for &.
OPEN: Feb–Nov.
FACILITIES: ramp, lounge, sun lounge, bar lounge, restaurant, sun terrace, 3-acre grounds (woodland).
BACKGROUND MUSIC: none.
LOCATION: 3¾ miles S of Keswick.
CHILDREN: not under 15.
DOGS: not allowed.
CREDIT CARDS: MasterCard, Visa.
PRICES: D,B&B £76.95–£115.95 per person, set dinner £32.95, special breaks, 1-night bookings refused at weekends.

**25% DISCOUNT VOUCHERS**

# BORROWDALE Cumbria

Map 4: inset C2

## SEATOLLER HOUSE

'From the outside, it is simple, without pretension; inside, the rooms are unexpectedly spacious though the door lintels are low. Seldom have we had such a warm welcome.' Visitors returning after 20 years 'enjoyed their stay greatly' at this guest house that has been welcoming walkers and ramblers for more than a century. Owned by a private company, it is managed by Daniel Potts and Lynne Moorehouse, 'ebullient and hard-working'. The furniture 'still has a shabby, dependable air'; there is a 'welcome indifference to frivolities like TV, radio and newspapers'. Dinner is taken with 'a degree of do-it-yourself conviviality at two good oak tables; after the gong sounds, a freshly baked loaf arrives at each; a guest sees to the cutting. The cooking is plain, but Lynne Moorehouse has a sure touch with spices. Large dishes and bowls of enjoyable, nourishing food are passed around the table.' At the head of the Borrowdale valley, the house is 'an excellent base for serious walkers: fellow guests are knowledgeable about the different routes'. Local weather forecasts are provided. (*T and SM*)

Borrowdale
Keswick CA12 5XN

T: 017687-77218
F: 017687-77189
E: seatollerhouse@btconnect.com
W: www.seatollerhouse.co.uk

BEDROOMS: 10, 2 on ground floor, 1 in garden bungalow, all with shower.
OPEN: 11 Mar–27 Nov, dining room closed midday, Tues night.
FACILITIES: lounge, library, tea bar, dining room, drying room, 1-acre grounds (beck), unsuitable for &.
BACKGROUND MUSIC: none.
LOCATION: on B5289, 7 miles S of Keswick.
CHILDREN: not under 5 (unless in a private group).
DOGS: not allowed in public rooms.
CREDIT CARDS: MasterCard, Visa.
PRICES: [2010] B&B £43 per person, D,B&B £64, reductions for longer stays, 1-night bookings sometimes refused.

# BOSCASTLE Cornwall

Map 1:C3

## THE OLD RECTORY

In an 'exceptional setting' in a valley above
Boscastle, this handsome stone house 'is well
looked after' by owners Chris and Sally Searle.
Due homage is paid to its history: here Thomas
Hardy met his future wife Emma Gifford, the
rector's sister. Hardy memorabilia and historical
pictures of the house are displayed in the dining
room. 'Sally greeted us warmly and sat down
over a cup of tea and biscuits to tell us about
the house and area,' say inspectors this year.
'Our room, Emma's, had large sash windows
overlooking the delightful south-facing garden.
The details were good: a panic box with
"anything you have forgotten"; a basket for
recyclable items; tea-making with fresh milk in
a fridge downstairs.' One bedroom, Old Stables,
has its own entrance. Sally Searle has won an
award for her 'superb' breakfast (taken at a time
agreed the evening before). 'A wonderful home-
made compote with plums, strawberries and
raspberries from the garden; freshly squeezed
orange and apple juice; golden scrambled eggs,
French toast with nectarines; slabs of butter,
delicious blackberry preserve.'

St Juliot, nr Boscastle PL35 0BT

T: 01840-250225
E: sally@stjuliot.com
W: www.stjuliot.com

BEDROOMS: 4, 1 in stables (linked to
house).
OPEN: mid-Feb–mid-Nov, 3 days
Christmas, 3 days New Year.
FACILITIES: sitting room, breakfast
room, 3-acre garden (croquet lawn,
'lookout'), unsuitable for &.
BACKGROUND MUSIC: none.
LOCATION: 2 miles NE of Boscastle.
CHILDREN: not under 12.
DOGS: only allowed in stables.
CREDIT CARDS: MasterCard, Visa.
PRICES: [2010] B&B £35–£49 per
person, 1-night bookings refused
weekends, 'busy periods'.

# BOSHAM West Sussex

Map 2:E3

## THE MILLSTREAM

'Strongly recommended' again this year, this converted manor house stands in manicured gardens near the harbour of this 'lovely' village. It has long been managed by Antony Wallace, who is 'courteous and efficient'; the staff are 'well trained'. A visitor in a wheelchair found 'the welcome and extra help simply astounding; every consideration was given to my disability, without intrusion'. This year, the public areas have been renovated (there is a new automatic front door) and eight bedrooms restyled. A ground-floor room with French doors opening on to the garden was liked. A smaller room was 'adequate, comfortable'. Neil Hiskey, who has been in the kitchen for ten years, has been promoted to head chef. His style is modern, eg, seared scallops, foie gras sauce; slow-roasted belly of pork, apple jus, celeriac and potato purée. 'The food used to be good; now it is exceptional,' says a returning visitor. Early suppers are provided for guests attending the Chichester theatre. Breakfast has an extensive choice. (*Mrs Blethyn Elliott, Dr JMR Irving, Rachel Macdonald*)

Bosham Lane
Bosham, nr Chichester PO18 8HL

T: 01243-573234
F: 01243-573459
E: info@millstream-hotel.co.uk
W: www.millstream-hotel.co.uk

BEDROOMS: 35, 2 in cottage, 7 on ground floor, 1 suitable for &.
OPEN: all year.
FACILITIES: lounge, bar, restaurant (pianist Fri and Sat), conference room, civil wedding licence, 1½-acre garden (stream, gazebo), Chichester Harbour (sailing, fishing) 300 yards.
BACKGROUND MUSIC: classical 10.30 am–10.30 pm.
LOCATION: 4 miles W of Chichester.
CHILDREN: all ages welcomed.
DOGS: only guide dogs allowed.
CREDIT CARDS: all major cards.
PRICES: [2010] B&B £72.50–£82.50 per person, D,B&B (min. 2 nights) £75–£112, set dinner £23.50–£30, Christmas/New Year packages, 1-night bookings refused Sat.

# BOURTON-ON-THE-HILL Gloucestershire    Map 3:D6

## THE HORSE AND GROOM

'Just how a gastropub should be: outstanding staff and food; friendly, informative; correct in all the details. They made us want to be English.' Praise from American visitors for Tom and Will Greenstock's Grade II listed Georgian building at the top of a hill in a honey-stone village. 'Tom greeted us warmly and took us straight to our room,' said visitors arriving 'guiltily early in the afternoon'. 'Our room was spacious, contemporary; quality furnishings and a wonderfully comfortable bed. Although it faced the road, traffic noise was not a problem, thanks to luxurious curtains.' Dinner, served in the 'unpretentious' old public bar, 'was a treat'. Readers enjoyed 'exceptional duck on polenta with chorizo and pancetta'; 'lemon sole cooked to perfection'. Puddings are 'simple and wonderfully presented'. The brothers 'were in evidence throughout the evening'. Breakfast is cooked to order, including freshly squeezed orange juice, 'delicious' bacon and 'creamy' scrambled egg. 'Good coffee' and 'unhurried relaxed service'. 'We loved our stay and will return without a doubt.' (*Stuart W Gardner, Christopher Butterworth, and others*)

Bourton-on-the-Hill
nr Moreton-in-Marsh GL56 9AQ

T/F:01386-700413
E: greenstocks@horseandgroom.info
W: www.horseandgroom.info

BEDROOMS: 5.
OPEN: all year except 25/31 Dec, restaurant closed Sun eve.
FACILITIES: bar/restaurant, 1-acre garden, unsuitable for &.
BACKGROUND MUSIC: none.
LOCATION: village centre.
CHILDREN: all ages welcomed.
DOGS: allowed in garden only.
CREDIT CARDS: MasterCard, Visa.
PRICES: [2010] B&B £44–£80 per person, full alc £30, midweek discounts, 1-night bookings refused weekends.

# BOWNESS-ON-WINDERMERE Cumbria   Map 4: inset C2

## FAYRER GARDEN HOUSE HOTEL

'I felt pampered,' says a visitor to Claire and Eric Wildsmith's 'very comfortable and well looked-after' hotel in a 'fine position' above Lake Windermere. Mark Jones is the 'helpful' manager. The Edwardian house stands in 'attractive' gardens with panoramic views of the lake: 'It was a real bonus to sit out here on a sunny weekend. Our spacious and well-equipped bedroom had a distant view over the garden to the water.' A single room was 'luxurious; lovely curtains and cushions'. Ground-floor rooms are good for people with a mobility problem. The public rooms have the views. The 'lovely' lounge is 'full of squashy chairs and sofas'; there are original oil paintings, flowers from the award-winning garden. In the air-conditioned *Terrace Restaurant*, the service by 'smiley staff who aim to please' is praised again this year. Head chef Eddie Wilkinson serves a daily-changing five-course menu of modern dishes using local produce, eg, loin of Cumberland pork, boulangère potatoes, green beans, sweetcorn pancake. Vegetarian options are available. (*DB, Dr and Mrs G Collingham*)

Lyth Valley Road
Bowness-on-Windermere LA23 3JP

T: 015394-88195
F: 015394-45986
E: lakescene@fayrergarden.com
W: www.fayrergarden.com

BEDROOMS: 29, 5 in cottage in grounds, 7 on ground floor.
OPEN: all year except first 2 weeks Jan.
FACILITIES: 2 lounges, lounge bar, restaurant, civil wedding licence, 5-acre grounds.
BACKGROUND MUSIC: classical, 'easy listening'.
LOCATION: 1 mile S of Bowness on A5074.
CHILDREN: not under 5.
DOGS: allowed in cottage rooms only.
CREDIT CARDS: MasterCard, Visa.
PRICES: B&B £53–£110 per person, D,B&B £62–£140, set dinner £40, Christmas/New Year packages, 1-night bookings sometimes refused Sat.

# BOWNESS-ON-WINDERMERE Cumbria    Map 4: inset C2

## LINDETH FELL

♛*César award in 2009*

'We have never seen a hotel where the individual needs of guests are given so much attention.' Trusted *Guide* readers 'very much enjoyed' their 2010 return to Diana Kennedy's Edwardian gentleman's residence above Lake Windermere. Mrs Kennedy works closely with Linda Hartill, the long-serving manager: the staff are 'well trained and unobtrusive, going quietly about their duties'. Other returning visitors found 'standards as high as ever; everything was immaculate and well serviced'. The house is 'cosy, distinctly old-fashioned, and obviously patronised by an older generation'. 'Our bedroom at the top overlooked the roof with a glimpse of the lake on one side, the garden on the other. Everything was replenished at night and in the morning.' Laura Hannigan is the new chef, serving a traditional menu with daily and seasonal changes. Dishes, perhaps pan-fried salmon, baby fennel, crushed new potatoes, are 'well presented without being precious'. 'Breakfast is as satisfying as ever, the cold buffet supplemented by cooked dishes, and hot croissants and toast.' (*Francine and Ian Walsh, and others*)

Lyth Valley Road
Bowness-on-Windermere LA23 3JP

T: 015394-43286
F: 015394-47455
E: kennedy@lindethfell.co.uk
W: www.lindethfell.co.uk

BEDROOMS: 14, 1 on ground floor.
OPEN: all year except 3 weeks in Jan.
FACILITIES: ramp, hall, 2 lounges, dispense bar, 3 dining rooms, 7-acre grounds (gardens, croquet, putting, bowls, tarn, fishing permits).
BACKGROUND MUSIC: none.
LOCATION: 1 mile S of Bowness on A5074.
CHILDREN: all ages welcomed.
DOGS: only assistance dogs allowed.
CREDIT CARDS: MasterCard, Visa.
PRICES: [2010] B&B £60–£95 per person, D,B&B £92–£130, set dinner £36, Christmas/New Year packages, special breaks, 1-night bookings sometimes refused Sat, bank holidays.

**25% DISCOUNT VOUCHERS**

# BOWNESS-ON-WINDERMERE Cumbria    Map 4: inset C2

## LINTHWAITE HOUSE

The owner, Mike Bevans, has 'sensitively' extended his timbered, creeper-covered, white and stone house which stands in 'lovely gardens' overlooking the middle stretch of Lake Windermere. Andrew Nicholson is the manager; his staff are 'friendly, professional'. The 'welcoming' lounge has colonial furniture, ornaments, potted plants; a log fire in winter, and an enclosed veranda facing the lake. Housekeeping is 'faultless' in the bedrooms, some of which have lake views. One room, which overlooked the garden, was 'large, with a comfortable bed, good sitting space and well-equipped bathroom'. Five contemporary rooms, each with a private terrace, are in an extension; the loft suite has a separate lounge, a telescope and a sliding glass roof (which closes automatically if it rains). The chef, Richard Kearsley, 'shows great attention to detail' in his modern dishes, perhaps pressing of pork belly and quince; roasted sea bass, braised beef shin, Puy lentils. A 'tasty and hearty' breakfast has 'the bonus of home-made damson jam'. There is good walking from the door; a tarn in the grounds. (*Roger and Margaret Murton, and others*)

Crook Road
Bowness-on-Windermere LA23 3JA

T: 015394-88600
F: 015394-88601
E: stay@linthwaite.com
W: www.linthwaite.com

BEDROOMS: 31, some on ground floor.
OPEN: all year.
FACILITIES: ramp, lounge/bar, conservatory, 3 dining rooms, function facilities, civil wedding licence, 14-acre grounds (croquet, tarn, fly-fishing).
BACKGROUND MUSIC: in bar all day, dining room during meals.
LOCATION: ¾ mile S of Bowness.
CHILDREN: no under-7s in dining rooms after 7 pm.
DOGS: allowed in two bedrooms only (also outdoor kennel).
CREDIT CARDS: Amex, MasterCard, Visa.
PRICES: [2010] B&B £66–£248 per person, D,B&B £106–£288, set dinner £49, special breaks, Christmas/New Year packages, 1-night bookings refused some weekends, bank holidays.

**25% DISCOUNT VOUCHERS**

## BRADPOLE Dorset

Map 1:C6

## ORCHARD BARN

At the house which they built on the site of an old Dorset farm on the banks of the River Asker, Nigel and Margaret Corbett welcome B&B visitors, many of whom knew the couple when they ran *Summer Lodge* at Evershot (see entry). The Corbetts, who have been involved with hotels for more than 50 years, live in a separate wing. Visitors have their own large, vaulted-ceilinged lounge with an open fire and gallery. Afternoon tea with home-made cake and shortbread is served here or, in summer, in the peaceful south-facing garden. Two of the 'comfortable' bedrooms lead directly off the sitting room; one of these (the Mews Room) has its own front door and lobby. The Gallery Room, on the first floor, is spacious and has a well-appointed bathroom with shower. Mrs Corbett's jams and marmalade are served at breakfast, which has Fairtrade teas and coffee, interesting yogurts, home-baked wholemeal toast, free-range eggs, local bacon and sausages. Light snacks (Quiche Lorraine, West Bay crab salad) can be provided on a tray in the evening (at 24 hours' notice); many eating places are nearby. (*MK*)

Bradpole
nr Bridport DT6 4AR

T/F: 01308-455655
E: enquiries@
   lodgeatorchardbarn.co.uk
W: www.lodgeatorchardbarn.co.uk

BEDROOMS: 3, 1 on ground floor.
OPEN: all year except Christmas/New Year.
FACILITIES: lounge, dining room.
BACKGROUND MUSIC: none.
LOCATION: off A35, via Lee Lane, in village adjoining Bridport.
CHILDREN: all ages welcomed.
DOGS: allowed in public rooms subject to other guests' approval.
CREDIT CARDS: none accepted.
PRICES: [2010] B&B £52.50–£90 per person, snack supper £5–£15, 1-night bookings sometimes refused.

# BRAITHWAITE Cumbria

Map 4: inset C2

## THE COTTAGE IN THE WOOD

In a 'beautiful' setting within the forest on Whinlatter Pass, looking down to the Skiddaw mountain range, Kath and Liam Berney run their 17th-century coaching inn as a restaurant-with-rooms. 'A wonderful place in an amazing location,' says a visitor in 2010. 'Excellent service, delicious food.' A regular correspondent found it 'a simply lovely place to stay and eat'. The Berneys tell us they have added a 'garden' bedroom in 2010, 'our best room'. A room in the attic has a roll-top bath and a separate shower. Oak and Sycamore are deluxe rooms, with king-size bed and mountain views. 'Cosy' cottage rooms are smaller. The large, white restaurant has a conservatory extension with forest views. Rupert Willday is the chef, cooking modern British dishes. 'We enjoyed the potted shrimps, mullet and wild trout; an excellent cheese plate and delicious white chocolate mousse with raspberries.' Guests can take tea or evening meals on the terrace. Breakfast has fresh grapefruit, local bacon and eggs, home-made jam and marmalade. 'Ideal for walkers and mountain bikers; good value.' (*Elaine Magnani, Hilary Blakemore, Sarah Tricks*)

Magic Hill
Whinlatter Forest
Braithwaite CA12 5TW

T: 017687-78409
E: relax@thecottageinthewood.co.uk
W: www.thecottageinthewood.co.uk

BEDROOMS: 10, 1 on ground floor.
OPEN: Feb–Dec, restaurant closed Mon.
FACILITIES: lounge, bar, restaurant, 5-acre grounds (terraced garden).
BACKGROUND MUSIC: popular, classical in restaurant.
LOCATION: 5 miles NW of Keswick.
CHILDREN: not under 10.
DOGS: not allowed.
CREDIT CARDS: MasterCard, Visa.
PRICES: B&B £48–£75 per person, D,B&B £76–£103, set dinner £28, midweek breaks, Christmas/New Year packages, 1-night bookings refused weekends.

# BRAMPTON Cumbria

Map 4:B3

## FARLAM HALL

*César award in 2001*

Approached up a sweeping drive past an ornamental lake, this old house, mainly Victorian, has been run as a traditional hotel (Relais & Châteaux) by the Quinion family for 35 years. 'We are a genuine family team working with enthusiastic local people; we pride ourselves on being staunchly English,' they say. Readers have long liked the 'sense of humour' that runs alongside old-fashioned service. Smart dress is preferred at dinner, served at 8 pm in the large dining room, which has floor-to-ceiling windows that overlook the garden and lake. Barry Quinion supervises the kitchen that produces a daily-changing menu of 'English country house dishes', eg, pheasant breast with herb mousse, smoked bacon mashed potatoes, red wine sauce. Ornately Victorian public rooms have an open fire, patterned wallpaper, fresh flowers, ornaments. The bedrooms, also with floral designs, vary in size and are priced accordingly. A 'classic' cooked breakfast is served in the restaurant; a continental breakfast can be taken in your room. More reports, please.

Brampton CA8 2NG

T: 01697-746234
F: 01697-746683
E: farlam@farlamhall.co.uk
W: www.farlamhall.co.uk

BEDROOMS: 12, 1 in stables, 2 on ground floor.
OPEN: all year except 24–30 Dec, 3–13 Jan, restaurant closed midday (light lunches for residents by arrangement).
FACILITIES: ramps, 2 lounges, restaurant, 10-acre grounds (croquet lawn), unsuitable for &.
BACKGROUND MUSIC: none.
LOCATION: on A689, 2½ miles SE of Brampton (not in Farlam village).
CHILDREN: not under 5.
DOGS: not allowed unattended in bedrooms.
CREDIT CARDS: Amex, MasterCard, Visa.
PRICES: [2010] B&B £102–£132 per person, D,B&B £145–£175, set dinner £43–£45, special breaks, New Year package.

**25% DISCOUNT VOUCHERS**

# BRANCASTER STAITHE Norfolk

Map 2:A5

## THE WHITE HORSE

'A super place to stay, with great views across the salt marshes and the sea.' 'Lovely, highly recommended for the excellent food and superb ambience.' Cliff Nye's relaxed inn on the marshland coast of north Norfolk 'didn't disappoint' visitors this year. The interior is open plan, with a linked bar (wall settles and plain tables); a lounge area with sofas and Lloyd Loom chairs; and a conservatory restaurant facing the sea. Outside is a landscaped sunken garden with a sun canopy over the eating area for alfresco dining. The best of the bedrooms in the main building is the Room at the Top, on two levels. 'It was spacious, well equipped; the telescope by a small balcony helped us make the most of the views.' Eight ground-floor rooms in the garden are architecturally designed with grass and sedum roofing, to blend in with the landscape. Each has a terrace with direct access to the Norfolk Coast Path. In the restaurant, chef Rene Llupar offers 'amazing local mussels and fish dishes of a high order'. There is also a bar menu and a children's menu. (*Dr and Mrs G Collingham, Elizabeth Tyrrell*)

Brancaster Staithe
PE31 8BY

T: 01485-210262
F: 01485-210930
E: reception@
   whitehorsebrancaster.co.uk
W: www.whitehorsebrancaster.co.uk

BEDROOMS: 15, 8 on ground floor in annexe, 1 suitable for ♿.
OPEN: all year.
FACILITIES: 2 lounge areas, public bar, conservatory restaurant, dining room, ½-acre garden (covered sunken garden), harbour sailing.
BACKGROUND MUSIC: 'easy listening' at quiet times.
LOCATION: centre of village just E of Brancaster.
CHILDREN: all ages welcomed.
DOGS: allowed in annexe rooms (£10) and bar.
CREDIT CARDS: MasterCard, Visa.
PRICES: [2010] B&B £45–£120 per person, D,B&B £65–£120, full alc £39, off-season breaks, Christmas/New Year packages.

# BRANSCOMBE Devon

Map 1:C5

## THE MASONS ARMS

'A pleasant place to stay, in a lovely location,' say visitors this year to this creeper-covered 14th-century inn, which was bought by St Austell Brewery in July 2010. 'Service, by the cheerful staff, was just right,' write visitors in 2010. The peaceful National Trust village, surrounded by hills, reminded some American visitors of Switzerland. Grade II listed, the inn attracts many locals for meals or drinks, and is in easy walking distance of Branscombe's pebble beach. Some bedrooms are in the pub, but the majority are in cottages on a raised terrace nearby. Some are huge. 'Ours had a pleasant view over the garden and a nice sitting-out area. Soft furnishings were a little faded, but the bathroom had been recently renovated and was enormous.' Guests can eat in the restaurant (three cosy small rooms) or in the bar. 'My husband enjoyed his seafood grill (he still mentions it) as I did my chargrilled rib-eye steak.' Breakfast has been praised. Booking is advised for meals in both restaurant and pub. Popular with dog owners. (*Jenny Buckley, Marc and Margaret Wall, and others*)

Branscombe EX12 3DJ

T: 01297-680300
F: 01297-680500
E: reception@masonsarms.co.uk
W: www.masonsarms.co.uk

BEDROOMS: 21, 14 in cottages.
OPEN: all year.
FACILITIES: ramps, lounge, 2 bars, 2 dining rooms, large terraced gardens, pebble beach ½ mile, unsuitable for &.
BACKGROUND MUSIC: none.
LOCATION: village centre.
CHILDREN: all ages welcomed.
DOGS: allowed in some bedrooms, bar.
CREDIT CARDS: Diners, MasterCard, Visa.
PRICES: [2010] B&B £28–£87.50 per person, D,B&B £48.50–£117, set dinner £29.95, full alc £37.50, Christmas/New Year packages, 1-night bookings refused weekends.

# BRAY Berkshire

## THE WATERSIDE INN

In a 'superb' Thames-side setting in a 16th-century village, Alain and Michel Roux's restaurant-with-rooms is thought 'first class'. The father and son owner/chefs have held three *Michelin* stars for 25 years for their French haute cuisine. A set menu is available at lunchtime; in the evening visitors can choose from a carte (only the host is given the prices) or a five-course menu exceptionnel (to be ordered by the whole table). Sample dishes: poached sole, tarragon, morels, vin jaune sauce; spit-roasted Challandais duck, lightly spiced prunes, green Puy lentils, Grande Chartreuse jus. Pre-dinner drinks can be taken on a terrace by the river, or on an electric launch which is available for hire. Michel Roux's wife, Robyn, designed the 'sybaritic' bedrooms in elegant French style; all have linen sheets, flat-screen TV, Wi-Fi and access to a kitchenette. The two best rooms open on to a terrace with 'stunning' river views. Breakfast, brought to the bedroom on a large wicker tray, has fresh orange juice, yogurt, croissants; good coffee and a newspaper. (*MB*)

Ferry Road
Bray SL6 2AT

T: 01628-620691
F: 01628-784710
E: reservations@
   waterside-inn.co.uk
W: www.waterside-inn.co.uk

BEDROOMS: 9, 1, plus 2 apartments, in nearby cottage.
OPEN: all year except 26 Dec–3 Feb, Mon/Tues (except Tues evening June–Aug).
FACILITIES: restaurant, private dining room (with drawing room and courtyard garden), civil wedding licence, riverside terrace (launch for drinks/coffee), unsuitable for &.
BACKGROUND MUSIC: none.
LOCATION: 3 miles SE of Maidenhead.
CHILDREN: not under 12.
DOGS: not allowed.
CREDIT CARDS: all major cards.
PRICES: [2010] B&B £100–£220 per person, suite/apartment £440–£675, set lunch £56.50–£112.50.

# BRIGHTON East Sussex

Map 2:E4

## DRAKES

'A great candidate for a romantic weekend,' writes a visitor this year to this seafront boutique hotel. Close to The Lanes and the Pavilion, this conversion of a double-fronted Georgian town house is owned by Andy Shearer and managed by Richard Hayes. The bedrooms have an extravagant modern decor ('with a touch of decadence', says the brochure). 'Ours was a splendid room, small but beautifully appointed; we had the ridiculous pleasure of taking a bath while overlooking the sea.' Those without a sea view look over the back gardens of other houses towards the town. All rooms have air conditioning, flat-screen TV, broadband Internet access. Public areas are 'surprisingly sparse, but you want to spend most of your time in the bedroom'; 24-hour service is available in the ground-floor lounge. The restaurant in the basement has been taken in-house. Andrew MacKenzie stays on as chef, serving modern dishes, eg, tempura frogs' legs, garlic purée; pan-roast cod, pommes Anna, spinach soubise. A five-course tasting menu can be taken, with a different wine for each course.

43/44 Marine Parade
Brighton BN2 1PE

T: 01273-696934
F: 01273-684805
E: info@drakesofbrighton.com
W: www.drakesofbrighton.com

BEDROOMS: 20, 2 on ground floor.
OPEN: all year.
FACILITIES: ramp, lounge/bar/Reception, restaurant, meeting room, civil wedding/partnership licence, unsuitable for &.
BACKGROUND MUSIC: 'easy listening' in bar/Reception.
LOCATION: ½ mile from centre, on seafront.
CHILDREN: all ages welcomed.
DOGS: not allowed.
CREDIT CARDS: Amex, MasterCard, Visa.
PRICES: room £105–£325, breakfast £5–£12.50, tasting menu £50–£85, full alc £47.50 (*12.5% 'discretionary' service charge added*), midweek packages, 3-night min. stay bank holidays, Christmas/New Year packages, 1-night bookings refused Sat.

**25% DISCOUNT VOUCHERS**

# BRIGHTON East Sussex

Map 2:E4

## HOTEL DU VIN BRIGHTON  **NEW**

Between The Lanes (cobbled streets, antique shops and tea houses) and the seafront, the Brighton branch of the Hotel du Vin chain is a clever conversion of Gothic revival/mock Tudor buildings. 'Simply a great place,' says a trusted reporter this year restoring it to a full *Guide* entry. 'Interesting, trendy; good food and wine,' is another comment. Original features (a heavily carved staircase, bizarre gargoyles) are retained in the vaulted bar/lounge; here and in the bistro the ambience is 'lively and informal'. 'We very much enjoyed the cooking': chef Rob Carr presents bistro dishes (smoked eel; braised lamb shank, etc). An 'excellent' breakfast, which costs extra, has a buffet of cereals, fresh fruit, croissants, freshly baked bread; cooked dishes. 'We were upgraded to a great room overlooking the sea; twin bathtubs at the windows.' All rooms have a large bed, freestanding bath, walk-in drench shower. Six rooms, presented as beach huts, face an inner courtyard. Internet access is free for the first 30 minutes; charges apply thereafter. Despite this, 'there is no other hotel for me in Brighton'. (*Wolfgang Stroebe, David Charlesworth*)

2–6 Ship Street
Brighton BN1 1AD

T: 01273-718588
F: 01273-718599
E: info@brighton.hotelduvin.com
W: www.hotelduvin.com

BEDROOMS: 37, 6 in courtyard, 2, on ground floor, suitable for &.
OPEN: all year.
FACILITIES: lounge/bar, bistro, billiard room, function rooms, civil wedding licence.
BACKGROUND MUSIC: 'easy listening' all day in public areas.
LOCATION: 50 yds from beach front.
CHILDREN: all ages welcomed.
DOGS: not allowed in public rooms.
CREDIT CARDS: all major cards.
PRICES: [2010] room £170–£345, breakfast £10.95–£13.95, full alc £45, special breaks.

# BRIGHTON East Sussex

Map 2:E4

## PASKINS TOWN HOUSE

'A marvellous, slightly eccentric place in a great location yards from the sea, and an easy walk to everything.' More praise this year for Susan and Roger Marlowe's environmentally friendly B&B in two tall Grade II listed 19th-century houses in a conservation area. An earlier visitor (a hotelier) said: 'A positive, unusual experience where owners and staff genuinely care for their guests.' There is an Art Deco breakfast room, and an adjoining small sitting room with 'comfortable armchairs, a splendid 1930s gramophone, and newspapers'. They can be crowded at busy times. 'The choice at breakfast is massive: fruits (dried and compote), a selection of juices (not freshly squeezed), and various cooked dishes. The scrambled eggs were just the right texture.' Sandwiches and drinks are served in the lounge or bedroom. The rooms have been given a dramatic decor. 'Ours, at the front, was small but well equipped; the decoration was odd, dark hessian and 1960s psychedelic. A smart bathroom.' Another room with black-and-white wallpaper left a visitor feeling 'dizzy'. All rooms have 'interesting environmental toiletries, and a comprehensive information folder'. (*David Nutt, RR*)

18–19 Charlotte Street
Brighton BN2 1AG

T: 01273-601203
F: 01273-621973
E: welcome@paskins.co.uk
W: www.paskins.co.uk

BEDROOMS: 19.
OPEN: all year.
FACILITIES: lounge, breakfast room.
BACKGROUND MUSIC: none.
LOCATION: 10 mins' walk from centre.
CHILDREN: all ages welcomed.
DOGS: not allowed in public rooms.
CREDIT CARDS: Amex, MasterCard, Visa.
PRICES: B&B £40–£75 per person, 3-night breaks, 1-night bookings refused weekends, bank holidays.

# BRISTOL

Map 1:B6

## HOTEL DU VIN BRISTOL

In a 'great location' close to the centre of town, 'this lovely old industrial building' has been imaginatively converted to house the Bristol branch of the Hotel du Vin chain. Lorraine Jarvie is the manager. Just off a busy road (and beside an ugly 1960s office block), the building has a glass canopy entrance leading to spacious public areas and a sweeping steel and oak staircase. 'We had a fantastic spacious room on two levels; stylish modern decor, a huge bed. On the upper level, a big freestanding bath by the window. No real view but it didn't matter as the room was light and airy.' Bedrooms at the front have secondary double glazing to eliminate traffic noise. Earlier visitors enjoyed the buzz of the brasserie restaurant (dishes like rib-eye steak, pommes frites, Béarnaise sauce). There might be a 'slightly impersonal feel'. Breakfast (charged extra) has an extensive choice ('delicious bacon rolls and coffee were a good deal'). Parking is limited in the hotel's secure car park (there are parking spaces outside the building). (*Anna Raphael, and others*)

The Sugar House
Narrow Lewins Mead
Bristol BS1 2NU

T: 0117-925 5577
F: 0117-925 1199
E: info@bristol.hotelduvin.com
W: www.hotelduvin.com

BEDROOMS: 40.
OPEN: all year.
FACILITIES: lift, ramp, lounge, library/billiard room, 2 bars, bistro, 3 private dining rooms, civil wedding licence.
BACKGROUND MUSIC: 'easy listening' in bar.
LOCATION: city centre.
CHILDREN: all ages welcomed.
DOGS: allowed.
CREDIT CARDS: Amex, MasterCard, Visa.
PRICES: [2010] room £125–£205, breakfast £9.95–£13.95, set dinner £25, full alc £65, special breaks, Christmas/New Year packages.

**25% DISCOUNT VOUCHERS**

# BROAD CAMPDEN Gloucestershire

Map 3:D6

## THE MALT HOUSE

In 'charming' gardens in a quiet Cotswold village, this conversion of a Grade II listed malt house with two adjacent cottages is run as a B&B by Judi Wilkes. She is 'very friendly and welcoming', say returning visitors this year. The 'attention to detail and level of help' were praised by other guests. There are two comfortable sitting rooms with open fires, armchairs, plenty of newspapers and magazines. In fine weather, afternoon tea (with home-made biscuits) and evening drinks may be served in the garden, which has a summer house and croquet lawn. There are lovely views over the countryside. The 'beautifully furnished' bedrooms, all different, have many 'nice touches': umbrellas, torches, spare toothbrushes, scissors, fresh milk for tea-making. 'Ours was comfortable and well appointed.' All overlook the garden; three have a private entrance. The 'generous' breakfasts are praised. A map with local eating places is in each room; the *Horse and Groom*, Bourton-on-the-Hill (see entry), is recommended this year. House parties are catered for. You can walk on the Cotswold Way from the gate. (*Michael and Eithne Dandy, Christopher Butterworth*)

Broad Campden
nr Chipping Campden
GL55 6UU

T: 01386-840295
F: 01386-841334
E: info@malt-house.co.uk
W: www.malt-house.co.uk

BEDROOMS: 7, 2 on ground floor, 3 with own entrance.
OPEN: all year except Christmas.
FACILITIES: 2 lounges, dining room, 3-acre garden (croquet, orchard, stream), unsuitable for &.
BACKGROUND MUSIC: none.
LOCATION: 1 mile S of Chipping Campden.
CHILDREN: all ages welcomed.
DOGS: allowed in 1 bedroom only.
CREDIT CARDS: MasterCard, Visa.
PRICES: B&B £67.50–£85 per person, special breaks, 1-night bookings sometimes refused weekends high season.

**25% DISCOUNT VOUCHERS**

# BROADWAY Worcestershire

## RUSSELL'S RESTAURANT

♥ *César award in 2006*

'A sense of well-being, thanks to high standards of service, food, comfort and style,' was enjoyed by visitors returning to Barry Hancox and Andrew Riley's chic conversion of this honey-stoned building on the High Street of the pretty Cotswold village. 'They keep an attentive eye on the needs of guests and diners.' Their painstaking restoration of furniture designer Sir Gordon Russell's former showroom into a restaurant-with-rooms has added contemporary touches while retaining attractive original features. The individually designed bedrooms have air conditioning, good linen, flat-screen TV and broadband Internet access. A room on two levels has 'a window on nearly every wall'. Some rooms face the village (windows double glazed). In the public areas are inglenook fireplaces, beams, an old oak staircase. In the smart L-shaped dining room, chef Matthew Laughton serves modern British dishes (perhaps confit belly of sucking pig, mustard mash, sage gravy); set menus are available at lunchtime and from 6 to 7 pm; thereafter you eat à la carte. In fine weather, meals may be taken in the courtyard or on the front patio. (*Tom and Sarah Mann*)

The Green, 20 High Street
Broadway WR12 7DT

T: 01386-853555
F: 01386-853964
E: info@russellsofbroadway.co.uk
W: www.russellsofbroadway.co.uk

BEDROOMS: 7, 3 in adjoining building, 2 on ground floor.
OPEN: all year, restaurant closed Sun night except bank holidays.
FACILITIES: ramp, residents' lobby, bar, restaurant, private dining room, patio (heating, meal service).
BACKGROUND MUSIC: 'ambient'.
LOCATION: village centre.
CHILDREN: all ages welcomed.
DOGS: not allowed.
CREDIT CARDS: all major cards.
PRICES: [2010] B&B £47.50–£147.50 per person, full alc £45, seasonal breaks on website, 1-night bookings refused weekends.

**25% DISCOUNT VOUCHERS**

# BROXTON Cheshire

Map 3:A5

## FROGG MANOR

♥ *César award in 1997*

'We were transported into a world of make-believe, a perfect interlude from a mad, mad world.' More praise this year for John Sykes's eccentric hotel dedicated to frogs and 1930s music. 'Exceptional, the hospitality is second to none,' says another guest. The frogs come in all manner of forms: ceramic, brass, straw and wood. The background music in the public rooms, which are generously furnished with antiques and ornaments, is from the 1930s, in keeping with the style. Bedrooms are also decorated with flamboyance. The Wellington Suite has a centrally placed four-poster with drapes to the ceiling giving an impression of a campaign tent; Lady Guinevere is a tree house with an exuberant panel behind the bedhead; Mountbatten is light and airy, with pastel shades. 'Our room boasted every luxury, fluffy white towels in abundance, clean linen sheets every day and from our window we looked down onto an array of frogs, floodlit at night.' Mr Sykes is also the chef: 'Superb food; an exquisite combination of tastes.' (*Anthony James, Olive Murray*)

Nantwich Road (A534)
Broxton, Chester CH3 9JH

T: 01829-782629
F: 01829-782459
E: info@froggmanorhotel.co.uk
W: www.froggmanorhotel.co.uk

BEDROOMS: 8, 1 in tree house, 1 suitable for &.
OPEN: all year.
FACILITIES: ramp, lounge, bar lounge, restaurant, private dining room, conference/function facilities, civil wedding licence, 12-acre grounds (tennis).
BACKGROUND MUSIC: 1930s/40s CDs in lounge, restaurant and bar lounge.
LOCATION: 12 miles SE of Chester.
CHILDREN: all ages welcomed.
DOGS: allowed in bedrooms, bar lounge.
CREDIT CARDS: all major cards.
PRICES: [2010] B&B (continental) £49–£135 per person, D,B&B £86–£172, set dinner £37–£42, full alc £51, midweek discounts.

**25% DISCOUNT VOUCHERS**

# BRYHER Isles of Scilly

## HELL BAY HOTEL

On the westerly frontier of Britain, Bryher is the smallest of the inhabited Scilly Isles. The hotel, built in the style of cottages, faces Hell Bay, where jagged rocks reach out to the warning light of Bishop Rock. It is owned by Robert Dorrien-Smith, the leaseholder of neighbouring Tresco, who has filled it with his 'enchanting' collection of modern British art (works by Roger Hilton, Ivon Hitchens, Barbara Hepworth). The suites are decorated in seaside style, a blend of Cornwall and New England. All have a sitting area, some have two bedrooms and a lounge; many face the bay, and have a door opening on to the garden or, on the first floor, to a small balcony. The bathrooms are large and bright (with notes about the conservation policy). The large lounges have plenty of comfortable seating, and art books as well as the paintings. In the panoramic dining room, Glenn Gatland serves a sophisticated modern menu (dishes like fillet of beef, miniature cottage pie). More reports, please.

Bryher, Isles of Scilly
Cornwall TR23 0PR

T: 01720-422947
F: 01720-423004
E: contactus@hellbay.co.uk
W: www.hellbay.co.uk

BEDROOMS: 25 suites, in 5 buildings, some on ground floor, 1 suitable for &.
OPEN: 15 Mar–30 Oct.
FACILITIES: lounge, games room, bar, 2 dining rooms, gym, sauna, large grounds (heated swimming pool, 15 by 10 metres, children's playground, par 3 golf course), beach 75 yds.
BACKGROUND MUSIC: none.
LOCATION: W coast of island, boat from Tresco (reached by boat/helicopter from Penzance) or St Mary's.
CHILDREN: all ages welcomed (high tea at 5.30).
DOGS: not allowed in public rooms.
CREDIT CARDS: MasterCard, Visa.
PRICES: [2010] D,B&B £135–£300 per person, 4-night breaks.

# BUCKDEN Cambridgeshire

Map 2:B4

## THE GEORGE

Owners Anne, Richard and Becky Furbank say they have 'brought a slice of London' to this historic Cambridgeshire village, creating a 'fashionably stylish' hotel from a 19th-century coaching inn. The decor and 'well-chosen furnishings' have been admired by guests. Colours are neutral, there are leather tub chairs and sofas. The bedrooms, all named after famous Georges, have Internet access, satellite TV and a safe. Hanover and Gershwin (premier rooms) have mahogany furniture and a 'very comfortable' bed with brass bedhead. Handel has twin beds. A standard room (Mallory, 'perhaps because of the climb') has a patchwork counterpane. Waiters wear grey shirt and tie in the light and airy ground-floor brasserie where all meals are served. This year there is a new chef, Chris Cheah; his style is modern, eg, quail, pearl barley risotto, root vegetables. Summer meals can be taken on the terrace. The sensibly priced wine list has 20 by the glass. Breakfast includes 'good coffee', brown bread toast, croissants, fruit, cheese and any variation of a full British. More reports, please.

High Street
Buckden PE19 5XA

T: 01480-812300
F: 01480-813920
E: mail@thegeorgebuckden.com
W: www.thegeorgebuckden.com

BEDROOMS: 12.
OPEN: all year.
FACILITIES: lift, bar, lounge, restaurant, private dining room, civil wedding licence, courtyard.
BACKGROUND MUSIC: jazz/contemporary in all public areas.
LOCATION: village centre.
CHILDREN: all ages welcomed, baby-changing facilities.
DOGS: allowed in bedrooms and foyer.
CREDIT CARDS: Amex, MasterCard, Visa.
PRICES: [2010] B&B £45–£70 per person, D,B&B £60–£100, full alc £40.

**25% DISCOUNT VOUCHERS**

# BUCKLAND MARSH Oxfordshire

Map 2:C2

## THE TROUT AT TADPOLE BRIDGE

The 'warm atmosphere and outstanding food' were enjoyed by inspectors this year at Gareth and Helen Pugh's old stone pub/restaurant. It has a 'cracking position' by a narrow bridge over the Thames. Lawns run down to riverside moorings; boating visitors are encouraged. 'The bedrooms, breakfast room and kitchen are in a neat extension to the rear, meaning no disturbance from traffic noise.' The bar (busy with locals) and eating areas are in the old part of the building, with stone walls, part-flagged and part-carpeted floors, original fireplaces, 'unusual pictures'. 'Helen Pugh was very much in charge at dinner, taking orders, showing an interest.' Pascal Clavaud serves a seasonal menu with blackboard specials: 'Standout dishes were juicy scallops wrapped in crispy pancetta, with chorizo, black olive mash; a generous rack of pink lamb, parsnip dauphinoise, beetroot.' The bedrooms vary in style: 'Our cosy room had a huge sleigh bed, an antique wooden dressing table, an ornate mirror and a smallish sitting area.' Breakfast has 'toast from home-made bread, good local bacon and sausage'. Check in before 3 pm or after 6 pm.

Buckland Marsh SN7 8RF

T: 01367-870382
F: 01367-870912
E: info@trout-inn.co.uk
W: www.trout-inn.co.uk

BEDROOMS: 6, 3 in courtyard.
OPEN: all year except 25 Dec, restaurant closed Sun night Nov–Apr.
FACILITIES: bar, dining area, breakfast area, 2-acre garden (river, moorings), unsuitable for &.
BACKGROUND MUSIC: none.
LOCATION: 2 miles N of A420, halfway between Oxford and Swindon.
CHILDREN: all ages welcomed.
DOGS: allowed.
CREDIT CARDS: MasterCard, Visa.
PRICES: [2010] B&B £60–£80 per person, D,B&B £90–£110, full alc £28, New Year package, 1-night bookings refused weekends.

# BURFORD Oxfordshire

Map 2:C2

## BURFORD HOUSE

**NEW**

On the high street of an attractive Cotswolds town, this half-timbered early 17th-century building returns to the *Guide* under the ownership of Ian Hawkins, who runs it with Stewart Dunkley (the chef). An inspector in 2010 thought it 'relaxing, well managed by friendly staff'. There are two sitting rooms: one facing the high street, with a cream and dark red colour scheme, has good chairs and settees; the other opens on to the pretty courtyard garden. 'Our first-floor bedroom at the back was nicely furnished with a huge bed (sheets and blankets), plenty of hangers in the wardrobe; the bathroom, fresh and clean, had a door leading down steps to the courtyard.' The dining room has dark red walls, candlelit tables, theatrical posters (background music from shows in the evening). 'We were delighted with the food from a sensibly short menu: delicious asparagus and poached egg with Parmesan shavings and truffle oil; rack of lamb with dauphinoise potatoes; coffee and home-made nougat in the lounge. Breakfast is of equal quality (especially good unsmoked bacon). Ian insisted on carrying our case to the car.'

99 High Street
Buford OX18 4QA

T: 01993-823151
F: 01993-823240
E: stay@burfordhouse.co.uk
W: www.burfordhouse.co.uk

BEDROOMS: 8, 2 in adjoining coach house, 1 on ground floor.
OPEN: all year except 1 week in Jan.
FACILITIES: 2 lounges, restaurant, small courtyard garden, unsuitable for ♿.
BACKGROUND MUSIC: in 1 lounge and restaurant.
LOCATION: central.
CHILDREN: all ages welcomed.
DOGS: only guide dogs allowed.
CREDIT CARDS: all major cards.
PRICES: [2010] B&B £57.50–£130 per person, D,B&B (Thurs–Sat) £72–£185, full alc £40, special offers, Christmas/New Year packages, 1-night bookings normally refused weekends.

**25% DISCOUNT VOUCHERS**

# BURFORD Oxfordshire

Map 2:C2

## THE LAMB INN   `NEW`

'A lovely place', this old inn, on a leafy side street of the medieval town, has flagstoned floors, beamed ceilings, log fires, copper and brass. Managed by Paul Heaver, it is part of a small Cotswold hotel group (see also *The Manor House*, Moreton-in-Marsh). Visitors this year 'were made to feel wanted'. Inspectors agreed: 'The mainly European staff were without exception attentive, friendly.' Summer drinks and meals are served in an enclosed garden (well-spaced seating amid gravel paths, lawns, borders). 'Our large room was attractively furnished with antiques; a half-tester bed; bold floral fabrics; lots of storage; a big, light bathroom. Mineral water replenished during turn-down.' The dining room, overlooking the garden, has 'well-dressed' tables, fresh flowers. 'The cooking [Sean Ducie is chef] was imaginative; highlights from the seasonal menu were a meaty ham hock terrine, and pan-fried cod with a delicious squid-ink risotto; a small pistachio brûlée came as a dessert pre-starter.' Breakfast had big jugs of freshly squeezed juice, honeycomb, chunky toast, a fresh loaf of bread; 'splendid' cooked dishes. (*David Nicholls, and others*)

Sheep Street
Burford OX18 4LR

T: 01993-823155
F: 01993-822228
E: info@lambinn-burford.co.uk
W: www.cotswold-inns-hotels.
co.uk/lamb

BEDROOMS: 17.
OPEN: all year.
FACILITIES: 2 lounges, bar, restaurant, courtyard, ½-acre garden, unsuitable for &.
BACKGROUND MUSIC: 'gentle' throughout.
LOCATION: 500 yds from centre.
CHILDREN: all ages welcomed.
DOGS: allowed.
CREDIT CARDS: all major cards.
PRICES: [2010] B&B £75–£87.50 per person, D,B&B £110–122.50, set meals £35, full alc £41 (*10% service added to restaurant bills*), special breaks, Christmas/New Year packages, 1-night bookings sometimes refused Sat.

**25% DISCOUNT VOUCHERS**

# CANNINGTON Somerset

Map 1:B5

## BLACKMORE FARM

In open countryside overlooking the Quantock hills, Ann and Ian Dyer's large 15th-century Grade I listed manor house is on their working dairy farm. Many period features are retained: oak beams, stone archways and open fireplaces. The massive front door is several centuries old. The impressive Great Hall has a long oak refectory table (an 'excellent' breakfast is taken here), large open fireplace and a full suit of armour. The small sitting room has books, board games and brochures. One bedroom, The Gallery, has original wall panelling, wide, comfortable bed, sitting room up a steep flight of steps, small bathroom (lavatory in a medieval garderobe). The Solar has a large double bedroom, a single bed in a closet leading off it, and bathroom. Tea and 'delicious home-made cake' are served free to arriving guests. Children are made welcome and will enjoy the farm animals. For 'basic pub grub', the *Maltshovel* pub is friendly; there are plenty of restaurants within easy driving distance. More reports, please.

Blackmore Lane
Cannington
nr Bridgwater TA5 2NE

T: 01278-653442
E: dyerfarm@aol.com
W: www.dyerfarm.co.uk

BEDROOMS: 5, 2 in ground-floor barn, suitable for &.
OPEN: all year.
FACILITIES: lounge/TV room, hall/breakfast room, 1-acre garden (stream, coarse fishing).
BACKGROUND MUSIC: none.
LOCATION: 3 miles NW of Bridgwater.
CHILDREN: all ages welcomed.
DOGS: not allowed.
CREDIT CARDS: Diners, MasterCard, Visa.
PRICES: B&B £40–£55 per person, 1-night bookings refused bank holiday weekends.

# CARTMEL Cumbria

## AYNSOME MANOR

*César award in 1998*

Between the fells and the sea in the lovely Vale of Cartmel, this traditional hotel has been run for more than 30 years by two generations of the Varley family. Christopher and Andrea are the 'hard-working' owner/managers, helped by his parents, Tony and Margaret. They have a loyal following. First-time visitors in 2010 were impressed: 'It was so good we stayed an extra night. Excellent service and housekeeping. Good food.' The public areas have been redecorated and given new carpets this year. Smart casual dress is required in the oak-panelled restaurant where Gordon Topp's daily-changing five-course dinner menu highlights local produce, perhaps roast Holker venison on spiced red cabbage, rösti potato. Coffee, with petits fours, is served in the lounge. A traditional lunch is served on Sunday, followed by a lavish buffet supper in the evening. At busy times there are two sittings for dinner. Bedrooms in the main house are on two floors; they vary in size; some are suitable for a family. Two rooms are in a cottage across the cobbled courtyard, converted from a 16th-century stone stable. *(Ken and Mildred Evans)*.

Cartmel
nr Grange-over-Sands
LA11 6HH

T: 01539-536653
F: 01539-536016
E: aynsomemanor@btconnect.com
W: www.aynsomemanorhotel.co.uk

BEDROOMS: 12, 2 in cottage (with lounge) across courtyard.
OPEN: all year except 25/26 Dec, 2–28 Jan, lunch served Sun only, Sun dinner for residents only.
FACILITIES: 2 lounges, bar, dining room, ½-acre garden, unsuitable for &.
BACKGROUND MUSIC: none.
LOCATION: ½ mile outside village.
CHILDREN: no under-5s at dinner.
DOGS: not allowed in public rooms.
CREDIT CARDS: Amex, MasterCard, Visa.
PRICES: B&B £49–£67.50 per person, D,B&B £65–£89, set dinner £27, New Year package, 1-night bookings sometimes refused weekends.

**25% DISCOUNT VOUCHERS**

# CHADDESLEY CORBETT Worcestershire    Map 3:C5

## BROCKENCOTE HALL

'In lovely parkland with a serene lake', this 'amazing pseudo-Regency pile' is run as a small hotel by Joseph and Alison Petitjean. 'It is a good place and lives up to its reputation; we would go again,' say trusted *Guide* correspondents in 2010. 'They continue to get everything right,' adds a returning visitor. The Victorian building was remodelled in the style of a French château in 1939. The high-ceilinged entrance hall has a log fire, 'most welcome on a winter's day'; free Internet access is available on a computer (no Wi-Fi). 'Our bedroom was huge, immaculate, with a large, comfy sofa, a tea tray, fresh fruit, a carafe of sherry; an encased spa bath in the superb bathroom.' Tables are well spaced in the oak-panelled restaurant where the chef, John Sherry, serves 'classic French dishes with modern influences'. His elaborate dishes (eg, skate wing, pork belly, Cumbrian ham, wilted greens, fondant potatoes, Pommery mustard sauce) might have 'too many ingredients fighting for attention'. Delicious desserts: 'A passion fruit soufflé stayed beautifully risen.' Breakfast has 'good coffee and croissants'. (*Francine and Ian Walsh, Gordon Hands*)

Chaddesley Corbett
nr Kidderminster DY10 4PY

T: 01562-777876
F: 01562-777872
E: info@brockencotehall.com
W: www.brockencotehall.com

BEDROOMS: 17, some on ground floor, 1 suitable for &.
OPEN: all year.
FACILITIES: lift, ramp, hall, 3 lounges, bar, conservatory, restaurant, function facilities, civil wedding licence, 70-acre grounds (gardens, lake, fishing, croquet, tennis).
BACKGROUND MUSIC: in restaurant, lounges.
LOCATION: 3 miles SE of Kidderminster.
CHILDREN: all ages welcomed.
DOGS: not allowed.
CREDIT CARDS: all major cards.
PRICES: [2010] B&B £60–£145 per person, D,B&B £99.50–£184.50, set dinner £39.50, full alc £45, short breaks, midweek discounts, Christmas/New Year packages.

# CHAGFORD Devon

Map 1:C4

## GIDLEIGH PARK

The North River Teign runs through the extensive grounds of this luxurious country house hotel (Relais & Châteaux) which is owned by Andrew and Christina Brownsword (who also own *The Bath Priory*, Bath, see entry). 'Many happy hours can be spent' enjoying the grounds, which have formal gardens, an 'interesting' kitchen garden, marked walks, a croquet lawn, putting, bowling, etc. The cooking, under executive chef Michael Caines, is 'accomplished as would be expected of a *Michelin* two-starred establishment'; his classic French menus might include dishes like rosé veal, button onions, broad beans and morels. 'Terrific; we had the tasting menu and did not think the portions were too small; the best ever foie gras.' One visitor this year praised the 'attentive' staff; other guests found it 'as hard to understand the overseas staff as they did us'. The bedrooms have 'supremely comfortable' beds, 'a superb bathroom'; fresh fruit, mineral water and a decanter of Madeira or port are 'welcoming touches'. The largest suite has a sauna and steam room. (*Martin Landy, and others*)

Chagford TQ13 8HH

T: 01647-432367
F: 01647-432574
E: gidleighpark@gidleigh.co.uk
W: www.gidleigh.com

BEDROOMS: 24, 2 in annexe (75 yds), 2 in cottage (375 yds), some, on ground floor, suitable for &.
OPEN: all year.
FACILITIES: ramps, drawing room, hall, bar, loggia, conservatory, 3 dining rooms, civil wedding licence, 107-acre grounds (gardens, tennis, river, fishing).
BACKGROUND MUSIC: none.
LOCATION: 2 miles from Chagford.
CHILDREN: no under-8s at dinner.
DOGS: allowed in 3 bedrooms, not in public rooms.
CREDIT CARDS: all major cards.
PRICES: B&B £155–£577.50 per person, D,B&B £250–£672.50, set meals £35–£45, full alc £95, special breaks, Christmas/New Year packages, 1-night bookings refused at weekends.

# CHAGFORD Devon

Map 1:C4

## MILL END HOTEL

Endorsed in 2010 for its 'comfort and friendliness', Keith Green's white-walled former corn mill has a 'superb position' by a bridge over the River Teign. The house has a 'homely charm, comfy sofas, books to dip into, and good local walks'. There have been changes front-of-house and in the kitchen this year. Tristan Denman has been appointed manager; Wayne Pearson has returned as the chef. Early reports on his modern cooking are mixed. Typical dishes: pigeon breast and butternut squash risotto; ragout of seafood with saffron. 'No music in the dining room, what a bonus.' Each of three south-facing rooms has a private patio; a first-floor suite is liked; standard rooms face the road. 'Our comfortable room was well equipped; the refurbished bathroom was all one could wish for.' Another visitor was less sure of the 'bizarre' decor in his room. Breakfast has 'good toast, very fresh eggs'. There are large grounds to explore, and good walking on the river. 'We would go back.' More reports, please.

Sandy Park
nr Chagford TQ13 8JN

T: 01647-432282
F: 01647-433106
E: info@millendhotel.com
W: www.millendhotel.com

BEDROOMS: 14, 3 on ground floor.
OPEN: all year.
FACILITIES: 3 lounges, bar, restaurant, 15-acre grounds (river, fishing, bathing), unsuitable for &.
BACKGROUND MUSIC: none.
LOCATION: village on A382, 1½ miles NE of Chagford.
CHILDREN: all ages welcomed, no under-12s in restaurant in evening.
DOGS: not allowed in public rooms.
CREDIT CARDS: MasterCard, Visa.
PRICES: [2010] B&B £50–£85 per person, D,B&B £75–£115, set dinner £42, full alc £52, Christmas/New Year packages, 1-night bookings sometimes refused.

**25% DISCOUNT VOUCHERS**

## CHAGFORD Devon

Map 1:C4

### PARFORD WELL

'A beautifully furnished small house in a perfectly manicured walled garden', Tim Daniel's B&B is near a small village in the Dartmoor national park. 'Go when the rhododendron are flowering,' says a returning visitor this year. A 'light and airy' lounge has original paintings, sculptures, fresh flowers, books and a fire. The 'high-quality' small bedrooms upstairs are well equipped; bathrooms have 'lovely fluffy towels'. One room has its bathroom across the hall. Second helpings are offered at breakfast, normally taken communally round a farmhouse table in an attractive room with Georgian furniture. Porridge is served 'however you like it'; orange juice is freshly squeezed; eggs are free range; bread, with home-made preserves, is from the local baker. Guests wanting privacy may eat at a table for two across the hall, in a small room hung with luxurious drapes that once belonged to the late Queen Mother. Mr Daniel, once the co-owner of *Number Sixteen* in South Kensington, London (see entry), lives in an adjoining cottage. There is good walking from the doorstep. (*David Charlesworth*)

Sandy Park
nr Chagford TQ13 8JW

T: 01647-433353
E: tim@parfordwell.co.uk
W: www.parfordwell.co.uk

BEDROOMS: 3.
OPEN: all year except Christmas.
FACILITIES: sitting room, 2 breakfast rooms, ½-acre garden, unsuitable for &.
BACKGROUND MUSIC: none.
LOCATION: in hamlet 1 mile N of Chagford.
CHILDREN: not under 8.
DOGS: not allowed.
CREDIT CARDS: none.
PRICES: [2010] B&B £37.50–£47.50 per person, 1-night bookings sometimes refused weekends in season.

# CHETTLE Dorset

Map 2:E1

## CASTLEMAN

'Full marks for intelligent, charming staff and efficient service,' say regular *Guide* correspondents visiting this Queen Anne dower house, which is run as an informal restaurant-with-rooms by Barbara and Edward Bourke. 'It might not suit everyone; nothing happens until early evening, when everything comes alive. Lights go on, a fire is lit in the bar, drinks and menus appear and the place fills up with locals from miles around.' The chef, Richard Morris, uses seasonal produce for his modern menus: 'Partridges and pears in many guises; huge and chunky scallops; the fish ragout was something special.' Small housekeeping 'blips' (flickering lights, missing bulbs, a stain on the ceiling) are 'forgiven' because 'they are so thoughtful in all departments: two hot-water bottles, fresh milk in the bedrooms, plenty of books and magazines. Our room was huge and had a new sofa, masses of storage. We were very comfortable.' Breakfast is served until 10 am: 'No set menu but anything you asked for was available: yogurt, dried fruit compote, excellent kippers and scrambled eggs.' (*Janet and Dennis Allom*)

Chettle
nr Blandford Forum DT11 8DB

T: 01258-830096
F: 01258-830051
E: enquiry@castlemanhotel.co.uk
W: www.castlemanhotel.co.uk

BEDROOMS: 8 (1 family).
OPEN: Mar–Jan, except 25/26 Dec, 31 Dec, restaurant closed midday except Sun.
FACILITIES: 2 drawing rooms, bar, restaurant, 2-acre grounds (stables for visiting horses), riding, fishing, shooting, cycling nearby, only restaurant suitable for &.
BACKGROUND MUSIC: none.
LOCATION: village, 1 mile off A354 Salisbury–Blandford, hotel signposted.
CHILDREN: all ages welcomed.
DOGS: not allowed.
CREDIT CARDS: MasterCard, Visa.
PRICES: B&B £42.50–£60, full alc £32.50, discount for 3 or more nights.

# CHICHESTER West Sussex

Map 2:E3

## ROOKS HILL  `NEW`

Close to Goodwood, this brick-and-flint former farmhouse (Grade II listed) has been restored 'with ingenuity' by Ron and Lin Allen who run it as a B&B. 'They are a charming couple,' says an inspector in 2010. 'She greeted us warmly, offering help with our luggage, and tea or coffee after we had unpacked.' Original oak beams (from old ship timbers) are preserved throughout the house. There are six bedrooms: 'Goodwood, on the first floor, overlooks the road, and has lovely views of the South Downs. It was furnished in dark wood (from Java), with a sleigh bed, large wardrobe, chest of drawers, dressing table; modern fittings and a large shower cabinet in the bathroom. The road is busy, but windows are triple glazed; noise was not a problem.' There are lots of books (many connected with racing) in the lounge. The double-aspect breakfast room has patio doors opening on to a 'charming courtyard garden'. 'We enjoyed fresh fruit, yogurts, and good cooked dishes with ingredients from local suppliers. Jams and marmalade are home made.'

Lavant Road
Mid Lavant, Chichester PO18 0BQ

T: 01243-528400
E: info@rookshill.co.uk
W: www.rookshill.co.uk

BEDROOMS: 6, 2 on ground floor.
OPEN: all year.
FACILITIES: lounge, breakfast room, courtyard garden.
BACKGROUND MUSIC: classical in breakfast room.
LOCATION: 2 miles N of city centre.
CHILDREN: not under 12.
DOGS: not allowed.
CREDIT CARDS: Amex, MasterCard, Visa.
PRICES: [2010] B&B £37.50–£82.50 per person, special offers, 1-night bookings refused weekends Apr–Oct.

**25% DISCOUNT VOUCHERS**

# CHILLATON Devon

Map 1:D3

## TOR COTTAGE

In a private and secluded mid-Devon valley 'where you will feel you have escaped from the rest of the world', Maureen Rowlatt's upmarket B&B is surrounded by hillsides where deer roam amid the cover of gorse. There is much wildlife in the large wooded grounds. A trug containing sparkling wine, home-made truffles, fresh fruit awaits arriving visitors. Four bedrooms, each with private terrace, are in the garden. The Garden Room, a conversion of a stone cart house, has a vaulted ceiling with original beams, antique double bed and sitting area with a log fire. Laughing Waters, furnished in New England style, has maple furnishings, a black stove, a gypsy caravan, a hammock and a barbecue. The Cottage Wing is upstairs in the main house. All rooms have CD- and DVD-player. Recent praise: 'We enjoyed lazy days by the glorious swimming pool.' 'Wonderful' breakfasts are ordered the evening before. A light supper tray may also be pre-ordered (chicken or ham salad, soup and pasty). (*LN*)

Chillaton, nr Lifton
PL16 0JE

T: 01822-860248
F: 01822-860126
E: info@torcottage.co.uk
W: www.torcottage.co.uk

BEDROOMS: 5, 4 in garden.
OPEN: Feb–mid-Dec, do not arrive before 4 pm.
FACILITIES: sitting room, large conservatory, breakfast room, 28-acre grounds (2-acre garden, heated swimming pool (13 by 6 metres) May–Sept, barbecue, stream, bridleway, walks), river (fishing ½ mile), unsuitable for &.
BACKGROUND MUSIC: in breakfast room.
LOCATION: ½ mile S of Chillaton.
CHILDREN: not under 14.
DOGS: only guide dogs allowed.
CREDIT CARDS: MasterCard, Visa.
PRICES: B&B (min. 2 nights) £70–£98 per person, tray supper £24, autumn and spring breaks, 1-night bookings sometimes refused.

# CHILLINGTON Devon

Map 1:D4

## WHITEHOUSE 🏅

*César award: Devon hotel of the year*

'A peaceful rear garden with trees, shrubs and a lawn is just one of the surprises at this Georgian house on a busy road in a South Hams village. It has been given a swanky 21st-century interior by the owners, Tamara Costin, Matthew Hall and Ally Wray. They run it in informal style, quickly on first-name terms with guests. The bedrooms have been decorated with flamboyance: exposed brickwork, fancy wallpapers, much use of natural wood; chandeliers and retro lamps. All rooms have a large handmade bed, plasma TV and DVD, free Wi-Fi. Visitors are welcomed with complimentary afternoon tea, which can be taken in one of the lounges (wooden floors, log fires, large leather chairs and sofas) or in the garden, which has beanbags for children to play on. Beatus Elscholtz is the new head chef, serving modern dishes (eg, chicken livers, polenta, spinach, onion and thyme conserve) in the conservatory dining room. An Aga-cooked breakfast, until 11-ish, has daily-changing buffet specials (spicy fruit compote, Bircher muesli); home-made jams; cooked dishes include Salcombe smokie, crispy bacon. (*GT*)

Chillington TQ7 2JX

T: 01548-580505
E: frontofhouse@
   whitehousedevon.com
W: www.whitehousedevon.com

BEDROOMS: 6.
OPEN: all year.
FACILITIES: bar, sitting room, study, dining room, restaurant, meeting room, civil wedding licence, terrace, garden, unsuitable for &.
BACKGROUND MUSIC: 'chill out' in public areas.
LOCATION: on edge of village, 4 miles E of Kingsbridge.
CHILDREN: all ages welcomed.
DOGS: allowed, must be on a lead in public rooms.
CREDIT CARDS: all major cards.
PRICES: [2010] B&B £90–£125 per person, full alc £45, Christmas/New Year packages.

# CLEE STANTON Shropshire

Map 3:C5

## TIMBERSTONE

'A charming place, with charming people.' In deep countryside in the hills above Ludlow ('no noise or light pollution at night'), this 'charming' house has been renovated and extended by Alex Read and Tracey Baylis. Two of the bedrooms are in the old house: a visitor this year found his 'comfortable, adequate, in a rustic setting'. Earlier visitors 'loved our large bedroom, with original beams, big bed, and a window seat'. Two newer bedrooms in an extension have hand-crafted oak fittings; one has a freestanding bath in the room. A 'light connecting room' serves as lounge and dining room: it has floor-to-ceiling windows, sofas and chairs, books, games, DVDs. The hostess, who worked with the chef Shaun Hill when he was in Ludlow, cooks dinner, served communally, by arrangement: 'We ate in both nights, and enjoyed generous portions of pork with mustard sauce, and sea bream; well cooked and presented; honey and figs were a good pudding.' Breakfast has home-made preserves, chunky toast, eggs from the owners' hens. (*David Bartley, Gordon Franklin*)

Clee Stanton
Ludlow SY8 3EL

T: 01584-823519
E: enquiry@timberstoneludlow.co.uk
W: www.timberstoneludlow.co.uk

BEDROOMS: 4 (plus summer house retreat in summer).
OPEN: all year except 25 Dec.
FACILITIES: lounge/dining room, ½-acre garden, treatment room, unsuitable for &.
BACKGROUND MUSIC: in lounge/dining room ('but guests may turn it off').
LOCATION: 5 miles NE of Ludlow.
CHILDREN: all ages welcomed.
DOGS: not allowed in public rooms.
CREDIT CARDS: MasterCard, Visa.
PRICES: [2010] B&B £44–£65 per person, D,B&B £67–£88, set menu £25, full alc £31, winter breaks.

## CLIPSHAM Rutland

Map 2:A3

### BEECH HOUSE & OLIVE BRANCH

In a tree-lined lane in a village near Stamford, Sean Hope and Ben Jones's informal pub/restaurant-with-rooms is 'perfect for a romantic break', says a visitor this year. The bedrooms are in 'pretty' *Beech House* opposite the restaurant. 'We loved it. Our charming room, Double Cream, was nicely decorated, with welcome touches like home-made biscuits in a jar.' In the bathroom, a claw-footed bath is positioned to give 'nice views while soaking'. Aubergine has an upholstered 1920s double bed with mirrored furniture and bold floral fabrics; Berry, on the ground floor, has a separate dressing room with daybed. A fridge, CDs, DVDs, magazines, books and local information are on the landing (the only public area). In the *Olive Branch*, Sean Hope has a *Michelin* star for his 'flavoursome, modern' cooking. Dishes on a daily-changing menu might include salmon terrine, pickled fennel; braised shoulder of lamb, rosemary fondant. 'We had a wonderful dinner; the young staff provided delightful service.' Breakfast, in the *Barn*, adjacent, has freshly squeezed juice, a buffet and cooked dishes. (*Catrin Treadwell*)

Main Street
Clipsham LE15 7SH

T: 01780-410355
F: 01780-410000
E: beechhouse@
   theolivebranchpub.com
W: www.theolivebranchpub.com

BEDROOMS: 6, 2 on ground floor, family room (also suitable for &) in annexe.
OPEN: all year except 25/26 Dec, 1 Jan.
FACILITIES: ramps, pub, dining room, breakfast room, small front garden.
BACKGROUND MUSIC: in pub.
LOCATION: in village 7 miles NW of Stamford.
CHILDREN: all ages welcomed.
DOGS: allowed in downstairs bedrooms and bar.
CREDIT CARDS: MasterCard, Visa.
PRICES: B&B £85–£95 per person, D,B&B £97.50–£110, set meals £25, full alc £45, seasonal breaks, 1-night bookings refused bank holidays, Burghley Horse Trials.

# COLN ST ALDWYNS Gloucestershire

Map 3:E6

## THE NEW INN

Renovated without any loss of its traditional feel, this 400-year-old inn is in a pretty Cotswold village away from the main tourist routes. 'It looks the part, with flagstone and wooden floors, oak beams,' said an inspector. The inn belongs to the small Hillbrooke group (see also *The Elephant*, Pangbourne); Stuart Hodges is the manager. 'We strive for quirkiness not quaintness,' they say. This is evident in the bedrooms, which have bold colours, eccentric touches. 'Our spacious first-floor room had a black bedcover and furniture, a bright red back wall and carpet.' A room in the eaves has a chocolate carpet, a brass bed; a flat-screen TV attached to an old beam. There are black leather sofas, wooden tables in the bar; bright red and cream walls in the dining areas. The chef, Oliver Addis, serves a modern British menu with dishes like slow-braised pork belly, honey glaze, five spices. Outside are wooden benches and tables, popular with walkers at weekends. A four-mile path along the river leads to Bibury.

nr Cirencester GL7 5AN

T: 01285-750651
F: 01285-750657
E: info@thenewinnatcoln.co.uk
W: www.new-inn.co.uk

BEDROOMS: 13, 1 on ground floor, 5 in annexe.
OPEN: all year.
FACILITIES: bar, restaurant, terrace, unsuitable for &.
BACKGROUND MUSIC: in public areas.
LOCATION: in village 8 miles E of Cirencester.
CHILDREN: all ages welcomed.
DOGS: allowed in 1 bedroom, not in restaurant.
CREDIT CARDS: MasterCard, Visa.
PRICES: [2010] B&B £47.50–£155 per person, D,B&B £75–£210, full alc £40, special breaks on website, Christmas/New Year packages, 1-night bookings sometimes refused weekends.

**25% DISCOUNT VOUCHERS**

# COLWALL Worcestershire

Map 3:D5

## COLWALL PARK HOTEL

On the sunny western side of the Malvern hills (good walking), this large Edwardian house in the middle of a pretty village is run as a traditional hotel by owners Iain and Sarah Nesbitt. The 'high standards' are praised by visitors, who received a 'good, informative' welcome. The bar, frequented by locals as well as guests, 'has a nice pubby atmosphere; we enjoyed canapés in soft armchairs in front of a blazing fire. Two ales on tap were an added pleasure.' In the *Seasons* restaurant, panelled with light oak, James Garth's 'excellent' modern cooking is served on 'immaculate' tables with white linen cloths. A typical dish: herb-crumbed loin of Longdon Marsh lamb, Mediterranean vegetables, thyme mash. The bedrooms vary in size: 'Our room was furnished in old-fashioned dark wood; the large, comfy bed had proper sheets and blankets; tea- and coffee-making, mineral water, and home-made biscuits were provided.' In the bathroom, a large bath with shower above, 'plentiful hot water'. Breakfast, with home-made jams and full English, 'made an excellent start to the day'. (*IM*)

Colwall, nr Malvern
WR13 6QG

T: 01684-540000
F: 01684-540847
E: hotel@colwall.com
W: www.colwall.co.uk

BEDROOMS: 22.
OPEN: all year.
FACILITIES: ramp, 2 lounges (1 with TV), library, bar, restaurant, ballroom, business facilities, 1-acre garden, only public rooms suitable for &.
BACKGROUND MUSIC: blues in bar, jazz in restaurant.
LOCATION: halfway between Malvern and Ledbury on B4218, train Colwall.
CHILDREN: all ages welcomed.
DOGS: not allowed.
CREDIT CARDS: MasterCard, Visa.
PRICES: [2010] B&B £62.50–£90 per person, D,B&B £97.50, full alc £40, gourmet breaks, Christmas/New Year packages.

**25% DISCOUNT VOUCHERS**

# CONSTANTINE BAY Cornwall

Map 1:D2

## TREGLOS HOTEL

'The very model of what a good family-run hotel should be. Everything is well planned, well chosen, and it works.' Praise this year for Jim and Rose Barlow's traditional hotel on the north Cornish coast. Their staff are 'attentive, helpful but not intrusive, addressing guests correctly by name'. *Treglos* stands in landscaped gardens overlooking Constantine Bay; the public rooms and many of the bedrooms have fine views. 'We would happily have stayed on and on in our sea-view room with a balcony. The details are good: you can read in bed without straining the eyes.' In the formal restaurant, men are asked to wear a jacket and tie (jackets optional in July and August) in the evening. The dishes on Paul Becker's daily-changing three-course menu are 'well balanced, presented, and delicious', perhaps sea bass with crayfish tails, leeks, tarragon mayonnaise. Families are welcomed, but not children under seven in the restaurant (they have supper at 5.30 pm). Breakfasts are 'first class, the soft herring roes being especially good'. The Barlows also own Merlin Golf and Country Club (ten minutes' drive). (*Sir Patrick Cormack*)

Constantine Bay
Padstow PL28 8JH

T: 01841-520727
F: 01841-521163
E: stay@tregloshotel.com
W: www.tregloshotel.com

BEDROOMS: 42, 1 on ground floor, 2 suitable for &.
OPEN: end Feb–end Nov.
FACILITIES: ramps, 2 lounges (pianist twice weekly), bar, restaurant, children's den, snooker room, beauty treatments, indoor swimming pool (10 by 5 metres), 3-acre grounds.
BACKGROUND MUSIC: piano in restaurant Tues/Thurs.
LOCATION: 3 miles W of Padstow.
CHILDREN: no under-7s in restaurant after 6.30 pm.
DOGS: not allowed in public rooms.
CREDIT CARDS: MasterCard, Visa.
PRICES: [2010] B&B £68–£94 per person, D,B&B £84–£113, full alc £40, 4 nights for the price of 3 Mar, Apr, May, Oct, 1-night bookings sometimes refused.

# CORNHILL ON TWEED Northumberland    Map 4:A3

## COLLINGWOOD ARMS `NEW`

Local craftsmen worked 'inside and out' to
renovate this Grade II listed Georgian posting
inn in a small village in 'magnificent
countryside' near Flodden Field. Owned by
John Cook and managed by Kevin Kenny, it is
'highly recommended' this year. 'A real find,'
says a fellow *Guide* hotelier, who had a 'faultless'
stay en route to Edinburgh. 'Log fires were
burning in the library/sitting room and front
hall. You make your own tea in a small guest
kitchen, slightly strange. The staff are extremely
friendly.' The 'comfortable' bedrooms, each
named after a ship in Vice Admiral
Collingwood's 'van' at the Battle of Trafalgar,
have antique furnishings; 'many extras' in the
period bathrooms. There are adjoining rooms
for families (cots available). In the bar/brasserie
and a separate restaurant, Derek Weekley serves
'well-cooked' dishes on a short menu (perhaps
rare breed pork cutlet, baby roast potatoes).
'Breakfast was exceptional: the best kipper I
have ever had; on the buffet, a large honeycomb
from a local producer.' Fishermen have use of a
rod room; there are kennels for dogs. (*Richard
Bright, Chris Davy*)

Main Street
Cornhill on Tweed TD12 4UH

T: 01890-882424
F: 01890-883098
E: enquiries@collingwoodarms.com
W: www.collingwoodarms.com

BEDROOMS: 15, 1 on ground floor.
OPEN: all year.
FACILITIES: hall, library,
bar/brasserie, dining room, small
garden.
BACKGROUND MUSIC: in bar.
LOCATION: village centre.
CHILDREN: all ages welcomed.
DOGS: allowed in kennels.
CREDIT CARDS: MasterCard, Visa.
PRICES: [2010] B&B £55–£77.50 per
person, D,B&B £22.50 added, set
meal £30, full alc £45–£50.

# CORSE LAWN Gloucestershire

Map 3:D5

## CORSE LAWN HOUSE

*César award in 2005*

Set back from the village green and a busy road near Tewkesbury, this red brick Queen Anne Grade II listed building is run in personal style by Baba Hine; many of her staff are long serving. 'A delightful hotel; Baba was present as ever,' says a reader this year. 'The staff were welcoming, pleasant, helpful,' is another comment. Visitors can eat in the restaurant, where smart casual dress is preferred, or in the brightly decorated bistro. Andrew Poole's French/British cooking is thought 'outstanding'. When he was away, 'Baba Hine prepared a fine dish of pigeon breast with red cabbage and seasonal vegetables'. Bar lunches are also good. Bedrooms, mostly large, are traditionally furnished, 'well equipped' with good storage, biscuits, fresh tea and coffee; 'fresh milk in the fridge is a nice touch'. A large first-floor room was liked. A spacious room at the back was quiet, without traffic noise. The swimming pool, tennis court and croquet lawn are popular. Dogs are welcomed. (*Stuart Smith, John Barnes, John Shrimpton, and others*)

Corse Lawn GL19 4LZ

T: 01452-780771
F: 01452-780840
E: enquiries@corselawn.com
W: www.corselawn.com

BEDROOMS: 18, 5 on ground floor.
OPEN: all year except 24–26 Dec.
FACILITIES: lounge, bar lounge, bistro/bar, restaurant, 2 conference/private dining rooms, civil wedding licence, 12-acre grounds (croquet, tennis, covered heated swimming pool, 20 by 10 metres).
BACKGROUND MUSIC: none.
LOCATION: 5 miles SW of Tewkesbury on B4211.
CHILDREN: all ages welcomed.
DOGS: allowed in bedrooms, on a lead in drawing rooms.
CREDIT CARDS: all major cards.
PRICES: B&B £80–£100 per person, D,B&B £100–£120, set dinner £20–£32.50, short breaks, New Year package.

**25% DISCOUNT VOUCHERS**

## COVERACK Cornwall

Map 1:E2

### THE BAY HOTEL

In an attractive fishing village on a 'wonderful' bay (beaches, rock pools, a little harbour), this small hotel is run by its owners, Ric (the chef) and Gina House. A visitor this year praised the 'happy, friendly and positive attitude' of the family. 'Such good hosts,' is another comment. The white-painted building is decorated in coastal tones. The bedrooms have full or partial views of the sea: 'Our pleasant top-floor room was exactly as described by Mrs House and her daughter when we booked. The west-facing window overlooked the village and part of the bay; plenty of storage space, a large bathroom.' A 'noisy' ground-floor room was less liked. Cream teas can be taken on a garden terrace. The outlook is spectacular from the conservatory restaurant. Visitors staying for seven nights praised the host's cooking: 'The food was fantastic and the service faultless. We enjoyed the wide range of seafood; a shellfish gratinée was exquisite.' The daily-changing menu might include seared king scallops, bacon, shallots, white wine and cream; whole Cornish sole with anchovy butter. (*Dr Alec Frank, Mrs Tricia Mugridge*)

North Corner, Coverack
nr Helston TR12 6TF

T: 01326-280464
E: enquiries@thebayhotel.co.uk
W: www.thebayhotel.co.uk

BEDROOMS: 13, some on ground floor.
OPEN: Mar–Nov, Christmas/New Year.
FACILITIES: reception lounge, lounge, bar lounge, restaurant, 1-acre garden.
BACKGROUND MUSIC: none.
LOCATION: village centre, 10 miles SE of Helston.
CHILDREN: not under 8.
DOGS: not allowed in public rooms.
CREDIT CARDS: MasterCard, Visa.
PRICES: [2010] B&B £57–£95 per person, D,B&B £67–£115, full alc £42.95, special offers, Christmas/New Year house parties.

**25% DISCOUNT VOUCHERS**

# COWAN BRIDGE Lancashire

Map 4: inset D2

## HIPPING HALL

❦ *César award in 2008*

'One of our favourite places,' say trusted reporters returning in 2010 to Andrew Wildsmith's small hotel/restaurant in a village near Kirkby Lonsdale. Other praise this year: 'Andrew is always around; his staff are most helpful; a splendid friendly welcome, and assistance with luggage.' 'Fantastic; great room, delicious dinner.' The 17th-century house stands amid mature trees in 'immaculate' grounds. The sitting room has cream patterned wallpaper, framed pictures, comfortable chairs and settee. Meals are taken in the 15th-century Great Hall with tapestries, a minstrels' gallery, a 'huge' fireplace with log fire. Brent Hulena is the new chef serving modern dishes (eg, veal shin ravioli; plaice, fennel, tagliatelle nero, mussel chowder). 'The food is still good.' In the bedrooms, white walls, white rustic furniture and white carpets give a sense of 'lightness and space'; the bathrooms are 'smart'. The 'great' breakfast has freshly squeezed juices, smoothies, eggs, carefully sourced bacon and sausages, a basket of pastries and fresh bread. (*David and Kate Wooff, Gordon Murray, and others*)

Cowan Bridge
nr Kirkby Lonsdale LA6 2JJ

T: 015242-71187
E: info@hippinghall.com
W: www.hippinghall.com

BEDROOMS: 9, 3 in cottage, 1, on ground floor, suitable for &.
OPEN: all year except 3–6 Jan.
FACILITIES: lounge, bar, restaurant, civil wedding licence.
BACKGROUND MUSIC: classical in restaurant, jazz in lounge and bar.
LOCATION: 2 miles SE of Kirkby Lonsdale, on A65.
CHILDREN: all ages welcomed.
DOGS: allowed in cottage Room 7 only.
CREDIT CARDS: MasterCard, Visa.
PRICES: B&B £85–£155 per person, D,B&B £110–£170, set dinner £49.50–£62.50, Christmas/New Year packages, 1-night bookings normally refused Sat.

# CROFT-ON-TEES Co. Durham

## CLOW BECK HOUSE

🏆 *César award in 2007*

'After a stressful journey, the welcome we received was little short of fantastic.' A visitor this year to David and Heather Armstrong's small hotel in open country outside Croft-on-Tees had a 'relaxing and stress-busting stay'. 'David immediately offered us a seat in the lounge and a cup of tea (or something stronger).' The Armstrongs 'are such lovely people', says another guest. 'They always make you feel special.' Eccentricity abounds, from the giant pigs in the flowerbeds to the flamboyant bedrooms (in stone-walled buildings around the gardens). 'Our delightful room was spacious and well equipped.' 'They keep decorating and improving.' Mr Armstrong, the chef, describes his style as 'British with flair': visitors enjoy rustic portions of 'wonderful' dishes, perhaps lamb and pastry spiral, blackcurrant compote; cod chunk, light Mediterranean tomato sauce. Vegetarians have a separate menu with extensive choice. Breakfast, 'a feast', includes Doreen's black pudding; fruit-and-nut bread, home-made preserves. Warning: satnav leads to an unmade road at the back; follow the brown signs from the village. (*Averil Wilkinson, and others*)

Monk End Farm
Croft-on-Tees
nr Darlington DL2 2SW

T: 01325-721075
F: 01325-720419
E: david@clowbeckhouse.co.uk
W: www.clowbeckhouse.co.uk

BEDROOMS: 13, 12 in garden buildings, 1 suitable for ♿.
OPEN: 4 Jan–23 Dec.
FACILITIES: ramps, lounge, restaurant, small conference facilities, 2-acre grounds in 100-acre farm.
BACKGROUND MUSIC: classical in restaurant.
LOCATION: 3 miles SE of Darlington.
CHILDREN: all ages welcomed.
DOGS: not allowed.
CREDIT CARDS: Amex, MasterCard, Visa.
PRICES: [2010] B&B £67.50–£85 per person, full alc £37.

# CROOKHAM Northumberland

## THE COACH HOUSE AT CROOKHAM

Near Flodden Field and the Scottish border, Toby and Leona Rutter run their guest house in a Grade II listed 17th-century dower house and a series of renovated farm buildings. A visitor in 2010 enjoyed 'a good experience; the welcome was warm; our spacious room was well furnished.' The residents' lounge has a vaulted ceiling, large open fire, an honesty bar and views over the terrace and orchard (Shetland ponies graze here). There are three traditional bedrooms in the house, one with its own private staircase. Others are in the courtyard, linked by paved paths. One is dual aspect; another has exposed beams, and a former stone bread oven. Most have facilities en suite (some have a private bathroom). Three are adapted for disabled guests to whom 'great consideration is given'. A traditional three-course dinner is served at 7.30 pm in the dining room; no choice of main course, which might be chicken with white wine, cream, tarragon sauce. Breakfast has a wide selection of fruits, yogurt, cereals and cooked dishes (kippers, smoked haddock and kedgeree available if ordered the evening before). (*Max Lickfold*)

Crookham
Cornhill-on-Tweed TD12 4TD

T: 01890-820293
F: 01890-820284
E: stay@coachhousecrookham.com
W: www.coachhousecrookham.com

BEDROOMS: 11, 7 around courtyard, 3 suitable for &.
OPEN: all year except Christmas/New Year.
FACILITIES: lounge, 2 dining rooms, terrace, orchard.
BACKGROUND MUSIC: none.
LOCATION: On A697, 3 miles N of Milfield.
CHILDREN: all ages welcomed.
DOGS: not allowed in public rooms or main house bedrooms.
CREDIT CARDS: MasterCard, Visa (*2% surcharge*).
PRICES: [2010] B&B £39–£64 per person, set dinner £22.95, 1-night bookings refused Fri/Sat.

# CROSTHWAITE Cumbria

Map 4: inset C2

## THE PUNCH BOWL INN

🐦 *César award in 2010*

Beside a handsome church in 'one of the last unspoilt valleys' in the Lake District, this 300-year-old inn has been carefully restored by the owners Paul Spencer and Richard Rose. 'They have modernised to a high standard without losing any of the traditional appeal,' said *Guide* inspectors. 'Housekeeping throughout is immaculate; the inn gleams and shines.' A reporter this year found it 'low-key without being laid-back; lacking pretension'. Even the smaller bedrooms have 'ample space'; bathrooms are well equipped. 'My high-ceilinged room was well decorated with silk curtains, hand-blocked wallpaper, and a vast ornate mirror.' A free cream tea is served in the afternoon in the lounge. The busy bar has slate-flagged floor and traditional furniture; there are polished floorboards, leather chairs in the 'smartly set' restaurant. Chris Meredith is the new chef: his modern menus use local ingredients (eg, braised shoulder of Borrowdale lamb, mashed potato, cockles, tomato and basil jus). Bar meals, sandwiches and snacks are served until 6 pm. Breakfast is 'terrific'. (*Tony and Josephine Green, and others*)

Crosthwaite, Lyth Valley
LA8 8HR

T: 01539-568237
F: 01539-568875
E: info@the-punchbowl.co.uk
W: www.the-punchbowl.co.uk

BEDROOMS: 9.
OPEN: all year.
FACILITIES: lounge, 2 bar rooms, restaurant, civil wedding licence, 2 terraces, only restaurant suitable for &.
BACKGROUND MUSIC: in bar and restaurant.
LOCATION: 5 miles W of Kendal, via A5074.
CHILDREN: all ages welcomed.
DOGS: only allowed in bar.
CREDIT CARDS: Amex, MasterCard, Visa.
PRICES: [2010] B&B £71.25–£155 per person, full alc £37, Christmas/New Year packages.

# CRUDWELL Wiltshire

Map 3:E5

## THE RECTORY HOTEL

In large stone-walled gardens in a classic Cotswold village, this 18th-century rectory has been given a fresh look by Julian Muggridge (antique dealer) and Jonathan Barry (formerly with Hotel du Vin). The high-ceilinged lounge has an ornate Regency fireplace, leather chairs, white walls, stripped floors, antiques, alongside Perspex tables, glass-shelved alcoves. An eco-friendly wood-pellet boiler is new this year. Visitors in 2010 had 'a pleasant experience; a good welcome from the able staff'. The 'comfortable' bedrooms are individually designed; there are washed-out colours, hand sprung mattresses, Egyptian linen. A 'fine' dinner was enjoyed in the 'lovely' wood-panelled restaurant which looks over a sunken Victorian baptism pool. Chef Peter Fairclough uses local produce (suppliers listed) for his seasonal menu of modern British dishes, eg, chump of lamb, beetroot dauphinoise, cabbage and bacon. Children have their own menu from 6.15 to 7 pm. Guests can also eat at *The Potting Shed*, a pub opposite under the same ownership. Meals can be taken in the garden in summer. There's an open-air heated swimming pool, a croquet lawn. (*Stuart Smith*)

Crudwell, nr Malmesbury
SN16 9EP

T: 01666-577194
F: 01666-577853
E: info@therectoryhotel.com
W: www.therectoryhotel.com

BEDROOMS: 12.
OPEN: all year, restaurant closed lunchtime.
FACILITIES: lounge, bar, dining room, civil wedding licence, 3-acre garden (heated 20-metre swimming pool), unsuitable for &.
BACKGROUND MUSIC: 'light jazz' in bar and dining room, evenings.
LOCATION: 4 miles N of Malmesbury.
CHILDREN: all ages welcomed.
DOGS: not allowed in dining room.
CREDIT CARDS: MasterCard, Visa.
PRICES: B&B £57.50–£107.50 per person, full alc £36.50, midweek breaks, Christmas/New Year packages, 1-night bookings refused bank holidays.

## DARTMOUTH Devon

Map 1:D4

### DART MARINA   **NEW**

'A thoroughly pleasant hotel in a fabulous location.' 'One of our favourites; delightful staff, well-appointed rooms, good food.' Praise from two regular reporters brings a full *Guide* entry for this large hotel by the 'higher' ferry across the River Dart. Owned by Richard Seton, who has made 'radical improvements', it is managed by Chris Jones. The welcome is 'enthusiastic': 'John, the porter, is noticeably helpful to visitors with disabilities, and is a mine of information.' The bedrooms, which overlook the river, have 'a stylish modern decor with muted colours'. 'Our room was beautifully presented; a modern bathroom with fluffy towels and robes.' In the *River* restaurant, which has 'one of the best views in town', table settings are 'immaculate', the service 'friendly, attentive'. Mark Streeter's cooking is 'excellent': 'We had a good rump of lamb with ratatouille and fondant potatoes; a delicious plaice meunière.' Meals can also be taken in the *Wildfire* bistro (tempura prawns, lamb tagine, etc) and on a river terrace. 'Generous' breakfasts have 'interesting choices; a delicious apricot and prune compote; first-class cooked dishes'. (*Mary Woods, Ian Malone*)

Sandquay Road
Dartmouth TQ6 9PH

T: 01803-832580
F: 01803-835040
E: reception@dartmarina.com
W: www.dartmarina.com

BEDROOMS: 49, 3 on ground floor, 1 suitable for &.
OPEN: all year.
FACILITIES: lounge/bar, bistro, restaurant, river-front terrace, civil wedding licence, spa (heated indoor swimming pool, 8½ by 4 metres, gym, treatments).
BACKGROUND MUSIC: soft jazz in restaurant.
LOCATION: on waterfront.
CHILDREN: all ages welcomed.
DOGS: in ground-floor rooms (£10), not during meal times in public rooms.
CREDIT CARDS: all major cards.
PRICES: [2010] B&B £67.50–£147.50 per person, D,B&B £90–£170, set meals £35, special breaks, Christmas/New Year packages, 1-night bookings refused Sat.

# DARTMOUTH Devon

Map 1:D4

## NONSUCH HOUSE

❧ *César award in 2000*

On a steep hill ('providing good exercise for the reasonably fit'), Kit and Penny Noble's large Edwardian villa has panoramic views over the river to Dartmouth. Trusted reporters were impressed by the friendly welcome: 'Our bags were carried to our room and we were shown to the conservatory where we enjoyed tea and home-made cakes while watching the activity on the busy river.' Bedrooms have been redecorated this year. 'Ours had a bay window facing south, with armchairs set around it, and a very comfortable bed.' A visitor who arrived with a cold was so well cared for that she recommended it as 'the best place in which to be ill'. The cosy sitting room has relaxing chairs, books and magazines; a log fire in winter. New Zealander Kit is an excellent cook and discusses the menu beforehand: this uses many local ingredients, perhaps line-caught sea bass or rack of Blackawton lamb. No liquor licence; bring your own wine — whites will be chilled. 'There is proper' bread, freshly squeezed orange juice at breakfast. (*BB, CH*)

Church Hill, Kingswear
Dartmouth TQ6 0BX

T: 01803-752829
F: 01803-752357
E: enquiries@nonsuch-house.co.uk
W: www.nonsuch-house.co.uk

BEDROOMS: 4.
OPEN: all year, dining room closed midday, evening Tues/Fri/Sat.
FACILITIES: ramps, lounge, dining room/conservatory, ¼-acre garden (sun terrace), rock beach 300 yds (sailing nearby), membership of local gym and spa.
BACKGROUND MUSIC: none.
LOCATION: 5 mins' walk from ferry to Dartmouth.
CHILDREN: not under 10.
DOGS: not allowed.
CREDIT CARDS: MasterCard, Visa.
PRICES: [2010] B&B £55–£75 per person, D,B&B £90–£120, special breaks, Christmas/New Year packages, 1-night bookings usually refused weekends.

# DEDHAM Essex

Map 2:C5

## DEDHAM HALL & FOUNTAIN HOUSE RESTAURANT

With the 'feel of a family home', this group of 14th- and 15th-century buildings is run in informal style as a guest house, restaurant and art school by Jim and Wendy Sarton. In a 'quiet, peaceful location' in an area of outstanding natural beauty, it is reached down a bumpy lane in Constable country (Flatford Mill is a two-mile walk away along the River Stour). Artists attending painting courses (February to November) stay in large rooms around an old Dutch barn, now a studio. Other visitors stay in bedrooms without a key; the decor is traditional: dark wood, huge beds and Persian rugs. Walls in the residents' lounge are crammed with paintings by local artists and those attending the courses. The *Fountain House* restaurant is popular with locals; reservations are essential; the beamed dining room overlooks the pond and gardens of the hall. 'Imaginative' meals (perhaps salmon with spinach in puff pastry) are cooked on an Aga, and dinner is served communally by candlelight. (*CWMcK*)

Brook Street, Dedham
nr Colchester CO7 6AD

T: 01206-323027
F: 01206-323293
E: sarton@dedhamhall.demon.co.uk
W: www.dedhamhall.demon.co.uk

BEDROOMS: 20, 14 in annexe, some on ground floor.
OPEN: all year except Christmas/New Year, restaurant closed Sun/Mon.
FACILITIES: ramps, 2 lounges, 2 bars, dining room, restaurant, studio, 6-acre grounds (pond, gardens).
BACKGROUND MUSIC: none.
LOCATION: end of High Street.
CHILDREN: all ages welcomed.
DOGS: not allowed.
CREDIT CARDS: MasterCard, Visa.
PRICES: B&B £55–£65 per person, D,B&B £85–£95, full alc £40, painting holidays (Feb–Nov).

# DEDHAM Essex

Map 2:C5

## THE SUN INN

Opposite Dedham's church, Piers Baker's yellow-painted old coaching inn has established a following for the quality of the Italian cooking. 'Delicious lunch; worth seeking out by any serious food lover,' says one visitor this year. Jessica Savill is the 'young, friendly' manager. The open-plan dining room, on two levels, 'is furnished minimally, with the ancient beams of the house exposed and forming a partition with the bar'. There are open log fires, a display of work by local artists, for sale. The chef, Ugo Simonelli, serves a daily-changing menu using local and seasonal ingredients. Typical dishes: Tuscan bread soup, black cabbage; grilled Salt Marsh leg of lamb, roasted red and yellow beetroots, salsa verde. The bedrooms have 'character' furniture, a mix of antique and repro, 'divinely comfortable' beds, many quirky touches (old packing cases for bedside tables). At breakfast there is fresh orange juice, hand-cut wholemeal and soda bread toast; a wide choice of cooked dishes. There are special menus for children, and there is plenty to keep them occupied in the large walled garden. (*Robert Gower*)

High Street, Dedham
nr Colchester CO7 6DF

T: 01206-323351
E: office@thesuninndedham.com
W: www.thesuninndedham.com

BEDROOMS: 5.
OPEN: all year except 25/26 Dec.
FACILITIES: lounge, bar, dining room, ½-acre garden (covered terrace, children's play area), unsuitable for &.
BACKGROUND MUSIC: jazz/Latin/blues throughout.
LOCATION: central, 5 miles NE of Colchester.
CHILDREN: all ages welcomed.
DOGS: not allowed in bedrooms.
CREDIT CARDS: all major cards.
PRICES: B&B £40–£75 per person, D,B&B £50–£100, set meals £10.50–£13.50, full alc £37, see website for special offers.

# DURHAM Co. Durham

## FALLEN ANGEL    `NEW`

Overlooking the university cricket pitch and the River Wear, this Grade II listed Georgian townhouse has been given a 'beautifully eccentric' makeover as a restaurant-with-rooms by the owner, John Marshall. 'Highly recommended,' says a visitor this year, 'a perfect place to stay for a few days.' The bedrooms are themed. Le Jardin, one of three garden apartments (each with a hot tub on a balcony), has an AstroTurf carpet and palm trees. Cruella de Vil, decorated in black with a splash of diamante, has a velvet-clad sleigh bed, a ceramic Dalmatian; faux leather tiles and a canopied bath in the bathroom, Russian Bride, a top-floor suite with views over castle and cathedral, has hand-carved furniture, bamboo flooring and a glass-fronted sauna. Première has a cinema screen; a Tardis and Cyberman are found in Sci Fi. The restaurant also has 'quirky details': Philippe Starck 'ghost' chairs, portholes, parasols. The seasonal menus might include seared king scallops, pea purée; sea bass, pak choi, chilli ginger dressing. Breakfast, which can be taken in the room, is 'English at its best'. (*Christian Bartoschek*)

34 Old Elvet
Durham DH1 3HN

T: 0191-384 1037
F: 0191-384 3348
E: info@fallenangelhotel.com
W: www.fallenangelhotel.com

BEDROOMS: 10, 3 in garden apartments, 1 suitable for &.
OPEN: all year, restaurant closed Sun–Wed evenings.
FACILITIES: restaurant, small garden.
BACKGROUND MUSIC: clavinola (automatic piano) in restaurant.
LOCATION: in centre.
CHILDREN: all ages welcomed.
DOGS: not allowed.
CREDIT CARDS: all major cards.
PRICES: [2010] room £70–£260, breakfast £4.95–£12, set meals £25, full alc £40, special offers, Christmas/New Year packages.

# EAST HOATHLY East Sussex

Map 2:E4

## OLD WHYLY

**NEW**

In extensive grounds with a lake, topiary and statuary, this Grade II listed Georgian manor house is run by Sarah Burgoyne as 'the most elegant' B&B. 'My guests should feel as though they are staying in a home, not a house,' she says. A visitor this year was 'greeted with home-made cake and tea, served in exquisite china in a beautiful drawing room'. The bedrooms are individually decorated in country house style. 'Ours was small; there are larger and prettier ones, but the charm of the house was more than adequate compensation.' A 'passionate' cook, Mrs Burgoyne serves dinner by arrangement in the dining room. Typical dishes: wild mushroom risotto; skate wings with warm salsa. Breakfast, 'communal but cheery', has eggs from the hens and ducks in the garden, honey from bees in the orchard. In good weather, meals are taken under a vine-covered pergola on the terrace. Hampers can be provided for Glyndebourne (ten minutes' drive). Guests have access to a hard tennis court, and a wisteria-shaded swimming pool. There are many walks directly from the house. (*Catrin Treadwell*)

London Road
East Hoathly BN8 6EL

T: 01825-840216
E: stay@oldwhyly.co.uk
W: www.oldwhyly.co.uk

BEDROOMS: 4.
OPEN: all year.
FACILITIES: drawing room, dining room, 4-acre garden in 30-acre grounds, heated outdoor swimming pool (10 x 5 metres), tennis, unsuitable for &.
BACKGROUND MUSIC: none.
LOCATION: 1 mile N of village.
CHILDREN: all ages welcomed.
DOGS: not allowed in public rooms.
CREDIT CARDS: none.
PRICES: B&B £45–£85 per person, set dinner £30, Glyndebourne hamper £35, 1-night bookings sometimes refused Fri/Sat.

# EAST LAVANT West Sussex

Map 2:E3

## THE ROYAL OAK

In Goodwood country, close to the South Downs and Chichester, this 200-year-old flint-stone inn is in a pretty village. It is owned by Charles Ullmann, who has appointed a new manager this year, Marco Ruggieri. In the restaurant (popular with locals and Chichester theatre-goers), Steve Ferre has been promoted to head chef. His modern à la carte menu, which changes monthly, might include dishes like wild mushroom risotto; duo of Sussex pork (pan-roasted fillet and twice-cooked belly), dauphinoise potatoes. There are daily blackboard specials. On fine days, meals are also served on the front terrace or in the small side garden. Bedrooms, which vary in size, are in the main building and a converted barn and cottage. They combine traditional features (beams and flagstones) with modern facilities: under-floor heating in bathroom, powerful shower, flat-screen TV and DVD-player. Beds have been described as 'very comfortable'. Breakfast, served in the restaurant, has fresh fruit, and 'cooked dishes well up to standard'. Cots and high chairs are provided for children. More reports, please.

Pook Lane
East Lavant PO18 0AX

T: 01243-527434
E: info@royaloakeastlavant.co.uk
W: www.royaloakeastlavant.co.uk

BEDROOMS: 6, 3 in adjacent barn and cottage, 2 self-catering cottages nearby.
OPEN: all year.
FACILITIES: bar/restaurant, terrace (outside meals), small garden, unsuitable for &.
BACKGROUND MUSIC: jazz in restaurant.
LOCATION: 2 miles N of Chichester.
CHILDREN: all ages welcomed.
DOGS: guide dogs only allowed in bar area.
CREDIT CARDS: all major cards.
PRICES: [2010] B&B £45–£85, D,B&B £30 added, full alc £36, winter breaks, Christmas/New Year packages, 1-night bookings refused weekends.

**25% DISCOUNT VOUCHERS**

# EGTON BRIDGE North Yorkshire

Map 4:C5

## BROOM HOUSE   **NEW**

In a peaceful setting outside a pretty village in the North York Moors national park, this Victorian farmhouse has been 'transformed into a perfect guest house' by owners David and Maria White. 'It exceeded our expectations in every way,' say the nominators. The 'friendly, hard-working' couple have added bedrooms in an extension which also contains *Whites*, a bistro open to the public. 'She cooks; he is front-of-house, waiting at table with well-trained local girls. The bread, marmalade, yogurt, jams and muffins are all home made.' She uses local ingredients for her menus, which have 'a good choice on each course', eg, smoked trout cheesecake, orange and pine nut salad; chicken roulade, creamy mash, white wine and tarragon sauce. 'Our compact room in the extension had lovely views of the garden and woods beyond: a comfortable bed, good linen, a modern decor in grey, black and white. A good-sized bathroom with fluffy towels. Considerate hosts, they took our cases away for storage.' Much to do in the area; in the village you can catch the local trains that pass the perimeter of the garden. (*Janet and Dennis Allom*)

Broom House Lane
Egton Bridge YO21 1XD

T: 01947-895279
F: 01947-895657
E: mw@broom-house.co.uk
W: www.egton-bridge.co.uk

BEDROOMS: 9, 1 on ground floor, 2 in cottage.
OPEN: Feb–Dec except Christmas, restaurant closed Mon.
FACILITIES: lounge, dining room, restaurant, civil wedding licence, garden.
BACKGROUND MUSIC: in restaurant.
LOCATION: ½ mile W of village.
CHILDREN: all ages welcomed.
DOGS: not allowed.
CREDIT CARDS: MasterCard, Visa.
PRICES: [2010] B&B £43–£63 per person, D,B&B £61.75–£81.75, full alc £38, New Year package, 1-night bookings sometimes refused.

# EMSWORTH Hampshire

Map 2:E3

## RESTAURANT 36 ON THE QUAY ♟

*César award: restaurant-with-rooms of the year*

'Everything is harmonious and tasteful' at Ramon and Karen Farthing's restaurant-with-rooms. The 17th-century building overlooks the harbour of a small fishing village. He is the *Michelin*-starred chef; she is a 'gracious hostess of many talents' (says an inspector). Five bedrooms are above the restaurant; a cottage across the road has a bedroom, lounge and kitchen. Saffron, a new suite accessed by a side door, is 'furnished with understated elegance; low glass tables, white leather and metal chairs, handsome objets d'art and pictures; impeccable bedroom; fresh milk in a fridge in the mini-kitchen'. In the dining room, 'beautifully laid tables are a splendid backdrop for top-class cooking; Ramon is not afraid of contrasting textures and seasonings. Highlights were a pre-starter of wild mushroom soup; mouth-watering serrano ham with a roundel of hot duck liver pâté; lemon sole paupiettes, crab, creamed leek lasagne; a delicious trio of lemon desserts. Service, by charming, well-trained girls, was leisurely.' A 'faultless' continental breakfast (cereals, strawberries, home-made jams, two kinds of brioche, croissants, etc) is brought to the room.

47 South Street
Emsworth PO10 7EG

T: 01243-375592
E: info@36onthequay.co.uk
W: www.36onthequay.co.uk

BEDROOMS: 6, 1 in cottage (with lounge) across road (can be let weekly).
OPEN: all year except 3 weeks Jan, 1 week May, 1 week Oct, restaurant closed Sun/Mon.
FACILITIES: lounge area, bar area, restaurant, terrace, only restaurant suitable for ♿.
BACKGROUND MUSIC: none.
LOCATION: on harbour.
CHILDREN: all ages welcomed.
DOGS: only allowed in cottage, by arrangement.
CREDIT CARDS: Diners, MasterCard, Visa.
PRICES: [2010] B&B £47.50–£100 per person, set dinner £48.95.

# ERMINGTON Devon

## PLANTATION HOUSE

'Highly recommended' in 2010, this cream-painted Georgian rectory (Grade II listed) has been renovated by Richard and Magdalena Hendey. The four-year project has been completed, they tell us, with the redesign of the final two bedrooms; all the public areas 'have been under the surgeon's knife', and the gardens have been developed to supply vegetables, fruit and herbs for the kitchen (as well as eggs from their own hens). The Hendeys are 'warm and welcoming', says a visitor. Richard Hendey is a 'talented' chef: his five-course menu, served in the newly decorated dining room, might include a tasting of nettle and lettuce soup; wild rabbit cooked four ways, ginger wine sauce, potato purée, baby beetroot. One of the new bedrooms has a separate dressing area; both have king-size bed, bathroom with under-floor heating, walk-in shower and recliner bath. All rooms have fresh flowers, fruit, mineral water, cafetière coffee. Breakfast has fresh fruit salad, home-made muesli; smoked salmon and scrambled eggs, dry-cured bacon; toast from home-made bread. (*Gaye and Garth Allen, and others*)

Totnes Road
Ermington, nr Plymouth
PL21 9NS

T: 01548-831100
E: info@plantationhousehotel.co.uk
W: www.plantationhousehotel.co.uk

BEDROOMS: 9.
OPEN: all year, restaurant closed midday, generally closed Sun.
FACILITIES: lounge/bar, 2 dining rooms, terrace, garden, unsuitable for &.
BACKGROUND MUSIC: if required.
LOCATION: 10 miles E of Plymouth.
CHILDREN: 'well-behaved' children welcomed.
DOGS: allowed in 1 bedroom, not in public rooms.
CREDIT CARDS: Amex, MasterCard, Visa.
PRICES: [2010] B&B £55–£100 per person, set dinner £35–£39, New Year package, 1-night bookings occasionally refused.

## EVERSHOT Dorset

Map 1:C6

### SUMMER LODGE

In large grounds, this country retreat for the Earl of Ilchester was enlarged by Thomas Hardy, who adopted the pretty village as the setting for *Tess of the d'Urbervilles*. It is now run as a hotel (Relais & Châteaux) by the Red Carnation group, which has 'spent a fortune on the house and gardens'. 'Really luxurious; wonderful service; expensive but worth it,' says a visitor returning after many years. Public rooms have gilt mirrors, brass fenders, needlepoint cushions, swags. The 'excellent, comfortable' bedrooms, decorated in country house style, have fine fabrics, patterns, heavy drapes, many extras (eg, fleece hot-water bottles). Room One remains as Hardy designed it, a suite with an open fireplace, two bathrooms. In the dining room, chef Steven Titman serves a seasonal menu of modern dishes with French influences, perhaps lasagne of Cornish brill, creamed baby spinach, razor clams. In summer, meals can be taken on a terrace. The spa has a large indoor swimming pool. The *Acorn Inn* in the village is also owned by Red Carnation. (*Mrs Blethyn Elliott, EJT Palmer*)

9 Fore Street
Evershot DT2 0JR

T: 01935-482000
F: 01935-482040
E: summer@relaischateaux.com
W: www.summerlodgehotel.com

BEDROOMS: 24, 9 in coach house and courtyard house, 4 in lane, 1 on ground floor suitable for &.
OPEN: all year.
FACILITIES: ramps, drawing room, lounge/bar, restaurant, indoor swimming pool (11 by 6 metres), civil wedding licence, 4-acre grounds (garden, croquet, tennis).
BACKGROUND MUSIC: 'contemporary' in lounge/bar.
LOCATION: 10 miles NW of Dorchester.
CHILDREN: all ages welcomed.
DOGS: allowed in some bedrooms, some public rooms.
CREDIT CARDS: all major cards.
PRICES: [2010] B&B £100–£225 per person, D,B&B £160–£285, full alc £75, website offers, Christmas/New Year packages, 1-night bookings refused weekends July–Oct.

# EVESHAM Worcestershire

Map 3:D6

## THE EVESHAM HOTEL

♦ *César award in 1990*

'A feeling of relaxation and humour' runs through John and Sue Jenkinson's family-friendly and quirky hotel. A guest in 2010 (on his 12th visit) was 'treated to the wonderful sight of John Jenkinson in his inimitable way telling a visitor not to use his mobile phone in the lounge'. The guest pack advises: 'Only oiks may use mobile phones in public areas. We do not cater for oiks.' The jokey theme is reflected in Mr Jenkinson's selection of 'humorous' ties, the 'smile-enforcing loos' (fart machines, mirrors that speak), silly books, key fobs attached to teddy bears. Regulars love the attention to detail (bedrooms have a silent fridge with soft drinks, milk and wine; double doors eliminate corridor noise; 'more storage space in our beautifully decorated room than we have ever seen'. Children are 'genuinely welcomed'; they will enjoy the themed bedrooms (Alice in Wonderful, Safari, etc), the swimming pool and play areas. In May 2010, long-serving cooks Andrea Walker and Rachel Grove were promoted to share the position of head chef. (*Frank G Millen, and others*)

Cooper's Lane, off Waterside
Evesham WR11 1DA

T: 01386-765566
F: 01386-765443
FP: 0800-716969 (reservations only)
E: reception@eveshamhotel.com
W: www.eveshamhotel.com

BEDROOMS: 40, 11 on ground floor, 2 suitable for &.
OPEN: all year except 25/26 Dec.
FACILITIES: 2 lounges, bar, restaurant, private dining room, indoor swimming pool (5 by 12 metres), 2½-acre grounds (croquet, putting, swings, trampoline).
BACKGROUND MUSIC: none.
LOCATION: 5 mins' walk from centre, across river.
CHILDREN: all ages welcomed.
DOGS: only guide dogs allowed in public rooms.
CREDIT CARDS: all major cards.
PRICES: [2010] B&B £60–£85 per person, full alc £37.50, New Year package, 1-night bookings refused Sat, for Cheltenham Gold Cup, New Year.

## EXFORD Somerset

Map 1:B4

### THE CROWN

'Recommended to anyone seeking a wonderfully situated country retreat, without wishing to sacrifice comfort to rusticity.' A regular reporter was 'very taken' with this much-extended 17th-century coaching inn on the green of this picturesque village in Exmoor national park. The 'welcoming' owners, Chris Kirkbride and Sara and Dan Whittaker, are 'doing a splendid job and deserve to succeed. The service is impeccable, friendly but not over-familiar.' 'Well-appointed' bedrooms are individually styled: 'Ours was tastefully furnished, with a spacious bathroom.' A double-aspect second-floor room was 'comfortably furnished': two armchairs, a desk, built-in wardrobe, large chest of drawers. In the attractive restaurant (dark red walls, crisp white cloths, 'eye-catching' table settings) the cooking of chef Darren Edwards 'is beautifully presented, the wild sea bass as good as I have ever eaten'. Good wines by the glass. There are blackboard specials on a bar menu, also curry nights. On fine evenings, dinner may be served on the terrace. A stream runs through the large grounds. (*Sir Patrick Cormack, SJ Smith*)

Exford
Exmoor National Park
TA24 7PP

T: 01643-831554
F: 01643-831665
E: info@crownhotelexmoor.co.uk
W: www.crownhotelexmoor.co.uk

BEDROOMS: 17.
OPEN: all year.
FACILITIES: lounge, cocktail bar, public bar, restaurant, meeting room, 3½-acre grounds (trout stream, water garden, terrace garden), stabling for visiting horses, unsuitable for &.
BACKGROUND MUSIC: in bar and restaurant.
LOCATION: on village green.
CHILDREN: all ages welcomed.
DOGS: not allowed in restaurant.
CREDIT CARDS: MasterCard, Visa.
PRICES: [2010] B&B £62.50–£72.50 per person, D,B&B £99–£109, full alc £50, special breaks, Christmas/New Year packages, 1-night bookings refused holiday weekends.

# FAVERSHAM Kent

Map 2:D5

## READ'S

♥ *César award in 2005*

'A delightful house and a warm welcome; many nice little touches,' says a visitor this year to David and Rona Pitchford's *Michelin*-starred restaurant-with-rooms. The elegant Georgian manor house stands amid gardens and lawns near an old market town, close to Canterbury. 'Perfect' cooking and service, says another guest. The small dining room may become crowded when visitors gather for dinner. But everyone praises the 'unfussy' service, under Mrs Pitchford's direction, in the candlelit restaurant. Her husband uses vegetables and herbs from the walled gardens for his 'excellent' modern dishes, perhaps terrine of ham hock and chicken, home-made piccalilli; caramelised pork, lemon thyme stuffing, pak choi, red onion marmalade. The wine list has some rare bottles, a good best buys selection. The spacious bedrooms are furnished in period style, with traditional English fabrics; there are 'comfortable' beds; a decanter of sherry. Guests have access, on an honesty basis, to the Pantry, which has a well-stocked fridge, tea and coffee-making facilities. Breakfast has 'delicious' home-made jams, good cooked dishes. (*David Birnie, Mrs Blethyn Elliott*)

Macknade Manor
Canterbury Road
Faversham ME13 8XE

T: 01795-535344
F: 01795-591200
E: enquiries@reads.com
W: www.reads.com

BEDROOMS: 6.
OPEN: all year except 25/26 Dec, 1st week Jan, 2 weeks Sept, restaurant closed Sun/Mon.
FACILITIES: sitting room/bar, restaurant, private dining room, civil wedding licence, 4-acre garden (terrace, outdoor dining), only restaurant suitable for &.
BACKGROUND MUSIC: none.
LOCATION: ½ mile SE of Faversham.
CHILDREN: all ages welcomed.
DOGS: not allowed.
CREDIT CARDS: all major cards.
PRICES: [2010] room £125–£195, D,B&B £130–£145 per person, set dinner £52.

# FLEET Dorset

Map 1:D6

## MOONFLEET MANOR

'Beautifully situated', between the Fleet lagoon and the shingle Chesil Beach, this 'friendly' Georgian manor house belongs to von Essen's Luxury Family Hotels group. 'A lovely stay' was enjoyed by a visitor this year: 'Our children loved the swimming pool and facilities.' Small children can be left in the Four Bears' Den, which is Ofsted-registered. Their older siblings have the run of a large indoor play area which has a trampoline, table tennis, soft tennis, table football, computer games, etc; 'some of the kit needs replacing'. There are play areas, swings and slides in the large grounds. Adults can book holistic therapies and other spa treatments. Children sharing a room with their parents are charged only for their meals. High tea is served at 5 pm ('our five-year-old was not too impressed'). In the evening, Tony Smith, who has been chef for ten years, cooks 'excellent' meals; his style is British/French, with dishes like crab cake with gazpacho sauce; corn-fed chicken, smoked bacon, pine kernels, cauliflower purée. 'Our beautiful interconnecting bedrooms in the main house were well appointed.' (*Jill Cripps*)

Fleet Road, Fleet
nr Weymouth DT3 4ED

T: 01305-786948
F: 01305-774395
E: info@moonfleetmanorhotel.co.uk
W: www.moonfleetmanorhotel.co.uk

BEDROOMS: 36, 6 in 2 annexes, 3 on ground floor.
OPEN: all year.
FACILITIES: lift, 2 lounges with dispense bar, restaurant, meeting room, games room/nursery, disco, indoor 10-metre swimming pool, sauna, solarium, sunbed, aromatherapy, snooker, 5-acre grounds (children's play areas, tennis, bowls, squash, badminton).
BACKGROUND MUSIC: none.
LOCATION: 7 miles W of Weymouth.
CHILDREN: all ages welcomed.
DOGS: not allowed in restaurant.
CREDIT CARDS: all major cards.
PRICES: [2010] B&B £80–£215 per person, D,B&B £85–£230, special offers, Christmas/New Year packages, 1-night bookings refused weekends, bank holidays.

# GATESHEAD Tyne and Wear

Map 4:B4

## ESLINGTON VILLA

Within easy reach of the attractions of the Gateshead area, Nick and Melanie Tulip's imposing Victorian villa stands in extensive gardens in a quiet, tree-lined suburb of Gateshead. It is liked by readers for the ambience, style and friendly service. Bedrooms in the older part of the house are traditionally furnished. Chestnut has a four-poster bed and a large bathroom with corner bath; Lilac has windows looking over the garden. Rooms in an extension have a lighter, more contemporary touch. The airy restaurant with a conservatory extension is popular with locals. The chef, Andy Moore, serves a modern menu, perhaps Cumbrian air-dried ham, truffled Camembert; seared salmon, crispy chilli salad, sticky rice. Breakfast has a wide choice including smoked haddock risotto and 'tasty' kippers. Wi-Fi is available throughout. There is background music in the public rooms. Seminars, private meetings and functions are often held. More reports, please.

8 Station Road, Low Fell
Gateshead NE9 6DR

T: 0191-487 6017
F: 0191-420 0667
E: home@eslingtonvilla.co.uk
W: www.eslingtonvilla.co.uk

BEDROOMS: 18, 3 with separate entrance on ground floor.
OPEN: all year except 25/26 Dec, 1 Jan.
FACILITIES: ramp, lounge/bar, conservatory, restaurant, private dining room, conference/function facilities, 2-acre garden (patio).
BACKGROUND MUSIC: jazz/popular throughout.
LOCATION: 2 miles from centre, off A1.
CHILDREN: all ages welcomed.
DOGS: not allowed.
CREDIT CARDS: Amex, MasterCard, Visa.
PRICES: B&B [2010] £74.50–£79.50 per person, set dinner £22.50–£24.50.

**25% DISCOUNT VOUCHERS**

# GILLINGHAM Dorset

Map 2:D1

## STOCK HILL HOUSE

In lovely landscaped grounds on the Somerset/
Dorset border, this late Victorian mansion has
long been liked for its friendly atmosphere
and 'excellent' food. It has been run as a small
hotel/restaurant (Relais & Châteaux) for 25
years by owners Nita and Peter Hauser; she is a
'wonderful hostess'; he is the chef, cooking in
a classic French style with a 'hint of Austria' to
reflect his birthplace. In the formal dining room,
which faces the garden, he presents a daily-
changing menu which might include home-cured
ox tongue; Aga-roasted duckling, sour black
cherries and cassis. A vegetarian menu is also
available. There are two lounges, one formal in
period style with striped fabrics, china figurines;
the other cosy with a log fire. The bedrooms
vary greatly in size (which is reflected in the
price). They are individually decorated with
bold colours, stripes and patterns, and furnished
with antiques and curios; extras include
bathrobes. Breakfast is taken in the Lancaster
room, named after the cartoonist Osbert
Lancaster, whose grandfather lived here. 'Highly
recommended.' (*Pamela Sandford*)

Stock Hill
Gillingham SP8 5NR

T: 01747-823626
F: 01747-825628
E: reception@stockhillhouse.co.uk
W: www.stockhillhouse.co.uk

BEDROOMS: 9, 3 in coach house.
OPEN: all year, restaurant closed
Mon lunch.
FACILITIES: ramp, 2 lounges,
restaurant, breakfast room, private
dining room, 11-acre grounds
(tennis, croquet, small lake),
unsuitable for &.
BACKGROUND MUSIC: none.
LOCATION: 1 mile W of Gillingham.
CHILDREN: not under 6.
DOGS: not allowed.
CREDIT CARDS: MasterCard, Visa.
PRICES: [2010] D,B&B £120–£160 per
person, set lunch £17.50–£30, dinner
£45, Christmas/New Year packages,
1-night bookings sometimes refused
bank holidays.

# GITTISHAM Devon

Map 1:C5

## COMBE HOUSE

*César award in 2007*

'We enjoyed every moment.' 'One of the best
breaks for years.' 'We were very well looked
after.' Much praise for Ken and Ruth Hunt's
Grade I listed Elizabethan manor house in a
large estate of woodland and pastures. 'There
was a warm feeling throughout; the staff were
lovely,' says a visitor in 2010. The 'excellent'
ratio of staff to guests is liked. 'All four
bedrooms taken by our party were recently
refurbished; each one different. We liked the
special touches: beds turned down (with two
hot-water bottles); free-range coat-hangers;
toiletries replaced.' Another comment: 'The
view from the windows of our superior room
took the breath away.' Bedrooms in the former
servants' wings have a country look. A thatched
cottage in the grounds has a walled garden, good
'for doggy friends'. Redecoration has continued
this year: the Great Hall has been freshened; a
kitchen garden and Victorian potting sheds have
been restored. The gardens supply 40 per cent of
the produce for chef Hadleigh Barrett's modern
cooking. (*Zara Elliott, Mr and Mrs Harry
Medcalf, Richard Bright*)

Gittisham
nr Honiton EX14 3AD

T: 01404-540400
F: 01404-46004
E: stay@combehousedevon.com
W: www.combehousedevon.com

BEDROOMS: 16, 1 in cottage.
OPEN: all year except first 2 weeks
Jan.
FACILITIES: ramp, sitting room,
Great Hall, bar, restaurant, private
dining rooms, civil wedding licence,
10-acre garden in 3,500-acre estate
(helipad), coast 9 miles, only public
rooms suitable for &.
BACKGROUND MUSIC: in hall and bar
'as appropriate'.
LOCATION: 2 miles SW of Honiton.
CHILDREN: all ages welcomed.
DOGS: allowed in public rooms,
some bedrooms.
CREDIT CARDS: MasterCard, Visa.
PRICES: [2010] B&B £179–£199 per
person, set dinner £27–£32, full alc
£48, special breaks, Christmas/New
Year packages, 1-night bookings
sometimes refused Fri/Sat.

**25% DISCOUNT VOUCHERS**

# GREAT DUNMOW Essex

## STARR RESTAURANT WITH ROOMS

Owned by Terence and Louise George for 30 years, this 15th-century, timber-clad building is on the marketplace of a little Essex town. They run it as a restaurant-with-rooms; Stephanie Etienne is the manager. The welcome is 'perfect'. The smart, colourful and quiet restaurant (no mobile phones, no background music) is in two sections, one with old stripped beams, the other a conservatory extension. The chef, Adam Rigden, serves modern British and European dishes, eg, ham hock and pig's trotter croquette; lightly spiced halibut, chickpea gremolata. A good choice of wines by the glass. Monthly cookery demonstrations are held. The bedrooms, in a converted stable block in the rear courtyard, vary in size. The Oak Room has a four-poster bed and a freestanding bath. A recent visitor's room had a patterned carpet, checked bedspread; a 'smart' bathroom with a large bath and separate shower cubicle. A smaller room was 'immaculate'. Breakfast has leaf tea, freshly squeezed orange juice, 'good' croissants, a choice of cooked items. More reports, please.

Market Place
Great Dunmow CM6 1AX

T: 01371-874321
F: 01371-876642
E: starrrestaurant@btinternet.com
W: www.the-starr.co.uk

BEDROOMS: 8, in stable block in courtyard, 2 on ground floor.
OPEN: all year except 26 Dec–5 Jan, restaurant closed Sun night/Mon.
FACILITIES: bar/lounge, restaurant, 2 private dining rooms, unsuitable for &.
BACKGROUND MUSIC: none.
LOCATION: central.
CHILDREN: all ages welcomed.
DOGS: not allowed.
CREDIT CARDS: all major cards.
PRICES: B&B £65–£90 per person, set dinner £25–£39.50, full alc £59.

**25% DISCOUNT VOUCHERS**

# GREAT MILTON Oxfordshire

Map 2:C3

## LE MANOIR AUX QUAT'SAISONS

♦ *César award in 1985*

'A really superb hotel for the special occasion,' says a visitor this year to Raymond Blanc's famous domain (Relais & Châteaux). 'The food may be the main reason for wanting to go, but if you decide to stay, the staff show all the attention to detail exemplified by the cooking.' It is co-owned with Orient Express Hotels; Philip Newman-Hall has returned as general manager. Within gardens of 'stunning beauty', it stands in a pretty Oxfordshire village. M. Blanc has redesigned four of the suites this year with Emily Todhunter: Blanc de Blanc, with a private garden, is layered in shades of white; L'Orangerie has Italian palazzo-style walls, a limed oak and heated stone floor. 'There's no need to splash out on a suite: all the standard rooms are huge, with a luxurious bathroom,' says a returning visitor. In the conservatory restaurant (two *Michelin* stars), the 'service is impeccable, the meals memorably good', says the *Guide*'s founding editor. The only disappointment: 'Nudging for a gratuity on the credit card handset.' (*David Young, HR*)

Church Road
Great Milton OX44 7PD

T: 01844-278881
F: 01844-278847
E: lemanoir@blanc.co.uk
W: www.manoir.com

BEDROOMS: 32, 22 in garden buildings, some on ground floor.
OPEN: all year.
FACILITIES: ramps, 2 lounges, champagne bar, restaurant, private dining room, cookery school, civil wedding licence, 27-acre grounds (gardens, croquet, lake).
BACKGROUND MUSIC: in the lounges.
LOCATION: 8 miles SE of Oxford.
CHILDREN: all ages welcomed.
DOGS: not allowed in house (free kennels).
CREDIT CARDS: all major cards.
PRICES: [2010] B&B (French breakfast) £230–£510 per person, set dinner £100–£130, full alc £140, special breaks, cookery courses, Christmas/New Year packages, 1-night bookings refused Sat May–July.

## GREENWAY Devon

Map 1:D4

### OLD MILL FARM

In a 'wonderful' position 'with constantly changing light' on the River Dart, this old mill has been renovated by Robert and Kate Chaston. 'Charming hosts, great ambience,' says a visitor this year. Natural materials have been used throughout; Kate Chaston's paintings are on display. 'Everything is tastefully chosen and presented.' The 'lovely touches' are liked: 'Home-made cake offered every day, fresh fruit and flowers in the bedroom.' Three rooms have 'stunning' views of the river. Kingfisher has a huge bed, two armchairs by the window; 'a floor-to-ceiling window in the bathroom, which has an oversized tub, a walk-in shower'; extras include 'spare toothbrushes, an excellent skin lotion'. Breakfast is served overlooking the water in the *River Room*, or outside on the terrace in warm weather. Highlights are 'Robert's apple juice from the orchard, and Kate's home-made marmalade'. In the extensive grounds is a natural spring water swimming pool. A 20-minute walk leads to Agatha Christie's former home, now owned by the National Trust. (*Carol Ann Hydes, WA*)

Greenway, Galmpton
Brixham TQ5 0ER

T: 01803-842344
F: 01803-843750
E: enquiries@oldmillfarm-dart.co.uk
W: www.oldmillfarm-dart.co.uk

BEDROOMS: 3.
OPEN: all year except Jan.
FACILITIES: 2 sitting rooms, *River Room*, 'natural swimming pond' (45 by 15 metres), unsuitable for &.
BACKGROUND MUSIC: none.
LOCATION: 3 miles S of Paignton.
CHILDREN: all ages welcomed.
DOGS: not allowed.
CREDIT CARDS: none.
PRICES: B&B £47.50–£67.50 per person, midweek off-season rates, 1-night bookings refused at weekends.

# GRENDON UNDERWOOD Buckinghamshire Map 2:C3

## SHAKESPEARE HOUSE

Interior designers Nick Hunter and Roy Elsbury spent five years renovating this beautiful Elizabethan Grade II listed former coaching inn in the Chilterns. In 2010 they added three more bedrooms in an adjacent converted barn (also Grade II listed). The style is theatrical (Shakespeare is reputed to have stayed here when travelling to London). The drawing room in the main house is an 'inviting place', with large black-and-white-patterned settees, oak beams and a blazing fire. The colours are 'imaginative'; there is a sense of opulence throughout. Five of the bedrooms (including one of two family rooms with two bedrooms) are in the main house. The barn has a separate entrance, and linked living and dining areas on the ground floor. 'Our room had gold-framed mirrors, pretty lamps, antique furniture.' Some rooms have a private bathroom across the corridor. Barn visitors have a continental breakfast (cooked is extra); in the main house there is a choice of cooked dishes, and a help-yourself buffet. Mr Elsbury will cook a set dinner by arrangement ('delicious').

Main Street, Grendon Underwood
nr Bicester HP18 0ST

T: 01296-770776
F: 01296-771058
E: enquiries@
   shakespeare-house.co.uk
W: www.shakespeare-house.co.uk

BEDROOMS: 8, 3 in barn conversion, 1 on ground floor.
OPEN: all year, except 19 Dec–1 Jan, exclusive lets only Christmas/New Year.
FACILITIES: 2 drawing rooms, 2 dining rooms, ½-acre garden, unsuitable for &.
BACKGROUND MUSIC: in 1 drawing room and 1 dining room ('at guests' discretion').
LOCATION: in village, 8 miles E of Bicester.
CHILDREN: all ages welcomed.
DOGS: allowed in some bedrooms and 1 drawing room.
CREDIT CARDS: Amex, MasterCard, Visa.
PRICES: [2010] B&B £49.75–£125 per person, D,B&B £84.75–£160, full alc £40–£50.

**25% DISCOUNT VOUCHERS**

# HALNAKER West Sussex

Map 2:E3

## THE OLD STORE

Close to the Goodwood estate and within easy reach of Chichester, Patrick and Heather Birchenough's Grade II listed Georgian building was once the village store and bakery. Now it is a B&B, long been liked for the warmth of the welcome and the 'excellent value'. 'They gave us tea and cake in the sitting room when we arrived. Heather's breakfast is the best we know,' says a visitor this year. The 'spotless' bedrooms, on two floors, have mineral water, a tea-maker, fresh milk in a Thermos flask. Wi-Fi is available free of charge in all rooms. Some have views of Chichester cathedral and, on clear days, across to the Isle of Wight. Breakfast has Sussex Orchards apple juice, freshly made porridge (ask in advance for it), wholemeal or white toast (served in folded linen), English muffins with scrambled eggs and smoked salmon, organic eggs cooked to order, local sausages and bacon. *The Anglesey Arms*, just across the road, is open for evening meals; the Birchenoughs can advise on other places to eat. The village name is pronounced 'Hannaka'. (*Mary Woods*)

Stane Street, Halnaker, nr Chichester PO18 0QL

T: 01243-531977
E: theoldstore4@aol.com
W: www.theoldstoreguesthouse.com

BEDROOMS: 7, 1 on ground floor.
OPEN: all year except Christmas, Jan, Feb.
FACILITIES: lounge, breakfast room, ¼-acre garden with seating, unsuitable for &.
BACKGROUND MUSIC: none.
LOCATION: 4 miles NE of Chichester.
CHILDREN: all ages welcomed (under-5s free).
DOGS: not allowed.
CREDIT CARDS: MasterCard, Visa.
PRICES: [2010] B&B £35–£65 per person (higher for Goodwood 'Festival of Speed' and 'Revival' meetings), 1-night bookings often refused weekends.

# HAMBLETON Rutland

Map 2:B3

## HAMBLETON HALL

♛*César award in 1985*

On a peninsula jutting into Rutland Water, this imposing Victorian mansion has been run for 30 years as a luxury hotel (Relais & Châteaux) by Tim and Stefa Hart. Regular visitors admire the old-world charm and 'intoxicating' setting: 'Nothing much changes, thank goodness,' said trusted *Guide* reporters. Stefa Hart oversees the decor with Nina Campbell. The style is classical (fine fabrics, antiques, open fires): a visitor this year praised the 'sumptuous sofas and cushions, plumped up like a politician's ego'. The spacious bedrooms have floral fabrics; the best overlook Rutland Water. In the candlelit dining room, 'an oasis of peace', the chef, Aaron Patterson, has long held a *Michelin* star. 'An evening of delight,' says a visitor this year. 'The food was divine; wonderful canapés (Parmesan, chicken liver, blue cheese), divine bread. Everything was cooked and presented to perfection.' Bread from Mr Hart's Hambleton bakery is also served at breakfast along with home-made granola, fruit compotes, yogurt and freshly squeezed juices. Mr Hart also owns *Hart's* in Nottingham (see entry). (*Robert Gower, Dr Alec Frank*)

Hambleton, Oakham LE15 8TH

T: 01572-756991
F: 01572-724721
E: hotel@hambletonhall.com
W: www.hambletonhall.com

BEDROOMS: 17, 2-bedroomed suite in pavilion.
OPEN: all year.
FACILITIES: lift, ramps, hall, drawing room, bar, restaurant, 2 private dining rooms, small conference facilities, civil wedding licence, 17-acre grounds (swimming pool, heated May–Sept, tennis, cycling, lake with fishing, windsurfing, sailing).
BACKGROUND MUSIC: none.
LOCATION: 3 miles SE of Oakham.
CHILDREN: only children 'of a grown-up age' in restaurant, except at breakfast.
DOGS: not allowed in public rooms, nor unattended in bedrooms.
CREDIT CARDS: all major cards.
PRICES: [2010] B&B (continental) £102.50–£300 per person, set dinner £37–£65, full alc £85, seasonal breaks, Christmas/New Year packages, 1-night bookings sometimes refused.

# HAROME North Yorkshire

## THE PHEASANT

The welcome is 'warm' at this small hotel, a conversion of a blacksmith's shop, the village smithy and barns overlooking a duck pond. It is owned by Andrew and Jacquie Pern, who also own the *Star Inn* (see next entry), and their former head chef, Peter Neville. There is a rustic, stone-floored bar with an 'impressive' open fireplace, a sitting room with an outdoor terrace, and a conservatory breakfast room. Dinner is taken at smart circular tables in the elegant dining room. Mr Neville emphasises 'fresh, clean flavours' on his market and tasting menus, which might include steak tartare, poached duck egg, pickled beetroot purée; roast lamb saddle, curried parsnips, coriander, silverskins. Bedrooms, set around a courtyard of fruit trees, have an 'unostentatious' contemporary feel: 'Ours had Shaker-style furniture, a two-seater sofa and a modern four-poster without drapes.' Breakfast has a buffet with fruit salad, charcuterie, home-smoked salmon, local cheeses, home-made bread and croissants; 'interesting egg dishes', Whitby kippers. There is a kidney-shaped heated indoor pool and a beauty treatment room. (*Gordon Murray, and others*)

Harome, nr Helmsley
YO62 5JG

T: 01439-771241
F: 01439-771744
E: reservations@
   thepheasanthotel.com
W: www.thepheasanthotel.com

BEDROOMS: 12, 2 courtyard suites.
OPEN: all year.
FACILITIES: lounge, bar, dining room, conservatory, indoor swimming pool, courtyard, garden, 10-acre deer park.
BACKGROUND MUSIC: in bar and restaurant.
LOCATION: village centre.
CHILDREN: all ages welcomed.
DOGS: not allowed.
CREDIT CARDS: MasterCard, Visa.
PRICES: [2010] B&B £75 per person, D,B&B £105, set dinner £30, full alc £39, Christmas package.

# HAROME North Yorkshire

## THE STAR INN

*❦César award in 2004*

Derelict until acquired by Andrew and Jacquie Pern in 1996, this 14th-century thatched longhouse in a pretty Yorkshire village is now a *Michelin*-starred restaurant-with-rooms. The Perns announced in April, 2010, that they have had 'an amicable parting of the ways, but we are totally committed to working together. Only a fool would give up what we have created, and we are not fools.' Mr Pern, who says that he normally lets his food do the talking, cooks 'superb' modern dishes reflecting his northern roots, perhaps Harome-reared 'loose birds duck', Yorkshire sauce, sage and onion mash. The large sitting room has an open fire, comfortable settees and chairs. Breakfast is taken communally. The bedrooms are split between the shooting lodge-styled *Cross House Lodge* opposite, *Black Eagle Cottage* close by, and a farmhouse (for group bookings). Rooms in *Cross House Lodge* are decorated in rustic, modern style; all have TV, CD/DVD-player, home-made biscuits, fruit and fudge. *Black Eagle Cottage* has three suites, each with its own entrance; the room rate includes a breakfast hamper. (*JH, and others*)

Harome, nr Helmsley YO62 5JE

T: 01439-770397
F: 01439-771833
E: reservations@
   thestarinnatharome.co.uk
W: www.thestaratharome.co.uk

BEDROOMS: 14, 8 in *Cross House Lodge* opposite, others in separate buildings.
OPEN: all year except 1 Jan, restaurant closed Mon lunch.
FACILITIES: 2 lounges, coffee loft, bar, breakfast room, restaurant, private dining room, civil wedding licence, 2-acre garden, unsuitable for ♿.
BACKGROUND MUSIC: varied CDs.
LOCATION: village centre.
CHILDREN: all ages welcomed (children's menu).
DOGS: not allowed.
CREDIT CARDS: MasterCard, Visa.
PRICES: [2010] B&B £70–£115 per person, full alc £45.

# HARTINGTON Derbyshire

Map 2:A2

## CHARLES COTTON HOTEL

'Strongly recommended' by returning visitors in 2010, this renovated stone-built 17th-century coaching inn is in an attractive village. 'A bargain for the Peak District', it is owned by Ray and Carolyn Cook; Clive Nichols is now the manager. There is a tea room which serves light meals during the day, a small residents' lounge, and a large bar with a simply furnished dining room adjacent. 'The food is excellent and imaginative. We particularly enjoyed deep-fried soft shell crab, and pheasant terrine; roast salmon with chorizo casserole. The service, by friendly local staff, was excellent.' The simple bedrooms, in the main house and a converted stable block, have original beams, white-painted walls, pine furnishings. 'Our large room at the front, with a view of the square, had a four-poster bed, plenty of storage space; lots of hot water in a good-sized bathroom with a corner bath. Housekeeping is of the highest standard.' A 'good' breakfast is taken in the tea room. Children are welcomed (family rooms have bunk beds), as are dogs and walkers. (*Richard and Jean Green*)

Hartington SK17 0AL

T: 01298-84229
F: 01298-84301
E: info@charlescotton.co.uk
W: www.charlescotton.co.uk

BEDROOMS: 17, 3 on ground floor.
OPEN: all year except 25 Dec.
FACILITIES: lounge, bar, restaurant, tea room.
BACKGROUND MUSIC: 'soft' in bar.
LOCATION: centre of village, 9 miles N of Ashbourne.
CHILDREN: all ages welcomed.
DOGS: allowed in 6 bedrooms, bar.
CREDIT CARDS: MasterCard, Visa.
PRICES: B&B £45–£55 per person, D,B&B £70–£80, full alc £30, special breaks.

# HARWICH Essex

Map 2:C5

## THE PIER AT HARWICH

On the quayside of this busy port, Paul Milsom's hotel/restaurant is a stylish adaptation of two historic buildings: one built in the mid-19th century to accommodate passengers travelling to Europe, the other the former *Angel* pub, built in the 17th century. Seven of the bedrooms and two restaurants are in the large blue-and-white main building; the other bedrooms and a beamed lounge are in the pub. Many of the rooms face the harbour (a recent visitor enjoyed watching the ships sail past). All rooms have been redecorated this year; they have a minibar and a hospitality tray. The first-floor *Harbourside* restaurant has a minimalist decor, a polished pewter champagne bar. Chef Chris Oakley specialises in seafood, much of which is landed in the harbour opposite. Typical dishes: lobster bisque with cream and brandy; halibut, leek mash, tomato and herb salsa. The brasserie-style *Ha'Penny Bistro* is on the ground floor. Breakfast has freshly squeezed orange juice, 'thick slices' of cheese and ham. Mr Milsom also owns *Le Talbooth* restaurant in Dedham and two hotels: *milsoms*, and *Maison Talbooth*, Dedham (see Shortlist). (*LW*)

The Quay
Harwich CO12 3HH

T: 01255-241212
F: 01255-551922
E: pier@milsomhotels.com
W: www.milsomhotels.com

BEDROOMS: 14, 7 in annexe, 1 on ground floor.
OPEN: all year.
FACILITIES: ramps, lounge (in annexe), restaurant, bistro, civil wedding licence, small front terrace.
BACKGROUND MUSIC: 'easy listening' in bar.
LOCATION: on quay.
CHILDREN: all ages welcomed.
DOGS: only guide dogs allowed.
CREDIT CARDS: all major cards.
PRICES: [2010] B&B £55–£140 per person, full alc £42.50, special breaks, Christmas/New Year packages.

**25% DISCOUNT VOUCHERS**

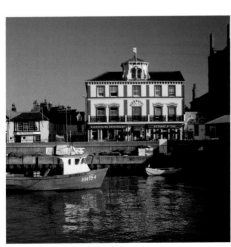

# HASTINGS East Sussex

Map 2:E5

## SWAN HOUSE

The owners, Brendan McDonagh and fashion designer Lionel Copley, have given their white-painted, oak-beamed, 15th-century cottage a 'restful, pleasing' look. They run it as a small, stylish B&B. They have furnished it with antiques, paintings, and bric-a-brac from their online business, an 'interiors emporium'. The long lounge has an inglenook fireplace, two large settees. Bedrooms vary in size: the Garden Room, on the ground floor, is the smallest; it has dark wood flooring and an ornate French bed. Artisan, at the rear of the house, in a former Victorian bakery, has a stained-glass ceiling window; the Renaissance Suite has two large rooms with a shared en suite shower room (with private access for both). The house is on a narrow street ('bring a small car,' said an inspector) of medieval houses in the 'delightful' old town. Nearby are antique shops, booksellers, quirky art galleries and a good bakery (which supplies the house). The 'excellent' breakfast ('freshly squeezed orange juice, superb bacon') can be taken in the lounge or the bedroom. The owners will assist with parking.

1 Hill Street
Hastings, TN34 3HU

T: 01424-430014
E: res@swanhousehastings.co.uk
W: www.swanhousehastings.co.uk

BEDROOMS: 4, 1 on ground floor.
OPEN: all year except Christmas.
FACILITIES: lounge/breakfast room, courtyard garden, civil wedding licence, unsuitable for &.
BACKGROUND MUSIC: none.
LOCATION: in old town, near seafront.
CHILDREN: not under 5.
DOGS: not allowed.
CREDIT CARDS: all major cards.
PRICES: B&B £35–£75 per person, website offers, 1-night bookings refused weekends.

**25% DISCOUNT VOUCHERS**

# HATCH BEAUCHAMP Somerset

Map 1:C6

## FARTHINGS

**NEW**

On a quiet country road, John Seeger's white-painted 200-year-old hotel/restaurant has a 'welcoming and relaxed atmosphere', says an inspector in 2010. 'There was a blazing log fire in the lounge; nice sofas, coffee table and magazines, good flower arrangements.' A 'lovely' spaniel 'did a diligent job meeting and greeting guests at pre-dinner drinks'. There are lots of flowers in the 'intimate' restaurant, 'not all real'. The chef, Simon Clewlow, uses local produce (including eggs from their own hens) for his traditional menus: 'The food was good: haddock and scallops in a ramekin with home-baked rolls; fresh lemon sole and rump lamb (lacking in vegetables); pleasant, if inexperienced, service.' The Bay bedroom was 'spacious, with a sitting area in the bay window which looked over the large garden. Decor was traditional; chintzy fabric, duck-egg blue walls; good lighting; a comfortable but squeaky sleigh bed. A quirky wooden spiral staircase led to the old-fashioned bathroom (carpeted; apricot suite).' The 'excellent' breakfast had freshly squeezed orange, apple and grapefruit juices; 'delicious yogurt; up-to-standard cooked English; good fresh coffee'.

Hatch Beauchamp
nr Taunton TA3 6SG

T: 01823-480664
F: 01823-481118
E: farthingshotel@yahoo.co.uk
W: www.farthingshotel.co.uk

**BEDROOMS:** 12, 2 on ground floor.
**OPEN:** all year.
**FACILITIES:** bar, lounge, 3 restaurants, civil wedding licence, 3-acre garden.
**BACKGROUND MUSIC:** in bar and restaurant.
**LOCATION:** in village.
**CHILDREN:** all ages welcomed.
**DOGS:** not allowed in restaurant.
**CREDIT CARDS:** Amex, MasterCard, Visa.
**PRICES:** B&B £35–£95 per person, D,B&B £65–£125, full alc £40, special breaks, Christmas/New Year packages.

**25% DISCOUNT VOUCHERS**

# HATHERSAGE Derbyshire

Map 3:A6

## THE GEORGE HOTEL

The Duke of Devonshire sold *The George* to James Eyre in 1839, and Charlotte Brontë (a patron) used the family name and the setting of Hathersage as the model for *Jane Eyre*. The 14th-century grey-stone inn is owned by Eric Marsh, who also runs *The Cavendish* in nearby Baslow (see entry); Philip Joseph is the manager of both. 'Most enjoyable: the staff are a delight, the decor is spruce and welcoming,' says a visitor this year. There are stone walls, oak beams, open fires and antique furniture. The chef, Helen Heywood, serves an 'imaginative' modern British menu, featuring local produce. 'A moist rabbit loin on a bed of egg tagliatelle in a chanterelle cream sauce was beautifully balanced; a good selection of breads baked in the kitchen.' Eight of the bedrooms have recently been refurbished in stylish modern palettes, and given a power shower in the en suite bathroom. Front bedrooms face a busy road, but double glazing ensures that noise is kept to a minimum. Breakfast is a hearty affair; 'Helen's home-made marmalade' is recommended. (*Padi Howard*)

Main Road
Hathersage S32 1BB

T: 01433-650436
F: 01433-650099
E: info@george-hotel.net
W: www.george-hotel.net

BEDROOMS: 22.
OPEN: all year.
FACILITIES: lounge/bar, restaurant, 2 function rooms, civil wedding licence, courtyard, Wi-Fi, only restaurant suitable for &.
BACKGROUND MUSIC: light jazz in restaurant.
LOCATION: in village centre, parking.
CHILDREN: all ages welcomed.
DOGS: not allowed.
CREDIT CARDS: all major cards.
PRICES: [2010] B&B £64.50–£92 per person, set dinner £28.65–£40.50, full alc £44.25, special breaks, Christmas/New Year packages, 1-night bookings occasionally refused weekends.

**25% DISCOUNT VOUCHERS**

# HELMSLEY North Yorkshire

Map 4:C4

## THE FEVERSHAM ARMS

In a 'delightful' market town on the edge of the North Yorkshire moors, Simon and Jill Rhatigan have much extended their former coaching inn, adding a spa in a poolside wing. 'Accommodation, food and service were excellent,' says a regular reporter this year. A dissenter found the new areas 'bland'. The bedrooms vary greatly in size and style. Traditionally furnished poolside suites are decorated in green and beige; they have a double-ended bath and separate walk-in shower. Three have a connecting bedroom for children. French windows open on to the swimming pool. Suites in the main house have a sitting area or a separate sitting room. The smallest rooms face the street. In the high-ceilinged conservatory restaurant, chef Simon Kelly has a modern style, eg, lobster ravioli, pea shoots; sirloin of Yorkshire beef, celeriac, braised shin, bone marrow, Madeira jus. Children have their own menu. The 'exceptional' breakfast has toast from organic breads, the usual range of cooked dishes; a 'proper bacon sandwich' (ciabatta, back bacon, home-made Yorkshire relish). (*Colin and Dorothy Powell, and others*)

1 High Street
Helmsley YO62 5AG

T: 01439-770766
F: 01439-770346
E: info@fevershamarmshotel.com
W: www.fevershamarmshotel.com

BEDROOMS: 33, 5 in garden, 12 by pool, 8 on ground floor.
OPEN: all year.
FACILITIES: 2 lounges, bar, conservatory restaurant, private dining room, library, boardroom, terrace (outside dining), civil wedding licence, 1-acre garden (heated 13-metre swimming pool, spa).
BACKGROUND MUSIC: in restaurant, private dining room, boardroom.
LOCATION: central, safe parking.
CHILDREN: all ages welcomed.
DOGS: not allowed in public rooms.
CREDIT CARDS: Amex, MasterCard, Visa.
PRICES: [2010] B&B £72.50–£212.50 per person, D,B&B £112.50–£250, set dinner £33, special breaks, Christmas/New Year packages, 1-night bookings sometimes refused weekends.

# HETTON North Yorkshire

Map 4:D3

## THE ANGEL INN

'Highly popular; run by friendly enthusiasts. A place where enjoyment is above average.' New praise this year from a long-standing *Guide* reporter for Juliet Watkins's former drovers' inn, in a pretty Dales village. It claims to have been one of the first fine-dining pubs. 'Although it was buzzing with trade, we received prompt service from the smart young staff. It was a picture-postcard scene, sitting by a blazing fire, enveloped in excited gossip.' Bruce Elsworth is the chef/director; Simon Farrimond the 'young, smartly dressed' manager. Pascal Watkins (Juliet's son) runs a wine 'cave' in a converted barn opposite. The five bedrooms are in the barn. They have brass bed fittings and bright fabrics; a suite has a Victorian half-tester bed, and a sitting room with views of Rylstone Fell. The bar/brasserie menu (topped up by daily blackboard specials) is Anglo-French, eg, Provençal fish soup; Bolton Abbey mutton and ale pie. 'Food was delicious, generous in quantity, perfectly cooked.' Breakfast, served until 10 am, has 'very good' fresh juices and an 'immense' Yorkshire platter. (*Robert Gower, and others*)

Hetton, nr Skipton BD23 6LT

T: 01756-730263
F: 01756-730363
E: info@angelhetton.co.uk
W: www.angelhetton.co.uk

BEDROOMS: 5 in barn across road, 1, on ground floor, suitable for ♿.
OPEN: all year except 25 Dec, 1 week Jan.
FACILITIES: bar/brasserie, restaurant (2 rooms), civil wedding licence, terrace (outside dining), wine shop.
BACKGROUND MUSIC: none.
LOCATION: off B6265, 5 miles N of Skipton, car park.
CHILDREN: all ages welcomed.
DOGS: not allowed in public rooms.
CREDIT CARDS: Amex, MasterCard, Visa.
PRICES: [2010] B&B £70–£95 per person, D,B&B £97.50–£127.50, full alc £36–£50, midweek breaks.

**25% DISCOUNT VOUCHERS**

# HINTON ST GEORGE Somerset

Map 1:C6

## THE LORD POULETT ARMS

◊ *César award in 2008*

Owners Stephen Hill and Michelle Paynton have created a 'self-consciously stylish' retreat at their 17th-century inn in a pretty Somerset village. They have restored the building 'in the modern idiom': bare flag and wooden floors throughout, open fires, oak tables, antique chairs; 'splashy wallpaper/fabrics', muted paint colours. There is a 'good warm atmosphere' in the bar/dining room; the snug bar is popular with locals, perhaps playing dominoes; dogs asleep under the tables. The bedrooms have a touch of eccentricity, with exposed walls, antique beds; two have a slipper bath in the room; two bathrooms are across a corridor. Readers like the absence of a television: instead, you can listen to a Roberts radio, read magazines. Chef Gary Coughlan serves a seasonal menu, using fruit and vegetables from the local allotment holders, eg, forced rhubarb and roasted beetroot salad; fish and chips, gribiche sauce. Bar meals are served all day. There is no background music. Breakfast has 'good coffee, and home-made preserves from the village shop' (across the street). (*BG, QH*)

High Street
Hinton St George TA17 8SE

T: 01460-73149
E: reservations@
    lordpoulettarms.com
W: www.lordpoulettarms.com

BEDROOMS: 4.
OPEN: all year except 25/26 Dec, 1 Jan.
FACILITIES: bar, restaurant, private dining room, 1-acre grounds, unsuitable for &.
BACKGROUND MUSIC: none.
LOCATION: village centre.
CHILDREN: all ages welcomed.
DOGS: allowed in snug bar, not in bedrooms.
CREDIT CARDS: MasterCard, Visa.
PRICES: B&B £42.50–£65 per person, full alc £35, 1-night bookings sometimes refused Sat.

# HOLT Norfolk

## BYFORDS

'The smiley, friendly staff made me feel genuinely welcome,' says a visitor this year to Iain and Clair Wilson's 'higgledy-piggledy' conversion of Grade II listed houses on the square of this charming Norfolk town. They run it as a delicatessen, café/bistro and 'posh B&B'. Local materials have been used for the bedrooms, which have exposed brickwork, oak floorboards. 'Our beautifully furnished room had a good selection of coffees and teas, home-made shortbread, magazines; fresh flowers in the bathroom, candles beside the bath, and a huge drench shower. The only downside was the sound of a kitchen extractor fan.' The restaurant, a series of 'cheerfully rustic rooms', has 'a buzzy feel': an all-day menu has pastas, pizzas, etc; in the evening a short prix-fixe menu might include smoked haddock chowder; braised lamb and lentil salad. Breakfast has a buffet with 'freshly baked breads, juices, cereals and fruits; warm croissants were brought to the table; my husband appreciated the full English, especially the thick-cut bacon'. The generous picnic basket is recommended. (*Katharine Chater*)

1–3 Shirehall Plain
Holt NR25 6BG

T: 01263-711400
F: 01263-714815
E: queries@byfords.org.uk
W: www.byfords.org.uk

BEDROOMS: 16, 3 on ground floor, 1 suitable for &.
OPEN: all year.
FACILITIES: ramps, 5 internal eating areas, deli.
BACKGROUND MUSIC: jazz/'easy listening', live jazz on last Wed of every month.
LOCATION: central, private secure parking.
CHILDREN: all ages welcomed.
DOGS: only guide dogs allowed.
CREDIT CARDS: all major cards.
PRICES: B&B £70–£100 per person, D,B&B £87–£116, full alc £35, winter offers, Christmas/New Year packages, 1-night bookings usually refused Sat.

# HOPE Derbyshire

Map 3:A6

## UNDERLEIGH HOUSE

'We are pleased to invite you to our home,' say Vivienne and Philip Taylor, who greet visitors with a friendly handshake and the offer of tea and cake. Their long, low, creeper-clad conversion of a late 19th-century barn and cottages is near a Domesday-old village in the Hope valley, excellent walking country. All bedrooms have fine views over the garden and surrounding countryside. The Thornhill Suite has direct access from outside via a stone staircase, an adjoining lounge. Aston, on the first floor, has double-aspect windows and a king-size bed. All rooms have tea/coffee-making equipment, hairdryer, TV with DVD- and CD-player; good toiletries. Breakfast, served communally at a large oak table in the beamed and flagstoned hall, has jugs of orange or apple juice, home-recipe muesli, fruit compote; the 'full works' (with local sausage, bacon and black pudding), smoked haddock; home-made bread and croissants. The Taylors serve drinks in a large lounge with a log fire, or in summer on a terrace. They will provide menus for local eating places; the information pack is comprehensive. More reports, please.

Losehill Lane
off Edale Road
Hope S33 6AF

T: 01433-621372
F: 01433-621324
E: info@underleighhouse.co.uk
W: www.underleighhouse.co.uk

BEDROOMS: 5.
OPEN: Feb–Dec, except Christmas/New Year/most of Jan.
FACILITIES: lounge, breakfast room, ¼-acre garden, unsuitable for &.
BACKGROUND MUSIC: none.
LOCATION: 1 mile N of Hope.
CHILDREN: not under 12.
DOGS: allowed by arrangement.
CREDIT CARDS: MasterCard, Visa (*both 3% surcharge*).
PRICES: [2010] B&B £41–£82 per person, 3-night rates, 1-night bookings refused Fri/Sat, bank holidays.

# HUNTINGDON Cambridgeshire

Map 2:B4

## THE OLD BRIDGE

By a medieval bridge over the River Ouse, John Hoskins's town house hotel, in an ivy-clad building dating from the 1700s, doubles as a busy inn popular with the local community. Nina Beaumond is the manager. Mr Hoskins, a Master of Wine, also runs a wine shop in the hotel (it has 24 bottles available for tasting). The 'well-thought-out' bedrooms have been individually designed by Julia Hoskins in contemporary style; there are comfortable beds, hypo-allergenic duvets and flat-screen TVs. 'Our large and light room had plenty of mirrors, good hanging space and a magnificent bathroom.' In the 'lovely' restaurant, with its large oval cupola, chef Simon Cadge serves a monthly-changing menu of traditional and modern dishes (perhaps calf's liver with bacon; slow-roast pork belly, sesame and spiced parsnip purée). The building is surrounded by a busy traffic system, but bedrooms have triple glazing and air conditioning. Early morning tea and a free newspaper are delivered to the room. Breakfast has 'plenty of choice, good orange juice, good service'. (*RB, and others*)

1 High Street
Huntingdon PE29 3TQ

T: 01480-424300
F: 01480-411017
E: oldbridge@huntsbridge.co.uk
W: www.huntsbridge.com

BEDROOMS: 24, 2 on ground floor.
OPEN: all year.
FACILITIES: ramps, lounge, bar, restaurant, private dining room, wine shop, business centre, civil wedding licence, 1-acre grounds (terrace, garden), river (fishing, jetty, boat trips), unsuitable for &.
BACKGROUND MUSIC: none.
LOCATION: 500 yds from centre, parking, station 10 mins' walk.
CHILDREN: all ages welcomed.
DOGS: allowed.
CREDIT CARDS: all major cards.
PRICES: B&B £65–£99.50 per person, D,B&B £85–£125, full alc £40, Christmas/New Year packages.

# HURSTBOURNE TARRANT Hampshire    Map 2:D2

## ESSEBORNE MANOR

Sympathetically extended, this late Victorian house is run as a traditional hotel by owners Lucilla and Ian Hamilton; their son, Mark, is the manager. Visitors, who found it 'invitingly snug', praised the 'family-run atmosphere and efficient service'. In the North Wessex Downs, an area of outstanding natural beauty, it is approached by a long drive flanked by sheep meadows. In the landscaped garden, there is a tennis court and croquet lawn (some noise from the adjacent busy road). Bedrooms vary; some in the main house have a spa bath, some a four-poster. The honeymoon suite has a carved rococo bed, sunken double spa bath, and separate lounge. Children are welcomed (though there are no special facilities): six rooms around a courtyard are good for a family. Pre-dinner drinks and canapés are taken in the bar or on the terrace. There is a new chef this year, Charles Murray. His short menu might include local pork three ways, spiced Bramley apple, butter fondant. Weddings (marquee on the lawn) and meetings are catered for. More reports, please.

Hurstbourne Tarrant,
nr Andover SP11 0ER

T: 01264-736444
F: 01264-736725
E: info@esseborne-manor.co.uk
W: www.esseborne-manor.co.uk

BEDROOMS: 20, 6 in courtyard, 3 in cottages.
OPEN: all year.
FACILITIES: 2 lounges, bar, restaurant, function room, civil wedding licence, 3-acre grounds (formal gardens, tennis, croquet), arrangements with nearby golf club and fitness céntre.
BACKGROUND MUSIC: in bar.
LOCATION: on A343, 7 miles N of Andover.
CHILDREN: all ages welcomed.
DOGS: not allowed in public rooms.
CREDIT CARDS: all major cards.
PRICES: [2010] B&B £62.50–£125 per person, D,B&B £30 added, set meals £16–£19, full alc £34, special breaks, Christmas/New Year packages.

**25% DISCOUNT VOUCHERS**

## ILSINGTON Devon

Map 1:D4

### ILSINGTON COUNTRY HOUSE

In a 'stunning' position high on the edge of the Dartmoor national park, the Hassell family's country hotel was nominated by a long-time *Guide* reader for its 'friendly staff, comfortable rooms and superb food'. The public rooms are furnished in traditional style with much 'comfortable' seating; a large, south-facing conservatory is 'warm enough for afternoon teas in late March'. The bedrooms, individually styled, have a flat-screen TV, tea- and coffee-making facilities; Wi-Fi is available for an extra charge. 'Lots of hot water in our bathroom.' There is a smart casual dress code in the restaurant, which has 'beautiful views'. Chef Mike O'Donnell serves a 'superb' modern menu, which might include assiette of rabbit, rösti potato, rosemary sauce; the wine list is 'interesting'. Guests have access to a spa with a swimming pool, sauna, steam room and gymnasium. Weddings and conferences are often held. Fly- and sea-fishing, mountain biking, and walking on the moors are among the many activities in the area. (*GJ*)

Ilsington
nr Newton Abbot
Dartmoor TQ13 9RR

T: 01364-661452
F: 01364-661307
E: hotel@ilsington.co.uk
W: www.ilsington.co.uk

BEDROOMS: 25, 8 on ground floor.
OPEN: all year.
FACILITIES: ramp, lift, bar, lounge, library, conservatory, indoor swimming pool (4 by 11 metres), civil wedding licence, 10-acre grounds.
BACKGROUND MUSIC: in restaurant.
LOCATION: in village 4 miles NE of Ashburton.
CHILDREN: all ages welcomed.
DOGS: allowed in ground-floor rooms, not in public rooms.
CREDIT CARDS: Amex, MasterCard, Visa.
PRICES: [2010] B&B £45–£105 per person, D,B&B (min. 2 nights) £70–£130, set dinner £33.95, full alc £50, special offers, Christmas/New Year packages, 1-night bookings refused weekends.

**25% DISCOUNT VOUCHERS**

# IPSWICH Suffolk

## SALTHOUSE HARBOUR HOTEL   **NEW**

A 'hip, sought-after hotel', Robert Gough's stylish conversion of a Victorian warehouse on the waterfront has been extended this year. The *eaterie* restaurant has been given a 'well-conceived' make-over (with the bar on an island in the middle), and 27 bedrooms have been added in an adjacent building. 'High standards have been maintained,' says a returning visitor. Lynn Cowan is the new manager: the staff are 'young, friendly, efficient'. All bedrooms are 'stylishly furnished, with a clean minimalist look'. A new room was 'well lit, air conditioned; a comfortable bed, nice ornaments, leather armchair and stool. The excellent bathroom has a walk-in monsoon shower and tub bath. Ask for a front-facing room for the marina view.' Downstairs, the lounge has specially commissioned artwork, Moroccan tables. The chef, Simon Barker, sources 80 per cent of the ingredients for his modern Mediterranean menus from local markets. 'The cooking is excellent: intense flavours: roast partridge, black pudding and celeriac mash; beautifully rare steak.' The Gough family also owns *The Angel*, Bury St Edmunds (see Shortlist). (*Robert Gower*)

Neptune Quay
Ipswich IP4 1AX

T: 01473-226789
F: 01473-226927
E: staying@salthouseharbour.co.uk
W: www.salthouseharbour.co.uk

BEDROOMS: 70, 4 suitable for &.
OPEN: all year.
FACILITIES: lounge, bar, *eaterie*, conference rooms.
BACKGROUND MUSIC: contemporary in lounge, brasserie.
LOCATION: on waterfront.
CHILDREN: all ages welcomed.
DOGS: in lounge, bedrooms (£5).
CREDIT CARDS: all major cards.
PRICES: [2010] B&B £50–£150 per person, full alc £40, special offers.

# IREBY Cumbria

## OVERWATER HALL

'Recommended: friendly, informal; high standards. No reception desk here, just a warm welcome.' Praise in 2010 for this castellated Grade II listed Georgian mansion in an isolated part of the northern Lake District. It is run in personal style by the owners. Stephen Bore and Angela Hyde are 'hands-on' front-of-house (she also supervises housekeeping); her husband, Adrian, is the chef. Children and dogs are welcomed: the house stands in extensive gardens and nursery woodland in which they can freely roam. The public rooms have an 'opulent' decor in keeping with the house. There's a bright yellow ceiling in the dining room, and the bedrooms are equally bold. Extras include bathrobes, flowers, a fruit bowl, mineral water. Bathrooms are well equipped, some have a walk-in shower. In the elegantly laid dining room, smart casual dress is required. Adrian Hyde's daily-changing menu of modern dishes might include pear poached in cassis and cinnamon; Cumbrian game three ways (venison, wood pigeon, rabbit). There is high tea for under-fives at 5.30 pm. Breakfast has locally smoked kippers, eggs Benedict, etc. (*Barbara and Daniel McDowell*)

Overwater, nr Ireby
CA7 1HH

T: 017687-76566
F: 017687-76921
E: welcome@overwaterhall.co.uk
W: www.overwaterhall.co.uk

BEDROOMS: 11, 1 on ground floor, restaurant closed Mon lunch.
OPEN: all year.
FACILITIES: drawing room, lounge, bar area, restaurant, civil wedding licence, 18-acre grounds, Overwater tarn 1 mile.
BACKGROUND MUSIC: light jazz, 'easy listening', in restaurant.
LOCATION: 2 miles NE of Bassenthwaite Lake.
CHILDREN: not under 5 in restaurant (high tea at 5.30 pm).
DOGS: allowed except in 1 lounge.
CREDIT CARDS: MasterCard, Visa.
PRICES: [2010] B&B £60–£110 per person, D,B&B £30 added, set dinner £40, full alc £50, 4-night breaks all year, Christmas/New Year packages, 1-night bookings refused Sat.

**25% DISCOUNT VOUCHERS**

# KESWICK Cumbria

Map 4: inset C2

## DALEGARTH HOUSE

'An intimate and informal atmosphere' is created by Bruce and Pauline Jackson at their white-fronted, traditional Edwardian guest house just a 'stone's throw' from Derwentwater. 'Exceptional quality in an outstanding location,' says a visitor this year. In an elevated position above the lake, it has immediate access to the fells, making a 'carless' holiday possible. The owners, both born locally, are happy to advise visitors about the area. Bedrooms are 'spacious, well furnished'; 'spotlessly clean'. Mr Jackson, the 'only chef in the kitchen', asks visitors to make their dinner choice on arrival or after breakfast. Meals, taken in a red-carpeted, chandelier-lit dining room, are 'a tasty treat'; 'Bruce attended to every idiosyncratic whim of our vegetarian son'. Non-vegetarians might have selected herb-crusted roast rack of lamb, bubble and squeak, red wine sauce. The 'outstanding' breakfast has fruit compotes and cereals and a 'first-class' cooked selection. 'Our only gripe (a minor one) was the single CD which provided background music.' The garden has a 'profusion of flowers', which appear in the house. (*KA McCallum, Arthur G Boon*)

Portinscale
Keswick CA12 5RQ

T: 017687-72817
E: allerdalechef@aol.com
W: www.dalegarth-house.co.uk

BEDROOMS: 10, 2 on ground floor.
OPEN: Mar–Nov.
FACILITIES: lounge, bar, dining room, garden, unsuitable for &.
BACKGROUND MUSIC: in public rooms ('only if quiet').
LOCATION: 1½ miles W of Keswick.
CHILDREN: not under 12.
DOGS: not allowed.
CREDIT CARDS: MasterCard, Visa.
PRICES: [2010] B&B £42–£50 per person, D,B&B £62–£70, set dinner £25, special breaks, 1-night advance bookings sometimes refused.

# KING'S LYNN Norfolk

Map 2:A4

## THE BANK HOUSE   `NEW`

On the quayside in the 'rich historic centre' of
King's Lynn, this Grade II listed Georgian
merchant's house (later the first bank of a
founding father of Barclays) has been extensively
renovated by Jeannette and Anthony Goodrich
who also own *The Rose & Crown*, Snettisham
(see entry). 'It is a good hotel which could
become very good,' say regular correspondents
this year. 'Some of the rooms are spacious, each
has its own individual characteristic.' An
inspector's room on the top floor was
'satisfactorily equipped, except that it lacked
cupboard and shelf space for storage; a fine view
of the River Purfleet'. Stuart Deuchars, who
worked at *St John's*, London ('the cooking shows
the influence'), serves a brasserie menu in three
dining areas. The *River Room* has leather-seated
wooden chairs, a mix of tables; the *Main Room*
(once the banking hall) has tub chairs and round
tables; the high-ceilinged *Old Kitchen* has
contemporary black furnishings. 'A thoroughly
satisfactory dinner; the staff were friendly,
attentive. Breakfast was equally good: the best
kipper I've had in a long while.' (*John and
Theresa Stewart, and others*)

King's Staithe Square
King's Lynn PE30 1RD

T: 01553-660492
E: info@thebankhouse.co.uk
W: www.thebankhouse.co.uk

BEDROOMS: 11.
OPEN: all year.
FACILITIES: bar, 3 dining rooms,
private dining room, terrace, only
dining rooms suitable for &.
BACKGROUND MUSIC: none.
LOCATION: central, opposite Custom
House.
CHILDREN: all ages welcomed.
DOGS: not allowed.
CREDIT CARDS: Diners, MasterCard,
Visa.
PRICES: [2010] B&B £50–£110 per
person, full alc £30, Christmas/New
Year packages.

# KIRKBY STEPHEN Cumbria

Map 4:C3

## AUGILL CASTLE

At their family home, a restored Victorian fantasy-Gothic castle in the upper Eden valley, Simon and Wendy Bennett and their children are 'wonderful hosts who make guests very welcome'. The castle is run in informal style. 'There's plenty for children to do,' says a visitor this year. 'They have fun in the evening with films and popcorn, while adults enjoy a quiet drink in the bar.' Outdoors, there's a playground, a fort in the forest, a tree house. Many of the bedrooms are big enough for a family. 'Ours was beautifully furnished with lovely finishing touches: fresh milk for tea, sherry to enjoy before supper, a scrumptious home-made flapjack.' Three rooms have been added this year in a converted stable and an orangery. Children are given an early supper; meals are taken (by arrangement) communally; at weekends there is a four-course house-party-style dinner. Seasonal dishes might include halibut with cockle broth. 'His cooking is good; her puddings are delicious.' Breakfast, usually from 9 am, has 'lovely home-made bread and preserves', eggs from the resident hens. (*Stella Bridle*)

South Stainmore
nr Kirkby Stephen CA17 4DE

T: 01768-341937
E: enquiries@stayinacastle.com
W: www.stayinacastle.com

BEDROOMS: 14, 2 on ground floor, 3 in Stable House, 1 in Orangery, 1 in Little Castle.
OPEN: all year, dinner by arrangement, lunch for groups, by arrangement.
FACILITIES: hall, drawing room, library (honesty bar), music (sitting) room, dining room, civil wedding licence, 15-acre grounds (landscaped garden, tennis).
BACKGROUND MUSIC: none.
LOCATION: 3 miles W of Kirkby Stephen.
CHILDREN: all ages welcomed.
DOGS: not allowed.
CREDIT CARDS: Amex, MasterCard, Visa.
PRICES: B&B £80 per person, D,B&B £120, New Year package, 2-night bookings preferred weekends.

**25% DISCOUNT VOUCHERS**

# KIRKBY STEPHEN Cumbria

Map 4:C3

## A CORNER OF EDEN

Down a narrow lane in 'beautiful' farmland bordered by 'dramatic countryside', Debbie and Richard Temple run the Grade II listed farmhouse which they have carefully restored as a B&B. They have furnished the bedrooms with antiques and second-hand furniture. Rooms have a Georgian feel; one has a dark wood bedside cabinet (made by Richard Temple from an old wardrobe); all have a decanter of home-made blackcurrant gin. Planning restrictions dictated that the four rooms share two bathrooms. Thick towelling robes are provided for visits to 'the lovely bathroom and the shower room'. Guests are encouraged to take a candlelit champagne bath. There are books and magazines in the lounge. At weekends, the Temples may provide, by arrangement, a no-choice three-course dinner (dishes like grilled goat's cheese; salmon fillet with a pesto dressing). An old inn serving pub food is three fields away. For those still hungry, there is a complimentary butler's pantry with an array of snacks. The 'very good breakfast' is a leisurely affair, with home-made marmalade and muesli; eggs from the Temples' own hens. House-party bookings are taken. (*OH*)

Low Stennerskeugh
Ravenstonedale
Kirkby Stephen CA17 4LL

T: 015396-23370
E: enquiries@acornerofeden.co.uk
W: www.acornerofeden.co.uk

BEDROOMS: 4.
OPEN: all year except 1 week at Christmas, house party only at New Year.
FACILITIES: lounge, dining room, pantry, 5-acre grounds, unsuitable for &.
BACKGROUND MUSIC: none.
LOCATION: 4 miles S of Kirkby Stephen.
CHILDREN: not under 12 except for house parties.
DOGS: not allowed in dining room, 1 bedroom (£5 per night charge).
CREDIT CARDS: none.
PRICES: B&B £65 per person, set dinner £30.

# LACOCK Wiltshire

Map 2:D1

## AT THE SIGN OF THE ANGEL

🍷 *César award in 1989*

'A good experience; we particularly enjoyed dinner in the garden under an apple tree, in the company of a fine black hen.' Again this year there is enthusiasm for this 'enchanting' 15th-century half-timbered inn, one of the oldest buildings in a famous National Trust village (recently used as the setting for TV's *Cranford*). 'The food was delicious, the staff were friendly and helpful,' is another comment. Owner/managers Lorna and George Hardy say that 'doorways are low, floorboards creak, walls are uneven, but character abounds'. Bedrooms in the old building are furnished with antiques. A ground-floor room was thought small, but its bathroom was 'delightfully large'. Four 'excellent' rooms in a cottage in the garden have under-floor heating, and an 'all-important car-parking space at the door'. Tables are laid with silverware in the three dining rooms where 'delicious' English dishes are served. 'The kidneys and monkfish with Mediterranean vegetables were excellent.' Breakfast has stewed fruit, home-made bread and marmalade; Wiltshire bacon, eggs from the hens in the garden. (*Mr SJ Smith, Pamela Sandford*)

6 Church Street
Lacock, nr Chippenham SN15 2LB

T: 01249-730230
F: 01249-730527
E: angel@lacock.co.uk
W: www.lacock.co.uk

BEDROOMS: 11, 3 on ground floor, 5 in cottage.
OPEN: all year except 24–27 Dec (open for dinner 31 Dec), restaurant closed Mon except bank holidays.
FACILITIES: ramps, lounge, bar, restaurant, civil wedding licence, ground-floor rooms suitable for &.
BACKGROUND MUSIC: none.
LOCATION: village centre, 4 miles S of Chippenham.
CHILDREN: all ages welcomed.
DOGS: not allowed in dining rooms.
CREDIT CARDS: all major cards.
PRICES: [2010] B&B £60–£82 per person, set dinner (2 courses) £16.95, full alc £40.

# LANGAR Nottinghamshire

Map 2:A3

## LANGAR HALL

🦢 *César award in 2000*

'Anyone needing reassurance that the great British hotel is alive and well should head immediately for Langar.' A ringing endorsement this year for Imogen Skirving's informal hotel, a Georgian mansion owned by her family since the mid-19th century. 'Imogen continues to preside over timeless, understated perfection. It is an example of the country house hotel at its very best.' Family portraits line the stairs that lead to the themed bedrooms, named after people associated with the house. They are 'splendidly comfortable, decidedly quirky'. Edwards, the largest, overlooks the garden and park; it has the original four-poster bed. Mark's Room is twin-bedded, with views over ancient yew trees to the moat. Cartland, dedicated to the novelist who stayed here, is 'romantic, but not pink'. In the drawing room there are paintings by and of the Bloomsbury Group. The daily-changing menu of the chef, Gary Booth, might include Langar lamb, champ mash, roast carrot, grain mustard. 'Faultless food from genuinely local ingredients.' Service is 'excellent'. There is a chapel in the 'lovely' grounds. (*Peter Jowitt*)

Langar NG13 9HG

T: 01949-860559
F: 01949-861045
E: info@langarhall.co.uk
W: www.langarhall.co.uk

BEDROOMS: 12, 1 on ground floor, 1 garden chalet.
OPEN: all year.
FACILITIES: ramps, sitting room, study, library, bar, garden room, restaurant, civil wedding licence, 30-acre grounds (gardens, children's play area, croquet, ponds, fishing), unsuitable for ♿.
BACKGROUND MUSIC: none.
LOCATION: 12 miles SE of Nottingham.
CHILDREN: all ages welcomed.
DOGS: small dogs on a lead allowed by arrangement, not unaccompanied in bedrooms.
CREDIT CARDS: MasterCard, Visa.
PRICES: [2010] B&B £40–£110 per person, set dinner £20, special offers, Christmas/New Year packages.

**25% DISCOUNT VOUCHERS**

# LASTINGHAM North Yorkshire

Map 4:C4

## LASTINGHAM GRANGE

♔ *César award in 1991*

'How nice to stay in a hotel where the owners
are genuinely hands-on and pleased to see you.'
Renewed praise this year for this traditional
hotel on the North Yorkshire Moors, which is
run by Bertie Wood, helped by his mother, Jane,
and brother, Tom. 'We were warmly welcomed,
helped with luggage, and given tea with scones
and cream,' say other visitors. Some might find
the decor 'overpowering': 'a riot of floral pattern
on curtains, bedspread and carpet'. Everyone
likes the 'peace and friendliness'. In the bedrooms,
'comfortable' beds have sheets and blankets;
lighting is 'excellent'. The traditional cooking of
Paul Cattaneo is also liked; his daily-changing
menu might include cream of watercress; roast
partridge with bread sauce. Portions are generous:
'Two plates of vegetables were appreciated,
sometimes with a second potato dish. The Woods
clearly like to feed up their guests, making
walking on the moors compulsory.' The converted
17th-century farmhouse stands in large gardens
with an adventure playground for children.
(*David Fisher, Jill and Mike Bennett*)

Lastingham YO62 6TH

T: 01751-417345
F: 01751-417358
E: reservations@
   lastinghamgrange.com
W: www.lastinghamgrange.com

BEDROOMS: 11, also cottage in
village.
OPEN: all year except Dec, Jan, Feb.
FACILITIES: ramps, hall, lounge,
dining room, laundry facilities,
12-acre grounds (terrace, garden,
adventure playground, croquet,
boules), limited assistance for ♿.
BACKGROUND MUSIC: none.
LOCATION: 5 miles NE of
Kirkbymoorside.
CHILDREN: all ages welcomed.
DOGS: not allowed in public rooms.
CREDIT CARDS: MasterCard, Visa.
PRICES: [2010] B&B £60–£130 per
person, D,B&B £120–£160, set
dinner £37.75.

**25% DISCOUNT VOUCHERS**

# LAVENHAM Suffolk

Map 2:C5

## THE GREAT HOUSE

*César award in 2009*

'Heartily endorsed' this year, Régis and Martine Crépy's 'outstanding' restaurant-with-rooms adds a Gallic flourish to the main square of the most English of towns. 'The setting is superb, the welcome warm,' says one visitor. In the candlelit dining room, with its bare-boarded contemporary decor, the service by the 'attentive, immaculately dressed French staff' is widely praised: 'Formal, but not at all snooty.' So is the cooking of the chef, Enrique Bilbault: 'We enjoyed halibut, duck, bream and salmon; in each case the fish was perfectly timed and admirably designed.' 'A rare place, where the wines are not a rip-off.' Four of the bedrooms have a sitting room. 'Our room overlooking the marketplace was spacious, well appointed; a good bathroom down a few steps.' A room in the roof space was 'smart with a three-cornered sofa, a leather writing desk; because of the roof timbers, the bathroom was partitioned off'. The breakfast buffet might be 'a bit meagre', but the full English was 'exemplary'. Children are welcomed. (*Brian MacArthur, Dr Trevor Roberts, Robert Gower, David Grant, Dan Allen*)

Market Place
Lavenham CO10 9QZ

T: 01787-247431
F: 01787-248007
E: info@greathouse.co.uk
W: www.greathouse.co.uk

BEDROOMS: 5.
OPEN: Feb–Dec, restaurant closed Sun night, Mon, Tues midday.
FACILITIES: lounge/bar, restaurant, ½-acre garden (patio, swings), unsuitable for &.
BACKGROUND MUSIC: French.
LOCATION: by Market Cross, near Guildhall, public car park.
CHILDREN: all ages welcomed.
DOGS: not allowed in public rooms.
CREDIT CARDS: MasterCard, Visa.
PRICES: [2010] room £120–£250, D,B&B £110–£160 per person, breakfast £9.50–£15, dinner £31.95, full alc £48, midweek breaks, 1-night bookings refused Sat.

# LAVENHAM Suffolk

## LAVENHAM PRIORY

'What a wonderful place. It was like being a lord of the manor; we were made to feel extremely welcome.' Praise again in 2010 for Tim and Gilli Pitt's beautiful half-timbered house, originally owned by Benedictine monks, later an Elizabethan merchant's house, in lovely gardens in the medieval village. The Pitts have imaginatively furnished the Grade I listed building in keeping with its Elizabethan heritage. Oak beams and floors feature throughout. The Great Hall is dominated by a huge inglenook fireplace; visitors can relax in comfortable chairs and sofas. There are two lounge areas, with a library, a selection of games and open fires. A Jacobean staircase leads to the 'bed chambers' which have creaking floorboards, sloping ceilings. The beds (three four-posters, a lit bateau and a polonaise) were made by a local cabinetmaker; all rooms have been given a 32-inch LCD TV and Wi-Fi access this year. Breakfast in the Merchants dining room is 'superb', with sausages and Manx kippers, fruit compotes, yogurts and muesli. (*Andy Fisher*)

Water Street
Lavenham CO10 9RW

T: 01787-247404
F: 01787-248472
E: mail@lavenhampriory.co.uk
W: www.lavenhampriory.co.uk

BEDROOMS: 6.
OPEN: all year except Christmas/New Year.
FACILITIES: Great Hall/sitting room, snug, breakfast room, 3-acre garden (medieval courtyard, herb garden), unsuitable for &.
BACKGROUND MUSIC: none.
LOCATION: central.
CHILDREN: not under 12.
DOGS: not allowed.
CREDIT CARDS: MasterCard, Visa.
PRICES: [2010] B&B £52–£85 per person, winter midweek discount for 2 nights or more, 1-night bookings refused Sat, some holidays.

# LEDBURY Herefordshire

Map 3:D5

## THE FEATHERS

The black-and-white Tudor exterior of *The Feathers* dominates the cobblestoned centre of this 'genuine old market town'. The 16th-century coaching inn is owned by David Elliston and managed by Mary Diggins. 'They go the extra mile to anticipate every need,' says a visitor in 2010. A 'characterful' old staircase leads to the bedrooms, which are individually furnished and vary in size, style and historical influence. They have 'period charm': beamed walls and ceilings, antique furniture are evident throughout. Double glazing 'keeps outside noise to a minimum'. Radio, satellite TV and broadband are standard in all rooms. A small spa has an indoor, heated swimming pool, a steam room and a gym. The hotel has two dining areas. *Fuggles Brasserie* 'strives to bring exotic flavours to fine local ingredients' in dishes like Marches beef, Stilton-glazed Portobello mushrooms, roasted vine tomatoes. *Quills* is the more formal dining option. Simpler meals are served in *The Top Bar* which has exposed beams and brickwork. Breakfast is 'well presented'. (*Mrs D Broomfield*)

High Street
Ledbury HR8 1DS

T: 01531-635266
F: 01531-638955
E: mary@feathers-ledbury.co.uk
W: www.feathers-ledbury.co.uk

BEDROOMS: 22, 1 suite in cottage, also self-catering apartments.
OPEN: all year.
FACILITIES: lounge, bar, brasserie, restaurant, function/conference/wedding facilities, spa (swimming pool, 11 by 6 metres, whirlpool, gym), civil wedding licence, courtyard garden (fountain, alfresco eating), unsuitable for &.
BACKGROUND MUSIC: none.
LOCATION: town centre, parking.
CHILDREN: all ages welcomed.
DOGS: allowed, only guide dogs in restaurant and brasserie.
CREDIT CARDS: all major cards.
PRICES: [2010] B&B £79.50–£125 per person, full alc £45, New Year package.

**25% DISCOUNT VOUCHERS**

# LEDBURY Herefordshire

Map 3:D5

## VERZON HOUSE

Experienced hoteliers Peter and Audrey Marks have restored this imposing red brick Georgian farmhouse close to this charming market town. They run it as a small hotel with their daughter, Jane, the manager. 'No sign of chintz in the modern bedrooms,' said a visitor who was impressed by the restoration ('no expense has been spared'). Original cornices and an inlaid staircase have been preserved; there are open fires in the public rooms. Bedrooms, each named after a local apple variety (Bloody Turk, Chisel Jersey and Court Royal, etc), are individually designed. All have a fridge with water, apple juice, milk. Jason Orsi has been appointed chef this year. His à la carte menu might include twice-baked Montgomery cheddar cheese soufflé; sweet herb marinated lamb cutlets, dauphinoise potatoes. A table d'hôte Italian menu is available during the week. On fine days, lunch (which has a selection of British tapas), afternoon tea and dinner can be taken on the brasserie terrace. Breakfast has 'the best' scrambled eggs. Weddings and parties are catered for. (*RB*)

Hereford Road, Trumpet
Ledbury HR8 2PZ

T: 01531-670381
F: 01531-670830
E: info@verzonhouse.com
W: www.verzonhouse.com

BEDROOMS: 8.
OPEN: all year.
FACILITIES: bar, lounge, dining room, civil wedding licence, terrace, 5-acre grounds, only public areas suitable for &.
BACKGROUND MUSIC: 'occasionally' in bar.
LOCATION: 2 miles W of Ledbury.
CHILDREN: welcomed, not under 8 at dinner.
DOGS: only guide dogs allowed.
CREDIT CARDS: Amex, MasterCard, Visa.
PRICES: [2010] B&B £72.50–£105 per person, full alc £39.50, winter breaks, Christmas/New Year/ Cheltenham Festival packages, 1-night bookings subject to availability at weekends.

# LEONARD STANLEY Gloucestershire

Map 3:E5

## THE GREY COTTAGE

♔ *César award in 1999*

'We love going back to stay with Rosemary Reeves in the homely guest house she keeps so well.' One of the many tributes to the 'inimitable' hostess whose Cotswold stone house remains popular with long-standing *Guide* readers. 'Rosie rushed to greet us with an umbrella,' says a returning visitor in 2010. 'We were swept into the sitting room for tea and cookies.' The 'attention to detail' is appreciated. 'Our bedroom was immaculate, and all needs were catered for: a torch, hair dryer, hospitality tray with fresh milk, lots of extras; the large bathroom had lots of smellies and large towels.' Mrs Reeves cooks dinner by arrangement. 'I admitted to being an extremely fussy eater; this did not deter Rosie and she cooked everything that I love.' The dining table has 'proper linen napkins, good glass and china'. There is an honesty bar, or you can bring your own wine. Breakfasts are 'a feast': freshly squeezed orange juice; Craster kippers which 'will linger in the memory'. (*Gordon Franklin, PW Townend, Sue and Colin Raymond, Richard Knight*)

Bath Road, Leonard Stanley
Stonehouse GL10 3LU

T: 01453-822515
E: rosemary.reeves@
   btopenworld.com
W: www.greycottage.ik.com

BEDROOMS: 3.
OPEN: all year except Christmas/
New Year, occasional holidays.
FACILITIES: sitting room with TV,
conservatory, dining room, ¼-acre
garden, unsuitable for &.
BACKGROUND MUSIC: 'no, never!'
LOCATION: 3 miles SW of Stroud.
CHILDREN: not under 10.
DOGS: not allowed.
CREDIT CARDS: none.
PRICES: [2010] B&B £30–£55 per
person, set dinner £23–£25, discount
for 3-night stays.

# LETCOMBE REGIS Oxfordshire

Map 2:C2

## BROOK BARN

**NEW**

Letcombe Brook, a protected chalk stream, runs through the garden of this 'amazing conversion of two ancient barns' outside a village near Wantage. The owners, Mark and Sarah-Jane Ashman, 'have preserved the wooden features, and enhanced them with immaculate furnishings', says the nominator. The sitting room has a double-height ceiling, huge French windows on two sides, a wood-burning stove, 'squashy sofas everywhere', a 'good selection of drinks' in an honesty bar. There is a library with newspapers, and an office area; free Wi-Fi. A monthly-changing dinner menu with daily specials is served at separate tables. 'I enjoyed a flavourful venison and pheasant pie with the lightest pastry; an indulgent bread-and-butter pudding.' Bedrooms, 'beautifully furnished', include 'lots of extras'; they have beams, rugs on oak floorboards. Four rooms have a private terrace; one has a separate bathroom. Breakfast has toast from home-baked bread, 'wonderful' eggs from hens that roam the garden; 'sausages and bacon from a local farm were so good that I went to the farmers' market to buy more'. (*Matthew Caminer*)

Letcombe Regis
nr Wantage OX12 9JD

T: 01235-766502
F: 0118-329 0452
E: info@brookbarn.com
W: www.brookbarn.com

BEDROOMS: 5, 4 on ground floor.
OPEN: all year except Christmas.
FACILITIES: library, drawing room, dining room, 1½-acre garden, unsuitable for &.
BACKGROUND MUSIC: 'easy listening' occasionally.
LOCATION: edge of village, 1½ miles SW of Wantage.
CHILDREN: not under 16.
DOGS: not allowed.
CREDIT CARDS: Amex, MasterCard, Visa.
PRICES: [2010] B&B £50–£125 per person, full alc £41.

## LIFTON Devon

Map 1:C3

### THE ARUNDELL ARMS

*César award in 2006*

After 50 years, Anne Voss-Bark has handed over the running of her sporting hotel to her son, Adam Fox-Edwards; Heather Measey is the new manager. 'Going back to this old friend, we were pleased to find all is well,' say inspectors in 2010. Fishing is an important attraction (there are 20 miles on the Tamar and tributaries, and a well-stocked lake): a non-fishing visitor felt equally welcome this year. 'Strongly endorsed: the facade gives no sense of the cosiness of the public rooms; staff are delightful.' The best bedrooms are in a rear extension. A small room on the second floor was 'homey; it had two armchairs, which we like. The wallpaper, bedhead and curtains had a Chinese pattern; at night it felt like a pretty tent.' The atmosphere in the 'elegant' dining room is 'genteel, no hint of stuffiness'. Steven Pidgeon's cooking is 'interesting but not fussy; we enjoyed a salad of asparagus, ham and olives; delicious sea bream with lentils, leeks and saffron; a very good rack of lamb; superlative crème brûlée'. An 'excellent kipper' at breakfast. (*Richard Parish, and others*)

Fore Street
Lifton PL16 0AA

T: 01566-784666
F: 01566-784494
E: reservations@arundellarms.co.uk
W: www.arundellarms.co.uk

BEDROOMS: 21, 4 on ground floor.
OPEN: all year.
FACILITIES: ramp, lounge, cocktail bar, public bar, 2 dining rooms, conference/meeting rooms, games room, skittle alley, civil wedding licence, ½-acre garden, 20 miles fishing rights on River Tamar and tributaries, fishing school.
BACKGROUND MUSIC: 'subtle' classical in restaurant and bar.
LOCATION: 3 miles E of Launceston.
CHILDREN: all ages welcomed.
DOGS: not allowed in restaurant.
CREDIT CARDS: MasterCard, Visa.
PRICES: [2010] B&B £37.50–£112.50 per person, set dinner £34.95, full alc £55, off-season breaks, sporting, gourmet, etc, New Year package.

**25% DISCOUNT VOUCHERS**

# LITTLE PETHERICK Cornwall

Map 1:D2

## MOLESWORTH MANOR

In a tiny village near Padstow, Jessica and Geoff French run their 17th-century former rectory as a B&B. They have two young children and welcome families; children are encouraged to play in the 'attractive' gardens. Readers like the 'comfortable accommodation', with 'plenty of space in the sitting room and bedroom'. There are three lounges, with log fires and comfortable chairs; complimentary tea on arrival may be taken here or, on fine days, on the terrace. The bedrooms, now with flat-screen TV, are named according to their earlier use or position: Butler's, Housekeeper's, Lordship's, etc. All except Cook's have en suite facilities. The 'superb' breakfast has fresh orange juice, Cornish apple juice, organic smoked salmon, free-range eggs, fresh fruit salads and compotes, freshly baked muffins; also full English. The Frenches belong to the Green Tourism Business Scheme: where possible, all food is organic and locally sourced. There is a wide range of eating places in Padstow. The whole house can be booked for special occasions. Newquay airport is nine miles away. More reports, please.

Little Petherick
nr Padstow PL27 7QT

T/F: 01841-540292
E:  molesworthmanor@aol.com
W:  www.molesworthmanor.co.uk

BEDROOMS: 9, plus 3 in self-catering cottage in grounds.
OPEN: Feb–Oct.
FACILITIES: 3 lounges, 1 with home cinema, breakfast conservatory, terrace, garden (children's play area), unsuitable for &.
BACKGROUND MUSIC: none.
LOCATION: 1½ miles SE of Padstow off A389 to Wadebridge.
CHILDREN: all ages welcomed.
DOGS: not allowed.
CREDIT CARDS: none.
PRICES: [2010] B&B £35–£55 per person, Christmas/New Year packages (self-catering), 1-night bookings sometimes refused.

**25% DISCOUNT VOUCHERS**

# LIVERPOOL Merseyside

Map 4:E2

## HOPE STREET HOTEL

Owned and managed by David Brewitt, this striking modern hotel has 'a good feel, and extremely friendly staff', says a visitor in 2010. Opposite the Philharmonic Hall, it spreads across two buildings: a 19th-century carriage works in the style of a Venetian palazzo, and an adjacent conversion, which has sixth-floor conference facilities with panoramic views over the city. The bedrooms in both buildings have wooden floor, under-floor heating, cherry wood furniture. 'Ours was large, clean and well equipped; a firm bed, as I prefer.' Noise in the corridors is dampened by under-laid seagrass matting, but a visitor commented on the nuisance of guests slamming their doors. The restaurant, *The London Carriage Works*, is a dramatic space with floor-to-ceiling glass sculptures, bare oak, and yellow brickwork. The chef, Paul Askew, cooks modern dishes, perhaps flash-fried chilli squid; confit shoulder, pan roast loin and kidney of new season lamb, caramelised onion. Breakfast can be continental (home-cured meats, regional cheese, fruit, pastries), full Liverpool, or taken from a carte (including bacon sandwiches, beans on toast). (*Carl Moore*)

40 Hope Street
Liverpool L1 9DA

T: 0151-709 3000
F: 0151-709 2454
E: sleep@hopestreethotel.co.uk
W: www.hopestreethotel.co.uk

BEDROOMS: 89, some suitable for &.
OPEN: all year.
FACILITIES: lift, ramps, lobby, reading room, bar, restaurant, function rooms, gym, treatment rooms, civil wedding licence.
BACKGROUND MUSIC: none.
LOCATION: opposite Philharmonic Hall.
CHILDREN: all ages welcomed.
DOGS: allowed.
CREDIT CARDS: Amex, MasterCard, Visa.
PRICES: [2010] room £130–£350, breakfast £14–£16.50, set meals £15–£20, full alc £40, Christmas/New Year packages.

# LODDISWELL Devon

Map 1:D4

## HAZELWOOD HOUSE

In an 'idyllic' setting, on a hillside surrounded by trees in a designated area of outstanding natural beauty, this early Victorian house is run in informal style by the owners, Jane Bowman, Gillian Kean and Anabel Farnell-Watson. 'Many visitors feel it is like staying in a private house,' they say. The drawing room and dining room have French windows looking on to a wisteria-laden veranda. The public rooms are decorated in bright colours; they have log fires, antiques and local paintings. The bedrooms are all different: those on the first floor are large with en suite facilities; simpler rooms with bathrooms nearby are on the second floor. Many rooms on both floors have 'stunning' views over the valley. The chef, Chris Scantlebury, uses local, organic ingredients for his menus in the attractive candlelit dining room (a typical dish: rack of lamb with a rosemary and redcurrant jus). The absence of background music is 'such bliss', said inspectors. Weddings, cultural courses and concerts are held. Children are welcomed. More reports, please.

Loddiswell
nr Kingsbridge TQ7 4EB

T: 01548-821232
F: 01548-821318
E: info@hazelwoodhouse.com
W: www.hazelwoodhouse.com

BEDROOMS: 14, 7 with facilities en suite.
OPEN: all year.
FACILITIES: hall with piano, drawing room, study/TV room, dining room, function/conference facilities, civil wedding licence, 67-acre grounds (river, boathouse, chapel), only restaurant suitable for &.
BACKGROUND MUSIC: on request.
LOCATION: 2 miles N of Loddiswell.
CHILDREN: all ages welcomed.
DOGS: not in dining room, on leads elsewhere.
CREDIT CARDS: MasterCard, Visa.
PRICES: [2010] B&B £45–£80 per person, D,B&B £63–£108, set dinner £20–£25, full alc £31.50, special breaks, Christmas/New Year packages.

**25% DISCOUNT VOUCHERS**

# LONGHORSLEY Northumberland

Map 4:B3

## THISTLEYHAUGH FARM

*César award: Farm guest house of the year*

'A lovely place and people.' 'Memorable.' The Nelless family who have farmed in this remote corner of Northumberland for three generations win more praise this year. Enid Nelless presides in the house with daughters-in-law Zoë and Janice; her husband, Henry, runs the organic cattle and sheep farm with their sons. 'We were warmly greeted by all the family plus dogs; even the orphan lambs and calves were welcoming.' There is a choice between duvet and blankets and sheets in the bedrooms, which are priced according to size. 'Our lovely large room had a superb bathroom, lots of goodies.' The tea tray has a china jar with home-made biscuits; fresh milk and bottled water are in a small fridge. The public rooms have grandfather clocks, antiques, pictures and prints. Visitors are invited to help themselves to sherry before dinner, a communal affair at 7 pm (not available on a Saturday): 'Good home cooking' of the farm's produce (eg, free-range organic roast duck, seasonal vegetables). Wine is 'incredible value' at £9 a bottle. (*Gordon Murray, and others*)

Longhorsley,
nr Morpeth NE65 8RG

T: 01665-570629
E: thistleyhaugh@hotmail.com
W: www.thistleyhaugh.co.uk

BEDROOMS: 5.
OPEN: all year except 20 Dec–1 Feb.
FACILITIES: 2 lounges, dining room, 720-acre farm, ¾-acre garden (summer house), fishing, shooting, golf, riding nearby, unsuitable for &.
BACKGROUND MUSIC: on request.
LOCATION: 10 miles N of Morpeth, W of A697.
CHILDREN: all ages welcomed.
DOGS: not allowed (kennels nearby).
CREDIT CARDS: MasterCard, Visa.
PRICES: B&B £40–£75 per person, D,B&B £20 added, 1-night bookings often refused.

# LOOE Cornwall

Map 1:D3

## THE BEACH HOUSE

On the seafront, looking out to Whitsand Bay and Looe Island, Rosie and David Reeve's white-fronted B&B is liked for the warmth of the welcome and the 'splendid' views. 'They are helpful and understanding,' say visitors returning in 2010. 'She remembered that we prefer blankets and sheets to a duvet; when I was unwell, breakfast was brought to the bedroom.' Three bedrooms face the sea. 'Our spotless room had French windows opening on to a small balcony, perfect for enjoying a glass of wine on a summer's evening.' Two rooms at the back have use of a garden room across the hall to enjoy the sea view. All bedrooms have king-size bed, flat-screen TV and a guest fridge; double glazing has been fitted this year. Cooked dishes at breakfast, ordered the evening before for an agreed time, include French toast (sweet with fruits), pancakes (with fruits and maple syrup) and scrambled eggs with smoked salmon. Details of local restaurants, including menus and prices, are available. The private parking 'is a blessing in Looe'. (*Sue and Colin Raymond*)

Marine Drive, Hannafore
Looe PL13 2DH

T: 01503-262598
F: 01503-262298
E: enquiries@
   thebeachhouselooe.co.uk
W: www.thebeachhouselooe.co.uk

BEDROOMS: 5.
OPEN: all year except Christmas.
FACILITIES: garden room, breakfast room, terrace, garden, beach opposite, unsuitable for &.
BACKGROUND MUSIC: classical in breakfast room.
LOCATION: ½ mile from centre.
CHILDREN: not under 16.
DOGS: dogs not allowed.
CREDIT CARDS: Diners, MasterCard, Visa.
PRICES: [2010] B&B £50–£65 per person, New Year package, 1-night bookings refused high season.

# LORTON Cumbria

## NEW HOUSE FARM

'Ideal for those who wish to avoid pretentiousness, and enjoy comfort and welcoming hospitality.' Praise from a regular correspondent this year for this 'well-maintained' 17th-century Grade II listed farmhouse, which is 'ideally situated for visiting the northern lakes'. Period features include oak beams and rafters, flagged floors and open stone fireplaces; Wi-Fi caters for more modern needs, but there is no TV (reception is poor). Bedrooms vary in size and decor: the Old Dairy, on the ground floor, has a solid oak four-poster and a large bathroom with double-ended slipper bath; Swinside, on the first floor, has a queen-size brass bed. There may be some traffic noise from the country road to the front; the rear bedrooms are quiet. The owner, Hazel Thompson, cooks traditional English dishes (eg, pheasant casserole; local poached salmon). 'Meals are fairly simple and conventional (a godsend to many of us), but both cooking and ingredients are good.' Guests are asked to register likes and dislikes in advance. Breakfasts have freshly squeezed orange juice, fresh-baked croissants, fruit, porridge, dishes cooked to order. 'Pets are allowed – and welcomed.'

Lorton
nr Cockermouth CA13 9UU

T: 01900-85404
F: 01900-85478
E: hazel@newhouse-farm.co.uk
W: www.newhouse-farm.com

BEDROOMS: 5, 1 in stable, 1 in Old Dairy.
OPEN: all year.
FACILITIES: 3 lounges, dining room, 17-acre grounds (garden, hot tub, streams, woods, field, lake and river, safe bathing, 2 miles), unsuitable for &.
BACKGROUND MUSIC: none.
LOCATION: on B5289, 2 miles S of Lorton.
CHILDREN: not under 6.
DOGS: not allowed in public rooms.
CREDIT CARDS: MasterCard, Visa.
PRICES: B&B £65–£90 per person, D,B&B £30 added, Christmas/New Year packages, 1-night bookings sometimes refused.

# LOWER BOCKHAMPTON Dorset

Map 1:C6

## YALBURY COTTAGE

At their small hotel/restaurant in peaceful
Hardy country, Jamie and Ariane Jones 'work
hard to please visitors' (praise in 2010). 'They are
hands-on hoteliers offering high standards and
a friendly welcome,' is another comment. 'She
takes good care front-of-house, while he is an
excellent cook.' The bedrooms overlook the
gardens or fields ('where horses graze'). A
ground-floor room was 'well presented in pastel
colours, with two comfy chairs, a good built-in
wardrobe; housekeeping was immaculate.
Thoughtful touches were a generous hospitality
tray and a useful information pack. The
compact bathroom had tiled floor and walls.'
The lounge and restaurant are in the oldest
part of the hotel, with low beams, inglenook
fireplaces, exposed stone walls. 'We enjoyed a
delicious dinner; local lamb was tender and
perfectly cooked, fine Lyme Bay seared scallops,
a flavourful board of Dorset cheeses, and lovely
desserts. Breakfast was as good, with fresh-cut
orange and grapefruit, home-made rhubarb
jam, freshly baked croissants; a varied cooked
choice.' (*Ian Malone, Michael and Betty Hill*)

Lower Bockhampton
nr Dorchester DT2 8PZ

T: 01305-262382
E: enquiries@yalburycottage.com
W: www.yalburycottage.com

BEDROOMS: 8, 6 on ground floor.
OPEN: all year except 23–29 Dec,
3–24 Jan, restaurant closed Sun/Mon
night.
FACILITIES: lounge, restaurant,
unsuitable for &.
BACKGROUND MUSIC: 'easy listening'
in lounge.
LOCATION: 2 miles E of Dorchester.
CHILDREN: welcomed on request.
DOGS: allowed in lounge, some
bedrooms.
CREDIT CARDS: MasterCard, Visa.
PRICES: [2010] B&B £47.50–£57.50
per person, D,B&B £77.50–£87.50,
full alc £45.

**25% DISCOUNT VOUCHERS**

# LOWER VOBSTER Somerset

## THE VOBSTER INN   NEW

The owners, Rafael and Peta Davila, are 'hard-working, charming and attentive', say visitors who made 'this remarkable find', a traditional inn, dating back to the 17th century, in a 'lovely, quiet' village. The Davilas have decorated the rustic bar and dining room 'in excellent taste, seamlessly merging old and new, with well-chosen original artefacts'. A separate entrance leads to the bedrooms: 'Light streamed from four windows into our spacious room, which had a cool modern look: a wonderfully comfortable bed, a brushed-leather sofa, modern paintings; a well-equipped bathroom.' Mr Davila's modern dishes are served in an 'attractively laid' eating area. 'Very good cooking: my starter of black pudding, seared calf's liver, bubble and squeak was delicate, well presented; lobster risotto was generous and delicious. Desserts are clearly his passion: an amazing pastry cup held a generous portion of chocolate ganache.' Breakfast, chosen the night before, is 'simple but excellent: fresh fruit salad; traditional cooked any way you like; an Arbroath smokie; large mugs of good coffee'. Children are welcomed. Two new bedrooms were being added for 2011. (*Ian and Francine Walsh*)

Lower Vobster
nr Radstock BA3 5RJ

T: 01373-812920
E: info@vobsterinn.co.uk
W: www.vobsterinn.co.uk

BEDROOMS: 3, 2 to be added in 2011.
OPEN: all year, restaurant closed Sun night/Mon.
FACILITIES: bar/dining room, 4-acre garden.
BACKGROUND MUSIC: 'easy listening' in bar.
LOCATION: in village 4 miles W of Frome.
CHILDREN: all ages welcomed.
DOGS: allowed in 1 bar area.
CREDIT CARDS: Diners, MasterCard, Visa.
PRICES: [2010] B&B £34.50–£48 per person, full alc £30.

**25% DISCOUNT VOUCHERS**

# LUDLOW Shropshire

Map 3:C4

## MR UNDERHILL'S

♨ *César award in 2000*

The announcement by Christopher and Judy Bradley that they have postponed their retirement from their popular restaurant-with-rooms is 'good news' for loyal followers. 'A delightful place, run to high standards,' says a regular visitor. Readers on their first visit were as enthusiastic. 'The welcome left nothing to be desired; the well-trained staff are friendly.' The setting, by a weir on the River Teme below Ludlow Castle, is 'delightful'. Christopher Bradley's *Michelin*-starred cooking is much praised: 'Sheer perfection: it is hard to believe he is self taught.' The eight-course set menu 'kicks off' with three tiny dishes (perhaps sorrel velouté; a cone of marinated salmon; duck liver custard). 'Sea bream with couscous and orange was delicately spicy; slow-roast magret de canard was served in thin rose-pink slices; venison with elderberries and black pudding crumb is a favourite; top-drawer dessert.' A suite with a 'fair-sized sitting room' overlooks the river. A small room was 'functional, light and airy; everything we needed'. 'Your five portions of fruit are neatly packed into breakfast', which also has a 'sinful brioche'. (*Padi Howard, Ken and Priscilla Winslow*)

Dinham Weir
Ludlow SY8 1EH

T: 01584-874431
W: www.mr-underhills.co.uk

BEDROOMS: 6, 1 in annexe.
OPEN: all year except Christmas, 10 days June, 10 days Nov, restaurant closed Mon/Tues.
FACILITIES: small lounge, restaurant, function facilities, ½-acre courtyard, riverside garden (fishing, swimming), unsuitable for &.
BACKGROUND MUSIC: none.
LOCATION: below castle, on River Teme, station ½ mile, parking.
CHILDREN: not 2–8.
DOGS: not allowed.
CREDIT CARDS: MasterCard, Visa.
PRICES: [2010] B&B £65–£150 per person, set dinner £50–£57.50, New Year packages, 1-night bookings sometimes refused Sat.

# LYDFORD Devon

Map 1:C4

## THE DARTMOOR INN

🞧 *César award in 2007*

On the western fringes of Dartmoor national park, Karen and Philip Burgess have converted this old inn on a busy road into a 'charming' restaurant-with-rooms. She has furnished it in 'charismatic' style; readers admire the 'care, flair, dedication and talent'. 'It is welcoming and cosy: open fires create a warm atmosphere,' says a visitor in 2010. There is a small bar, with log fire, local ales and a weekday menu of pub classics (fish and chips; steak sandwich). 'It comes to life in the evenings, when food and service are well up to standard.' Philip Burgess and Andrew Honey cook modern British dishes, eg, devilled sprats with a mustard dressing; rump of lamb with Indian spices, saffron sauce. Bedrooms are 'light and spacious', with antique hand-painted furniture. Toile, the largest, has a king-size bed; Ticking has a vaulted roof and a crystal-drop chandelier. Each has a Roberts radio; TV is available on request. Breakfast, 'taken really seriously', must be 'one of the best anywhere'. Mrs Burgess runs a boutique selling handmade French quilts, handbags and jewellery by local designers. (*John Rowlands, and others*)

Moorside
Lydford, nr Okehampton
EX20 4AY

T: 01822-820221
F: 01822-820494
E: info@dartmoorinn.co.uk
W: www.dartmoorinn.com

BEDROOMS: 3.
OPEN: all year, restaurant closed Sun evening for non-residents.
FACILITIES: 2 bars, restaurant, small sunken garden, unsuitable for &.
BACKGROUND MUSIC: none.
LOCATION: 6 miles E of Tavistock on A386 to Okehampton, train Exeter/Plymouth, parking.
CHILDREN: all ages welcomed.
DOGS: not allowed in bedrooms.
CREDIT CARDS: Amex, MasterCard, Visa.
PRICES: B&B from £57.50 per person, set dinner £21.50, full alc £40, special breaks, 1-night bookings sometimes refused bank holidays.

# LYMINGTON Hampshire

Map 2:E2

## BRITANNIA HOUSE

'As good as ever', this B&B is formed from two houses opposite each other on a street a short walk from the marina and smart shops. Owner/manager Tobias Feilke is 'charming to all his guests', say visitors in 2010. Earlier guests praised the 'excellent value for money', and the comprehensive information folder provided, 'as good as any we have seen'. The sitting room, in the older building (which dates from 1865), is decorated in blue and yellow, and has wide views of the harbour and marina; the sofas are 'enveloping', the lighting is good. The 'immaculate' bedrooms are all different. The largest is the ground-floor Forest Suite in the older building, which has king-size bed, plain walls, patterned soft furnishings. In the modern three-storey building, rooms are plainer, and have pine furnishings. All rooms have anti-allergic duvet and pillows, and a flat-screen TV. Mr Feilke's breakfasts, served at a 'convivial' communal table in the large pine kitchen, are 'excellent, with good ingredients'. (*Clair and David Stevens*)

Station Street
Lymington SO41 3BA

T: 01590-672091
E: enquiries@britannia-house.com
W: www.britannia-house.com

BEDROOMS: 6.
OPEN: all year.
FACILITIES: lounge, kitchen/breakfast room, courtyard garden, unsuitable for &.
BACKGROUND MUSIC: none.
LOCATION: 2 mins' walk from High Street/quayside, parking.
CHILDREN: not under 12.
DOGS: not allowed.
CREDIT CARDS: MasterCard, Visa.
PRICES: B&B £37.50–£45 per person, midweek discount, 1-night bookings refused weekends.

# LYNDHURST Hampshire

Map 2:E2

## LIME WOOD    `NEW`

In extensive grounds in the New Forest, this Regency manor house has been given a £30 million make-over and reopened as a 'relaxed' country house hotel. The nominator, a long-standing *Guide* correspondent, encountered some service glitches, but liked 'the lack of airs and graces, the entrancing public rooms and the flexible dining arrangements'. The lounges 'have been styled with flair and humour, with antiques and quirky, oversized modern furniture. They felt cosy except for the horrible muzak; we discovered peace in the intimate library.' The bedrooms are in the main house and three 'beautifully designed' new buildings in the grounds. 'Our lovely coach house room was light and airy, with emphasis on texture in the design (a beautiful bedspread); everything was well thought out, with good lighting and great comfort; a double-ended bath in the bathroom.' Two eating options: a 'beautiful' *Fine Dining* room, and the *Scullery*, which is open all day with an 'innovative menu of sorts of nursery/comfort food and a good selection of fish'. A spa was due to open as the *Guide* went to press. (*Wendy Ashworth*)

Beaulieu Road
Lyndhurst SO43 7FZ

T: 02380-287177
F: 02380-287199
E: info@limewood.co.uk
W: www.limewood.co.uk

BEDROOMS: 29, 5 on ground floor, 2 suitable for ♿, 5 in Crescent, 5 in Coach House, 5 in Pavilion.
OPEN: all year, *Fine Dining* restaurant closed Mon.
FACILITIES: bar, 2 lounges, library, 2 restaurants, private dining rooms, civil wedding licence, 14-acre gardens.
BACKGROUND MUSIC: live/recorded in public areas.
LOCATION: in New Forest, 12 miles SW of Southampton.
CHILDREN: all ages welcomed.
DOGS: allowed in selected bedrooms, not in public rooms.
CREDIT CARDS: Amex, MasterCard, Visa.
PRICES: [2010] room £122.50–£345, set meals £40, full alc £70, special breaks, Christmas/New Year packages, 1-night bookings sometimes refused.

# MALVERN WELLS Worcestershire

Map 3:D5

## THE COTTAGE IN THE WOOD

High on the side of the Malvern hills, with a panoramic view of the Severn valley, this early Victorian house is owned by John and Sue Pattin, who run it with son Dominic (chef) and son-in-law Nick Webb (manager). Guests like the 'friendly welcome'. In the original *Dower House*, bedrooms are traditional and have 'a country feel'. *The Pinnacles*, a converted coach house 100 yards from the main building, has 19 'pleasant, well-equipped' rooms, some with a patio or small balcony. *Beech Cottage*, also in the grounds, has four 'homely' rooms, each with its own front door. Binoculars are supplied; the information pack is comprehensive. The *Outlook* restaurant has tall French windows and a small terrace, ideal for aperitifs before meals. It has been renovated this year (one returning visitor thought the noise levels were higher). Dominic Pattin's menus might include marinated venison saddle, fondant potato, red cabbage; orange and cardamom brûlée. Pets are welcomed in ground-floor rooms in *The Pinnacles*. You can walk from the door to the top of the hills. (*C and LB, JM*)

Holywell Road
Malvern Wells WR14 4LG

T: 01684-588860
F: 01684-560662
E: reception@
   cottageinthewood.co.uk
W: www.cottageinthewood.co.uk

BEDROOMS: 30, 4 in *Beech Cottage*, 70 yds, 19 (1 suitable for &) in *The Pinnacles*, 100 yds.
OPEN: all year.
FACILITIES: lounge, bar, restaurant, function facilities, 7-acre grounds (terrace), leisure facilities nearby.
BACKGROUND MUSIC: none.
LOCATION: 3 miles S of Great Malvern.
CHILDREN: all ages welcomed.
DOGS: guide dogs welcomed, other dogs in *The Pinnacles* only.
CREDIT CARDS: Amex, MasterCard, Visa.
PRICES: [2010] B&B £49.50–£109 per person, D,B&B £64.50–£123, full alc £33, Christmas/New Year packages, 1-night bookings sometimes refused Sat.

**25% DISCOUNT VOUCHERS**

# MARAZION Cornwall

Map 1:E1

## MOUNT HAVEN HOTEL & RESTAURANT

'Staff are attentive, very helpful. You won't be disappointed,' writes a visitor in 2010. An inspector agreed, above all admiring the food. The long, low, white-painted hotel is on the edge of a village overlooking St Michael's Mount. Owners Mike and Orange Trevillion have given it a flavour of the East (incense, tapestries from Jaipur, figurines from Nepal and Bali). 'The lounge is large: a bar at the back, a super seating area by big glass doors leading on to a terrace. The furniture is cosy, dark reds, leather and velvet upholstery; pity about the rather fey muzak.' The 14 sea-facing bedrooms were given a facelift this year; there are floor-to-ceiling sliding windows, large balconies. 'My room was big, attractively decorated in pale aqua blue, beige and white; restful and modern; a luxurious shower room (no bath).' Dinner, prepared by new chef James Morris, was 'truly delicious; poached John Dory on spinach, with three tiny quail's eggs and a fine ravioli'. Breakfast has a buffet (prunes, cereals, fresh fruit, etc); 'lovely poached egg with mushrooms'. (*Steven Hur, and others*)

Turnpike Road
Marazion TR17 0DQ

T: 01736-710249
F: 01736-711658
E: reception@mounthaven.co.uk
W: www.mounthaven.co.uk

BEDROOMS: 18, some on ground floor.
OPEN: mid-Jan–mid-Dec.
FACILITIES: lounge/bar, restaurant, healing room (holistic treatments), sun terrace, ½-acre grounds (rock/sand beaches 100 yds), unsuitable for &.
BACKGROUND MUSIC: 'chill-out' music all day, bar, lounge.
LOCATION: 4 miles E of Penzance, car park.
CHILDREN: all ages welcomed.
DOGS: allowed on terrace only.
CREDIT CARDS: MasterCard, Visa.
PRICES: [2010] B&B £55–£105 per person, D,B&B £85–£135, full alc from £35, 3-night breaks spring/autumn, min. 2 nights on bank holidays.

**25% DISCOUNT VOUCHERS**

# MARCHAM Oxfordshire

Map 2:C2

## B&B RAFTERS **NEW**

On the edge of a village near Abingdon, this half-timbered house is run as B&B by its owners, Sigrid and Arne Grawert. 'She greeted us warmly and provided lovely fresh coffee,' say visitors this year. 'A welcome change to the corporate chains close to Oxford. Excellent value for money.' The decor is contemporary: 'Our room was lovely; the bathroom fantastic.' The largest bedroom has a king-size bed, a 'love' sofa, a private balcony; a free-standing bath and walk-in shower in the bathroom. A single room has a waterbed. In all rooms there are fresh flowers, a hospitality tray with mineral water, bathrobes, and iron and ironing board. Organic ingredients from local farms are used where possible for the 'delicious' breakfast ('part of the South Oxfordshire Big Breakfast initiative'). Bread is home baked, orange juice freshly squeezed, jams and marmalade are home made; the whisky porridge ('not for the faint-hearted') is recommended. Vegetarians are catered for. Several eating places are within a few miles. Buses to Abingdon and Oxford pass through the village. (*Deborah Roberts, Vicky Vyse*)

Abingdon Road
Marcham
nr Abingdon OX13 6NU

T: 01865-391298
F: 01865-391173
E: enquiries@bnb-rafters.co.uk
W: www.bnb-rafters.co.uk

BEDROOMS: 4.
OPEN: all year.
FACILITIES: lounge, breakfast room, garden, unsuitable for &.
BACKGROUND MUSIC: none.
LOCATION: edge of village, 3 miles W of Abingdon.
CHILDREN: all ages welcomed.
DOGS: not allowed.
CREDIT CARDS: MasterCard, Visa.
PRICES: [2010] B&B £45–£60 per person.

# MARKINGTON North Yorkshire

Map 4:D4

## HOB GREEN

'Staff and service are first class,' say visitors in 2010 to the Hutchinson family's traditional hotel, an 18th-century house in 'a lovely setting, very quiet and peaceful'. There are extensive views across a valley, and 'wonderful' woodland walks from the award-winning gardens. The public rooms, 'beautifully furnished and very comfortable', have original features, paintings, marquetry furniture and a log fire. The 'well-equipped' bedrooms are traditionally decorated, with patterned wallpaper, flowery fabrics. 'Ours was a good size, with two lovely big windows overlooking the countryside. It was nice to have a small fridge with fresh milk.' There is an evening turn-down service. In the 'attractive' dining room, Chris Taylor cooks 'excellent dishes, traditional with a modern twist', eg, lamb's kidneys, red wine and spring onion sauce; rack of Nidderdale lamb, rosemary, Marsala and ginger jus. The Victorian kitchen garden provides the ingredients for the chef's vegetable selection. Breakfast has home-made preserves and a wide choice of cooked dishes. Wi-Fi is available. There are good walks in the grounds and the village. Fountains Abbey is three miles away. (*CLH, DB*)

Markington
nr Harrogate HG3 3PJ

T: 01423-770031
F: 01423-771589
E: info@hobgreen.com
W: www.hobgreen.com

BEDROOMS: 11.
OPEN: all year.
FACILITIES: hall, drawing room, sun lounge, restaurant, civil wedding licence, 2½-acre garden (children's play area), 800-acre grounds, unsuitable for &.
BACKGROUND MUSIC: classical in public rooms.
LOCATION: 1 mile SW of Markington, 5 miles SW of Ripon.
CHILDREN: all ages welcomed.
DOGS: not allowed in public rooms.
CREDIT CARDS: all major cards.
PRICES: [2010] B&B £60–£100 per person, D,B&B £82.50–£125, set dinner £29.50, full alc £35, special breaks, Christmas/New Year packages, 1-night bookings refused weekends.

# MARTINHOE Devon

Map 1:B4

## HEDDON'S GATE HOTEL

'Enthusiastically endorsed' in 2010, this small hotel on this 'beautiful' part of the north Devon coast is much liked by *Guide* readers. The owners, Anne and Eddie Eyles, are 'extremely friendly, welcoming, showing a great attention to detail', says one visitor. The former Victorian hunting lodge has an 'exceptional' setting in woodland on the slopes of the Heddon valley. 'The decor is very English, a little eccentric in the nicest possible way; not for modernists or style fascists.' The bar has stags' antlers, black leather furniture. 'Free afternoon tea every day provides a good opportunity to talk to other guests.' 'Furnishing is original, even outré, in the bedrooms; everything clean throughout.' 'The dinners are the highlight of a stay: consistently delicious soups with warm rolls; imaginative second courses, eg, warm salad of pigeon breast with beetroot; a choice of a fish or a meat main course, perhaps sirloin steak with whisky sauce, or salmon with dill. Make room for the desserts like an incredibly light chocolate tart.' There are 'well-signposted circular walks' from the grounds. (*Stephen and Pauline Glover, Jeanette Cottrell, Martin Arnold*)

Martinhoe, Parracombe
Barnstaple EX31 4PZ

T: 01598-763481
E: hotel@heddonsgate.co.uk
W: www.heddonsgate.co.uk

BEDROOMS: 9.
OPEN: Mar–Oct, dining room closed midday.
FACILITIES: 2 reception halls, 2 lounges, library, bar, dining room, 2½-acre grounds, river, fishing, riding, pony trekking nearby, sea ¾ mile, unsuitable for &.
BACKGROUND MUSIC: none.
LOCATION: 6 miles W of Lynton.
CHILDREN: not under 12 (except in parties taking exclusive use).
DOGS: not allowed in dining room, not unattended in bedrooms.
CREDIT CARDS: MasterCard, Visa.
PRICES: [2010] B&B £50–£80 per person, D,B&B £80–£110, set dinner £34, special breaks, 1-night bookings occasionally refused.

**25% DISCOUNT VOUCHERS**

# MASHAM North Yorkshire

Map 4:D4

## SWINTON PARK ♨

*César award: Family hotel of the year*

'Luxurious yet relaxed, personal and unfussy', this Gothic castle (Grade II* listed) is the family home of Mark and Felicity Cunliffe-Lister. 'You could tell that it is run by people who have children,' said inspectors in 2010, impressed that nappies, wipes, bath powder were provided and a small teddy bear was left in their baby's cot. In the 'wonderful grounds' are deer, lakes, woods; 'lots to do, fishing, falconry displays, etc'. Reception staff are 'smiley, welcoming'. Indoors, there are 'sunny corners to sit in'; a 'beautiful' semicircular drawing room has family portraits, floor-to-ceiling windows, huge sofas, newspapers, magazines. 'A great playroom: ping-pong, billiards, lots of toys.' Lovely views from the bedrooms, which have decanters of whisky and gin, tea, coffee, biscuits. 'The tasting menu at dinner was innovative, delicious. Breakfast also very good: a huge vat of freshly squeezed orange juice, good cooked dishes. No eyebrows were raised when our toddler threw his cereal over the floor. We liked the green initiatives; a woodchip boiler, reusable water bottles in the room.' (*Derek Eastham, and others*)

Masham, nr Ripon
HG4 4JH

T: 01765-680900
F: 01765-680901
E: reservations@swintonpark.com
W: www.swintonpark.com

BEDROOMS: 30, 4 suitable for &.
OPEN: all year, restaurant closed midday Mon/Tues.
FACILITIES: lift, ramps, 3 lounges, library, bar, restaurant, banqueting hall, spa, games rooms, cinema, civil wedding licence, 200-acre grounds (many activities).
BACKGROUND MUSIC: in bar and dining room.
LOCATION: 1 mile SW of Masham.
CHILDREN: all ages welcomed.
DOGS: not allowed in public rooms, unattended in bedrooms.
CREDIT CARDS: all major cards (*Amex 3% service charge*).
PRICES: [2010] B&B £87.50–£185 per person, D,B&B £122.50–£220, set dinner £45–£55, special breaks, Christmas/New Year packages, 1-night bookings sometimes refused Sat.

# MATLOCK BATH Derbyshire

Map 3:B6

## HODGKINSON'S HOTEL

Cut into the cliff face, this Georgian building was once part of a larger inn, the first built for visitors to the town's spa. It became a small stand-alone hotel in the 1830s; the owner, Dianne Carrieri, now presides over a quirky atmosphere dedicated to Victoriana. Furniture and ornaments 'fit the period of the building well'. The 'comfortable' lounge has William Morris-patterned wallpaper, floral curtains, portraits, a variety of figurines. 'The friendly owners make all the difference,' said a reader who liked the 'excellent value'. Most bedrooms are 'a good size and full of character', though the single room is small. The Riber and Mayfield rooms have been redecorated this year, the former with dark woods, an ornate antique bed and plush velvet soft furnishings. In the small restaurant (only five tables), 'food is good, albeit quite simple'. Breakfasts, 'highly recommended', have a selection of cereals and porridge; cooked options including a full English or vegetarian; smoked haddock kedgeree. The building stands on the busy A6: rear rooms are the quietest. (*DV*)

150 South Parade
Matlock Bath, Matlock DE4 3NR

T: 01629-582170
F: 01629-584891
E: enquiries@
   hodgkinsons-hotel.co.uk
W: www.hodgkinsons-hotel.co.uk

BEDROOMS: 8.
OPEN: all year except 25/26 Dec.
FACILITIES: lounge, bar, restaurant, meeting/private dining room, 1-acre garden (opposite River Derwent, fishing, day ticket), unsuitable for &.
BACKGROUND MUSIC: blues/jazz/classical in restaurant.
LOCATION: central, parking for 5 cars.
CHILDREN: all ages welcomed.
DOGS: not allowed in restaurant.
CREDIT CARDS: Amex, MasterCard, Visa.
PRICES: [2010] B&B £45–£70, set dinner £28–£30.50, full alc £75, 2- to 3-night breaks, New Year package, 1-night bookings refused Sat July–Oct.

**25% DISCOUNT VOUCHERS**

# MAWGAN PORTH Cornwall

Map 1:D2

## BEDRUTHAN STEPS HOTEL

'Everything was spruce; it looked good and confident,' says an observer this year. High above a golden beach (with sandy coves, rock pools, good surfing), this large white hotel is owned and managed by three sisters, Emma Stratton, Deborah Wakefield and Rebecca Whittington. It has welcomed families for 40 years. There are children's clubs, indoor and outdoor play areas, and 'lovely' heated outdoor swimming pools. In the evening, children have their own tea room; older children 'on their best behaviour' can dine with their parents. In the *Indigo Bay* restaurant, chef Adam Clark serves a modern menu, eg, braised beef faggots, smoked bacon savoy cabbage, caramelised onion jus. He seeks to source up to 70 per cent of the ingredients from Cornwall. Light lunches are served in the *Café Indigo*. There are large suites for families; cheaper rooms have no sea view. Adults can retreat to the Ocean Spa which has a thermal suite, a hammam. A staff 'green team' meets monthly to discuss environmental initiatives. A sister hotel, *The Scarlet* (see next entry), has opened nearby. More reports, please.

Mawgan Porth TR8 4BU

T: 01637-860860
F: 01637-860714
E: stay@bedruthan.com
W: www.bedruthan.com

BEDROOMS: 101, 1 suitable for &.
OPEN: all year except 20–28 Dec.
FACILITIES: lift, 2 lounges, 2 bars, 3 dining rooms, ballroom, 4 children's clubs, spa (indoor swimming pool), civil wedding licence, 5-acre grounds (heated swimming pools, tennis, playing field).
BACKGROUND MUSIC: 'relaxing' in bar and restaurant.
LOCATION: 4 miles NE of Newquay.
CHILDREN: all ages welcomed.
DOGS: only guide dogs allowed.
CREDIT CARDS: Amex, MasterCard, Visa.
PRICES: [2010] B&B £67–£133 per person, D,B&B £79–£145, set dinner £29.50, special breaks, New Year package, 1-night bookings sometimes refused in season.

# MAWGAN PORTH Cornwall

Map 1:D2

## THE SCARLET [NEW]

With strong green credentials and a 'youthful appeal', this design hotel has been built by sisters Emma Stratton, Deborah Wakefield and Rebecca Whittington down the hillside from their other hotel, the *Bedruthan Steps* (see previous entry). 'The exterior is ugly, but once inside you have a dramatic view across a shallow sheet of water to the sea,' say inspectors, who enjoyed their stay despite 'a few flaws, some mild chaos'. Muzak is played all day in the public areas. The young staff, mainly English, 'were willing, helpful'. There are five grades of bedroom, the majority categorised as 'just right'. 'Our large room had a pale wooden floor, a bath in the room, and a large wet room; tricky technology. Huge windows facing the beach led to a balcony with rocking chairs.' There is a natural outdoor swimming pool and a chlorine-free indoor one. 'Excellent if elaborate' dishes provided by Ben Tunnicliffe included 'superb asparagus soup and a complicated dish with mullet'. Breakfast, brought to the table, 'was exceptional; a different dish every day, eg, poached pears with yogurt'. 'A spa offers all manner of New Age treatments.'

Tredragon Road
Mawgan Porth TR8 4DQ

T: 01637-861800
F: 01637-861801
E: stay@scarlethotel.co.uk
W: www.scarlethotel.co.uk

BEDROOMS: 37, 2 suitable for &.
OPEN: all year except 2 Jan–4 Feb.
FACILITIES: lift, lobby, bar, lounge, library, restaurant, civil wedding licence, spa (indoor swimming pool 4 by 13 metres, steam room, hammam, treatment room), heated natural outdoor swimming pool (40 sq metres), seaweed baths.
BACKGROUND MUSIC: all day in bar and restaurant.
LOCATION: 4 miles NE of Newquay.
CHILDREN: normally not under 16.
DOGS: not allowed.
CREDIT CARDS: Amex, MasterCard, Visa.
PRICES: [2010] B&B £90–£197.50 per person, D,B&B £115–£215, full alc £62, special offers, Christmas/New Year packages, 1-night bookings generally refused.

**25% DISCOUNT VOUCHERS**

# MAWNAN SMITH Cornwall

Map 1:E2

## BUDOCK VEAN

'Standards continue to improve' at this family-run hotel with 'long-serving and attentive staff'. More praise this year from returning visitors to Martin and Amanda Barlow's traditional hotel in a tranquil setting on the River Helford. A wide range of activities is available in the grounds including tennis, golf, water sports, boat trips. There is a health spa and a covered swimming pool. Fans admire the traditional services: room turn-down, overnight shoe cleaning, valet parking. Bedrooms are 'very well appointed', housekeeping is 'impossible to fault'. It's worth paying extra for a superior room, with 'wonderful views over the golf course or gardens'. Men are requested to wear a jacket and tie after 7 pm in the bar and the main restaurant, but there is less formality and the same menu in the *Country Club*. The chef is Darren Kelly: 'Our five-course dinners were jaw-dropping, and no magnifying glasses are needed to spot the food.' 'You could stay a week and eat a different Cornish fish every evening.' (*David RW Jervois, CM Brook, Mary Woods*)

Helford Passage, Mawnan Smith
nr Falmouth TR11 5LG

T: 01326-252100
F: 01326-250892
E: relax@budockvean.co.uk
W: www.budockvean.co.uk

BEDROOMS: 57, 4 self-catering cottages.
OPEN: all year except 2–22 Jan.
FACILITIES: lift, ramps, 3 lounges, conservatory, 2 bars, restaurant, snooker room, civil wedding licence, 65-acre grounds (covered heated swimming pool), *Country Club*, health spa, tennis, 9-hole golf course, river frontage, unsuitable for &.
BACKGROUND MUSIC: live in restaurant.
LOCATION: 6 miles SW of Falmouth.
CHILDREN: no under-7s in dining room after 7 pm.
DOGS: allowed in some bedrooms, not in public rooms.
CREDIT CARDS: Diners (*2% surcharge*), MasterCard, Visa.
PRICES: [2010] B&B £56–£118 per person, D,B&B £68–130, set dinner £39, full alc £34, various packages.

# MAWNAN SMITH Cornwall

Map 1:E2

## MEUDON

'Everything is done to a consistently high standard' at the Pilgrim family's traditional hotel. It stands in 'lovely' gardens in a valley leading down to a private beach. Harry Pilgrim, the chairman, and his son, Mark, 'give personal attention to guests'. The manager, Mike Evans, leads a 'caring' staff: 'We were addressed by name from the moment we arrived,' says a visitor in 2010. In a 'slight time warp', *Meudon* appeals to those who like turn-down service at night, shoe cleaning, a formal dress code in the restaurant. 'Bedrooms are more modern now, with very good beds, slightly faded chintz,' says a returning visitor. Another comment: 'Lovely to have two chairs in the room, and a handrail in the bathroom.' 'Fabulous cream teas with the best-ever strawberry jam' are served in the lounge. The chef, Alan Webb, uses local produce for his 'classic English' cooking on a menu that changes on an eight-day cycle, eg, chump of Cornish lamb, cinnamon and apricot red cabbage: 'Super lobster with a fine butter sauce.' (*LM Mayer-Jones, and others*)

Mawnan Smith
nr Falmouth TR11 5HT

T: 01326-250541
F: 01326-250543
E: wecare@meudon.co.uk
W: www.meudon.co.uk

BEDROOMS: 29, 16 on ground floor, 2 suitable for &, self-catering cottage.
OPEN: all year except Jan.
FACILITIES: lift, ramps, 3 lounges, bar, restaurant, 8½-acre grounds (gardens, private beach, yacht), golf, riding, windsurfing nearby.
BACKGROUND MUSIC: none.
LOCATION: 4 miles SW of Falmouth.
CHILDREN: all ages welcomed.
DOGS: allowed in bridge lounge, bedrooms.
CREDIT CARDS: all major cards.
PRICES: [2010] B&B £88–£110 per person, set dinner £39, special breaks, Christmas package.

# MEVAGISSEY Cornwall

Map 1:D2

## TREVALSA COURT

**NEW**

Built as an Arts and Crafts holiday home in 1937, this small hotel stands on a cliff on the edge of a Cornish village. The owners, John and Susan Gladwin, have 'wonderful taste in furnishings, and understand that attention to detail is important', according to an inspector. The 'relaxed atmosphere' is liked, so is the 'personal' welcome: 'bags carried to our room'. The house has mullioned windows, a sweeping staircase, a wood-panelled dining room. 'Lots of space in the sitting areas, newspapers, magazines; like staying with a well-heeled friend.' 'Everything fresh and contemporary; the young staff engaging without being obsequious.' Most of the bedrooms face the sea: 'Our bright room had a terrific view of the bay.' Colin Grigg's cooking is 'above average': 'A super dinner: delicious gurnard, an ambrosial steak; lovely celeriac chips; home-made bread, good local cheeses.' Breakfast has a 'healthy' buffet, 'good smoked salmon and scrambled eggs'. In the garden there is a 'dinky little summer house'. A steep winding path leads down to a small private beach. Good walking from the grounds. (*Anthony Karger, and others*)

School Hill
Mevagissey PL26 6TH

T: 01726-842468
E: stay@trevalsa-hotel.co.uk
W: www.trevalsa-hotel.co.uk

BEDROOMS: 14, 2 on ground floor.
OPEN: Feb–Nov.
FACILITIES: lounge, bar, restaurant, 2½-acre garden.
BACKGROUND MUSIC: mixed in bar and restaurant in evening.
LOCATION: edge of village.
CHILDREN: all ages welcomed.
DOGS: allowed by arrangement.
CREDIT CARDS: all major cards.
PRICES: B&B £75–£112.50 per person, D,B&B £22.50 added, set dinner £30, website offers, 1-night bookings refused high season weekends, bank holidays.

# MIDSOMER NORTON Somerset

Map 2:D1

## THE MOODY GOOSE AT THE OLD PRIORY

'Lovely rooms, excellent food, welcoming staff,' says a visitor to this restaurant-with-rooms. The Grade II listed 12th-century building is said to be the oldest in Somerset. The honey-stoned house stands within a walled garden by the church in a former mining village near Bath. The lounges have inglenook fireplaces, flagstone floors, rugs, deep sofas and oak beams. The restaurant has exposed brick walls, white linen on wooden tables, French watercolours on the wall. The owner, Stephen Shore, is an 'exceptional' cook, wrote earlier visitors; he serves a market menu (and a carte) of modern dishes, perhaps creamed celeriac velouté, crisp chorizo; slow-cooked chicken with lemon and thyme. Herbs, fruit and vegetables are grown in the kitchen garden. The 'lovely' bedrooms have antique furniture, bright colours. Mary Bell, which has a bateau lit, faces the garden; Chapel overlooks the church. Breakfast, taken in the rear dining room, has home-baked pastries, freshly squeezed juice; cooked dishes include smoked haddock. Guests can take tea in the mature walled garden. Mr Shore offers 'one-to-one tuition' for aspiring cooks. (*SE*)

Church Square
Midsomer Norton
nr Bath BA3 2HX

T: 01761-416784
F: 01761-417851
E: info@theoldpriory.co.uk
W: www.theoldpriory.co.uk

BEDROOMS: 6.
OPEN: all year, except Christmas, restaurant closed Sun.
FACILITIES: 2 lounges, 2 dining rooms, private dining/function room, ¼-acre garden, unsuitable for &.
BACKGROUND MUSIC: classical in restaurants.
LOCATION: 9 miles SW of Bath.
CHILDREN: all ages welcomed.
DOGS: not allowed.
CREDIT CARDS: Amex, MasterCard, Visa.
PRICES: [2010] B&B £60–£95 per person, set dinner £32.50, full alc £59.

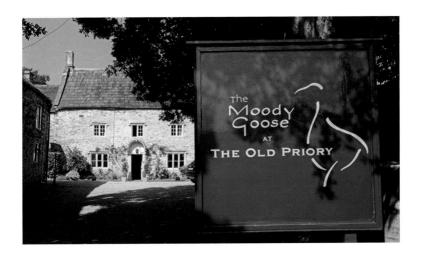

## MILTON ABBOT Devon

Map 1:D3

### HOTEL ENDSLEIGH

Built in 1810 by Georgina, Duchess of Bedford, this shooting and fishing lodge has been restored 'in the spirit of the Regency period' as a luxurious country hotel by Olga Polizzi of *Hotel Tresanton*, St Mawes (see entry). It stands in extensive grounds with streams and waterfalls that run down to the wide River Tamar (on which the *Endsleigh* has seven rods). The gardens, designed by Humphry Repton, are well maintained, and have many rare trees. Readers find the atmosphere 'relaxed'. Roland Jaletzk is the new manager this year. The public rooms have a 'modern' country house feel; Regency panelling, contemporary art, log fires. The bedrooms have antique furniture and original features. All but one are in the main house; Room 17 ('a thatched romantic hideaway with wood-burning stove and private garden') is the former gatekeeper's lodge. In the dining room, Christopher Dyke is now the chef, cooking modern English dishes on a daily-changing menu, eg, organic salmon tartar, pickled white radish; free-range Crediton duck breast, pommes Anna, turnips and orange. More reports, please.

Milton Abbot
nr Tavistock PL19 0PQ

T: 01822-870000
F: 01822-870578
E: mail@hotelendsleigh.com
W: www.hotelendsleigh.com

BEDROOMS: 16, 1 on ground floor, also 1 in lodge (1 mile from main house).
OPEN: all year except 2 weeks Jan.
FACILITIES: drawing room, library, card room, bar, 2 dining rooms, civil wedding licence, terraces, 108-acre estate (fishing, ghillie available).
BACKGROUND MUSIC: evenings only, during dinner.
LOCATION: 7 miles NW of Tavistock, train/plane Plymouth.
CHILDREN: all ages welcomed.
DOGS: not allowed in restaurant, eating terrace.
CREDIT CARDS: all major cards.
PRICES: B&B £90–£180 per person, D,B&B £130–£200, set dinner £40, full alc £50, 1-night bookings refused weekends.

**25% DISCOUNT VOUCHERS**

# MISTLEY Essex

Map 2:C5

## THE MISTLEY THORN

In a 'lovely' coastal village on the River Stour, Sherri Singleton and David McKay's restaurant-with-rooms is 'welcoming, with good food; exceptional value'. The yellow-painted 18th-century coaching inn 'has a real buzz', busy with locals and visitors. Sherri Singleton and Chris Pritchard have a *Michelin* Bib Gourmand for their menus, which specialise in seafood. 'Our meals had fresh local ingredients and were well presented. Mersea rock oysters were as good as we've tasted; new season's lamb was perfectly cooked.' Children have their own menu; the vegetarian dishes are praised. The bedrooms are decorated in taupe and cream; some have views over the Stour estuary, all have large bed, good storage space; a double-ended bath and a shower in the bathroom. Free Wi-Fi is available throughout the building. The 'good, freshly cooked' breakfasts have Buck's Fizz, eggs Benedict on toasted focaccia, kippers; cooked dishes are ordered the evening before. There is a small sitting area for residents. The hostess also runs cookery workshops, and owns an Italian restaurant, *Lucca Enoteca*, in nearby Manningtree. (*SP, JB*)

High Street
Mistley, nr Manningtree
CO11 1HE

T: 01206-392821
F: 01206-390122
E: info@mistleythorn.co.uk
W: www.mistleythorn.com

BEDROOMS: 7.
OPEN: all year.
FACILITIES: ramp, small sitting area, bar, restaurant, bedrooms unsuitable for &.
BACKGROUND MUSIC: light pop/jazz in restaurant.
LOCATION: village centre, 9 miles W of Harwich.
CHILDREN: all ages welcomed.
DOGS: allowed, if small and well behaved.
CREDIT CARDS: MasterCard, Visa.
PRICES: [2010] B&B £45–£60 per person, D,B&B £60–£77.50, cookery courses, New Year package.

# MOCCAS Herefordshire

Map 3:D4

## MOCCAS COURT

♥*César award in 2008*

One of Herefordshire's great houses, Grade I listed with original designs by the Adam brothers, this is the family home of Ben and Mimi Chester-Master. They create a 'deliberately informal atmosphere' (visitors are greeted on first-name terms and there is no dress code). 'We have no spa or gym,' they say. The house stands by the River Wye in an immaculate park designed by Capability Brown and Humphry Repton. A magnificent cantilevered staircase below a glass dome leads to the bedrooms, which have fine fabrics, period furnishings. The Pleasure Ground, the largest with the best views over the park, is popular with honeymooners. Two smaller rooms are on the second floor (reached by 64 steps). Bathrooms are modern with 'piping hot' water. Ben Chester-Master ('a farmer and chef of 18 years', who is passionate about local ingredients) cooks a no-choice dinner by arrangement. It is taken communally at an 'exquisite' circular table in the Round Room (visitors can request a separate table when they book). (*DB, UM, TH*)

Moccas, nr Hereford
HR2 9LH

T: 01981-500019
F: 01981-500095
E: info@moccas-court.co.uk
W: www.moccas-court.co.uk

BEDROOMS: 5.
OPEN: Tues–Sat (Thurs–Sat Jan–Mar), closed Christmas.
FACILITIES: 2 lounges, music room, library, dining room, civil wedding licence, 75-acre grounds (river, fishing), unsuitable for &.
BACKGROUND MUSIC: none.
LOCATION: 10 miles W of Hereford.
CHILDREN: not under 16 except by arrangement.
DOGS: not allowed in house.
CREDIT CARDS: Amex, MasterCard, Visa.
PRICES: B&B £68.50–£137 per person, set dinner £45.

# MORETON-IN-MARSH Gloucestershire
Map 3:D6

## THE MANOR HOUSE **NEW**

'Our welcome could not have been better,' say
inspectors visiting this old sandstone building,
parts of which date back to the 15th century, in
the market town. Badly damaged by flooding,
it has been restored by the small Cotswold Inns
and Hotels group (see entry for *The Lamb*,
Burford); Simon Stanbrook is the manager.
Bedrooms are reached by winding corridors
leading from a spacious lobby. 'Our large room
had arched windows facing the lovely garden.
It was thoughtfully furnished; antique bedside
tables, two large armchairs, a dressing table with
a hospitality tray.' Rooms at the front are double
glazed against traffic noise. There are two
dining areas: a conservatory brasserie with
Lloyd Loom chairs, and the formal *Mulberry*
restaurant. The chef, Nick Orr, uses seasonal
produce for his menus: 'This is food as theatre,
served with ceremony. The highlights were a
meaty ravioli of lobster, delicious pork served
three ways; a wonderful strawberry dessert.'
Breakfast was 'just right'; jugs of juice on a
sideboard; a good choice of cooked dishes.
Popular with weddings at weekends (check
when booking). (*Helen Beach, and others*)

High Street
Moreton-in-Marsh GL56 0LJ

T: 01608 650501
F: 01608-651481
E: info@manorhousehotel.info
W: www.cotswold-inns-hotels.co.uk

BEDROOMS: 35, 1 on ground floor
suitable for &.
OPEN: all year.
FACILITIES: library, lounge, bar,
brasserie, restaurant, function
rooms, civil wedding licence, ½-acre
garden.
BACKGROUND MUSIC: in public
areas.
LOCATION: on edge of market town.
CHILDREN: all ages welcomed.
DOGS: allowed in designated rooms.
CREDIT CARDS: all major cards.
PRICES: [2010] B&B £72.50–£160 per
person, D,B&B £27.50 added, set
dinner £37.50 (*10% service charge*),
special offers, Christmas/New Year
packages.

**25% DISCOUNT VOUCHERS**

# MORETON-IN-MARSH Gloucestershire

Map 3:D6

## THE REDESDALE ARMS

Co-owner and manager, Robert Smith, runs a 'well-oiled establishment', says a visitor returning in 2010 to this centuries-old coaching inn on the main street of an attractive Cotswold market town. 'My disabled husband finds the public rooms and the bedrooms easily accessible. Rooms are clean and modern; service is outstanding. Highly recommended.' The bars and restaurant have original beams, and there are quaint passages. The best bedrooms are in a converted stable block at the back, a short walk outdoors (umbrellas are provided). Front windows are double glazed. Some rooms have a whirlpool bath, suites have a king-size bed. Earlier visitors liked their country-style room, with good extra touches (fresh flowers and a complimentary decanter of sherry). There is a residents' lounge, which has dark wood and leather furniture, an open fire in a stone surround. Chef Craig Mallins's modern menu (with a short list of daily specials) is served in the restaurant and bars (dishes like Gloucester Old Spot sausages with bacon and parsley mash). (*Mrs A Davey, DB*)

High Street
Moreton-in-Marsh
GL56 0AW

T: 01608-650308
F: 01608-651843
E: info@redesdalearms.com
W: www.redesdalearms.com

BEDROOMS: 23, 16 in annexe across courtyard, 1 suitable for &.
OPEN: all year.
FACILITIES: 3 lounge bars, 2 restaurants, heated open dining area.
BACKGROUND MUSIC: in all public areas.
LOCATION: town centre.
CHILDREN: all ages welcomed.
DOGS: allowed in some bedrooms, some public rooms but not restaurant.
CREDIT CARDS: Amex, MasterCard, Visa.
PRICES: [2010] B&B £42.50–£70 per person, D,B&B £67.50–£95, full alc £30, special breaks, Christmas/New Year packages, 1-night bookings refused Sat Apr–Sept.

# MORSTON Norfolk

Map 2:A5

## MORSTON HALL

*César award in 2010*

Behind high walls in well-maintained grounds and gardens, Tracy and Galton Blackiston's Jacobean flint-and-brick mansion stands amid a stirring landscape of sandbanks and salt marshes on the north Norfolk coast. They run it as a restaurant-with-rooms (*Michelin* star); she is front-of-house, he the chef, working with Samantha Wegg. 'It's a winning formula; the place was heaving on a Friday night,' says a reporter this year. In the evening, guests gather for drinks and canapés in lounges with log fire and candles. There is no choice on the four-course dinner menu: likes and dislikes are discussed in advance. In Mr Blackiston's absence, inspectors thought the cooking 'lived up to its reputation', with 'distinctive flavours, well-balanced ingredients'. Dishes might include braised neck of lamb, haricot beans; roasted loin of veal, potato gnocchi, braised onions, tomato fondue and Buccaneers sauce. Bedrooms in the main house are traditionally furnished, the spacious garden suites have a hi-tech bathroom. Breakfast reflects the standards of dinner: 'The first time I've enjoyed porridge for 25 years.'

Morston, Holt
NR25 7AA

T: 01263-741041
F: 01263-740419
E: reception@morstonhall.com
W: www.morstonhall.com

BEDROOMS: 13, 6 in garden pavilion on ground floor.
OPEN: all year except Christmas, 3 weeks Jan, restaurant closed midday.
FACILITIES: hall, lounge, conservatory, restaurant, 3½-acre garden (pond, croquet).
BACKGROUND MUSIC: none.
LOCATION: 2 miles W of Blakeney.
CHILDREN: all ages welcomed.
DOGS: not allowed in public rooms.
CREDIT CARDS: all major cards.
PRICES: D,B&B £150–£180 per person, set dinner £55, New Year package, 1-night bookings sometimes refused Sat.

## MORTEHOE Devon

Map 1:B4

### THE CLEEVE HOUSE

'Really good value in these hard times', this small, unpretentious, 'welcoming' hotel is in a village on the north Devon coast above a three-mile Blue Flag beach. The 'personal touch' of the owners, David and Anne Strobel, was praised by a visitor in 2010. 'The welcome is excellent, the atmosphere is quiet and peaceful.' The 'fairly small' bedrooms, simply furnished in pine, are equipped with 'everything you might need'. 'Ours was warm and comfortable.' Good country views from the rear rooms. The Strobels share the cooking (he does the main course, she the puddings). 'The food gets better every year.' 'Imaginative' dishes include seared venison steaks with pears and red wine sauce. There is a good range of vegetarian alternatives. The dining room closes during the school summer holidays ('most guests say they don't want to eat in, but we will cook for a minimum of six if asked'). Breakfast has home-made bread, preserves and yogurt; a wide range of cooked choices includes kippers and poached haddock. 'We never tire of the various coastal walks from the door.' (*J Hemmings, CM*)

North Morte Road
Mortehoe, nr Woolacombe
EX34 7ED

T: 01271-870719
E: info@cleevehouse.co.uk
W: www.cleevehouse.co.uk

BEDROOMS: 6, 1, on ground floor, suitable for &.
OPEN: Apr–Sept, restaurant closed Wed, and evenings 21 July–31 Aug.
FACILITIES: ramp, lounge, bar area, dining room, ½-acre garden (patio), golf nearby, Woolacombe beach 1½ miles.
BACKGROUND MUSIC: none.
LOCATION: 4 miles W of Ilfracombe, train/coach Barnstaple.
CHILDREN: not under 12.
DOGS: not allowed.
CREDIT CARDS: MasterCard, Visa (*both 1% charge*).
PRICES: B&B £41–£46 per person, D,B&B £64–£70, full alc £40, 1-night bookings sometimes refused Sat.

# NEAR SAWREY Cumbria

Map 4: inset C2

## EES WYKE COUNTRY HOUSE

In 'a fine location' amid pristine farmland with lake and mountain views, this attractive Georgian building was once the holiday retreat for Beatrix Potter. Run by chef/proprietor Richard Lee, with his wife, Margaret, it has two 'nicely decorated' lounges with comfortable chairs and sofas, and open fires in winter. It was 'highly recommended' by a visitor who liked 'the friendly country house atmosphere' and 'excellent cooking'. Another guest was less happy with his 'old-fashioned' room and 'tiny bathroom'. Two bedrooms have their private bathroom across a landing (dressing gown provided). Dinner is served at 7.30 pm: guests make their choice at 6.30 from a daily-changing five-course menu (main courses like sea bass roasted with red onion, pancetta, tarragon and garlic). 'Richard Lee is obviously a good cook; the wine list is comprehensive and good value. Everything is perfect at breakfast, from the leaf tea with strainer to the embossed butter pats.' It has an extensive buffet of cereals, freshly squeezed juice, yogurt; good cooked dishes; honey in the comb. (*GEG, and others*)

Near Sawrey
Ambleside LA22 0JZ

T: 015394-36393
E: mail@eeswyke.co.uk
W: www.eeswyke.co.uk

BEDROOMS: 8, 1 on ground floor.
OPEN: all year.
FACILITIES: 2 lounges, restaurant, veranda, 1-acre garden, unsuitable for &.
BACKGROUND MUSIC: none.
LOCATION: edge of village 2½ miles SE of Hawkshead on B5286.
CHILDREN: not under 12.
DOGS: not allowed.
CREDIT CARDS: MasterCard, Visa.
PRICES: B&B £56–£66 per person, D,B&B £89–£99, set dinner £33, full alc £43, Christmas/New Year packages, 1-night bookings refused some bank holidays.

# NETLEY MARSH  Hampshire

Map 2:E2

## HOTEL TERRAVINA

❦ *César award in 2009*

At their contemporary hotel in the New Forest, the hosts, Gérard and Nina Basset, are 'very hands-on'; their staff are 'pleasant, professional, helpful', say visitors in 2010. The interiors are open and modern, with glass panels, natural wood or slate flooring. One visitor felt that 'comfort was sacrificed for effect' in the low chairs and sofas of the small lounge. Alan Haughie is the head chef; his modern cooking 'with a California influence' is admired. 'We enjoyed some delicious dishes, particularly a truffle cappuccino and chestnut and parsnip pithiviers. The offer of a second selection of bread was refreshing.' Gérard Basset was named the world's best sommelier in 2010; his eclectic wine list has 'surprisingly reasonable prices'. The bedrooms have lots of wood, neutral colours, generous bathroom; most have a patio or terrace. A room in the extension had 'state-of-the-art fittings, desk, free Wi-Fi and a mini-espresso machine'. Breakfast (charged extra) has a continental buffet, and cooked dishes to order. A colonial-style roofed terrace overlooks the large garden.

174 Woodlands Road
Netley Marsh
nr Southampton SO40 7GL

T: 02380-293784
F: 02380-293627
E: info@hotelterravina.co.uk
W: www.hotelterravina.co.uk

BEDROOMS: 11, some on ground floor, 1 suitable for ♿.
OPEN: all year, except 2 days between Christmas/New Year.
FACILITIES: ramp, lounge, bar, restaurant, private dining room, civil wedding licence, 1-acre grounds (swimming pool, heated in summer).
BACKGROUND MUSIC: none.
LOCATION: NW of Southampton, 2 miles W of Totton.
CHILDREN: all ages welcomed.
DOGS: not allowed.
CREDIT CARDS: Amex, MasterCard, Visa.
PRICES: [2010] room £145–£245, breakfast £9.50–£12.50, full alc £55, 2-night bookings preferred at weekends (check with hotel).

# NEW ROMNEY Kent

## ROMNEY BAY HOUSE

With 'the feel of a home, not a hotel', this red-roofed, white-fronted 1920s mansion stands in an isolated position by a pebble beach on the Kent coast. Designed by Sir Clough Williams-Ellis of Portmeirion fame for American actress/journalist Hedda Hopper, it is now owned by Clinton and Lisa Lovell and their family. Visitors are greeted in 'friendly, personal fashion'. The 'colourful' bedrooms, facing the sea (and, on a clear day, France) or a golf course, have large windows, four-poster or half-tester bed. The house is furnished with antiques and pictures; log fires burn and candles are lit at night. A seaside-themed lookout room has a telescope. Mr Lovell cooks a no-choice dinner on four nights a week, with dishes like hot home-smoked salmon, sweet ginger; rump of Romney Marsh lamb with celeriac and leek gratin. Breakfast is full English or continental (cold meats, cheese, fruits, croissants, toast). The house is not easy to find: ask for directions rather than trusting in satnav, say the Lovells, who prefer to take bookings by phone. More reports, please.

Coast Road, Littlestone
New Romney TN28 8QY

T: 01797-364747
F: 01797-367156

BEDROOMS: 10.
OPEN: all year except 1 week Christmas, 1 week early Jan, dining room closed midday, Sun/Mon/Thurs evenings.
FACILITIES: 2 lounges, bar, conservatory, dining room, small function facilities, 1-acre garden (croquet, boules), opposite sea (sand/pebble beach, safe bathing, fishing), unsuitable for &.
BACKGROUND MUSIC: none.
LOCATION: 1½ miles from New Romney.
CHILDREN: not under 14.
DOGS: not allowed.
CREDIT CARDS: Amex, MasterCard, Visa.
PRICES: B&B £47.50–£95 per person, set menu £45 (*optional' 5% service charge added to bill*), winter breaks, New Year package, 1-night advance bookings refused weekends.

**25% DISCOUNT VOUCHERS**

# NEWCASTLE UPON TYNE Tyne and Wear   Map 4:B4

## JESMOND DENE HOUSE

In a suburb colonised by students, this Arts and Crafts mansion in a wooded valley is run as a luxury hotel by a consortium of local businessmen. Original features (ornate fireplaces, stained glass, oak panelling) have been preserved in the Great Hall and the two smart lounges, one formerly a billiard room; they stand alongside more modern touches including retro leather chairs, contemporary artwork. Readers (and inspectors) have liked the 'calm and excellence', the 'friendly service' and 'quality furnishings'. Bedrooms in the mansion have muted colours; magazines, a fruit bowl, a plasma TV. Suites in the recently built *New House* have a sitting room, big bed, bolder colours. A choice of dining areas: informal in a former music room with delicate plasterwork; and, more formal, an oak-floored garden room with a summer terrace. The chef, Pierre Rigothier, cooks modern dishes, eg, loin of Kielder venison, confit quince, celeriac and coffee sauce. Children have a separate dining menu and a pets' corner, with pot-bellied pigs and peacocks. More reports, please.

Jesmond Dene Road
Newcastle upon Tyne NE2 2EY

T: 0191-212 3000
F: 0191-212 3001
E: info@jesmonddenehouse.co.uk
W: www.jesmonddenehouse.co.uk

BEDROOMS: 40, 8 in adjacent annexe, 2 suitable for &.
OPEN: all year.
FACILITIES: lift, 2 lounges, cocktail bar, restaurant, conference/function facilities, civil wedding licence, 2-acre garden.
BACKGROUND MUSIC: in public areas.
LOCATION: 5 mins' drive from centre via A167.
CHILDREN: all ages welcomed.
DOGS: only guide dogs allowed.
CREDIT CARDS: all major cards.
PRICES: [2010] room £150–£450, breakfast £16, set dinner £26, Christmas/New Year packages.

# NEWENT Gloucestershire

Map 3:D5

## THREE CHOIRS VINEYARDS

In attractive, undulating Gloucestershire countryside, this restaurant-with-rooms at an award-winning vineyard, one of the largest in Britain, is recommended by a visitor this year. The restaurant is on the crest of a hill above the south-facing vines, which thrive in the shelter of the Malvern hills and the Brecon Beacons. 'The views were wonderful, the environment was relaxing, the service excellent.' Chef Darren Leonard serves modern British dishes (perhaps seared breast of duck, butternut squash confit, dauphinoise potatoes) on a short seasonal menu which has 'enough choice to allow variety' on a three-night stay. Eight of the bedrooms are in a single-storey building beside the restaurant. 'Our large room was comfortably furnished; French windows opened on to a terrace with a table and chairs, a pleasant place to sit.' Three newer rooms, designed to be warm in winter and cool in summer, are in a lodge among the vines; they have private parking. Breakfast has a large buffet, 'lovely scrambled eggs and smoked salmon'. Guests in the lodge rooms are given a breakfast hamper. (*Gordon Turner, L Michael Mayer-Jones*)

Newent GL18 1LS

T: 01531-890223
F: 01531 890877
E: info@threechoirs.com
W: www.three-choirs-vineyards.
   co.uk

BEDROOMS: 11, 3 in lodges 500 yds from restaurant, all on ground floor, 1 suitable for &.
OPEN: all year, except Christmas/New Year.
FACILITIES: lounge, restaurant, 100-acre grounds.
BACKGROUND MUSIC: none.
LOCATION: 2 miles N of Newent.
CHILDREN: all ages welcomed.
DOGS: not allowed.
CREDIT CARDS: MasterCard, Visa.
PRICES: [2010] B&B £57.50–£87.50 per person, D,B&B £92.50–£117.50 (min. 2 nights), full alc £45, wine-tasting breaks, 1-night bookings sometimes refused weekends.

# NEWLANDS Cumbria

## SWINSIDE LODGE　**NEW**

At the foot of Cat Bells in a silent and scenic stretch of Derwentwater, this Regency house returns to a full entry in the *Guide* under the ownership of Mike and Kath Bilton. 'The house is spotless and the service is obliging,' says a visitor in 2010. 'We were greeted by Kath Bilton; our cases were carried to our refurbished bedroom by a helpful French factotum/waiter. It was beautifully appointed, with a bath and separate shower.' There are three sizes of bedroom; each has a hospitality tray, mineral water, flat-screen TV/DVD-player. Turn-down is available. In the candlelit dining room, the chef, Clive Imber, who has stayed from the previous regime, serves a set four-course daily-changing menu of classic English and French dishes, eg, fillet of Cumbrian beef, caramelised balsamic onions, fondant potato. 'Perfectly cooked and presented; table linen and cutlery were immaculate; the service was efficient and courteous.' The lodge is surrounded by wooded fields and hills. A five-minute trail leads to a jetty on the lake where ferries can be caught. (*John Harrop*)

Grange Road
Newlands
nr Keswick CA12 5UE

T: 017687-72948
F: 017687-73312
E: info@swinsidelodge-hotel.co.uk
W: www.swinsidelodge-hotel.co.uk

BEDROOMS: 7.
OPEN: all year except Christmas.
FACILITIES: 2 lounges, dining room, ½-acre garden, unsuitable for &.
BACKGROUND MUSIC: in reception, dining room.
LOCATION: 2 miles SW of Keswick.
CHILDREN: not under 12.
DOGS: not allowed in house (dry store available).
CREDIT CARDS: all major cards.
PRICES: [2010] D,B&B £82–£102 per person, set dinner £45, special offers, New Year package.

# NORTH MOLTON Devon

Map 1:B4

## HEASLEY HOUSE

☙ *César award in 2010*

'A find,' say visitors in 2010. In a quiet hamlet on the southern edge of Exmoor national park, Jan and Paul Gambrill run their Georgian dower house as a small hotel/restaurant. A seasoned reporter called it 'a *Guide* classic'. An inspector thought it 'wonderful; they love what they are doing and are making a great go of it. Paul carried my bag to my eyrie room with cheerful chat.' The rooms are individually styled; all have large bed, 'quality' cotton bedlinen. 'Mine was vast, plenty of hanging and drawer space, deep comfy armchair; tea tray with a fast cordless kettle.' 'Ours had two televisions. A good selection of DVDs is available.' Mr Gambrill is the chef; he describes his style as 'unpretentious, using local sources'. His cooking is mostly admired: 'A delicious minted broad bean, pea and watercress soup with home-baked bread; quail with game chips, bread sauce and perfect roast potatoes.' The wine list is 'short, well balanced'. 'Great breakfast: fresh orange juice, perfect cooked full English.' (*Ken and Priscilla Winslow, and others*)

Heasley Mill
North Molton EX36 3LE

T: 01598-740213
E: enquiries@heasley-house.co.uk
W: www.heasley-house.co.uk

BEDROOMS: 7.
OPEN: all year except Christmas, Feb (private parties only at New Year).
FACILITIES: lounge, bar, restaurant, ½-acre garden, unsuitable for &.
BACKGROUND MUSIC: in bar on request ('eclectic, not Lloyd Webber').
LOCATION: N of N Molton.
CHILDREN: all ages welcomed.
DOGS: not allowed in restaurant.
CREDIT CARDS: MasterCard, Visa.
PRICES: B&B £70–£105 per person, D,B&B £30 added, set meals £24–£30.

**25% DISCOUNT VOUCHERS**

# NORTH WALSHAM Norfolk

Map 2:A6

## BEECHWOOD HOTEL

Once Agatha Christie's East Anglian hideaway, this Georgian house, 'with Victorian character', is run as a small 'homely' hotel by Lindsay Spalding and Don Birch. It has many devotees. The staff 'made us feel welcome', says a visitor this year. 'We always try to entertain our guests,' says Mr Birch. 'We guarantee a restful stay because we don't take large groups.' The chef, Steven Norgate, has a daily-changing short menu of 'modern British cuisine with a Mediterranean influence', eg, duo of salmon and crayfish; pork fillet, herb mash, turned carrots, crispy pancetta. All ingredients are sourced, where possible, within ten miles. Bedrooms come in three sizes: small doubles ('cosy, with shower'); half-tester rooms; more spacious garden and four-poster rooms have a freestanding slipper bath, a walk-in shower. Wi-Fi is now available throughout the building. Coffee and tea are served in a lounge bar; a garden lounge opens on to a terrace. Dogs are welcomed in three bedrooms. Harry Potter and Tess, rescue Airedale terriers, join visitors in the lounge after their evening walk. (*Christine Saunderson, and others*)

20 Cromer Road
North Walsham NR28 0HD

T: 01692-403231
F: 01692-407284
E: info@beechwood-hotel.co.uk
W: www.beechwood-hotel.co.uk

BEDROOMS: 17, some on ground floor, 1 suitable for ♿.
OPEN: all year, except Christmas, restaurant closed midday Mon–Sat.
FACILITIES: 2 lounges, bar, restaurant, 1-acre garden (croquet).
BACKGROUND MUSIC: none.
LOCATION: near town centre.
CHILDREN: not under 10.
DOGS: allowed (3 'dog' bedrooms).
CREDIT CARDS: MasterCard, Visa.
PRICES: B&B £45–£75 per person, D,B&B £55–£95, set dinner £36, short breaks, New Year package, 1-night bookings sometimes refused Sat.

**25% DISCOUNT VOUCHERS**

# NORTHAM Devon

Map 1:B4

## YEOLDON HOUSE

The owners, Jennifer and Brian Steele, are 'friendly, available and helpful' at this 19th-century gabled house in a peaceful setting overlooking the River Torridge. 'We could lie in bed and watch the morning mists rising from the river,' say visitors this year. Inspectors were impressed by the cooking of Brian Steele, formerly an executive chef at a large London hotel. 'The food is the main reason for coming: his sea bass was wonderful, succulent and tasting of the sea; generous vegetables.' Bedrooms vary: a four-poster room was 'refurbished to a high standard, very clean'. 'Our room was nicely decorated in shades of pale yellow; a lot of furniture; a small bathroom with little storage.' The popular Crow's Nest overlooks the estuary and has a battlemented balcony. There are teddy bears everywhere; a large lounge. The gardens are 'maintained to a high standard'. Breakfast has 'good' porridge, smoked haddock, 'perfect poached eggs'. 'All the guests were of a certain age and friendly; we enjoyed the interaction,' said a visitor in autumn. (*AE Silver, and others*)

Durrant Lane
Northam, nr Bideford
EX39 2RL

T: 01237-474400
F: 01237-476618
E: yeoldonhouse@aol.com
W: www.yeoldonhousehotel.co.uk

BEDROOMS: 10.
OPEN: all year except 21–26 Dec, restaurant closed midday and Sun evening.
FACILITIES: lounge/bar, restaurant, civil wedding licence, 2-acre grounds, beach 5 mins' drive, unsuitable for &.
BACKGROUND MUSIC: classical evenings in public rooms.
LOCATION: 1 mile N of Bideford.
CHILDREN: all ages welcomed.
DOGS: allowed, but not left unattended and not in restaurant.
CREDIT CARDS: Amex, MasterCard, Visa.
PRICES: B&B £60–£67.50 per person, D,B&B £85–£100, set menu £35, short breaks, New Year package, 1-night bookings sometimes refused.

# NORWICH Norfolk

## BY APPOINTMENT

❦ *César award in 1999*

A 'theatrical experience', presided over like an impresario by the owner, Robert Culyer, this restaurant-with-rooms was given its *César* in 1999 for 'utterly enjoyable mild eccentricity'. A decade later, *Guide* inspectors were entranced. The entrance may be unprepossessing, through a side gate into the kitchen, but the 'welcome was warm; a chef carried our bags'. The bedrooms, reached by a maze of narrow corridors and steep stairs in three 15th-century buildings, are 'wonderfully cluttered with antiques and artefacts'. Queen Consort is 'a large light room with two huge chandeliers and a coal fire'. Queen Elizabeth, in the eaves, has sheets and blankets on the bed, a dressing table, pictures and curios; a claw-footed bath and a separate power shower in the bathroom. A single room, Queen Eleanor, was added in 2010. In the equally flamboyant dining rooms 'Robert recites the menus'. The chef, Ellery Powell, uses good ingredients with robust sauces in dishes like rack of lamb, crushed new potatoes, caper jus. Breakfast is 'as good'.

25–29 St George's Street
Norwich NR3 1AB

T/F: 01603-630730
E:   puttii@tiscali.co.uk
W:
www.byappointmentnorwich.co.uk

BEDROOMS: 6.
OPEN: all year except 25 Dec/1 Jan, restaurant closed midday, and Sun and Mon evenings.
FACILITIES: 2 lounges, restaurant, small courtyard, unsuitable for &.
BACKGROUND MUSIC: classical/jazz in restaurant.
LOCATION: city centre.
CHILDREN: not under 12.
DOGS: not allowed.
CREDIT CARDS: MasterCard, Visa.
PRICES: B&B £60–£80 per person, full alc £40.

# NORWICH Norfolk

Map 2:B5

## 38 ST GILES `NEW`

On a street of independent shops and Georgian houses, Jeanette and William Cheeseman's 'boutique B&B' is reached by a private courtyard shared with a nursery school. The red brick town house, built for a banking family in the 18th century, has an elegant hall with a striking chandelier, two flights of stairs with galleried landings. Paintings by local artists are displayed throughout. Home-made cake, fresh milk and water are left in the bedrooms with tea- and coffee-making facilities for arriving visitors. All rooms have silk curtains, handmade mattress; a state-of-the-art TV; Internet access. The Brown Room has wooden floors, Persian rugs, colourful drapes; a sofa bed in a separate sitting room makes it good for a family. The Blue Room ('although the smallest, probably our favourite') has an antique Chinese wardrobe, a vintage wing armchair. The Green Room has calm colours, a chaise longue, an original fireplace. Breakfast includes fresh croissants, pastries, home-made jams, fruit, honey on the comb; you can try the full cooked or perhaps buttermilk pancakes with bacon. The Cheesemans will recommend local eating places.

38 St Giles Street
Norwich NR2 1LL

T: 01603-662944
E: 38stgiles@gmail.com
W: www.38stgiles.co.uk

BEDROOMS: 5, 1 on ground floor.
OPEN: all year except 23–27 Dec.
FACILITIES: breakfast room.
BACKGROUND MUSIC: radio at breakfast.
LOCATION: central.
CHILDREN: all ages welcomed.
DOGS: not allowed in public rooms.
CREDIT CARDS: all major cards.
PRICES: B&B £65–£90 per person, 2-night bookings 'encouraged' at weekends.

# NOTTINGHAM Nottinghamshire

Map 2:A3

## HART'S HOTEL

🏛 *César award in 2007*

'A very enjoyable city hotel, with high standards; good for business and leisure.' Praise this year from inspectors for Tim Hart's purpose-built hotel. It is on the site of Nottingham's medieval castle in a cul-de-sac five minutes' walk from the centre ('steepish on return'). The interiors are contemporary: 'Lots of art on the walls, brightly coloured seating, a vast window in the lobby. Our garden room had its own outdoor space with table and chairs. Decor was plain, fairly masculine, but good-quality, goose-down duvet and pillows. The lighting throughout is well planned.' One niggle: 'Lots of extra charges, £8 for parking, £5 for internet use, £1 for two small biscuits.' Tom Earle is the chef at *Hart's*, the contemporary restaurant (banquette seating in brown velvet, original art, wood floors, plenty of space between tables). 'The food is simple, with twists; we had gravadlax with a lovely dressing, red snapper, and wonderful desserts.' Light meals are served all day in Park's Bar. Breakfast can be continental or cooked. Mr Hart also owns *Hambleton Hall*, Hambleton (see entry).

Standard Hill, Park Row
Nottingham NG1 6GN

T: 0115-988 1900
F: 0115-947 7600
E: reception@hartshotel.co.uk
W: www.hartsnottingham.co.uk

BEDROOMS: 32, 2 suitable for ♿.
OPEN: all year, restaurant closed 1 Jan.
FACILITIES: lift, ramps, reception/lobby, bar, restaurant (30 yds), conference/banqueting facilities, small exercise room, civil wedding licence, small garden, private car park with CCTV.
BACKGROUND MUSIC: light jazz in bar.
LOCATION: city centre.
CHILDREN: all ages welcomed.
DOGS: not allowed in public rooms, or unattended in bedrooms.
CREDIT CARDS: Amex, MasterCard, Visa.
PRICES: [2010] room £120–£260, breakfast £8.50–£13.50, set dinner £25, full alc £50.

**25% DISCOUNT VOUCHERS**

# OBORNE Dorset

Map 1:C6

## THE GRANGE AT OBORNE

In a 'charming' hamlet near Sherborne, this 200-year-old manor house is managed by Jennifer and Jonathan Fletcher who, with their staff, are 'pleasant, helpful'. Dinner in the candlelit dining room, which overlooks the garden, is formal, with silver service and dessert trolley. The chef, Nick Holt, cooks modern dishes using local and seasonal ingredients, eg, Dorset woodland venison, wild mushrooms, rum jus. The vegetarian choices are commended. The older bedrooms are traditional in style with silk throws and original fireplace; the newer rooms have a contemporary decor. Beds have sheets and blankets and a choice of pillows. 'Our large room had direct access to the well-manicured garden.' Breakfast has 'generous' cooked dishes. Games are available in the lounge area. The hotel's owners (Mrs Fletcher's parents) spent a year researching their personal guide to the attractions of Wessex to give guests an 'unbiased' insight into local attractions such as Stonehenge, Hardy Country and Cadbury Castle. Weddings and functions are held in the ballroom. (*John and Elspeth Gibbon*)

Oborne, nr Sherborne
DT9 4LA

T: 01935-813463
F: 01935-817464
E: reception@thegrange.co.uk
W: www.thegrangeatoborne.co.uk

BEDROOMS: 18, 1 suitable for ♿.
OPEN: all year.
FACILITIES: lounge, bar, restaurant, 2 function rooms, civil wedding licence, ¾-acre garden.
BACKGROUND MUSIC: 'easy listening' all day, in public rooms.
LOCATION: 2 miles NE of Sherborne by A30.
CHILDREN: all ages welcomed.
DOGS: only guide dogs allowed.
CREDIT CARDS: all major cards.
PRICES: B&B £49.50–£80 per person, D,B&B (min. 2 nights) £71.80–£102, set dinner £25–£34, hibernation breaks Oct–Mar, Christmas/New Year packages, 1-night bookings refused Sat in summer.

**25% DISCOUNT VOUCHERS**

# OLD HUNSTANTON Norfolk

Map 2:A5

## THE NEPTUNE

A short walk from the beach, this red brick, creeper-clad 18th-century coaching inn has been redecorated with a nautical feel by chef Kevin Mangeolles and his wife, Jacki, who run it as a restaurant-with-rooms. There is a small lounge and bar, but the action centres on the smart dining room with its well-spaced, 'nicely laid' tables and Lloyd Loom chairs. Mr Mangeolles has a *Michelin* star for his 'refined, unfussy' cooking on an evolving menu, eg, roast quail and chorizo, sweetcorn sauce; sea bass, chicken wings, baby turnip, watercress sauce. Inspectors admired the excellence of the food, and the 'careful, thoughtful' presentation. Ten wines and two champagnes are available by the glass. Bedrooms are furnished with white New England-style furniture; all have a shower (no baths), a flat-screen TV, Wi-Fi. A room up steep steps was 'thoughtfully equipped: pale blue carpet, excellent bed, magazines'; a small shower room was 'like a ship's galley'. Breakfast has freshly squeezed orange juice, fruit yogurt, two types of toast, home-made croissants, 'delicious scrambled eggs'. More reports, please.

85 Old Hunstanton Road
Old Hunstanton PE36 6HZ

T: 01485-532122
E: reservations@theneptune.co.uk
W: www.theneptune.co.uk

BEDROOMS: 6, all with shower.
OPEN: all year, except 25/26 Dec, 3 weeks Jan, 2 weeks Nov, Mon off-season.
FACILITIES: residents' lounge, bar, restaurant, unsuitable for &.
BACKGROUND MUSIC: jazz in bar.
LOCATION: village centre, on A149.
CHILDREN: not under 10.
DOGS: not allowed.
CREDIT CARDS: MasterCard, Visa.
PRICES: [2010] B&B £50–£75, D,B&B £30 added, full alc £50–£55, website offers, New Year package, 1-night bookings refused Sat in season.

# ORFORD Suffolk

Map 2:C6

## THE CROWN AND CASTLE

'The staff are friendly and helpful; the food is good and varied.' Praise this year for this old red brick inn in a peaceful village near Aldeburgh. It is owned and run by Ruth Watson (cookery writer and TV presenter), with her husband, David, and Tim Sunderland (partner/manager). 'We are alwlays made to feel welcome and valued,' is the comment of a visitor returning in 2010. The 'attractive' modern paintings in the public rooms and bedrooms are admired. The sea-facing bedrooms in the main house are recommended: 'Our newly refurbished suite was modern with high-quality fittings (flat-screen TV in both sitting room and bedroom); a lovely spacious bathroom.' Garden rooms have a 'fine interior, huge bed, good bathroom'. Mrs Watson oversees the cooking in the bistro-style *Trinity* restaurant (*Michelin* Bib Gourmand for dishes like venison, chestnut and red wine stew); Nick Thacker has been promoted to head chef. Breakfast has freshly squeezed orange juice, hand-cut toast; eggs Benedict among the cooked choices. A 'smart' pub lunch is served (more formal on Sunday). (*Peter Whiteley, Helen Cruickshank*)

Orford, nr Woodbridge IP12 2LJ

T: 01394-450205
E: info@crownandcastle.co.uk
W: www.crownandcastle.co.uk

BEDROOMS: 19, 10 (all on ground floor) in garden, 1 in courtyard.
OPEN: all year except 3–7 Jan.
FACILITIES: lounge/bar, restaurant, private dining room, gallery (with Wi-Fi), ½-acre garden.
BACKGROUND MUSIC: none.
LOCATION: market square.
CHILDREN: not under 4, not under 8 in *Trinity* restaurant.
DOGS: allowed in bar, 5 garden rooms (£5).
CREDIT CARDS: MasterCard, Visa.
PRICES: B&B £62.50–£112.50 per person, D,B&B £85–£135, special breaks, Christmas/New Year packages, 1-night bookings refused Sat.

# OSWESTRY Shropshire

Map 3:B4

## PEN-Y-DYFFRYN

♥ *César award in 2003*

Standing in extensive grounds with no passing traffic, this silver-stone Georgian rectory is run as a small country hotel by owners Miles and Audrey Hunter. 'They are friendly and involved, visible at meal times,' says a visitor in 2010. *Pen-y-Dyffryn* was built a few hundred yards on the English side of the border for a Welsh parish church. *Guide* readers have long liked the 'peace and tranquillity', and the excellent service by 'well-trained young staff'. The public rooms have fresh flowers, log fires in winter. In summer, the complimentary tea on arrival can be taken on a terrace with splendid views over the hills. Many of the bedrooms are south facing. Each of the four rooms in the coach house has a stone-walled patio opening on the garden; these rooms are popular with dog owners. The rooms in the main house vary in size. In the dining room, chef David Morris serves modern British dishes, perhaps guineafowl, smoked pancetta, champ potatoes. 'Excellent food, with good choice; a fine wine list.' Breakfast is 'excellent', too. Good walking from the door, including the circular Offa's Dyke Path. (*Carol Jackson*)

Rhydycroesau
Oswestry SY10 7JD

T: 01691-653700
F: 01978-211004
E: stay@peny.co.uk
W: www.peny.co.uk

BEDROOMS: 12, 4, each with patio, in coach house, 1 on ground floor.
OPEN: all year except Christmas.
FACILITIES: 2 lounges, bar, restaurant, 5-acre grounds (dog-walking area), unsuitable for &.
BACKGROUND MUSIC: light classical in evening.
LOCATION: 3 miles W of Oswestry.
CHILDREN: not under 3.
DOGS: not allowed in public rooms after 6 pm.
CREDIT CARDS: Diners, MasterCard, Visa.
PRICES: [2010] B&B £59–£86 per person, D,B&B £84–£122, set dinner £36, full alc £50, New Year package, 1-night bookings sometimes refused Sat.

**25% DISCOUNT VOUCHERS**

# OXFORD Oxfordshire

Map 2:C2

## MALMAISON

An imaginative conversion of the city's Victorian castle gaol, the Oxford branch of this contemporary chain has metal walkways, cell doors with spy holes (reversed for today's guests). Some of the jokes may seem laboured ('We're taking no prisoners,' says the brochure) but the 'sheer drama' wins fans. Bedrooms in the A-wing atrium, built around a huge oblong space, are created from three cells (two for the sleeping area, one for the bathroom). 'They are cosy, with decent beds and the usual stylish bathroom fittings,' says a visitor in 2010. The governor's old house has a mini-cinema; mezzanine rooms with four-poster bed. In C-wing, 'Love Suite Love' suites have champagne on ice, chocolate-dipped strawberries, aromatic oils and candles. The open-plan Governor's suite is spacious; it has a 'fabulous' bathroom. In the candlelit brasserie (below ground), 'the food is fine, and the service excellent'. Breakfast has 'plenty of choice'. 'Many things are done well, but *Malmaison* lacks heart; nothing seems individual enough.' (*DB*)

3 Oxford Castle
New Road
Oxford OX1 1AY

T: 01865-268400
E: oxford@malmaison.com
W: www.malmaison.com

BEDROOMS: 94, 16 in *House of Correction*, some in *Governor's House*, 3 suitable for &.
OPEN: all year.
FACILITIES: ramps, *Visitors' Room* lounge, 2 bars, brasserie, 2 private dining rooms, gym, free Wi-Fi, outside seating.
BACKGROUND MUSIC: in public areas.
LOCATION: central, pre-booked parking (£20 a night).
CHILDREN: all ages welcomed.
DOGS: allowed.
CREDIT CARDS: all major cards.
PRICES: [2010] room £160–£385, breakfast from £13.95, set menu £16.50.

# OXFORD Oxfordshire

Map 2:C2

## OLD BANK 🏆

*César award: City hotel of the year*

'A stylish, well-run and discreetly luxurious hotel in the middle of a lovely city.' 'A big place with a personal feel, well deserving endorsement.' Praise again in 2010 for Jeremy Mogford's modern conversion of three stone buildings (one a former bank) opposite All Souls on the High. Ben Truesdale is the manager: 'The staff are helpful, never intrusive.' 'Our superior room was peaceful, spacious, nicely decorated; a lovely view of Merton tower; an excellent marble bathroom.' A small room was 'cosy and lacked for nothing'. Mr Mogford's extensive collection of contemporary art is displayed in public areas and bedrooms. 'Tables are tightly packed, but service is prompt' in *Quod*, the 'lively' bar/restaurant, 'an excellent Oxford meeting place'. The 'reasonably priced' menu (pastas, omelettes, steaks, daily specials) 'was of a high standard, well presented'. Breakfast (7 to 11 am, charged extra) had 'a good range of buffet items, very good bread, proper marmalade'. Also recommended: the complimentary walking tour of the city by a 'pleasant and knowledgeable' guide. (*Mary Wilmer, Stuart W Gardner, Robert Gower, Michael and Eithne Dandy*)

92–94 High Street
Oxford OX1 4BN

T: 01865-799599
F: 01865-799598
E: info@oldbank-hotel.co.uk
W: www.oldbank-hotel.co.uk

BEDROOMS: 42, 1 suitable for ♿.
OPEN: all year.
FACILITIES: lift, residents' lounge/bar, bar/grill, dining terrace, 2 meeting/private dining rooms, small garden.
BACKGROUND MUSIC: jazz in library/bar in evenings.
LOCATION: central (windows facing High St double glazed), access to rear car park.
CHILDREN: all ages welcomed.
DOGS: not in bedrooms, public rooms.
CREDIT CARDS: Amex, MasterCard, Visa.
PRICES: [2010] room £185–£230, breakfast £11.95–£12.95, set lunch £9.95, full alc £30, 'last-minute rates', Christmas/New Year packages, 1-night bookings sometimes refused weekends.

# OXFORD Oxfordshire

Map 2:C2

## OLD PARSONAGE

'We enjoyed our stay and would go back.' An endorsement from a trusted correspondent this year for Jeremy Mogford's wisteria-covered 17th-century building beside St Giles's church. Deniz Bostanci is the manager. 'The strong points are an outside sitting area within the walls; the limited but free parking; the good food.' The club-like lounge (red walls with original cartoons and prints, and a small library) and bar/restaurant with year-round log fire are popular with students and visiting parents. 'Both lunch and dinner were good.' Chef Simon Cottrell 'adapts traditional recipes and devises new ones' for dishes like breaded langoustines with caper mayonnaise; lemon and coriander lamb tagine. Bar meals are available; children have their own menu; the 'very high' tea is recommended. A first-floor bedroom to the side of the building had a small bed, 'noisy air conditioning' on a hot day; 'fortunately, it was quiet and we were able to leave the window open'. A 'characterful' ground-floor room was found 'more spacious'. The 'excellent' breakfast has 'a great deal of choice on the continental buffet'. Mr Mogford also owns *Old Bank* (see previous entry). (*Wolfgang Stroebe*)

1 Banbury Road
Oxford OX2 6NN

T: 01865-310210
F: 01865-311308
E: reservations@
    oldparsonage-hotel.co.uk
W: www.oldparsonage-hotel.co.uk

BEDROOMS: 30, 10 on ground floor, 1 suitable for &.
OPEN: all year.
FACILITIES: lounge, bar/restaurant, civil wedding licence, terrace, roof garden, small walled garden.
BACKGROUND MUSIC: modern jazz in bar/restaurant area.
LOCATION: NE end of St Giles, some traffic noise, windows double glazed, small car park.
CHILDREN: all ages welcomed.
DOGS: allowed.
CREDIT CARDS: Amex, MasterCard, Visa.
PRICES: [2010] room £179–£210, breakfast £12.95–£14, set supper £13.50, full alc £40, special breaks, Christmas/New Year packages, 1-night bookings refused weekends.

# PADSTOW Cornwall

Map 1:D2

## THE SEAFOOD RESTAURANT

The writ of celebrity chef Rick Stein runs wide in this north Cornish fishing port. The business empire he has created (and still runs) with his ex-wife, Jill, has bedrooms in six separate buildings across the village, and four distinct dining options. Mrs Stein designed the bedrooms: the three simplest rooms are above *Rick Stein's Café* on a quiet side street (no views). *St Petroc's Hotel*, a wisteria-clad white Georgian building, has ten rooms. Two of the four rooms in *Prospect House* are equipped for disabled visitors. The most expensive, in *St Edmund's House*, have views across the Camel estuary; most rooms above the *Seafood Restaurant* also have the view. The one-bedroom *Bryn Cottage* has a private garden. David Sharland is the executive chef for the flagship *Seafood Restaurant*, where dishes might include chargrilled Dover sole with sea salt and lime. A 'from-the-grill' menu (28-day dry-aged steaks, etc) has been introduced at *St Petroc's*; the *Café* has a *Michelin* Bib Gourmand for its dishes (Thai fishcakes, mussels with crème fraîche and saffron). Or try the fish and chip shop. More reports, please.

Riverside, Padstow PL28 8BY

T: 01841-532700
F: 01841-532942
E: reservations@rickstein.com
W: www.rickstein.com

BEDROOMS: 40, in 6 buildings, some on ground floor, 2 suitable for &.
OPEN: all year except 24–26 Dec, restaurants also closed 1 May.
FACILITIES: ramps, *Seafood*: lift, conservatory bar, restaurant, *St Petroc's*: lounge, reading room, bar, bistro, *Café* unsuitable for &.
BACKGROUND MUSIC: *St Petroc's* and *Café*.
LOCATION: *Seafood Restaurant* on harbour, other buildings nearby.
CHILDREN: all ages welcomed, but no under-3s in *Seafood Restaurant*.
DOGS: allowed in public rooms except restaurants, most bedrooms.
CREDIT CARDS: MasterCard, Visa.
PRICES: [2010] B&B £45–150 per person, *Restaurant* tasting menu £65.50, full alc £60, *St Petroc's Bistro* winter set meal £17.50, full alc £40, *Café* set meals £21.75, special breaks, 1-night bookings refused Sat.

# PANGBOURNE Berkshire

Map 2:D3

## THE ELEPHANT

*César award in 2010*

Christoph Brooke's small Hillbrooke group has renovated this late 19th-century hotel with oriental references: the spacious public rooms have an elephant theme; there are overstuffed sofas, big, quirky furniture and polished floorboards. In a busy village ('that needs a bypass'), it is managed by Annica Eskelius. It is 'a professional and well-run hotel, thoughtfully decorated', says an inspector in 2010. 'Service was impressive and always friendly. Our bedroom in the main building, overlooking the pretty garden, had a beautiful, large Indian bed (cream-painted carved wood), interesting furnishings and fittings; a good hospitality tray and information pack. We would have loved to stay longer.' Rooms at the front face the main crossroads in the village; an annexe room was thought 'characterless'. *Christoph's* dining room has big bay windows, wooden tables and floor. 'The dining experience was generally good: imaginative starters (beetroot and goat's cheese salad; scallops), slightly disappointing main courses. The desserts were impressive.' *The New Inn*, Coln St Aldwyns (see entry), belongs to the same group.

Church Road
Pangbourne RG8 7AR

T: 01189-842244
F: 01189-767346
E: reception@elephanthotel.co.uk
W: www.elephanthotel.co.uk

BEDROOMS: 22, 8 in annexe, 4 on ground floor, 1 suitable for &.
OPEN: all year.
FACILITIES: bar, 2 lounges, restaurant, conference rooms, civil wedding licence, garden.
BACKGROUND MUSIC: 'soft'.
LOCATION: in village, 6 miles NW of Reading.
CHILDREN: all ages welcomed.
DOGS: allowed in 1 bedroom, not in restaurant.
CREDIT CARDS: Amex, MasterCard, Visa.
PRICES: [2010] B&B £70–£100 per person, D,B&B from £100, full alc £37.50, website offers, Christmas/New Year packages.

**25% DISCOUNT VOUCHERS**

# PENZANCE Cornwall

Map 1:E1

## THE ABBEY HOTEL

*César award in 1985*

On a quiet, narrow street that leads down to the harbour, this bright blue Georgian town house is 'an antidote to blandness'. Owned by Jean Shrimpton and managed in relaxed style by her son, Thaddeus Cox, it is liked for its 'mild eccentricity'. The listed building is decorated 'with character and attitude'. The 'magnificent' 19th-century drawing room, full of curios, has high ceilings, peach walls, deep-green velvet curtains for the huge arched windows, which open on to an exotically planted walled garden. There are scarlet walls and carpets in the corridors; a 'wonderful' collection of contemporary art throughout. The largest bedroom has a canopied bed, floor-to-ceiling windows looking out towards St Michael's Mount. A smaller room at the top of the house had 'huge bedside tables, big ceramic reading lights; a small shower room across the corridor'. All rooms have flat-screen TV and free Wi-Fi. An 'excellent' breakfast is taken in an oak-panelled dining room (with antique dresser and old brick fireplace). Summer teas and drinks can be taken in the garden. Evening meals are no longer served.

Abbey Street
Penzance TR18 4AR

T: 01736-366906
E: hotel@theabbeyonline.co.uk
W: www.theabbeyonline.co.uk

BEDROOMS: 6, also 2 apartments in adjoining building.
OPEN: all year.
FACILITIES: drawing room, dining room, garden, unsuitable for &.
BACKGROUND MUSIC: none.
LOCATION: 300 yds from centre, parking.
CHILDREN: all ages welcomed.
DOGS: allowed.
CREDIT CARDS: Amex, MasterCard, Visa.
PRICES: [2010] B&B £37.50–£100 per person, midweek offers.

# PENZANCE Cornwall

Map 1:E1

## HOTEL PENZANCE

The owners, Stephen and Yvonne Hill, have
converted two Edwardian merchants' houses on a
hill above the harbour into a small hotel. Andrew
Griffiths is the manager; the staff are 'attentive,
accommodating'. The 'attractive' bedrooms
are furnished with dark and blonde woods,
traditional patterns on the bedspreads. The best
rooms have views over St Michael's Mount and
the Lizard. Food in the *Bay Restaurant* is 'first
class'; the chef, Ben Reeves, cooks 'imaginative
dishes', eg, south coast scallops, butternut squash
ravioli; free-range duck, chicory with prosciutto,
pickled plum. There is a vegan menu, and an
extensive Cornish farmhouse cheese selection.
Floor-to-ceiling windows open on to a deck,
where guests may dine in good weather. The
restaurant has an art gallery displaying
contemporary Cornish artists. Breakfast has a
buffet with seasonal fruits, compote, porridge
with Rodda's clotted cream, organic muesli,
croissants; cooked choices include scrambled eggs
with smoked trout. A visitor this year complained
of loud background music (it was turned down).
In the Mediterranean gardens, there is a heated
swimming pool. (*Fiona Owen-Jones, and others*)

Britons Hill
Penzance TR18 3AE

T: 01736-363117
F: 01736-350970
E: enquiries@hotelpenzance.com
W: www.hotelpenzance.com

BEDROOMS: 25, 2 on ground floor,
1 suitable for &.
OPEN: all year, restaurant closed Sat
lunch.
FACILITIES: ramps, 3 lounges,
bar/restaurant, ½-acre garden,
terrace, 15-metre swimming pool,
rock beach, safe bathing nearby.
BACKGROUND MUSIC: in restaurant.
LOCATION: on hill, ½ mile from
centre.
CHILDREN: all ages welcomed.
DOGS: not allowed in public rooms.
CREDIT CARDS: Amex (2½%
surcharge), MasterCard, Visa.
PRICES: [2010] B&B £75–£92.50 per
person, D,B&B £100–£117.50, set
dinner £24–£29.95, full alc £40,
special breaks, Christmas/New Year
packages.

**25% DISCOUNT VOUCHERS**

# PETERSFIELD Hampshire

Map 2:E3

## JSW

In a prosperous Hampshire town, this white-painted 17th-century former coaching inn is run as a restaurant-with-rooms by Jake Watkins, who has a *Michelin* star for his modern British cooking. There is an 'air of relaxation' in the beamed restaurant, where tables are well spaced, lighting is subdued. 'The cuisine is of the highest quality,' says a trusted reporter. Dishes might include scallops with lightly spiced mussels and razor clams; 18-hour-cooked ox cheek, curly kale and mash. Coffee comes with 'superb home-made truffles'. The three cream-and-brown bedrooms, off a wide landing on the first floor, overlook the street at the front of the building. All have Wi-Fi, a large flat-screen TV and good heating. 'Ours was very comfortable and clean.' One has a sitting room with a sofa bed. The modern bathrooms all have shower cabinets, no baths. A continental breakfast is brought to the bedroom: it has fresh orange juice, home-made muesli, toast, home-made marmalade. In warm weather, meals can be taken in a smart courtyard at the back. No guest lounge. (*J and SL, and others*)

20 Dragon Street
Petersfield GU31 4JJ

T: 01730-262030
E: jsw.restaurant@btinternet.com
W: www.jswrestaurant.com

BEDROOMS: 3.
OPEN: all year except Mon/Sun, 2 weeks summer, 2 weeks winter.
FACILITIES: restaurant, courtyard.
BACKGROUND MUSIC: NONE.
LOCATION: town centre.
CHILDREN: not allowed at dinner Fri/Sat.
DOGS: not allowed.
CREDIT CARDS: Diners, MasterCard, Visa.
PRICES: [2010] B&B £42.50–£55 per person, set meals £19.50–£29, tasting menu £40–£50.

# PETWORTH West Sussex

Map 2:E3

## THE OLD RAILWAY STATION

'The quaintness of the location and buildings adds a special charm' to this B&B with a difference, a Grade II* listed Victorian railway station, and its four Pullman carriages. 'We could make believe we were on a real journey,' say visitors who slept in a carriage this year. It is run by owners Gudmund Olafsson (Icelandic) and Catherine Stormont. The old waiting room, 'with a welcoming old-fashioned coal fire', is used for breakfast, afternoon tea and evening drinks. The station building also houses the biggest bedrooms. Others are in the Pullman cars (of the type used for the original Orient Express), each divided into two bedrooms. 'Ours, quite spacious, well decorated, had good furniture in keeping with the period and a large comfortable bed.' Bathroom facilities might have been 'a little tired' but 'we would return'. Breakfast was 'excellent, freshly cooked, tasty'. The pretty garden has ancient trees, a sunken lawn, and steep banks covered with shrubs. *The Badger*, a pub with a restaurant within walking distance, is recommended for evening meals. (*Max Lickfold*)

Petworth GU28 0JF

T: 01798-342346
F: 01798-343066
E: info@old-station.co.uk
W: www.old-station.co.uk

BEDROOMS: 10, 8 in Pullman carriages, 1 suitable for ♿.
OPEN: all year except Christmas/New Year.
FACILITIES: lounge/bar/breakfast room, platform/terrace, 2-acre garden.
BACKGROUND MUSIC: classical/soft 1940s in waiting room.
LOCATION: 1½ miles S of Petworth.
CHILDREN: not under 10.
DOGS: not allowed.
CREDIT CARDS: Amex, MasterCard, Visa.
PRICES: [2010] B&B £44.50–£97 per person, special breaks, 1-night bookings refused weekends and during Goodwood events.

# PICKERING North Yorkshire

Map 4:D4

## THE WHITE SWAN

On the main street of a 'nice old market town', this 'unpretentious' 16th-century coaching inn has been owned by the Buchanan family for 25 years. Victor and Marion Buchanan live nearby with their three small children; Alison Dunning manages the 'slick operation'. 'The welcome was excellent, bags carried, room explained,' say inspectors. Traditional bedrooms are in the main building; newer, contemporary rooms are in an annexe. 'Ours was smart and modern, of a reasonable size, with stone floor and rugs; the comfortable bed came with blankets and sheets as we requested. Storage was adequate for one night. A lovely white-and-cream bathroom.' In the 'cosy' red-walled dining room, chef Darren Clemmit serves 'honest food'. 'We enjoyed monkfish and mushroom sauce; a delicious dessert of poached pear and apple slices. The lack of muzak was a plus point.' Breakfast has 'very good marmalade' and 'delicious haddock with a poached egg'. A club room has a pool table, honesty bar and Wi-Fi. The information pack is 'a masterpiece of amusing comments'.

Market Place
Pickering YO18 7AA

T: 01751-472288
F: 01751-475554
E: welcome@white-swan.co.uk
W: www.white-swan.co.uk

BEDROOMS: 21, 9 in annexe.
OPEN: all year.
FACILITIES: ramps to ground-floor facilities, lounge, bar, club room, restaurant, private dining room, conference/meeting facilities, civil wedding licence, small terrace (alfresco meals), 1½-acre grounds.
BACKGROUND MUSIC: none.
LOCATION: central.
CHILDREN: all ages welcomed.
DOGS: not allowed in restaurant.
CREDIT CARDS: Amex, MasterCard, Visa.
PRICES: [2010] B&B £75–£130 per person, D,B&B £105–£157.50, full alc £35, Christmas/New Year packages, 1-night bookings sometimes refused weekends.

**25% DISCOUNT VOUCHERS**

# PICKHILL North Yorkshire

## THE NAG'S HEAD

'Everything an English inn should be.' Much praise comes this year for Edward and Janet Boynton's 18th-century former coaching inn on the main street of a pretty Domesday village. 'Well run; the staff are friendly, informative,' say visitors in 2010. A returning guest was given 'the warmest of welcomes'. Everyone admires the 'excellent' cooking of Mark Harris, served in the bar or the dining room, which has 'a huge bookcase crammed with books, large mirrors, an attractive old fireplace'. 'We enjoyed game soup and Whitby scampi in the lightest batter, enticing vegetarian tortellini. Delicious.' Another comment: 'A great find for wine buffs as it is run by a connoisseur.' The bedrooms are simple but 'perfectly adequate'. A suite, in an adjacent building, was 'a reasonable size with pine furniture, a large comfy bed and a sitting area through an archway. Plenty of hot water in the bathroom.' The 'good breakfast' includes a 'large buffet selection, proper butter, fruit and a cooked menu with lots of choice'. (*Ian Malone, Jo and Paul Pennington, Sir John B Hall, Robert Gower*)

Pickhill, nr Thirsk YO7 4JG

T: 01845-567391
F: 01845-567212
E: enquiries@nagsheadpickhill.co.uk
W: www.nagsheadpickhill.co.uk

BEDROOMS: 14, 6 in annexe, 2 in cottage, 3 on ground floor.
OPEN: all year except 25 Dec.
FACILITIES: ramps, lounge, bar, restaurant, meeting facilities, lawn (croquet, putting).
BACKGROUND MUSIC: in lounge, bar and restaurant.
LOCATION: 5 miles SE of Leeming.
CHILDREN: all ages welcomed.
DOGS: allowed in some bedrooms.
CREDIT CARDS: MasterCard, Visa.
PRICES: [2010] B&B £42.50–£80 per person, full alc £35, themed breaks, New Year package.

# PORLOCK Somerset

Map 1:B5

## THE OAKS

Surrounded by wide lawns and the oak trees from which it takes its name, this gabled Edwardian country house has a fine position overlooking the sea on the edge of a village. It has long been run 'with quiet efficiency' by owners Tim and Anne Riley. Visitors are greeted with tea and cakes on arrival; the atmosphere of 'old-fashioned courtesy' is valued by readers. The lounge, with a mainly pink decor, has an open fire; it is seen as the place for 'after-dinner coffee or after-walk collapse'. All the bedrooms have sea views, fresh flowers, Egyptian cotton bedlinen, extras like fresh milk and fruit. In the dining room, tables are arranged around the panoramic windows so that everyone is assured of views of the village or the sea. Anne Riley cooks a short four-course daily-changing dinner menu of classic dishes, perhaps cheese and crayfish pancake; tenderloin of Somerset pork with apples and cider. The hotel's entrance is at a sharp angle of the main road. Dunkery Beacon and Selworthy are within walking distance. (*M and JP*)

Porlock TA24 8ES

T: 01643-862265
F: 01643-863131
E: info@oakshotel.co.uk
W: www.oakshotel.co.uk

BEDROOMS: 8.
OPEN: Apr–Nov, Christmas/New Year.
FACILITIES: 2 lounges, bar, restaurant, 2-acre garden, pebble beach 1 mile, unsuitable for &.
BACKGROUND MUSIC: classical during dinner.
LOCATION: edge of village.
CHILDREN: not under 8.
DOGS: not allowed.
CREDIT CARDS: MasterCard, Visa.
PRICES: [2010] B&B £72.50 per person, D,B&B £100, set menu £32.50, special breaks, Christmas/New Year packages.

# PORT ISAAC Cornwall

Map 1:D2

## PORT GAVERNE HOTEL

'The perfect hideaway; a cheery pub in a beautiful little cove with a shingly beach.' Praise again this year for Graham and Annabelle Sylvester's unpretentious inn near Port Isaac. 'The staff are welcoming and friendly; the dinners wholesome,' is another comment. Once frequented by crews from the slate vessels trading in the port, it remains 'a pub at heart' and is popular with locals. There is no background music in the bar, which has slate floors, wooden beams and a log fire. Music is now played in the restaurant where the 'splendid' cooking of Ian Brodey is much enjoyed. Dishes on his daily-changing menu that were admired this year included 'excellent Dover sole'; 'superb lobster thermidor, as good as in the best restaurants in France'. The bar has a separate blackboard menu (fish and chips; crab salad, etc). Bedrooms, up steep staircases, are simple, bathrooms 'clean but fairly basic'. Breakfasts are 'substantial', with a buffet for cereals, etc, and good cooked dishes. Parking can be difficult at busy times. 'Very dog friendly.' (*Jonathan Mirsky, Sir Patrick Cormack, CM Brook*)

Port Gaverne
nr Port Isaac PL29 3SQ

T: 01208-880244
FP: 0500 657867
F: 01208-880151
E: graham@port-gaverne-hotel.co.uk
W: www.port-gaverne-hotel.co.uk

BEDROOMS: 15.
OPEN: all year except Christmas.
FACILITIES: lounge, 2 bars, restaurant, beer garden, golf, fishing, surfing, sailing, riding nearby, unsuitable for &.
BACKGROUND MUSIC: in restaurant.
LOCATION: ½ mile N of Port Isaac.
CHILDREN: all ages welcomed.
DOGS: not allowed in restaurant.
CREDIT CARDS: MasterCard, Visa.
PRICES: [2010] B&B £45–£65 per person, set dinner £27, New Year package.

# PORTSCATHO Cornwall

Map 1:E2

## DRIFTWOOD HOTEL

🎗*César award in 2010*

On a low cliff overlooking the sea, Paul and Fiona Robinson's upmarket hotel is appropriately 'light and airy with a seaside feel'. Visitors this year were 'delighted': 'The owners and staff were charming.' Mr Robinson runs the reception 'in a chatty, laid-back style'. The public areas have an 'elegant, understated' look; rugs on bare floorboards, colours of white and blue. This is mirrored in the bedrooms. 'French windows opened on to a deck from our ground-floor room. The lamps, mirror frames, and boats on the wall were made of driftwood; nothing twee, tastefully done.' 'Our lovely top-floor room had an almost Mediterranean view; not for tall guests because of low beams.' In the candlelit dining room, chef Chris Eden serves 'wildly inventive' dishes on a menu with five choices for each course, one changing nightly. Most visitors are impressed (one complained of lack of variety). Summer lunches are served on a terrace; picnics are supplied for the beach. Breakfast has freshly squeezed orange juice, 'accurately cooked eggs'. (*P and JL, and others*)

Rosevine
nr Portscatho TR2 5EW

T: 01872-580644
F: 01872-580801
E: info@driftwoodhotel.co.uk
W: www.driftwoodhotel.co.uk

BEDROOMS: 15, 4 in courtyard, also 2 in Cabin (2 mins' walk).
OPEN: 6 Feb–6 Dec.
FACILITIES: 2 lounges, bar, restaurant, children's games room, 7-acre grounds (terraced gardens, private beach, safe bathing), unsuitable for &.
BACKGROUND MUSIC: jazz in restaurant and bar.
LOCATION: N side of Portscatho.
CHILDREN: all ages welcomed.
DOGS: not allowed.
CREDIT CARDS: Amex, MasterCard, Visa.
PRICES: [2010] B&B £82.50–£127.50 per person, D,B&B (in low season) £102.50–£135, set dinner £42, tasting menu £55, website offers, 1-night bookings sometimes refused weekends.

# PURTON Wiltshire

Map 3:E5

## THE PEAR TREE AT PURTON

'Excellent hosts who engage with their guests', Francis and Anne Young are hands-on owners at their extended 16th-century sandstone former vicarage (Pride of Britain). It stands in 'thoughtfully developed' grounds (with a formal garden, a vineyard and a wild-flower meadow) on the outskirts of a Saxon village; 'a delightful spot'. It is endorsed this year by a large family group celebrating a golden wedding: 'All our children were pleased with the hotel and their rooms; a successful occasion.' The 'beautiful' building (with a 'dull' extension) has a 'pleasant entrance', a panelled library with an original stone fireplace, plenty of books and chairs. 'Our good-sized bedroom had an old-fashioned decor (a pink bathroom suite); lots of storage, good lighting, large, restful bed.' In the candlelit dining room, in two conservatories, the chef, Alan Postill, serves modern dishes: 'A pressed sole and langoustine terrine was well presented; good braised pork shoulder, smoked tenderloin, spring onion mash.' A 'routine' breakfast has a small buffet, proper jams and butter. The Youngs are proud of being 'consciously green'. (*Eric G Hinds, and others*)

Church End
Purton, nr Swindon SN5 4ED

T: 01793-772100
F: 01793-772369
E: stay@peartreepurton.co.uk
W: www.peartreepurton.co.uk

BEDROOMS: 17, some on ground floor.
OPEN: all year.
FACILITIES: ramps, lounge/bar, library, restaurant, function/conference facilities, civil wedding licence, 7½-acre grounds (vineyard, croquet, pond, jogging route).
BACKGROUND MUSIC: none.
LOCATION: 5 miles NW of Swindon.
CHILDREN: all ages welcomed.
DOGS: not unattended in bedrooms, not in public rooms.
CREDIT CARDS: all major cards.
PRICES: B&B £60–£140 per person, set dinner £34.50, full alc £42, special breaks.

**25% DISCOUNT VOUCHERS**

# RAMSGILL-IN-NIDDERDALE N. Yorkshire  Map 4:D3

## THE YORKE ARMS

♀ *César award in 2000*

In a 'beautiful, isolated' position by the green in a village below the moors, Bill and Frances Atkins's 17th-century former shooting lodge is popular with gourmet visitors. 'Very enjoyable, with superb food,' says a reporter this year. In the bar, which has old beams, log fires, wooden tables and settles, Bill Atkins is the busy host; his wife has a *Michelin* star for her innovative cooking. 'Gathering in the small lounge for pre-dinner drinks can be a scrum, but the canapés are beautiful.' Many of the herbs and vegetables are grown behind the inn. 'Thoughtful menus made the best of local produce: delicious halibut; Nidderdale lamb; perfect moist venison. Every dish was beautifully presented and prepared.' The bedrooms have high-tech fittings (LCD TV and DVD-player) but some rooms are small. 'Ours was quaint, though I am not sure that I approve of an en suite bathroom with no door.' Breakfast has 'undyed smoked haddock and perfect poached eggs'. The Gouthwaite Reservoir bird sanctuary is nearby. (*David Birnie, and others*)

Ramsgill-in-Nidderdale
nr Harrogate HG3 5RL

T: 01423-755243
F: 01423-755330
E: enquiries@yorke-arms.co.uk
W: www.yorke-arms.co.uk

BEDROOMS: 12, 2 in *Ghyll Cottage*.
OPEN: all year, Sun dinner for residents only.
FACILITIES: ramp, lounge, bar, 2 dining rooms, function facilities, 2-acre grounds, unsuitable for &.
BACKGROUND MUSIC: classical in dining rooms.
LOCATION: centre of village, train from Harrogate.
CHILDREN: not under 12.
DOGS: allowed by arrangement in 1 bedroom, not in restaurant.
CREDIT CARDS: Diners, MasterCard, Visa.
PRICES: [2010] B&B £75–£120 per person, D,B&B £150–£190, tasting menu £75, full alc £75, winter offers, Christmas/New Year packages.

# RAVENSTONEDALE Cumbria

Map 4:C3

## THE BLACK SWAN

'A good place to stay. Clean, welcoming, efficiently run.' Praise in 2010 for Alan and Louise Dinnes's restored Victorian pub in a 'beautiful' village. They have turned it into a hub of village life. The bar and restaurant are popular with locals as well as visitors; the village shop has been reopened in a downstairs room. Three new bedrooms have been added this year, including a four-poster room with a log-burning stove, a large bathroom with a roll-top bath and a walk-in shower. Inspectors liked their 'pleasant, well-equipped' room, which had a seating area with armchairs; 'a compact bathroom, good storage, lots of hot water'. Two rooms in a ground-floor annexe with direct outdoor access are equipped for disabled visitors; the owners warn of 'some noise from the bar'. Chef Tim Stevenson serves 'generous portions of straightforward food' on a menu of seasonal dishes (eg, venison in a chocolate and red wine sauce). Children are welcomed (family rooms, games, etc). A pick-up service is offered to walkers on the Howgill Fells. Guests can borrow golf clubs for the local course, or tennis rackets to play on the village court. (*C Trevor Lockwood*)

Ravenstonedale
Kirkby Stephen CA17 4NG

T/F: 015396-23204
E: enquiries@blackswanhotel.com
W: www.blackswanhotel.com

BEDROOMS: 14, 2 in ground-floor annexe suitable for &.
OPEN: all year except 25 Dec.
FACILITIES: bar, lounge, 2 dining rooms, beer garden, tennis and golf in village.
BACKGROUND MUSIC: optional 'easy listening'.
LOCATION: in village 5 miles SW of Kirkby Stephen.
CHILDREN: all ages welcomed.
DOGS: allowed in 2 bedrooms, not in restaurant.
CREDIT CARDS: MasterCard, Visa.
PRICES: [2010] B&B £37.50–£62.50 per person, full alc £26, New Year package.

**25% DISCOUNT VOUCHERS**

# REETH North Yorkshire

Map 4:C3

## THE BURGOYNE HOTEL

♦ *César award in 2002*

'Perfect, everything had been thought of,' say
visitors this year to this late Georgian Grade II
listed country house which has been run for 20
years by Derek Hickson. 'Dinner and breakfast
were outstanding as was the attitude of the staff.'
In a commanding position above the green of an
attractive village in the Yorkshire Dales national
park, the house is furnished in traditional style.
An inglenook fireplace is a feature of one of the
two 'comfortable' sitting rooms which have
'squashy sofas and armchairs' and a 'good supply
of up-to-date magazines'. Dinner is served at 8
pm in the green-walled restaurant. Paul Salonga
and Chris Harker's daily-changing four-course
dinner menu (six choices for each course) has
traditional dishes (eg, roast best end of lamb,
home-made mint sauce, redcurrant jelly.
Bedrooms are 'tasteful and well equipped', with
'all kinds of extras': those at the front have a
view over Swallowdale. A comfortable rear
room had antique pine furniture. Breakfast has
'nicely presented' cooked items. (*Gwyn Morgan,
and others*)

On the Green
Reeth, nr Richmond
DL11 6SN

T/F: 01748-884292
E: enquiries@theburgoyne.co.uk
W: www.theburgoyne.co.uk

BEDROOMS: 8, 1 suite, 1 suitable
for &.
OPEN: 11 Feb–2 Jan, restaurant
closed midday.
FACILITIES: ramp, 2 lounges, dining
room, ½-acre garden.
BACKGROUND MUSIC: jazz/classical
in dining room 'when required'.
LOCATION: village centre.
CHILDREN: not under 10.
DOGS: not allowed in 1 lounge,
dining room, or unattended in other
lounge, bedrooms.
CREDIT CARDS: MasterCard, Visa.
PRICES: [2010] B&B £67–£98 per
person, set dinner £33.50, midweek/
Christmas/New Year packages,
1-night bookings sometimes
refused Sat.

# RICHMOND North Yorkshire

Map 4:C3

## MILLGATE HOUSE

*César award: B&B of the year*

'Former teachers Austin Lynch and Tim Culkin have furnished their 'stunning' early Georgian stone house with imagination, filling the 'charming' public rooms with 'delightful' objects. Just off the town's cobbled square, the house has an award-winning walled garden renowned for its clever planting (it is open to the public from April to October). 'They are friendly and passionate about their home and the garden,' says a visitor in 2010. Two of the three bedrooms overlook the garden, and beyond to the River Swale and the Cleveland hills. 'Our huge room had double-aspect views; comfy chairs, a wonderful bed; a bookcase of tempting titles.' The Regency drawing room is packed with antiques, silverware, pictures and books. Breakfast is served until 9.45 am in a splendid dining room redecorated in pale grey. A 'magnificent' buffet has a wide selection of fresh fruit, cereals, seeds, yogurt and croissants; hot dishes are cooked to order and served at table. The proprietors, who have two whippets, welcome visiting dogs. A set dinner is available for groups of 16 or more. (*Bianca Emberson*)

Richmond DL10 4JN

T: 01748-823571
F: 01748-850701
E: oztim@millgatehouse.demon.co.uk
W: www.millgatehouse.com

BEDROOMS: 3, also self-catering facilities for 12.
OPEN: all year.
FACILITIES: hall, drawing room, dining room, ½-acre garden, unsuitable for &.
BACKGROUND MUSIC: occasional classical in hall.
LOCATION: town centre.
CHILDREN: not under 10.
DOGS: not in dining room.
CREDIT CARDS: none.
PRICES: B&B £55–£72.50 per person, Christmas/New Year packages.

# RIPLEY North Yorkshire

Map 4:D4

## THE BOAR'S HEAD

♥ *César award in 1999*

'We're already looking forward to our next stay,' says a visitor to this 18th-century former coaching inn within the Ripley Castle estate. Renovated by Sir Thomas and Lady Ingilby, whose family have lived on the estate for 700 years, it is a combination of pub and country hotel, 'elegant but not stuffy'. 'The management is cheerful, enlightened and inspirational,' say visitors in 2010. The owners write: 'Our staff are encouraged to wear a smile and make all guests feel welcome.' Lady Ingilby oversees the design of the bedrooms, each individually styled. Some look over the cobbled market square, superior rooms are across a courtyard in *Birchwood House*. 'Our double-aspect room was light and airy, beautifully presented with lots of storage space. Our daughter had an equally pleasant standard room.' Antique furniture and pictures come from the attics of Ripley Castle. In the smart restaurant, Kevin Kindland is the new chef, serving modern British dishes, perhaps noisettes of lamb, pan-fried lamb's liver, gratin potatoes. Simpler meals are available in the bistro. Hotel guests have access to the castle grounds. (*JB, and others*)

Ripley Castle Estate, Ripley
nr Harrogate HG3 3AY

T: 01423-771888
F: 01423-771509
E: reservations@
    boarsheadripley.co.uk
W: www.boarsheadripley.co.uk

BEDROOMS: 25, 10 in courtyard, 6 in *Birchwood House* adjacent, some on ground floor.
OPEN: all year.
FACILITIES: ramps, 2 lounges, bar/bistro, restaurant, civil wedding licence (in castle), 150-acre estate (deer park, lake, fishing, 20-acre garden).
BACKGROUND MUSIC: 'easy listening' in restaurant and bistro.
LOCATION: 3 miles N of Harrogate.
CHILDREN: all ages welcomed.
DOGS: allowed.
CREDIT CARDS: all major cards.
PRICES: [2010] B&B £62.50–£75 per person, D,B&B £85–£95, full alc £37, Christmas/New Year packages.

# RIPON North Yorkshire

Map 4:D4

## THE OLD DEANERY

'Very friendly and personal', this old building stands opposite England's oldest cathedral. 'The house is charming, with huge windows, wide corridors, and pale colours upstairs,' says an inspector this year. 'The owner, Linda Whitehouse, carried our bags to a spacious room facing the lovely garden with its huge willow tree. It had a pretty four-poster and a nice sofa. It was warm but lighting was dim; poor storage.' First-floor rooms have original pine shutters and panelling; old beams and sloping ceilings on the second floor. 'We had tea in the lounge/bar, which has black painted floorboards, black chairs; unfortunately there was muzak.' Mrs Whitehouse tells us music 'can be switched off to order'. In the candlelit dining room, chef Robert Harvey's cooking 'was very good indeed; a little fishcake as an amuse-bouche; my plaice with caper sauce was delicious, fresh to taste. The service was nicely paced.' Breakfast, in a room facing the garden, has a small buffet, 'good haddock with poached egg; pre-sliced toast'. In summer, teas, drinks and meals are served in the garden. Weddings are held.

Minster Road
Ripon HG4 1QS

T: 01765-600003
F: 01765-600027
E: reception@theolddeanery.co.uk
W: www.theolddeanery.co.uk

BEDROOMS: 11.
OPEN: all year except 24/25 Dec, 1 Jan, restaurant closed Sun evening.
FACILITIES: lounge, bar, restaurant, conference facilities, civil wedding licence, 1-acre garden, only restaurant suitable for &.
BACKGROUND MUSIC: in bar, restaurant ('can be switched off to order').
LOCATION: town centre.
CHILDREN: all ages welcomed.
DOGS: not allowed in restaurant.
CREDIT CARDS: MasterCard, Visa.
PRICES: B&B £60–£75 per person, set dinner £31.50, full alc £39, special breaks.

**25% DISCOUNT VOUCHERS**

# ROMALDKIRK Co. Durham

## THE ROSE AND CROWN

❦*César award in 2003*

Opposite the green of a Teesdale village, this 18th-century coaching inn has stone walls, oak beams and panelling, gleaming brass and copper, log fires, old farming implements, fresh flowers. It is owned by Alison and Christopher Davy; Jenny Hollando is the manager. Recent visitors were 'impressed' by the hospitality and the meals. Mr Davy is joint head chef with Andrew Lee, serving modern dishes with a regional influence in the intimate brasserie (redecorated this year) or the oak-panelled restaurant with candlelight and white linen. Dishes might include white onion, almond and truffle soup; rump of venison, Puy lentils, wild mushroom broth. A children's menu is available, and late suppers can be taken in the bar. Bedrooms in the main house (all now upgraded) have beams, antiques; flat-screen TV and a sound system. Two have a private sitting room. Those in the courtyard at the rear have a more contemporary decor; they are liked by dog owners and walkers for their direct access to the car park. Breakfast has home-made bread, jams and marmalade. A guide to the area, written by the Davys, is recommended. (*DS*)

Romaldkirk
nr Barnard Castle DL12 9EB

T: 01833-650213
F: 01833-650828
E: hotel@rose-and-crown.co.uk
W: www.rose-and-crown.co.uk

BEDROOMS: 12, 5 in rear courtyard, some ground floor.
OPEN: all year except 24–26 Dec.
FACILITIES: residents' lounge, lounge bar, *Crown Room* (bar meals), restaurant, fishing (grouse shooting, birdwatching) nearby.
BACKGROUND MUSIC: none.
LOCATION: village centre.
CHILDREN: all ages welcomed.
DOGS: allowed in bar, not unattended in bedrooms.
CREDIT CARDS: MasterCard, Visa.
PRICES: [2010] B&B £70–£120 per person, D,B&B £102.50–£152.50, set dinner £32.50, winter discounts, New Year package, 1-night bookings refused Sat 'except quiet periods'.

**25% DISCOUNT VOUCHERS**

# ROSS-ON-WYE Herefordshire

Map 3:D5

## WILTON COURT

On the banks of the River Wye facing the pretty market town, this small hotel/restaurant is liked for the 'warm, unobtrusive welcome from the staff and the owners'. 'A great venue in which to relax, eat and stay,' is another comment this year. Once a magistrates' court, the pink stone building (part Elizabethan) has many original features to which the owners, Helen and Roger Wynn, have added objets d'art from their time working in hotels in the Far East. There are leaded windows, uneven floors; the bar was the original courthouse. In the conservatory-style *Mulberry* restaurant (named after a 300-year-old tree in the garden), chef Michael Fowler uses local produce where possible for his 'imaginative and delicious' dishes (perhaps wild mushroom and chestnut ravioli; Herefordshire fillet of beef, smoked mashed potato, oxtail and Madeira jus). The bedrooms, traditionally furnished, are 'extremely comfortable with superb views'; three face the river, others overlook the gardens. The award-winning breakfast has good fruit salad and 'excellent' cooked dishes. (*MC Smith, Mrs E Britton, and others*)

Wilton Lane, Ross-on-Wye
HR9 6AQ

T: 01989-562569
F: 01989-768460
E: info@wiltoncourthotel.com
W: www.wiltoncourthotel.com

BEDROOMS: 10.
OPEN: all year except 2–15 Jan.
FACILITIES: sitting room, bar, restaurant, private dining room, conference facilities, civil wedding licence, 2-acre grounds (riverside garden, fishing), only restaurant suitable for &.
BACKGROUND MUSIC: at mealtimes in restaurant/bar.
LOCATION: ½ mile from centre.
CHILDREN: all ages welcomed.
DOGS: not allowed in restaurant.
CREDIT CARDS: Amex, MasterCard.
PRICES: [2010] B&B £52.50–£135 per person, D,B&B £72.50–£155, full alc £37.50, special breaks, Christmas/ New Year packages, 1-night bookings refused Sat in season.

**25% DISCOUNT VOUCHERS**

# ROSTHWAITE Cumbria

Map 4: inset C2

## HAZEL BANK

The atmosphere is 'friendly and relaxed' at Rob van der Palen and Anton Renac's 'solid' Lakeland grey stone house in large gardens and woodlands in the Borrowdale valley. They took over the hotel in late 2008: first-time visitors this year report that 'many of the guests had been regulars under previous owners and were happy with the new style'. 'They run the house with style and good taste. It is furnished beautifully but simply,' is another comment. Rob van der Palen is 'very efficient' in charge of front-of-house; 'Anton's cooking is excellent'. Dinner, served at 7 pm, has a daily-changing no-choice European menu, perhaps chestnut mushrooms with goat's cheese, tomato coulis; salmon fillet with a Cumberland ham crust. 'The individual flavours, often intense, combine splendidly.' The bedrooms vary in size from large to compact. 'We had a beautiful view of the peaceful garden and the fells from our bedroom window.' 'This used to be a hotel for people who want to explore the Lake District, but now I would visit just for the food.' There is good walking from the door. Local buses stop at the foot of the drive. (*John and Christine Moore, Peter Mahaffey*)

Rosthwaite
nr Keswick CA12 5XB

T: 017687-77248
E: info@hazelbankhotel.co.uk
W: www.hazelbankhotel.co.uk

BEDROOMS: 8, 2 on ground floor, also self-catering cottage.
OPEN: all year.
FACILITIES: ramp, lounge, honesty bar, dining room, drying room, 4-acre grounds (croquet, woods, becks).
BACKGROUND MUSIC: none.
LOCATION: 6 miles S of Keswick on B5289 to Borrowdale.
CHILDREN: not under 10.
DOGS: not allowed.
CREDIT CARDS: MasterCard, Visa.
PRICES: B&B £56–£65 per person, D,B&B £73–£85, special breaks, 1-night bookings sometimes refused.

# ROWSLEY Derbyshire

Map 3:A6

## THE PEACOCK AT ROWSLEY

Formerly the dower house for Haddon Hall, this Derbyshire stone building, with its mullioned windows and leaded lights, stands in grounds that run down to the River Derwent. The interior combines country antiques and original features (beams, stone fireplaces) with modern simplicity. Visitors who arrived 'on a freezing afternoon' were 'soothed by the cosiness and the warm welcome'. The bedrooms, designed by India Mahdavi, have colourful modern fabrics alongside antiques and old prints. One has a bed from Belvoir Castle. Rooms overlooking the garden are quiet; those at the front facing the road to Bakewell are double glazed. Wi-Fi is available throughout. In two dining rooms, with interesting Mouseman furniture, the chef, Dan Smith, serves modern dishes, eg, assiette of rabbit, tarragon gnocchi, mustard sauce. A simpler menu is available in the bar. Breakfast has a buffet (cereals, 'good' toast, waffles, etc): cooked dishes cost extra. Guests are given a 50% discount for admission to Haddon Hall. There is shooting on the estate and good fishing on the Wye. (*JB, C and PG*)

Bakewell Road
Rowsley DE4 2EB

T: 01629-733518
F: 01629-732671
E: reception@
   thepeacockatrowsley.com
W: www.thepeacockatrowsley.com

BEDROOMS: 16.
OPEN: all year except 24–26 Dec (open for lunch only), 3–11 Jan.
FACILITIES: lounge, bar, dining room, live classical guitar Fri, conference rooms, civil wedding licence, ½-acre garden on river, fishing Apr–Oct, unsuitable for &.
BACKGROUND MUSIC: none.
LOCATION: village centre.
CHILDREN: 'no children under 10 Fri/Sat.'
DOGS: not allowed in public rooms.
CREDIT CARDS: all major cards.
PRICES: [2010] B&B £75–£122.50 per person, D,B&B £105–£160, cooked breakfast £6.95, full alc £58, website offers, New Year package, 1-night bookings refused Sat.

## RUSHLAKE GREEN East Sussex

Map 2:E4

### STONE HOUSE

'Our family built this house in 1495 and has lived here ever since,' say Peter and Jane Dunn. A Tudor manor house, with Georgian additions, it sits in parkland on the Sussex Weald, with two lakes, a farm and extensive woodland. The attractive gardens provide flowers for the house and herbs and vegetables for the kitchen. The spacious public rooms have 'lovely log fires, but they were not lit before 5 pm'. An impressive double staircase rises from the black-and-white marble floor of the entrance hall to two grand bedrooms in the Georgian part of the house; they have a four-poster bed and lavish furnishings. In the Tudor wing, rooms are smaller, with beams, sloping ceilings, mullioned windows, antiques. On a cold March day, visitors would have preferred stronger heating. Jane Dunn has a *Michelin* Bib Gourmand for her 'good, enjoyable' cooking; her specialities include rare slices of Stone House venison rolled in rosemary and pepper, on red cabbage. A picnic can be provided for Glyndebourne, 20 minutes' drive away. (*CE, PEC, and others*)

Rushlake Green
Heathfield TN21 9QJ

T: 01435-830553
F: 01435-830726
W: www.stonehousesussex.co.uk

BEDROOMS: 6, plus 2 in coach house.
OPEN: all year except 21 Dec–1 Jan.
FACILITIES: hall, drawing room, library, dining room, billiard room, 1,000-acre estate (5½-acre garden, farm, woodland, croquet, shooting, pheasant/clay-pigeon shooting, 2 lakes, rowing, fishing), unsuitable for &.
BACKGROUND MUSIC: none.
LOCATION: 4 miles SE of Heathfield, by village green.
CHILDREN: not under 9.
DOGS: not allowed in public rooms.
CREDIT CARDS: MasterCard, Visa.
PRICES: [2010] B&B £62.50–£132.50 per person, set dinner £27.95, Glyndebourne hamper (no VAT) £39, weekend house parties, winter breaks, cookery courses, 1-night bookings sometimes refused Sat.

# RYE East Sussex

Map 2:E5

## THE GEORGE IN RYE

On Rye's quaint, narrow High Street, this 16th-century coaching inn is a 'thriving place', busy with locals and visitors. It has been 'kept in good nick', say inspectors in 2010 who liked the 'eclectic mix of traditional wooden furniture, with splashes of vibrant colours on walls otherwise painted in light greys and beige'. It is owned by Alex and Katie Clarke (a film set designer); their staff were 'friendly, if low-key'. 'Our bedroom was impeccably clean and decorated to a high standard. The large, comfortable bed had a dramatic wall-size padded bedhead with fabric featuring a Victorian pastoral scene; a spacious and light bathroom.' Some rooms are in the main building, others across a courtyard. Downstairs, there is a cosy lounge near Reception, with 'plenty of newspapers and magazines' and a lively, beamed bar. The bistro-style restaurant, busy on a Saturday evening, has a 'romantic atmosphere'. 'We enjoyed scallops with red lentil dhal and coriander; rare venison Wellington; portions were generous.' Breakfast included 'delicious home-made yogurt' and 'beautifully cooked egg dishes'.

98 High Street
Rye TN31 7JT

T: 01797-222114
F: 01797-224065
E: stay@thegeorgeinrye.com
W: www.thegeorgeinrye.com

BEDROOMS: 24, 6 in annexe.
OPEN: all year.
FACILITIES: sitting room, lounge/bar, restaurant, ballroom, civil wedding licence, terrace, courtyard garden, unsuitable for &.
BACKGROUND MUSIC: 'easy listening' in public rooms.
LOCATION: town centre, pay-and-display car park nearby.
CHILDREN: all ages welcomed.
DOGS: 'well-behaved' dogs allowed in bar/lounge/courtyard.
CREDIT CARDS: all major cards (3% surcharge for Amex).
PRICES: [2010] B&B £67.50–£110.50 per person, full alc £35, special breaks, Christmas/New Year packages, supplement for 1-night bookings Sat.

## RYE East Sussex

Map 2:E5

### JEAKE'S HOUSE

❧ *César award in 1992*

'Quiet, welcoming, and with good views from
the windows', Jenny Hadfield's B&B has long
been liked by *Guide* readers for the friendly,
unfussy service. Created from adjoining
buildings (including a wool store, and a chapel
which became a men's club) on one of Rye's
ancient cobbled streets, it was once owned by
American poet Conrad Aitken. The larger
bedrooms are named after the writer friends
who visited him. They are 'spotless', with either
a mahogany or a brass bed; some are up narrow
staircases; some have low beams, furniture may
stand at odd angles due to sloping floors.
Breakfast is taken in the red-walled former
chapel, with high windows, good paintings and
china, plants. It has a self-service buffet (freshly
squeezed orange juice and live yogurt available);
cooked options might be oak-smoked haddock
with poached egg; the choice for vegetarians
includes boiled eggs with Marmite soldiers;
preserves are home made. Evening drinks are
served in the book-lined bar, furnished with old
chapel pews; a folder of sample menus from
nearby restaurants is available. (*RR*)

Mermaid Street
Rye TN31 7ET

T: 01797-222828
E: stay@jeakeshouse.com
W: www.jeakeshouse.com

BEDROOMS: 11.
OPEN: all year.
FACILITIES: parlour, bar/library,
breakfast room, unsuitable for &.
BACKGROUND MUSIC: classical in
breakfast room.
LOCATION: central, car park (£3 per
24 hours, advance booking needed).
CHILDREN: not under 8.
DOGS: allowed.
CREDIT CARDS: MasterCard, Visa.
PRICES: [2010] B&B £45–£64 per
person, 2-night midweek breaks
Nov–Mar, 1-night bookings
sometimes refused busy weekends.

# ST ALBANS Hertfordshire

Map 2:C3

## ST MICHAEL'S MANOR **NEW**

The Newling Ward family has owned and run this 16th-century manor house for more than 45 years. David Newling Ward (of the third generation) is in charge; the manager is Olivier Delaunoy. The setting is 'difficult to beat', in extensive gardens with a lake, close to the cathedral, on a 'centuries-old' street. The public rooms are 'handsome and elegant, with attractive paintings and the occasional oriental influence'. 'We ate well in the romantic, candlelit conservatory restaurant overlooking the floodlit garden.' The chef, Erick Moboti, serves 'tasty' modern dishes (eg, confit pork belly with chorizo, wild mushroom and butter bean fricassée). 'Breakfasts challenged us with the gluttonous delights of eggs royale and eggs Benedict, as well as an extensive cold table.' The rooms in the main house have a period decor; Japanese is the theme in a modern wing. 'Our modern room had every amenity, quality furnishings, a very comfortable bed.' Weddings and functions are often held. 'Visitors might feel overwhelmed; it could be useful to escape, for a breather, to a nearby pub.' (*David Nicholls*)

Fishpool Street
St Albans AL3 4RY

T: 01727-864444
F: 01727-848909
E: reservations@
    stmichaelsmanor.com
W: www.stmichaelsmanor.com

BEDROOMS: 30, 8 in garden wing, some on ground floor, 1 suitable for &.
OPEN: all year.
FACILITIES: ramps, 2 lounges, bar, restaurant, conservatory, 2 private dining rooms, civil wedding licence, 5-acre gardens (croquet, lake).
BACKGROUND MUSIC: classical/contemporary in public areas.
LOCATION: old St Albans, near cathedral.
CHILDREN: all ages welcomed.
DOGS: not allowed.
CREDIT CARDS: all major cards.
PRICES: B&B £72.50–£172.50 per person, set meals £16.50–£20.50, full alc £47.50, website offers, Christmas/New Year packages.

# ST HILARY Cornwall

Map 1:E1

## ENNYS

On a Georgian estate near Penzance, this historic manor house, creeper-clad and imposing, is run as a smart B&B by travel writer Gill Charlton. At the end of a long private drive, it is surrounded by fields leading down to the River Hayle. Exotic plants grow in the pretty garden, which also has a swimming pool (available to visitors in mornings and late afternoons). This year two former family suites in a Grade II listed granite barn beside the main house have been rebuilt as one-bedroom suites, each with its own kitchenette, luxury bathroom (with walk-in shower and separate bathtub), and a private entrance. Bedrooms in the main house have large, 'super-comfortable' beds, furniture commissioned from local craftsmen. Reception rooms are 'nice and bright with interesting works of art'; the main sitting room has a roaring log fire on chilly evenings and a selection of books on the area. Breakfast has freshly squeezed orange juice, good toast, 'lovely' marmalade, 'scrumptious' cooked dishes on an extensive menu based on local produce, much of it organic.

Trewhella Lane, St Hilary
nr Penzance TR20 9BZ

T: 01736-740262
F: 01736-740055
E: ennys@ennys.co.uk
W: www.ennys.co.uk

BEDROOMS: 5, 2 in barn, 3 self-catering apartments (can be B&B off-season).
OPEN: 1 Apr–1 Nov.
FACILITIES: sitting room, breakfast room, 3-acre grounds (tennis, 13-metre heated swimming pool, not available to residents 1–4 pm), unsuitable for &.
BACKGROUND MUSIC: none.
LOCATION: 5 miles E of Penzance.
CHILDREN: not under 16.
DOGS: not allowed.
CREDIT CARDS: MasterCard, Visa.
PRICES: B&B £50–£90 per person, 1-night bookings refused high season, bank holidays.

# ST IVES Cornwall

## BOSKERRIS HOTEL

In a suburban setting above Carbis Bay, this 1930s building has been given a bright modern feel that matches the panoramic view to St Ives. 'Even on a gloomy day, the scene is compelling,' says a visitor this year. 'The restrained decor is beautifully done; the lounge is a relaxing place to be.' The 'delightful' staff are 'attentive, never intrusive'. The owners, Jonathan and Marianne Bassett, have renovated the exterior this year, refurnished the lounge and bar, and added a larger bed to most of the rooms. A large map of Cornwall in the lobby, with recommendations of where to eat and visit, has been updated; daily suggestions for trips are made, tailored to the weather. 'Our bedroom at the back was well furnished, with proper hangers, good drawer space; a sea view.' A 'new team' has taken over in the kitchen; we would welcome reports on the seasonal menus. Breakfast has 'imaginative combinations of good ingredients'; French toast, pan-fried bananas, dry-cured bacon; ricotta hot cakes with a berry compote. St Ives is a five-minute train ride away. (*Bob Lloyd, Colin and Jennifer Beales*)

Boskerris Road
Carbis Bay
St Ives TR26 2NQ

T: 01736-795295
E: reservations@boskerrishotel.co.uk
W: www.boskerrishotel.co.uk

BEDROOMS: 15, 1 on ground floor.
OPEN: Feb–Nov, restaurant closed Tues.
FACILITIES: lounges, bar, restaurant, private dining/meeting room, decked terrace, 1½-acre garden.
BACKGROUND MUSIC: jazz/Latin.
LOCATION: 1½ miles from centre (5 mins by local train), car park.
CHILDREN: not under 7.
DOGS: not allowed.
CREDIT CARDS: Amex (5% *surcharge*), MasterCard, Visa.
PRICES: [2010] B&B £52.50–£117.50 per person, full alc £38, 1-night bookings refused in high season.

**25% DISCOUNT VOUCHERS**

# ST LEONARDS-ON-SEA East Sussex

Map 2:E4

## HASTINGS HOUSE  NEW

On a garden square by the seafront, Seng and
Elizabeth Loy have given their white stuccoed
Victorian house a modern make-over into an
imaginative B&B. 'Seng is a friendly host, and
always has a smile and a few words when you
pass,' says a visitor this year. 'The lovely touches:
flowers in the bedrooms, beautiful sheets and
towels, complimentary refreshments,' impressed
another guest. The bedrooms are done in
striking colours. Room 7, at the top of the house,
with a bay window overlooking the sea, has
'sumptuous' dusky pinks, and Sahara browns;
floor-to-ceiling slate grey tiles in the shower
room. Room 3 ('spacious, immaculate and
bright') has high bay windows, drop-down
curtains; it is decorated in aubergine, brown,
cream and gold. 'Fruit, juice, coffee and tea
were constantly replenished' at breakfast, which
has fresh local breads, 'a great choice of eggs and
cooked breakfast'. 'We ordered a picnic to take
to the battlefield: beautiful fillings for the
sandwiches, chicken satay, fresh fruit, olives,
mixed salads, plates, napkins, even a table cloth.'
(*Linzi and Paul Cook, Helen Paris*)

9 Warrior Square
St Leonards-on-Sea TN37 6BA

T: 01424-422709
F: 01424-420592
E: info@ hastingshouse.co.uk
W: www.hastingshouse.co.uk

BEDROOMS: 8.
OPEN: all year.
FACILITIES: bar/lounge, dining
room, unsuitable for &.
BACKGROUND MUSIC: in bar/lounge.
LOCATION: 1 mile from town centre.
CHILDREN: all ages welcomed.
DOGS: not allowed.
CREDIT CARDS: MasterCard, Visa.
PRICES: B&B £49.50–£67.50 per
person, 1-night bookings refused
high season, weekends.

**25% DISCOUNT VOUCHERS**

# ST LEONARDS-ON-SEA East Sussex

Map 2:E4

## ZANZIBAR INTERNATIONAL HOTEL

'It's a bit unusual,' says an inspector in 2010 visiting Max O'Rourke's upmarket B&B. It is in a terrace of Victorian houses 'of faded grandeur' on the seafront of St Leonards, a 'satellite' of Hastings. 'Words like eclectic, eccentric, exotic might set the scene. The youthful Max, and his manager, Ian Taylor, run a friendly ship and go out of their way to make guests enjoy their stay.' The house was 'in a mess' when Mr O'Rourke bought it. 'Now all is spic and span, freshly painted in white; pine floors polished.' The bedrooms are styled after countries he visited on his travels: 'Ours was Egypt, with the Nile woven on a giant wall-hanging, an overstuffed satin sofa.' Antarctica is 'startlingly white'; India has 'colourful silk fabrics'. All rooms have 'top-of-the-range bathroom fittings' but poor storage. Downstairs has a 'crazy mix of furniture; an old upright piano, lofty tree ferns'. Breakfast, ordered the evening before, is taken at a large table; a 'fruity' continental and 'the full English' were enjoyed. Parking permits are provided for a secure underground car park, 'a fair step from the hotel'.

9 Eversfield Place
St Leonards-on-Sea TN37 6BY

T: 01424-460109
E: info@zanzibarhotel.co.uk
W: www.zanzibarhotel.co.uk

BEDROOMS: 9, 1 on ground floor.
OPEN: all year.
FACILITIES: lounge, bar, breakfast room, conservatory, small garden, beach across road, unsuitable for &.
BACKGROUND MUSIC: none.
LOCATION: seafront, 650 yds W of Hastings pier, free parking vouchers issued.
CHILDREN: all ages welcomed.
DOGS: allowed ('for a nominal charge').
CREDIT CARDS: Amex, MasterCard, Visa.
PRICES: [2010] B&B £59.50–£154.50 per person, special breaks, Christmas/New Year packages, 1-night bookings often refused Sat.

**25% DISCOUNT VOUCHERS**

# ST MARY'S Isles of Scilly

Map 1: inset C1

## STAR CASTLE

⚫*César award in 2009*

In an imposing position above Hugh Town with views across all the islands, this star-shaped Tudor fortress, with additional buildings in gardens, is run in hands-on fashion by Robert Francis and his son, James. 'A lovely place; friendly staff, fantastic food,' says a visitor this year. Another comment: 'Reception staff always found time for a chat.' The old building has been furnished with antiques, tapestries, portraits and other historical memorabilia; the dungeon is now a bar. Bedrooms are in the castle (furnished in keeping with its character), and in two single-storey garden buildings (some have fine views). The chef, Gareth Stafford, serves 'consistently delicious food' in the *Castle* dining room (perhaps pan-roasted fillet of beef, bone marrow bonbons) or, in summer, in the more informal *Conservatory*, which specialises in seafood. Vegetables come from the kitchen garden. At breakfast, which has a buffet and generous cooked dishes (a 'plateful of kippers'), a family member is present to discuss the times of boat trips and other activities. (*Sue Hedges, Mrs VE Barnett, Antony Griew*)

The Garrison, St Mary's
Isles of Scilly
Cornwall TR21 0JA

T: 01720-422317
F: 01720-422343
E: info@star-castle.co.uk
W: www.star-castle.co.uk

BEDROOMS: 38, 27 in 2 garden wings.
OPEN: all year except 1–22 Dec,
4 Jan–12 Feb.
FACILITIES: lounge, bar, 2 restaurants, 3-acre grounds (covered swimming pool, 12 by 3 metres, tennis), beach nearby, unsuitable for &.
BACKGROUND MUSIC: none.
LOCATION: ¼ mile from town centre, boat (2¾ hours)/helicopter (20 mins) from Penzance, air links.
CHILDREN: not under 5 in restaurants.
DOGS: not allowed in restaurants.
CREDIT CARDS: Amex, MasterCard, Visa.
PRICES: [2010] B&B £65–£160 per person, D,B&B £81–£181, set dinner £28.50, short breaks, Christmas/New Year packages.

# ST MAWES Cornwall

Map 1:E2

## TRESANTON

*♧César award in 2009*

'From the moment you pull up in your car, which is unloaded far quicker than you packed it, you get the impression that service is one of the hotel's outstanding selling points.' Praise from a regular correspondent for Olga Polizzi's luxurious yet informal hotel. Federica Bertolini is the manager. 'The staff are friendly, unstuffy, extremely professional.' Most bedrooms have sea views: 'Our spacious double reflected the Italianate/marine theme. No mass-produced furniture; just carefully selected pieces, assembled with flair and imagination to create a simple, elegant style. Everything was immaculately maintained.' The all-white restaurant has full-length doors opening on to a large terrace where guests can dine (rugs and patio heaters provided). The chef, Paul Wadham, serves modern dishes with a Mediterranean influence, eg, sea bass with monk cheeks, Maxim potatoes, artichokes and pancetta. 'The meals are good, though hearty eaters might find portions small.' Children are welcomed. 'An enjoyable, sophisticated experience; expensive, but worth it.' Mrs Polizzi also owns *Hotel Endsleigh*, Milton Abbot (see entry). (*Jenny Buckley*)

27 Lower Castle Road
St Mawes TR2 5DR

T: 01326-270055
F: 01326-270053
E: info@tresanton.com
W: www.tresanton.com

BEDROOMS: 29, in 4 houses.
OPEN: all year.
FACILITIES: 2 lounges, bar, restaurant, cinema, playroom, conference facilities, civil wedding licence, terrace, ¼-acre garden, by sea (shingle beach, safe bathing, 15-metre yacht), unsuitable for &.
BACKGROUND MUSIC: none.
LOCATION: on seafront, valet parking (car park up hill).
CHILDREN: all ages welcomed.
DOGS: allowed in 2 bedrooms, not in public rooms.
CREDIT CARDS: Amex, MasterCard, Visa.
PRICES: [2010] B&B £95–£180 per person, set dinner £42, special breaks, Christmas/New Year packages, 1-night bookings refused weekends.

## SALCOMBE Devon

Map 1:E4

### THE TIDES REACH

At the mouth of the Salcombe estuary across the road from South Sands beach, this traditional seaside hotel has been owned and managed for three generations by the Edwards family. Its appeal is mainly to mature visitors (children under eight are not welcomed). No beauty, but functional, the 1960s building has angular balconies and bright blue awnings. Its bar and lounge and eight bedrooms have been redecorated this year; 12 balconies have been rebuilt. 'The staff are obliging; the food is good,' says a visitor in 2010. The colours are bright in the bedrooms, most of which have a large window that faces the sheltered garden. The sun lounge, where lunch can be taken, has a water feature; a sea-water aquarium is the main feature in the cocktail bar. There are sea views from some tables of the dining room where the chef, Finn Ibsen, serves modern dishes, eg, Dartmoor lamb with creamed Jerusalem artichoke. Breakfast has fresh fruit, yogurts and cereals; cooked dishes include a daily fish option. Snack lunches can be taken in the garden by a large duck pond. (*PL Hamlyn*)

South Sands
Salcombe TQ8 8LJ

T: 01548-843466
F: 01548-843954
E: enquire@tidesreach.com
W: www.tidesreach.com

BEDROOMS: 32.
OPEN: Feb–Nov.
FACILITIES: lift, ramps, 3 lounges, 2 bars, restaurant, leisure centre (indoor swimming pool, 13 by 6 metres, gym, games room, beauty treatments), ½-acre grounds (pond), sandy beach 10 yds, unsuitable for &.
BACKGROUND MUSIC: none.
LOCATION: on Salcombe estuary, 1 mile from town.
CHILDREN: not under 8.
DOGS: allowed in some bedrooms, 1 lounge.
CREDIT CARDS: all major cards.
PRICES: [2010] B&B £50–£142 per person, D,B&B £70–£162, set dinner £32.50, 1-night bookings sometimes refused.

**25% DISCOUNT VOUCHERS**

# SCOTBY Cumbria

## WILLOWBECK LODGE

Run by its 'friendly and informative' owners, John and Liz McGrillis, this architect-designed house has a 'beautiful' setting by a pond amid 'peaceful' woodland on the edge of a village near Carlisle. The large lounge has a vaulted roof, with floor-to-ceiling windows, deep red sofas, velvet cushions and a wood-burning stove. Visitors can choose from a selection of DVDs to watch on the communal TV or take to their room. Bedrooms are 'spotless', bathrooms are 'bright and modern'; 'housekeeping is superb'. There are no telephones in the rooms, but you can borrow a cordless phone from reception. Mrs McGrillis cooks a fixed menu in the evenings (phone ahead to discuss preferences), with dishes like mushrooms with garlic and parsley; smoked haddock, mashed potato, wilted spinach, poached egg, saffron cheese sauce. Mr McGrillis provides the 'tasty' breakfast, ordered the evening before; it has fresh fruit salad in summer, fruit compote in winter. The house is well placed for visitors breaking their journey to and from Scotland, but it 'has no motorway aura'. (*Kristian Lord*)

Lambley Bank
Scotby, nr Carlisle CA4 8BX

T: 01228-513607
F: 01228-501053
E: info@willowbeck-lodge.com
W: www.willowbeck-lodge.com

BEDROOMS: 6, 2 in annexe.
OPEN: all year except 20–28 Dec, restaurant closed Sun.
FACILITIES: lounge, lounge/dining room, conference/function facilities, 1½-acre garden (stream, pond), unsuitable for &.
BACKGROUND MUSIC: 'when guests choose'.
LOCATION: 2½ miles E of Carlisle.
CHILDREN: not under 12.
DOGS: not allowed.
CREDIT CARDS: MasterCard, Visa.
PRICES: [2010] B&B £55–£125 per person, set dinner £30.

# SEAVIEW Isle of Wight

## THE SEAVIEW

Endorsed again this year, Brian Gardener's hotel/restaurant is on a quiet part of the Solent coast, in the north-east of the Isle of Wight, 'a pleasant spot with a yacht club, a boat builder, dinghies in most front gardens, people in nautical paraphernalia'. The hotel's public rooms reflect this heritage, with seafaring memorabilia, ship's lamps, photographs of warships. Bedrooms in the main building have luxurious fabrics, natural seagrass carpets. A room in 'a rather stark brick building across the car park' had 'a good bed, dimming lights; no unnecessary minibar or trouser press but welcome robes and slippers; the bathroom had a bath with internal blue lights and a TV; the water cascaded vertically (slightly alarmingly) from a hole in the ceiling'. Housekeeping was 'slightly erratic' but turn-down 'worked like clockwork'. David Etchell-Johnson was appointed chef in April 2010; he serves seasonal menus, using produce from the hotel's farm, in the small dining room or the larger *Sunshine* restaurant with a conservatory, and the bar. Families are actively welcomed. (*Nigel and Jennifer Jee*)

High Street
Seaview PO34 5EX

T: 01983-612711
F: 01983-613729
E: reception@seaviewhotel.co.uk
W: www.seaviewhotel.co.uk

BEDROOMS: 28, 10 in annexe, 4 on ground floor, 1 suitable for &.
OPEN: all year except 21–27 Dec.
FACILITIES: lift, ramps, lounge, 2 bars, 2 dining rooms, treatment room, function room, patio, access to local sports club (swimming pool, gym, tennis, etc).
BACKGROUND MUSIC: none.
LOCATION: village centre.
CHILDREN: all ages welcomed.
DOGS: allowed in some bedrooms.
CREDIT CARDS: all major cards.
PRICES: [2010] B&B £62.50–£110 per person, full alc £35, 1-night bookings refused weekends Mar–Oct.

# SHAFTESBURY Dorset

Map 2:D1

## LA FLEUR DE LYS

In the centre of a historic town in the Vale of Blackmore, this former girls' boarding house has been run for 20 years as a restaurant-with-rooms by David Shepherd, Mary Griffin and Marc Preston. 'Still the perfect place for us to stay,' is this year's endorsement. Mary Griffin, 'who seems to run everything', is a cat enthusiast (feline ornaments are everywhere). The smart dining room overlooks a courtyard garden, where pre-dinner drinks (and afternoon tea) can be taken in warm weather. David Shepherd and Marc Preston serve modern dishes, eg, lime-marinated smoked salmon, smoked haddock mousse; honey-roasted breast of duck, broad beans, spring onions, piquant sauce. The bedrooms, each named after a grape variety (Shiraz, Riesling, etc), vary in style; one has a four-poster; another is suitable for a family. Superior rooms have flat-screen TV, sofa and laptop computer (Internet access is free). A visitor this year found a bed 'hard'. Breakfast has fresh orange juice, porridge, butter and marmalade in pots. Wine-tasting evenings are held. (*Peter Rogers, and others*)

Bleke Street
Shaftesbury SP7 8AW

T: 01747-853717
F: 01747-853130
E: info@lafleurdelys.co.uk
W: www.lafleurdelys.co.uk

BEDROOMS: 7, some on ground floor.
OPEN: all year, restaurant closed Sun night, midday Mon and Tues.
FACILITIES: lounge, bar, dining room, conference room, small courtyard.
BACKGROUND MUSIC: none.
LOCATION: edge of centre, car park.
CHILDREN: all ages welcomed.
DOGS: not allowed.
CREDIT CARDS: Amex, MasterCard, Visa.
PRICES: [2010] B&B £50–£75 per person, D,B&B £85–£100, set meals £25–£30, full alc £45, Christmas package.

# SHAFTESBURY Dorset

Map 2:D1

## HOTEL GROSVENOR    `NEW`

'Recommended without hesitation' by a regular correspondent, this Grade II listed Georgian coaching inn stands in the centre of the market town. Reopened in December 2009 after two years' renovation, it 'is now very "designer" modern, with excellent bedrooms and bathrooms, and a first-class restaurant'. John Crompton is the manager; 'staff are very helpful'. There is an intimate lounge; French doors open from the bar on to a courtyard with raised evergreen borders and olive trees: drinks can be taken here in warm weather. The bedrooms are individually designed: there are handmade beds, bespoke furniture, flat-screen TVs, iPod docks, free Wi-Fi access, coffee machines. Several rooms have fabrics by Cecil Beaton in homage to his Dorset connections. The Cranbourne Suite has the original fireplace, a lounger, and a bay window overlooking the courtyard. There are powerful rain showers; larger bedrooms have a freestanding bath. In the L-shaped *Greenhouse* restaurant (painted floorboards, modern art), Mark Treasure serves 'traditional European food for the modern palate', eg, ox cheek terrine; halibut, baby artichokes, aïoli, pesto. (*Richard Baker*)

The Commons
Shaftesbury SP7 8JA

T: 01747-850580
F: 01747-851883
E: reception@hotelgrosvenor.com
W: www.hotelgrosvenor.com

BEDROOMS: 16, 1 suitable for &.
OPEN: all year.
FACILITIES: lift, bar, lounge, restaurant, private dining room, ballroom, courtyard garden.
BACKGROUND MUSIC: in bar.
LOCATION: town centre.
CHILDREN: all ages welcomed.
DOGS: allowed, in bedrooms upon request.
CREDIT CARDS: Amex, MasterCard, Visa.
PRICES: [2010] B&B £62.50–£125 per person, full alc £35, website offers.

**25% DISCOUNT VOUCHERS**

# SHANKLIN Isle of Wight

## RYLSTONE MANOR

Within a small public park on a cliff-top above Sandown Bay, this Victorian gentleman's residence is run as a small traditional hotel by owners Mike and Carole Hailston. He handles bookings and 'will even sort out your ferry; she greeted us wearing an apron labelled "domestic goddess". Her kindness shines through this popular if old-fashioned place,' says a visitor this year. The green-walled lounge has books and ornaments; there are basket chairs in a Victorian covered patio. The well-furnished bedrooms, each named after an English tree, vary in size: they have 'chintz, striped wallpaper, teddy bears, magazines; a comfortable bed'. Mr Hailston, the chef, serves a short daily-changing menu of modern European dishes in the small dining room, perhaps porcini mushroom ravioli; sea bass with ratatouille. *Rylstone* has a 'secluded private garden, a pleasant place to sip wine on a summer afternoon'. Or you can join locals 'out for a stroll' in the park; a brass band might play in the nearby bandstand. Steep cliff steps lead down to fine beaches; the town is 20 minutes' walk away. (*David Berry*)

Rylstone Gardens
Popham Road, Shanklin
PO37 6RG

T/F: 01983-862806
E: rylstone.manor@btinternet.com
W: www.rylstone-manor.co.uk

BEDROOMS: 9.
OPEN: all year.
FACILITIES: drawing room, bar lounge, dining room, terrace, 1-acre garden in 4-acre public gardens, direct access to sand/shingle beach, unsuitable for &.
BACKGROUND MUSIC: classical, 'easy listening', in bar, restaurant.
LOCATION: Shanklin old village.
CHILDREN: not allowed.
DOGS: not allowed.
CREDIT CARDS: MasterCard, Visa.
PRICES: [2010] B&B £62.50–£67.50 per person, D,B&B £90–£95, set menu £27.50, website offers, Christmas package, 1-night bookings refused June–Aug (unless space permits).

**25% DISCOUNT VOUCHERS**

# SNETTISHAM Norfolk

Map 2:A4

## THE ROSE & CROWN

'A lovely old country pub in a pleasant Norfolk village', this 14th-century inn is owned by Jeannette and Anthony Goodrich; Kim Tinkler is the manager. 'The atmosphere is warm and relaxed; staff, although often busy, are unfailingly efficient,' says a visitor this year. 'The pub is crowded in the evenings, yet spotless in the mornings.' There are uneven floors, low beamed ceilings and a warren of twisting corridors. The bedrooms have been renovated in contemporary style. A room in the oldest section was 'spacious, thoughtfully decorated, with good lighting to compensate for the small windows. The carefully laid out bathroom had an excellent shower.' A room in an extension was 'nice, bright and clean; good notes by the owners on local attractions'. There is a residents' lounge with a log fire, three bars and three dining areas. 'We had delicious duck, perfectly cooked fish. Our vegetarian daughter found plenty of choice.' Breakfasts are 'generous and varied'. 'They were very caring of my mother's limited walking abilities.' The Goodriches also own *The Bank House*, King's Lynn (see entry). (*Michael and Eithne Dandy, Mary Hewson, Vivien Whitaker*)

Old Church Road, Snettisham
nr King's Lynn PE31 7LX

T: 01485-541382
F: 01485-543172
E: info@
  roseandcrownsnettisham.co.uk
W: www.roseandcrownsnettisham.
  co.uk

BEDROOMS: 16, 2 suitable for &.
OPEN: all year.
FACILITIES: ramp, garden room with guests' seating area, lounge, 3 bars, 3 dining areas, large walled garden (play fort, barbecue, heat lamps), beaches 5 and 10 mins' drive.
BACKGROUND MUSIC: none.
LOCATION: village centre, 4 miles S of Hunstanton.
CHILDREN: all ages welcomed.
DOGS: 'well-behaved' dogs allowed (extra charge).
CREDIT CARDS: Diners, MasterCard, Visa.
PRICES: [2010] B&B £47.50–£65 per person, D,B&B £67.50–£72.50, full alc £30, website breaks, Christmas/New Year packages, 1-night bookings occasionally refused Sat (supplement charged July/Aug).

# SOAR MILL COVE Devon

Map 1:E4

## SOAR MILL COVE HOTEL

Set in large grounds on the south Devon coast, and surrounded by 2,000 acres of National Trust land above an isolated cove, Keith Makepiece's single-storey hotel has long been popular with *Guide* readers. This year all the bedrooms have been refurbished, with new beds throughout and a 'lighter, fresher look'. They are equipped with DVD-player, flat-screen TV and free broadband Internet access. 'You tell us and we'll get it,' Mr Makepiece says about pillows and blankets. Forty new pieces of original artwork are on display. All the bedrooms open on to a terrace. Standards of welcome, housekeeping and food remain 'as high as ever', says a recent visitor. In the formal *Serendipity* restaurant, chef Ian MacDonald's menu might include fillet of turbot steamed over a lemon and ginger infusion. *Castaways*, a coffee bar, is for muddy paws and younger guests. Breakfast has an extensive choice; 'beautiful' marmalade. Families are welcome (small swimming pools, play areas, activity packs); the hotel is popular with older visitors off-season. (*Margaret H Box, and others*)

Soar Mill Cove
nr Salcombe TQ7 3DS

T: 01548-561566
F: 01548-561223
E: info@soarmillcove.co.uk
W: www.soarmillcove.co.uk

BEDROOMS: 22, all on ground floor.
OPEN: Mar–Nov.
FACILITIES: lounge, 2 bars, restaurant (pianist), coffee shop, indoor swimming pool (10 by 6 metres), treatment room (hairdressing, reflexology, aromatherapy, etc), civil wedding licence, 10-acre grounds (swimming pool, 10 by 7 metres, tennis, children's play area), sandy beach, 600 yds.
BACKGROUND MUSIC: occasional.
LOCATION: 3 miles SW of Salcombe.
CHILDREN: all ages welcomed.
DOGS: well-behaved small dogs allowed, but not in public rooms.
CREDIT CARDS: MasterCard, Visa.
PRICES: B&B £60–£120 per person, D,B&B £79–£149, full alc £45, Christmas/New Year packages, 1-night bookings sometimes refused.

# SOUTH ZEAL Devon

Map 1:C4

## THE OXENHAM ARMS

'We enjoyed our stay: the owner is welcoming, the public rooms are full of history and character; a good place for exploring Dartmoor.' Praise from an inspector in 2010 for Mark Payne's refurbished 500-year-old coaching inn (a scheduled ancient monument) in a pretty village. He has renovated with 'great attention to detail'. A granite Tudor porch opens into the white-painted interior; there is a beamed and panelled bar with log fire, mullioned windows; real ales. An oak staircase leads to the six bedrooms, each named after a rare-breed animal (Hebridean, Buff Orpington, Berkshire, etc). Three have a four-poster bed; all have Egyptian cotton sheets; the bed throws are woven from the wool of the owner's Hebridean sheep. This year there is a new beauty therapy room (the Green Room) with a variety of treatments. The Great Hall, with its huge granite fireplace, is the setting for *Burgoyne's* restaurant, where the daily-changing menu might include grilled garlic sardines, Provençal sauce; coq au vin with mashed potato. When possible, meat and vegetables are from the hotel's own farm, its new kitchen garden, and local producers.

South Zeal EX20 2JT

T: 01837-840244
F: 01837-840791
E: relax@theoxenhamarms.co.uk
W: www.theoxenhamarms.co.uk

BEDROOMS: 6.
OPEN: all year.
FACILITIES: 2 bar areas, 2 dining rooms, terrace, 3-acre garden, unsuitable for &.
BACKGROUND MUSIC: classical/soul/blues.
LOCATION: village centre, off A30 Exeter–Okehampton.
CHILDREN: all ages welcomed.
DOGS: not allowed in some bedrooms.
CREDIT CARDS: Amex, MasterCard, Visa.
PRICES: [2010] B&B £42.50–£120 per person, D,B&B £62.50–£140, full alc £30, Christmas/New Year packages.

**25% DISCOUNT VOUCHERS**

# STAMFORD Lincolnshire

Map 2:B3

## THE GEORGE

🏆 *César award in 1986*

'I frequently come here to relax, eat well, and be spoiled by attentive staff.' This year's praise for Lawrence Hoskins's 16th-century coaching inn in the centre of a lovely old market town long since bypassed by the A1. The busy public rooms have mullioned windows, antique oak panelling, creaking floorboards, cosy corners; good flower arrangements. Individually designed bedrooms have oak panels and furniture, patterned rugs, china plates on walls. A courtyard room has 'space for everything', a modern bathroom with power shower and bath. Early morning tea is delivered to the rooms, shoes are shined. Chris Pitman is manager and executive chef, supervising a range of meal styles. Men are asked to wear a jacket and tie in the oak-panelled *George* restaurant where the dishes are 'mainly traditional but with modern ideas', eg, fillet of beef, oxtail faggot, caramelised onion purée. The *Garden Room* has an extensive, more informal menu (fishcakes, pastas, curries), which in warmer weather can be taken in a courtyard with plants. (*Teresa Rubnikowicz*)

71 St Martins
Stamford PE9 2LB

T: 01780-750750
F: 01780-750701
E: reservations@
   georgehotelofstamford.com
W: www.georgehotelofstamford.com

BEDROOMS: 47.
OPEN: all year.
FACILITIES: ramps, 2 lounges, 2 bars, 2 restaurants, 4 private dining rooms, business centre, civil wedding licence, 2-acre grounds (courtyard, herb garden, monastery garden, croquet), only public areas suitable for ♿.
BACKGROUND MUSIC: none.
LOCATION: ½ mile from centre (front windows double glazed).
CHILDREN: all ages welcomed.
DOGS: allowed, but not unattended in bedrooms, only guide dogs in restaurants.
CREDIT CARDS: all major cards.
PRICES: [2010] B&B £70–£135 per person, full alc £55, seasonal breaks, 1-night bookings refused Sat.

# STANTON WICK Somerset

Map 1:B6

## THE CARPENTERS ARMS

'Much enjoyed' in 2010, this 'friendly' pub with rooms is in a peaceful hamlet in the Chew valley south of Bristol. The bar has 'a lovely big fire and large leather sofas; three real ales on tap and a good wine list'. The 'attractive' restaurant has 'good place settings', a traditional menu. 'The manager, Simon Pledge, took our order. The steaks were cooked as we had requested.' An 'immaculate' corridor lined with pictures leads to the modern bedrooms. 'Everything was pristine in our large room; light wood furnishings, a two-seater sofa, a tea tray with a Thermos of fresh milk (what a joy). Fluffy towels and a large bath in the bathroom.' The generous breakfast has 'freshly squeezed juices, cereals, yogurts, fresh fruit, and a well-presented full English'. Guests' cars are locked in a yard at night ('a bonus'). Children under 12 stay free in their parents' room. 'Good value; we will return.' (*Ian Malone*)

Stanton Wick, nr Pensford
BS39 4BX

T: 01761-490202
F: 01761-490763
E: carpenters@buccaneer.co.uk
W: www.the-carpenters-arms.co.uk

BEDROOMS: 12.
OPEN: all year except 25/26 Dec, 1 Jan at night.
FACILITIES: bar, 2 restaurants, function room, patio, unsuitable for &.
BACKGROUND MUSIC: none.
LOCATION: 8 miles S of Bristol, 8 miles W of Bath.
CHILDREN: all ages welcomed.
DOGS: allowed in bar and on patio only.
CREDIT CARDS: all major cards.
PRICES: [2010] B&B £52.50–£72.50 per person, D,B&B £69–£90, full alc £30, New Year package.

# STRATFORD-UPON-AVON Warwickshire     Map 3:D6

## CHERRY TREES     **NEW**

'Perfectly situated', south of the River Avon near a footbridge to the theatre, Gill and Phil Leonard's modern house is a 'revelation', says an inspector who has been searching 'for a decent B&B in the town' for 25 years. 'A friendly welcome from Gill, who gave us tea and delicious home-made cream scones.' The three bedrooms are all on the ground floor; two have direct access to the 'pretty, private' garden. 'Our room was positively huge; a large wardrobe with padded hangers, two armchairs, a small chaise longue and a flat-screen TV; off the bedroom was a small conservatory with a coffee table, chairs, a fridge with fresh milk. Patio doors opened on to the garden, a suntrap with a swing seat. Housekeeping could not have been better.' Breakfast, ordered the evening before, is served on the first floor: 'the usual cereals, yogurts and cooked dishes (very good bacon and scrambled eggs)'. The 'many thoughtful touches' were liked, eg, a notepad and pen for detailing any faulty items. Gill Leonard offers advice on local restaurants; *Malbec* on Union Street is recommended.

Swan's Nest Lane
Stratford-upon-Avon CV37 7LS

T: 01789-292989
E: gotocherrytrees@aol.com
W: www.cherrytrees-stratford.co.uk

BEDROOMS: 3, all on ground floor.
OPEN: all year.
FACILITIES: breakfast room, garden.
BACKGROUND MUSIC: in breakfast room.
LOCATION: central, near river.
CHILDREN: not under 16.
DOGS: not allowed.
CREDIT CARDS: (*5% surcharge*) MasterCard, Visa.
PRICES: [2010] B&B £47.50–£57.50 per person, special offers, 1-night bookings refused Sat.

# STRATFORD-UPON-AVON Warwickshire　　Map 3:D6

## WHITE SAILS　**NEW**

Recommended for its 'unassuming excellence', this former nursing home has been rejuvenated by Roy and Janet Emerson as an upmarket B&B. They are 'particularly helpful and have good local knowledge', says the nominator. The four bedrooms are 'of first-class quality, luxuriously fitted, comfortable bed, spotlessly clean'. The largest, Superb Stratford, is decorated in cream and white; its bathroom has a freestanding Victorian bath, and a walk-in deluge shower. Warwick, in burgundy and cream, has a four-poster bed, a black-and-white bathroom with a freestanding bath and a separate power shower. All rooms have a fridge with fresh milk, mineral water; air conditioning, double glazing (two face the road at the front). Original paintings and bronze sculptures are displayed throughout. Complimentary sherry is available in the guest lounge. The award-winning breakfast ('the best ever') has a lavish buffet with cereals, yogurt, home-baked bread, and fruit (plums with honey and cinnamon). Cooked dishes include toasted raisin bread with cinnamon sugar and apple slices. The town centre is a 15-minute walk (buses pass the door). (*John and Sara Leathes*)

85 Evesham Road
Stratford-upon-Avon CV37 9BE

T: 01789-264326
E: enquiries@white-sails.co.uk
W: www.white-sails.co.uk

BEDROOMS: 4.
OPEN: all year except Jan, Feb.
FACILITIES: lounge, dining room, garden (summer house).
BACKGROUND MUSIC: none.
LOCATION: 1 mile W of centre.
CHILDREN: not under 12.
DOGS: not allowed.
CREDIT CARDS: MasterCard, Visa (*1½ % surcharge*).
PRICES: B&B £47.50–£60 per person, 1-night bookings sometimes refused.

# STUCKTON Hampshire

## THE THREE LIONS INN

'Charming people', Mike and Jayne Womersley run their restaurant-with-rooms in a quiet rural setting on the northern boundary of the New Forest national park. He is the 'superb' chef; her 'friendly and welcoming manner permeates through to the staff', says a visitor this year. Originally a farmhouse, the main building has a bar, a narrow lounge area and a 'pretty' dining room with a 'wonderful' conservatory; oak tables, tulles chairs; a 'beautiful Turkish carpet'. Mr Womersley's 'delicious' French/English dishes are chosen from a portable blackboard menu; these might include galette of smoked haddock; local venison and chanterelles. Bedrooms, some on the ground floor, are in adjacent buildings. Four are in a chalet-style building with easy access to the pleasant garden. 'Our room, recently refurbished and with a new carpet, was most comfortable.' Continental breakfast is included in the room rate; full English ('one of the best ever') is available for an extra charge. Readers advise confirming your arrival time, as access is limited outside restaurant opening times. The Womersleys say 'children will find a genuine welcome'. (*Miranda Mackintosh, Michael John Cross, and others*)

Stuckton, nr Fordingbridge
SP6 2HF

T: 01425-652489
F: 01425-656144
E: the3lions@btinternet.com
W: www.thethreelionsrestaurant.
   co.uk

BEDROOMS: 7, 4 in courtyard block on ground floor.
OPEN: all year except last 2 weeks Feb, restaurant closed Sun night/Mon.
FACILITIES: ramps, conservatory, meeting/sitting room, public bar, restaurant, 2½-acre garden (sauna, whirlpool).
BACKGROUND MUSIC: in bar.
LOCATION: 2 miles E of Fordingbridge.
CHILDREN: all ages welcomed.
DOGS: not allowed in bar, restaurant.
CREDIT CARDS: MasterCard, Visa.
PRICES: B&B £40–£79 per person, cooked breakfast £7.75, set dinner £24.50, full alc £45–£50, special breaks.

**25% DISCOUNT VOUCHERS**

# STURMINSTER NEWTON Dorset

Map 2:E1

## PLUMBER MANOR

*César award in 1987*

The Dawlish stream, a tributary of the River Stour, runs through the grounds of this mellow brick-and-stone manor house, which has been the family home of the Prideaux-Brunes since it was built in the early 17th century. It has long been run as a restaurant-with-rooms by Richard Prideaux-Brune, his wife, Alison, and brother, Brian (the chef). The public rooms are furnished in traditional style (one visitor this year thought them dated) with antiques, contemporary works of art, open fires. A daily-changing menu of English/French dishes is served in three dining rooms: it might include wild mushroom millefeuille, brandy, basil and cream; guineafowl, black cherries and cinnamon. 'Excellent food and good service,' said a recent report. Bedrooms in the main house are approached from a gallery hung with family portraits. Others (newer and larger) are in a converted barn around a courtyard; these have window seats overlooking the river and the topiary garden. The Hardy Way leads from the door. Pets can stay in four courtyard rooms. (*Roger Rowson, JC, and others*)

Sturminster Newton DT10 2AF

T: 01258-472507
F: 01258-473370
E: book@plumbermanor.co.uk
W: www.plumbermanor.co.uk

BEDROOMS: 16, 10 on ground floor in courtyard.
OPEN: all year except Feb.
FACILITIES: lounge, bar, 3 dining rooms, gallery, 5-acre grounds (garden, tennis, croquet, stream).
BACKGROUND MUSIC: none.
LOCATION: 3 miles SW of Sturminster Newton.
CHILDREN: all ages welcomed.
DOGS: allowed in 4 bedrooms, not in public rooms.
CREDIT CARDS: all major cards.
PRICES: [2010] B&B £62.50–£95 per person, set dinner £26–£30.

# SWAFFHAM Norfolk

Map 2:B5

## STRATTONS

♔ *César award in 2003*

Very green, 'but at the opposite end of the scale to spartan', Vanessa and Les Scott's Grade II listed Palladian-style villa has a rural feel though it is near the centre of the old market town. The Scotts' daughter Hannah is the manager with Dominic Hughes. In 2010 they added two bedrooms and two self-contained apartments in a conversion of an old print workshop near the entrance. This building also houses *CoCoes*, a café/deli serving light meals from 8 am to 7 pm. The bedrooms have exotic themes: Opium has a bed flanked with Doric columns, and a bath big enough for two; Boudoir is sensual with a Parisian feel; the Red Room has rich fabrics. In the lounge are original paintings, sculptures and ornaments. In the *Rustic* restaurant, new chef Simon Linacre-Marshall serves modern dishes, eg, Tuscan bean risotto; beef fillet with a morel mushroom ragout. The 'excellent' breakfast has freshly squeezed juices, free-range eggs (from bantams in the garden), home-made breads. More reports, please.

4 Ash Close
Swaffham PE37 7NH

T: 01760-723845
F: 01760-720458
E: enquiries@strattonshotel.com
W: www.strattonshotel.com

BEDROOMS: 12, 4 in annexes, 2 on ground floor, plus 2 self-contained apartments.
OPEN: all year except 24–26 Dec.
FACILITIES: drawing room, reading room, restaurant, terrace, 1-acre garden, unsuitable for &.
BACKGROUND MUSIC: in restaurant.
LOCATION: central, parking.
CHILDREN: all ages welcomed.
DOGS: allowed in some bedrooms but not unaccompanied, not allowed in restaurant, and 'must be kept on lead' in grounds.
CREDIT CARDS: MasterCard, Visa.
PRICES: [2010] B&B £67.50–£125 per person, D,B&B £107.50–£150, full alc £50, special breaks, New Year package, 1-night bookings refused weekends, bank holidays.

# TARRANT LAUNCESTON Dorset

Map 2:E1

## LAUNCESTON FARM  `NEW`

On a working farm with an organic beef herd, Sarah Worrall and her family welcome visitors to their farmhouse, which has been stylishly renovated. Her son, Jimi, runs the farm; her daughter, Eve, is 'gardener, forager and grower of all things delicious'. 'It stands out because of the quality of the experience,' says the nominator. 'We were given home-made cakes and tea by an open fire on arrival. Our lovely bedroom had a slipper bath at the end of a gilt-framed bed; there were Fairtrade teas and coffee, organic toiletries. My husband was happy with the flat-screen TV and Wi-Fi access.' Mrs Worrall serves a two-course meal of 'wholesome' dishes (eg, venison pie, farm vegetables) on two evenings a week: a communal affair in the dining room. Breakfast, also communal, is taken in a converted cart shed. 'Gorgeous: home-pressed apple juice; locally produced bacon and sausages; farm eggs and mushrooms.' Jimi Worrall gives tours of the property ('we came away understanding how an organic farm works'). In summer visitors may use a heated outdoor swimming pool. (*Lynn Mason*)

Tarrant Launceston
nr Blandford Forum DT11 8BY

T: 01258-830528
E: info@launcestonfarm.co.uk
W: www.launcestonfarm.co.uk

BEDROOMS: 6.
OPEN: all year except 19–26 Dec.
FACILITIES: 2 lounges, dining room, breakfast room, terrace, 1-acre walled garden, heated outdoor swimming pool (5 by 10 metres, summer only), unsuitable for &.
BACKGROUND MUSIC: classical during breakfast.
LOCATION: 5 miles NE of Blandford Forum.
CHILDREN: not under 12.
DOGS: not allowed in house.
CREDIT CARDS: none.
PRICES: [2010] B&B £37.50–£100 per person, set meals (2 courses) £20, full alc £45, 1-night bookings refused weekends May–Sept.

# TAUNTON Somerset

Map 1:C5

## THE CASTLE AT TAUNTON

*César award in 1987*

A West Country institution, this wisteria-covered, castellated hotel, once a Norman fortress, and an inn since the 12th century, has been in the Chapman family's hands for more than 60 years. Kit and Louise Chapman are in charge; Kevin McCarthy is the long-serving manager. The bedrooms, reached by a fine wrought iron staircase, have been individually decorated by Mrs Chapman to create 'warmth and a sense of welcome; throw off your shoes and put your feet up'. A penthouse terrace has a suite with a roof garden; all rooms have flat-screen TV, free Wi-Fi, tea/coffee-making facilities. There are fresh flowers, tapestries, paintings and old oak furniture in the public rooms. In the formal L-shaped restaurant the chef, Richard Guest, sources ingredients from West Country suppliers for his seasonal menus, perhaps seared Brixham scallops, apple and blood orange salad; Woolley Farm guineafowl, red cabbage. *Brazz*, an 'unbuttoned' brasserie/bar/café, has lighter dishes (fishcakes, pasta, salads, etc). Regular events, including musical evenings and an annual garden party, are held. More reports, please.

Castle Green
Taunton TA1 1NF

T: 01823-272671
F: 01823-336066
E: reception@the-castle-hotel.com
W: www.the-castle-hotel.com

BEDROOMS: 44.
OPEN: all year, restaurant closed Sun and Mon.
FACILITIES: lift, ramps, lounge, bar, restaurant, brasserie, private dining/meeting rooms, civil wedding licence, 1-acre garden, shop.
BACKGROUND MUSIC: in bar and brasserie.
LOCATION: central.
CHILDREN: all ages welcomed.
DOGS: small 'well-behaved' dogs allowed, not in public rooms.
CREDIT CARDS: all major cards.
PRICES: [2010] B&B £97.50–£150.50 per person, D,B&B £124.50–£147.50, full alc £55, special breaks, Christmas/New Year packages.

**25% DISCOUNT VOUCHERS**

## TEFFONT EVIAS Wiltshire

Map 2:D1

### HOWARD'S HOUSE

*César award in 2010*

In a fold between high Wiltshire hills, this mellow stone dower house is in a village of Hansel and Gretel houses reached by small bridges across the River Neff. Independently owned, and managed by Noële Thompson, it is 'delightful, peaceful, relaxing, personal', says a visitor this year. 'The staff are courteous, public rooms are welcoming,' say other guests. The good-sized bedrooms are 'like a spare room in a private home, not at all designery'; they have pastel colours, floral curtains. 'Not my sort of pigeon, but I can understand its appeal,' said a visitor who thought his room 'average, with (to be fair) a great outlook'. Bathrooms have been renovated this year. There are log fires, fresh flowers in the beamed lounge. The chef, Nick Wentworth, serves modern dishes: 'Our meals were interesting, beautifully cooked; wonderful local venison, delicious orange soufflé.' 'Background music was turned off when we asked.' Breakfast 'was first rate – especially the mushroom tartlet and kippers'. (*Susi Batty, John and Cherry Hopkins, and others*)

Teffont Evias
nr Salisbury SP3 5RJ

T: 01722-716392
F: 01722-716820
E: enq@howardshousehotel.co.uk
W: www.howardshousehotel.co.uk

BEDROOMS: 9.
OPEN: all year, exclusive bookings in Christmas week.
FACILITIES: lounge, restaurant, 2-acre grounds (croquet), river, fishing nearby, unsuitable for &.
BACKGROUND MUSIC: 'easy listening' ('requests when possible').
LOCATION: 10 miles W of Salisbury.
CHILDREN: all ages welcomed.
DOGS: allowed (£10 surcharge in rooms).
CREDIT CARDS: Amex, MasterCard, Visa.
PRICES: [2010] B&B £87.50–£137.50 per person, full alc £45, winter breaks, New Year package.

**25% DISCOUNT VOUCHERS**

# TEIGNMOUTH Devon

Map 1:D5

## THOMAS LUNY HOUSE

Built by the marine artist Thomas Luny, this attractive Georgian house in the town centre is run as a B&B by the 'charming' owners, John and Alison Allan. Set back from the street, it stands in a walled courtyard reached by an archway that requires care when driving through. Readers have long liked the elegance and continuing high standards. Visitors are greeted with afternoon tea with home-baked cake, which can be taken in the bedroom, in the drawing room (with open fires, antique furniture, comfortable sofas) or in summer in the walled garden. Each of the bedrooms has a theme: the Luny Room is nautical, mirroring the artist; the Clairmont has an Edwardian feel; the Chinese has hand-painted oriental furniture and a canopy bed; the smaller Bitton is dominated by a four-poster. Old wooden chests are used as luggage racks, and also hold spare blankets. Breakfast has freshly squeezed orange juice, home-made bread, toast and preserves, leaf tea; cooked dishes include often-praised scrambled eggs. Early morning tea and a newspaper can be delivered to the room. More reports, please.

Teign Street
Teignmouth TQ14 8EG

T: 01626-772976
E: alisonandjohn@
   thomas-luny-house.co.uk
W: www.thomas-luny-house.co.uk

BEDROOMS: 4.
OPEN: all year, except early Jan–mid-Feb.
FACILITIES: 2 lounges, breakfast room, small walled garden, sea (sandy beach 5 mins' walk), unsuitable for &.
BACKGROUND MUSIC: none.
LOCATION: town centre.
CHILDREN: not under 12.
DOGS: not allowed.
CREDIT CARDS: MasterCard, Visa.
PRICES: [2010] B&B £37.50–£70 per person, 1-night bookings sometimes refused.

# TEMPLE SOWERBY Cumbria

Map 4: inset C3

## TEMPLE SOWERBY HOUSE

'Cumbria's best-kept secret,' according to a visitor this year, is Paul and Julie Evans's popular country hotel in the Eden valley between the Pennines and the Lake District. Originally the principal residence in this conservation village, the Grade II listed brick-fronted house has thick walls and a Georgian wing. The Evanses are 'exceptional hosts; the delightful staff make it an enjoyable place. We couldn't have been better looked after.' The conservatory-style restaurant faces the walled garden which yields herbs and vegetables for the imaginative menus of the chef, Ashley Whittaker. He offers a choice of six dishes (perhaps pan-roasted topside, beetroot mash, chocolate, orange and port sauce) for each course. 'Everything was perfectly prepared and utterly delicious.' The interesting wine list has 'sensible' prices. The bedrooms are in the house or a coach house, where dogs are welcome. 'Superior' ones have views; 'classic' rooms are smaller. 'Breakfast is superb; none of this buffet nonsense.' It includes 'delicious bread and rolls', 'unwrapped butter'. (*Jennifer Black, and others*)

Temple Sowerby
Penrith CA10 1RZ

T: 017683-61578
F: 017683-61958
E: stay@templesowerby.com
W: www.templesowerby.com

BEDROOMS: 12, 2 on ground floor, 4 in coach house (20 yds).
OPEN: all year except 19–29 Dec.
FACILITIES: 2 lounges, bar, restaurant, conference/function facilities, civil wedding licence, 2-acre garden (croquet).
BACKGROUND MUSIC: in restaurant at night.
LOCATION: village centre.
CHILDREN: not under 12.
DOGS: by prior arrangement, not allowed in public rooms.
CREDIT CARDS: Amex, MasterCard, Visa.
PRICES: [2010] B&B £62.50–£75 per person, D,B&B £80–£110, alc £48, special breaks, New Year package, 1-night bookings occasionally refused.

**25% DISCOUNT VOUCHERS**

# TETBURY Gloucestershire

Map 3:E5

## CALCOT MANOR

*César award in 2001*

'All is serene and orderly,' says a visitor in 2010 to this 'civilised' Cotswold hotel with extensive facilities for adults and children. The converted 14th-century farmhouse, with surrounding cottages and outbuildings, is run by Richard Ball, managing director. His wife, Cathy, is in charge of the spa, which has a large indoor swimming pool and an outdoor hot tub. Couples have 'lovely' bedrooms in the manor. Families stay in courtyard suites which have a double bedroom and a sitting room with bunks or a sofa bed. There is an Ofsted-registered playzone for the very youngest; older children have *Mez* in a converted barn with games and a small cinema. Special times are allocated for children in the spa. There are two styles of dining. Chef Michael Croft serves modern British food in the 'light and airy' *Conservatory*, eg, wood-roasted brill, red wine sauce. Families are more likely to gather in the *Gumstool Inn* which has a more informal atmosphere and menu. *Barnsley House*, in nearby Barnsley (see entry), is now under the same ownership. (*Dr Alec Frank*)

nr Tetbury GL8 8YJ

T: 01666-890391
F: 01666-890394
E: reception@calcotmanor.co.uk
W: www.calcotmanor.co.uk

BEDROOMS: 35, 10 (family) in cottage, 11 around courtyard, on ground floor.
OPEN: all year.
FACILITIES: ramps, lounge, 2 restaurants, 2 bars, private dining room, cinema, crèche, civil wedding licence, 220-acre grounds (tennis, heated outdoor 8-metre swimming pool, children's play area, spa with 16-metre swimming pool).
BACKGROUND MUSIC: in restaurants.
LOCATION: 3 miles W of Tetbury.
CHILDREN: all ages welcomed.
DOGS: allowed in courtyard bedrooms.
CREDIT CARDS: all major cards.
PRICES: [2010] B&B £120–£220 per person, D,B&B (min. 2 nights midweek) £150–£262.50, 2-day breaks, Christmas/New Year packages, 1-night bookings sometimes refused weekends.

# TITCHWELL Norfolk

Map 2:A5

## TITCHWELL MANOR

Close to the RSPB reserve at Titchwell Marsh, Margaret and Ian Snaith's small hotel/restaurant is popular with birdwatchers (including the BBC *Springwatch* team who stay when filming). The bar was redesigned in 2010 to create a new informal dining area, the *Eating Rooms*, with bright patterns, gilt mirrors and retro chairs. In the conservatory restaurant, which faces the walled garden, the Snaiths' son, Eric, has a seven-course modern European menu using local produce for his seasonal dishes. We would welcome reports on the new style of cooking. A recent visitor praised the 'excellent hands-on management' of the owners, and the 'efficient' staff. The public rooms have Lloyd Loom chairs, mosaic tiled floor, dark woodwork. The bedrooms are decorated in a seaside style, with painted slatted wood walls and earthy colours, patterned wallpapers, seascape art and modern lamps. 'Our room was comfortable and clean; it was well equipped with thoughtful extras.' The newest rooms are around the pretty garden; two are equipped for disabled visitors. Midweek birdwatching breaks are organised. (*DV*)

Titchwell, nr Brancaster
PE31 8BB

T: 01485-210221
F: 01485-210104
E: reception@titchwellmanor.com
W: www.titchwellmanor.com

BEDROOMS: 27, 16 on ground floor, in herb garden, 2 suitable for &.
OPEN: all year.
FACILITIES: 2 lounges, bar, restaurant, civil wedding licence, ½-acre garden (beaches, golf nearby).
BACKGROUND MUSIC: in public rooms.
LOCATION: on coast road, 5 miles E of Hunstanton.
CHILDREN: all ages welcomed except under-14s at Christmas.
DOGS: allowed in bar, bedrooms.
CREDIT CARDS: MasterCard, Visa.
PRICES: [2010] B&B £55–£125 per person, D,B&B (min. 2 nights) £75–£97.50, full alc £40, midweek breaks, Christmas/New Year packages, 1-night bookings sometimes refused Sat.

# TITLEY Herefordshire

Map 3:C4

## THE STAGG INN

In a small, straggling village in lovely Herefordshire countryside, this white-fronted old inn was one of the first pubs in Britain to be awarded a *Michelin* star. It is 'thoroughly civilised' but also unpretentious. The hosts, Steve and Nicola Reynolds, are 'thoughtful', their welcome is 'warm'. Three bedrooms above the bar are 'bright, heavily beamed'. Three 'spacious' rooms are down the road, in a listed Georgian ex-vicarage backed by a garden where chickens and pets roam. Vegetables and herbs come from the vicarage garden, and pigs are kept on nearby land. The restaurant is spread across a series of stepped areas with country-style wooden tables and simple upholstered chairs. There is no background music ('you can join the conversation,' say the Reynoldses). The cooking style is modern (eg, belly of Middle-White pork, bean and chorizo casserole). The sausages, black pudding, chorizo and salamis are made on the premises. A bar snack menu is also available. Breakfast has home-baked bread, home-made preserves, 'a large chunk of butter', 'excellent scrambled eggs'. (*JAF, JM*)

Titley, nr Kington HR5 3RL

T: 01544-230221
F: 01544-231390
E: reservations@thestagg.co.uk
W: www.thestagg.co.uk

BEDROOMS: 6, 3 at *Old Vicarage* (300 yds).
OPEN: all year except Sun night/Mon, 25/26 Dec, 2 weeks Jan/Feb, first 2 weeks Nov.
FACILITIES: (*Old Vicarage*) sitting room, 1½-acre garden, (*Stagg Inn*) bar, restaurant areas, small garden, unsuitable for &.
BACKGROUND MUSIC: none.
LOCATION: on B4355 between Kington (3½ miles) and Presteigne.
CHILDREN: all ages welcomed.
DOGS: allowed in pub only.
CREDIT CARDS: MasterCard, Visa.
PRICES: B&B £45–£65 per person, full alc £32, 1-night bookings sometimes refused Sat.

25% DISCOUNT VOUCHERS

# ULLSWATER Cumbria

Map 4: inset C2

## HOWTOWN HOTEL

*César award in 1991*

For more than a century, the Baldry family have welcomed visitors to their unsophisticated hotel in a small hamlet on the quiet eastern shore of Lake Ullswater. Jacquie Baldry runs it in relaxed style with her son, David. Some of the house's style may border on the quirky, but *Guide* readers have long liked the simple virtues and the lack of frills. 'We still maintain our traditional ways,' says Mrs Baldry, 'though mobile phone reception is getting ever nearer.' There is no phone, TV or radio in the simple bedrooms, most of which have lake views. All have a private bathroom; four are across a corridor. A gong summons guests to dinner at 7 pm for traditional food from a short four-course menu: 'No surprises, but generally good,' is a recent comment. On Sunday there is a set lunch and a cold supper. The 'generous' breakfast, also announced by a gong, is at 9 am. Popular with walkers (a car-free holiday is possible), who can ask for a substantial picnic. (*PEC, and others*)

Ullswater, nr Penrith CA10 2ND

T: 01768-486514
W: www.howtown-hotel.com

BEDROOMS: 13, 4 in annexe, 4 self-catering cottages for weekly rent.
OPEN: Mar–1 Nov.
FACILITIES: 3 lounges, TV room, 2 bars, dining room, 2-acre grounds, 200 yds from lake (private foreshore, fishing), walking, sailing, climbing, riding, golf nearby, unsuitable for &.
BACKGROUND MUSIC: none.
LOCATION: 4 miles S of Pooley Bridge, bus from Penrith station 9 miles.
CHILDREN: all ages welcomed (no special facilities).
DOGS: not allowed in public rooms.
CREDIT CARDS: none.
PRICES: [2010] D,B&B £71–£80 per person, set dinner £23.50, 1-night bookings sometimes refused.

# ULVERSTON Cumbria

Map 4: inset C2

## THE BAY HORSE

*♥César award in 2009*

'Wonderfully situated, with ever-changing views' across tidal Morecambe Bay, this old inn is liked for the 'good value' and friendly staff. The owner/chef, Robert Lyons, and manageress, Lesley Wheeler, are 'unobtrusive, professional'. They tell us that several bedrooms have been redecorated this year; all have been given a new bed, wall-mounted flat-screen TV and tea-making facilities ('we still give the option of a freshly prepared tray'). The rooms are small; six front ones open on to a terrace overlooking the bay ('a great asset'). Guests take drinks in the busy bar (popular with locals) before dining in the panoramic conservatory restaurant (also redecorated this year). The cooking is much admired: Mr Lyons offers a fixed-price menu or a seasonal carte with dishes like Lakeland lamb shank braised with orange, ginger and red wine. 'We were struck by the wide choice of vegetarian courses. Much use is made of cream.' Nothing is packaged for the 'exemplary' breakfast menu (no buffet): 'fruit, good cooked dishes, leaf tea'. (*John and Theresa Stewart, and others*)

Canal Foot
Ulverston LA12 9EL

**T:** 01229-583972
**F:** 01229-580502
**E:** reservations@
     thebayhorsehotel.co.uk
**W:** www.thebayhorsehotel.co.uk

BEDROOMS: 9.
OPEN: all year, restaurant closed Mon midday (light bar meals available).
FACILITIES: bar lounge, restaurant, picnic area, unsuitable for &.
BACKGROUND MUSIC: classical/'easy listening'.
LOCATION: 8 miles NE of Barrow-in-Furness.
CHILDREN: not under 10.
DOGS: not allowed in restaurant.
CREDIT CARDS: Amex, MasterCard, Visa.
PRICES: B&B £45–£60 per person, full alc £45, bargain breaks, cookery courses, Christmas/New Year packages.

**25% DISCOUNT VOUCHERS**

# VENTNOR Isle of Wight

Map 2:E2

## THE HAMBROUGH

**NEW**

High above the harbour, this three-storey Victorian villa has been restored as a restaurant-with-rooms with 'confidence and panache' by chef/patron Robert Thompson. With a *Michelin* star for his cooking, he is a 'hands-on owner', says a visitor this year. 'Dinner, the main reason to come, did not disappoint: a foie gras starter was a revelation; a symphony of grouse brought out the unusual taste of the bird. Breads were wonderful, as were the breakfasts.' A small guest lounge at the back faces an 'uninspiring' garden. The large bedrooms are decorated in contemporary neutral colours. 'We stayed in one of the two rooms at the front with a balcony. The view was splendid with the Channel glistening in the sun. The bedlinen was good, the mattress firm.' Two rooms have large sea-facing windows; other rooms have restricted views. All have espresso machines, free Wi-Fi; impeccable bathrooms. 'The youngish staff seem proud of their work. When we returned late, they delivered a glass of wine and a pot of tea to our room.' (*David Berry*)

Hambrough Road
Ventnor PO38 1SQ

T: 01983-856333
F: 01983-857260
E: info@thehambrough.com
W: www.thehambrough.com

BEDROOMS: 7, plus five-bedroom villa.
OPEN: all year except New Year, 10 days April, 2 weeks Nov, restaurant closed Mon, certain Sundays.
FACILITIES: lounge, restaurant, small patio garden, unsuitable for &.
BACKGROUND MUSIC: mellow in restaurant and lounge.
LOCATION: S end of Ventnor Bay.
CHILDREN: all ages welcomed.
DOGS: not allowed.
CREDIT CARDS: MasterCard, Visa.
PRICES: [2010] B&B £85–£150 per person, D,B&B £140–£205, tasting menu £70, full alc £70, Christmas package.

# VERYAN-IN-ROSELAND Cornwall

Map 1:D2

## THE NARE

◊ *César award in 2003*

'It's good to find such service and cheerfulness in a hotel,' says a visitor this year about Toby Ashworth's luxury hotel (Pride of Britain) above a beach on Gerrans Bay. He is 'attentive, charming'. Other praise: 'As we drew up outside, the car's passenger door was opened by a young lady who greeted my wife by name.' The sea-facing bedrooms are generally spacious; some have a balcony or terrace. 'Country view' rooms tend to be smaller. 'Our suite was well appointed, with lovely furniture and a comfortable bed; the bath was too short for a six-footer.' 'It was nice to find a decanter of our favourite sherry in our room,' said returning visitors. 'The only snag is the cost, though you get what you pay for.' Men are asked to wear a jacket and tie in the main dining room, which has sea views on three sides. Richard James offers a daily-changing set dinner menu with hors d'oeuvres from a trolley. The less formal *Quarterdeck* has a carte with dishes like turbot fillet, celeriac purée, cèpes and pancetta. Children are welcomed. (*JR Shrimpton, Joanna Russell, HJM Tucker, and others*)

Carne Beach
Veryan-in-Roseland
nr Truro TR2 5PF

T: 01872-501111
F: 01872-501856
E: reservations@narehotel.co.uk
W: www.narehotel.co.uk

BEDROOMS: 37, some on ground floor, 1 in adjoining cottage, 5 suitable for &.
OPEN: all year.
FACILITIES: lift, ramps, lounge, drawing room, sun lounge, bar, billiard room, light lunch/supper room, 2 restaurants, conservatory, indoor swimming pool, gym, 2-acre grounds (heated swimming pool, tennis, safe sandy beach), concessionary golf at Truro golf club.
BACKGROUND MUSIC: none.
LOCATION: S of Veryan, on coast.
CHILDREN: all ages welcomed.
DOGS: not allowed in public rooms.
CREDIT CARDS: MasterCard, Visa.
PRICES: [2010] B&B £125–£356 per person, D,B&B £140–£371, set dinner £48, special breaks, Christmas/New Year packages.

# WADDESDON Buckinghamshire

Map 2:C3

## THE FIVE ARROWS　NEW

Built in 1887 to house the craftsmen working on Waddesdon Manor for the Rothschild family, this Grade II listed hotel is owned (like the Manor) by the National Trust, and managed by Alex McEwen. 'It is a delight,' says an inspector, 'with relaxed and welcoming service by helpful staff of various nationalities.' The exterior is striking: a patterned tiled roof, half-timbering, wrought ironwork, ornate chimney stacks. 'Our bedroom was reasonably sized, painted in subtle yellow, with a comfortable large bed, white-painted fitted wardrobes, cupboards and dressing table. The shower room was tiled from floor to ceiling; a huge shower with a raindance shower head.' The dining room is divided into three sections: 'Ours, with high-backed tapestry chairs, and a wall covered with books, felt like an intimate library. The main courses were superb; succulent sea bream and linguine; tender rib-eye steak with wild mushrooms and roasted garlic. Handmade chips in a mini-copper pan were the best ever. After these delights, breakfast seemed ordinary: unpackaged butter and jams; good coffee; dry toast and muffins.' National Trust members qualify for a 10% discount on B&B rates.

High Street
Waddesdon HP18 0JE

T: 01296-651727
F: 01296-655716
E: five.arrows@nationaltrust.org.uk
W: www.thefivearrows.co.uk

BEDROOMS: 11, 3, in courtyard, on ground floor.
OPEN: all year.
FACILITIES: bar, restaurant, civil wedding licence, garden.
BACKGROUND MUSIC: none.
LOCATION: in village.
CHILDREN: all ages welcomed.
DOGS: not allowed in bedrooms.
CREDIT CARDS: Amex, MasterCard, Visa.
PRICES: [2010] B&B £63–£175 per person, D,B&B £80–£250, full alc £40–£50, special offers, 1-night bookings sometimes refused.

**25% DISCOUNT VOUCHERS**

# 25%
## DISCOUNT VOUCHER

### THE GOOD HOTEL GUIDE 2011
Use this voucher to claim a 25% discount off the normal price for bed and breakfast at hotels with a `25% DISCOUNT VOUCHERS` sign at the end of the entry. **You must request a voucher discount at the time of booking and present this voucher on arrival. Further details and conditions overleaf.** Valid to 18th October 2011.

# 25%
## DISCOUNT VOUCHER

### THE GOOD HOTEL GUIDE 2011
Use this voucher to claim a 25% discount off the normal price for bed and breakfast at hotels with a `25% DISCOUNT VOUCHERS` sign at the end of the entry. **You must request a voucher discount at the time of booking and present this voucher on arrival. Further details and conditions overleaf.** Valid to 18th October 2011.

# 25%
## DISCOUNT VOUCHER

### THE GOOD HOTEL GUIDE 2011
Use this voucher to claim a 25% discount off the normal price for bed and breakfast at hotels with a `25% DISCOUNT VOUCHERS` sign at the end of the entry. **You must request a voucher discount at the time of booking and present this voucher on arrival. Further details and conditions overleaf.** Valid to 18th October 2011.

# 25%
## DISCOUNT VOUCHER

### THE GOOD HOTEL GUIDE 2011
Use this voucher to claim a 25% discount off the normal price for bed and breakfast at hotels with a `25% DISCOUNT VOUCHERS` sign at the end of the entry. **You must request a voucher discount at the time of booking and present this voucher on arrival. Further details and conditions overleaf.** Valid to 18th October 2011.

# 25%
## DISCOUNT VOUCHER

### THE GOOD HOTEL GUIDE 2011
Use this voucher to claim a 25% discount off the normal price for bed and breakfast at hotels with a `25% DISCOUNT VOUCHERS` sign at the end of the entry. **You must request a voucher discount at the time of booking and present this voucher on arrival. Further details and conditions overleaf.** Valid to 18th October 2011.

# 25%
## DISCOUNT VOUCHER

### THE GOOD HOTEL GUIDE 2011
Use this voucher to claim a 25% discount off the normal price for bed and breakfast at hotels with a `25% DISCOUNT VOUCHERS` sign at the end of the entry. **You must request a voucher discount at the time of booking and present this voucher on arrival. Further details and conditions overleaf.** Valid to 18th October 2011.

**CONDITIONS** **CONDITIONS**

1. Hotels with a **25% DISCOUNT VOUCHERS** sign have agreed to give readers a discount of 25% off their normal bed-and-breakfast rate.
2. One voucher is good for a single-night stay only, at the discounted rate for yourself alone or for you and a partner sharing a double room.
3. Hotels may decline to accept a voucher reservation if they expect to be fully booked at the full room price.

---

**CONDITIONS**

1. Hotels with a **25% DISCOUNT VOUCHERS** sign have agreed to give readers a discount of 25% off their normal bed-and-breakfast rate.
2. One voucher is good for a single-night stay only, at the discounted rate for yourself alone or for you and a partner sharing a double room.
3. Hotels may decline to accept a voucher reservation if they expect to be fully booked at the full room price.

---

**CONDITIONS**

1. Hotels with a **25% DISCOUNT VOUCHERS** sign have agreed to give readers a discount of 25% off their normal bed-and-breakfast rate.
2. One voucher is good for a single-night stay only, at the discounted rate for yourself alone or for you and a partner sharing a double room.
3. Hotels may decline to accept a voucher reservation if they expect to be fully booked at the full room price.

---

**CONDITIONS**

1. Hotels with a **25% DISCOUNT VOUCHERS** sign have agreed to give readers a discount of 25% off their normal bed-and-breakfast rate.
2. One voucher is good for a single-night stay only, at the discounted rate for yourself alone or for you and a partner sharing a double room.
3. Hotels may decline to accept a voucher reservation if they expect to be fully booked at the full room price.

---

**CONDITIONS**

1. Hotels with a **25% DISCOUNT VOUCHERS** sign have agreed to give readers a discount of 25% off their normal bed-and-breakfast rate.
2. One voucher is good for a single-night stay only, at the discounted rate for yourself alone or for you and a partner sharing a double room.
3. Hotels may decline to accept a voucher reservation if they expect to be fully booked at the full room price.

---

**CONDITIONS**

1. Hotels with a **25% DISCOUNT VOUCHERS** sign have agreed to give readers a discount of 25% off their normal bed-and-breakfast rate.
2. One voucher is good for a single-night stay only, at the discounted rate for yourself alone or for you and a partner sharing a double room.
3. Hotels may decline to accept a voucher reservation if they expect to be fully booked at the full room price.

# WAREHAM Dorset

## THE PRIORY

🏆 *César award in 1996*

'Recommended for ambience, comfort and good staff', this 16th-century former priory, in gardens on the River Frome, is owned by Anne Turner with her brother-in-law, Stuart; her son, Jeremy Merchant, is the manager. 'The staff have remained essentially the same, and addressed us by name,' say returning visitors this year. The flagstoned courtyard is approached across a green. The beamed drawing room, where pre-dinner drinks are taken, has a country house decor. In the candlelit *Abbot's Cellar* dining room, Stephan Guinebault, who has been promoted to head chef this year, serves modern English/European dishes, perhaps truffled goat's cheese in filo; breast of guineafowl, pistachio and apricot stuffing. The bedrooms are individually furnished and vary in size: 'Our mini-suite in the Boathouse was slightly OTT, with a four-poster bed, dark beams and baronial fittings.' Another room, in the main building, was 'comfortable, with glorious views across the river'. A 'good' breakfast is taken in a garden room, or in summer on a terrace. (*EJT Palmer, Nigel and Jennifer Jee, Michael and Jennifer Price*)

Church Green
Wareham BH20 4ND

T: 01929-551666
F: 01929-554519
E: reservations@theprioryhotel.co.uk
W: www.theprioryhotel.co.uk

BEDROOMS: 18, some on ground floor (in courtyard), 4 suites in Boathouse.
OPEN: all year.
FACILITIES: ramps, lounge, drawing room, bar, 2 dining rooms, 4-acre gardens (croquet, river frontage, moorings, fishing), unsuitable for ♿.
BACKGROUND MUSIC: pianist in drawing room Sat night.
LOCATION: town centre.
CHILDREN: not under 14.
DOGS: only guide dogs allowed.
CREDIT CARDS: all major cards.
PRICES: [2010] B&B £117.50–£172.50 per person, D,B&B £142.50–£197.50, set dinner £42.50, off-season breaks, Christmas/New Year packages, 1-night bookings sometimes refused.

# WARMINSTER Wiltshire

Map 2:D1

## CROCKERTON HOUSE

'Everything is immaculate, not a blade of grass out of place' at Christopher and Enid Richmond's restored Grade II listed house, once part of the Longleat estate. 'Chris came out to meet us and help with baggage,' say inspectors this year. 'The interior is beautifully decorated, painted walls in restful colours, pleasant furniture, some antiques.' Visitors arriving before 5 pm are given free afternoon tea and cake in a 'lovely' sitting room or, in summer, under a tree in the garden. All three bedrooms are spacious and have a large bed. The Heytesbury Suite is large and light, with a window overlooking the garden. A hospitality tray has fresh coffee and milk. The Officer's Room has an adjacent bathroom with bath and walk-in shower, and a separate lavatory. Enid Richmond serves an Aga-cooked dinner by arrangement from Monday to Thursday; the set menu might include West Country cheese soufflé, slow-cooked beef. Breakfast has freshly squeezed orange juice, organic cereals, fresh fruit salad, organic bacon, sausage and eggs, toasted home-made bread.

Crockerton Green
Warminster BA12 8AY

T: 01985-216631
E: stay@crockertonhouse.co.uk
W: www.crockertonhouse.co.uk

BEDROOMS: 3.
OPEN: all year except Christmas, dining room closed Fri–Sun.
FACILITIES: drawing room, dining room, 1-acre garden, unsuitable for &.
BACKGROUND MUSIC: none.
LOCATION: 1½ miles S of Warminster.
CHILDREN: not under 12.
DOGS: not allowed.
CREDIT CARDS: MasterCard, Visa.
PRICES: [2010] B&B £34–£67.50 per person, set dinner £30, reduced rates for longer stays, 1-night bookings refused weekends Apr–Oct.

# WARTLING East Sussex

Map 2:E4

## WARTLING PLACE

On a hill near the church for which it was once the rectory, this white-painted Grade II listed B&B is kept 'spick and span' by the owners, Barry and Rowena Gittoes. It stands in attractive gardens on the edge of the Pevensey Levels nature reserve. The elegant lounge has 'comfortable' settees and chairs, antiques, an honesty bar, and a long polished table (where breakfast is taken) in front of the windows. Prints and pictures hang on the walls. Bedrooms are individually furnished; two have an antique four-poster bed. A garden-facing room had 'nice bits and pieces, heavy curtains, plenty of chairs'. All rooms have TV and DVD-player, tea- and coffee-making facilities; Wi-Fi is available. An 'exceptional' breakfast has yogurt, cereals, pastries; a wide range of cooked dishes includes kedgeree, omelettes, waffles with maple syrup, scrambled eggs. 'Classical music played softly.' An evening meal is available by arrangement; for dining out, *The Lamb*, an 'excellent' gastropub almost opposite, is recommended; so is the *Sundial* in Herstmonceux. More reports, please.

Wartling, Herstmonceux
nr Eastbourne BN27 1RY

T: 01323-832590
E: accom@
     wartlingplace.prestel.co.uk
W: www.wartlingplace.co.uk

BEDROOMS: 4, also self-catering cottage.
OPEN: all year.
FACILITIES: lounge/dining room with honesty bar and CD-player, 3-acre garden, unsuitable for &, except ground floor of cottage.
BACKGROUND MUSIC: none.
LOCATION: 3 miles N of Pevensey.
CHILDREN: all ages welcomed.
DOGS: allowed in cottage only.
CREDIT CARDS: Amex, MasterCard, Visa.
PRICES: B&B £62.50–£80 per person, set dinner £35, Christmas/New Year packages, 1-night bookings sometimes refused weekends.

# WATERMILLOCK Cumbria

Map 4: inset C2

## RAMPSBECK

At this elegant, 18th-century country house, Tracey McGeorge has been promoted to joint manager alongside the ever-popular Marion Gibb, whose 'work rate is phenomenal'. Their 'efficient, friendly' staff are praised by a visitor this year. In extensive parkland and gardens, the house has spectacular views of Lake Ullswater and the fells. Public rooms are 'comfortable': the panelled hall has settees, a log fire in winter; the drawing room has an original marble fireplace and an ornate ceiling. The lounge bar opens on to a terrace where tea and light meals are served in summer. Bedrooms vary in size and aspect; most have lake views; the best have a sitting area. 'Ours was well appointed, and had a new-looking bathroom.' In the recently renovated candlelit dining room the chef, Andrew McGeorge, cooks sophisticated dishes on a daily-changing menu, eg, braised pig's cheek, parsnip purée, apple jelly; Dover sole, seared queen scallops, white asparagus, tomato dressing. 'We are happy to cook any of our dishes more simply,' says the menu. One caveat: 'The background music repeated itself a little too often.' (*HJ Martin Tucker, CJ Bell*)

Watermillock on Ullswater
nr Penrith CA11 0LP

T: 01768-486442
F: 01768-486688
E: enquiries@rampsbeck.co.uk
W: www.rampsbeck.co.uk

BEDROOMS: 19.
OPEN: early Feb–31 Dec.
FACILITIES: 2 lounges, bar, restaurant, civil wedding licence, 18-acre grounds (croquet), lake frontage (fishing, sailing, windsurfing, etc), unsuitable for &.
BACKGROUND MUSIC: occasionally in bar and restaurant.
LOCATION: 5½ miles SW of Penrith.
CHILDREN: young children not allowed in restaurant at night.
DOGS: allowed in 3 bedrooms, hall lounge.
CREDIT CARDS: MasterCard, Visa.
PRICES: [2010] B&B £70–£145 per person, D,B&B £90–£190, set dinner £47–£52.50, special breaks, Christmas/New Year packages, 1-night bookings occasionally refused.

# WEM Shropshire

Map 3:B5

## SOULTON HALL `NEW`

On a 500-acre estate with a working farm, this 'impressive' Tudor manor house has been in the hands of the same family since 1556. 'It remains very much the home of John and Ann Ashton,' say inspectors in 2010. 'They are hard-working hosts, happy to advise on local places of interest.' The hall has a 'remarkable' collection of antiques from various periods, old family portraits, original fireplaces, and 'a happy mix of comfortable sofas and armchairs'. Four of the bedrooms are in the main house; others are in the *Carriage House* and *Cedar Lodge* close by. 'Our room in the main house was a generous space with stone mullioned windows. An immense Victorian wardrobe provided ample storage. Armchairs and a desk in an alcove encouraged relaxation.' Dinner is served in a small candlelit room by the host. His wife cooks traditional meals: 'She delivers spot-on seasoning in dishes like spinach timbale with crunchy elements of other vegetables; main courses came with vegetables from local producers, which were full of flavour and cooked with care. The cooked breakfast was of prime quality.'

nr Wem SY4 5RS

T: 01939-232786
F: 01939-234097
E: enquiries@soultonhall.co.uk
W: www.soultonhall.co.uk

BEDROOMS: 8, 2 on ground floor, 2 in *Carriage House*, 2 in *Cedar Lodge*.
OPEN: all year except 24–26 Dec, house parties only at New Year.
FACILITIES: lounge, bar/study, dining room, conference rooms, civil wedding licence, 2-acre gardens on 500-acre estate.
BACKGROUND MUSIC: in dining room 'when necessary'.
LOCATION: 2 miles E of Wem.
CHILDREN: all ages welcomed.
DOGS: allowed in annexes only.
CREDIT CARDS: Amex, MasterCard, Visa.
PRICES: [2010] B&B £41.50–£67.50 per person, D,B&B £77–£103, full alc £40, 1-night bookings sometimes refused.

# WEST STOKE West Sussex

## WEST STOKE HOUSE

♥ *César award in 2008*

At the foot of the South Downs, this white-painted, former dower house to the Goodwood estate has been sympathetically restored by Rowland and Mary Leach. They run it as a restaurant-with-rooms in an unstuffy and relaxed style: no dress code is enforced (the host might well appear in a pair of baggy shorts). The manager, Richard Macadam, is 'professional and puts you at your ease', say trusted reporters in 2010. In the dining room (the original ballroom with a small musicians' gallery), Darren Brown has a *Michelin* star for his 'superb' cooking: his modern English menu might include pressed terrine of foie gras, Madeira reduction; rolled and poached saddle of rabbit, bulgar wheat, baby artichokes, broad beans, chervil. The bedrooms (all different) are 'beautifully decorated': The Gregory, which overlooks the gardens, has 'French Hollywood'-style furniture and a round bed; Bridge can be expanded into a family suite; Jean's Attic is timber-framed with exposed beams. The house is popular for weddings and other celebrations. (*JR, and others*)

West Stoke, nr Chichester
PO18 9BN

T: 01243-575226
F: 01243-574655
E: info@weststokehouse.co.uk
W: www.weststokehouse.co.uk

BEDROOMS: 8.
OPEN: all year except Christmas, restaurant closed Sun evening/Mon/Tues.
FACILITIES: lounge, restaurant, civil wedding licence, 5-acre grounds (garden games), only restaurant suitable for &.
BACKGROUND MUSIC: soft, in restaurant and lounge.
LOCATION: 2 miles NW of Chichester.
CHILDREN: all ages welcomed.
DOGS: not allowed in public rooms.
CREDIT CARDS: Amex, MasterCard, Visa.
PRICES: [2010] B&B £75–£125 per person, set dinner £45, full alc £60, see website for special breaks, New Year package, 1-night bookings refused weekends.

# WHITEWELL Lancashire

Map 4:D3

## THE INN AT WHITEWELL

'A delightful place in a beautiful setting', Charles Bowman's quirky 300-year-old inn stands high in the Hodder valley with 'glorious' views of the Forest of Bowland. The building is filled with antiques, prints and paintings. Reception doubles as a wine shop ('reasonable prices'); books in cases in the corridors are for sale. There is 'plenty of room to relax in the public areas beside blazing fires'. Guests can eat in the bar, which occupies most of the ground floor ('excellent choices, reasonably priced'). In the more formal riverside dining room, chef Jamie Cadman uses local produce for his dishes, perhaps 'a memorable thick pea and ham soup'; roast loin of lamb, smoked bacon and cabbage polenta cake. Bedrooms have wool and horsehair mattresses with hand-sewn springs; many bathrooms have a Victorian bathing machine. 'Our room was small and comfortable, with a view over the rooftops.' 'I had a great view of the hunt meeting from my large, front-facing room.' The breakfast porridge is recommended. The inn owns seven miles of fishing. (*Mrs J Deeming, Diana Holmes, Sara Price*)

Whitewell, Forest of Bowland
nr Clitheroe BB7 3AT

T: 01200-448222
F: 01200-448298
E: reception@innatwhitewell.com
W: www.innatwhitewell.com

BEDROOMS: 23, 4 (2 on ground floor) in coach house, 150 yds.
OPEN: all year.
FACILITIES: 2 bars, restaurant, boardroom, orangery, civil wedding licence, 5-acre garden, 7 miles fishing (ghillie available), unsuitable for &.
BACKGROUND MUSIC: none.
LOCATION: 6 miles NW of Clitheroe.
CHILDREN: all ages welcomed.
DOGS: not allowed in dining room.
CREDIT CARDS: MasterCard, Visa.
PRICES: [2010] B&B £83–£177 per person, full alc £30.

# WILMINGTON East Sussex

## CROSSWAYS HOTEL

'The generosity and conviviality of the owners and their staff remain exemplary,' says a returning visitor to David Stott and Clive James's restaurant-with-rooms in a small Georgian country house in the Cuckmere valley. Close to Glyndebourne, it attracts many opera fans (a special package is offered). Six of the bedrooms have now been renovated in contemporary style and three new bathrooms have been installed. The remaining room was due for renovation in late 2010. The 'only drawback of this entirely delightful and idiosyncratic place is the busy main road' at the end of the large garden (bedrooms are double glazed). There is no guest lounge, but bedrooms are well equipped with 'every imaginable appliance': some have a sofa, one has a balcony. The four-course fixed-price dinner menu 'included a much-appreciated crab and Wensleydale cheesecake and a Parmesan-coated pork fillet'. A 'copious' breakfast is served in a sunny room with a collection of cheese plates. It is 'fresh and delicious'. Picnics for Glyndebourne can be arranged from 'an excellent local deli'. (*Richard Parish*)

Lewes Road
Wilmington BN26 5SG

T: 01323-482455
F: 01323-487811
E: stay@crosswayshotel.co.uk
W: www.crosswayshotel.co.uk

BEDROOMS: 7, also self-catering cottage.
OPEN: all year except 22 Dec–29 Jan, restaurant closed Sun/Mon evening.
FACILITIES: breakfast room, restaurant, 2-acre grounds (duck pond), unsuitable for &.
BACKGROUND MUSIC: light classical/popular in restaurant.
LOCATION: 2 miles W of Polegate on A27.
CHILDREN: not under 12.
DOGS: not allowed.
CREDIT CARDS: Amex, MasterCard, Visa.
PRICES: B&B £62.50–£79 per person, D,B&B £90–£99, set dinner £37.95.

# WINCHELSEA East Sussex

Map 2:E5

## THE STRAND HOUSE

'Quaint, and with a wealth of history', these two Grade II listed buildings (one 13th century, the other Tudor) are run as a small hotel by owners Mary Sullivan and Hugh Davie. Some of the bedrooms are up steep steeps; many have low beams. A six-foot visitor this year was 'kindly upgraded' from a low-ceilinged room. One 'delightful' room has flowery fabrics, an inglenook fireplace, brass bedhead. Two bathrooms have been upgraded this year. The attractive lounge has sofas, a log fire; 'alas dreadful background music'. Afternoon tea, with strawberries, scones, smoked salmon sandwiches and home-made cake is 'a real treat'. 'Full of energy', Mary Sullivan is around the house most of the day. In the evening, she takes orders for dinner then 'disappears into the kitchen' to prepare her 'unpretentious' meals, perhaps tomato and mozzarella salad; Rye Bay gurnard with a mustard cream sauce. Breakfast has a wide range of cooked choices; packed lunches are available upon request. (*RW Baker, and others*)

Tanyards Lane
Winchelsea TN36 4JT

T: 01797-226276
F: 01797-224806
E: info@thestrandhouse.co.uk
W: www.thestrandhouse.co.uk

BEDROOMS: 10, 1 on ground floor.
OPEN: all year.
FACILITIES: reception, lounge, bar, breakfast room, civil wedding/partnership licence, 1-acre garden, unsuitable for &.
BACKGROUND MUSIC: jazz/big bands/crooners in public rooms.
LOCATION: 300 yds from centre, 2 miles SW of Rye.
CHILDREN: not under 5.
DOGS: allowed by arrangement, but not in public rooms.
CREDIT CARDS: MasterCard, Visa.
PRICES: [2010] B&B £35–£67.50 per person, D,B&B £62.50–£95, set dinner £27–£29.50, special breaks, Christmas/New Year packages, 1-night bookings refused summer weekends.

# WINCHESTER Hampshire

## THE WYKEHAM ARMS    **NEW**

'A uniquely hospitable town pub that gives satisfaction to hotel guests', this 250-year-old inn between the college and the cathedral returns to a full *Guide* entry after a period without reports. Now owned by Fuller's brewery, it is managed by Jon and Monica Howard. 'Our room in the main building was small, but well provided with essentials like a minibar, a fridge with fresh milk and a television,' said an inspector. 'Insulation was not perfect (a draughty window) and the bathroom was so small that the towels (first class) had to be stored in the bedroom.' Seven more expensive bedrooms are in a 16th-century building across the street; it has a suite on two floors, and a courtyard. Tables must be booked in advance for the dining rooms which are often busy. Nick Funnell joined as chef in March 2010, cooking modern dishes, perhaps grilled Brie and onion marmalade tartlet; caramelised Barbary duck, mangetout, mashed potato, orange and juniper berry jus. We would welcome reports on the food. 'Breakfast was the usual buffet, well served.' (*Ann and Sidney Carpenter, and others*)

75 Kingsgate Street
Winchester SO23 9PE

T: 01962-853834
F: 01962-854411
E: wykehamarms@fullers.co.uk
W: www.fullershotels.com

BEDROOMS: 14, 7 in annexe.
OPEN: all year.
FACILITIES: 2 bars, 2 dining rooms, function room, small garden, unsuitable for &.
BACKGROUND MUSIC: light classical in breakfast room.
LOCATION: central.
CHILDREN: not under 12.
DOGS: allowed in bars, 1 bedroom.
CREDIT CARDS: all major cards.
PRICES: [2010] B&B £50–£60 per person, D,B&B £65–£75, set meals £20–£35, full alc £36, Christmas/New Year packages.

**25% DISCOUNT VOUCHERS**

## WINDERMERE Cumbria

Map 4: inset C2

### GILPIN HOTEL AND LAKE HOUSE

**♦** *César award in 2000*

'All in order and as good as ever. Staff outstanding; never stuffy, always pleasant and efficient.' Returning visitors in 2010 again praise this country house hotel (Relais & Châteaux), run by John and Christine Cunliffe with son Barney and his wife, Zoë. The hands-on family create a 'warm atmosphere'. The Edwardian building has extensive grounds with terrace, pond, waterfall, croquet lawn and llama paddock. New this year: the *Lake House*, for a group, small wedding or conference. Attention to detail is commended: 'Rooms made up twice a day; towels big and soft; always fresh milk in the refrigerator, a carafe of water on the shelf. Our lovely big room had a sitting area opening on to the garden.' In the restaurant, chef Russell Plowman offers two menu styles: 'signature' dishes with 'rich combinations' (eg, roast loin and braised shank of rosé veal, butternut squash purée); and 'classics' with 'comfort' flavours (fillet and cheek of beef, red wine sauce). 'Small, elegant portions, perfectly cooked.' (*David and Bridget Reed, Robert Gower, Wolfgang Stroebe*)

Crook Road
nr Windermere LA23 3NE

T: 015394-88818
F: 015394-88058
E: hotel@gilpinlodge.co.uk
W: www.gilpinlodge.co.uk

BEDROOMS: 26, 6 in orchard wing, 6 in *Lake House* (½ mile from main house).
OPEN: all year.
FACILITIES: ramps, bar, 2 lounges, 4 dining rooms, 22-acre grounds (ponds, croquet), free access to nearby country club (swimming pool, sauna, squash), golf course opposite, unsuitable for &.
BACKGROUND MUSIC: none.
LOCATION: on B5284, 2 miles SE of Windermere.
CHILDREN: not under 7.
DOGS: not allowed (kennels at nearby farm).
CREDIT CARDS: all major cards.
PRICES: [2010] D,B&B £145–£260 per person, set dinner £52.50, Christmas/ New Year packages, min. 2 nights weekends.

**25% DISCOUNT VOUCHERS**

# WOLD NEWTON East Yorkshire

## THE WOLD COTTAGE

Once a gentleman's retreat, this stylish red brick Georgian country house stands in landscaped grounds, with views to the Yorkshire Wolds. The 'friendly' owners, Katrina and Derek Gray, have 'lovingly restored' it. 'Wonderful: we could not have been made more welcome; the location is stunning,' is a recent comment. Two of the bedrooms have a four-poster bed; a large family suite has twin beds as well as a double; two rooms are in a converted barn. The house is heated by a straw burner (using straw from the farm). Breakfast and evening meals (preceded by complimentary sherry) are served in the elegant candlelit dining room, communally or at separate tables. Mrs Gray places importance on the provenance of the produce. Fruit and vegetables are grown in the garden. 'Like the best home cooking on dinner-party days.' The 'excellent' breakfast includes locally smoked fish (salmon, haddock and kippers), cereals, fresh fruit and yogurt, variations of full English, and home-made bread and raspberry and strawberry jam. Honey comes from Bobby's Bees, two miles away. (*YB*)

Wold Newton, nr Driffield
YO25 3HL

T/F: 01262-470696
E: katrina@woldcottage.com
W: www.woldcottage.com

BEDROOMS: 5, 2 in converted barn, 1 on ground floor.
OPEN: all year.
FACILITIES: lounge, dining room, 3-acre grounds (croquet) in 240-acre farmland.
BACKGROUND MUSIC: at mealtimes, 'easy listening'.
LOCATION: just outside village.
CHILDREN: all ages welcomed.
DOGS: not allowed.
CREDIT CARDS: MasterCard, Visa.
PRICES: B&B £50–£75 per person, D,B&B £75–£100, set dinner £25.

# WOOKEY HOLE Somerset

Map 1:B6

## MILLER'S AT GLENCOT HOUSE

Antiques dealer Martin Miller has filled this 19th-century mansion with a wealth of curiosities and eccentric paraphernalia. It stands in extensive grounds in the Mendip hills, where the River Axe emerges from Wookey Hole. Built in Jacobean style, it has mullioned windows, carved ceilings and wood panelling. Second-hand books are piled everywhere, alongside stuffed peacocks, paintings, candlesticks, prints, huge Chinese vases. 'Wonderfully quirky and great fun,' is a recent comment. There is a small cinema with seating on sofas and a chaise longue. Bedrooms are lavishly furnished; some have a four-poster, all have colourful drapes and fabrics. A window table is recommended for the *Riverview* restaurant, which has beamed ceilings, a huge chandelier. In keeping with the house, Jonathan Elvin's menus have modern British dishes 'with an eccentric twist', eg, whipped goat's cheese, pickled beets and walnut; wild sea bass, shellfish and coconut bisque. 'Breakfast has a help-yourself continental buffet; hot dishes cost extra.' There's a cricket pitch in the grounds. Mr Miller also owns *Miller's Residence*, London (closed for refurbishment). More reports, please.

Glencot Lane
Wookey Hole, nr Wells BA5 1BH

T: 01749-677160
F: 01749-670210
E: relax@glencothouse.co.uk
W: www.glencothouse.co.uk

BEDROOMS: 15, some on ground floor.
OPEN: all year, restaurant closed Sun evening.
FACILITIES: 2 lounges, restaurant, small cinema, snooker room, library, 18-acre grounds (garden, river (fishing), croquet, cricket pitch).
BACKGROUND MUSIC: jazz/'easy listening' in public rooms.
LOCATION: 2 miles NW of Wells.
CHILDREN: all ages welcomed.
DOGS: not allowed in some bedrooms, in restaurant.
CREDIT CARDS: all major cards.
PRICES: [2010] B&B (continental) £82.50–£147.50 per person, set dinner £34.50, full alc £55, 2-day half-board rates, seasonal breaks, Christmas/New Year packages, min. 2 nights for summer weekends.

# WOOLACOMBE Devon

Map 1:B4

## WATERSMEET

Returning after many years to Michael and Amanda James's traditional hotel on Woolacombe Bay, trusted *Guide* reporters were 'astounded by the improvements'. 'The setting, on the side of a cliff, has always been stunning; the additions – a wonderful dining room with 90-degree views, a lovely swimming pool – have added an extra dimension. The decor might be considered "unfashionable", but it is classic, and correct for the Edwardian building.' All but three of the bedrooms have the views: 'Our huge room had a glimpse of the sea; everything was immaculate in the superb bathroom; smart tiling and an excellent shower over the bath.' Men are asked to wear a jacket or a tie in the dining room, which has 'beautifully set' tables on two levels. The chef, John Prince, uses local produce for his dishes: 'Tian of smoked salmon and shrimps with a gazpacho coulis and avocado mousse was good; we enjoyed collops of rare venison with red cabbage, vanilla potato purée. The service was charming; the background music relatively unobtrusive.' Breakfast has a small buffet, 'fine' cooked dishes. (*Francine and Ian Walsh*)

Mortehoe
Woolacombe EX34 7EB

T: 01271-870333
F: 01271-870890
E: info@watersmeethotel.co.uk
W: www.watersmeethotel.co.uk

BEDROOMS: 29, 3 on ground floor, 1 suitable for &.
OPEN: all year.
FACILITIES: lift, lounge, bar, function room, civil wedding licence, terrace, 3-acre gardens, heated indoor and outdoor swimming pools, sandy beach below.
BACKGROUND MUSIC: classical/romantic in restaurant.
LOCATION: by sea, 4 miles SW of Ilfracombe.
CHILDREN: not under 8 in restaurant in evening.
DOGS: not allowed.
CREDIT CARDS: MasterCard, Visa.
PRICES: [2010] B&B £65–£128 per person, D,B&B £78–£161, set dinner £36, full alc £50, midweek breaks, Christmas/New Year packages, 1-night bookings sometimes refused.

# WORFIELD Shropshire

Map 3:C5

## THE OLD VICARAGE

The setting of Sarah and David Blakstad's hotel in a red brick Edwardian former parsonage is 'lovely, with wide views across open country', says a visitor this year. There is a manicured lawn, and statues and seats around old elms. Bedrooms vary in size and style; most have antique furniture, one has a Victorian four-poster bed, another a walnut half-tester. All contain a decanter of sherry, fresh milk and fruit. Each of the four rooms in the coach house has a private garden ('we could sit outside with a complimentary glass of sherry in the evening'). 'Our large room had a comfortable sitting area, a good-sized bed. The bathroom, which had a separate shower as well as a bath, was well equipped.' In the *Orangery* restaurant, the chef, Simon Diprose, serves a 'very good' seasonally changing menu of British dishes, eg, pork fillet with morels, garlic and marjoram ravioli. Breakfasts were 'extremely good, with tasty cooked dishes and freshly squeezed orange juice'. On Sunday evenings dinner is by arrangement only. (*Mary Hewson, and others*)

Worfield
nr Bridgnorth WV15 5JZ

T: 01746-716497
F: 01746-716552
E: admin@oldvicarageworfield.com
W: www.oldvicarageworfield.com

BEDROOMS: 14, 4 in coach house, 2 on ground floor, 2 suitable for &.
OPEN: all year, restaurant sometimes closed on Sun evening.
FACILITIES: ramps, lounge, bar, restaurant, 2 private dining rooms, small conference facilities, civil wedding licence, 2-acre grounds (patio, croquet).
BACKGROUND MUSIC: 'very low' in public areas.
LOCATION: 2 miles NE of Bridgnorth.
CHILDREN: all ages welcomed.
DOGS: not allowed in public rooms.
CREDIT CARDS: MasterCard, Visa.
PRICES: [2010] B&B £44.75–£60 per person, D,B&B £75–£100, set dinner £35, full alc £42.25, special breaks.

**25% DISCOUNT VOUCHERS**

# YARM North Yorkshire

## JUDGES

'What a lovely hotel; reasonable prices, excellent food, friendly staff.' Praise from a reader in 2010 for the Downs family's Victorian house (Pride of Britain) which was once a residence for circuit judges. A stream runs through large wooded grounds with landscaped gardens; a gazebo was added in 2010. Many of the bedrooms have been refurbished, bathrooms upgraded. 'Our superb room even had a TV in the bathroom. All rooms have feather mattress, footbath, and a goldfish in a small bowl 'with a request to feed it'. The old-fashioned values are appreciated: shoes are shined, beds turned down at night: 'there are quiet lounges where a proper cup of tea is served'. No mobile phones or intrusive muzak. New carpets have been laid in the public areas this year. A couple who married at *Judges* praised the 'helpful staff'; visitors during another wedding said staff 'seemed to be overstretched'. The chef, John Schwarz, serves 'excellent' modern dishes (poached seafood, potato and sweetcorn chowder) in the conservatory dining room. (*WK Wood, and others*)

Kirklevington Hall
Yarm TS15 9LW

T: 01642-789000
F: 01642-782878
E: reservations@judgeshotel.co.uk
W: www.judgeshotel.co.uk

BEDROOMS: 21, some on ground floor.
OPEN: all year.
FACILITIES: ramps, lounge, bar, restaurant, private dining room, function facilities, business centre, civil wedding licence, 36-acre grounds (paths, running routes), access to local spa and sports club.
BACKGROUND MUSIC: none.
LOCATION: 1½ miles S of centre.
CHILDREN: all ages welcomed.
DOGS: only guide dogs allowed.
CREDIT CARDS: all major cards.
PRICES: [2010] B&B £62.50–£107.50 per person, D,B&B £95–£140, set menu £32.50, full alc £42.50, Christmas/New Year packages.

**25% DISCOUNT VOUCHERS**

# YORK North Yorkshire

Map 4:D4

## DEAN COURT

In 'a wonderful position, right by the Minster', this city hotel (Best Western) is 'effortlessly run' by manager David Brooks. A visitor this year, at first disappointed by the shape and size of her bedroom, 'was slowly seduced by the Minster bells, the superb location and the outstanding breakfasts'. Superior rooms, decorated in contemporary colours, face the Minster (the bells fall silent at night). Lunch was enjoyed in the *Court* bistro this year: 'Delicious leek and potato soup, and a bacon butty. A nice atmosphere apart from awful piped music. Good service.' A seasonal menu of modern French/English dishes is served in the *D.C.H.* restaurant, with dishes like pressed confit of rabbit; red snapper, Thai-spiced coconut broth, wilted curly kale. Extra beds can be supplied for children, who have their own menu and 'can plunder our toy box'. Trusted *Guide* reporters liked the extras in the bedrooms, fruit and bathrobes, free Wi-Fi. Valet parking is available. A French family found the staff adaptable about breakfast. 'Three days were not long enough to explore York; we will return to *Dean Court*.' (*Val Ferguson, and others*)

Duncombe Place
York YO1 7EF

T: 01904-625082
F: 01904-620305
E: sales@deancourt-york.co.uk
W: www.deancourt-york.co.uk

BEDROOMS: 37, 3 suitable for &.
OPEN: all year.
FACILITIES: ramp, 2 lounges, bar, restaurant, bistro/bar, conference/function facilities, civil wedding licence.
BACKGROUND MUSIC: in public areas, not in restaurant at breakfast.
LOCATION: central, opposite Minster.
CHILDREN: all ages welcomed.
DOGS: guide dogs only.
CREDIT CARDS: all major cards.
PRICES: B&B £44.50–£117.50 per person, D,B&B (min. 2 nights) £100–£147.50, full alc £45, website offers, Christmas/New Year packages, 1-night bookings sometimes refused.

# YORK North Yorkshire

## MIDDLETHORPE HALL & SPA

Bishopthorpe Road
York YO23 2GB

T: 01904-641241
F: 01904-620176
E: info@middlethorpe.com
W: www.middlethorpe.com

In a large park with a lake beside York's ring road, this 'beautiful' William III mansion 'combines access to the city with all the space and comfort of a country house'. Owned by the National Trust, it is managed by Lionel Chatard. The staff are 'helpful, friendly', says a visitor this year. The best bedrooms, in the main house, have a sitting room and gas coal fire. A junior suite in the courtyard also has a separate sitting room 'traditionally furnished with sofas and a bureau'. The public rooms have leather Chesterfields, antiques, gilded mirrors and historic paintings. In the dark-panelled candle-lit dining room facing the walled garden, Nicholas Evans serves a modern menu (eg, slow-roasted fillet of beef, pease pudding). A spa in two converted estate houses across the drive is 'bright and spotless with a nice pool', but a disabled visitor found access to it difficult. The Trust holds regular events and may open *Middlethorpe* to the public. (*Bianca Emberson, and others*)

BEDROOMS: 29, 17 in coach house, 2 in garden, 1 suitable for &.
OPEN: all year.
FACILITIES: drawing room, sitting rooms, library, bar, restaurant, private dining rooms, function facilities, civil wedding licence, 20-acre grounds, spa (health and beauty facilities, heated indoor swimming pool, 13 by 6 metres).
BACKGROUND MUSIC: none.
LOCATION: 1½ miles S of centre, by racecourse.
CHILDREN: not under 6.
DOGS: only in garden suites, not in public rooms.
CREDIT CARDS: Amex, MasterCard, Visa.
PRICES: [2010] B&B (continental) £99.50–£134.50 per person, Yorkshire breakfast £6.95 extra, full alc £60, Christmas/New Year packages.

## ZENNOR Cornwall

Map 1:D1

### THE GURNARD'S HEAD

🏆 *César award in 2009*

'A wonderfully relaxing and enjoyable place', Charles and Edmund Inkin's pub/restaurant has a 'lovely, isolated' position on the north Cornish coast near Land's End. 'They have just the right recipe for keeping guests happy,' says a visitor this year. 'The welcome is immediate, from the young staff,' say other guests. 'Their informality of dress and manner add greatly to the experience.' Most of the interior has been repainted. The bar and restaurant have wooden floors, log fires, 'lots of interesting art work'. A room above the bar was 'unfussy, comfortable; no television (thank heavens)'. One reader found his room 'disappointingly small' but 'reasonable value'. A larger room at the back was 'lovely and light; a supremely comfortable bed; a large bathroom with bath'. Bruce Rennie was promoted to head chef in 2010; he promises more vegetarian choices. Breakfast is simple but good: rustic breads, home-made jam, local apple juice; kippers or full English. The Inkin brothers also own *Felin Fach Griffin*, Felin Fach, in Wales (see entry). (*Simon Rodway, Canon and Mrs MA Bourdeaux, and others*)

Treen, nr Zennor
St Ives TR26 3DE

T: 01736-796928
E: enquiries@gurnardshead.co.uk
W: www.gurnardshead.co.uk

BEDROOMS: 7.
OPEN: all year except 24/25 Dec, 4 days in Jan.
FACILITIES: bar area, small connecting room with sofas, dining room, ½-acre garden, unsuitable for &.
BACKGROUND MUSIC: at mealtimes and part of day.
LOCATION: 7 miles SW of St Ives, on B3306.
CHILDREN: all ages welcomed.
DOGS: not allowed in dining room.
CREDIT CARDS: MasterCard, Visa.
PRICES: [2010] B&B £45–£77.50 per person, full alc £34, midweek offers, 'Sunday sleepover' rates, 1-night bookings 'occasionally' refused, particularly for guests not eating in.

# SCOTLAND

Hotels in Scotland are flourishing, thanks
to rising standards of hospitality and cooking.
Our Scottish award winner, *Killiecrankie House*,
Killiecrankie, is an outstanding example of a
personally run country hotel. As in other
chapters, we offer a breadth of choice, ranging
from simple B&Bs to hospitable inns and
delightful island hotels.

# ABERFELDY Perth and Kinross

Map 5:D2

## FORTINGALL HOTEL

'Charming, with plenty of character', this privately owned hotel has a 'wonderful' position in a small Arts and Crafts conservation village in a landscape dominated by Glen Lyon and Loch Tay. It is managed by Roddy Jamieson ('hands on and ubiquitous'). 'The staff are pleasant, and educated in all aspects of the hotel,' say visitors in 2010. The main hall has 'an appropriately Scottish theme of muted tartans and well-polished furniture'. 'Our bedroom was bright, clean and comfortable, with all the expected facilities, and some extras.' Earlier visitors commented on an 'exceptional' hospitality tray with ground coffee beans, leaf tea, fresh milk, good china. 'Good housekeeping.' In the 'agreeable' dining room, the chef, Darin Campbell, serves modern dishes, eg, seared sea bass, lemongrass risotto, confit tomato, olive and micro-herb salad. Simpler food (eg, lamb stew) is available in the 'cosy' bar. Children have their own menu. Breakfast has 'standard sideboard starters'; 'very good toast from home-made bread, decent butter and good marmalade'. Shooting, fishing, cycling and walking for all abilities are all available locally. (*Lesley Anne Ritchie, and others*)

Fortingall
Aberfeldy PH15 2NQ

T: 01887-830367
E: hotel@fortingallhotel.com
W: www.fortingall.com

BEDROOMS: 10, 2 in annexe.
OPEN: all year.
FACILITIES: lounge, library, bar, dining room, function room, wedding facilities, garden.
BACKGROUND MUSIC: in restaurant, live fiddle music in bar Friday.
LOCATION: in village 7 miles W of Aberfeldy.
CHILDREN: all ages welcomed.
DOGS: allowed.
CREDIT CARDS: MasterCard, Visa.
PRICES: [2010] B&B £80–£105 per person, D,B&B £125–£150, set dinner £45, full alc £60, special breaks, New Year package.

# AULDEARN Highland

Map 5:C2

## BOATH HOUSE

**NEW**

Once on the Historic Scotland endangered list, this pale stone Regency mansion was stylishly restored by Wendy and Don Matheson. It stands in extensive grounds with an ornamental lake, woodland, a wild flower meadow and streams. The original marbled hallway, circular staircase and fireplaces have been retained. The work of 30 Highland artists is displayed in the public rooms. 'Lovely, relaxed; I rated it highly,' said a visitor this year restoring it to the *Guide* after a period without reports. The spacious bedrooms are smartly furnished, some with half-tester bed. Superior rooms have a sitting area (two occupy a wing of the house each). In the oval dining room, chef Charles Lockley has a *Michelin* star for his six-course menu of 'Scottish dishes with strong French influences', perhaps Tongue oysters, anise, carrots; red deer, wheat grain, bacon, parsley root. Breakfast, served at table, has home-made herb muesli, Golspie organic porridge; cooked choices include truffled scrambled eggs. Children are welcomed. There is a health and beauty spa in the basement. (*JS Waters*)

Auldearn, nr Nairn IV12 5TE

**T:** 01667-454896
**F:** 01667-455469
**E:** info@boath-house.com
**W:** www.boath-house.com

**BEDROOMS:** 8, 1 in cottage (30 yds) suitable for &.
**OPEN:** all year.
**FACILITIES:** 2 drawing rooms, library, orangery, restaurant, health/beauty spa, wedding facilities, 20-acre grounds, lake, rivers, woods, fishing.
**BACKGROUND MUSIC:** none.
**LOCATION:** 2 miles E of Nairn.
**CHILDREN:** all ages welcomed.
**DOGS:** not allowed in public rooms.
**CREDIT CARDS:** Diners, MasterCard, Visa.
**PRICES:** [2010] B&B £110–£250 per person, D,B&B £160–£210, dinner £65, winter breaks, Christmas/New Year packages.

# AVIEMORE Highland

Map 5:C2

## CORROUR HOUSE

At their B&B, a former dower house of 'real
antique character', Carol and Robert Still 'take
immense trouble to make sure that guests have
all they need'. The four-square stone house stands
in large gardens with 'outstanding' views across
to the Lairig Ghru pass and the Cairngorms.
Guests are given tea and shortbread on arrival.
The public rooms are 'beautifully decorated':
an open fire burns much of the time in the
lounge. Original features include fine cornices,
stained-glass windows in the hall. Malt whisky
is available from the bar; advice is given on
the many eating places in the area. 'Chintzy'
bedrooms vary in size. 'The bathroom was well
equipped.' 'A very good breakfast' is taken in a
'stunning' room. Red squirrels are often to be
seen, and red deer. As well as the usual sporting
activities, including skiing in Aviemore, a ten-
minute walk away, there are steam and
funicular railways nearby. (*MH*)

Rothiemurchus
Inverdruie
by Aviemore PH22 1QH

T: 01479-810220
F: 01479-811500
E: enquiries@corrourhouse.co.uk
W: www.corrourhouse.co.uk

BEDROOMS: 8.
OPEN: New Year–mid-Nov.
FACILITIES: lounge, cocktail bar,
dining room, 4-acre gardens and
woodland, unsuitable for &.
BACKGROUND MUSIC: none.
LOCATION: ¾ mile S of Aviemore.
CHILDREN: all ages welcomed
(under-4s stay free).
DOGS: not allowed in public rooms
or unsupervised in bedrooms.
CREDIT CARDS: Amex, MasterCard,
Visa.
PRICES: [2010] B&B £45–£58 per
person, reductions for 3 or more
nights, New Year package, 1-night
bookings refused in season at
weekends.

# BALLANTRAE South Ayrshire

Map 5:E1

## COSSES COUNTRY HOUSE

'We knew it was a great place from the moment we were greeted by Susan and her Labradors.' This pretty white building, once a shooting lodge, is run as a guest house (Wolsey Lodge) by owners Robin and Susan Crosthwaite. It stands in flower-filled gardens and woodland in a peaceful valley just outside an old fishing village. Two of the bedrooms are in converted byres and stables across a courtyard. They are traditionally furnished, with floral patterns; each has a sitting room with antique furniture, books, maps, etc. A smaller (and cheaper) bedroom is in the main house. All the bathrooms have been renovated this year, with stone tiles and under-floor heating. Mrs Crosthwaite provides tea with home-made cakes and scones for arriving visitors. She uses produce from the garden for her daily-changing menus, served communally; dishes might include Ballantrae Bay lobster, green mayonnaise, new potatoes, peach and ginger salad. She has published a book of local recipes. Breakfast, which is full Scottish with healthy options, eg, fresh fruit salad, may be taken on the patio in good weather. (*Mr and Mrs J Teed*)

Ballantrae KA26 0LR

T: 01465-831363
F: 01465-831598
E: staying@cossescountryhouse.com
W: www.cossescountryhouse.com

BEDROOMS: 3, on ground floor, 2 across courtyard.
OPEN: Mar–Dec.
FACILITIES: drawing room, dining room, games room, utility room, 12-acre grounds.
BACKGROUND MUSIC: none.
LOCATION: 2 miles E of Ballantrae.
CHILDREN: not under 12 in dining room for dinner.
DOGS: allowed by arrangement in 1 suite, not in public rooms.
CREDIT CARDS: MasterCard, Visa.
PRICES: [2010] B&B £42.50–£75 per person, set dinner £30–£35, special breaks.

# BALLANTRAE  South Ayrshire

## GLENAPP CASTLE

The term Scottish baronial could have been invented to describe Glenapp, designed by the doyen of Victorian castle architects, David Bryce. Once the seat of the earls of Inchcape, the castle and its 'magnificent' gardens were restored over six years by Graham and Fay Cowan. They run it as a country hotel (Relais & Châteaux). 'Professional attentive service by caring staff'; 'luxury is standard,' are comments this year. There are fine paintings, Middle Eastern rugs, intricate plasterwork and an oak-panelled entrance and staircase. The parquet-floored library has floor-to-ceiling bookshelves. Spacious bedrooms have an open fire, and views of the gardens or over the Irish Sea to Ailsa Craig. In an elegant dining room, the chef, Adam Stokes, serves 'imaginative, beautifully presented' dishes (eg, venison with walnuts, Szechuan and hotpot) on his daily-changing dinner menu. Guests 'can wander at will' through wooded grounds with 'superb views'; there is a lake, a walled garden and a 150-foot Victorian glasshouse. Golf, fishing and shooting can be arranged. (*Tony Green, Natasha Green*)

Ballantrae KA26 0NZ

T: 01465-831212
F: 01465-831000
E: info@glenappcastle.com
W: www.glenappcastle.com

BEDROOMS: 17, 7 on ground floor.
OPEN: 26 Mar–22 Dec, 30 Dec–2 Jan.
FACILITIES: ramp, lift, drawing room, library, 2 dining rooms, wedding facilities, 36-acre gardens (tennis, croquet), fishing, golf nearby, access to spa.
BACKGROUND MUSIC: none.
LOCATION: 2 miles S of Ballantrae.
CHILDREN: not under 5 in dining room after 7 pm.
DOGS: allowed in 1 bedroom, not in public rooms.
CREDIT CARDS: Amex, MasterCard, Visa.
PRICES: [2010] B&B £172.50–£275 per person, D,B&B £202.50–£305, set dinner £60, website offers, New Year package, 1-night bookings refused bank holiday Sat, New Year.

**25% DISCOUNT VOUCHERS**

# BALLATER Aberdeenshire

Map 5:C3

## DEESIDE HOTEL

Run as a 'home from home' by owners Gordon Waddell (chef) and Penella Price ('unfailingly pleasant'), this Victorian house is on the outskirts of an attractive resort burgh on the River Dee. It is liked for its 'good value', 'charm' and 'consistently good food'. Bedrooms, with king-size or twin beds, are 'inoffensively decorated' and have generous storage, books and home-made shortbread. There are log fires in the 'small, comfortable' library and lounge, and in the restaurant in winter. In summer, meals are taken in the conservatory area overlooking the walled garden, which yields herbs, vegetables and soft fruit for Mr Waddell's menus. These might include rack of lamb with rosemary, flageolet vert, mint barley risotto. The 'good wine list, reasonably priced', has a 'more interesting – and expensive –' supplement. The bar has over 40 whiskies. A children's menu is available. Breakfast has free-range eggs, home-made marmalade, 'fine kippers'. Several shops in Ballater have a royal warrant (Balmoral is nearby). (*A and EW, AW*)

45 Braemar Road
Ballater AB35 5RQ

T: 013397-55420
F: 0871 989 5933
E: mail@deesidehotel.co.uk
W: www.deesidehotel.co.uk

BEDROOMS: 9, 2 on ground floor.
OPEN: Feb–Nov.
FACILITIES: ramp, lounge, library, bar, restaurant, 1-acre garden.
BACKGROUND MUSIC: Mozart in bar and restaurant.
LOCATION: village outskirts.
CHILDREN: all ages welcomed.
DOGS: not allowed in upstairs bedrooms or public rooms.
CREDIT CARDS: MasterCard, Visa.
PRICES: [2010] B&B £40–£50 per person, D,B&B £60–£75, set dinner £17.95, full alc £30, reductions for 3 or more nights, 1-night bookings sometimes refused Sat in season.

# BALQUHIDDER Stirling

Map 5:D2

## MONACHYLE MHOR

On a large working estate, this 'friendly, relaxed' restaurant-with-rooms is run by siblings Tom, Dick and Melanie Lewis. The 18th-century converted stone farm buildings are in a 'remote, peaceful, beautiful' setting at the end of a four-mile track skirting Loch Voil. Recent visitors were greeted by a local girl who helped them with their bags. Tom Lewis uses meat from the farm ('we could see the pigs from the kitchen window'), vegetables and herbs from the walled garden for his modern dishes, eg, guineafowl breast, herbed pistachio farci, leeks fondue, dauphinoise potatoes, mustard sauce. The innovative vegetarian dishes have been praised. No tartan in sight in the smallish sitting room and bar (log fires, contemporary and antique furniture and paintings – Melanie is an artist and designer). The bedrooms vary in size: a small room was 'nicely decorated; it had proper coffee and a large bathroom'. Two luxury suites in converted stables have a steam room; there are plenty of 'audio-visual gadgets'. The breakfast menu is extensive, both hot and cold. Many food-related courses are run. (*KS*)

Balquhidder
Lochearnhead FK19 8PQ

**T:** 01877-384622
**F:** 01877-384305
**E:** monachyle@mhor.net
**W:** www.mhor.net

**BEDROOMS:** 14, 2 on ground floor, 8 in courtyard.
**OPEN:** all year.
**FACILITIES:** sitting room, bar, conservatory restaurant, wedding facilities, garden, unsuitable for &.
**BACKGROUND MUSIC:** classical/jazz in bar/restaurant.
**LOCATION:** 11 miles NW of Callander.
**CHILDREN:** all ages welcomed (under-2s free).
**DOGS:** allowed in 2 bedrooms.
**CREDIT CARDS:** all major cards.
**PRICES:** [2010] B&B £64–£132.50 per person (only available Mon–Thurs), D,B&B £166–£357, set dinner £46, 1-night bookings refused Sat in season.

# BLAIRGOWRIE Perth and Kinross

## KINLOCH HOUSE

'It is the epitome of luxury,' say *Guide* regulars this year of the Allen family's Victorian mansion (Relais & Châteaux) near Dunkeld. 'We left reluctantly and will return at the earliest opportunity.' Another comment: 'Food and service excellent.' Set 'high on a slope' in the gentle Perthshire hills, the house 'looked stunning, with its red creeper in full autumn colour'. 'It is a treat to visit, with the atmosphere of a family home; the well-furnished lounges have comfortable chairs, fine china and ornaments, paintings of quality.' The manager is Paul Knott. Visitors felt 'pampered' by his helpful staff. 'Our bedroom was huge, warm, and with every conceivable extra.' Many rooms are spacious, some have a four-poster bed and a large Victorian bath. Most showers are hand held. Steven MacCallum, previously at *Airds*, Port Appin (see entry), joined as chef in October 2009. 'His cooking is outstanding: delicious sauces, succulent beef and venison, unusual desserts.' Breakfast has 'excellent kippers'. There is a health centre. Shooting and fishing can be arranged. (*Val Ferguson, Robert Gower, and others*)

Dunkeld Road
by Blairgowrie PH10 6SG

**T:** 01250-884237
**F:** 01250-884333
**E:** reception@kinlochhouse.com
**W:** www.kinlochhouse.com

**BEDROOMS:** 18, 4 on ground floor.
**OPEN:** all year except 14–29 Dec.
**FACILITIES:** ramp, drawing room, 2 lounges, conservatory, bar, dining room, private dining room, health centre (swimming pool), wedding facilities, 25-acre grounds.
**BACKGROUND MUSIC:** none.
**LOCATION:** 3 miles W of Blairgowrie, on A923.
**CHILDREN:** no under-7s in dining room at night.
**DOGS:** allowed by arrangement (dog units available).
**CREDIT CARDS:** Amex, MasterCard, Visa.
**PRICES:** [2010] B&B £85–£155 per person, D,B&B £133–£203, set dinner £48, full alc £62.50, see website for offers, New Year package, 1-night bookings sometimes refused.

# BROADFORD Highland

## TIGH AN DOCHAIS    `NEW`

In a 'wonderful situation' on Broadford Bay, Neil
Hope and Lesley Unwin's striking contemporary
house has uninterrupted sea, island and mountain
views. It enters the *Guide* thanks to an
enthusiastic report from award-winning retired
B&B owners: 'On an island with a multitude of
grim B&Bs, this place shines out.' The architect-
designed house is entered by a bridge to the upper
floor where the guest lounge and dining room
have full-length picture windows. There is solid
oak flooring throughout; contemporary art. The
bedrooms are on the ground floor: 'They are
well furnished and fully equipped for everything
you might need to pass the time in bad weather.'
Guests can sit out on a decking with chairs
'midges permitting'. Mr Hope provides a no-
choice set meal (must be booked in advance when
likes and dislikes are discussed). 'He is a keen and
accomplished cook; the poached sea trout with
fresh vegetables was memorable. Outstanding
value; bring your bottle.' Breakfast, served
communally, has fresh fruit salad, house yogurt,
home-made muffins; locally smoked haddock
and kippers are among the cooked choices. (*Fiona
and Colin Mitchell-Rose*)

13 Harrapool, Broadford
Isle of Skye IV49 9AQ

T: 01471-820022
E: hopeskye@btinternet.com
W: www.skyebedbreakfast.co.uk

BEDROOMS: 3, all on ground floor.
OPEN: Apr–Nov.
FACILITIES: lounge, dining room,
½-acre garden, unsuitable for &.
BACKGROUND MUSIC: Celtic at
breakfast.
LOCATION: 1 mile E of Broadford.
CHILDREN: all ages welcomed.
DOGS: not allowed.
CREDIT CARDS: Amex, MasterCard,
Visa.
PRICES: [2010] B&B £40 per person,
set dinner £25, 2-night bookings
preferred July/Aug.

# BRODICK North Ayrshire

Map 5:E1

## KILMICHAEL COUNTRY HOUSE

Visitors in 2010 'had a delightful stay at this well-appointed hotel in beautiful gardens; such a warm welcome'. The small hotel stands in wooded grounds with fine views of Goat Fell, the island's highest mountain. The owners, Geoffrey Botterill and Antony Butterworth, who are much in evidence, have filled the house with furniture and pictures collected on their travels. 'A very special place,' says another visitor. 'The two first-floor lounges are good places to relax in.' Five of the bedrooms are in the main house; three are in converted stables a short walk away. 'Our room was cosy, with a separate sitting room and large bathroom.' Visitors like the thoughtful extra touches in the rooms: a china tea set, Ordnance Survey map, history of the island. In the 'spacious, properly lit' conservatory dining room 'the service was just right, professional, friendly and not over-attentive'. Mr Butterworth cooks a daily-changing set menu: 'We take account of allergies and intolerances, but we are reluctant to modify our entire menu to suit those who were startled by a piece of broccoli as a child,' he says. (*Derek Lambert, Simon Tonking*)

Glen Cloy, by Brodick
Isle of Arran KA27 8BY

T: 01770-302219
F: 01770-302068
E: enquiries@kilmichael.com
W: www.kilmichael.com

BEDROOMS: 8, 3 in converted stables (20 yds), 7 on ground floor, 4 self-catering cottages.
OPEN: Easter–Oct, restaurant closed Mon and Tues.
FACILITIES: 2 drawing rooms, dining room, 4½-acre grounds (burn).
BACKGROUND MUSIC: light classical background music during meals.
LOCATION: 1 mile SW of village.
CHILDREN: not under 12.
DOGS: not allowed in public rooms.
CREDIT CARDS: MasterCard, Visa.
PRICES: [2010] B&B £64–£99.50 per person, dinner £44, various packages, 1-night bookings refused Sat.

# CARRADALE Argyll and Bute

Map 5:E1

## DUNVALANREE IN CARRADALE

Above a beach with 'breathtaking' views across Kilbrannan Sound to the Isle of Arran, this small hotel/restaurant is run by owners Alan and Alyson Milstead, who are 'warm and delightful'. 'It is old-fashioned in a good way, which is part of the charm,' says a visitor in 2010. A 'superb' cook, Mrs Milstead is listed in the *Good Food Guide* for her short, daily-changing table d'hôte menu. She uses local produce and seafood (Carradale is a fishing village) in her dishes, perhaps Gigha halibut, Arran mustard, buttered samphire. 'David serves cocktails of the day from his impressive bar.' The bedrooms are 'comfortable, well presented'. A ground-floor room has French doors leading on to a patio with a table and chairs. 'Our adequate room had a comfortable bed; lots of extras.' Bunk beds can be provided for children. 'Quality tea and decent coffee were to hand, as was a tin of Alyson's delicious home-made biscuits.' Breakfast includes freshly squeezed orange juice, grapefruit grilled with ginger and brown sugar, Loch Fyne kippers, a full fry-up with potato scone. Distilleries, archaeology, golf, sea tours and wildlife are all nearby. (*CLH, Pauline Macdonald*)

Port Righ, Carradale
PA28 6SE

T: 01583-431226
E: book@dunvalanree.com
W: www.dunvalanree.com

BEDROOMS: 5, 1 on ground floor suitable for &.
OPEN: all year except Christmas.
FACILITIES: lounge, dining room, ½-acre garden.
BACKGROUND MUSIC: radio at breakfast, Scottish/jazz in evening in dining room.
LOCATION: on edge of village 15 miles N of Campbeltown.
CHILDREN: all ages welcomed.
DOGS: allowed in 1 ground-floor bedroom only.
CREDIT CARDS: MasterCard, Visa.
PRICES: [2010] D,B&B £55–£87.50, set menus £22.50–£27, full alc £28, New Year package, 1-night bookings sometimes refused.

**25% DISCOUNT VOUCHERS**

# CHIRNSIDE Borders

Map 5:E3

## CHIRNSIDE HALL

Built as a holiday retreat for an Edinburgh businessman, this 'beautifully restored' late Georgian mansion in the Borders is run by Tessa and Christian Korsten. 'We are more like a private house than a hotel,' they say. Visitors delighted by the warmth of the welcome 'were made to feel at home' by the 'hands-on' owners. 'She seemed able to read our minds; not once did we have to chase for assistance,' is a recent comment. There are 'inspiring' views of the Cheviot hills from the large 'attractive' public rooms, 'pleasantly' decorated with bold colours, rich fabrics; there are open fires in marble fireplaces; lots of seating in the lounge. The well-equipped bedrooms have heavy drapes, dark colours. 'Our south-facing room was large and warm.' One room has a four-poster bed and a sofa. Several first-floor rooms have been given a new bathroom this year. We would welcome reports on chef Mark Wilkinson's daily-changing menu which might include sea bass grilled with sea salt and lime, basil-crushed potatoes. Popular with hunting and fishing parties in winter. (*A McM*)

Chirnside, nr Duns TD11 3LD

**T:** 01890-818219
**F:** 01890-818231
**E:** reception@chirnsidehallhotel.com
**W:** www.chirnsidehallhotel.com

**BEDROOMS:** 10.
**OPEN:** all year except Mar.
**FACILITIES:** 2 lounges, dining room, private dining room, billiard room, fitness room, library/conference rooms, wedding facilities, 5-acre grounds, unsuitable for &.
**BACKGROUND MUSIC:** 'easy listening' and classical.
**LOCATION:** 1½ miles E of village, NE of Duns.
**CHILDREN:** all ages welcomed.
**DOGS:** not allowed in public rooms, unattended in bedrooms.
**CREDIT CARDS:** Amex, MasterCard, Visa.
**PRICES:** [2010] B&B £75–£105 per person, D,B&B £100–£125, set dinner £30, short breaks.

# COLONSAY Argyll and Bute

Map 5:D1

## THE COLONSAY

Visitors to the only hotel on this 'idyllic' eight-mile-long Hebridean island were picked up from the ferry and 'well looked after' by the manager, Scott Omar, and his 'courteous, efficient' staff. The unpretentious hotel is owned by a group headed by the laird and his wife, Alex and Jane Howard. Bedrooms are simply furnished, 'comfortable, spotless'. The largest room, with views across to the harbour, has Designers Guild fabrics. The bar, which has three log fires, has spacious sitting areas, 'lots of books and games'. There are harbour views from the informal restaurant (abstract art, wood-burning stove), which is 'more gastropub than formal dining'. The short seasonal menu, with much local fish and shellfish, might include smoked mackerel pâté; roast hake, haricot beans with chorizo and mussels. Vegetables are from the hotel's organic garden. 'Outstanding' breakfasts have home-baked bread, home-made jams; cooked dishes cost extra. Packed lunches are provided if you want to spend the day exploring. There are archaeological remains, or 'you can bask on a splendid golden beach', play golf, tennis and go fishing. (*KC, and others*)

Isle of Colonsay
PA61 7YP

T: 01951-200316
F: 01951-200353
E: hotel@colonsayestate.co.uk
W: www.colonsayestate.co.uk

BEDROOMS: 9.
OPEN: Mar–Jan, no Monday check-in.
FACILITIES: conservatory lounge, log room, bar, restaurant, accommodation unsuitable for &.
BACKGROUND MUSIC: none.
LOCATION: 400 yds W of harbour.
CHILDREN: all ages welcomed.
DOGS: not allowed in bedrooms.
CREDIT CARDS: Amex, MasterCard, Visa.
PRICES: [2010] B&B £42.50–£72.50 per person, D,B&B £24 added, full alc £25–£35, 1 free night for a 3-night stay at certain times, Christmas/New Year packages.

# CONTIN Highland

Map 5:C2

## COUL HOUSE

There are splendid views of the Strathconon valley from this spacious 1820s hunting lodge. It stands in mature woodland outside a small village on the River Conon. Built for Sir George Mackenzie in 1821, it has fine public rooms with ornate ceilings, log fires. Stuart and Susannah Macpherson are the 'hard-working' owners, supported by 'unendingly helpful' staff. The bedrooms, individually decorated, are 'clean, comfortable, with good pillows'; some have a four-poster. The Macphersons plan further renovation of bedrooms and bathrooms 'in quieter periods'. The chef, Garry Kenley, cures and smokes fish using traditional Highland techniques for his contemporary Scottish dishes, perhaps pickled herring with sour cream, aubergine caviar; saddle of venison, celeriac and beetroot pavé. Dinner is served in a high-ceilinged, octagonal dining room, with full-height windows. Bread is home baked at breakfast, which has much choice of cereals and cooked dishes. Children are welcomed, and have their own menu; there's a Wendy house in the trees. 'This is a great place to bring your four-legged friend, with miles of forest walks, and log fires to curl up to.' More reports, please.

Contin IV14 9ES

T: 01997-421487
F: 01997-421945
E: stay@coulhousehotel.com
W: www.coulhousehotel.com

BEDROOMS: 21, some on ground floor.
OPEN: all year except 24–26 Dec.
FACILITIES: ramp, 2 lounges, restaurant, conference/wedding facilities, 8-acre garden (children's play area, 9-hole pitch and putt).
BACKGROUND MUSIC: in lounge bar and restaurant.
LOCATION: rural, 17 miles NW of Inverness.
CHILDREN: all ages welcomed.
DOGS: allowed (£5 per day).
CREDIT CARDS: MasterCard, Visa.
PRICES: B&B £77.50–£95 per person, full alc £50, special breaks, New Year package, 1-night bookings refused New Year.

**25% DISCOUNT VOUCHERS**

# CRINAN Argyll and Bute

## CRINAN HOTEL

A hotel for more than two centuries, this white-painted building has a 'superb position' overlooking the Straits of Jura. It has been owned and run for the last 40 years by Nick and Frances Ryan. Fans commend the charm, the informal ambience, and Mr Ryan's 'hands-on style'. Some find the decor of the public rooms dated and 'in need of an overhaul'. All bedrooms have the 'marvellous views'; some have a balcony. 'Ours was simply furnished, which we like, clean and comfortable, with large bed and soft pillows.' In the 'well-proportioned' *Westward* restaurant, seafood is a feature of the menus of chef Gregor Bara, 'though not exclusively so'. He uses fresh local produce for his traditional French/Scottish dishes, eg, crab risotto; rack of Argyll hill lamb, Pommery mustard sauce. Traditional bar meals are available in the panelled *Mainbrace* bar. Mrs Ryan (the artist Frances Macdonald) exhibits her paintings in a gallery on the top floor, where there is a bay-windowed lounge with 'squashy sofas'. Children and dogs are welcomed. (*ST, and others*)

Crinan
by Lochgilphead PA31 8SR

**T:** 01546-830261
**F:** 01546-830292
**E:** reservations@crinanhotel.com
**W:** www.crinanhotel.com

**BEDROOMS:** 20.
**OPEN:** all year except 20–27 Dec.
**FACILITIES:** lift, ramps, 10 public rooms including observation lounge, coffee shop, art gallery, treatment room (health and beauty), wedding facilities, patio, ¼-acre garden, safe, sandy beaches nearby.
**BACKGROUND MUSIC:** none.
**LOCATION:** village centre, waterfront.
**CHILDREN:** all ages welcomed.
**DOGS:** not allowed in some public rooms.
**CREDIT CARDS:** MasterCard, Visa.
**PRICES:** B&B £65–£105 per person, D,B&B £85–£150, set dinner £45, full alc (*Mainbrace*) £26, short breaks, courses, various packages.

# DORNOCH Highland

## 2 QUAIL

Enthusiastic golfers, Michael and Kerensa Carr run their Victorian stone house in this seaside town as a licensed B&B. They no longer have a restaurant, as Mr Carr has taken the position of executive chef at the historic Royal Dornoch championship golf course. 'Golfing visitors will still be able to sample my style of cooking,' he says. Readers find the Carrs 'delightful hosts, friendly and helpful'. Mrs Carr is an award-winning picture framer and restorer. Guests are encouraged to use the cosy lounge/library, where they can 'enjoy a glass of wine or a wee dram'. The 'clean, comfortable' bedrooms are well proportioned, traditionally furnished. Housekeeping is 'exemplary'. Breakfast, served at an agreed time from 7 am ('for those with early tee times'), has home-made yogurts and muesli, croissants; cooked dishes include kippers and smoked salmon from Golspie. Advice is given on places to eat in Dornoch 'for a variety of budgets'. The house is close to the small cathedral; long sandy beaches are nearby. Royal Dornoch is one of the oldest and finest links courses in the world.

Castle Street
Dornoch IV25 3SN

T: 01862-811811
E: ghg@2quail.com
W: www.2quail.com

BEDROOMS: 3.
OPEN: all year except Christmas, 2 weeks Feb/Mar, advance booking only for Sun/Mon.
FACILITIES: lounge, dining room, unsuitable for &.
BACKGROUND MUSIC: occasional.
LOCATION: central.
CHILDREN: not under 10 except for 'babes in arms'.
DOGS: only guide dogs allowed.
CREDIT CARDS: Amex, MasterCard, Visa.
PRICES: [2010] B&B £35–£55 per person.

# DRUMBEG Highland

## BLAR NA LEISG AT DRUMBEG HOUSE

'Something special is going on here: a rare combination of supremely comfortable accommodation and top-notch food in a heart-stoppingly beautiful place.' Enthusiasm from *Guide* inspectors for Anne and Eddie Strachan's small restaurant-with-rooms, a renovated laird's house by a loch on the Assynt peninsula. She is the 'gifted' cook; he runs front-of-house 'with courtesy and grace'. They have 'gutted and redesigned' the interiors of the stone dwelling. 'They have decorated with flair: the impression is of lightness (pale walls, oak floors) brought alive by vivid colours (curtains, pictures).' The sitting room is 'simply furnished, with elegant, squashy sofas'. No choice on the dinner menu (tastes are discussed when booking). 'A delicious appetiser; a glorious haddock soufflé; an amazing bream dish with piquant sauce; the most tender fillet steak; moist juicy pear on a biscuit base with a meringue sheaf; culinary heaven.' Two of the bedrooms have loch views: 'The colours in our room were restful, the fabrics of the highest quality; a large, extremely comfortable bed.' Breakfast, 'served at a time to suit us', has extensive choice: it is 'wonderful'.

Drumbeg IV27 4NW

T/F: 01571-833325
E: info@blarnaleisg.com
W: www.blarnaleisg.com

BEDROOMS: 4, plus self-catering studio.
OPEN: all year.
FACILITIES: lounge, library, day room, dining room, 4-acre grounds, unsuitable for &.
BACKGROUND MUSIC: none.
LOCATION: outskirts of village.
CHILDREN: all ages welcomed (by arrangement).
DOGS: allowed in cottage only.
CREDIT CARDS: none.
PRICES: D,B&B £105–£125 per person, set meals £45, various courses, Christmas/New Year packages.

**25% DISCOUNT VOUCHERS**

# DUNVEGAN Highland

Map 5:C1

## THE THREE CHIMNEYS AND THE HOUSE OVER-BY

♥ *César award in 2001*

Despite the remote setting by Loch Dunvegan, food lovers have been coming for 25 years to Eddie and Shirley Spear's acclaimed restaurant-with-rooms. 'The long journey is worthwhile; it has a special combination of a fine location, good food and superb service,' say *Guide* hoteliers making a 'pilgrimage' in 2010. The restaurant is in a white-painted crofter's cottage; the split-level bedrooms are in *The House Over-By* (next door). The bedrooms have been upgraded in contemporary style this year; each has sea views, six-foot bed, new carpets and soft furnishings, Freeview TV and a sofa. The morning room in *The House Over-By* has been reconfigured with new sofas, to allow the service of pre-dinner drinks. The candlelit restaurant has also been given a make-over, the entire space now devoted to dining tables. Michael Smith, the acclaimed chef, uses local meat and fish in dishes like steamed monkfish, sea bass and squid, saffron potatoes, carrots, winkle and sorrel butter. Breakfast has freshly squeezed orange juice, fruit salad, cheeses, porridge, smoked fish, a hot dish of the day. (*Phillip Gill and Anton van der Horst*)

Colbost, Dunvegan
Isle of Skye IV55 8ZT

T: 01470-511258
F: 01470-511358
E: eatandstay@threechimneys.co.uk
W: www.threechimneys.co.uk

BEDROOMS: 6, all on ground floor in separate building, 1 suitable for &.
OPEN: all year except Jan and early Feb, restaurant closed midday in winter.
FACILITIES: ramps, 3 public rooms, garden on loch.
BACKGROUND MUSIC: in lounge evenings.
LOCATION: 4 miles W of Dunvegan.
CHILDREN: no under-5s at lunch, no under-8s at dinner, tea at 5 pm.
DOGS: not in bedrooms.
CREDIT CARDS: Amex, MasterCard, Visa.
PRICES: B&B from £142.50 per person, D,B&B from £202.50, set lunch from £27.50, set dinner £55, 7-course tasting menu £80, special offers, Christmas/New Year packages.

# DUROR Argyll and Bute

Map 5:D1

## BEALACH HOUSE

♦ *César award in 2009*

Up a 'challenging' one-and-a-half-mile forestry track, this 'handsome, well-maintained' building is the only dwelling in 'stunning' Salachan Glen. Much liked by readers and endorsed again this year, it is run as a small guest house by Jim and Hilary McFadyen. 'They work hard and are superb hosts,' says a visitor in 2010. Visitors are greeted on first-name terms and given complimentary tea with 'delicious' cakes by a log fire in the lounge (recent guests arriving at 11 pm received an equally warm welcome). Bedrooms, though not large, are 'warmly furnished, extremely comfortable'. Bathrooms have a power shower (one also has a bath). Hilary McFadyen's 'superb' dinner, on a daily-changing menu (three courses with three choices for each), always has a vegetarian option (eg, red pepper and onion tartlet with a rarebit topping). No licence but guests may bring their own wine. Breads, chutneys, jams and ice creams are home made. Breakfasts are 'heartbreakingly delicious', and 'innovative' with 'unusual cereals and two kinds of marmalade'. 'Always freshly made juice.' (*Marc and Margaret Wall, Jean and Michael Clunas, and others*)

Salachan Glen, Duror
Appin PA38 4BW

T: 01631-740298
E: enquiries@bealachhouse.co.uk
W: www.bealachhouse.co.uk

BEDROOMS: 3.
OPEN: Feb–Oct.
FACILITIES: lounge, conservatory, dining room, 8-acre grounds, unsuitable for &.
BACKGROUND MUSIC: none.
LOCATION: 2 miles S of Duror, off A828.
CHILDREN: not under 14.
DOGS: not allowed.
CREDIT CARDS: MasterCard, Visa.
PRICES: B&B £40–£55 per person, set dinner £28.

# EDINBANE Highland

Map 5:C1

## GRESHORNISH HOUSE

'An archetypal country house hotel: squashy sofas, log fires, billiard room, candlelit dinners.' Praise this year for this listed, white-painted building (18th-century with Victorian additions) in a remote corner of Skye. Overlooking a sea loch, it stands in extensive and 'beautiful' grounds. The owners, Neil and Rosemary Colquhoun, were 'exceptionally kind and considerate' to another visitor who muddled his booking. 'The young staff were friendly,' is a typical comment. Some of the bedrooms are spacious; those in the eaves have a sloping ceiling. 'Our large room overlooking the gardens had the most comfortable bed.' In the restaurant (open to non-residents), the 'fine' cooking (three- and five-course options) of head chef Mac Browning was enjoyed. He uses local produce for traditional Scottish dishes, eg, mussels, white wine, parsley and cream sauce; breast of Barbary duck, orange and lemon glaze. A seafood lunch menu is served in summer. 'Good breakfast.' Children get reduced rates, high chairs, etc. Mrs Colquhoun tells us that she has withdrawn the option of playing background music: 'Guests seem more than happy with the peace and quiet.' (*GC, Robert Chandler*)

Edinbane, by Portree
Isle of Skye IV51 9PN

**T:** 01470-582266
**F:** 01470-582345
**E:** info@greshornishhouse.com
**W:** www.greshornishhouse.com

**BEDROOMS:** 8.
**OPEN:** 1 Mar–6 Jan except Christmas, restaurant closed Mon/Tues in winter.
**FACILITIES:** drawing room, bar, billiard room, dining room, conservatory, wedding facilities, only public rooms accessible for &.
**BACKGROUND MUSIC:** none.
**LOCATION:** 17 miles NW of Portree.
**CHILDREN:** all ages welcomed.
**DOGS:** not allowed in public rooms, or unaccompanied in bedrooms.
**CREDIT CARDS:** Amex, MasterCard, Visa.
**PRICES:** [2010] B&B £60–£102.50 per person, D,B&B £90–£132.50, set dinner £38–£45, seasonal and 3-day breaks, 1-night bookings sometimes refused at weekends in high season.

**25% DISCOUNT VOUCHERS**

# EDINBURGH

## THE BONHAM   **NEW**

In a quiet square near the West End, this conversion of three Victorian town houses is part of Peter Taylor's Town House Collection. It returns to the *Guide* after a positive report from visitors this year: 'It was well positioned for our activities; a relaxed and pleasant base.' Johanne Falconer is the manager: 'The service by a courteous staff was excellent.' Paintings by contemporary Scottish artists hang throughout the building. The decor is modern, colourful. 'We were pleased with our bedroom with an outlook over the gardens; lighting was inadequate for reading. The well-equipped bathroom was of reasonable size.' Some rooms have a bay window with views across to the Firth of Forth. One has a freestanding Edwardian copper bath. In the oak-panelled dining room, the cooking of Michel Bouyer was found 'well up to standard'. Trained in Paris, he serves 'modern classics', perhaps seared hand-dived scallops, crab cannelloni, pear and caper dressing. 'We particularly liked the 24-hour Lite Bite menu available in the room or the lounge.' Free car parking was 'a bonus'. (*Elspeth Jervie and John Gibbon*)

35 Drumsheugh Gardens
Edinburgh EH13 7RN

T: 0131-274 7400
F: 0131-274 7405
E: reserve@
    thetownhousecollection.com
W: www.thebonham.com

BEDROOMS: 48, 1 suitable for &.
OPEN: all year.
FACILITIES: reception lounge, restaurant.
BACKGROUND MUSIC: in public areas all day.
LOCATION: central.
CHILDREN: all ages welcomed.
DOGS: not allowed in public rooms.
CREDIT CARDS: all major cards.
PRICES: [2010] B&B £70–£230 per person, D,B&B £30 added, full alc £38, special breaks, Christmas/New Year packages, 1-night bookings refused Sat.

# EDINBURGH

## INGRAMS

Just over the hill from Princes Street and George Street on the northern slopes of the New Town is David and Theresa Ingram's B&B. Their Regency town house (no sign outside) is a Grade A listed building. It has a handsome flying stone staircase lit by an oval cupola, and is furnished with antiques (the 'eloquent' Mr Ingram is also an antique dealer). His 'pleasant' breakfasts are served round a large table in the 'beautiful, formal' dining room: there is fresh fruit salad with rose water, home-made muesli, and 'fine coffee'; the 'amazing porridge' is recommended. On the lower ground floor (one guest mentioned overhead noise) there are two twin-bedded bedrooms, and a double which faces the garden. Each has a private bathroom, though not necessarily en suite. 'My room,' said one visitor, 'was simple, well laid out and comfortable.' Convenient for all that Edinburgh has to offer in the way of food and culture. (*J and KP, and others*)

24 Northumberland Street
Edinburgh EH3 6LS

T: 0131-556 8140
F: 0131-556 4423
E: info@ingrams.co.uk
W: www.ingrams.co.uk

BEDROOMS: 3.
OPEN: all year except Christmas.
FACILITIES: sitting room, dining room, garden.
BACKGROUND MUSIC: baroque at breakfast if required.
LOCATION: 5 mins' walk from centre, limited parking.
CHILDREN: not under 15.
DOGS: not allowed.
CREDIT CARDS: Diners, MasterCard, Visa.
PRICES: B&B £50–£65 per person.

## EDNAM Borders

### EDENWATER HOUSE

By a 17th-century kirk in a peaceful hamlet near Kelso, this old stone manse is run as a small private hotel by owners Jeff and Jacqui Kelly. It has glorious views, across fields bisected by the Eden Water, to the Cheviot hills. Readers have given it the 'highest marks' for the 'attention to detail' and the quality of Mrs Kelly's cooking (she formerly ran a restaurant in Edinburgh). In an attractive candlelit dining room which has the views, she serves a three-course no-choice menu (likes and dislikes and dietary requirements are discussed in advance). Typical dishes: medallions of monkfish, Parmesan crust, pickled vegetables; guineafowl with cèpe and foie gras mousse. The bedrooms are well equipped; two face the river; one has a small single room adjacent. The public rooms have 'collections everywhere, beautiful furniture'. A wine-tasting/function room has been added this year. 'Delicious' breakfasts have a range of juices, fruit and yogurts; cooked options. There is good walking all around; fishing, shooting and golf can be arranged. More reports, please.

Ednam, nr Kelso TD5 7QL

T: 01573-224070
E: jeffnjax@hotmail.co.uk
W: www.edenwaterhouse.co.uk

BEDROOMS: 4.
OPEN: 1 Feb–31 Oct, dining room closed Sunday.
FACILITIES: lounge, drawing room, study, dining room, wedding facilities, 1-acre grounds, unsuitable for &.
BACKGROUND MUSIC: none.
LOCATION: 2 miles N of Kelso on B6461.
CHILDREN: not under 10.
DOGS: not allowed.
CREDIT CARDS: MasterCard, Visa.
PRICES: B&B £40–£65 per person, set dinner £36, full alc £50.

# ERISKA Argyll and Bute

## ISLE OF ERISKA

♥*César award in 2007*

'Still a wonderful, civilised haven from everyday life,' says a visitor returning this year to Beppo and Chay Buchanan-Smith's Scottish baronial mansion (Pride of Britain). 'We were pleased to find everything as well run as ever; exemplary service from well-trained staff, who remembered us from previous visits.' An earlier comment: 'The brothers watch over everything in a discreet and understated way.' Reached by a wrought iron vehicle bridge, the hotel is on a 'peaceful and beautiful' private island with a nine-hole golf course. Inside are grand panelled lounges, log fires, large comfortable sofas. 'Immaculate' bedrooms in the main house have a mix of traditional and contemporary design. Each of the modern spa suites in the grounds has a conservatory and private garden with hot tub. Robert MacPherson's six-course dinners 'seemed better than ever': the Scottish dishes might include roasted Oban turbot, local cockles, poached lettuce, celery and cider sauce. Male guests wear a jacket and tie to dinner. Light meals are served on a veranda. 'Limitless fresh orange juice' at breakfast. (*Roland Cassam, JR*)

Benderloch, Eriska
by Oban PA37 1SD

T: 01631-720371
F: 01631-720531
E: office@eriska-hotel.co.uk
W: www.eriska-hotel.co.uk

**BEDROOMS:** 25, including 5 spa suites and 2 garden cottages, some on ground floor.
**OPEN:** all year except Jan.
**FACILITIES:** ramp, 5 public rooms, leisure centre, swimming pool (17 by 6 metres), gym, sauna, treatments, wedding facilities, tennis, 9-hole golf course.
**BACKGROUND MUSIC:** none.
**LOCATION:** 12 miles N of Oban.
**CHILDREN:** all ages welcomed, but no under-5s in leisure centre.
**DOGS:** not allowed in public rooms or some bedrooms.
**CREDIT CARDS:** Amex, MasterCard, Visa.
**PRICES:** [2010] B&B £150–£225 per person, D,B&B £155–£270, set dinner £42.50, Christmas/New Year packages, 2-night min. stay.

# FORT AUGUSTUS Highland

Map 5:C2

## THE LOVAT

Experienced hoteliers David and Geraldine Gregory, and their daughter Caroline, the managing partner, have 'made a good job' of their renovation of this former railway hotel on the southern shore of Loch Ness. They have a gold award in the Green Tourism Business Scheme for their comprehensive environmental policy. Guests arriving by public transport get a discount; a biomass woodchip burner provides heating and hot water; a rocket composter takes all food waste. The decor is a mix of traditional and modern. All bedrooms have a hospitality tray, a flat-screen TV, an iron and ironing board, Internet access. Each of six studio rooms in an annexe has a private parking space; an open-plan wet room; 'an umbrella for a rainy day'. Colin Clark, the chef, serves a brasserie menu (eg, grilled halibut with caper butter) and more formal restaurant dishes, perhaps smoked lamb loin, plum chutney, pork syrup. 'The staff, mainly female, are attentive.' Breakfasts have fresh and dried fruits, muesli, kippers and smoked haddock. The Gregorys' other daughter, Rohaise, runs *The Torridon*, Torridon (see entry). (*M and MH*)

Fort Augustus PH32 4DU

T: 0845-4501100
F: 01320-366677
E: info@thelovat.com
W: www.thelovat.com

BEDROOMS: 28, 6 in annexe, 2 suitable for &.
OPEN: all year.
FACILITIES: lounge, 2 bars, 4 dining rooms, wedding facilities, 2¾-acre grounds.
BACKGROUND MUSIC: in bar.
LOCATION: in village SW of Inverness by A82.
CHILDREN: all ages welcomed.
DOGS: allowed in 1 bedroom only.
CREDIT CARDS: Amex, MasterCard, Visa.
PRICES: [2010] B&B £42.50–£132.50 per person, D,B&B £78.25–£152.50, set dinner £40, special breaks, Christmas/New Year packages.

# FORT WILLIAM Highland

Map 5:C1

## THE GRANGE

In a peaceful garden with lovely views across Loch Linnhe, this white-painted Victorian Gothic house is run as a B&B by owners Joan and John Campbell. 'She is charming and helpful, booking restaurants, suggesting walks and providing maps,' says a visitor this year. There are log fires, antiques and 'fresh flowers from the garden'. Just three bedrooms: 'Our garden room, beautifully designed by Joan, had a sleeping area and, through an arch, a sitting room with chaise longue and armchairs. The bathroom was spacious, well lit, with pedestal bath and walk-in shower.' Of the other rooms, Rob Roy, with colonial-style bed, is where Jessica Lange stayed while filming; the Turret Room has a window seat with garden and loch views and a Louis XV king-size bed. Earlier guests liked 'the little extras: towels tied up with a ribbon; decanter of sherry with lovely glassware'. Breakfast (ordered the evening before) is served on white china in a room overlooking the loch. 'My poached eggs arrived with a flower; porridge came with whisky, cream, brown sugar and honey.' (*Dale and Krystina Vargas, and others*)

Grange Road
Fort William PH33 6JF

T: 01397-705516
E: info@thegrange-scotland.co.uk
W: www.thegrange-scotland.co.uk

BEDROOMS: 3.
OPEN: Mar–Nov.
FACILITIES: lounge, breakfast room, 1-acre garden, unsuitable for &.
BACKGROUND MUSIC: none.
LOCATION: edge of town.
CHILDREN: not under 12.
DOGS: not allowed.
CREDIT CARDS: MasterCard, Visa.
PRICES: [2010] B&B £55–£59 per person, 1-night bookings sometimes refused.

# GATESIDE Fife

Map 5:D2

## EDENSHEAD STABLES

In wooded grounds bordered by the River Eden, these pink stone stables have been converted into a modern B&B by owners Gill and John Donald. It is recommended by readers for the 'air of relaxed comfort', and the good value. The interior is 'immaculate', filled with 'beautiful furnishings, lovely paintings'. A large sitting room leads on to a patio; there is much local information, maps and books. The bedrooms have an 'upmarket' bathroom with an 'excellent' shower. Guests sit at a large table in the 'elegant' dining room for breakfast, served from 7.45 to 8.45 am (earlier by arrangement). It has local soft fruits in season, oatmeal porridge; the usual cooked choices and three kinds of fish. A three-course dinner is offered by arrangement for groups of four to six (dishes like mixed game pie, rowan jelly). Bring your own wine (free corkage). There are pubs and restaurants nearby. Secure storage is provided for golf clubs (many good courses in the area). No visiting dogs, but the owners' Hungarian vizslas, Rosa and Zeta, are 'very much part of the team'. (*J and AK*)

Gateside, by Cupar
KY14 7ST

T/F:01337-868500
E:  info@edensheadstables.com
W:  www.edensheadstables.com

BEDROOMS: 3, all on ground floor.
OPEN: March–end Nov.
FACILITIES: lounge, dining room, patio, courtyard, 3-acre grounds bordering River Eden, unsuitable for &.
BACKGROUND MUSIC: none.
LOCATION: on edge of village 12 miles SE of Perth.
CHILDREN: not under 12.
DOGS: not allowed.
CREDIT CARDS: Amex, MasterCard, Visa.
PRICES: [2010] B&B £40–£55 per person, set dinner £25, off-season breaks, 1-night bookings occasionally refused weekends and July/Aug.

# GIFFORD East Lothian

## EAGLESCAIRNIE MAINS

Off the beaten track 18 miles east of Edinburgh, but easily accessible if you have a car, *Eaglescairnie* is an 'impeccable' white-painted Georgian house run as a B&B 'on very personal lines' by owners Michael and Barbara Williams. 'Full of character', it sits at the centre of a 350-acre award-winning farm that is 'an example of best practice in combining agriculture with wildlife and landscape diversity, and the advancement of bio-diversity'. The 'tranquil' house is 'tastefully and comfortably furnished': the drawing room has chintz sofas, an open fire, maps, guides, board games, television. There is Wi-Fi. Spacious bedrooms have a tea and coffee tray, a radio and good views; a shower over the bath in the en suite or private bathroom. In summer, breakfast is taken in a conservatory. Mrs Williams uses farm and local produce for dishes that are cooked to order. No evening meal, but there are two pubs in Gifford, a mile away. Eight golf courses are within a few miles. More reports, please.

Gifford, nr Haddington EH41 4HN

**T/F:** 01620-810491
**E:** williams.eagles@btinternet.com
**W:** www.eaglescairnie.com

**BEDROOMS:** 3.
**OPEN:** all year except Christmas week.
**FACILITIES:** sitting room, conservatory, large garden (tennis), unsuitable for &.
**BACKGROUND MUSIC:** none.
**LOCATION:** 1 mile W of Gifford.
**CHILDREN:** all ages welcomed.
**DOGS:** allowed by prior arrangement.
**CREDIT CARDS:** MasterCard, Visa.
**PRICES:** [2010] B&B £35–£50 per person, discount for 4-night stay, 1-night bookings refused Fri and Sat in July/Aug, bank holiday weekends.

**25% DISCOUNT VOUCHERS**

# GLENFINNAN Highland

Map 5:C1

## GLENFINNAN HOUSE

Across the water from the Glenfinnan Monument where Bonnie Prince Charlie raised the standard at the start of the 1745 Jacobite Rebellion, this handsome Victorian mansion has 'a hint of small medieval French château'. Owned by Jane MacFarlane-Glasow, it is managed by Manja and Duncan Gibson. Popular with locals for celebrations and weddings, the house is also liked by visitors for the Highland atmosphere and the warmth of the welcome (extended to children, who have their own short menu). The decor is traditional with wood panelling but no tartan. Bedrooms vary in size. Those at the front have 'superb views'; the Jacobite suite, with a four-poster and an adjoining room for children, is new this year. There are two other family rooms. In the 'relaxing' dining room, Duncan Gibson serves 'traditional Scottish food with a French twist'. 'Good meals' are served in the bar. Children have a playroom, and can enjoy the lawns which run down to Loch Shiel. Breakfast is a buffet breakfast. (*MR, and others*)

Glenfinnan
by Fort William PH37 4LT

T/F: 01397-722235
E:   availability@
     glenfinnanhouse.com
W:  www.glenfinnanhouse.com

BEDROOMS: 12.
OPEN: end Mar–early Nov.
FACILITIES: ramps, drawing room, playroom, bar, restaurant, wedding facilities, 1-acre grounds, playground, unsuitable for &.
BACKGROUND MUSIC: Scottish in bar and restaurant.
LOCATION: 15 miles NW of Fort William.
CHILDREN: all ages welcomed.
DOGS: not in restaurant.
CREDIT CARDS: Amex, MasterCard, Visa.
PRICES: [2010] B&B £60–£95 per person, full alc £38–£40, special breaks (see website).

**25% DISCOUNT VOUCHERS**

# GRANTOWN-ON-SPEY Highland

Map 5:C2

## CULDEARN HOUSE

At their Victorian granite house in a 'peaceful' setting on the edge of a pretty Speyside town, William and Sonia Marshall are 'charming hosts'. It is liked for its 'homely heart': 'The moment you walk through the door after a day out, Sonia appears with trays of tea and cake.' There is plenty of seating in the panelled lounge, watercolours, antique maps, a log fire (and a choice of more than 50 malt whiskies). Bedrooms are 'comfortably furnished': 'Our room, overlooking the front garden, was spotless. Fresh flowers were a thoughtful touch.' A visitor in November 'could have been warmer'. Much praise again this year for Mrs Marshall's daily-changing four-course dinner served in a candlelit room. 'Her Culdearn steak was melt in the mouth'; a vegetarian enjoyed oven-baked mushroom risotto with Parmesan. 'Splendid' breakfasts include 'porridge, fruits, delicious potato scones' and 'scrambled eggs cooked to perfection'. The Marshalls 'know the area well' and will guide visitors to interesting local attractions. (*Anike Whelan, Rebecca Overy, and others*)

Woodlands Terrace
Grantown-on-Spey PH26 3JU

T: 01479-872106
F: 01479-873641
E: enquiries@culdearn.com
W: www.culdearn.com

BEDROOMS: 6, 1 on ground floor.
OPEN: all year.
FACILITIES: lounge, dining room, ¾-acre garden.
BACKGROUND MUSIC: pre-dinner classical in lounge.
LOCATION: edge of town.
CHILDREN: not under 10.
DOGS: only guide dogs allowed.
CREDIT CARDS: Diners, MasterCard, Visa.
PRICES: [2010] B&B £56–£83 per person, D,B&B £89–£110, set dinner £34, spring/autumn breaks, reduced rates for 4–7 nights, Christmas/New Year packages.

# GRULINE Argyll and Bute

## GRULINE HOME FARM

On a wild and beautiful peninsula, this handsome converted farmhouse (no longer working) stands amid gardens and pastureland overlooking Ben More. Regular visitors will be pleased to learn that the owners, Angela and Colin Boocock, have extended their opening season for 2011 and postponed 'for a couple of years' plans to retire. The Boococks are 'warmly welcoming' (except to children); arriving guests are given afternoon tea in the conservatory. The house is traditionally decorated with antique and modern furniture; all bedrooms were recently refurbished. A dinner-party atmosphere is encouraged in the dining room (with Mouseman furniture), open to non-residents. Mrs Boocock, responsible for front-of-house, is meticulous with 'presentation and service', using fine china and crystal. Her husband's 'excellent' four-course dinner might include fillet steak Diane, sweet potato dauphinoise. No licence (bring your own wine; no corkage charged), but visitors are offered complimentary sherry. Breakfast has 'outstanding' warm fruit compote, home-made jam and muesli; cooked dishes include Loch Fyne kippers, black pudding and haggis. (*J and DM*)

Gruline, Isle of Mull
PA71 6HR

T: 01680-300581
E: boo@gruline.com
W: www.gruline.com

**BEDROOMS:** 3, 1, on ground floor, 5 yds from main house.
**OPEN:** Jan–Nov.
**FACILITIES:** lounge, conservatory, dining room, 2½-acre garden.
**BACKGROUND MUSIC:** light classical.
**LOCATION:** 2½ miles from Salen village, 14 miles S of Tobermory.
**CHILDREN:** not under 16.
**DOGS:** allowed in annexe bedroom only.
**CREDIT CARDS:** none.
**PRICES:** [2010] B&B £60 per person, D,B&B £100, set dinner £40.

# INVERGARRY Highland

Map 5:C2

## TOMDOUN HOTEL

'An interesting, quirky place in a stunning setting', Michael Pearson's simple, sporting hotel is recommended for 'an authentic Highland lodge experience'. It stands in woodland overlooking the Upper Garry river, off the single-track drovers' road leading to Skye. Squashy sofas in front of log fires, ancient leather luggage in the hall, dogs wandering about the public rooms, contribute to the charm. Facilities are limited (no TV, telephone in the bedroom). Two rooms have been amalgamated in 2010, to create a new superior room with a walk-in wardrobe; a claw-foot bath in the bathroom. 'Our fine room had a wonderful view.' Three simpler, cheaper rooms share a bathroom. Residents can eat until 6 pm in the bar, a popular local, which has two log fires. In the dining room, David Errington's 'excellent' menu might include red mullet with olives, tomatoes, rosemary and anchovy mash. 'We encourage our guests to mingle in the bar and dining room,' says Mr Pearson. There is much fishing, stalking, shooting, mountain biking, and good walking, both light and serious. (*Alan and Edwina Williams, and others*)

Invergarry PH35 4HS

T: 01809-511218
E: enquiries@tomdoun.com
W: www.tomdoun.com

BEDROOMS: 9, 6 with facilities en suite.
OPEN: all year.
FACILITIES: drawing room, bar, dining room, wedding facilities, 80-acre grounds.
BACKGROUND MUSIC: none.
LOCATION: 10 miles W of Invergarry; 6 miles off A87.
CHILDREN: all ages welcomed.
DOGS: not allowed in public rooms.
CREDIT CARDS: Amex, MasterCard, Visa.
PRICES: [2010] B&B £40–£75 per person, full alc £35.

**25% DISCOUNT VOUCHERS**

# INVERNESS Highland

## TRAFFORD BANK GUEST HOUSE

Once the home of the Bishop of Moray and Ross-shire, this stone, bay-windowed house has been renovated by interior designer Lorraine Freel. She runs it as a 'superb' B&B with Koshal Pun: 'The best accommodation we have found in Inverness,' said the nominators (regular *Guide* correspondents). 'The welcome, the bedroom and the breakfast were of the highest quality,' is a comment in 2010. In mature gardens (plenty of places to sit), the house is a short walk from the centre of town. It has been furnished with a mix of antiques and contemporary pieces (some of which the owner designed). Most of the 'luxurious' bedrooms are large. The Thistle Room has dramatic handmade Grand Thistle wallpaper and furnishings. The Floral Suite has a large, modern half-tester bed. The Green Room is suitable for a small family. Spacious bathrooms have a roll-top bath or a shower. All rooms have a hospitality tray, decanter of sherry, silent fridge, flat-screen TV, iPod docking. Breakfast, ordered the evening before, is taken in a conservatory overlooking the garden. It has 'excellent choices, served piping hot'. Free Wi-Fi is available throughout. (*Fiona McEwan, and others*)

96 Fairfield Road
Inverness IV3 5LL

T: 01463-241414
F: 01463-241421
E: info@
  traffordbankguesthouse.co.uk
W: www.traffordbankguesthouse.
  co.uk

BEDROOMS: 5.
OPEN: all year except 15 Nov–8 Dec.
FACILITIES: ramps, 2 lounges, conservatory, garden, unsuitable for &.
BACKGROUND MUSIC: none.
LOCATION: 10 mins' walk from centre.
CHILDREN: all ages welcomed.
DOGS: only guide dogs allowed.
CREDIT CARDS: MasterCard, Visa.
PRICES: [2010] B&B £40–£95 per person.

# IONA Argyll and Bute

Map 5:D1

## ARGYLL HOTEL

The smaller of the two hotels on this mystical Hebridean island is run by Daniel Morgan and Claire Bachellerie, whose ecological commitment is driven by the location. When possible, produce and resources are acquired locally; waste is recycled or composted; vegetables and herbs are grown organically in their garden. The 'imaginative' food is praised by readers. The chatty menus of the chef, Peter Janicina, might include Cullen Skink ('the staple diet of big bearded men in fishing smocks'); Loch Etive salmon ('with a tangy wasabi and walnut crème dressing'). A hotel for 140 years, the *Argyll* sits in a row of 19th-century houses in the main village, a short walk from the jetty where the ferry from Mull docks. There are 'idyllic' views from book-filled lounges and conservatory. Manager Jann Simpson is assisted by 'delightful' local staff. Children are welcomed (early supper available). So are dogs, 'but local crofters insist they be exercised on a lead'. The best rooms are in the main house: cheaper annexe rooms are small, but have 'good storage and a well-planned bathroom'. (*RM, and others*)

Isle of Iona PA76 6SJ

T: 01681-700334
F: 01681-700510
E: reception@argyllhoteliona.co.uk
W: www.argyllhoteliona.co.uk

BEDROOMS: 16, 7 in annexe.
OPEN: Mar–Oct.
FACILITIES: 2 lounges, conservatory, restaurant, unsuitable for &.
BACKGROUND MUSIC: in restaurant.
LOCATION: village centre.
CHILDREN: all ages welcomed.
DOGS: not allowed in dining room, £10 charge per stay.
CREDIT CARDS: MasterCard, Visa.
PRICES: [2010] B&B £26–£87.50 per person, full alc £32, 1-night bookings sometimes refused.

# KILBERRY Argyll and Bute

Map 5:D1

## KILBERRY INN

♥ *César award in 2010*

In a 'wild magical place at the edge of the world', David Wilson and Clare Johnson's unpretentious restaurant-with-rooms on the Kintyre peninsula 'justly deserved' the *Guide*'s *César* award in 2010, say returning visitors. 'We still have nothing but praise.' Mr Wilson is 'chatty but discreet, filling the peat-fired dining room with mirth', says a reporter this year. Clare Johnson, assisted by Tom Holloway and John McNulty, has a *Michelin* Bib Gourmand for modern cooking on a short, seasonal menu. 'Our favourites were heavenly potted crab, the best we have ever eaten; melt-in-the mouth venison; and honey and mascarpone crème brûlée.' The ingredients are local (the seafood is landed at nearby Tarbert). Beams and bare stone walls with local artwork 'give plenty of character' to the two dining rooms (there is no lounge). The small bedrooms, in adjacent single-storey 'cottages', have their own hallway, a shower. 'Nothing grand, but wonderfully cosy.' 'Extremely good' breakfasts include smoothies, scrambled eggs with smoked salmon. (*Marc and Margaret Wall, GC, and others*)

Kilberry, by Tarbert
PA29 6YD

T: 01880-770223
E: relax@kilberryinn.com
W: www.kilberryinn.com

BEDROOMS: 5, all on ground floor.
OPEN: Tues–Sun 18 March–end Oct, weekends only Nov–Dec, except Christmas.
FACILITIES: bar/dining room, smaller dining room, small grounds.
BACKGROUND MUSIC: in larger dining room, lunch and dinner.
LOCATION: 16 miles NW of Tarbert, on B8024.
CHILDREN: no under-12s.
DOGS: not allowed in public rooms, 4 bedrooms.
CREDIT CARDS: MasterCard, Visa.
PRICES: [2010] D,B&B £92.50 per person, full alc £39.50, winter breaks, New Year package, 1-night bookings sometimes refused weekends in summer.

# KILCHRENAN Argyll and Bute

Map 5:D1

## ARDANAISEIG

In 'a wonderful spot' down a ten-mile track by Loch Awe, this late Georgian stone baronial mansion stands in extensive wooded grounds with an amphitheatre. It is owned by Bennie Gray of Gray's Antiques Market in London; the manager is Peter Webster. Unsurprisingly, the interior has a playful Gothic look, with rich furnishings, tapestries, bold colour schemes. Open fires burn in the long, gold-papered drawing room and the more intimate library bar. The bedrooms are opulently furnished with pieces from the owner's collection. The best have loch views ('I saw an osprey'). A boathouse overlooking the water has been converted into a 'romantic' suite with modern decor. Gary Goldie serves a no-choice four-course dinner of modern dishes, eg, best end of lamb, wild garlic, confit tomatoes, aubergine caviar, herb jus. A dairy-intolerant visitor praised the chef's 'flair and imagination in working around this restriction'. Breakfast ('plenty of choice') has brown toast, and honey and preserves in jars. Guests can sail in a hotel boat to a private island. The neglected walled garden 'would make a great kitchen garden'. (*Robert Chandler, J and GM*)

Kilchrenan
by Taynuilt PA35 1HE

T: 01866-833333
F: 01866-833222
E: ardanaiseig@clara.net
W: www.ardanaiseig.com

**BEDROOMS:** 18, some on ground floor, 1 in boat house, 1 self-catering cottage.
**OPEN:** all year except Jan.
**FACILITIES:** drawing room, library/bar, restaurant, wedding facilities, 360-acre grounds on loch (open-air theatre, tennis, bathing, fishing).
**BACKGROUND MUSIC:** in restaurant.
**LOCATION:** 4 miles E of Kilchrenan.
**CHILDREN:** all ages welcomed, but no under-12s at dinner.
**DOGS:** not allowed in public rooms.
**CREDIT CARDS:** all major cards.
**PRICES:** [2010] B&B £64–£212 per person, set dinner £50, special offers, Christmas/New Year packages.

**25% DISCOUNT VOUCHERS**

# KILLIECRANKIE Perth and Kinross

## KILLIECRANKIE HOUSE ♟♟

*César award: Scottish hotel of the year*

'The feel-good factor was instantaneous; the welcome warm and sincere from courteous young staff dressed in elegant tartan trousers, a charming Scottish touch.' There is much enthusiasm this year for Henrietta Fergusson's 'charming small hotel', a white dower house in 'enchanting' gardens at the entrance to the Pass of Killiecrankie. 'It was a joy to stay here; she is a real expert,' is the comment of a fellow *Guide* hotelier. All the bedrooms have now been renovated: 'Our small but pleasant room was spotless.' 'Such attention to detail: a hot-water bottle at turn-down; shortbread and good coffee; luxurious bathroom products.' The service in the 'cosy' dining room 'was elegant without being too formal as in many country house hotels'. Chef Mark Easton's modern British cooking was 'exceptional, with local produce; good red lamb; perfect partridge, in a magnificent jus'. A vegetarian enjoyed 'tasty, original dishes'. 'Breakfast was another exquisite Scottish affair with beautiful linen and crockery; freshly squeezed juice, great coffee, porridge, stewed fruit, good hot dishes.' (*Gill Allen, Dennis Marler, Mark Crichton, Robert Gower*)

Killiecrankie
by Pitlochry PH16 5LG

T: 01796-473220
F: 01796-472451
E: enquiries@killiecrankiehotel.co.uk
W: www.killiecrankiehotel.co.uk

BEDROOMS: 10, 2 on ground floor.
OPEN: 19 Mar–3 Jan.
FACILITIES: ramp, sitting room, bar with conservatory, dining room, breakfast conservatory, 4½-acre grounds, unsuitable for &.
BACKGROUND MUSIC: none.
LOCATION: hamlet 3 miles W of Pitlochry.
CHILDREN: all ages welcomed.
DOGS: not allowed in eating areas, some bedrooms.
CREDIT CARDS: MasterCard, Visa.
PRICES: [2010] B&B £80–£90 per person, D,B&B £90–£125, set dinner £38, special breaks, Christmas/New Year packages, 1-night bookings sometimes refused.

# KINGUSSIE Highland

Map 5:C2

## THE CROSS AT KINGUSSIE

'Hands-on' owners David and Katie Young are 'welcoming and professional' at their restaurant-with-rooms in the Cairngorm national park, says a visitor this year. 'Very enjoyable; we had an excellent, roomy bedroom, and loved the Highlands location.' The converted tweed mill stands in large wooded riverside grounds with abundant wildlife. Mr Young shares the cooking with Becca Henderson, using Scottish produce on a short 'first-class' menu, eg, hot smoked organic sea trout, Eyemouth crab, avocado and soya bean salad; seared fillet of roast chicken breast, tomato risotto, wilted wild garlic leaves. Guests with dietary requirements, including vegetarians, are asked to give advance warning. The award-winning wine list has many half bottles and wines by the glass. 'Light and bright' interiors have modern Scottish art. Drinks are served on a pretty terrace in summer. Most bedrooms are spacious; some have river views; tea-making facilities on request. Breakfast includes freshly squeezed juices, seasonal fruit salad, home-made bread and jams; the hot dish of the day might be French toast with cinnamon and maple syrup. (*Dennis Marler, and others*)

Tweed Mill Brae, Ardbroilach Road
Kingussie PH21 1LB

T: 01540-661166
F: 01540-661080
E: relax@thecross.co.uk
W: www.thecross.co.uk

BEDROOMS: 8.
OPEN: early Feb–end Dec except Christmas, normally closed Sun/Mon.
FACILITIES: 2 lounges, restaurant, 4-acre grounds, only restaurant suitable for &.
BACKGROUND MUSIC: none.
LOCATION: 440 yds from village centre.
CHILDREN: 'generally' not under 9.
DOGS: not allowed.
CREDIT CARDS: Amex, MasterCard, Visa.
PRICES: [2010] B&B £50–£90 per person, D,B&B £100–£140, set dinner £50, special breaks, New Year package.

# KIRKCUDBRIGHT Dumfries and Galloway    Map 5:E2

## GLADSTONE HOUSE

'We were very well looked after,' say visitors this year to Gordon and Hilary Cowan's guest house in a Grade II listed Georgian building in the centre of this lovely little town (pronounced Kircoobrie). The 'cosy' bedrooms are 'comfortable with good views over the rooftops'; there may be 'some neighbourly noise'. Bathrooms have 'quality towels, changed every two days'. A double room with window seats facing the High Street and a maze of gardens is recommended by readers. The house has a fine drawing room, which 'takes up most of the first floor'. Mr Cowan cooks an evening meal by arrangement, served at separate tables in the pretty dining room (typical dishes: game terrine, home-made chutney; trout with almonds and beurre blanc). 'Cooked to perfection and served with panache.' No licence; bring your own wine. 'Great breakfasts' have a huge selection of fresh and dried fruits; traditional cooked of your choice; home-made marmalade and proper toast from home-baked bread. Guests may use the secluded garden. (*Jean and Michael Clunas*)

48 High Street
Kirkcudbright DG6 4JX

T: 01557-331734
E: hilarygladstone@aol.com
W: www.kirkcudbrightgladstone.com

BEDROOMS: 3.
OPEN: all year except for occasional holidays.
FACILITIES: drawing room, dining room, ½-acre garden, unsuitable for &.
BACKGROUND MUSIC: none.
LOCATION: town centre.
CHILDREN: normally not allowed under 14 ('but we are flexible').
DOGS: not allowed.
CREDIT CARDS: MasterCard, Visa.
PRICES: [2010] B&B £36–£55 per person, set dinner (by arrangement) £25, 3-night breaks or longer.

# KIRKWALL Orkney

Map 5:A3

## LYNNFIELD HOTEL

'Laid-back and helpful', Malcolm Stout and Lorna Reid own and run this small hotel with 'friendly', mainly local, staff. It stands in Orkney's capital beside the Highland Park distillery, which supplies many of the malt whiskies for the small bar. The restaurant, which has spectacular views over the water to Kirkwall and the north isles, also has a whisky theme (barrels, flasks, copper stills, malt shovels, etc). Recent visitors were impressed by the cooking: 'Fish and seafood dishes are particularly delicious' (perhaps steamed halibut on crispy vegetables, herb butter sauce). The 'good-sized' residents' lounge has 'comfortable sofas and well-stocked bookcases'; coffee and 'home-made sweeties' are taken here after dinner. The bedrooms vary in size and shape. Two suites have a separate lounge with good seating (and the views). Some rooms have a four-poster or half-tester bed. A large room had armchairs, a walk-in closet, spa bath and big shower. From October to March, a six-course 'Lynnfield Lux' gourmet dinner is held on several Friday evenings. Archaeology, wildlife and sailing all nearby. (*MH, D and JS*)

Holm Road
Kirkwall KW15 1SU

**T:** 01856-872505
**F:** 01856-870038
**E:** office@lynnfield.co.uk
**W:** www.lynnfieldhotel.com

**BEDROOMS:** 10, 1 suitable for ♿.
**OPEN:** all year except 25/26 Dec, 1–7 Jan.
**FACILITIES:** residents' lounge, bar lounge, restaurant, business/small conference/wedding facilities, small garden.
**BACKGROUND MUSIC:** Scottish in restaurant.
**LOCATION:** ½ mile from centre, parking.
**CHILDREN:** not under 12.
**DOGS:** not allowed in public rooms.
**CREDIT CARDS:** MasterCard, Visa.
**PRICES:** [2010] B&B £45–£90 per person, full alc £40, winter D,B&B rates.

# LANARK South Lanarkshire

Map 5:E2

## NEW LANARK MILL

At a 'lovingly restored' World Heritage Site ('which needs a weekend to explore'), this 18th-century cotton mill is run as a hotel by the New Lanark Trust. It may not be a typical *Guide* hotel, but a regular correspondent, stopping off on the road to the Highlands in 2010, had 'a good experience at a fair price'. The staff are 'friendly, helpful'. In a wooded valley below the Falls of Clyde, the 'impressive building has been beautifully decorated'; most of the bedrooms have a river view. 'We were upgraded to a suite, which was enormous and luxurious, a rare treat at the price.' Smaller rooms have been found 'comfortable, clean, well furnished'. The style of cooking in the river-view restaurant is 'traditional Scottish with a Mediterranean influence', eg, rack of garlic-marinated Border lamb, Provence organic potato, rosemary jus. Light meals are available in the 'jolly' bar. 'The tasty food was well cooked and presented.' Breakfast has a buffet of cooked dishes ('disappointing, the menu of cooked-to-order choices is a better choice'). Popular with weddings (check before booking). (*CLH, and others*)

Mill One, New Lanark Mills
Lanark ML11 9DB

T: 01555-667200
F: 01555-667222
E: hotel@newlanark.org
W: www.newlanark.org

BEDROOMS: 38, 4 suitable for &.
OPEN: all year.
FACILITIES: lounge, bar, restaurant, heated indoor swimming pool (16 by 7 metres), free access to leisure club, function/conference/wedding facilities.
BACKGROUND MUSIC: varied, in public areas.
LOCATION: 1 mile S of Lanark.
CHILDREN: all ages welcomed.
DOGS: allowed in some bedrooms, only guide dogs in public rooms.
CREDIT CARDS: all major cards.
PRICES: [2010] B&B £59.50–£84.50 per person, D,B&B £74.50–£99.50, set dinner £27.50, special breaks, website offers, Christmas/New Year packages.

# LOCHEPORT Western Isles

Map 5: inset A1

## LANGASS LODGE

Niall and Amanda Leveson Gower have created an 'elegant' modern hotel by sympathetically extending this former hunting lodge by a sea loch. It has an isolated setting above an ancient stone circle, with 'lovely views; sight of Skye on a good day'. They run it with John and Anne Buchanan, who are responsible for the cooking and hospitality. The bedrooms are split between the main house and the new hillside wing, which enjoys 'fabulous' views. 'Ours was comfortable and spacious, with doors opening to the garden; the bathroom was rather OTT: modern taps, basin, etc.' There is 'plenty of storage, a king-size bed, wooden floors with rugs'. Seafood (often gathered from the owners' pots) predominates on John Buchanan's menus. Guests can dine in the bar (dishes like calamari, sweet chilli sauce; North Uist game pie) or the two-tier restaurant, where a short daily-changing menu might include Grimsay crab tart; seared loin of cod, chorizo, red onions. Children are 'positively encouraged': there are high chairs, a special menu, toys in the lounge. 'Dogs can come, too.' (*Brenda and Bob Halstead, and others*)

Isle of North Uist
Locheport HS6 5HA

T: 01876-580285
F: 01876-580385
E: langasslodge@btconnect.com
W: www.langasslodge.co.uk

BEDROOMS: 11, 1 suitable for &.
OPEN: Mar–Jan.
FACILITIES: lounge, sitting room, 2 dining rooms, wedding facilities, 14-acre grounds.
BACKGROUND MUSIC: in bar.
LOCATION: 7½ miles W of Lochmaddy.
CHILDREN: all ages welcomed.
DOGS: allowed 'everywhere'.
CREDIT CARDS: MasterCard, Visa.
PRICES: [2010] B&B £45–£82.50 per person, set meals £28–£34.

# LOCHINVER Highland

## THE ALBANNACH

'A marvel; not just for the food (deserving its
*Michelin* star), but also for the beauty of the
position and the luxury of the accommodation.'
Praise this year for Lesley Crosfield and Colin
Craig's white-painted house high above
Lochinver's working harbour. 'The food is as
good as one gets'; 'Perfect,' are other comments
this year. Joint chefs, they serve a 'well-balanced'
five-course hand-written menu (no choice,
preferences are discussed; dishes like saddle of
roe deer, candy beetroot, truffled squash, game
port sauce). 'We loved the oysters and mezes
with our pre-dinner drink; everything was
beautifully served without the flummery that
can spoil such restaurants.' The restaurant is
closed to non-residents on Monday evenings,
when a seafood supper can be pre-booked by
hotel guests. All but one of the bedrooms have
views across the sea loch. The loft suite has a
deck terrace, and 'the most elegant modern
bathroom; a huge bath with pillow rests, separate
large power shower. Stunning, even if it took me
ages to work out how to use all the gadgets.'
'Good breakfasts.' (*Sarah Curtis, Charles Grant,
JS Waters*)

Baddidarroch
Lochinver IV27 4LP

**T:** 01571-844407
**E:** info@thealbannach.co.uk
**W:** www.thealbannach.co.uk

**BEDROOMS:** 5, 1 in byre.
**OPEN:** mid-Mar–early Jan.
**FACILITIES:** ramp, snug,
conservatory, dining room, ½-acre
garden, unsuitable for &.
**BACKGROUND MUSIC:** none.
**LOCATION:** ½ mile from village.
**CHILDREN:** not under 12.
**DOGS:** not allowed.
**CREDIT CARDS:** MasterCard, Visa.
**PRICES:** [2010] D,B&B £130–£200 per
person, set dinner £55, off-season
breaks, Christmas/New Year
packages, 1-night bookings
refused Sat.

# LOCHRANZA North Ayrshire

Map 5:D1

## APPLE LODGE

🍎*César award in 2000*

The homely atmosphere brings many returning visitors to John and Jeannie Boyd's guest house near the sea and the ferry to Kintyre. The white-painted, grey-roofed former manse is decorated with handmade artefacts, family photographs, books, teddy bears. It has wonderful views. 'Warm and comfortable', 'chintzy' bedrooms, all with an apple name, have antique fireplace, paintings, home-made biscuits; bathrooms are 'beautifully fitted'. Pippin, above the living room, may be subject to noise. Pearmain has a four-poster. Apple Cottage has a small sitting room and kitchen, and French doors on to the garden where red squirrels might be seen. Mrs Boyd ('a first-class all-rounder') serves a three-course, no-choice dinner menu (not in July and August) at 7 pm. Dishes are normally discussed with guests beforehand and served with candlelight, crystal and flowers. She calls her cooking 'best of British', eg, oak-smoked breast of chicken with celeriac mayonnaise. No licence; bring your own wine. Golf, walking and wildlife (deer and eagles) nearby. (*J and DM, and others*)

Lochranza
Isle of Arran KA27 8HJ

T/F: 01770-830229
W: www.a1tourism.com/uk/
applelodge2.html

BEDROOMS: 4, 1 on ground floor.
OPEN: all year except Christmas/New Year, dining room closed midday, for dinner Tues and July/Aug.
FACILITIES: lounge, dining room, ¼-acre garden, unsuitable for &.
BACKGROUND MUSIC: none.
LOCATION: outside village on N side of island.
CHILDREN: not allowed.
DOGS: not allowed.
CREDIT CARDS: none.
PRICES: B&B £40–£56 per person, set dinner £26, usually min. 3-night booking.

# MUIR OF ORD Highland

Map 5:C2

## THE DOWER HOUSE

❦*César award in 2008*

A 'miniature treasure chest' in a 'large, beautiful', wooded garden bordered by two rivers, *The Dower House* continues to attract praise. The pretty Georgian single-storey cottage-orné, once a shooting lodge for Lord Gladstone in the later 19th century, is the family home of Robyn and Mena Aitchison. They are 'nice people', 'friendly without being interfering'. Inside, it is filled with Persian rugs, Chinese vases and other antiques, flowery fabrics, potted plants and stacked bookcases, which create a 'much-loved' feel that extends to the 'cosy' bedrooms. 'Our suite had a small Edwardian piano and a Victorian bath, very long and narrow, curiously comfortable once you were in it.' Guests usually dine in: Mr Aitchison is a 'skilled, self-taught chef', whose no-choice menu (discussed in advance) was found 'imaginative and excellent' this year (typical dish: fillet of beef, port and anchovy sauce). Fishing, boat trips and the whisky trail are all nearby. Children are welcomed – there are swings and a tree house in the garden. (*Sarah Curtis, JS Waters*)

Highfield
Muir of Ord IV6 7XN

T/F: 01463-870090
E: info@thedowerhouse.co.uk
W: www.thedowerhouse.co.uk

BEDROOMS: 4, all on ground floor.
OPEN: all year except Christmas Day.
FACILITIES: lounge, dining room, TV room with Internet access, 4½-acre grounds, unsuitable for &.
BACKGROUND MUSIC: none.
LOCATION: 14 miles NW of Inverness.
CHILDREN: no under-5s at dinner (high tea at 5).
DOGS: not allowed in public rooms.
CREDIT CARDS: MasterCard, Visa.
PRICES: B&B £65–£85 per person, set dinner £42.

# MUTHILL Perth and Kinross

## BARLEY BREE `NEW`

French chef Fabrice Bouteloup and his wife, Alison, have revamped this 18th-century coaching inn in a conservation village near Crieff. They run it as a restaurant-with-rooms. 'The welcome is warm, the rooms are tastefully decorated, and the food is memorable,' says the nominator. There is a lounge 'with a log fire, comfortable sofas, sporting papers'. M. Bouteloup 'takes advantage of all that Perthshire has to offer' for his weekly-changing menus (with game during the shooting season). 'We had a great meal: a mouth-watering halibut with bisque in a little cup; venison cooked to perfection; a delicious individual tarte Tatin with home-made ice cream.' A tasting menu is available on request. There is a three-course lunch menu or you can ask for a bowl of soup with home-made bread. The bedrooms are decorated in neutral colours: 'Our newly done-up room had a good shower and under-floor heating in the bathroom. Fabrice cooked a good breakfast in the morning: it was served by a lovely lady.' The Bouteloups, parents themselves, welcome families: there is a dedicated room and a children's menu. (*Jackie Tunstall-Pedoe*)

6 Willoughby Street
Muthill PH5 2AB

**T:** 01764-681451
**E:** info@barleybree.com
**W:** www.barleybree.com

**BEDROOMS:** 6.
**OPEN:** all year except Christmas, 2 weeks Feb, 2 weeks in autumn, restaurant closed Mon/Tues.
**FACILITIES:** lounge, restaurant, small terrace, unsuitable for &.
**BACKGROUND MUSIC:** none.
**LOCATION:** village centre.
**CHILDREN:** all ages welcomed.
**DOGS:** not allowed.
**CREDIT CARDS:** MasterCard, Visa.
**PRICES:** [2010] B&B £50–£65 per person, full alc £38, special offers.

# NEWTON STEWART Dumfries and Galloway   Map 5:E1

## KIRROUGHTREE HOUSE

♀ *César award in 2003*

'One feels cared for at this comfortable hotel with old-fashioned, courteous service.' Praise again this year for this imposing, white, bow-windowed Georgian mansion with Victorian additions. It is owned by the small McMillan group and managed by Jim Stirling ('who takes great pride in looking after his guests'). His staff are 'well trained, friendly and attentive': visitors are met in the car park, cases collected. Afternoon tea with silver service is taken in one of the elegant public rooms. 'We had the largest room we've ever slept in, with a good bathroom and a huge comfortable bed; sherry and fruit are supplied.' In the formal dining room, men are asked to wear a jacket and tie in the evening. Rolf Mueller's 'modern European' four-course menus might include loin of venison, fondant potato, red cabbage, redcurrant sauce ('genteel portions, rich flavours'). 'The lemon posset was a dream.' The large grounds adjoin the Galloway Forest Park; the 'book town' of Wigtown is nearby. (*Marian Lampert, Ciaran Hydes*)

Newton Stewart DG8 6AN

**T:** 01671-402141
**F:** 01671-402425
**E:** info@kirroughtreehouse.co.uk
**W:** www.kirroughtreehouse.co.uk

**BEDROOMS:** 17.
**OPEN:** mid-Feb–2 Jan.
**FACILITIES:** lift, 2 lounges, 2 dining rooms, 8-acre grounds (gardens, tennis, croquet, pitch and putt).
**BACKGROUND MUSIC:** none.
**LOCATION:** 1½ miles NE of Newton Stewart.
**CHILDREN:** not under 10.
**DOGS:** allowed in lower ground-floor bedrooms only, not in public rooms.
**CREDIT CARDS:** Amex, MasterCard, Visa.
**PRICES:** [2010] B&B £90–£125 per person, set dinner £35, special breaks, Christmas/New Year packages, 1-night bookings sometimes refused.

# OBAN Argyll and Bute

## LERAGS HOUSE

'In a wonderful setting with Loch Feochan at the bottom of the garden', this handsome Georgian house drew more praise this year. Returning visitors 'were treated like old friends' by Australian owners Bella and Charlie Miller. 'They are charming hosts,' say first-time guests. Her cooking ('Scottish with Australian flair') is 'excellent and sophisticated: she does everything from making breakfast yogurt to after-dinner mint chocolates'. There is no choice on the three-course menu, but 'Bella is flexible to guests' preferences' (vegetarians enjoyed 'wonderful' meals). Typical dishes include smoked mackerel pâté; supreme of guineafowl, preserved lemon, green olives, potato rösti. Public rooms and bedrooms are stylishly furnished in pastel or neutral shades, with splashes of colour. A 'spacious' suite had lovely views; a 'best-ever' bed, with 'crisp, white linen'. 'I would have liked a shower fitting for the bath.' The garden is 'a peaceful place to watch herons and other wildlife as the tide races in'. Visitors with 'limited disability' can be accommodated. No dogs, but Rex and Libby, Hungarian vizslas, contribute to the welcome. (*Dale and Krystina Vargas, Kate Colgrave*)

Lerags, by Oban
PA34 4SE

T: 01631-563381
E: stay@leragshouse.com
W: www.leragshouse.com

BEDROOMS: 5.
OPEN: Easter–Nov.
FACILITIES: sitting room, dining room, wedding facilities, 1-acre grounds, unsuitable for &.
BACKGROUND MUSIC: in dining room.
LOCATION: 5 miles S of Oban.
CHILDREN: not under 12.
DOGS: not allowed.
CREDIT CARDS: MasterCard, Visa.
PRICES: D,B&B £95–£105 per person, 1-night bookings sometimes refused.

# OBAN Argyll and Bute

## THE MANOR HOUSE

On a rocky headland on the south shore of Oban bay ('a superb location'), this listed Georgian stone house was once the principal residence on the Duke of Argyll's estate. It is run as a small hotel/restaurant by owners Lesley and Margaret Crane; Gregor MacKinnon is the manager. Readers find it well run, with good food. The house has period features, and fine views over Oban's busy harbour to the Morven hills. In the candlelit dining room, chefs Patrick Freytag and Shaun Squire serve a daily-changing menu of seasonal dishes, perhaps West Coast scallops with Stornoway black pudding, orange vinaigrette; corn-fed chicken supreme, wild mushrooms, bacon sauce, spring onion mash. Most of the bedrooms have the view (binoculars are provided); all have fresh fruit, bottled water, chocolate and biscuits; free Wi-Fi. A small room was 'sparkling clean', with a 'soft, comfortable bed'; bar lunches are recommended; drinks and light meals can also be taken in summer on a panoramic terrace. Oban harbour is the ferry head for Mull, Iona and Fingal's Cave. (*CHH, RL, and others*)

Gallanach Road
Oban PA34 4LS

**T:** 01631-562087
**F:** 01631-563053
**E:** info@manorhouseoban.com
**W:** www.manorhouseoban.com

**BEDROOMS:** 11, 1 on ground floor.
**OPEN:** all year except 25/26 Dec.
**FACILITIES:** 2 lounges, bar, restaurant, wedding facilities, 1½-acre grounds, unsuitable for &.
**BACKGROUND MUSIC:** traditional in bar and dining room.
**LOCATION:** ½ mile from centre.
**CHILDREN:** not under 12.
**DOGS:** not allowed in public rooms.
**CREDIT CARDS:** all major cards.
**PRICES:** [2010] B&B £60–£100 per person, D,B&B £93–£140, set dinner £37, full alc £55, off-season breaks, New Year package.

# PEAT INN Fife

## THE PEAT INN

At his former coaching inn at the crossroads of a tiny village near St Andrews, owner/chef Geoffrey Smeddle has been awarded a *Michelin* star for his classic cooking (with a hint of modern); his wife, Katherine, is the 'charming' front-of-house. 'Passionate about fresh local produce', he serves a seasonal menu with dishes like feuilleté of langoustines, scallop and smoked haddock; roast rump and confit breast of lamb, wild mushrooms, flageolet beans, oregano. It is served by 'keen young waiters' in three dining rooms (big windows, widely spaced tables, cream and brown decor). Pre-dinner drinks are served in a sitting room with log fire. The Smeddles have renovated the bedrooms in the adjacent *Residence*. Seven are a split-level suite, with a gallery living room with magazines, board games; a good marble bathroom. They overlook a lovely garden at the back of the house (very quiet). The continental breakfast, delivered to the room at an agreed time, has freshly squeezed juice, boiled eggs, ham, cheeses, a variety of toasted breads and croissants, preserves. More reports, please.

Peat Inn, by Cupar
**KY15 5LH**

**T:** 01334-840206
**F:** 01334-840530
**E:** stay@thepeatinn.co.uk
**W:** www.thepeatinn.co.uk

**BEDROOMS:** 8 suites, all on ground floor in annexe.
**OPEN:** all year except 1 week Nov, Christmas, 2 weeks Jan, and Sun/Mon.
**FACILITIES:** ramp, lounge, restaurant, 1-acre garden.
**BACKGROUND MUSIC:** none.
**LOCATION:** 6 miles SW of St Andrews.
**CHILDREN:** all ages welcomed.
**DOGS:** only guide dogs allowed.
**CREDIT CARDS:** Amex, MasterCard, Visa.
**PRICES:** [2010] B&B £87.50–£95 per person, set dinner £32, tasting menu £55, full alc £42, special breaks, New Year package.

# PITLOCHRY Perth and Kinross

Map 5:D2

## CRAIGATIN HOUSE AND COURTYARD **NEW**

'A magical setting with fairy lights in the trees to welcome us on a wild November evening.' In wooded grounds close to the town centre, Martin and Andrea Anderson's B&B gains a full entry after two positive reports this year. 'The hosts are charming, the house is warm and inviting,' says one visitor. Another comment: 'A lovely place, well appointed, spotless; the owners and their staff were courteous. Very good value.' Seven of the bedrooms are in the main house; the others in converted stables behind. 'Our first-floor room was decorated in modern style; excellent towels and good toiletries. We woke to birdsong and views of the misty mountains.' All rooms have a hospitality tray with mineral water, tea and coffee, local biscuits. Breakfast is served in two dining rooms, one in an extension completed in 2010, which also has a guest lounge. 'Delicious locally sourced produce, home cooked and simple.' A buffet has porridge with whisky, compote of apricots, fresh fruit salad. Cooked dishes include a full Scottish, 'a divine omelette Arnold Bennett'. (*Tessa Allen, John and Lin Williams*)

165 Atholl Road
Pitlochry PH16 5QL

T: 01796-472478
E: enquiries@craigatinhouse.co.uk
W: www.craigatinhouse.co.uk

BEDROOMS: 13, 6 in courtyard, 2 on ground floor, 1 suitable for &.
OPEN: all year except Christmas.
FACILITIES: lounge, 2 dining rooms, 1-acre garden.
BACKGROUND MUSIC: jazz occasionally.
LOCATION: central.
CHILDREN: not under 8.
DOGS: not allowed.
CREDIT CARDS: MasterCard, Visa.
PRICES: [2010] B&B £39–£52.50 per person (single prices by arrangement), New Year package, 1-night bookings often refused Sat.

**25% DISCOUNT VOUCHERS**

# PORT APPIN Argyll and Bute

Map 5:D1

## THE AIRDS HOTEL

In a 'peaceful and pretty' position with fine views over Loch Linnhe, this former ferry inn is run as a luxury hotel (Relais & Châteaux) by Shaun (the manager) and Jenny McKivragan. The two large lounges have 'log fire, books and magazines, and lots of paintings, some of them rather good'. Pre-dinner drinks are served in a 'light and airy' conservatory at the front. The bedrooms vary in size and decoration: an attic room was 'cosy; a couple would have to co-ordinate their movements'. They have a mix of plain and floral fabrics, antiques, flat-screen TV, fresh fruit. 'Good bathroom fittings, and assiduous housekeeping.' The chef, Paul Burns, serves modern French dishes 'with a hint of Scotland', eg, tapenade crusted cod, wilted greens, wild garlic froth. Presentation is 'meticulous', 'service is formal, spot-on attention to detail'. We are told, in answer to a comment last year, that the staff are mostly British. Breakfast, served at the table, has 'good porridge', a 'first-class grill'. (*T and MH, and others*)

Port Appin PA38 4DF

T: 01631-730236
F: 01631-730535
E: airds@airds-hotel.com
W: www.airds-hotel.com

BEDROOMS: 11, 2 on ground floor, also self-catering cottage.
OPEN: all year except 2 days a week Nov, Dec, Jan.
FACILITIES: 2 lounges, conservatory, snug bar, restaurant, wedding facilities, ¾-acre garden (croquet, putting), unsuitable for &.
BACKGROUND MUSIC: none.
LOCATION: 25 miles N of Oban.
CHILDREN: all ages welcomed, but no under-9s in dining room after 7.30 (high tea at 6.30).
DOGS: allowed by prior agreement; not in public rooms.
CREDIT CARDS: Amex, MasterCard, Visa.
PRICES: [2010] D,B&B £122.50–£227.50 per person, off-season breaks, Christmas/New Year packages.

# PORTPATRICK Dumfries and Galloway

Map 5:E1

## KNOCKINAAM LODGE

In the Rhins (headlands) of Galloway, 'one of the last unspoilt parts of the UK', David and Sian Ibbotson's grey stone 19th-century hunting lodge stands 'virtually on the seashore', down a long, bumpy track. 'The setting is idyllic. The owners and staff are charming,' says a visitor in 2010. 'It demonstrates the value of hands-on management.' 'Beautifully decorated', the house has rich fabrics, antiques, oak panelling, open fires in the public rooms. In the candlelit dining room, chef Tony Pierce has a *Michelin* star for his 'superb' four-course menu. There is no choice; 'subtle changes allow diets to be catered for, individual requests are acted on'. Portions are 'small but satisfying' for dishes like paupiette of chicken, basil mousse, thyme pomme fondant, confit garlic, rosemary-scented jus. The largest bedroom, South (where Churchill stayed), is 'comfortable, airy; the large bathroom and walk-in shower looked out to sea'. Early risers get to sit at the window at breakfast, also 'well presented'. (*ST, and others*)

Portpatrick DG9 9AD

T: 01776-810471
F: 01776-810435
E: reservations@
   knockinaamlodge.com
W: www.knockinaamlodge.com

BEDROOMS: 10.
OPEN: all year.
FACILITIES: 2 lounges, 1 bar, restaurant, wedding facilities, 30-acre grounds, only restaurant suitable for &.
BACKGROUND MUSIC: classical in restaurant.
LOCATION: 3 miles S of Portpatrick.
CHILDREN: no under-12s in dining room after 7 pm (high tea at 6).
DOGS: allowed in some bedrooms (£20 per stay), not in public rooms.
CREDIT CARDS: Amex, MasterCard, Visa.
PRICES: [2010] D,B&B £130–£210 per person, set dinner £55, reductions for 3 or more nights off-season, midweek breaks, Christmas/New Year packages, 1-night bookings sometimes refused.

# PORTREE Highland

Map 5:C1

## VIEWFIELD HOUSE

🏵 *César award in 1993*

In large wooded grounds on the outskirts of Portree, this baronial pile is 'an agreeable place in a lovely setting'. The hands-on owner, Hugh Macdonald, whose family has lived in the house for two centuries, is 'hands-on, caring and likeable'; his two assistants are 'unselfconsciously charming, determined that guests should be made welcome'. The 'pleasing' drawing room has a 'brightly burning' log fire, grand piano, family photographs, chairs and sofas ('some needing re-springing'), lots of books. Inspectors were given free afternoon tea with 'delicious' scones and jam. A 'huge' bedroom on the first floor was 'clean and polished; a massive wardrobe, two writing desks, twin beds with a shared bedside table (inadequate lighting); the wallpaper, with dense, dark-coloured flowers, was just right for the setting; beautiful fabric curtains; lots of hot water in the large bathroom'. Breakfast has cereals in bowls on a sideboard, 'generous slabs of butter; fine scrambled eggs; service never faded.' Dinner is no longer served; simple dishes can be provided. There is Wi-Fi Internet access throughout. Children are welcomed.

Portree
Isle of Skye IV51 9EU

**T:** 01478-612217
**F:** 01478-613517
**E:** info@viewfieldhouse.com
**W:** www.viewfieldhouse.com

**BEDROOMS:** 11, 1, on ground floor, suitable for ♿.
**OPEN:** Easter–mid-Oct.
**FACILITIES:** ramp, drawing room, morning/TV room, dining room, 20-acre grounds (croquet, swings).
**BACKGROUND MUSIC:** none.
**LOCATION:** S side of Portree.
**CHILDREN:** all ages welcomed.
**DOGS:** not allowed in public rooms except with permission of other guests (except guide dogs).
**CREDIT CARDS:** MasterCard, Visa.
**PRICES:** B&B £55–£75 per person, full alc £30, 3- to 5-day rates, 1-night group bookings sometimes refused.

**25% DISCOUNT VOUCHERS**

# ST MARGARET'S HOPE Orkney

Map 5:A3

## THE CREEL  NEW

On the seafront of the pretty main village of South Ronaldsay, this cream-coloured house has been run for 25 years as a restaurant-with-rooms by Alan and Joyce Craigie. 'Excellent food and a nice room overlooking the harbour,' say visitors this year, restoring it to the *Guide* after a period without reports. All three of the spacious bedrooms have the views over St Margaret's Hope bay; they have recently been renovated with light wood fittings and floors. Mr Craigie's cooking is renowned in Orkney and further afield. He specialises in seafood for his short menus, eg, grilled mackerel, rhubarb chutney, toasted oatmeal; pan-fried scallops and steamed haddock, red pepper and onion marmalade. All vegetables are locally grown; Orkney beef and seaweed-fed lamb from North Ronaldsay also feature. There is a selection of Orkney ales and island malt whiskies. Breakfast, served in a large sunny room (which doubles as private dining room), has home-made muesli and porridge; grilled local kippers or smoked haddock; home-made bannocks, soda bread and preserves. (*Josie and Guy Mayers*)

Front Road
St Margaret's Hope KW17 2SL

T: 01865-831311
E: alan@thecreel.freeserve.co.uk
W: www.thecreel.co.uk

BEDROOMS: 3.
OPEN: Apr–Oct, restaurant closed Mon/Tues.
FACILITIES: small lounge, 2 dining rooms, only restaurant suitable for &.
BACKGROUND MUSIC: none.
LOCATION: on seafront of village, 15 miles from Kirkwall.
CHILDREN: not under 5.
DOGS: not allowed.
CREDIT CARDS: MasterCard, Visa.
PRICES: [2010] B&B £57.50 per person, D,B&B £95.50, set meals £30–£36.

# ST OLA Orkney

## FOVERAN

In a 'delightful' setting with 'wonderful views across Scapa Flow', this simple, single-storey hotel was liked this year for the 'warm welcome' and 'good cooking'. The owners, Paul and Helen Doull, 'run a very efficient operation', say visitors. The building might be 'undistinguished' but the interior is 'fine'. 'Our well-furnished bedroom was small, but perfectly adequate', decorated in blond woods. A 'good bathroom had places for putting things'. The bedrooms do not share the views enjoyed by the public rooms. Pre-dinner drinks are served by a fire in the lounge. Window tables in the restaurant, 'large, light and airy', are provided with binoculars. Paul Doull's 'consistently good' cooking is popular with locals. The emphasis is on the island's excellent produce, eg, sea bass on linguini with tomato and basil butter. The service is from 'a splendid team of youngsters'. Breakfast is 'excellent'. 'There is a good walk to the beach, with plenty of wildlife to see'; also important archaeological sites nearby. (*Dale and Krystina Vargas, Josie and Guy Mayers*)

St Ola
Kirkwall KW15 1SF

**T:** 01856-872389
**F:** 01856-876430
**E:** foveranhotel@aol.com
**W:** www.foveranhotel.co.uk

**BEDROOMS:** 8, all on ground floor.
**OPEN:** mid-Apr–early Oct, by arrangement at other times, only restaurant Christmas/New Year, restaurant closed Sun evening end Sept–early June.
**FACILITIES:** lounge, restaurant, wedding facilities, 12-acre grounds (private rock beach).
**BACKGROUND MUSIC:** Scottish, in evening, in restaurant.
**LOCATION:** 3 miles SW of Kirkwall.
**CHILDREN:** all ages welcomed.
**DOGS:** not allowed.
**CREDIT CARDS:** MasterCard, Visa.
**PRICES:** [2010] B&B £52.50–£72.50 per person, D,B&B £77.50–£97.50, full alc £35, 1-night bookings sometimes refused.

# SHIELDAIG Highland

Map 5:C1

## TIGH AN EILEAN

🏵 *César award in 2005*

In a pretty village of white-washed cottages on the shores of Loch Torridon, Christopher and Cathryn Field's 'charming' small hotel has long been liked by *Guide* readers. Most of the bedrooms have fine views across the sea to Shieldaig Island. They vary in size; some are small (one at the back was not liked this year). The renovation of all the bathrooms (new showers) was completed for 2010. The Fields tell us they have new duvets this year, though visitors can opt for sheets and blankets. Free tea, coffee and shortbread are available in the cosy bar/library. Mr Field sources fish and meat locally for his four-course dinner menus which might include langoustines with a truffle-scented pea risotto; juniper-crusted saddle of Highland venison, braised wild leeks, game jus. There is an extensive range of Scottish cheeses. *The Coastal Kitchen*, an informal first-floor restaurant, has pizzas from a wood-fired oven and seafood. Breakfasts are generous, with freshly squeezed juice; dishes of the day might include locally smoked haddock, eggs Benedict. (*B and BH, J and GM, and others*)

Shieldaig, Loch Torridon
IV54 8XN

T: 01520-755251
F: 01520-755321
E: tighaneilean@keme.co.uk
W: www.tighaneilean.co.uk

BEDROOMS: 11.
OPEN: mid-Mar–late Oct.
FACILITIES: 2 lounges, bar/library, village bar (separate entrance), 2 restaurants, roof terrace, unsuitable for ⅃.
BACKGROUND MUSIC: none.
LOCATION: on village seafront.
CHILDREN: all ages welcomed (under-8s stay free, under-16s half price).
DOGS: not allowed in public rooms.
CREDIT CARDS: Amex, MasterCard, Visa.
PRICES: [2010] B&B £80 per person, D,B&B £120, bar meals, set dinner £40, full alc in *The Coastal Kitchen* £25, discounts for 3 or more nights.

**25% DISCOUNT VOUCHERS**

# SKIRLING Borders

## SKIRLING HOUSE

*❦César award in 2004*

'All-round excellence combines with informality to create a wonderfully relaxed experience' at Bob and Isobel Hunter's 'delightful' Arts and Crafts house (Wolsey Lodge) on the green of a tiny village in lovely Borders countryside. Other praise this year: 'Our favourite place just seems to get better; the hosts are not at all intrusive but always quickly available to answer questions.' Built as the summer retreat by the art collector Sir Gibson Carmichael, the house has a fine collection of china, books and posters. Visitors are greeted with tea and cakes in the drawing room, with its 16th-century carved Florentine ceiling, full-height windows. The large bedrooms are 'beautifully fitted with every conceivable extra'; carpets are custom designed. Mr Hunter's four-course no-choice menu (preferences discussed) is 'outstanding' (typical dish: spiced chicken breast, wild apricots). 'Excellent' breakfasts (fresh orange juice, French toast with caramelised apples and black pudding, home-made jams). Children are welcomed. 'It is like staying with good friends who are entertaining other interesting house guests.' (*Simon James, Bob and Deborah Steel*)

Skirling, by Biggar ML12 6HD

T: 01899-860274
F: 01899-860255
E: enquiry@skirlinghouse.com
W: www.skirlinghouse.com

BEDROOMS: 5, plus 1 single available if let with a double, 1 on ground floor suitable for ♿.
OPEN: Mar–Dec, closed Christmas.
FACILITIES: ramps, drawing room, library, conservatory, dining room, 5-acre garden (tennis, croquet) in 100-acre estate with woodland.
BACKGROUND MUSIC: none.
LOCATION: 2 miles E of Biggar, by village green.
CHILDREN: all ages welcomed.
DOGS: allowed by arrangement, not in public rooms or unattended in bedrooms.
CREDIT CARDS: MasterCard, Visa.
PRICES: [2010] B&B £50–£80 per person, D,B&B £80–£110, set dinner £30–£45.

**25% DISCOUNT VOUCHERS**

# SLEAT Highland

## TORAVAIG HOUSE

In a beautiful setting on the coast road close to the Armadale ferry, this white-painted building has been renovated by Anne Gracie and Kenneth Gunn. 'A very welcoming hostelry,' says a visitor this year. The bedrooms, refreshed in contemporary style, vary in size; some have sea views, all have bath and/or power shower. The Eriska Room has a sleigh bed. The drawing room has a marble fireplace, log fire, grand piano, comfortable seating. Ritchie Gilfinnan was appointed chef in 2010: we would welcome reports on his modern Scottish cooking. Kenneth Gunn was formerly captain of a cruise ship: from April to September, visitors can take full- or half-day trips on his 42-foot yacht, *Solus na Mara*. They can also get married on it. Mr Gunn and Ms Gracie also own *Duisdale House,* Sleat (see Shortlist). (*MC Clark, and others*)

Knock Bay, Sleat
Isle of Skye IV44 8RE

**T:** 01471-820200
**F:** 01471-833231
**E:** info@skyehotel.co.uk
**W:** www.skyehotel.co.uk

**BEDROOMS:** 9.
**OPEN:** all year.
**FACILITIES:** lounge, dining room, wedding facilities, 2-acre grounds, unsuitable for &.
**BACKGROUND MUSIC:** gentle Scottish.
**LOCATION:** 7 miles S of Broadford.
**CHILDREN:** not under 12.
**DOGS:** not allowed.
**CREDIT CARDS:** MasterCard, Visa.
**PRICES:** [2010] B&B £74.50–£99.55 per person, D,B&B £119.50–£144.50, set dinner £45.50, full alc £63, seasonal offers, midweek breaks, Christmas/New Year packages.

# STRONTIAN Highland

## KILCAMB LODGE

By the shore of Loch Sunart (with its own beach), this 'wonderful' hotel stands amid woodlands and hills. '*Kilcamb* has become a very special place for us,' say visitors this year. The old stone building (dating back to the early 1700s), with two Victorian wings, is run as a luxury hotel by the 'friendly' owners, Sally and David Fox. Their manager, Phillip Fleming, leads a 'cheery' team. The drawing room, in yellow and blue, has an open fire, fresh flowers and 'comfortable period furnishings'. Six of the bedrooms, decorated in country house style, have loch views; three face the gardens. Recent visitors liked their large room, with 'an enormous bed and a window seat'. Chef Tammo Siemers smokes and cures his own meats and fish for his seasonal menus, with dishes like white balsamic-poached chicken, seared foie de canard. Breakfast includes fresh croissants and free-range eggs. 'Doggy treats' await canine visitors who can roam in the grounds ('no flowerbeds to worry about'). (*Jill and Peter Bickley*)

Strontian PH36 4HY

T: 01967-402257
F: 01967-402041
E: enquiries@kilcamblodge.co.uk
W: www.kilcamblodge.co.uk

BEDROOMS: 10.
OPEN: Feb–early Jan.
FACILITIES: drawing room, lounge bar, dining room, wedding facilities, 22-acre grounds (loch frontage, beach with safe bathing, fishing, boating), unsuitable for &.
BACKGROUND MUSIC: jazz/classical in bar, dining room.
LOCATION: edge of village.
CHILDREN: not under 10.
DOGS: welcomed.
CREDIT CARDS: Amex (with surcharge), MasterCard, Visa.
PRICES: [2010] D,B&B £119.50–£254, off-season breaks, Christmas/New Year packages.

# TARBERT Western Isles

Map 5:B1

## CEOL NA MARA

Above a rocky tidal loch, this old stone house was renovated and extended by John and Marlene Mitchell, 'friendly and hard-working hosts'. 'This was the find of our holiday,' said the nominators. 'Lovely views from all windows, and rooms equipped as well as any hotel.' The large lounge is filled with books and 'family treasures'; guests can sit in a sun lounge or, in good weather, outside on a terrace. 'Our large, comfortable room was without a blemish; it had a flat-screen TV, silent fridge, masses of storage; a good bathroom with a shower.' An 'exceptionally generous' breakfast is served from 8 to 8.30 am: 'The porridge has to be sampled; home-made breads and yogurt, a wide selection of fish and fruit.' The cooked dishes include 'Ceol na Mara cairn' (black pudding, potato scone, bacon, with a poached egg). No dinner: the Mitchells recommend eating at the *Pierhouse* restaurant at the nearby *Hotel Hebrides*. Mr Mitchell will advise on the attractions of the island, which include white-sand beaches, archaeological sites and birdwatching. (*J and DA*)

7 Direcleit, Tarbert
Isle of Harris HS3 3DP

T: 01859-502464
E: midgie@madasafish.com
W: www.ceolnamara.com

BEDROOMS: 4.
OPEN: all year.
FACILITIES: 2 lounges, sun lounge, dining room, unsuitable for &.
BACKGROUND MUSIC: soft Highland/Celtic at breakfast.
LOCATION: ½ mile S of Tarbert.
CHILDREN: all ages welcomed.
DOGS: not allowed.
CREDIT CARDS: all major cards (*3% surcharge*).
PRICES: B&B £30–£45 per person.

# TIRORAN Argyll and Bute

## TIRORAN HOUSE

On the shores of Loch Scridain, near Mull's highest mountain, Laurence and Katie Mackay seek to create a 'relaxed house-party atmosphere' at their white-painted Victorian hunting lodge. They tell us they have redecorated every room in the house this year. There are two sitting rooms with 'comfortable chairs, books, log fire', a vine-draped conservatory. The host is front-of-house in the evening, introducing guests to each other as he serves drinks before dinner. In the candlelit dining room, Katie Mackay's three-course menus (three options each course; order by 6 pm) might include Aga-baked sea bass, crispy herb crust, chard and fennel. Vegetables and herbs come from the organic kitchen garden. The bedrooms vary in size and style; all have a hospitality tray with island bakery biscuits. A door from the garden room opens on to a patio. Breakfast has full Scottish options with free-range eggs, home-made muesli, breads, marmalade and preserves. A burn tumbles past the house; the garden leads to a private beach. Much wildlife; good walking. No mobile phone signal, but there is Wi-Fi. (*AB*)

Tiroran, Isle of Mull
PA69 6ES

**T:** 01681-705232
**F:** 01681-705240
**E:** info@tiroran.com
**W:** www.tiroran.com

**BEDROOMS:** 8, 2 on ground floor, 1 in annexe.
**OPEN:** Apr–Oct, groups only at New Year.
**FACILITIES:** 2 sitting rooms, dining room, conservatory, 17½-acre grounds (burn, beach with mooring).
**BACKGROUND MUSIC:** traditional/'easy listening'.
**LOCATION:** N side of Loch Scridain.
**CHILDREN:** all ages welcomed, usually no under-14s in dining room.
**DOGS:** allowed in 2 bedrooms, not normally in public rooms.
**CREDIT CARDS:** MasterCard, Visa.
**PRICES:** B&B £50–£87.50 per person, set dinner £42, New Year package, 1-night bookings sometimes refused.

# TOBERMORY Argyll and Bute

Map 5:D1

## HIGHLAND COTTAGE   **NEW**

In the main village of the Island of Mull, David and Josephine Currie offer a 'wonderful personal service' at their purpose-built small hotel/restaurant. They supervised the construction in 1998, to 'incorporate everything a small hotel needs'; they promise 'a lack of stuffiness'. Guests have the use of a computer in the reading room/library. The bedrooms vary in size. There is a four-poster bed in two sea-facing rooms; a room on the ground floor has level access to the street. 'Our room had everything we could hope for; our daughter enjoyed the DVD-player.' All rooms have an iPod dock and a hospitality tray. The hotel's real strength is the cuisine: 'Dinner is a treat.' Booking is essential in the dining room, where Josephine Currie serves a four-course menu with much local fish, eg, Inverlussa mussels French style, garlic and breadcrumbs; sea bass, butterbean and olive mash, sauce vierge. 'David is helpful in booking trips; he knows the boat owners and can advise on what is available.' There are whale-watching trips, wildlife cruises, fishing charters, and boats to Staffa and Iona. (*Mark Abrol*)

Tobermory
Isle of Mull PA75 6PD

T: 01688-302030
E: davidandjo@
   highlandcottage.co.uk
W: www.highlandcottage.co.uk

**BEDROOMS:** 6, 1 on ground floor.
**OPEN:** 12 Mar–mid-Oct.
**FACILITIES:** 2 lounges, restaurant.
**BACKGROUND MUSIC:** in 1 lounge, restaurant.
**LOCATION:** village centre.
**CHILDREN:** not under 10.
**DOGS:** not allowed in public rooms.
**CREDIT CARDS:** MasterCard, Visa.
**PRICES:** [2010] B&B £77.50–£95 per person, D,B&B £120–£140, set meals £49.50, special breaks, 1-night bookings refused weekends.

**25% DISCOUNT VOUCHERS**

# TORRIDON Highland

## THE TORRIDON

'Everything superb, just as we remembered,' say visitors returning after five years to this former shooting lodge on the shores of Loch Torridon. It is run as a 'romantic' luxury hotel (Pride of Britain) by Rohaise and Daniel Rose-Bristow; Robert Ince is the manager. The traditionally furnished interior retains its 'sense of Victorian grandeur', with decorative plaster ceilings, panelling, big open fireplaces and leather couches. The 'warm, spacious' bedrooms are individually furnished; all have a king-size bed; two have a four-poster and a claw-footed freestanding bath. A recent visitor enjoyed 'spectacular' mountain views while having a cup of tea in the bath. Jason 'Bruno' Birkbeck is now the chef: *Guide* readers found his cooking 'impressive' when he was at *Hipping Hall*, Cowan Bridge, Lancashire (see entry). His style is modern, eg, braised daube of beef, crispy tongue, horseradish pomme purée. Breakfasts are traditionally 'leisurely and substantial'. 'We were given an upgrade although they didn't know this was a birthday treat; expensive, but worth it for special occasions.' A popular wedding venue. (*Florence and Russell Birch*)

Torridon, by Achnasheen IV22 2EY

T: 01445-791242
F: 01445-712253
E: info@thetorridon.com
W: www.thetorridon.com

BEDROOMS: 19, 1, on ground floor, suitable for &, 1 suite in adjacent cottage.
OPEN: all year except Jan, Mon/Tues Nov–Mar.
FACILITIES: ramp, lift, drawing room, library, whisky bar, dining room, wedding facilities, 58-acre grounds.
BACKGROUND MUSIC: classical at night in dining room.
LOCATION: On W coast, 10 miles SW of Kinlochewe.
CHILDREN: no under-10s in dining room in evening (high tea provided).
DOGS: allowed in cottage only.
CREDIT CARDS: Amex, MasterCard, Visa.
PRICES: [2010] B&B £87–£207 per person, D,B&B £125–£252, set dinner £45, special breaks, Christmas/New Year packages.

# ULLAPOOL Highland

Map 5:B2

## THE CEILIDH PLACE

'We loved this place; the atmosphere is warm and welcoming.' In a Highland fishing village of whitewashed cottages, this unusual undertaking, a combination of an arts centre, a bookshop, a coffee house and a hotel/restaurant, is owned by Jean Urquhart and managed by Effie MacKenzie. It is liked for its 'intimate feel' and 'chatty, friendly' staff. The simple, spacious bedrooms, recently renovated, are 'perfectly adequate'. There is no television but each room has a radio and a small library of books selected by Scottish authors; extras include thick bathrobes. There are more basic bunk-bedded rooms for two to four people in the Clubhouse across the road. Chef Scott Morrison serves a 'superb' menu of 'Scottish eclectic' dishes (eg, fish pie, venison casserole). Vegetarian dishes are a speciality, perhaps broccoli, red onion and Cheddar pie. In summer, the café serves meals all day; in winter, food and drink are taken in the parlour. A pantry with free tea and coffee and an honesty bar are available in the guests' living room, which has more books, games, Wi-Fi. Ceilidhs, concerts, literary events and plays are often held. (*Alan and Edwina Williams, and others*)

14 West Argyle Street
Ullapool IV26 2TY

T: 01854-612103
F: 01854-613773
E: stay@theceilidhplace.com
W: www.theceilidhplace.com

BEDROOMS: 13, 10 with facilities en suite, plus 11 in Clubhouse across road.
OPEN: all year except 2 weeks mid-Jan.
FACILITIES: bar, parlour, café/bistro, restaurant, bookshop, conference/function/wedding facilities, 2-acre garden, only public areas suitable for &.
BACKGROUND MUSIC: 'eclectic' in public areas.
LOCATION: village centre, large car park.
CHILDREN: all ages welcomed.
DOGS: not allowed in public rooms where food is served.
CREDIT CARDS: MasterCard, Visa.
PRICES: [2010] B&B £50–£73 per person, full alc £38, reductions for stays of more than 2 nights, Christmas/New Year packages.

**25% DISCOUNT VOUCHERS**

# WALKERBURN Borders

## WINDLESTRAW LODGE

'Superb' was the succinct appraisal of a *Guide* regular this year of Alan and Julie Reid's 'stunning' pink stone Edwardian house in the Borders. The Reids 'balance friendly interest with efficiency', said an earlier visitor. The house was built by a Tweed mill-owner as a wedding present for his Austrian bride. There are family photographs and objets d'art in the candlelit open-plan public rooms; open fires, 'breathtaking' views. In the wood-panelled dining room, the host's daily-changing menus of seasonal local produce are admired by readers for the 'intense flavours' and presentation. A typical menu might include wood pigeon shot by Mr Reid in the surrounding fields; game from nearby estates. Children under 12 take an early high tea. 'Smart, comfortable' bedrooms vary in size: McIntosh has a king-size bed, the original bathtub; Willison has a walk-in shower, roll-top bath and valley views. Cooked breakfast dishes include scrambled eggs with smoked salmon. The Reids cater for house parties and small weddings. Hill walking, historic Borders towns, abbeys and castles are all nearby. (*Geoffrey Bignell, and others*)

Galashiels Road
Tweed Valley
Walkerburn EH43 6AA

T: 01896-870636
E: reception@windlestraw.co.uk
W: www.windlestraw.co.uk

BEDROOMS: 6, all on first floor.
OPEN: all year except 2 days Christmas, 2 days New Year, 1 week June.
FACILITIES: bar lounge, sun lounge, drawing room, dining room, 'exclusive use for small weddings', 1-acre grounds, unsuitable for &.
BACKGROUND MUSIC: none.
LOCATION: outskirts of village, 2 miles E of Innerleithen.
CHILDREN: not under 12 at dinner (high tea 5–6 pm).
DOGS: allowed in some bedrooms, not in public rooms.
CREDIT CARDS: MasterCard, Visa.
PRICES: B&B £70–£110 per person, D,B&B £110–£155, set dinner £46, 2-night midweek breaks.

# WHITHORN Dumfries and Galloway

Map 5:E2

## THE STEAM PACKET INN

Whithorn is not an island and the *Steam Packet* is not a boat but a 'delightful' inn, where the Scoular family have been offering 'remarkably good value' for nearly 30 years. On the quay of a pretty village at the tip of the Machars peninsula, it is run by the 'quietly dedicated', 'ever helpful' Alastair Scoular, who promises that visitors will not be disturbed by piped music. The chefs, Chris Mills and Peter Martin, serve 'big portions' from a blackboard menu, often including fish landed at the doorstep, eg, skate wing, slowly baked with white wine, peppercorns, herbs and lemon. Meals are served in the 'small, busy' bars, the 'bright, cheerful' dining room and the conservatory. Tea and coffee are available all day. 'Satisfactory' breakfasts include Mrs Scoular senior's home-made marmalade. The best bedroom has picture windows, seating area, modern bathroom, a big bed. Seven of the rooms are in the family's neighbouring pub. Children are welcomed. The 'book town' of Wigtown is nearby, as are 'wonderful coastal walks'. (*GM, and others*)

Harbour Row
Isle of Whithorn
Newton Stewart DG8 8LL

T: 01988-500334
F: 01988-500627
E: steampacketinn@btconnect.com
W: http://home.btconnect.com/
   steampacketinn/

BEDROOMS: 14, 7 in adjacent pub.
OPEN: all year except 25 Dec.
FACILITIES: 2 bars, 2 restaurant areas, small garden, unsuitable for &.
BACKGROUND MUSIC: none.
LOCATION: village centre, 9 miles S of Wigtown.
CHILDREN: all ages welcomed.
DOGS: not allowed in front restaurant.
CREDIT CARDS: MasterCard, Visa.
PRICES: B&B £30–£35 per person, full alc £25, off-season 2 nights-for-1 packages.

# WALES

Many of our Welsh hotels take great pride in their national identity. Menus are often written in Welsh as well as English, and visitors are encouraged to embrace the local culture. Our Welsh country hotel of the year, *Tŷ Mawr*, Brechfa, is a fine example of a country place where the simple things are done well.

## ABERAERON Ceredigion

### HARBOURMASTER HOTEL

*César award in 2005*

'Bright and engaging, inside and out', this handsome old house, painted a vivid French blue, is 'superbly located' among smaller candy-coloured houses on the quay of a 'lovely little' west Wales town. Its bilingual owners, Glyn and Menna Heulyn, are 'hands-on' hosts. A combination of 'local pub with restaurant and rooms', it has a 'real buzz', and is often 'full and happy' (the background music might be 'drowned by Welsh voices'). There is no residents' lounge, but the bar is 'spacious, with different types of seating from comfy sofas to high bar stools'. Scott Davis, the new chef this year, has a modern style, using local ingredients, eg, sea bream, crab risotto, sweet chilli sauce. We would welcome reports on his cooking. All bedrooms have views. 'Ours was very comfortable, with a good bathroom, and a balcony with steamer chairs from which to watch the sunset.' A 'fine' breakfast, taken in the bar, has bacon in a bap, organic porridge with honey, Welsh rarebit. Good local walking. (*Peter Stoakle, and others*)

Pen Cei, Aberaeron
SA46 0BT

T: 01545-570755
F: 01545-570762
E: info@harbour-master.com
W: www.harbour-master.com

BEDROOMS: 13, 2 in cottage, 1 suitable for &.
OPEN: all year except 25 Dec.
FACILITIES: bar, restaurant, pebble beach (safe bathing nearby).
BACKGROUND MUSIC: 'modern, relaxed'.
LOCATION: central, on harbour.
CHILDREN: under-5s in cottage only.
DOGS: not allowed.
CREDIT CARDS: MasterCard, Visa.
PRICES: [2010] B&B £55–£125 per person, D,B&B £70–£150, full alc £40, special breaks, 1-night bookings refused weekends.

# ABERDYFI Gwynedd

## TREFEDDIAN HOTEL   `NEW`

On a bluff above a golf course with 'glorious views' across Cardigan Bay, this 'rather grand hotel' has been run by three generations of the Cave family. 'Their personal involvement shows in the comfortable, well-equipped bedrooms and lounges, and in the welcoming and efficient approach of the staff,' says a regular visitor, restoring it to the *Guide* after a period without reports. Popular with families during the holidays, it is busy with retired guests on special off-season breaks (in these periods a one-night booking may not be accepted). Men are asked to wear a jacket and tie in the dining room in the evening; 'good food and a blissful absence of muzak'. There are three lounges with 'fine old furnishings'; one is reserved for adults; a large one is for families; dogs are allowed in the third. 'When the sun came out, we swarmed into the garden', which has 'plenty of seats, hidden nooks, a pitch-and-putt course'. There are reduced rates for children, who have playrooms and a playground, a supper menu, baby-monitoring. (*Jelly Williams*)

Tywyn Road
Aberdyfi LL35 0SB

T: 01654-767213
F: 01654-767777
E: info@trefwales.com
W: www.trefwales.com

BEDROOMS: 59.
OPEN: Jan–Nov.
FACILITIES: lift, 3 lounges, bar lounge, restaurant, fitness centre, indoor swimming pool (6 by 12 metres), beauty salon, 15-acre grounds (tennis).
BACKGROUND MUSIC: none.
LOCATION: ½ mile N of village.
CHILDREN: all ages welcomed.
DOGS: allowed in 1 lounge, some bedrooms.
CREDIT CARDS: MasterCard, Visa.
PRICES: D,B&B £62–£105, set dinner £28.50, special breaks, 1-night bookings sometimes refused.

## ABERSOCH Gwynedd

Map 3:B2

### PORTH TOCYN HOTEL

*❦César award in 1984*

'A lovely place', Nick Fletcher-Brewer's family-friendly hotel has a magnificent setting above Cardigan Bay in sight of Snowdonia. Several beautiful beaches are nearby; in the grounds are a heated swimming pool and a 'makeshift football pitch'. Adults can find quiet corners outdoors for taking tea: indoors are sitting rooms with fine furniture, books and knick-knacks. Their offspring can 'escape' to a dedicated snug with books, TV and a video, and a conservatory with table tennis and games. Mr Fletcher-Brewer's son, Richard, and his girlfriend, Emma, have updated three more bedrooms this year and the bar has been 'given a make-over'. Several bedrooms are interconnected; extra beds and cots are provided without surcharge. Children can take high tea at 5.30 pm; Mr Fletcher-Brewer tells us he sees a trend towards en famille dining. In the restaurant Louise Fletcher-Brewer and Mike Green serve a modern British menu 'with a dinner-party edge'. The fish dishes are admired, perhaps halibut with sun-blushed tomato blini. At breakfast, cooked dishes are charged extra. (*Richard Creed, Derek Lambert*)

Bwlch Tocyn
Abersoch LL53 7BU

T: 01758-713303
F: 01758-713538
E: bookings@porthtocyn.fsnet.co.uk
W: www.porthtocynhotel.co.uk

BEDROOMS: 17, 3 on ground floor.
OPEN: week before Easter–early Nov.
FACILITIES: ramp, sitting rooms, children's rooms, cocktail bar, dining room, 25-acre grounds (swimming pool, 10 by 6 metres, heated May–end Sept, tennis), telephone to discuss disabled access.
BACKGROUND MUSIC: none.
LOCATION: 2 miles outside village.
CHILDREN: no tiny children at dinner (high tea at 5.30 pm).
DOGS: by arrangement, not allowed in public rooms.
CREDIT CARDS: MasterCard, Visa.
PRICES: [2010] B&B (continental) £47.50–£85 per person, cooked breakfast £6.50, set dinner £33.50–£40, off-season breaks, walking breaks, 1-night bookings sometimes refused.

**25% DISCOUNT VOUCHERS**

# ABERYSTWYTH Ceredigion

## GWESTY CYMRU

'With sympathy and flair', Huw and Beth Roberts have converted their Grade II listed Georgian terrace house on Aberystwyth's Victorian seafront promenade into a restaurant-with-rooms. It is 'sleek, modern and oozing quality'. The bedrooms have hand-crafted furniture, inlaid with Welsh slate, made by a local craftsman. Bold colours are augmented by specially commissioned artwork by Ceredigion artist Bethan Clwyd. They are well equipped; bedside lighting has been upgraded this year. Two rooms can interconnect for family use. Those in the eaves are a 'long climb'. A 'first-class dinner at a reasonable price' is served by Tim Morris in the small restaurant with its dramatic decor. He serves modern dishes with a Welsh twist, perhaps Pantmawr goat's cheese toasted with walnuts; fillet of Welsh beef, fondant potatoes, wilted spinach. Service is 'friendly and efficient'. There is no guest lounge; guests may sit in the cellar bar, or on the restaurant's sea-facing terrace which also provides outdoor dining.

19 Marine Terrace
Aberystwyth SY23 2AZ

T: 01970-612252
F: 01970-623348
E: info@gwestycymru.co.uk
W: www.gwestycymru.co.uk

BEDROOMS: 8, 2 on ground floor.
OPEN: all year except Christmas/New Year, restaurant closed for lunch Tues in winter.
FACILITIES: bar, restaurant, terrace, secure parking (book in advance), unsuitable for &.
BACKGROUND MUSIC: in Reception and restaurant.
LOCATION: central, on seafront.
CHILDREN: 'well-behaved' children welcomed.
DOGS: only guide dogs allowed.
CREDIT CARDS: MasterCard, Visa.
PRICES: [2010] B&B £42.50–£70 per person, full alc £35.

## BALA Gwynedd

Map 3:B3

### BRYNIAU GOLAU

'Natural hosts' Katrina Le Saux and Peter Cottee 'will do everything' to help visitors to their Victorian home, built as a summer house and overlooking Bala Lake on the edge of Snowdonia national park. In the gardens are 'spacious lawns and terraces with little corners to relax in', and take in the 'magical' views across to the Arenig Mountains. Visitors are welcomed with tea and home-made cakes, on the lawns in fine weather, or in an elegant spacious sitting room. Two of the 'impeccable' bedrooms have a four-poster bed; state-of-the-art bathrooms have a spa bath. A three-course evening meal is available, by arrangement, on two nights a week (typical dish: sea bass, beurre blanc, roasted winter vegetables); 'a fully stocked bar' is available. Breakfast, served at a long table in a room with a grand piano, 'is good, with freshly squeezed orange juice, local sausages and bacon'. Guests may use a barbecue in the grounds; the nearest restaurants are in Bala, less than two miles away. Walkers and cyclists are welcomed (drying facilities). (*JR*)

Llangower, Bala LL23 7BT

T: 01678-521782
E: katrinalesaux@hotmail.co.uk
W: www.bryniau-golau.co.uk

BEDROOMS: 3.
OPEN: Mar–Dec.
FACILITIES: sitting room, dining room, ½-acre garden, unsuitable for &.
BACKGROUND MUSIC: none.
LOCATION: 2 miles SE of Bala.
CHILDREN: not under 12.
DOGS: not allowed.
CREDIT CARDS: MasterCard, Visa.
PRICES: [2010] B&B £40–£65 per person, dinner £25, 1-night bookings refused weekends and peak times.

**25% DISCOUNT VOUCHERS**

# BEAUMARIS Isle of Anglesey

Map 3:A3

## YE OLDE BULLS HEAD

Once the staging post for coaches coming to this likeable little town for the ferries to Ireland, this 500-year-old inn has ancient beams and creaking staircases. 'One of my favourite hotels in the area,' said a visitor who liked the range of dining options. A 'buzzy' brasserie is in converted stables with stone walls and slate floors, where chef Stuart Briggs serves classic bistro dishes (moules marinière, steaks, etc). In the *Loft* restaurant, Hefin Roberts has a fine-dining menu of dishes like canon of lamb, leek porridge, shank ragout, coriander jus. There is a well-furnished lounge, and an 'atmospheric' bar with log fires. The 'smartly cosy' bedrooms in the old inn are named after Dickens's characters (the writer once stayed here). The bedrooms above the bar may suffer some noise. Rooms in the adjacent town house, a contemporary renovation of a 16th-century building, are filled with light and colour. One is suitable for a family; another is adapted for disabled visitors. A suite runs the length of the gabled roof. Breakfast has an extensive continental selection, a 'full range of cooked courses'. (*SOT*)

Castle Street
Beaumaris, Isle of Anglesey
LL58 8AP

T: 01248-810329
F: 01248-811294
E: info@bullsheadinn.co.uk
W: www.bullsheadinn.co.uk

BEDROOMS: 26, 2 on ground floor, 1 in courtyard, 13 in *The Townhouse* adjacent, 1 suitable for &.
OPEN: all year, except 25/26 Dec, 1 Jan, *Loft* restaurant closed lunch, Sun/Mon night.
FACILITIES: lift (in *Townhouse*), lounge, bar, brasserie, restaurant, sea 200 yds, only brasserie and *Townhouse* suitable for &.
BACKGROUND MUSIC: 'chill-out', jazz in brasserie.
LOCATION: central.
CHILDREN: no under-7s in restaurant or bedroom suites.
DOGS: only assistance dogs allowed.
CREDIT CARDS: Amex, MasterCard, Visa.
PRICES: [2010] B&B £45–£77.50 per person, set dinner (restaurant) £40, full alc £50, special breaks.

# BRECHFA Carmarthenshire

## TÝ MAWR

*César award: Welsh country hotel of the year*

In a 'tranquil spot with only the sound of running water from a stream in the garden', this 16th-century farmhouse is run as a country hotel and restaurant by the 'welcoming' Annabel Viney and Stephen Thomas. 'They looked after us well; it was more like staying in someone's home than a hotel,' one visitor wrote. Trusted correspondents enjoyed their 'best hotel experience for years'. The welcome is 'friendly, not matey; they are gracious hosts'. In a village on the edge of the Brechfa forest, the house has thick exposed-stone walls, fireplaces and beams. 'Our room was cosy and comfortable, overlooking the garden; in the bathroom a large claw-footed bath with shower over.' Stephen Thomas is the chef, producing 'good bistro-style cooking' using seasonal ingredients from 'local suppliers, all listed on menu'. 'The dishes ranged from simple with lots of flavour (gravadlax) to more complex but delicious plates (pork stuffed with date and pecan, berry jus). Wonderful home-made sorbets and bread.' 'In perfect weather, we sat on the patio with our drinks, watching the river.' Wi-Fi is available. (*Mrs J Stirrat, Sarah and Tony Thomas*)

Brechfa SA32 7RA

T: 01267-202332
E: info@wales-country-hotel.co.uk
W: www.wales-country-hotel.co.uk

BEDROOMS: 6, 2 on ground floor.
OPEN: all year.
FACILITIES: sitting room, bar, breakfast room, restaurant, 1-acre grounds, unsuitable for &.
BACKGROUND MUSIC: classical in restaurant.
LOCATION: village centre.
CHILDREN: not under 12.
DOGS: not allowed in restaurant.
CREDIT CARDS: Amex, MasterCard, Visa.
PRICES: [2010] B&B £54–£64 per person, D,B&B £75–£85, set meals £24–£29, alc £44, seasonal breaks, Christmas/New Year packages.

**25% DISCOUNT VOUCHERS**

# BROADHAVEN Pembrokeshire

## THE DRUIDSTONE

'Another fantastic week; as ever, a relaxed, friendly atmosphere.' Praise this year for Rod, Jane and Angus Bell's 'family holiday centre', which is recommended by regular visitors for travellers who look for 'character' rather than 'perfection'. It will not appeal to all: only five of the bedrooms have facilities en suite (the others share three bathrooms). 'Definitely more shabby chic than high-end luxury (a good thing),' says a fan. 'We felt they had upped their game this year with redecoration in the hotel.' Jane Bell tells us that she and her husband, Rod, have 'more or less' left their son, Angus, 'in sole charge' with his partner, Beth (who has opened 'possibly the smallest bookshop in the UK'). Angus also runs the kitchen, cooking 'tasty' bar dishes (pork and apple stew, vegetarian choices), and a 'fusion/instinctive' menu in the restaurant, eg, Moroccan-spiced leg of lamb, crushed chickpeas and chermoula. There are weekly 'feast' nights ('the best Asian buffet we've tasted'). The 'star attractions' are the 'unbeatable' view from the cliff-top location, and the huge sandy beach below. (*Melissa Midgen, and others*)

nr Broadhaven
Haverfordwest SA62 3NE

T: 01437-781221
E: enquiries@druidstone.co.uk
W: www.druidstone.co.uk

BEDROOMS: 11, also 5 holiday cottages.
OPEN: all year.
FACILITIES: sitting room, TV room, bar (occasional live music), farmhouse kitchen, restaurant, small conference/function facilities, civil wedding licence, 22-acre grounds, sandy beach, safe bathing 200 yds, unsuitable for &.
BACKGROUND MUSIC: in bar.
LOCATION: 7 miles W of Haverfordwest.
CHILDREN: all ages welcomed.
DOGS: not allowed in restaurant.
CREDIT CARDS: Amex, MasterCard, Visa.
PRICES: [2009] B&B £55–£90 per person, D,B&B £30 added, full alc £35, courses, conferences, Christmas/New Year/midweek packages, 1-night advance bookings refused Sat.

# CAPEL GARMON Conwy

Map 3:A3

## TAN-Y-FOEL COUNTRY HOUSE

In a 'wonderful, peaceful' setting, high on wooded hills in the Snowdonia national park, this 17th-century stone house is run by Peter and Janet Pitman and their daughter, Kelly. 'Highly professional', they work without any other help. This might explain the 'strict rules' noted by an inspector. Breakfast is between 8 and 9 am, dinner at 7.30 pm. 'We regret that we do not cater for vegetarians or late arrivals,' say the Pitmans. Drinks are served from 7 pm in the lounge (not available after 10.30 pm). Mrs Pitman's 'exceptionally good cooking' has consistently been given a high score by the *Good Food Guide*. She uses fruit and vegetables from her greenhouse for her short menu (two choices each course). It might include turbot, green speckled lentils, fennel cream, samphire, sweet beetroot syrup reduction. 'Very comfortable' bedrooms, in muted shades, have flat-screen TV, DVD/CD-player. Some have a 'magnificent view' of the valley; two have their own external entrance. There are 'spacious, well-equipped' bathrooms. 'A car is essential', but there is good local walking. More reports, please.

Capel Garmon
nr Betws-y-Coed LL26 0RE

T: 01690-710507
F: 01690-710681
E: enquiries@tyfhotel.co.uk
W: www.tyfhotel.co.uk

BEDROOMS: 5, 1 on ground floor, 2 in annexe.
OPEN: All year except Christmas/New Year, limited availability during winter, dining room closed midday.
FACILITIES: sitting room, breakfast room, dining room, 6-acre grounds, unsuitable for &.
BACKGROUND MUSIC: none.
LOCATION: 2 miles N of Betws-y-Coed.
CHILDREN: not under 12.
DOGS: not allowed.
CREDIT CARDS: MasterCard, Visa.
PRICES: [2010] B&B £67.50–£120 per person, set dinner £46, midweek breaks, 1-night bookings refused weekends, bank holidays.

# CARDIFF

Map 3:E4

## JOLYON'S

Opposite the Millennium Centre, home of the Welsh National Opera, Jolyon Joseph has converted this Georgian seamen's lodge into a small hotel. It is liked for the youthful, 'laid-back vibe' and hint of eccentricity. The manager is Gemma Saunders. The bedrooms are decorated in contemporary colours and have an eclectic mix of furnishings. A first-floor room at the front has an antique carved wooden bed with a matching armoire; a spa bath in the bathroom. A room on the top floor has a wrought iron bed and a balcony. All rooms have magazines, Freeview television, a pot of sweets, tea and coffee. A ground-floor room, with a wet bathroom, is not for light sleepers (especially at weekends) as it is above the busy basement *Bar Cwtch* (Welsh for a cuddle or a hug). This is a popular local venue for its 'Dishy Bits' menu (cured meats, flatbreads, stuffed mushrooms, etc) and an extensive range of pizzas from a wood-burning oven. Breakfast, served here until 10 am (later at weekends), has warm croissants, compote of seasonal fruits, scrambled eggs with bacon or smoked salmon. (*SOT, DB*)

5 Bute Crescent, Cardiff Bay
Cardiff CF10 5AN

T: 029-2048 8775
E: info@jolyons.co.uk
W: www.jolyons.co.uk

BEDROOMS: 7, 1 on ground floor.
OPEN: all year.
FACILITIES: residents' lounge, bar, live music sometimes, terrace, unsuitable for &.
BACKGROUND MUSIC: classical in lounge, mix in bar.
LOCATION: Cardiff Bay waterfront, under 2 miles from centre.
CHILDREN: not under 14.
DOGS: only assistance dogs allowed.
CREDIT CARDS: Amex, MasterCard, Visa.
PRICES: [2010] room £65–£200, breakfast £6.50–£11.50, special offers, Christmas/New Year packages.

# CONWY

Map 3:A3

## SYCHNANT PASS COUNTRY HOUSE

Above the medieval town of Conwy, within Snowdonia national park, Bre and Graham Carrington-Sykes are the 'enthusiastic' owners of this large Edwardian house. They have furnished it lavishly, covering the walls with pictures; the study has a large library of books. The bedrooms, named after TS Eliot's 'practical cats', vary greatly in size and style (visitors are encouraged to phone for advice on their choice). Mr Mistoffelees opens on to a terrace; Old Deuteronomy has an emperor bed and a balcony; head height is restricted in Grumbuskins, which has a sitting room in the eaves; McCavity's has a sofa bed for a 'little person'. Children are welcomed (swings in the grounds, games indoors), as are well-behaved pets (the owners have dogs of their own). Mr Carrington-Sykes is the chef, serving 'substantial' traditional dishes, eg, julienne pork fillet, rich mild curry cream. Breakfast is a buffet, with hot dishes cooked to order. A heated indoor swimming pool has French windows opening on to a terrace on sunny days. The family also offer accommodation in *Pentre Mawr*, Llandyrnog (see Shortlist). More reports, please.

Sychnant Pass Road
Conwy LL32 8BJ

T: 01492-596868
E: info@sychnantpasscountryhouse .co.uk
W: www.sychnantpasscountryhouse .co.uk

BEDROOMS: 12, 2 on ground floor.
OPEN: all year, except Christmas.
FACILITIES: sitting room, study, restaurant, indoor 12-metre swimming pool, gym, civil wedding licence, terraces (hot tub, sauna, tanning room), 3-acre garden.
BACKGROUND MUSIC: in restaurant.
LOCATION: 1½ miles SW of Conwy by A457.
CHILDREN: all ages welcomed.
DOGS: not allowed in restaurant.
CREDIT CARDS: MasterCard, Visa.
PRICES: [2010] B&B £50–£95 per person, D,B&B £82.50–£127.50, set meal £32.50, special offers, Christmas/New Year packages, 1-night bookings sometimes refused Sat.

# CRICKHOWELL Powys

## GLANGRWYNEY COURT

On a country estate with large walled gardens, this 'exceptional' Palladian house (Grade II listed) is the 'grand family home' of Christina and Warwick Jackson. 'Charming, attentive hosts', they run it as an upmarket B&B, providing evening meals to small groups. 'The ambience is perfect,' say recent visitors. The gardens, which are also listed, have ancient magnolias, acers, interesting shrubs. The spacious bedrooms are furnished in country house style. All rooms have antique furniture, full-length mirror, 'wonderful' tea tray; they face the garden with its views to the Black Mountains. The master suite has a steam shower; one twin room has a spa bath. Alex Polizzi, TV's hotel inspector, said: 'I had my best night's sleep away from home here.' Log fires burn in the winter in the lounge and library, which are furnished with period pieces. There is an honesty bar in the library, which has a large collection of books available to guests. The Jacksons will recommend places to eat locally, and organise taxis. Guests can discover sitting areas in the garden, or play tennis and croquet. (*P and MM*)

Glangrwyney, Crickhowell
NP8 1ES

T: 01873-811288
F: 01873-810317
E: info@glancourt.co.uk
W: www.glancourt.co.uk

BEDROOMS: 9, 1, on ground floor, in courtyard, also 3 self-catering cottages.
OPEN: all year.
FACILITIES: sitting room, library/honesty bar, dining room, civil wedding licence, 4-acre garden (croquet, boules, tennis) in 33-acre parkland, river 500 yds (fishing by arrangement), unsuitable for &.
BACKGROUND MUSIC: only if requested.
LOCATION: 2 miles SE of Crickhowell, off A40.
CHILDREN: all ages welcomed.
DOGS: allowed in cottages only.
CREDIT CARDS: MasterCard, Visa.
PRICES: [2010] B&B £45–£67.50 per person, special breaks, off-season discounts, 1-night bookings sometimes refused weekends, bank holidays.

# CRICKHOWELL Powys

Map 3:D4

## GLIFFAES

◊ *César award in 2009*

'Highly recommended' by readers again this year, this smart sporting hotel on a broad sweep of the River Usk has 'a homely feel, nothing formal or starchy'. The 19th-century Italianate building is owned and run by Susie and James Suter with her parents, Nick and Peta Brabner. It is decorated in country house style: there are comfortable seating areas and a conservatory with a view down the valley. The chef, Karl Cheetham, sources ingredients locally for his daily-changing modern menus, which might include piri-piri-spiced chicken livers; supreme of Bryn Derw chicken, sage and pancetta butter beans. 'The food was lovely; the quality of the produce was evident.' Most of the bedrooms are large. 'Our room had everything we needed; one of the best beds we've found in a hotel.' A small room was 'beautifully furnished'. *Gliffaes* owns a private stretch of the trout- and salmon-laden river (fishing courses arranged). Bicycles are available for hire; use of the hotel's tandem is free. (*Dr Rex Walters, Lynn Elliott*)

Crickhowell NP8 1RH

**T:** 01874-730371
**F:** 01874-730463
**E:** calls@gliffaeshotel.com
**W:** www.gliffaes.com

**BEDROOMS:** 23, 4 in annexe, 1 on ground floor.
**OPEN:** all year except 3–28 Jan, restaurant closed lunch (except Sun).
**FACILITIES:** ramp, 2 sitting rooms, conservatory, bar, dining room, civil wedding licence, 33-acre garden (tennis, croquet, fishing, ghillie available).
**BACKGROUND MUSIC:** jazz in bar.
**LOCATION:** 3 miles W of Crickhowell.
**CHILDREN:** all ages welcomed.
**DOGS:** not allowed indoors.
**CREDIT CARDS:** MasterCard, Visa.
**PRICES:** [2010] B&B £49–£119 per person, D,B&B £82–£148.50, set dinner £29–£37, fishing courses, website deals, Christmas/New Year packages, 1-night bookings refused weekends.

## DOLFOR Powys
Map 3:C4

### THE OLD VICARAGE

High in the hills of the Welsh Marches, this red
brick Victorian vicarage is run as a small guest
house by Tim and Helen Withers, who are
'friendly and informal, yet consummate
professionals'. The bedrooms have 'all modern
comforts'; there are excellent beds, flat-screen
TV. No tea-making: 'Water and sherry are
provided, and tea is brought in the morning.'
Bathrooms have under-floor heating, fluffy
towels. There is a lounge decorated in period
style; candles and antiques in the dining room.
The Witherses formerly ran a gastropub in
Wales; he is the chef, cooking 'wholesome, fresh'
food on a short menu, eg, Welsh Cheddar cheese
soufflé; roast organic Mochdre lamb, leeks and
red wine. 'He waited until he knew someone
wanted custard before making it, to ensure it
was fresh.' Breakfast ('equally good') has home-
made granola, fresh fruit, natural yogurt, local
apple juice on the dresser; Welsh mountain
honey and home-made preserves with Aga toast;
boiled eggs from the 'happy-looking hens we
passed on the way in', local sausage, bacon and
smoked salmon. Fans like the 'generous feel
about the place'. (*S and TT, and others*)

Dolfor, nr Newtown
SY16 4BN

T: 01686-629051
E: tim@theoldvicaragedolfor.co.uk
W: www.theoldvicaragedolfor.co.uk

BEDROOMS: 4.
OPEN: all year.
FACILITIES: drawing room, dining
room, 2-acre garden, unsuitable
for ♿.
BACKGROUND MUSIC: none.
LOCATION: 3 miles S of Newtown.
CHILDREN: not under 12.
DOGS: not allowed.
CREDIT CARDS: MasterCard, Visa.
PRICES: [2010] B&B £47.50–£65 per
person, D,B&B £77.50–£95, set
dinner £30, special breaks (walking,
etc), Christmas/New Year packages,
1-night bookings may be refused at
Christmas/New Year.

**25% DISCOUNT VOUCHERS**

# DOLYDD Gwynedd

Map 3:A2

## Y GOEDEN EIRIN

*❦César award in 2008*

'This is our home,' say John and Eluned Rowlands who emphasise 'a sense of place' at their informal guest house in a hamlet on the edge of the Snowdonia national park. The bilingual couple share their culture with guests. 'They gave us much attention,' say visitors in 2010. 'Eluned, a geography lecturer, guided us to interesting places. John's books line the walls.' Visitors like the 'personal welcome' and 'good value'. The renovated farm buildings have a mix of traditional and modern in decor and furnishings: Welsh granite, slate and old beams are featured. Among the 'beautiful objects' is a Bechstein grand piano, which John Rowlands might play (there is no other background music). A no-choice menu of Aga-cooked dishes is served by arrangement in the small dining room; ingredients are local and organic where possible for dishes like tagine of lamb. 'Excellent' breakfasts have freshly squeezed orange juice, home-made bread and preserves, a wide choice of cooked dishes. Green initiatives include solar panels, composting policies; use of local transport encouraged. (*John and Mary Hawes*)

Dolydd, Caernarfon LL54 7EF

T: 01286-830942
E: john_rowlands@tiscali.co.uk
W: www.ygoedeneirin.co.uk

BEDROOMS: 3, 2 in annexe.
OPEN: all year except Christmas/ New Year, dining room occasionally closed.
FACILITIES: lounge, dining room (occasional live piano music), Wi-Fi access, 20-acre pastureland, unsuitable for &.
BACKGROUND MUSIC: none.
LOCATION: 3 miles S of Caernarfon.
CHILDREN: not under 12.
DOGS: not allowed.
CREDIT CARDS: none, cash or cheque payment requested on arrival.
PRICES: [2010] B&B £40–£60 per person, set dinner £28, 1-night bookings sometimes refused weekends.

**25% DISCOUNT VOUCHERS**

# EGLWYSFACH Powys

## YNYSHIR HALL

In extensive landscaped gardens surrounded by an RSPB reserve, this small luxury hotel (Relais & Châteaux) has long been liked by readers for the beauty of the setting, the excellence of the service and the fine cooking. Rob and Joan Reen sold it to the von Essen group, but she remains as a hands-on manager, overseeing front-of-house, perhaps foraging for wood sorrel and wild garlic for the kitchen. The 'stunning' cooking of chef Shane Hughes (praised by a trusted reporter) was awarded a *Michelin* star in 2010. He uses fish landed locally and game from a nearby estate for his classic menus with dishes like squab pigeon and foie gras; paupiettes of lemon sole, gem lettuce, coriander, Thai-style nage. All the bread (brioche, olive, plain, rosemary focaccia) is home baked. The service throughout is 'exceptional; it is like being welcomed as a member of a family'. The public rooms are opulent, with stylish furnishings; Mr Reen's striking artwork is displayed throughout. Bedrooms, each named after a famous artist, are done in bold colours. (*RG*)

Eglwysfach
nr Machynlleth SY20 8PQ

T: 01654-781209
F: 01654-781366
E: info@ynyshirhall.co.uk
W: www.ynyshirhall.co.uk

BEDROOMS: 9, 2 in studio annexe, 1 on ground floor.
OPEN: all year.
FACILITIES: drawing room, bar lounge, breakfast room, restaurant, civil wedding licence, 14-acre gardens in 365-acre bird reserve (croquet, putting).
BACKGROUND MUSIC: classical in bar, restaurant.
LOCATION: 6 miles SW of Machynlleth.
CHILDREN: not under 9 (except for exclusive use).
DOGS: not allowed in public rooms.
CREDIT CARDS: all major cards.
PRICES: [2010] B&B £140–£197 per person, D,B&B £207.50–£283, set meals £70–£85, full alc £85, special breaks, Christmas/New Year packages, 1-night bookings refused weekends high season.

**25% DISCOUNT VOUCHERS**

# FELIN FACH Powys

Map 3:D4

## THE FELIN FACH GRIFFIN

On the road linking the Brecon Beacons and the Black Mountains, this old inn is run as a dining pub by brothers Charles and Edmund Inkin. Popular with locals, it has an informal 'youthful' atmosphere (background music is usually played); Julie Bell is the manager. Simon Potter was promoted to head chef in October 2009 with a brief to simplify the food, focusing on local suppliers and the inn's organic kitchen garden. His short supper menu might include smoked haddock chowder; braised pork cheeks, black pudding, garden pea risotto. Soda bread, the house speciality, is 'replenished on request'. Three of the simply furnished bedrooms have a four-poster bed. 'Our room was comfortable with lovely bedding.' A small room 'belied first impressions; plenty of storage, a firm bed; well-designed bathroom'. Radio 4's *Today* programme is played at breakfast at a communal table in the Aga room. 'Delicious' scrambled eggs, from hens which have a run in the garden; soda bread is served alongside white sliced. The brothers also own *The Gurnard's Head*, Zennor (see entry). (*J and MB, and others*)

Felin Fach, nr Brecon LD3 0UB

T: 01874-620111
E: enquiries@felinfachgriffin.co.uk
W: www.felinfachgriffin.co.uk

BEDROOMS: 7.
OPEN: All year except 24/25 Dec, 4 days Jan.
FACILITIES: bar area, dining room, breakfast room, private dining room, ½-acre garden (stream, kitchen garden), only bar/dining room suitable for &.
BACKGROUND MUSIC: CDs/radio most of the time (*Today* programme at breakfast).
LOCATION: 4 miles NE of Brecon, in village on A470.
CHILDREN: all ages welcomed.
DOGS: not allowed in dining room.
CREDIT CARDS: MasterCard, Visa.
PRICES: [2010] B&B £45–£75 per person, D,B&B £67.50–£95, set meals £21.50–£26.50, full alc £40, special breaks, 1-night bookings occasionally refused.

# FISHGUARD Pembrokeshire

Map 3:D1

## THE MANOR TOWN HOUSE  **NEW**

Near the town square of the ferry port, this Grade II listed Georgian house was bought by Helen and Chris Sheldon in 2009. 'Relaxed and warm', they run it as a B&B. 'We were pleased to be served coffee and warm Welsh cakes when we arrived,' say inspectors in 2010. The bedrooms have their original fireplace, 'homely furniture and wallpaper with a late Victorian/Edwardian feel'. 'Our large room had a good-sized bed, a dark wood dresser with ample mirrors, a winged armchair and a handsome sofa; a screen around the washbasin, which was in the room.' At breakfast, 'Helen served her speciality, home-made waffles with delicious toppings, with pride. The coffee was strong, the cereals were varied, and there was a good selection of other dishes.' Other visitors liked the bread from a local baker. No parking on the busy road outside: a public car park is five minutes' walk away. Many guests are on their way to the Irish ferries. Local eating places are limited; booking is recommended for nearby *BarFive*, under new management in 2010. (*Jill and Mike Bennett, and others*)

11 Main Street
Fishguard SA65 9HG

T: 01348-873260
E: enquiries@manortownhouse.com
W: www.manortownhouse.com

BEDROOMS: 6.
OPEN: all year except 24–28 Dec.
FACILITIES: 2 lounges, breakfast room, small walled garden, unsuitable for &.
BACKGROUND MUSIC: classical at breakfast.
LOCATION: central.
CHILDREN: all ages welcomed.
DOGS: not allowed.
CREDIT CARDS: MasterCard, Visa.
PRICES: B&B £35–£47.50 per person.

# HARLECH Gwynedd

Map 3:B3

## CASTLE COTTAGE

On the brow of a hill close to the castle of the 'quirky, historic' town, this 17th-century coaching inn has been restored as a restaurant-with-rooms by Glyn (the chef) and Jacqueline Roberts. 'They take pride in their work,' said the nominator. Dinner is the 'centrepiece of any stay': pre-starters (perhaps a 'delicious home-made Scotch egg') are taken in the bar, which has a log fire. The menu has an 'emphasis on local meat, game and fish', eg, breast of wild duck, creamed polenta, fine beans, port and chestnut sauce. The dishes are modern, the flavours strong, the portions large ('some simply too large to finish'). 'A study in simplicity,' said one visitor. The extensive wine list is 'well priced'. The bedrooms have been given a contemporary style. Three are in the main building, the others in a Grade II listed stone cottage next door, where a 'spacious' room was 'clean, modern (with atmospheric original roof beams); the bathroom had limestone tiles, a walk-in shower and a huge bath'. Parking is limited. (*SOT*)

Y Llech, Harlech LL46 2YL

T: 01766-780479
E: glyn@castlecottageharlech.co.uk
W: www.castlecottageharlech.co.uk

BEDROOMS: 7, 4 in annexe, 2 on ground floor.
OPEN: all year except Christmas and 3 weeks Nov.
FACILITIES: bar/lounge, restaurant.
BACKGROUND MUSIC: in dining room.
LOCATION: town centre.
CHILDREN: all ages welcomed.
DOGS: not allowed.
CREDIT CARDS: MasterCard, Visa.
PRICES: [2010] B&B £60–£80 per person, D,B&B £92–£112, set dinner £36.50, full alc £45, New Year package, 1-night bookings refused bank holidays.

**25% DISCOUNT VOUCHERS**

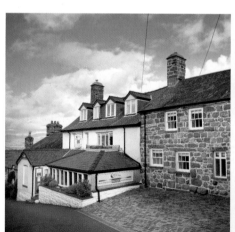

# HAVERFORDWEST Pembrokeshire

Map 3:D1

## CRUG-GLAS

**NEW**

On an 'immaculate' working farm near St David's, Perkin and Janet Evans welcome visitors with 'a pride in their house and their part of Wales that is reflected in their hospitality', say inspectors. 'Mrs Evans shook our hands, cheerfully introducing herself.' The guest lounge is a 'traditional and relaxing' room, with antiques, ornaments, games, books and magazines; an honesty bar. 'Our bedroom on the top floor was as big as a London flat. It had a mix of contemporary and antique furniture, exposed beams, a large bed, excellent storage; a separate sitting room, and a smartly tiled bathroom.' Janet Evans is the cook, displaying her dinner menu on the hall table at 4.40 pm (guests are asked to select in advance). 'In the smart dining room, we enjoyed an excellent Abercastle crab cake; tasty figs stuffed with cheese; a large portion of monkfish tails, blue cheese sauce and dishes of mashed and dauphinoise potatoes. The atmosphere was happy, conversation buzzed.' Breakfast has 'a super selection of fresh fruit; nice local cheeses. A hearty cooked dish of your choice: lovely scrambled eggs for us.'

nr Abereiddy
Haverfordwest SA62 6XX

T: 01348-831302
E: janet@crugglas.plus.com
W: www.crug-glas.co.uk

BEDROOMS: 7, 2 in coach house, 1 on ground floor.
OPEN: all year except Christmas.
FACILITIES: drawing room, dining room, 1-acre garden on 600-acre farm.
BACKGROUND MUSIC: classical in restaurant.
LOCATION: 3½ miles NE of St David's.
CHILDREN: not under 12.
DOGS: not allowed.
CREDIT CARDS: all major cards.
PRICES: B&B £50–£75 per person, full alc £40, special breaks, New Year package.

**25% DISCOUNT VOUCHERS**

# KNIGHTON Powys

## MILEBROOK HOUSE

A 'quintessential country hotel', this former dower house is owned and managed by Beryl and Rodney Marsden and their family. Mrs Marsden's kindness impressed a returning visitor this year; an earlier guest said that the house 'soothes and reassures'. Once the home of the explorer Sir Wilfred Thesiger, the stone building is surrounded by formal gardens with herbaceous borders, a croquet lawn and wildlife pond, and walks along the River Teme. Some visitors comment on the noise from the main road at the front. The kitchen garden supplies the vegetables for the menus of Chris Marsden, the grandson of the owners. His 'extremely competent' British dishes might include crispy slow-roasted pork belly, roast new potatoes. Many wines are served by the glass. The lounge has a log fire, fine art and plenty of books. The 'homely' bedrooms have thick carpets; rear rooms are the quietest. For walkers, some of the best stretches of Offa's Dyke path are nearby. A non-refundable deposit of £95 per room is required. (*Richard Creed*)

Milebrook
Knighton Powys LD7 1LT

T: 01547-528632
F: 01547-520509
E: hotel@milebrook.kc3ltd.co.uk
W: www.milebrookhouse.co.uk

BEDROOMS: 10, 2 on ground floor.
OPEN: all year except Sun night/Mon Nov–Jan, restaurant closed Mon lunch.
FACILITIES: lounge, bar, 2 dining rooms, 3½-acre grounds on river (terraces, pond, croquet, fishing).
BACKGROUND MUSIC: classical in bar and restaurant in evening.
LOCATION: on A4113, 2 miles E of Knighton.
CHILDREN: not under 8.
DOGS: not allowed.
CREDIT CARDS: MasterCard, Visa.
PRICES: [2010] B&B £55.50–£76.50 per person, set dinner £32.95, full alc £40, short breaks, Christmas/New Year packages.

**25% DISCOUNT VOUCHERS**

# LLANARMON DYFFRYN CEIRIOG Denbighshire Map 3:B4

## THE HAND AT LLANARMON

'A very well-run hotel which remains part of the community, run by friendly local staff.' Praise comes again in 2010 from returning visitors to Martin and Gaynor De Luchi's 'unpretentious' old drovers' inn in a village at the head of a pretty valley. 'The accommodation is comfortable and the prices are very reasonable.' The three bars are busy with locals ('there is usually someone willing to chew your ear off if talking is your game,' say the owners). Residents have their own lounge if they seek a quieter corner. The restaurant is in a converted dairy (stone walls and a large wood-burning stove). The cooking of the chef, Grant Mulholland, is 'consistently good; highlights were Welsh Black roast beef and superb confit of duck; desserts have moved up a notch, with a wonderful panna cotta with cream from a chocolate cup (eat after pouring)'. Three 'character' bedrooms are in the main house; 'country' rooms are in south-facing converted stables (wheelchair-users found access excellent). *Note*: Not to be confused with the *Hand Hotel* at Chirk, 11 miles away. (*Richard and Jenny Green*)

Llanarmon Dyffryn Ceiriog
Ceiriog Valley LL20 7LD

T: 01691-600666
F: 01691-600262
E: reception@thehandhotel.co.uk
W: www.thehandhotel.co.uk

BEDROOMS: 13, 4 on ground floor, 1 suitable for &.
OPEN: all year, accommodation closed at Christmas.
FACILITIES: ramp, lounge, bar, restaurant, games/TV room, civil wedding licence, terrace, ¾-acre grounds.
BACKGROUND MUSIC: none.
LOCATION: 10 miles W of Oswestry.
CHILDREN: all ages welcomed.
DOGS: not allowed in some bedrooms, public rooms except bar.
CREDIT CARDS: MasterCard, Visa.
PRICES: [2010] B&B £45–£62.50 per person, full alc £32, special breaks, New Year package.

**25% DISCOUNT VOUCHERS**

# LLANDOVERY Carmarthenshire

Map 3:D3

## THE NEW WHITE LION

In a small town of painted terrace houses near Brecon, Gerald and Sylvia Pritchard have converted this Grade II listed former pub into an upmarket guest house. 'Natural hosts', they are keen to introduce visitors to the heritage and wildlife of the area (in which they were born). The house has been renovated in contemporary style; there are fine fabrics, smart wallpaper, muted modern colours. The lounge has an open fire, a 'well-stocked' honesty bar. The bedrooms have antiques, a wide-screen television; a power shower. 'My room was small, but elegantly furnished; spotlessly clean.' Dinner must be booked in advance: Peter Devlin serves a short menu of 'no-frills' dishes, eg, smoked mackerel with horseradish cream; rack of lamb, dauphinoise potatoes, redcurrant/mint sauce. Vegetables are from the garden. 'It felt like Sunday supper at home, no higher praise.' Breakfast has a choice of 'hearty' full cooked Welsh or fish of the day; to finish, 'Mrs P's home-made Seville orange marmalade'. 'They were happy to serve me earlier than usual; Sylvia went out of her way to advise of a scenic route.' (*JG*)

43 Stone Street
Llandovery SA20 0BZ

T: 01550-720685
E: info@newwhitelion.co.uk
W: www.newwhitelion.co.uk

BEDROOMS: 6, 1 on ground floor.
OPEN: all year except Christmas, restaurant closed midday.
FACILITIES: lounge, dining room.
BACKGROUND MUSIC: assorted Welsh harp, 'easy listening'.
LOCATION: town centre, 17 miles W of Brecon.
CHILDREN: all ages welcomed (early supper available).
DOGS: not allowed.
CREDIT CARDS: Diners, MasterCard, Visa.
PRICES: [2009] B&B £50–£80 per person, set meals £20–£25, full alc £32.50, New Year package, 1-night bookings refused weekends.

**25% DISCOUNT VOUCHERS**

# LLANDRILLO Denbighshire

Map 3:B4

## TYDDYN LLAN

*César award in 2006*

'At the top of its game', Bryan and Susan Webb's elegant restaurant-with-rooms, a former shooting lodge, was awarded a *Michelin* star in 2010. 'This is surely the best food you'll find in Wales,' says a returning enthusiast. A first-time visitor agreed: 'A fantastic meal; like a top London restaurant but at an agreeable price.' Susan Webb runs front-of-house: 'Her bubbly personality belies a quiet authority and efficiency.' The house sits in 'manicured grounds' in the vale of Edeyrnion, facing the Berwyn Mountains. The public rooms have 'interesting colour schemes, a mix of antiques and modern sofas'; 'space to curl up with a book'. The bedrooms are 'thoughtfully furnished': 'Our room, in shades of dusky pink, had a comfortable bed (turn-down during dinner); good extras.' Dinner is served 'at just the right pace' in two candlelit dining rooms. Mr Webb cooks classic dishes on an extensive menu, eg, roast Bresse pigeon, wild garlic bubble and squeak, wild mushrooms. He also provides a 'great' breakfast ('perfect poached eggs'). (*Gordon Hands, Cy and Stanley Jones, and others*)

Llandrillo
nr Corwen LL21 0ST

T: 01490-440264
F: 01490-440414
E: enquiries@tyddynllan.co.uk
W: www.tyddynllan.co.uk

BEDROOMS: 14, 1, on ground floor, suitable for &.
OPEN: all year except 2 weeks Jan, restaurant closed midday Mon–Thurs.
FACILITIES: ramp, 2 lounges, bar, 2 dining rooms, civil wedding licence, 3-acre garden.
BACKGROUND MUSIC: none.
LOCATION: 5 miles SW of Corwen.
CHILDREN: all ages welcomed.
DOGS: allowed.
CREDIT CARDS: MasterCard, Visa.
PRICES: B&B £70–£140 per person, D,B&B £115–£185, set dinner £47.50–£67.50, full alc £60, special offers, gourmet dinners, Christmas/ New Year house parties.

**25% DISCOUNT VOUCHERS**

# LLANDUDNO Conwy

Map 3:A3

## BODYSGALLEN HALL AND SPA

*César award in 1988*

'This wonderful building, in a lovely location, remains a favourite. The staff are friendly, efficient.' Praise from a visitor this year to this Grade I listed, 17th-century mansion (Pride of Britain). 'Beautifully situated' with views of Snowdonia and Conwy Castle, it stands in a large park with woodland walks, knot garden and follies. Owned since 2008 by the National Trust, it is run by Historic House Hotels; Matthew Johnson is the manager. The house is filled with portraits, antiques; splendid fireplaces and stone mullioned windows, log fires. Modern features include a 'well-equipped' spa; also Wi-Fi. The best bedrooms (there are four suites) are 'large and elegant', furnished with chintz and soft colours; some have a four-poster. The cottage suites cater for families (provided the children are over six). In the restaurant (ask for a window table), the dress code is 'smart casual, no trainer shoes'. The chef, Gareth Jones, serves modern dishes, eg, seared fillet of sea bass, crab fritter, 'all things fennel'. The bistro has simpler dishes. (*Richard Mayou, Horst Stuiber, Sam Price*)

Llandudno LL30 1RS

T: 01492-584466
F: 01492-582519
E: info@bodysgallen.com
W: www.bodysgallen.com

BEDROOMS: 31, 16 in cottages, 1 suitable for ♿.

OPEN: all year, restaurant closed Sun lunch, all day Mon.

FACILITIES: hall, drawing room, library, bar, dining room, bistro, civil wedding licence, 220-acre park (gardens, tennis, croquet), spa (16-metre swimming pool, gym, sauna).

BACKGROUND MUSIC: in bistro.

LOCATION: 2 miles S of Llandudno.

CHILDREN: no children under 6 in hotel, under 8 in spa.

DOGS: not allowed.

CREDIT CARDS: Amex, MasterCard, Visa.

PRICES: [2010] B&B £82.50–£197.50 per person, D,B&B £115–£242.50, set dinner £39–£45, full alc £49, special breaks, Christmas/New Year packages, 1-night bookings sometimes refused.

## LLANDUDNO Conwy

Map 3:A3

### ST TUDNO HOTEL

❦ *César award in 1987*

Opposite the Victorian pier and gardens of the attractive seaside resort, this Grade II listed building has been run as a small, traditional hotel since 1972 by Martin Bland. 'He works very hard, and it shows,' says a returning visitor this year. Mr Bland 'makes a point of talking to his guests', is an earlier comment. Bedrooms have colourful wallpaper and furnishings. 'Our room at the back was a little faded; the large bed was comfortable, and housekeeping was first rate.' 'How nice to have fresh milk in the room fridge.' An Alice in Wonderland suite acknowledges 19th-century visits by Alice Liddell who inspired Lewis Carroll. Public rooms are traditionally decorated with swagged drapery, patterned wallpaper. In the *Terrace* restaurant, which has murals of Lake Como, stone fountains, and chandeliers, chef Ian Watson's 'classic modern British' dishes might include loin of roe deer, game pudding, truffled Welsh honey glaze. 'Delicious food, well presented and served.' 'An excellent Punch and Judy show on the seafront.' (*Richard Creed, and others*)

The Promenade
Llandudno LL30 2LP

T: 01492-874411
F: 01492-860407
E: sttudnohotel@btinternet.com
W: www.st-tudno.co.uk

BEDROOMS: 18.
OPEN: all year.
FACILITIES: lift, three lounges, restaurant, indoor heated swimming pool (8 by 4 metres), civil wedding licence, patio, 'secret garden', unsuitable for &.
BACKGROUND MUSIC: occasionally when quiet.
LOCATION: on promenade opposite pier, parking.
CHILDREN: all ages welcomed, under-5s have early supper.
DOGS: by arrangement (£10 per night), only in coffee lounge, not unattended in bedrooms.
CREDIT CARDS: all major cards.
PRICES: [2010] B&B £49.50–£150 per person, D,B&B £75–£175, set lunch £15–£20, full alc £40, special breaks, Christmas/New Year packages.

**25% DISCOUNT VOUCHERS**

# LLANDWROG Gwynedd

Map 3:A2

## RHIWAFALLEN

In extensive grounds surrounded by open countryside and distant views of the sea, this traditional granite farmhouse is run as a restaurant-with-rooms by 'charming hosts' Rob (the chef) and Kate John. Renovated 'to a high standard', the house stands well back from a main road. It has 'the feel of a modern city house': a large lounge, furnished with natural materials (slate, wood, subdued colours), 'is very comfortable, with lots of magazines to read'. The conservatory restaurant has been enlarged this year, and a small private dining room added. Mr John uses raw materials from local suppliers for his 'delicious' dishes ('classic with a modern twist'), eg, seared sea bass, porcini and bacon fricassée, candied celeriac. Some visitors would prefer not to be given a fixed-price three-course menu. Afternoon tea, included in the price, is 'a treat'. The contemporary bedrooms have oak flooring, rich fabrics, original artwork. The biggest has a seating area and a roof deck. Breakfast has freshly squeezed juices; 'fabulous home-made black pudding'. (*Rachael Keyues, JR, Clare Whitehurst*)

Llandwrog, nr Caernarfon LL54 5SW

T: 01286-830172
E: ktandrobjohn@aol.com
W: www.rhiwafallen.co.uk

BEDROOMS: 5, 1 on ground floor.
OPEN: all year, except 25/26 Dec, restaurant closed Sun night/Mon.
FACILITIES: ramps, lounge, restaurant, private dining room, 1-acre garden.
BACKGROUND MUSIC: modern ' chill-out'.
LOCATION: 6 miles S of Caernarfon.
CHILDREN: not under 12 (must have own room; standard rates).
DOGS: not allowed.
CREDIT CARDS: Amex, MasterCard, Visa.
PRICES: [2010] B&B £50–£75 per person, set dinner £35, special breaks, New Year package.

# LLANGAMMARCH WELLS Powys

Map 3:D3

## THE LAKE

❦*César award in 1992*

'Consistently good', Jean-Pierre Mifsud's mock-Tudor hotel has 'a fabulous setting' in 'magnificent' grounds with lawns that slope down to the River Irfon. 'Good food, friendly, efficient staff and comfortable rooms,' says a fan in 2010. Another comment: 'We enjoyed a well-prepared and presented lunch; the owner sat and chatted with us as we took coffee.' There are fresh flowers in the spacious lounges, which have log fires, rich furnishings, antiques. Welsh cream teas are served in the drawing room or, in good weather, under a chestnut tree in the grounds. An orangery is new this year. In the dining room (smart casual dress required), the chef, Sean Cullingford, has a modern style, eg, braised shin of Welsh beef, celeriac and Pommery mustard, red wine salsify. Bedrooms in the main house are decorated in country house style; suites in a new wing have a more contemporary look. The Kingfisher spa has a 'good-size' swimming pool, various treatments. 'Great walks around the lake; a small golf course is fun.' (*Annabel Viney, Peter Rogers*)

Llangammarch Wells
LD4 4BS

T: 01591-620202
F: 01591-620457
E: info@lakecountryhouse.co.uk
W: www.lakecountryhouse.co.uk

BEDROOMS: 30, 12 suites in adjacent lodge, 7 on ground floor, 1 suitable for ♿.
OPEN: all year.
FACILITIES: ramps, 3 lounges, orangery, restaurant, spa (20-metre swimming pool), civil wedding licence, 50-acre grounds (lake, fishing, tennis, par 3 golf course).
BACKGROUND MUSIC: none.
LOCATION: 8 miles SW of Builth Wells.
CHILDREN: no under-8s in spa, or in dining room after 7 pm.
DOGS: allowed in some bedrooms, only guide dogs in public rooms.
CREDIT CARDS: all major cards.
PRICES: B&B £92.50–£205 per person, D,B&B (min. 2 nights) £117.50–£230, set dinner £38.50, full alc £55, special breaks on website, Christmas/New Year packages.

**25% DISCOUNT VOUCHERS**

# LLANIDLOES Powys

Map 3:C3

## LLOYDS

**NEW**

In a small market town of timber-framed buildings on the eastern slopes of the Cambrian mountains, this 'modest' guest house in an 'unassuming building' is 'personal and quirky in a nice way', say the nominators. It is 'very well run' by the hands-on owners, Tom Lines and Roy Hayter. 'They are pleasantly high profile, helping with luggage and directions.' Steep, narrow stairs lead to traditionally furnished bedrooms: 'A most luxurious bed; the modern bathroom was well fitted.' Drinks are taken in a 'comfortable sitting room where chatting is encouraged'. Mr Hayter cooks a no-choice dinner (booking essential), which is 'more an event than a meal': The owners promise a 'leisurely paced' evening concluding after 11 pm. 'Tom carefully choreographs the occasion, providing an informal commentary on the five courses. We enjoyed roasted asparagus; savoury feta cheesecake; grape and grapefruit salad; roast guineafowl, carved at table, with delicious vegetables; three desserts on each plate included strawberry parfait. Breakfast was also good. The cooking shows great attention to detail; beautiful presentation.' Well placed for walking Glyndwr's Way. (*Stephen and Pauline Glover*)

6 Cambrian Place
Llanidloes SY18 6BX

T: 01686-412284
E: lloyds@dircon.co.uk
W: www.lloydshotel.co.uk

BEDROOMS: 7.
OPEN: 20 Mar–9 Jan, except Christmas.
FACILITIES: sitting room, dining room, unsuitable for &.
BACKGROUND MUSIC: none.
LOCATION: near the town centre.
CHILDREN: all ages welcomed.
DOGS: not allowed.
CREDIT CARDS: MasterCard, Visa.
PRICES: [2010] B&B £36–£57 per person, set dinner £37, special breaks.

**25% DISCOUNT VOUCHERS**

# LLANWRTYD WELLS Powys

## CARLTON RIVERSIDE

❦ *César award in 1998*

'Passionate about cooking', chef Mary Ann Gilchrist has long been praised by readers for the 'extraordinarily good food' at the restaurant-with-rooms she runs with her 'affable' husband, Alan, in this small spa town. The stone house (said to be the second oldest in the town) stands by the River Irfon. The best tables in the 'elegant' dining room face the river. The 'innovative, delicious meals' might include roast rack of Irfon valley lamb, new potatoes, buttered leeks, a sherried lamb jus. The 'superb' wine list has more than 80 wines. The basement bistro, which opens at weekends, has a blackboard menu of simpler dishes and pizzas. The four bedrooms vary in size. The twin-aspect Bridge Room has a sofa from which 'you can watch the river'; the Oriental Room may have 'no view to speak of', but it is large, and has antique chinoiserie lacquer furniture. Breakfast 'had fresh orange juice, very good scrambled eggs'. The Gilchrists live 175 yards away, but can be reached by intercom when not on the spot. (*JM, and others*)

Irfon Crescent
Llanwrtyd Wells LD5 4ST

**T:** 01591-610248
**E:** info@carltonriverside.com
**W:** www.carltonriverside.com

**BEDROOMS:** 5.
**OPEN:** all year except 19–30 Dec, restaurant closed Sun, bistro open Fri/Sat/Sun.
**FACILITIES:** reception, bar/lounge, restaurant, bar/bistro, unsuitable for &.
**BACKGROUND MUSIC:** classical piano in lounge.
**LOCATION:** town centre, no private parking.
**CHILDREN:** all ages welcomed.
**DOGS:** not allowed in public rooms.
**CREDIT CARDS:** MasterCard, Visa.
**PRICES:** B&B £25–£50 per person, D,B&B £40–£95, set meals £19.50–£39.50, full alc £100, gourmet breaks, New Year package, 1-night bookings occasionally refused.

**25% DISCOUNT VOUCHERS**

# NANT GWYNANT Gwynedd

Map 3:A3

## PEN-Y-GWRYD HOTEL

*César award in 1995*

An institution among the climbing and walking
fraternity for more than 50 years, this old inn is
run by brothers Rupert and Nicolas Pullee, who
have taken on day-to-day responsibility from
their parents, Brian and Jane. Regular visitors
enjoy the 'heart-warming' rituals established
by the brothers' grandparents: the house-party
style, the gong that summons guests to meals,
the Snowdon Club for children under 13 who
reach the top of the mountain. There are no
locks on the doors of the simple bedrooms,
which don't have TV or radio; only five have
facilities en suite, but the bathrooms have lots
of hot water. Everyone eats at the same time at
communal tables, with a choice of two main
courses on chef Lena Jensen's menus, perhaps
organic chicken with creamy pesto mushroom
sauce, or Welsh Black beef slow-cooked
goulash-style. Breakfast, served at table, has
porridge, prunes and fruit juices; eggs cooked
any way for the full Welsh. Walkers returning
from the hills gather in the beer garden at the
front; there are three other public rooms.

Nant Gwynant LL55 4NT

T: 01286-870211
W: www.pyg.co.uk

BEDROOMS: 16, 1 on ground floor.
OPEN: all year except Nov–Feb, but
open New Year, weekends Jan, Feb.
FACILITIES: lounge, bar, games
room, dining room, chapel, 2-acre
grounds (natural unheated 60-metre
swimming pool, sauna), unsuitable
for &.
BACKGROUND MUSIC: none.
LOCATION: between Beddgelert and
Capel Curig.
CHILDREN: all ages welcomed.
DOGS: allowed.
CREDIT CARDS: MasterCard, Visa.
PRICES: [2010] B&B £40–£50 per
person, set dinner £22–£28, 3-night
rates, 1-night bookings often
refused weekends.

# NEWPORT Pembrokeshire

## CNAPAN

On the main street of a seaside town beneath the Preseli hills (the larger Newport is in Gwent), this 'superb' sugar-pink restaurant-with-rooms is run 'with warmth' by owners Michael and Judith Cooper and Eluned Lloyd. They are proud of the house's 'lived-in and loved' interior, which is crammed with family treasures, books and games; a crowded Welsh dresser stands in the hall. In the afternoon, guests are given tea with Welsh scones in a 'comfortable little drawing room' with a log-burning stove. Judith Cooper is the chef; she champions local foods in her modern dishes, perhaps Cardigan Bay scallops, pea and mint purée, crispy chorizo; Welsh Black beef fillet, green peppercorn sauce, horseradish relish. The selection of Welsh cheeses is extensive, and puddings are a speciality. The small bedrooms have pine furniture, bright colours, tea/coffee-making facilities (a jug of fresh milk in the fridge). The shower rooms are compact; guests who want a bath have access to a shared bathroom. Huge breakfasts include home-made marmalade, free-range eggs, and kippers. More reports, please.

East Street, Newport
nr Fishguard SA42 0SY

T: 01239-820575
F: 01239-820878
E: enquiry@cnapan.co.uk
W: www.cnapan.co.uk

BEDROOMS: 5.
OPEN: 26 Mar–5 Jan, closed Christmas, restaurant closed Tues Easter–Oct.
FACILITIES: lounge, bar, restaurant, small garden, unsuitable for &.
BACKGROUND MUSIC: jazz/world music in evenings in dining room.
LOCATION: town centre.
CHILDREN: all ages welcomed (£10 for B&B in family room).
DOGS: only guide dogs allowed.
CREDIT CARDS: MasterCard, Visa.
PRICES: [2010] B&B £42–£52 per person, D,B&B £66–£82, full alc £43, 1-night bookings refused in season.

# NEWPORT Pembrokeshire

## LLYS MEDDYG

Once a coaching inn, then a doctor's house (Doctor's Court is the translation), this Georgian building is run as a restaurant-with-rooms by owners Ed and Lou Sykes. They have given it a contemporary interior. A trusted *Guide* correspondent found it a 'welcoming place with outstanding food'. The chef, Scott Davies, sources fish and meat locally for his 'inventive but not over-elaborate' dishes, eg, Bethesda farmhouse terrine, pear and saffron chutney; chump of Preseli lamb, cockles and cardamom. The service in the spacious dining room, by young Welsh-speaking girls, is 'cheerful and efficient'. There is a guest sitting room, and an 'atmospheric' cellar bar. Paintings by contemporary Welsh artists inspired by the surrounding landscape are displayed throughout (and are for sale). Each of the two larger bedrooms has a separate dressing room, a freestanding bath, and a walk-in shower. 'Our room had a very comfortable bed, and a sofa; a modish bathroom.' Three rooms can accommodate up to four people. There is a 'secret' garden at the back and a tented garden room for summer eating. (*DB, JR*)

East Street, Newport
nr Fishguard SA42 0SY

T: 01239-820008
E: contact@llysmeddyg.com
W: www.llysmeddyg.com

BEDROOMS: 8, 1 on ground floor.
OPEN: all year, restaurant closed Sun/Mon Oct–June.
FACILITIES: bar, restaurant, sitting room, civil wedding licence, garden.
BACKGROUND MUSIC: in bar and restaurant.
LOCATION: central.
CHILDREN: all ages welcomed.
DOGS: restricted access in public rooms and bedrooms.
CREDIT CARDS: MasterCard, Visa.
PRICES: [2010] B&B £50–£75 per person, D,B&B £75–£95, full alc £37, off-season midweek offers on website, 1-night bookings sometimes refused weekends.

# PENMAENPOOL Gwynedd

Map 3:B3

## PENMAENUCHAF HALL

In strikingly beautiful grounds with woodland and landscaped gardens, this imposing country house overlooks the Mawddach estuary. It is run by the 'hands-on' owners, Lorraine Fielding and Mark Watson, who tell us that renovation is ongoing ('a bit like the Forth Bridge'). An inspector found it 'a spacious, dependably comfortable place'; a recent visitor was unhappy with the 'number of rules'. The hall has polished oak floors and panelling, rugs, sofas, a log fire. There are oriental rugs on seagrass, armchairs and a period desk in the library; there are two well-furnished drawing rooms. Dinner is taken in a smart conservatory restaurant with oak panelling, slate flooring, well-dressed tables; views of Snowdonia from the Gothic windows. Chef Justin Pilkington, assisted by Tim Reeve, serves 'contemporary British' food, eg, seared scallops, pea purée; breast of Gressingham duck, creamed cabbage, roasted potatoes, thyme jus. Herbs, salads and vegetables are home grown. Bedrooms 'come in all shapes and sizes'; decor varies between contemporary and traditional; some rooms have a four-poster bed, some a sitting area with sofa. More reports, please.

Penmaenpool, nr Dolgellau
LL40 1YB

T: 01341-422129
F: 01341-422787
E: relax@penhall.co.uk
W: www.penhall.co.uk

BEDROOMS: 14.
OPEN: all year.
FACILITIES: ramps, six public rooms, restaurant, conference room, civil wedding licence, 21-acre grounds, unsuitable for &.
BACKGROUND MUSIC: classical/light jazz in restaurant.
LOCATION: 2 miles W of Dolgellau.
CHILDREN: over-6s welcome.
DOGS: allowed in hall/lounge area, by arrangement in 1 bedroom.
CREDIT CARDS: Diners, MasterCard, Visa.
PRICES: B&B £75–£145 per person, set dinner £40, various packages, 1-night bookings sometimes refused, Christmas/New Year packages.

**25% DISCOUNT VOUCHERS**

# PENMYNYDD Isle of Anglesey

Map 3:A3

## NEUADD LWYD

♥ *César award in 2010*

In a beautiful location amid farmland with views of Snowdonia, this 'handsome' early Victorian rectory is run as an upmarket guest house by Susannah and Peter Woods. These Welsh-speaking hosts are 'quite a double act', says a reporter this year. 'They run a kind of academy of their craft', demonstrating 'attention to detail and relentless pursuit of high standards'. Susannah Woods, who trained at *Ballymaloe* cookery school in Ireland, uses local ingredients for her four-course dinner (no choice: preferences are discussed, but 'the exact dishes remain a surprise'). 'She produced a delicious balanced meal of crab and slow-roasted Anglesey duck; the service was charming.' Binoculars are provided in the lounge, which has high-backed wooden chairs on each side of bay windows. The bedrooms are 'exquisitely' furnished. Owain 'was well proportioned, with solid, unshowy antiques and a vast French bed with a handmade mattress; in the bathroom a roll-top bath in front of the window'. Breakfast has fresh fruit juice of the day, home-made compotes, local honeys; interesting cooked dishes. (*AT, and others*)

Penmynydd,
nr Llanfairpwllgwyngyll
Isle of Anglesey LL61 5BX

T/F: 01248-715005
E: post@neuaddlwyd.co.uk
W: www.neuaddlwyd.co.uk

BEDROOMS: 4.
OPEN: 20 Jan–27 Nov, closed Sun/Mon/Tues except bank holidays.
FACILITIES: drawing room, lounge, dining room, 6-acre grounds, only dining room suitable for &.
BACKGROUND MUSIC: none.
LOCATION: 3 miles W of Menai Bridge, train to Bangor.
CHILDREN: not under 16.
DOGS: only guide dogs allowed.
CREDIT CARDS: MasterCard, Visa.
PRICES: B&B £75–£180 per person, D,B&B £100–£180, set dinner £42, see website for midweek rates.

# PENTREFOELAS Denbighshire

Map 3:A3

## HAFOD ELWY HALL

'We were greeted warmly and plied with tea and cake,' say visitors this year to Roger and Wendy Charles-Warner's working farm among hills and lakes in the Denbighshire mountains. The 'always attentive' host cooks meals 'country style and very well' (unfussy dishes, perhaps pork with Madeira and cream) using home-reared meat, and vegetables 'picked shortly before cooking'. No liquor licence: guests may bring their own wine. The hall has an Edwardian feel. Historic features include slate floors and a slate fireplace in the dining room, archways, architraves and a thunderbox bread oven. There are 'comfortable' chairs in the large sitting room; some visitors have commented on the 'peculiar knick-knackery'. There is 'everything you could wish for' in the bedrooms: two have a four-poster; one has a big cast iron bath in its bathroom, but 'no wall grips'. The eggs, sausages and bacon at breakfast come 'from our happy free-range animals'; muesli and preserves are home made. The Charles-Warners have won awards for their sustainable practice.

Hiraethog, nr Pentrefoelas
LL16 5SP

T: 01690-770345
F: 01690-770266
E: enquiries@hafodelwyhall.co.uk
W: www.hafodelwyhall.co.uk

BEDROOMS: 3, 1 on ground floor suitable for &.
OPEN: all year.
FACILITIES: 2 lounges, sun room, dining room, 60-acre grounds (private fishing).
BACKGROUND MUSIC: none.
LOCATION: 12 miles SE of Betws-y-Coed, 11 miles SW of Denbigh, 6½ miles N of Pentrefoelas off A543.
CHILDREN: normally not under 16.
DOGS: allowed in sun room and lounge 'if dry and clean and no other guest objects', not in bedrooms.
CREDIT CARDS: Diners, MasterCard, Visa.
PRICES: B&B £35–£65 per person, set dinner £18, Christmas/New Year packages, 1-night bookings refused weekends.

**25% DISCOUNT VOUCHERS**

# PORTMEIRION Gwynedd

## PORTMEIRION HOTEL

'The attentive and hospitable approach of the hotel staff (restaurant, bar, housekeeping, porters) is impressive; so consistent and sincere.' Praise from a returning visitor this year to Sir Clough Williams-Ellis's eccentric resort on the wooded hillside of a Snowdonia peninsula. The manager, Robin Llywelyn, grandson of Sir Clough, leads the long-serving staff. There has been much development this year. The public rooms have been renovated to restore the original furniture and fittings, layout and colour schemes; the curvilinear entrance lobby, destroyed by fire in 1981, was reinstated in 2010, creating more space for a new concierge desk, check-in, lavatories and a lift. The bedrooms are in buildings throughout the village: some in the restored hotel, others in *Castell Deudraeth* (an 1850s baronial folly with contemporary rooms), others in various eclectically designed cottages and villas. 'Breakfast and dinner were good' in the hotel's restaurant (modern Welsh dishes like poached turbot, Aberdaron crab, butternut squash). A light lunch was 'excellent' in *Castell Deudraeth*'s gastropub, which serves grills and seafood. The village is popular for weddings and functions. (*Deborah Starbuck-Edwards*)

Portmeirion LL48 6ER

T: 01766-770000
F: 01766-770300
E: stay@portmeirion-village.com
W: www.portmeirion-village.com

BEDROOMS: 14 in hotel, some on ground floor, 1 suitable for ♿, 11 in *Castell Deudraeth*, 28 in village.
OPEN: all year.
FACILITIES: hall, lift, 3 lounges, bar, restaurant, brasserie in *Castell*, children's supper room, function room, beauty salon, civil wedding licence, 170-acre grounds (garden), heated swimming pool (8 by 15 metres, May–Sept).
BACKGROUND MUSIC: harpist in bar, some nights, Sun lunch.
LOCATION: edge of Snowdonia national park, 2 miles from Porthmadog, free minibus from Minffordd station.
CHILDREN: all ages welcomed.
DOGS: only guide dogs allowed.
CREDIT CARDS: all major cards.
PRICES: B&B £85–£150 per person, D,B&B £110–£175, full alc £45, special offers/packages on website.

# PWLLHELI Gwynedd

## THE OLD RECTORY

In large wooded grounds near the church of a village on the beautiful Lleyn Peninsula, this small, pale yellow, former Georgian rectory is run as a B&B by owners Roger and Gabrielle Pollard. It has long been liked by *Guide* readers, who find them kind and considerate hosts, for the home-from-home atmosphere. The building has been thoughtfully restored. The public rooms are elegant, furnished with antiques, family pictures and original paintings; in cooler months a fire burns in the tall carved pine fireplace. All the bedrooms have views of the grounds (lawns, mature trees, paddocks): they are individually styled, and equipped with armchairs, radio, complimentary sherry, books and information on the area. Wi-Fi is available. In the dining room, which catches the morning sun, breakfast is 'well cooked and elegantly presented': compotes and jams are made from home-grown fruit; bread is also home made; the cooked choices include a traditional full English, or smoked salmon with local free-range scrambled eggs. The Pollards will advise on local eating places. There is much to see and do on the peninsula, which has Iron Age hill forts, sandy beaches, good walking. More reports, please.

Boduan
nr Pwllheli LL53 6DT

T/F:01758-721519
E: thepollards@theoldrectory.net
W: www.theoldrectory.net

**BEDROOMS:** 3, also self-catering cottage.
**OPEN:** all year except Christmas week.
**FACILITIES:** drawing room, dining room, 3½-acre grounds, walking, riding, sailing, unsuitable for &.
**BACKGROUND MUSIC:** none.
**LOCATION:** 4 miles NW of Pwllheli.
**CHILDREN:** all ages welcomed, under-1s stay free, babysitting by arrangement.
**DOGS:** allowed in grounds only.
**CREDIT CARDS:** none.
**PRICES:** B&B £45–£47.50 per person, seasonal offers, 1-night bookings refused bank holidays.

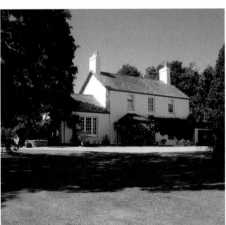

# PWLLHELI Gwynedd

## PLAS BODEGROES

*♧César award in 1992*

'What a lovely place; the food is superb, the rooms are delightful, the staff helpful.' Praise continues to come for Chris and Gunna Chown's restaurant-with-rooms in a white Georgian manor house in wooded grounds on the Lleyn peninsula. He is the talented chef; she runs front-of-house with warmth and professionalism. Everyone comes for his classic cooking, served in an attractive L-shaped dining room: 'We weren't disappointed: broccoli soup was delicious; the tender lamb had masses of flavour; I was even tempted by the light cinnamon shortbread with rhubarb and apple.' The bedrooms are decorated in Scandinavian style: 'Our room was spacious, with a really comfortable bed; the small bathroom was well designed, with a separate shower and a bath. It was a lovely change to be woken with a pot of tea in the morning rather than having to make our own.' Two smaller attic rooms are best for a one-night stay; two rooms are in a cottage, facing a tranquil courtyard garden. (*Mary and Rodney Milne-Day, Sara Price*)

Nefyn Road
Pwllheli LL53 5TH

T: 01758-612363
F: 01758-701247
E: gunna@bodegroes.co.uk
W: www.bodegroes.co.uk

BEDROOMS: 11, 2 in courtyard annexe.
OPEN: 14 Feb–end Nov, closed Sun and Mon except bank holidays.
FACILITIES: lounge, bar, breakfast room, restaurant, 5-acre grounds, unsuitable for &.
BACKGROUND MUSIC: in restaurant.
LOCATION: 1 mile W of Pwllheli.
CHILDREN: all ages welcomed.
DOGS: not allowed in public rooms, 1 bedroom.
CREDIT CARDS: MasterCard, Visa.
PRICES: B&B £55–£87.50 per person, D,B&B £97.50–£130, set dinner £42.50, full alc £55, midweek breaks, 1-night bookings refused bank holidays.

# REYNOLDSTON Swansea

Map 3:E2

## FAIRYHILL

'A delightful, small, country hotel with a calm, restful ambience; you feel at home and glad to be there.' Andrew Hetherington and Paul Davies's creeper-covered, 18th-century mansion is endorsed again this year. The house stands in 'superb' large grounds which have manicured lawns with sculptures, woodland, a trout stream and a lake with wild ducks. The manager is Audrey McMillan: 'Competent and friendly' service is by young men in black. The chef, James Hamilton, uses 'high-quality ingredients, cooked and presented very well and without pretension', eg, loin and belly of pork, braised red cabbage, black pudding mash, soya and sesame jus. All bedrooms (some are small) have modern furnishings (disliked by a dissenting reader this year), flat-screen TV/DVD/CD-player and free Wi-Fi. 'Our top-floor room was large, comfortable and well equipped.' Breakfast has 'proper bread with a toaster, lots of refrigerated and ambient goodies, the best cooked we've had for years'. Some visitors dislike the muzak played in the public areas. The hotel is near magnificent beaches of the Gower coast. (*Peter Stoakley, and others*)

Reynoldston, Gower
nr Swansea SA3 1BS

T: 01792-390139
F: 01792-391358
E: postbox@fairyhill.net
W: www.fairyhill.net

BEDROOMS: 8.
OPEN: all year except 26 Dec, first 3 weeks in Jan.
FACILITIES: lounge, bar, 3 dining rooms, meeting room, civil wedding licence, spa treatment room, 24-acre grounds (croquet, woodland, stream, lake), unsuitable for &.
BACKGROUND MUSIC: jazz/classical/pop in lounge, bar, dining room at mealtimes.
LOCATION: 11 miles W of Swansea.
CHILDREN: not under 8.
DOGS: allowed in bedrooms and grounds only.
CREDIT CARDS: MasterCard, Visa.
PRICES: [2010] B&B £87.50–£137.50 per person, D,B&B £132.50–£182.50, set dinner £35–£45, full alc £65, special breaks, New Year package, 1-night bookings sometimes refused Sat.

# SKENFRITH Monmouthshire

Map 3:D4

## THE BELL AT SKENFRITH

'A lovely country pub: comfortable and relaxed; great fun.' Praise in 2010 for Janet and William Hutchings's white-painted 17th-century coaching inn by an old stone bridge across the River Monnow in a delightful village in the Welsh Marches. Earlier visitors enjoyed the 'wonderfully quiet and beautiful' setting. The chef, Rupert Taylor, who has worked at *Fifteen* and the *Fat Duck*, 'takes his inspiration from the inn's organic kitchen garden and local produce' for his modern dishes, perhaps baby leek, garden herb and beetroot risotto; sirloin of Brecon beef, miniature cottage pie, horseradish mash, braised savoy cabbage, beef jus. We would welcome reports on his cooking. There is a 'splendid', wide-ranging wine list. There are flagstone floors, an inglenook fireplace, and 'simple yet sophisticated' bedrooms. A recent visitor loved his upgrade to a 'magnificent suite, with huge, stylish bathroom, very comfortable bed, large sofa'. All bedrooms have DVD/CD-player and free Internet access. Children are welcomed. The area is studded with ruined castles, including the 13th-century fortress in the village. (*Richard Mayou, Horst Stuiber*)

Skenfrith NP7 8UH

T: 01600-750235
F: 01600-750525
E: enquiries@skenfrith.co.uk
W: www.skenfrith.co.uk

BEDROOMS: 11.
OPEN: all year except last week Jan, first week Feb, also Tues Nov–Mar (not Christmas fortnight).
FACILITIES: large open sitting area, restaurant, private dining room, bar, 1-acre grounds, only restaurant suitable for &.
BACKGROUND MUSIC: none.
LOCATION: 9 miles W of Ross-on-Wye.
CHILDREN: all ages welcomed, no under-8s in restaurant in the evening.
DOGS: not unattended in bedrooms.
CREDIT CARDS: MasterCard, Visa.
PRICES: [2010] B&B £55–£120 per person, full alc £38, midweek breaks, Christmas package, 1-night bookings refused Sat, bank holidays.

**25% DISCOUNT VOUCHERS**

# TALSARNAU Gwynedd

Map 3:B3

## MAES-Y-NEUADD

🕊 *César award in 2003*

'A wonderful place in a peaceful setting; the staff are on the ball and the atmosphere is great.' A loyal fan explains why he returns annually to Peter and Lynn Jackson and Peter Payne's 14th-century 'mansion in the meadow'. 'Delighted' first-time visitors in 2010 wrote: 'We were warmly greeted, and pleased to find that so many of the staff could converse with us in Welsh.' Peter Jackson uses vegetables, herbs and fruit from the two walled kitchen gardens for his 'outstanding' daily-changing menus of modern dishes, eg, fillet of Welsh beef, potato rösti, braised root vegetable, port wine and shallot sauce. When he was on holiday, 'the chef in charge did an outstanding job'. The bedrooms vary considerably in size and style; the welcoming glass of sloe gin, and list of staff whom guests will encounter are liked. The public areas have 'lots of good space'; oak beams, antique and modern furniture, an inglenook fireplace. Mrs Jackson tells us that *Maes-y-Neuadd* is on the market, 'but we expect to be here for years'. (*Gordon Hands, Gareth Tilsley*)

Talsarnau LL47 6YA

T: 01766-780200
F: 01766-780211
E: maes@neuadd.com
W: www.neuadd.com

BEDROOMS: 15, 4 in coach house, 3 on ground floor.
OPEN: all year.
FACILITIES: lift, ramps, lounge, bar, conservatory, family dining room, main dining room, business facilities, civil wedding licence, terrace, 85-acre grounds (croquet, helipad).
BACKGROUND MUSIC: some traditional music in the restaurant.
LOCATION: 3 miles NE of Harlech off B4573.
CHILDREN: all ages welcomed but no under-8s in main dining room at night.
DOGS: allowed in 2 bedrooms only, on a leash in grounds.
CREDIT CARDS: MasterCard, Visa.
PRICES: [2010] B&B £49.50–£100, D,B&B £79–£135, set dinner £30–£39, full alc £48, special breaks, Christmas/New Year packages, 1-night bookings refused bank holidays.

**25% DISCOUNT VOUCHERS**

# TALYLLYN Gwynedd

Map 3:B3

## TYNYCORNEL

**NEW**

Talyllyn
Tywyn LL36 9AJ

On the shore of Lake Talyllyn, which it owns, this 'solid' white-fronted inn has been a fishing hostelry for two centuries. Phil Thomas is the general manager. It regains a full *Guide* entry thanks to a recommendation by regular contributors. 'It deserves its place for the location alone,' is a typical comment. Bedrooms are in the main building and an annexe. 'Our spacious "superior" room had its own patio with a stunning view over the lake; we advise taking one of these rooms for a visit of any length.' The lounge, which faces the lake, has an open fire. There is a new chef, Thomas Mansfield, whose menus might include duck hash with fried duck egg; sea trout with samphire, saffron potatoes. Breakfast has a wide choice: local cheeses, charcuterie, home-cooked ham; laver bread (seaweed) and oatmeal cakes with cured bacon; fresh haddock among the cooked dishes. There are fishing stories aplenty in the bar; guests have priority access to the waters, noted for the wild brown trout fishing. There is a drying room and freezer facilities. (*Alan and Edwina Williams*)

**T:** 01654-782282
**F:** 01654-782679
**E:** reception@tynycornel.co.uk
**W:** www.tynycornel.co.uk

**BEDROOMS:** 22, 9 in annexe, some on ground floor.
**OPEN:** all year.
**FACILITIES:** ramp, lounge, bar, restaurant, conservatory restaurant, conference facilities, drying room, civil wedding licence, ½-acre grounds.
**BACKGROUND MUSIC:** in restaurant.
**LOCATION:** 9 miles SW of Dolgellau.
**CHILDREN:** all ages welcomed.
**DOGS:** allowed in some annexe bedrooms, not in public rooms.
**CREDIT CARDS:** MasterCard, Visa.
**PRICES:** [to 31 Mar 2011] B&B £45–£70 per person, D,B&B £65–£90, special breaks.

# TREMADOG Gwynedd

Map 3:B3

## PLAS TAN-YR-ALLT

*César award in 2008*

'They make you feel at home without the drudgery.' More praise this year for Michael Bewick and Nick Golding, who receive visitors on a house-party basis at their Grade II listed mansion in a 'lovely setting' overlooking the Glaslyn estuary. The house is run with a 'theatrical' flourish: Percy the parrot breaks the ice in the bright red entrance hall. The bedrooms reflect aspects of its history. Miss Hilda is named after a former resident, a maiden aunt of Clough Williams-Ellis; you can enjoy the southerly views 'from the bed, or the bath'. Benson, named after the author EF Benson, is decorated in lavender Toile de Jouy. A new ground-floor suite has a private entrance. Guests dine together at 8.15 off a 'delicious' set menu, cooked by Nathan Jones, who has worked in the kitchen for four years. A typical dish: duck breast with fennel and apple and creamy mash. 'Preferences are taken into account without fuss.' Breakfast was 'especially enjoyed': a 'quality concoction of fresh fruits, cereals and hot dishes'. (*Judith Blechner, Dorothy Brining*)

Tremadog, nr Porthmadog
LL49 9RG

T: 01766-514545
E: info@tanyrallt.co.uk
W: www.tanyrallt.co.uk

BEDROOMS: 7, 1 on ground floor
OPEN: all year except Christmas, Mon/Tues Oct–Mar.
FACILITIES: drawing room, library, dining room, 47-acre grounds, unsuitable for ♿.
BACKGROUND MUSIC: none.
LOCATION: 1 mile N of Porthmadog, guests collected by car.
CHILDREN: not under 16.
DOGS: not allowed.
CREDIT CARDS: Amex, MasterCard, Visa.
PRICES: [2010] B&B £62.50–£160 per person, D,B&B £102–£199.50, set dinner £39.50, New Year package, 1-night bookings refused weekends.

# WHITEBROOK Monmouthshire

Map 3:D4

## THE CROWN AT WHITEBROOK

In a small village in the wooded Wye valley near Monmouth, this former 17th-century drovers' inn is run as a restaurant-with-rooms. The chef, James Sommerin, has a *Michelin* star for his 'original, flavoursome' dishes based on local ingredients (eg, butter roast beef, veal sweetbreads, butternut squash). A visitor this year thought the cooking was 'imaginative but not of star quality', a view at odds with earlier reports from an inspector, and a regular reporter who was impressed that the details of vegetarian cooking were understood. The 'comfortably small portions leave room for the little extras served between courses and the delicious bread'. The 'welcoming' lounge has large leather sofas. The contemporary bedrooms are in a modern extension. A 'small' executive room was 'pleasant and well equipped, with an excellent bathroom'. Another room, with a small sofa, was 'well furnished' with dressing table, writing desk, bookcase, tea tray and decanter of sherry. Breakfast was 'good, though service was slow'. (*JB, and others*)

Whitebrook, nr Monmouth
NP25 4TX

T: 01600-860254
F: 01600-860607
E: info@crownatwhitebrook.co.uk
W: www.crownatwhitebrook.co.uk

BEDROOMS: 8. Open: all year except Christmas/New Year, restaurant closed Sun night.
FACILITIES: ramp, lounge/bar, restaurant, business facilities, 6-acre garden, River Wye 2 miles (fishing), only restaurant suitable for &.
BACKGROUND MUSIC: soft jazz in lounge/bar.
LOCATION: 6 miles S of Monmouth.
CHILDREN: not under 12.
DOGS: only guide dogs allowed.
CREDIT CARDS: MasterCard, Visa.
PRICES: B&B [2010] £57.50–£100 per person, set meals £48–£70, full alc £75, special breaks.

# CHANNEL ISLANDS

Close to Normandy, these îles Anglo-Normandes, as the French call them, have a distinctly French flavour, notably in the cooking of lunch and dinner (breakfast tends to be boldly British). The hotels vary greatly in size and style; two are on small islands.

# BRAYE Alderney

## BRAYE BEACH HOTEL **NEW**

By a curving sandy beach sheltered by a Victorian breakwater, this 'relaxing' modern hotel gains a full entry this year after a strong recommendation by regular *Guide* readers. 'Most relaxing and comfortable; the young, enthusiastic staff showed much-appreciated personal touches.' Owned by Healthspan Leisure, a Guernsey group that runs Blue Islands (a low-cost airline), it is managed by Scott Chance, who is also the chef. Seventeen of the bedrooms have sea views; some have a small balcony. 'Our room was well laid out; a complimentary decanter of sherry was most welcome, as were the fresh milk and mineral water in the fridge (replenished daily). The excellent bathroom had plenty of shelf space.' Two large lounges, 'scrupulously clean and comfortable', lead to wrap-around decking. There's a small cinema with leather seats. 'The food was excellent, with a wide range of dishes, including good vegetarian choices.' Mr Chance cooks modern English/French dishes, perhaps goat's cheese croquante, spinach and tomato dressing; seared turbot, peas and baby leeks, orange flower butter sauce. 'Good value, especially with a package with flights.' (*John and Sara Leathes*)

Braye Street
Alderney GY9 3XT

T: 01481-824300
F: 01481-824301
E: reception@brayebeach.com
W: www.brayebeach.com

BEDROOMS: 27, 1 suitable for &.
OPEN: all year.
FACILITIES: lift, bar, 2 lounges, library, cinema, wedding facilities.
BACKGROUND MUSIC: 'easy listening' all day.
LOCATION: by harbour.
CHILDREN: all ages welcomed.
DOGS: not allowed.
CREDIT CARDS: all major cards.
PRICES: [2010] B&B £50–£90 per person, D,B&B £30 added, full alc £35, Christmas/New Year packages.

**25% DISCOUNT VOUCHERS**

# HERM

## THE WHITE HOUSE

❦ *César award in 1987*

The only intrusive sounds on this car-free island are 'the occasional tractor or the piping of oystercatchers at night'; radios are barred on beaches. There are no TVs, clocks or telephones in its sole hotel as 'they don't seem appropriate'; no background music, but a harp is played on Sunday. Sion Dobson Jones is the manager; the international young staff are 'friendly, helpful'. There has been much redecoration this year: the public rooms have new curtains, furniture and paintings 'to give a brighter feel'. Nine of the bedrooms and bathrooms have been upgraded in 'neutral colours in keeping with the character'. Recent visitors liked their 'light and airy room, with comfortable furnishings, plenty of hanging and storage space, and a well-equipped bathroom'. Smart dress (jacket and tie for men) is required in the dining rooms at night. There is a new chef, Nigel Waylen, who serves a short daily-changing menu of traditional dishes. 'His meals were excellent and nicely presented,' say returning visitors. Children have their own high tea menu; baby-listening is available. (*Nigel and Jennifer Lee*)

Herm, via Guernsey GY1 3HR

T: 01481-722159
F: 01481-710066
E: hotel@herm.com
W: www.herm-island.com

BEDROOMS: 40, 18 in cottages, some on ground floor.
OPEN: 26 Mar–30 Oct.
FACILITIES: 3 lounges, 2 bars, 2 restaurants, conference room, 1-acre garden (tennis, croquet, 7-metre solar-heated swimming pool), beach 200 yds, Herm unsuitable for &.
BACKGROUND MUSIC: none.
LOCATION: by harbour, air/sea to Guernsey, then ferry from Guernsey (20 mins).
CHILDREN: all ages welcomed, no under-9s in restaurant at night (high teas provided).
DOGS: allowed in 1 bedroom only.
CREDIT CARDS: Diners, MasterCard, Visa.
PRICES: [2010] D,B&B £88–£136 per person, set dinner £25, see website for special offers.

# ST BRELADE Jersey

Map 1: inset E6

## THE ATLANTIC HOTEL

'Recommended: a modern hotel but with character, in a wonderful quiet location.' Praise from returning visitors this year for Patrick Burke's luxury hotel overlooking the five-mile beach of St Ouen's Bay. The 'beautiful' bedrooms are 'very comfortable, and well equipped'. Some have full-length, sliding windows and a terrace or a Juliet balcony. 'Ours had an adjoining lounge with a second TV and a small private outside seating area.' The 'pleasant' public rooms have antique terracotta flagstones, a wrought iron staircase, rich carpeting, urns, fountains, antiques, specially designed furniture. 'Even the corridors are beautiful,' says a recent visitor. The *Ocean* restaurant, in blue, white and beige, reflects its coastal setting. Here, head chef Mark Jordan has a *Michelin* star ('fully justified') for his sophisticated cooking. Local ingredients are used wherever possible for his daily-changing set menu (butter-cooked Jersey sea bass with egg linguini is a typical dish). A seven-course tasting menu (for the entire table) is available for £70 per person or £120 including wines. Guests have free access to a leisure centre. (*Michael and Eithne Dandy*)

Le Mont de la Pulente
St Brelade JE3 8HE

T: 01534-744101
F: 01534-744102
E: info@theatlantichotel.com
W: www.theatlantichotel.com

BEDROOMS: 50, some on ground floor.
OPEN: 5 Feb–2 Jan.
FACILITIES: lift, lounge, library, cocktail bar, restaurant, private dining room, fitness centre (swimming pool, sauna), civil wedding licence, garden (tennis, indoor and outdoor heated swimming pools, 10 by 5 metres), golf club and beach ½ mile, unsuitable for &.
BACKGROUND MUSIC: in restaurant in evening.
LOCATION: 5 miles W of St Helier.
CHILDREN: all ages welcomed.
DOGS: not allowed.
CREDIT CARDS: all major cards.
PRICES: [2010] B&B £75–£275 per person, D,B&B £125–£325, set meal £50, full alc £85, special breaks, off-season rates, Christmas/New Year packages.

# ST SAVIOUR Jersey

Map 1: inset E6

## LONGUEVILLE MANOR

The Lewis family has owned and managed this extended 14th-century manor house, Jersey's grandest hotel (Relais & Châteaux), for 60 years. Malcolm Lewis, of the third generation, his wife, Patricia, and her brother-in-law, Pedro Bento, are now in charge. A family atmosphere is maintained amid the splendour (public rooms have antiques, original paintings, floral decorations); the family's pets are often seen (a soft-toy boxer dog in each bedroom is a reference to this). The spacious rooms, each named after a rose, are traditionally furnished and have fresh flowers, a bowl of fruit, home-made biscuits; each ground-floor room has a private patio. Dinner is served in the *Oak Room*, with panelling from ships of the Spanish Armada, or in the less formal *Garden Room*. Vegetables from the walled garden and fresh local produce are used by the chef, Andrew Baird, for his modern dishes (eg, upside-down crab soufflé; assiette of pork, ragout of vegetables, pancetta). Breakfast has a generous buffet, an extensive choice of cooked dishes. In summer, meals may be taken by the swimming pool in the gardens. More reports, please.

Longueville Road
St Saviour JE2 7WF

T: 01534-725501
F: 01534-731613
E: info@longuevillemanor.com
W: www.longuevillemanor.com

BEDROOMS: 31, 8 on ground floor, 2 in cottage.
OPEN: all year.
FACILITIES: lift, ramp, 2 lounges, cocktail bar, 2 dining rooms, function/conference/wedding facilities, 15-acre grounds (croquet, tennis, heated swimming pool, woodland), sea 1 mile.
BACKGROUND MUSIC: none.
LOCATION: 1½ miles E of St Helier.
CHILDREN: all ages welcomed.
DOGS: not allowed in public rooms.
CREDIT CARDS: all major cards.
PRICES: [2010] B&B £110–£230 per person, D,B&B £167.50–£287.50, set dinner £47.50–£55, full alc £80, special breaks, Christmas/New Year packages.

# SARK

## LA SABLONNERIE

'As wonderful as ever,' say visitors returning this year to this little hotel/restaurant on a delightful car-free island. It is best visited in summer. 'The glories are the lovely, large gardens,' said inspectors who also praised the 'excellent food'. Owner Elizabeth Perrée 'is around most of the time, on friendly terms with her guests; she and her staff always addressed us by name'. The attractive dining room has low beams, candles, elegant white china, 'smart' young waiters; 'no background music'. Colin Day's table d'hôte menu, 'different every day', might include ravioli of crab and scallops; ballottine of rabbit leg, caramelised lemon-shredded chicory. There is a separate lobster menu (in seven variations). The most spacious bedrooms are in cottages; others vary greatly; some may be basic. A 'lovely large room above the bar might be noisy'. Beds, with sheets and blankets, are 'comfortable'; at night all 'is beautifully quiet'. Breakfast has 'perfect' scrambled eggs; cereals and stewed fruit, 'so-so' toast and jams. In summer, meals and drinks can be taken in the gardens. 'Good walks from the door.' (*John Barnes, and others*)

Little Sark
Sark, via Guernsey GY9 0SD

T: 01481-832061
F: 01481-832408
E: lasablonnerie@cwgsy.net
W: www.lasablonnerie.com

BEDROOMS: 22, also accommodation in nearby cottages.
OPEN: Easter–Oct.
FACILITIES: 3 lounges, 2 bars, restaurant, wedding facilities, 1-acre garden (tea garden/bar, croquet), Sark unsuitable for &.
BACKGROUND MUSIC: classical/piano in bar.
LOCATION: S part of island, boat from Guernsey (hotel will meet).
CHILDREN: all ages welcomed.
DOGS: allowed at hotel's discretion, but not in public rooms.
CREDIT CARDS: MasterCard, Visa.
PRICES: B&B £40–£97.50 per person, D,B&B £59–£125, set meal £29.50, full alc £44.50 (*excluding 10% service charge*).

# IRELAND

The twin arts of conversation and hospitality remain vibrant in Ireland, which is why this chapter has some of our favourite hotels. Ireland is fruitful ground for the kind of small hotel we celebrate, where guests are received as friends of the family and given an insight into the local way of life.

# BAGENALSTOWN Co. Carlow

Map 6:D6

## LORUM OLD RECTORY

In the Barrow River valley, beneath the Blackstairs Mountains, Bobbie Smith's mid-Victorian former rectory is 'recommended without hesitation' again this year. 'The welcome was warm; we were made to feel like old friends,' say visitors. 'Sitting by the fire in the cosy study, full of books and family pictures, we felt like house guests,' is another comment. The house is filled with 'beautiful antiques, silver and brass, fine old prints'. All the bedrooms are spacious and high-ceilinged, and have good views of the rolling landscape. 'We slept in a very comfortable 16th-century four-poster.' 'Space was well utilised in our room, a shower room off one corner, the loo and wash basin off the other.' One bedroom has a separate bathroom. 'We dined in splendour in the lovely dining room across the corridor. The cooking was wonderful. The gorgeous home-made breads of different varieties were also served at breakfast with preserves made from home-grown fruit.' 'Bobbie Smith is a wonderful character and guide to all the best walks and sights in Carlow.' (*Robert J Delaney, Jill and Mike Bennett*)

Kilgreaney, Bagenalstown

T: 00 353 59-977 5282
F: 00 353 59-977 5455
W: www.lorum.com

BEDROOMS: 4.
OPEN: Mar–Nov.
FACILITIES: drawing room, study, dining room, 1-acre garden (croquet), unsuitable for &.
BACKGROUND MUSIC: none.
LOCATION: 4 miles S of Bagenalstown on R705 to Borris.
CHILDREN: welcomed by arrangement.
DOGS: allowed by arrangement.
CREDIT CARDS: Amex, MasterCard, Visa.
PRICES: B&B €75–€95 per person, D,B&B €123–€128, set dinner €48, 10% discount for stays of more than 2 nights.

**25% DISCOUNT VOUCHERS**

# BALLINGARRY Co. Limerick

Map 6:D5

## THE MUSTARD SEED AT ECHO LODGE

Once a convent, this Victorian lodge stands in large grounds above a quiet, pretty village. It is run as a restaurant-with-rooms by owner Daniel Mullane: 'Hotel-keeping is in his blood,' says the nominator, restoring it to the *Guide* after a long period without reports. 'He greeted me with tea and cake; from the moment I arrived his concern was that I should enjoy myself.' The decor is 'quirky and amusing': green walls in the living room are densely hung with prints, photographs, objets d'art 'gathered from around the world'. The bedrooms are done in period style; they are 'comfortable, with everything to hand; a delight to have fresh flowers'. The gardens are 'a joy to wander round, especially the kitchen garden with its greenhouse and polytunnel with herbs and soft fruits'. It supplies vegetables for the 'fine-dining' menus of the chef, David Rice, which might include smoked salmon with a prawn tempura; rack of lamb, confit lamb croquette, chargrilled aubergine, slow-roast tomato jus. Many outdoor activities are available in the surrounding hills and pastureland.

Ballingarry

T: 00 353 69-68508
F: 00 353 69-68511
E: mustard@indigo.ie
W: www.mustardseed.ie

BEDROOMS: 16, 1 on ground floor suitable for ♿.
OPEN: mid-Feb–mid-Jan, except 24–26 Dec, restaurant closed Sun/Mon off-season.
FACILITIES: lounge, library, dining room, wedding facilities, 12-acre grounds.
BACKGROUND MUSIC: in restaurant.
LOCATION: in village, 18 miles SW of Limerick.
CHILDREN: all ages welcomed.
DOGS: not allowed in public rooms.
CREDIT CARDS: Amex, MasterCard, Visa.
PRICES: [2010] B&B €65–€165 per person, D,B&B €128–€230, set dinner €63, full alc €76.

# BALLYCASTLE Co. Mayo

Map 6:B4

## STELLA MARIS

The hundred-foot conservatory along the front of this restored coastguard fortress has uninterrupted views across Bunatrahir Bay to Downpatrick Head. 'All you hear is the wind and the waves,' say visitors. Frances Kelly, who was born across the bay, and her American husband, Terence McSweeney, are 'convivial' hosts who create a 'relaxed' atmosphere (first-name terms). A sportswriter and keen golfer, he is happy to guide visitors to some of the fine links nearby. Each bedroom is named after a course; all but two have a sea view. There are antiques and leather sofas in the bar and the conservatory where pre-dinner drinks are dispensed with 'conversation'. Frances Kelly is the chef, serving local, organic ingredients in modern dishes like seared rib-eye of beef, thyme rösti, balsamic onion purée. Herbs and vegetables come from their own garden. The brief wine list is 'carefully chosen'. The award-winning breakfast has home-made preserves, freshly squeezed orange juice, a fruit platter, 'well-presented' cooked dishes. More reports, please.

Ballycastle

T: 00 353 96-43322
F: 00 353 96-43965
E: info@stellamarisireland.com
W: www.stellamarisireland.com

BEDROOMS: 11, 1, on ground floor, suitable for &.
OPEN: May–Sept, restaurant closed to non-residents on Mon.
FACILITIES: ramps, lounge, bar, restaurant, conservatory, wedding facilities, 2-acre grounds (golf), sea/freshwater fishing, sandy beach nearby.
BACKGROUND MUSIC: in public rooms.
LOCATION: 2 miles W of Ballycastle.
CHILDREN: all ages welcomed (limited availability).
DOGS: not allowed in house.
CREDIT CARDS: MasterCard, Visa.
PRICES: [2010] B&B €100–€185 per person, full alc €52.

**25% DISCOUNT VOUCHERS**

# BALLYLICKEY Co. Cork

## SEAVIEW HOUSE

In large grounds above Bantry Bay, this extended, white, bay-windowed Victorian building was the family home of Kathleen O'Sullivan, a 'hands-on, helpful and solicitous' hostess. It is a 'lovely place to stay', say recent visitors. There is a library with books in mahogany cases, and a lounge with antiques, flowers, an open fire (a television 'occupied by sports-loving guests' was not liked by visitors this year). Bedrooms, which vary in size, are in the old house and in an extension. Those at the front of the house have sea views (through the mature trees in the grounds). No background music in the bar, where conversation is the order of the day. The chef, Eleanor O'Donovan, serves organic country house dishes on her extensive dinner menus, eg, warm duck liver and bacon salad; pan-fried scallops, lemon butter. All meat and fish come from local sources. Guests can choose between taking three or four courses. Children are 'made to feel special'; they have their own high teas. Golf can be arranged at Bantry Park club. (*P and PP, and others*)

Ballylickey, Bantry Bay

T: 00 353 27-50073
F: 00 353 27-51555
E: info@seaviewhousehotel.com
W: www.seaviewhousehotel.com

BEDROOMS: 25, 2, on ground floor, suitable for &.
OPEN: mid-Mar–mid-Nov.
FACILITIES: bar, library, 2 lounges, restaurant/conservatory, wedding facilities, 3-acre grounds on waterfront (fishing, boating), riding, golf nearby.
BACKGROUND MUSIC: none.
LOCATION: 3 miles N of Bantry.
CHILDREN: all ages welcomed, special menus and babysitting available.
DOGS: not allowed in public rooms.
CREDIT CARDS: Amex, MasterCard, Visa.
PRICES: B&B €70–€120 per person, D,B&B €95–€130, set dinner €35–€45, special breaks.

**25% DISCOUNT VOUCHERS**

# BALLYVAUGHAN Co. Clare

Map 6:C4

## GREGANS CASTLE

On a hill above Galway Bay, this much-extended Georgian house, once the home of a local family, has long been run as a country house hotel by the Haden family. Simon Haden and his wife, Frederieke McMurray, are in charge. It stands amid trees and gardens on the edge of the almost lunar limestone landscape of the Burren. The elegant public rooms have interesting artefacts, paintings and photographs; flowers, books and magazines, open fires. The bedrooms are individually designed in country house style: 'Our room was light and airy.' No television (a 'bonus' for many), but free Wi-Fi access. A ground-floor suite has a four-poster bed, a separate sitting room. In the dining room, from which you can watch the sun set over the bay, the chef, Mickael Viljanen, serves an inventive modern menu (eg, terrine of moulard foie gras; John Dory, shellfish tortelloni, brown shrimp and verjus emulsion). 'Beautifully cooked, but oh so carefully arranged,' is this year's comment from visitors who would have preferred more choice. Light lunches and afternoon teas are served in the Corkscrew bar.

Ballyvaughan

T: 00 353 65-707 7005
F: 00 353 65-707 7111
E: stay@gregans.ie
W: www.gregans.ie

BEDROOMS: 20, some on ground floor.
OPEN: 11 Feb–26 Nov.
FACILITIES: hall, lounge/library, bar, dining room, 15-acre grounds (ornamental pool, croquet), wedding facilities, safe sandy beach 4½ miles, golf, riding, hill walking nearby.
BACKGROUND MUSIC: light jazz in bar.
LOCATION: 3½ miles SW of Ballyvaughan.
CHILDREN: no under-6s in dining room at night.
DOGS: allowed in 2 bedrooms, not in public rooms.
CREDIT CARDS: Amex, MasterCard, Visa.
PRICES: B&B €97.50–€117.50 per person, set dinner €65–€90, special breaks on website, 1-night bookings sometimes refused bank holiday weekends.

## BANGOR Co. Down

Map 6:B6

### CAIRN BAY LODGE

Overlooking Ballyholme Bay on the outskirts of a seaside resort town, this white, pebble-dashed house is run as a B&B by owners Chris and Jenny Mullen. They are 'welcoming, attentive': 'Even the dog who greets you on the drive is friendly.' An 'imaginative' welcome tray with tea, coffee and cake is among the many 'little treats'. There are DVDs, books, a telescope and binoculars for guests to study the view. The Ballyholme Bay room is 'worth the extra for the splendid view'. An 'excellent' breakfast taken in an oak-panelled dining room has a 'help-yourself' buffet with juices and cereals; organic porridge with seeds, cream and honey; home-made wheaten bread. Cooked choices include baked goat's cheese, duck eggs with soda bread soldiers, 'our own free-range' poached eggs, a full Ulster grill. Jenny Mullen, a beauty therapist, gives treatments in her salon. There is a small shop selling Irish linen, bric-a-brac, works by local artists. (*Susan O'Neill, and others*)

278 Seacliff Road
Ballyholme, Bangor BT20 5HS

T: 028-9146 7636
F: 028-9145 7728
E: info@cairnbaylodge.com
W: www.cairnbaylodge.com

BEDROOMS: 5.
OPEN: all year except 2–30 Jan.
FACILITIES: 2 lounges, dining room, beauty salon, small shop, ½-acre garden, unsuitable for &.
BACKGROUND MUSIC: in dining room during breakfast.
LOCATION: ¼ mile E of centre.
CHILDREN: all ages welcomed.
DOGS: not allowed.
CREDIT CARDS: MasterCard, Visa.
PRICES: B&B £37.50–£45 per person, special breaks, 1-night bookings sometimes refused.

**25% DISCOUNT VOUCHERS**

# BELFAST

Map 6:B6

## RAVENHILL HOUSE

In a leafy suburb of Victorian houses (good bus links to the city centre), Roger and Olive Nicholson's B&B in their family home is liked by *Guide* readers for the 'excellent value'. The sitting room has a piano, an open fire, a computer for guests' use, a CD-player with a library of albums ('Van Morrison is well represented'). Free Wi-Fi is available throughout the house. Fresh coffee is provided on the landing. The bedrooms have locally made ash and oak furniture. A small single room was 'clean, well equipped and well lit; sheets and blankets on the comfortable bed; a good shower in the bathroom'. Although the house is on a busy road, a recent visitor 'was not disturbed by traffic'. Guests are asked to make their choice for breakfast the evening before: it has freshly squeezed orange juice; organic oatmeal porridge; grilled organic bacon, sausages and potato bread; Ardglass kippers. The organic wheaten bread is home baked. Much information is available, including details of the many eating places nearby. More reports, please.

690 Ravenhill Road
Belfast BT6 0BZ

T: 028-9020 7444
F: 028-9028 2590
E: info@ravenhillhouse.com
W: www.ravenhillhouse.com

BEDROOMS: 5.
OPEN: all year except 2 weeks Christmas/New Year, 1 week in Aug.
FACILITIES: sitting room, dining room, unsuitable for &.
BACKGROUND MUSIC: occasional, with radio at breakfast.
LOCATION: 2 miles S of centre.
CHILDREN: all ages welcomed.
DOGS: not allowed.
CREDIT CARDS: MasterCard, Visa (3% surcharge).
PRICES: B&B £35–£50 per person, 1-night bookings sometimes refused.

**25% DISCOUNT VOUCHERS**

# CAPPOQUIN Co. Waterford

Map 6:D5

## RICHMOND HOUSE

'A wonderful visit; the atmosphere and food could not be faulted.' Paul and Claire Deevy's stately Georgian house, in parkland in the Blackwater valley, is 'excellent in every way' (the comment of a trusted reporter). 'The old house is charming, with appropriate antique furniture, flowers, homely, chintzy furnishings. This goes hand in hand with all mod cons, efficiency and comfort.' The house is family run: Claire Deevy is a 'delightful' host; 'her mother-in-law, Jean Deevy, is on hand to suggest excursions'. 'The staff, mostly local, many long serving, are helpful.' Paul Deevy is an accomplished cook, sourcing local chicken, fish and vegetables for his 'attractive' menus (sample dish: roast quail, mushroom stuffing, braised savoy cabbage, herb jus). The wine list is imaginative, with 'a good selection of half bottles'. The bedrooms, which vary considerably in size, are decorated in country house style. Housekeeping is meticulous. Breakfast, served on white china, has 'numerous fruit juice mixes, perfect poached eggs, chopped parsley trimmings, sausages which have to be tried to be believed'. (*Róisín Leahy, ES, and others*)

Cappoquin

T: 00 353 58-54278
F: 00 353 58-54988
E: info@richmondhouse.net
W: www.richmondhouse.net

BEDROOMS: 9.
OPEN: early Jan–23 Dec, restaurant closed Sun/Mon except July and Aug.
FACILITIES: lounge, restaurant, 12-acre grounds, fishing, golf, pony trekking nearby, unsuitable for &.
BACKGROUND MUSIC: 'easy listening' in restaurant.
LOCATION: ½ mile E of Cappoquin.
CHILDREN: all ages welcomed.
DOGS: not allowed.
CREDIT CARDS: MasterCard, Visa.
PRICES: B&B €50–€75 per person, set dinner €35–€55, special breaks.

**25% DISCOUNT VOUCHERS**

# CARRIGBYRNE Co. Wexford

## CEDAR LODGE

Well placed on the main road to Cork, 20 miles from Rosslare, Tom Martin's modern hotel is popular as a stopping-off point for ferry passengers. We were sorry to learn of the death in 2009 of Mr Martin's wife, Ailish. 'We are keeping up the good work. She's a hard act to follow; simplicity was her speciality,' he tells us. *Cedar Lodge* stands in award-winning gardens below the slopes of Carrigbyrne forest ('you don't notice the main road': rooms facing it are triple glazed). Readers have long liked the 'homely atmosphere', and the comfortable, well-equipped bedrooms. In the dining room with its exposed brick walls and large copper-canopied log fire, traditional dishes are served, eg, Dublin Bay prawn cocktail; brill, spinach, dill and mustard. The extensive wine cellar is admired. Mr Martin is an 'amusing, ebullient' host. More reports, please.

Carrigbyrne, Newbawn

T: 00 353 51-428386
F: 00 353 51-428222
E: info@cedarlodgehotel.ie
W: www.cedarlodgehotel.ie

BEDROOMS: 28, some on ground floor.
OPEN: 1 Feb–23 Dec.
FACILITIES: ramp, lounge, lounge/bar, restaurant, wedding facilities, 1½-acre garden.
BACKGROUND MUSIC: varied in bar and restaurant.
LOCATION: 14 miles W of Wexford.
CHILDREN: all ages welcomed.
DOGS: allowed by arrangement.
CREDIT CARDS: all major cards.
PRICES: B&B €80–€100 per person, set dinner €45.

25% DISCOUNT VOUCHERS

## CASHEL BAY Co. Galway

# Cashel House

*⚘César award in 2008*

At the head of Cashel Bay amid the wilds of
Connemara, the McEvilly family's civilised
19th-century manor house stands in lovely
rambling gardens. Kay McEvilly is 'at the centre
of things', supervising service in the dining room
and working in the garden in her few spare
moments. 'I was looked after supremely well,'
says a visitor in 2010. The house was put on the
map when General de Gaulle stayed for two
weeks in 1969. The decor and style may have
changed little since then, but the 'charm,
exceptional service and attention to detail'
continue to please visitors. Bedrooms vary in
size: some face the sea; others overlook the
gardens. A corner room had 'a large bed, neat
sitting area, traditional furnishings, heavy
drapes'. In the restaurant with a light
conservatory extension, Arturo Amit and
Arturo Tillo serve an extensive traditional menu
(main courses like braised lamb shank, creamy
mashed potatoes). An early bird menu, at almost
half the price, can be taken from 6 to 7 pm. Two-
night gardening courses are hosted by leading
Irish plantsman Ciaran Burke. (*MG Norkett*)

Cashel Bay

T: 00 353 95-31001
F: 00 353 95-31077
E: res@cashel-house-hotel.com
W: www.cashel-house-hotel.com

BEDROOMS: 30.
OPEN: all year.
FACILITIES: ramps, 2 lounges, bar,
library, dining room/conservatory,
wedding facilities, 50-acre grounds
(tennis, riding, small private beach).
BACKGROUND MUSIC: none.
LOCATION: 42 miles NW of Galway.
CHILDREN: all ages welcomed.
DOGS: not allowed in public rooms.
CREDIT CARDS: Amex, MasterCard,
Visa.
PRICES: (12½% service charge added)
B&B €85–€190 per person, early
bird dinner €32.50, set dinner €60,
winter breaks, Christmas/New Year
packages.

**25% DISCOUNT VOUCHERS**

# CASTLEHILL Co. Mayo

Map 6:B4

## ENNISCOE HOUSE

Set quietly on a large estate beside Lough Conn, this handsome Georgian mansion has been for centuries the home of the Kellett family. Susan Kellett runs it with her son, Donald John (known as DJ), as a private hotel. It is renowned for its fine plasterwork and the elliptical staircase that leads to the bedrooms. The three grandest rooms, at the front, have views over the lough. They have a four-poster or canopy bed. Winding corridors lead to the rooms at the back of the house, which have parkland views. The old nursery has a half-tester and twin beds, chintz chairs. Two large sitting rooms have log fire, original furniture, separate sitting areas, quiet corners. DJ serves dinner at well-spaced wooden tables in a candlelit dining room: two choices for each course, eg, baked cod with herb crust; venison casserole. Breakfast has a silver dish of porridge on the sideboard. Guests can explore the estate with Frodo, the yellow Labrador, who has been joined by Connie, a new 'working dog who is very much part of the establishment'. More reports, please.

Castlehill, Ballina

T: 00 353 96-31112
F: 00 353 96-31773
E: mail@enniscoe.com
W: www.enniscoe.com

BEDROOMS: 6, plus self-catering units behind house.
OPEN: Apr–Oct, groups only at New Year.
FACILITIES: 2 sitting rooms, dining room, 150-acre estate (garden, tea room, farm, heritage centre, conference centre, forge, fishing), unsuitable for &.
BACKGROUND MUSIC: none.
LOCATION: 2 miles S of Crossmolina.
CHILDREN: all ages welcomed.
DOGS: not allowed in public rooms.
CREDIT CARDS: MasterCard, Visa.
PRICES: B&B €98–€130 per person, D,B&B €146–€178, set dinner €50, 10% discount for 3 nights or more, New Year package, 1-night bookings refused bank holiday Sat.

**25% DISCOUNT VOUCHERS**

# CASTLELYONS Co. Cork

Map 6:D5

## BALLYVOLANE HOUSE

*César award in 2009*

At their family home, a fine Georgian house in large wooded grounds, the 'rather glamorous' Justin and Jenny Green welcome visitors as house guests. 'We were given a great welcome by Jenny Green, who showed us around and gave us tea by the fire,' say visitors this year. First-name terms are adopted, no room keys are issued. The four-course dinner is taken communally around a large mahogany table with a silver candlestick. Teena Mahon cooks country dishes (roast marinated butterflied leg of McGrath's lamb) with vegetables from the walled garden. No choice, but menus are discussed: 'We had no problems; delicious home cooking, fresh spinach, soda bread at its best.' In winter, the house might feel cold. Bedrooms have antique furniture, big beds, interesting bathrooms ('tricky to climb out of our splendid old bath on a wooden platform'). The 'highly professional' Greens' three children host visiting youngsters to high tea during half-term. There are three trout lakes in the grounds; six miles of fishing on the River Blackwater. (*Jill and Mike Bennett*)

Castlelyons, Fermoy

T: 00 353 25-36349
F: 00 353 25-36781
E: info@ballyvolanehouse.ie
W: www.ballyvolanehouse.ie

BEDROOMS: 6.
OPEN: 4 Jan–23 Dec.
FACILITIES: hall, drawing room, honesty bar, dining room, 15-acre grounds (garden, croquet, 3 trout lakes), unsuitable for &.
BACKGROUND MUSIC: none.
LOCATION: 22 miles NE of Cork.
CHILDREN: all ages welcomed.
DOGS: not allowed in bedrooms (outhouse provided).
CREDIT CARDS: Amex, MasterCard, Visa.
PRICES: B&B €95–€115 per person, set dinner €60, fishing school, monthly supper club, special breaks.

**25% DISCOUNT VOUCHERS**

## CLIFDEN Co. Galway

Map 6:C4

### THE QUAY HOUSE

♀ *César award in 2003*

On the small harbour below this interesting little town, this cluster of three buildings, once the harbourmaster's house, is run as a B&B by Paddy and Julia Foyle. 'Her friendly professionalism makes you feel immediately at home,' says one visitor. All but two of the bedrooms overlook the tidal harbour. Each room is different: Out of Africa has animal skins on the floor and walls, a leopard-print sofa. The 'quirky' Mirror Room has a large, gilded mirror behind the bed, a sofa, a good-sized bathroom. The newest section has studios, each with a small kitchen and a balcony. Peat fires burn in the sitting rooms, which have Napoleonic mementos, Irish paintings. Breakfast, taken in a conservatory, has a 'splendid' menu. 'I have never seen such choice': the seafood might include oysters; orange juice is freshly squeezed; brown bread and fruit brack are baked daily in the Aga. The Foyles have a licence, and sell a good selection of wines. They will recommend restaurants in the town, perhaps *Foyle's* ('yes, a relation'). (*David Berry, SS*)

Beach Road
Clifden

T: 00 353 95-21369
F: 00 353 95-21608
E: res@thequayhouse.com
W: www.thequayhouse.com

BEDROOMS: 14, 2 on ground floor, 1 suitable for &, 7 studios (6 with kitchenette) in annexe.
OPEN: Mid-Mar–end Oct.
FACILITIES: 2 sitting rooms, breakfast conservatory, ½-acre garden, fishing, sailing, golf, riding nearby.
BACKGROUND MUSIC: none.
LOCATION: harbour, 8 mins' walk from centre.
CHILDREN: all ages welcomed.
DOGS: not allowed.
CREDIT CARDS: MasterCard, Visa.
PRICES: B&B €70–€90 per person, special breaks, 1-night bookings refused bank holiday Sat.

# CLONES Co. Monaghan

Map 6:B6

## HILTON PARK

**NEW**

The home of the Madden family since 1734, this imposing Italianate mansion stands in a wooded park with three lakes, a golf course and pleasure gardens. It is run in house-party style by Johnny and Lucy Madden (of the eighth generation) with their son, Fred, and his wife, Joanna, 'whose youth and enthusiasm are reinvigorating the castle'. 'They offer the ultimate Irish country house experience,' says a recent visitor, a fellow *Guide* heritage house owner. The beautiful public rooms are furnished with period pieces, a fine fireplace was brought back from Naples by an ancestor; musical guests are encouraged to play an Erard grand piano. The main drawing room and dining room, on the first floor, have magnificent views of the parterre and park. Dinner can be taken communally or at separate tables. Lucy Madden has been joined by her son in the kitchen; they use seasonal produce, much of it from the estate, for dishes like wild garlic soup; roast loin of venison, red wine jus, braised red cabbage. Breakfast is taken in the vaulted former servants' hall. (*GG*)

Clones

T: 00 353 47-56007
F: 00 353 47-56033
E: mail@hiltonpark.ie
W: www.hiltonpark.ie

BEDROOMS: 6.
OPEN: Apr–Sept, groups only Oct–Mar.
FACILITIES: drawing room, sitting room, TV room, breakfast room, dining room, 600-acre grounds (3 lakes, golf course), unsuitable for &.
BACKGROUND MUSIC: none.
LOCATION: 4 miles S of Clones.
CHILDREN: not under 8.
DOGS: not allowed in bedrooms, public areas.
CREDIT CARDS: MasterCard, Visa.
PRICES: [2010] B&B €98–€135 per person, set dinner €55, special breaks, 1-night bookings sometimes refused.

## COBH Co. Cork

Map 6:D5

### KNOCKEVEN HOUSE  `NEW`

This harbour town was the *Titanic*'s final departure point on her ill-fated maiden voyage. It was also the last image of Ireland for many people who emigrated to America, and it has a 'wonderful' heritage centre. In large gardens five minutes' walk from the railway station, this 'very comfortable' early Victorian house is run as a B&B by John and Pam Mulhaire. 'Strongly recommended; they are friendly and helpful owners,' says the nominator. Other visitors 'were welcomed with home-made scones and tea' by the hostess. 'Staying here is like being in a private house.' The bedrooms, recently renovated, are richly decorated with floral patterns and toile de Jouy; one has long silk curtains and matching throws. 'Our beautiful room overlooked the gardens and beyond, the sea; an impressive power shower in the bathroom.' The 'delicious' breakfast, served at a mahogany table, has a buffet with muesli, fruit compotes, cheeses, home-baked breads and scones; full Irish, or scrambled eggs with smoked salmon. The Mulhaires, who have 'a wealth of local knowledge', will advise on places to eat in Cobh. (*Ian Luall Grant, Christopher and Sheila Richards*)

Rushbrooke
Cobh

T: 00 353 21-481 1778
F: 00 353 21-481 1719
E: info@knockevenhouse.com
W: www.knockevenhouse.com

BEDROOMS: 4.
OPEN: all year except 15–27 Dec.
FACILITIES: lounge, drawing room, dining room, 3-acre garden, unsuitable for &.
BACKGROUND MUSIC: none.
LOCATION: 1 mile W of centre.
CHILDREN: all ages welcomed.
DOGS: not allowed.
CREDIT CARDS: MasterCard, Visa.
PRICES: [2010] B&B €45–€55 per person, D,B&B €75, set dinner €49, New Year package.

# CONG Co. Mayo

Map 6:C4

## BALLYWARREN HOUSE

In attractive farming country between Lough Corrib and Lough Mask on the edge of Connemara, David and Diane Skelton's creeper-covered replica Georgian home is 'elegant but homely'. 'We were greeted with tea and home-baked goodies in a cosy sitting room,' says a visitor who enjoyed 'three wonderful days' this year. The bedrooms are 'decorated in rich colours appropriate to the style, and furnished with antiques and textiles'. They have magazines, chocolates and sherry. The Rose Room has an 'enormous' English oak four-poster, immaculate bedding; fluffy towels and a 'generous' bath. The Lavender Room has a French carved bed. Dinner is served in a 'lovely dusky pink and green room overlooking the garden'. Mrs Skelton posts her daily-changing menu on a blackboard; dishes are slow-cooked in her Aga: 'a velvety asparagus soup, generous helpings of tender meat dishes like a delicious lamb shank; flavoursome home-baked bread'. A choice of six cooked dishes at breakfast, a 'brilliant' buffet, home-made bread, jams and marmalades; eggs come from the hens which roam the grounds. (*Helen and David Daniel*)

Cross, Cong

T/F: 00 353 9495-46989
E: ballywarrenhouse@gmail.com
W: www.ballywarrenhouse.com

BEDROOMS: 3.
OPEN: all year.
FACILITIES: reception hall, 2 sitting rooms, dining room, 1-acre garden in 6-acre grounds (lake, fishing nearby), unsuitable for &.
BACKGROUND MUSIC: none.
LOCATION: 2 miles E of Cong.
CHILDREN: not under 14, except babies.
DOGS: not allowed in house.
CREDIT CARDS: Amex, MasterCard, Visa.
PRICES: B&B €62–€74 per person, set dinner €46, 1-night bookings occasionally refused.

# DUBLIN

Map 6:C6

## ABERDEEN LODGE

In a leafy residential area of south Dublin, Pat Halpin's small hotel is liked by visitors for the kindness of the staff, and the 'home comforts'. Ann Keane is the manager. The Victorian villa has a 'superb' garden (rear rooms overlook a cricket pitch). The bedrooms are decorated in contemporary colours; some have a four-poster bed. All have free Wi-Fi access. Breakfast is taken in an attractive room with floor-to-ceiling windows facing the garden (background music is played). A buffet table has jugs of freshly squeezed orange juice, fresh and stewed fruits, home-baked bread and muffins. The cooked dishes include the usual fry-up, buttermilk pancakes with maple syrup, scrambled eggs with smoked salmon. A short menu of sandwiches and simple meals can be taken in the bedroom or the drawing room. Good dining can be found in Sandymount, a short walk away. Free car parking is liked by visitors. There are good bus and train connections with the centre. One of the Halpin family's three other Dublin hotels, *Blakes*, reopened in 2010 after renovation. (*AT, JA*)

53–55 Park Avenue,
Ballsbridge, Dublin 4

T: 00 353 1-283 8155
F: 00 353 1-283 7877
E: info@aberdeenlodgedublin.com
W: www.aberdeenlodgedublin.com

BEDROOMS: 17.
OPEN: all year.
FACILITIES: ramps, drawing room, dining room, ½-acre garden, beach nearby.
BACKGROUND MUSIC: classical.
LOCATION: S of city, close to DART station.
CHILDREN: all ages welcomed.
DOGS: not allowed.
CREDIT CARDS: all major cards.
PRICES: B&B €69.50–€170 per person, set meals €25–€35, special offers, Christmas/New Year packages.

**25% DISCOUNT VOUCHERS**

# DUNFANAGHY Co. Donegal

Map 6:A5

## THE MILL

Overlooking a lake outside a small coastal village, this 19th-century former flax mill is run as an unpretentious restaurant-with-rooms by Derek (the chef) and Susan Alcorn. The mill was the home and studio of her grandfather, Frank Egginton, an acclaimed watercolour artist, whose work is displayed in the public rooms. 'Unusually for such establishments, there are spacious "lounging-about" facilities'; the 'atmospheric' drawing room has an open fire; there is comfortable seating, too, in a conservatory area. Susan Alcorn is the 'hard-working' front-of-house, taking orders in the lounges. Her husband's cooking has a loyal following: booking is essential for dinner, which is served in a two-tier restaurant. Seafood is a speciality in his modern menus. 'Excellent food: it is a treat to sit in the dining room looking out at the charming gardens,' said a visitor in 2010. The simple bedrooms have coffee/tea-making facilities; an 'adequate' bathroom; 'immaculate' housekeeping. Breakfast has 'particularly nice Guinness bread', carrageen milk mousse, and stewed rhubarb; 'super sausages and bacon'. Guests are asked not to check in between 1 and 4 pm. (*Karin Mackinnan*)

Figart
Dunfanaghy

T/F: 00 353 74-913 6985
E: themillrestaurant@oceanfree.net
W: www.themillrestaurant.com

BEDROOMS: 6.
OPEN: mid-Mar–mid-Dec, weekends only off-season, restaurant closed Mon.
FACILITIES: sitting room, conservatory, restaurant, 1-acre grounds (lake, beach ½ mile), only restaurant suitable for &.
BACKGROUND MUSIC: in lounge and restaurant.
LOCATION: at Figart, ½ mile W of Dunfanaghy.
CHILDREN: all ages welcomed.
DOGS: not allowed.
CREDIT CARDS: Amex, MasterCard, Visa.
PRICES: [2010] B&B €50–€70 per person, set dinner €43.50.

# DUNGARVAN Co. Waterford

Map 6:D5

## THE TANNERY RESTAURANT & TOWNHOUSE

'You check in at the restaurant and are taken to your room in the nearby *Townhouse*,' explain visitors this year to this restaurant-with-rooms in a small seaside town. It is run by celebrity chef Paul Flynn and his wife Máire (front-of-house). This year, the Flynns have doubled the number of bedrooms in the *Townhouse*, and launched a cookery school. The 'stylish' bedrooms are 'very 21st-century': 'Our room had a Scandinavian feel, with cool colours, boarded walls, comfortable beds, a good shower.' Guests entering the two-level restaurant, a converted leather warehouse, can see Mr Flynn cooking in an open kitchen on the ground floor. He uses vegetables and herbs from a recently created garden for his 'delicious' modern dishes, eg, Asian crab salad with pink grapefruit; seared lamb's liver, onion cream, parsnip and sage butter. A short 'early bird' menu is considered 'good value'. Breakfast is a DIY affair in the bedroom: 'Fresh pastries are hung outside the door; fresh milk, juice and yogurt are in the fridge.' Children are welcomed. (*Christopher and Sheila Richards*)

10 Quay Street
Dungarvan

T: 00 353 58-45420
F: 00 353 58-45814
E: bookings@tannery.ie
W: www.tannery.ie

BEDROOMS: 14, 2 on ground floor.
OPEN: all year except Christmas, 2 weeks in Jan, restaurant closed Sun evening, Mon.
FACILITIES: restaurant, private dining room.
BACKGROUND MUSIC: light jazz.
LOCATION: town centre.
CHILDREN: all ages welcomed.
DOGS: not allowed.
CREDIT CARDS: Amex, MasterCard, Visa.
PRICES: [2010] B&B €50 per person, D,B&B €100, early bird menu €28.50, full alc €75.

**25% DISCOUNT VOUCHERS**

# DUNKINEELY Co. Donegal

Map 6:B5

## CASTLE MURRAY HOUSE

Endorsed by returning visitors this year, this small hotel/restaurant has an elevated position above McSwyne's Bay overlooking the ruins of a castle (floodlit at night). It is owned and managed by Marguerite Howley; her staff (Irish and French) are 'warm and helpful'. Most of the 'comfortable' bedrooms, on the first and second floors, have fine sea views. In the absence of a lift, assistance is offered with luggage. Orders for dinner are taken in a 'splendid', long, narrow seating area facing the sea. Seafood is a speciality on chef Remy Dupuy's 'excellent' menu (French with a modern twist); perhaps prawns and monkfish in garlic butter; roast hake, ratatouille, red pepper coulis. A light lunch menu is available in summer months. Background music is played in the public rooms. Breakfast has freshly squeezed orange juice, fresh fruit salad, a 'substantial' fry. Cookery courses are held in the winter. 'Very good value.' (*Florence and Russell Birch*)

St John's Point
Dunkineely

T: 00 353 74-973 7022
F: 00 353 74-973 7330
E: info@castlemurray.com
W: www.castlemurray.com

BEDROOMS: 10.
OPEN: 14 Feb–5 Jan except Christmas, closed Mon/Tues except July, Aug.
FACILITIES: lounge, bar, restaurant, wedding facilities, ¼-acre garden, unsuitable for &.
BACKGROUND MUSIC: jazz, classical.
LOCATION: 1 mile SW of village.
CHILDREN: all ages welcomed.
DOGS: allowed in some bedrooms.
CREDIT CARDS: MasterCard, Visa.
PRICES: B&B €65–€95 per person, D,B&B €105–€115, set dinner €40, full alc €75, cookery courses, New Year package.

# ENNISCORTHY Co. Wexford

Map 6:D6

## BALLINKEELE HOUSE

'Highly recommended' by visitors from Austria
and France this year, this late Regency manor
house stands in a large park with three lakes,
ponds and woods. The fifth generation of the
family that built the house, the owners, John and
Margaret Maher, are 'friendly and helpful in
every way'. A pillared portico entrance opens on
to a spacious hall with Corinthian columns, a
decorated ceiling and large fireplace. Most of the
furniture is original ('like a living museum'):
'John and Margaret keep their house in
gorgeous shape while meeting modern
requirements.' The 'well-appointed' bedrooms
have an individual character, some with a four-
poster. Pre-dinner drinks are taken in front of
a fire in the drawing room. Dinner is taken
communally by candlelight in the rich-red
dining room. Margaret Maher is a 'homely yet
sophisticated' cook, using local produce in her
no-choice menu (vegetarians are catered for). 'A
delightful dinner, and breakfast with the best
cheese and honey we have found in Ireland,'
says a visiting chef from France. (*Winfried and
Edith König, Nelly Feuillette*)

Ballymurn
Enniscorthy

T: 00 353 91-38105
F: 00 353 91-38468
E: john@ballinkeele.ie
W: www.ballinkeele.ie

BEDROOMS: 5.
OPEN: Mar–Nov.
FACILITIES: 2 drawing rooms, dining
room, 6-acre gardens in 350-acre
estate, lakes, ponds, unsuitable
for &.
BACKGROUND MUSIC: none.
LOCATION: 6 miles SE of
Enniscorthy.
CHILDREN: all ages welcomed.
DOGS: not allowed.
CREDIT CARDS: MasterCard, Visa.
PRICES: [2010] B&B €75–€105 per
person, set dinner €48.

**25% DISCOUNT VOUCHERS**

# ENNISCORTHY Co. Wexford

Map 6:D6

## SALVILLE HOUSE

Overlooking the Slaney River valley and the Blackstairs Mountains, this Victorian country house stands in large grounds with mature trees. Run by owners Gordon and Jane Parker, it has long been popular with *Guide* readers for the 'warm ambience' and the skill of his cooking. It is a popular base for visitors attending the Wexford opera festival (early suppers are provided), and for motorists en route to the ferry harbour at Rosslare. Mr Parker, 'passionate about food', grows his own vegetables and herbs (organically) and sources local produce for his four-course no-choice dinner (it must be booked the evening before; 'let us know of any dislikes and allergies'). The menu might include white bean bruschetta, roasted peppers; beef, puréed horseradish and yogurt, rösti potatoes. Bring your own wine (no corkage charge). The three spacious bedrooms in the main house have the views. There is free Wi-Fi throughout. Breakfast has freshly squeezed orange juice, fruit compote, toasted oats and honey; full Irish, or locally produced smoked salmon with scrambled eggs. (*RR, S and PW*)

Salville
Enniscorthy

T/F: 00 353 53-923 5252
E:   info@salvillehouse.com
W:  www.salvillehouse.com

BEDROOMS: 5, 2 in apartment at rear.
OPEN: all year except Christmas.
FACILITIES: drawing room, dining room, 5-acre grounds ('rough' tennis, badminton, croquet), golf nearby, beach, bird sanctuary 10 miles, unsuitable for &.
BACKGROUND MUSIC: none.
LOCATION: 2 miles S of town.
CHILDREN: all ages welcomed.
DOGS: allowed by arrangement, but not in public rooms, bedrooms.
CREDIT CARDS: none.
PRICES: [2010] B&B €55–€65 per person, D,B&B €95–€105, set dinner €40, New Year package.

# GOREY Co. Wexford

Map 6:D6

## MARLFIELD HOUSE

In woodlands and lovely gardens, this fine
Regency mansion was once the Irish residence of
the earls of Courtown. It has been owned since
1978 by Ray and Mary Bowe whose daughters,
Margaret and Laura, run it as a sophisticated
country house hotel (Relais & Châteaux). The
gardens provide flowers for the house and fruit,
vegetables and herbs for the kitchen. There is a
wildfowl reserve, a lake with ducks, geese and
black swans. The entrance is impressive with
goldfish ponds, sometimes a peacock by the
house. In the dining room (frescoes, a domed
conservatory, and silver), service is formal. Paul
O'Loughlin, who joined as chef in March 2010,
serves intricate classic dishes, perhaps ravioli of
braised ham and foie gras; crab-crusted halibut,
purée of watercress, roasted Ratte potatoes,
beurre blanc. The best bedrooms have antiques,
dramatic wallpapers and curtains, marble
bathrooms. A large ground-floor room has 'a
welcoming coal-effect gas fire and French
windows opening on to the lovely grounds'.
The breakfast buffet has fruits from the garden.
Nearby are sandy beaches and golf. More
reports, please.

Courtown Road
Gorey

T: 00 353 53-942 1124
F: 00 353 53-942 1572
E: info@marlfieldhouse.ie
W: www.marlfieldhouse.com

BEDROOMS: 19, 8 on ground floor.
OPEN: Mar–Dec.
FACILITIES: reception hall, drawing
room, library/bar, restaurant with
conservatory, function/conference
facilities, wedding facilities, 36-acre
grounds (gardens, tennis, croquet,
wildfowl reserve, lake).
BACKGROUND MUSIC: classical in
library.
LOCATION: 1 mile E of Gorey.
CHILDREN: no under-8s at dinner,
high tea provided, babysitting
available.
DOGS: not allowed in public rooms.
CREDIT CARDS: all major cards.
PRICES: B&B €75–€250 per person,
D,B&B €140–€370, set dinner €59,
special breaks, Christmas package,
1-night bookings sometimes
refused Sat.

**25% DISCOUNT VOUCHERS**

# HOLYWOOD Co. Down

Map 6:B6

## RAYANNE HOUSE

In an elevated position above an attractive town on the Belfast Lough, this Victorian house has been modernised by owners Conor and Bernadette McClelland, who have given it a 'wonderful Art Deco theme'. Period features have been retained: there are wide landings, sweeping stairs, display cabinets and bookshelves. All the bedrooms have been renovated, using bold colours and fabrics against a neutral background. A ground-floor room is equipped for disabled visitors. Most rooms have views across to the Antrim hills. Conor McClelland, an accomplished cook who has worked in Germany and New York, has won awards for his breakfasts. Dishes must be chosen the evening before from an extensive menu which has 'starters' (prune soufflé on a purée of green figs, spicy fruit compote, etc), and 'mains' (pork and prune sausages, potato waffles, Dijon mustard, cider and honey sauce). He also serves evening meals 'of the highest standard', by arrangement, for a minimum of eight people. He uses local produce and seasonal ingredients in his modern dishes. Mrs McClelland was named 'friendliest landlady' in 2010. More reports, please.

60 Demesne Road
Holywood BT18 9EX

T/F:028-9042 5859
E:  info@rayannehouse.com
W:  www.rayannehouse.com

BEDROOMS: 11, 1, on ground floor, suitable for &.
OPEN: all year.
FACILITIES: 2 lounges, dining room, conference facilities, 1-acre grounds.
BACKGROUND MUSIC: light jazz in dining room.
LOCATION: ½ mile from town centre, 6 miles E of Belfast.
CHILDREN: all ages welcomed.
DOGS: not allowed.
CREDIT CARDS: MasterCard, Visa.
PRICES: [2010] B&B £45–£60 per person, D,B&B £44 added, full alc £50.

# INIS MEÁIN Co. Galway

Map 6:C4

## INIS MEÁIN RESTAURANT AND SUITES **NEW**

Inis Meáin (middle island) is the quietest of the Aran Islands off the Galway coast 'and has an atmosphere to match'. A stronghold of traditional culture (Irish is the first language of the 160 inhabitants), it has a rugged limestone landscape. Islander Ruairí de Blacam (the chef) runs this restaurant-with-rooms with his wife, Marie Thérèse (front-of-house); they have a 'gentle warmth and generosity of spirit', says the nominator. The building, designed to match the craggy surroundings, has 'rough stone walls and ceilings, timber floors and furniture, softened by woollen throws and cushions from the island's knitwear factory'. The three simple suites have a 'well-stocked' fridge, books about the island, fishing rods; and bicycles; 'wonderful views'. 'Ruairí's cooking is superb: fresh periwinkles from the island's shore are the appetizers; home-grown vegetables (delicious potatoes), much seafood including unparalleled lobster.' A breakfast tray is delivered to the suite with 'scones, brown soda bread, eggs, salamis, fresh fruit, yogurts, etc'. A packed lunch ('the best ever, crab salad, crème brûlée') is available. (*Sarah Goddard*)

Inis Meáin, Aran Islands
Galway

T: 00 353 86-826 6026
E: post@inismeain.com
W: www.inismeain.com

BEDROOMS: 3.
OPEN: Apr–Oct, hotel and restaurant closed Sun/Mon.
FACILITIES: restaurant, 3-acre grounds, unsuitable for &.
BACKGROUND MUSIC: Irish music in evening.
LOCATION: on island, 15 miles off Galway coast (45-minute ferry from Ros a' Mhíl, flights from Connemara airport).
CHILDREN: all ages welcome.
DOGS: not allowed.
CREDIT CARDS: MasterCard, Visa.
PRICES: [2010] B&B €125–€187 per person, full alc €50, min. stay 2 nights.

# KENMARE Co. Kerry

Map 6:D4

## SHELBURNE LODGE

In large grounds with a small orchard and lawns, Tom and Maura Foley's handsome 18th-century farmhouse is the oldest house in Kenmare. It has long been a favourite of *Guide* readers, who commend the attention to detail and 'continuing high standards'. A family member welcomes guests with a cup of tea and home-made cake in one of the elegant lounges. These have plenty of seating, log fires, antiques, books for guests to read. The bedrooms are individually decorated in traditional style; two rooms in an informal conversion of a coach house are suitable for a family. Wi-Fi is now available. In the large dining room, Mr Foley serves the 'best-ever' breakfast, explaining dishes to guests. It has freshly squeezed juice, fruit; yogurt, honey and nuts; home-baked bread and preserves. There is a daily fish dish as well as a full Irish plate. In the grounds are a grass tennis court and a pretty herb garden. The Foleys own *Packies*, a pub/restaurant in Kenmare, also noted for its fish dishes. Lighter daytime eating can be kept within the family; Maura Foley's sister runs the *Purple Heather* bistro. (*ES*)

Cork Road
Kenmare

T: 00 353 64-664 1013
F: 00 353 64-664 2135
E: shelburnekenmare@eircom.net
W: www.shelburnelodge.com

BEDROOMS: 10, 2 in coach house.
OPEN: mid-Mar–mid-Nov.
FACILITIES: drawing room, library, lounge in annexe, breakfast room, 3-acre garden (tennis), golf adjacent, unsuitable for &.
BACKGROUND MUSIC: none.
LOCATION: on R569 to Cork, ⅛ mile E of centre.
CHILDREN: all ages welcomed.
DOGS: not allowed.
CREDIT CARDS: MasterCard, Visa.
PRICES: B&B €50–€80 per person.

# KENMARE Co. Kerry

Map 6:D4

## VIRGINIA'S GUESTHOUSE

In the centre of a 'colourful little' resort town, this unpretentious guest house occupies the first and second floors above *Mulcahy's*, a popular restaurant. The hosts, Neil and Noreen Harrington, have an 'engaging charm'. 'He was delighted to give us whatever information we could wish for,' said one visitor. All the bedrooms and the breakfast room have been decorated and given new curtains this year. The furnishings are 'cheerful, homely'; bedrooms and bathrooms are 'bright and spotless'; earplugs are provided for light sleepers in front rooms. A time for breakfast is agreed when it is ordered the evening before. 'Noreen produces delicious cooked dishes from her tiny galley: everything is home made and organic, from the porridge, bread and preserves to the eggs, bacon, mushrooms, cheese and rhubarb.' Orange juice 'comes from real oranges squeezed by us every morning', say the Harringtons. No evening meals are served: there are 'many cheerful pubs just a few doors away'. *Fishy Fishy* (lunch only) on Market Place is recommended this year. (*TL*)

36 Henry Street
Kenmare

T: 00 353 64-664 1021
E: virginias@eircom.net
W: www.virginias-kenmare.com

BEDROOMS: 8.
OPEN: all year except 21–25 Dec.
FACILITIES: library, breakfast room, unsuitable for &.
BACKGROUND MUSIC: classical, 'easy listening' in breakfast room.
LOCATION: central.
CHILDREN: not under 12.
DOGS: not allowed.
CREDIT CARDS: MasterCard, Visa.
PRICES: B&B €30–€45 per person, 3-night off-season breaks, 1-night bookings refused New Year, bank holidays.

# KILCONNELL Co. Galway

## BALLINDERRY PARK

An attraction for any aficionado of the Irish country house, this beautifully proportioned Georgian building was found 'lonely and abandoned' by George and Susie Gossip, who have restored it with imagination. The yellow-painted house stands on a small hill in open countryside east of Galway. An impressive staircase, rising from the bow-fronted hall, leads to landings on both upper floors. The drawing room, painted and panelled in soft green, has comfortable chairs and sofas, cushioned window seats; prints and old porcelain. The dining room has rugs on unvarnished floors, dark blue walls; 17th-century oak and 18th-century mahogany furniture. Mr Gossip, who 'buzzes around dispensing bonhomie', is an 'excellent' cook, producing four-course no-choice dinners (likes and dislikes are discussed; he 'always enjoys the challenge of meeting his guests' requirements'). The preparation and cooking of game is his speciality. A recent visitor was served woodcock 'shot on the land by the man himself'; vegetarians are catered for. The two largest bedrooms are on the first floor; they are painted in strong colours and furnished with antiques. More reports, please.

Kilconnell
nr Ballinasloe

T/F: 00 353 90-968 6796
E: george@ballinderrypark.com
W: www.ballinderrypark.com

BEDROOMS: 4.
OPEN: 1 April–30 Sept, closed Christmas, groups only at New Year (other times by arrangement).
FACILITIES: hall, drawing room, dining room, 40-acre grounds, fishing, horse riding nearby, unsuitable for &.
BACKGROUND MUSIC: none.
LOCATION: 7 miles W of Ballinasloe.
CHILDREN: all ages welcomed.
DOGS: 'allowed if well behaved, must sleep in enclosed lobby outside bedroom'.
CREDIT CARDS: MasterCard, Visa.
PRICES: [2010] B&B €80–€100 per person, set dinner €55.

# KILMALLOCK Co. Limerick

Map 6:D5

## FLEMINGSTOWN HOUSE

*❦ César award in 2005*

On a working dairy farm beneath the
Ballyhoura Mountains, this 18th-century
building has been owned by the Sheedy family
for five generations. Imelda Sheedy-King has
'created an exceptional establishment; she is a
wonderful host', say visitors this year. Readers
have long admired her 'extraordinary warmth'
and 'attention to detail'. The house has a 'cosy'
lounge with 19th-century pieces. The spacious
bedrooms have a large bed; one has a crystal
chandelier. All have wide views. Mrs Sheedy-
King tells us that she has simplified her dinner
menu 'to give visitors what they want'. She
serves a three-course meal, by arrangement,
with traditional dishes, eg, hot cucumber soup,
Melba toast; chicken with mustard and crème
fraîche sauce, a selection of vegetables. There's
a good pub with food nearby for nights when
she is not cooking. Breakfast has home-made
breads, jams and cakes, cheeses (from her sister's
farm); fresh juices; cooked dishes might include
crepes filled with fruit, lemon butter sauce.
Visitors can explore the farm and watch the
cows being milked. (*Michael and Sue Callaghan*)

Kilmallock

T: 00 353 63-98093
F: 00 353 63-98546
E: info@flemingstown.com
W: www.flemingstown.com

BEDROOMS: 5, 1 self-catering lodge.
OPEN: Mar–Nov.
FACILITIES: lounge, dining room,
1-acre garden in 100-acre farm
(golf, riding, fishing, cycling
nearby), unsuitable for &.
BACKGROUND MUSIC: 'easy listening'
in dining room.
LOCATION: on R512, 2 miles SE of
Kilmallock.
CHILDREN: not under 10.
DOGS: not allowed in house.
CREDIT CARDS: MasterCard, Visa.
PRICES: B&B €50–€65 per person, set
dinner €35, special rates for stays of
more than 1 night.

# LETTERFRACK Co. Galway

## ROSLEAGUE MANOR 🏆

*César award in 2010*

'It's like being at home, only better.' Praise this year from a regular visitor to Edmund and Mark Foyle's Georgian manor house on Connemara's Atlantic coast. 'It doesn't matter that we know what to expect; we are never disappointed.' The setting is 'magnificent': the house looks across a sea loch to empty hills. Mark Foyle is the 'personable and hands-on manager': 'The welcome is warm; he and his staff, now mainly local, treat you more as friends than customers.' There are log and turf fires, paintings and antiques in the lounges. A conservatory and bar open on to a landscaped internal courtyard. The cooking of Pascal Marinot is 'simple, superbly done'; his short menus might include Atlantic seafood rillettes; grilled cod with orange risotto; 'perfectly cooked' Connemara lamb. Guests can now choose between two or four courses. The bedrooms are 'solid, spacious, comfy'. Fish (mackerel, plaice, bass) features on the breakfast menu, which also has freshly squeezed juice, plenty of fruit, home-baked scones and brown bread. (*Ann Walden, and others*)

Letterfrack

T: 00 353 95-41101
F: 00 353 95-41168
E: info@rosleague.com
W: www.rosleague.com

BEDROOMS: 20, 2 on ground floor.
OPEN: Mar–Nov.
FACILITIES: 2 drawing rooms, conservatory/bar, dining room, wedding facilities, 25-acre grounds (tennis), unsuitable for &.
BACKGROUND MUSIC: none.
LOCATION: 7 miles NE of Clifden.
CHILDREN: all ages welcomed.
DOGS: only 'well-behaved dogs' allowed in public rooms, with own bedding in bedrooms.
CREDIT CARDS: MasterCard, Visa.
PRICES: [2010] B&B €75–€125 per person, set dinner €32–€48, 1-night bookings refused bank holiday Sat.

**25% DISCOUNT VOUCHERS**

# LISDOONVARNA Co. Clare

Map 6:C4

## SHEEDY'S

The welcome is 'open and warm' at John and Martina Sheedy's hotel/restaurant in a building that has been owned by his family since the 18th century. He is the 'exceptional' chef; she runs front-of-house, 'a considerable presence at all times of day' (say inspectors in 2010). A bedroom in the main house was 'furnished in traditional style (curtains with tie rails, maroon-striped wallpaper); a small sitting area; an immaculate bathroom with the whitest of towels'. Some of the 'well-cared-for' bedrooms are in a modern extension. There is a turf fire in the cosy bar; a lounge with good seating, books and local information. 'We were served drinks in an extension at the front, which had picture windows, Lloyd Loom chairs. Martina took our dinner order and led us to the smartly laid dining room. We were brought grapefruit foam as a pre-starter; then came the freshest of crab salads; a huge helping of tender herb-crusted rack of lamb and confit shoulder with a dish of perfectly cooked vegetables.' Breakfast, served at table, is 'well done'.

Lisdoonvarna

T: 00 353 65-707 4026
F: 00 353 65-707 4555
E: info@sheedys.com
W: www.sheedys.com

BEDROOMS: 11, some on ground floor, 1 suitable for ♿.
OPEN: Easter–early Oct.
FACILITIES: ramp, sitting room/library, sun lounge, bar, restaurant, ½-acre garden (rose garden).
BACKGROUND MUSIC: light jazz at dinner.
LOCATION: 20 miles SW of Galway.
CHILDREN: all ages welcomed.
DOGS: not allowed.
CREDIT CARDS: MasterCard, Visa.
PRICES: [2010] B&B €50–€85 per person, D,B&B €99–€125, early bird menu €25.50, full alc €60, special breaks, 1-night bookings refused Sept weekends.

# MAGHERALIN Co. Armagh

## NEWFORGE HOUSE   `NEW`

'Accommodation, hospitality and food are of
the highest order.' Praise from a regular
correspondent brings a full entry for John and
Louise Mathers's family home. A fine Georgian
country house, it stands in 'extensive and well-
kept' grounds on the edge of a small village. It has
been 'sympathetically' converted as a guest house.
John Mathers, the sixth generation of his family
to live here, 'is a regular presence, greeting us on
first-name terms, offering advice on outings, and
tea when we returned from them'. The sitting
room and dining room have open log fires, 'good
antique furniture, decent paintings, current
magazines; good-quality fabrics with muted
tones have been used throughout'. A first-floor
bedroom had a 'comfortable bed, good storage,
fruit and flowers, tea-making facilities with fresh
milk; the impressive bathroom had a freestanding
bath, a separate shower'. Mr Mathers cooks a
'simple' three-course dinner: 'We enjoyed all we
tried: a perfectly rare fillet of local beef; duck
breast with mild oriental spices; fine artisan
cheeses.' A 'delicious' breakfast has fresh, stewed
and dried fruit, a 'fine' grill, 'delectable' scrambled
eggs. (*Andrew Wardrop*)

58 Newforge Road
Magheralin
Craigavon BT67 0QL

T: 028-9261 1255
F: 028-9261 2823
E: enquiries@newforgehouse.com
W: www.newforgehouse.com

BEDROOMS: 6.
OPEN: all year except 21 Dec–10 Jan.
FACILITIES: drawing room, dining
room, civil wedding licence, 4-acre
gardens (vegetable garden, orchard),
unsuitable for &.
BACKGROUND MUSIC: classical/Irish
in dining room.
LOCATION: edge of village, 3 miles
E of Craigavon.
CHILDREN: not under 10 (except for
under-1s).
DOGS: not allowed.
CREDIT CARDS: MasterCard, Visa.
PRICES: [2010] B&B £57.50–£105 per
person, D,B&B £91–£138.50, set
dinner £33.50, special breaks.

**25% DISCOUNT VOUCHERS**

## MILLSTREET Co. Waterford

Map 6:D5

### THE CASTLE COUNTRY HOUSE

Guests are welcome to watch, 'or indeed lend a hand if so inclined', during milking at Joan and Emmett Nugent's working dairy farm in pastureland in the Blackwater valley. It is built around a 16th-century fortified tower house (which protected farmers and their livestock). The 'beautifully decorated' bedrooms are in a restored wing; there are large beds, period furniture; tea- and coffee-making facilities. All rooms have country views. Mrs Nugent and her family 'made us feel truly at home', said the nominator. 'She arranged our daily excursions and provided tea and basketfuls of delicious scones at every encounter.' The dining room, in the oldest part of the castle, has five-foot-thick walls. Mrs Nugent tells us she now offers a simple supper (home-made soup with brown bread, smoked salmon) as an alternative to a three-course meal of 'delicious farm-fresh food' (eg, baked chicken with garlic cream and bacon). Breakfast has a buffet of home-grown fruit, cereals, breads; a wide range of cooked dishes, eg, grilled banana and bacon. This is the closest of three villages called Millstreet to Dungarvan. (*BW*)

Millstreet
Cappagh

T: 00 353 58-68049
F: 00 353 58-68099
E: castlefm@iol.ie
W: www.castlecountryhouse.com

BEDROOMS: 5.
OPEN: Mar–Nov.
FACILITIES: sitting room, dining room, 2-acre garden on 170-acre farm, unsuitable for &.
BACKGROUND MUSIC: classical in dining room.
LOCATION: 10 miles NW of Dungarvan towards Cappoquin.
CHILDREN: all ages welcomed.
DOGS: not allowed in house.
CREDIT CARDS: MasterCard, Visa.
PRICES: B&B €45–€55 per person, dinner €15–€30, 3-night breaks.

# MOUNTRATH Co. Laois

Map 6:C5

## ROUNDWOOD HOUSE

♕ *César award in 1990*

At their handsome Palladian villa at the foot of the Slieve Bloom Mountains, Rosemarie and Frank Kennan have been joined by their daughter, Hannah, and her husband, Paddy Flynn. The Kennans are gradually handing over the running of the house to the new generation: 'Assurances have been given that the new management will not introduce wide-screen televisions or trouser presses,' they promise. For more than 25 years, the family has been restoring the house they bought from the Irish Georgian Society. Run in a relaxed style, it has creaking floorboards, old furniture and books, 'a slightly shabby Irish charm'. Mrs Kennan has been joined by the Flynns in the kitchen to prepare the no-choice dinners. Dietary requirements are taken into account, then 'each course is a surprise', perhaps broccoli and cashew nut soup; peppered beef, brandy sauce, roast potatoes with garlic, balsamic and ginger red cabbage. Children are welcomed (there is a 'wet-day' nursery with toys). Self-catering is available in a converted coach house, forge and cottage. More reports, please.

Mountrath

T: 00 353 57-873 2120
F: 00 353 57-873 2711
E: info@roundwoodhouse.com
W: www.roundwoodhouse.com

BEDROOMS: 10, 4 in garden building.
OPEN: all year except Christmas.
FACILITIES: drawing room, study/library, dining room, playroom, table tennis room, wedding facilities, 20-acre grounds (garden, woodland), golf, walking, river fishing nearby, unsuitable for ♿.
BACKGROUND MUSIC: none.
LOCATION: 3 miles N of village.
CHILDREN: all ages welcomed.
DOGS: not allowed indoors.
CREDIT CARDS: all major cards.
PRICES: B&B €60–€80 per person, set dinner €50, special breaks.

**25% DISCOUNT VOUCHERS**

# MULTYFARNHAM Co. Westmeath

Map 6:C5

## MORNINGTON HOUSE

Owned by one family since 1858, this 'rather grand' old house stands amid extensive parkland with ancient trees near Lough Derravaragh, 60 miles north-west of Dublin. It remains much as it has been since it was remodelled in 1896, with original furniture and family portraits on the colourful walls. Visitors are entertained on house-party lines by Warwick and Anne O'Hara ('welcoming hosts'). '*Mornington* is not a hotel nor an inn, but a country family home,' they say. 'The house loves people and is never happier than when full of guests.' The 'idiosyncratic' bedrooms vary in size; front rooms are the best. French windows lend natural light to the drawing room, where visitors help themselves to drinks before dinner; a turf or log fire burns in colder weather. Many of the ingredients (vegetables, fruit and herbs) come from the walled garden for Mrs O'Hara's country house meals. Mr O'Hara cooks breakfast, which has freshly squeezed orange juice; home-made muesli and brown bread; a full Irish fry. More reports, please.

Multyfarnham

T/F: 00 353 44-937 2191
E:  stay@mornington.ie
W:  www.mornington.ie

BEDROOMS: 4.
OPEN: Apr–Oct.
FACILITIES: drawing room, dining room, 5-acre garden, 50-acre grounds (croquet, bicycle hire), unsuitable for &.
BACKGROUND MUSIC: none.
LOCATION: 9 miles NW of Mullingar.
CHILDREN: all ages welcomed.
DOGS: not allowed in house.
CREDIT CARDS: all major cards.
PRICES: B&B €75 per person, D,B&B €120, set dinner €45, 3-night breaks.

25% DISCOUNT VOUCHERS

# NEW QUAY Co. Clare

Map 6:C5

## MOUNT VERNON ⚜ [NEW]

*César award: Irish heritage house of the year*

On Flaggy Shore where the Burren meets the sea, this 18th-century villa was the summer home of Lady Gregory, the Irish cultural champion. It has been restored by Mark Helmore and Ally Raftery, who run it as 'a private country house and home'. 'Everything is excellent,' say inspectors. 'Mark welcomed us warmly and gave us a tour of the house, which is full of interesting objects.' Three of the bedrooms face the sea: 'Ours was beautifully furnished: a three-seater sofa at the end of the huge bed; gorgeous orange silk curtains; three steps down to a large, light bathroom.' Two rooms at the side have a door opening on to the garden. They have 'very comfortable antique bed, smart modern bathroom'. Guests gather for drinks from an honesty bar at 7.30 pm before dinner at a large table in the dining room. 'Faultless: delicious langoustine broth; a meaty Icelandic haddock on crunchy courgette slices. Breakfast, from 9 am, is 'just right'. The couple, 'friendly without being pushy', advise guests on exploration of the Burren.

Flaggy Shore
New Quay, Burren

T: 00 353 65-707 8126
F: 00 353 65-707 8118
E: info@mountvernon.ie
W: www.mountvernon.ie

BEDROOMS: 5, 2 on ground floor.
OPEN: Apr–Oct (by arrangement at other times), dining room closed Mon or Tues.
FACILITIES: sitting room, library, dining room, 5-acre gardens.
BACKGROUND MUSIC: none.
LOCATION: edge of hamlet, 5 miles NE of Ballyvaughan.
CHILDREN: not under 10.
DOGS: not allowed in public rooms or bedrooms.
CREDIT CARDS: MasterCard, Visa.
PRICES: [2010] B&B €100–€115 per person, set dinner €50, special breaks, 1-night bookings refused Sat.

**25% DISCOUNT VOUCHERS**

# NEWPORT Co. Mayo

## NEWPORT HOUSE

On an estuary looking over to Achill Island, this mellow mansion stands on the ancestral estate of the O'Donel family. Built on earlier foundations, it is Georgian in character. It is run 'like a large private home' by owners Thelma and Kieran Thompson (the manager is Catherine Flynn). Readers like the 'unstuffy' atmosphere; and the helpful local staff. The outstanding feature of the house is the elegant staircase and gallery with a lantern and dome; the drawing room on the first floor has Regency mirrors and a chandelier. In the formal dining room, chef John Gavin serves country house/French dishes on a short menu, eg, crab salad, tomato and brandy mayonnaise; brill, creamed leeks, vermouth sauce. The fish comes from the River Newport (on which the hotel has extensive rights) or the prolific waters of Lough Beltra West. The bedrooms in two courtyard houses are popular with angling visitors, who have access to a drying room; freezing and smoking of catches can also be arranged. Children are welcomed, as are dogs. (*MW*)

Newport

T: 00 353 98-41222
F: 00 353 98-41613
E: info@newporthouse.ie
W: www.newporthouse.ie

BEDROOMS: 16, 5 in courtyard, 4 on ground floor.
OPEN: 19 Mar–31 Oct.
FACILITIES: sitting room, bar, dining room, restaurant, billiard/TV room, table-tennis room, 15-acre grounds (walled garden, private fishing on River Newport), golf, riding, walking, shooting nearby, unsuitable for &.
BACKGROUND MUSIC: none.
LOCATION: in village 7 miles N of Westport.
CHILDREN: all ages welcomed.
DOGS: allowed in courtyard bedrooms, not in public rooms.
CREDIT CARDS: Amex, MasterCard, Visa.
PRICES: B&B €114–€164 per person, D,B&B €176–€226, set dinner €68, full alc €63, special breaks.

**25% DISCOUNT VOUCHERS**

# OUGHTERARD Co. Galway

Map 6:C4

## CURRAREVAGH HOUSE

🌣 *César award in 1992*

'The owners and staff have that perfect combination of friendliness and professionalism.' Guests on a second visit to the Hodgson family's early Victorian manor house in beautiful parkland and woodland on Lough Corrib met others who 'perfectly understandably return every year'. June Hodgson continues to assist her son, Henry, in running the front-of-house; his wife, Lucy, is the chef. 'When we arrived too early, Henry said "never too early" as he carried our bags to a lovely big room.' First-time visitors enjoyed 'the easy charm, the welcoming atmosphere, and the beauty of the setting. Despite the rain, we relaxed and felt at home.' Many of the bedrooms have views of the lough; they have fresh flowers and hot-water bottles, blankets and sheets. A lavish afternoon tea served in the drawing room has sandwiches, home-made scones and cakes. At dinner, the cooking had 'gone up several notches; interesting and adventurous, eg, pesto and goose breast; lovely fresh vegetables, great roast potatoes'. Henry Hodgson provides breakfast, a 'splendid' buffet. (*Jill and Michael Bennett, the Thomas family*)

Oughterard

T: 00 353 91-552312
F: 00 353 91-552731
E: rooms@currarevagh.com
W: www.currarevagh.com

BEDROOMS: 13.
OPEN: 1 Apr–15 Oct.
FACILITIES: sitting room/hall, drawing room, library/bar with TV, dining room, 180-acre grounds (lake, fishing, ghillies available, boating, swimming, tennis, croquet), golf, riding nearby, unsuitable for &.
BACKGROUND MUSIC: none.
LOCATION: 4 miles NW of Oughterard.
CHILDREN: all ages welcomed.
DOGS: allowed in all areas.
CREDIT CARDS: MasterCard, Visa.
PRICES: B&B €70–€95 per person, D,B&B €110–€135, set dinner €48.

**25% DISCOUNT VOUCHERS**

# RAMELTON Co. Donegal

Map 6:B5

## FREWIN

On the outskirts of a historic Georgian port on Lough Swilly, this former rectory has been unaltered since it was built in Victorian times. It has been renovated by Regina and Thomas Coyle, who ensured that the rich period features were preserved. These 'warm, welcoming' hosts have furnished their 'country house in miniature' with antiques (Mr Coyle is a collector); the old parish safe is embedded in the wall of the book-lined library; there is stained glass in the hall, an elegant staircase; croquet in the garden, wellington boots in the hall. The main bedroom has views on two sides over the mature gardens; and a small study/library, 'a lovely little nook'. Mrs Coyle will serve a 'simple but satisfactory' dinner by arrangement. Breakfast is taken communally around a large table: it has home-made muesli, bread straight from the oven, proper butter and preserves; a full fry-up. Ramelton is an interesting heritage town of merchant houses, old warehouses. On the River Lennon, it was an important port for the linen trade. More reports, please.

Rectory Road
Ramelton

T/F: 00 353 74-915 1246
E:  frewin.ramelton@gmail.com
W:  www.frewinhouse.com

BEDROOMS: 4, self-catering cottage for 2 in grounds.
OPEN: 1 Jan–20 Dec.
FACILITIES: sitting room, library, dining room, 2-acre garden, golf, horse riding, beaches nearby, unsuitable for &.
BACKGROUND MUSIC: none.
LOCATION: outskirts of town.
CHILDREN: 'not suitable for young children'.
DOGS: not allowed.
CREDIT CARDS: MasterCard, Visa.
PRICES: [2010] B&B €65–€100 per person, set dinner €50.

# RATHMULLAN Co. Donegal

## RATHMULLAN HOUSE

The Wheeler family are much in evidence at their 1800s mansion which stands in well-tended gardens on a two-mile sandy beach on Lough Swilly (an inlet of the sea). Brothers Mark (the manager) and William run it with their wives, Mary and Yvonne. 'Excellence and professionalism reign supreme,' says a visitor in 2010. 'It is just so comfortable,' is another comment. *The Weeping Elm* is a conservatory-style dining room with a tented ceiling. Kelan McMichael, who joined as chef in early 2010, is an advocate of the slow food movement; he sources fish from Donegal waters, and herbs and vegetables from the house's gardens, for dishes like seared Kilkeel wild halibut, slow-cooked fennel, tomato and salsa verde. We would welcome reports on his cooking (one visitor would have liked more vegetables). A series of interconnecting living rooms has chandeliers, sink-in sofas, log fires in marble fireplaces, butter-coloured walls. Ten spacious rooms in a Regency-style extension have restful colours; one has a 'room' for a dog. Bedrooms in the older part of the building are decorated in country house style. (*RWB, and others*)

Rathmullan

T: 00 353 74-915 8188
F: 00 353 74-915 8200
E: info@rathmullanhouse.com
W: www.rathmullanhouse.com

BEDROOMS: 32, some on ground floor, 2 suitable for &.
OPEN: 11 Feb–7 Jan except Christmas, midweek Nov, Dec.
FACILITIES: ramps, 4 sitting rooms, library, TV room, cellar bar/bistro, restaurant, 15-metre indoor swimming pool (steam room), small conference centre, wedding facilities, 7-acre grounds (tennis, croquet).
BACKGROUND MUSIC: none.
LOCATION: ½ mile N of village.
CHILDREN: all ages welcomed.
DOGS: allowed in 1 dog-friendly bedroom, but not in public rooms.
CREDIT CARDS: Amex, MasterCard, Visa.
PRICES: B&B €85–€150 per person, D,B&B €130–€195, set dinner €45–€55, full alc €80, special breaks, 1-night bookings refused at weekends, bank holidays.

# RIVERSTOWN Co. Sligo

Map 6:B5

## COOPERSHILL

🏛 *César award in 1987*

In 'pristine condition', this magnificent Palladian mansion has been home to the O'Hara family since it was built in 1774. It stands on a large estate, traversed by the River Arrow, with a sizeable farm and woodland. Simon O'Hara is in charge: the hospitality of the 'engaging family' has long been liked by readers. The magnificent public rooms have the original Georgian furniture 'that has never been anywhere else'. There are family portraits, stags' heads, gilded mirrors. Bedrooms retain their original dimensions. In the elegant dining room, dinner, a relaxed affair, is served around 8.30 pm. The chef, Christina McCauley, uses ingredients from the estate for her country house dishes (spinach soup and rosemary 'direct from the garden'; estate venison medallions, juniper sauce). At breakfast, 'juices, coffee and dishes are all squeezed, ground, and cooked to order to guarantee freshness'. *Coopershill* has been awarded an EU Eco-Label for its environment policy. Among the initiatives: wind-blown timber heats public rooms; 80 per cent of power is from renewable sources (primarily wind). More reports, please.

Riverstown

T: 00 353 71-916 5108
F: 00 353 71-916 5466
E: ohara@coopershill.com
W: www.coopershill.com

BEDROOMS: 8.
OPEN: Apr–Oct, off-season house parties by arrangement.
FACILITIES: 2 halls, drawing room, TV room, dining room, snooker room, wedding facilities, 500-acre estate (garden, tennis, croquet, woods, farmland, river with trout fishing), unsuitable for &.
BACKGROUND MUSIC: none.
LOCATION: 11 miles SE of Sligo.
CHILDREN: all ages welcomed.
DOGS: allowed in 1 bedroom, not in public rooms.
CREDIT CARDS: MasterCard, Visa.
PRICES: [2010] B&B €99–€122 per person, D,B&B €136–€167, set dinner €45, discounts for 3 or more nights.

**25% DISCOUNT VOUCHERS**

# ROSSLARE Co. Wexford

Map 6:D6

## CHURCHTOWN HOUSE

Popular with visitors attending the Wexford Opera Festival or catching the ferry at Rosslare, this white Georgian house has a 'beautiful' setting in mature parkland. The 'open and approachable' owners, Austin and Patricia Cody, create a 'calm atmosphere'. There are traditional fabrics, thick carpets, a big comfortable bed in the bedrooms; a ground-floor room was liked for the ample storage and good lighting. Irish paintings hang on the walls, and modern objets d'art are displayed in the elegant public rooms. Breakfast, served at separate tables, has home-made jams, bread baked in the kitchen. There is cold ham and cheeses; local sausages and bacon, white and black pudding, eggs any way: 'Guests tell us what they would like and we will cook it for them,' says Mrs Cody. A simpler early breakfast is provided for those taking the ferry to Fishguard. The Codys tell us that they will not be serving evening meals in 2011; they are happy to advise on restaurants in Rosslare. More reports, please.

Tagoat
Rosslare

T: 00 353 53-913 2555
F: 00 353 53-913 2577
E: info@churchtownhouse.com
W: www.churchtownhouse.com

BEDROOMS: 12, 5 on ground floor.
OPEN: mid-Mar–31 Oct.
FACILITIES: 2 lounges, dining room, 8-acre grounds (golf, fishing, riding), beaches nearby, unsuitable for &.
BACKGROUND MUSIC: none.
LOCATION: 2½ miles S of Rosslare.
CHILDREN: all ages welcomed.
DOGS: not allowed in house.
CREDIT CARDS: MasterCard, Visa.
PRICES: [2010] B&B €55–€75 per person, website offers, 2- to 3-night breaks.

## SCHULL Co. Cork

Map 6:D4

### ROCK COTTAGE

♀ *César award in 2004*

'After a while, you notice the systematic care that has been paid to make this a lovely, relaxing place to be.' Praise for this 'much-loved' house whose owner, Barbara Klötzer, 'knows how to make a hotel personal without it feeling that you are a guest in someone's home'. The 'truly beautiful' slate-sided Georgian hunting lodge stands in large grounds among grassy hillocks, one of which has 'stunning' views of Dunmanus Bay. The furniture and pictures are a 'mix of Victorian portraits and contemporary artists', fine furnishings, prints and ornaments. The patio is an 'appealing place to enjoy your own wine or beer, watch the animals which roam freely'. The 'light, airy' bedrooms are decorated in bright Tyrolean style; two have a sitting area. Ms Klötzer's cooking, based on her own farm ingredients, is much admired; she might serve a warm lamb's liver salad. Breakfast (ordered the night before) 'was the best we had in Ireland; a fresh berry milkshake was glorious. Her egg, bacon, sausage and white and black pudding were a delight.' (*DB*)

Barnatonicane
Schull

T/F: 00 353 28-35538
E: rockcottage@eircom.net
W: www.rockcottage.ie

BEDROOMS: 3, also 1 self-catering cottage.
OPEN: all year (advance notice essential for Sun night).
FACILITIES: lounge, dining room, 17-acre grounds, unsuitable for &.
BACKGROUND MUSIC: when guests want it.
LOCATION: 8 miles NW of Schull.
CHILDREN: not under 10.
DOGS: only disability dogs allowed.
CREDIT CARDS: MasterCard, Visa.
PRICES: B&B €70–€100 per person, set dinner €50, 1-night bookings refused in winter, bank holidays.

# SHANAGARRY Co. Cork

Map 6:D5

## BALLYMALOE HOUSE

❦*César award in 1984*

'As lovely as ever', the Allen family's renowned hotel/restaurant is 'so relaxed', say inspectors this year. 'No rules, flexible mealtimes, no dress code; and no muzak.' The ivy-covered Georgian mansion retains the 'atmosphere of a civilised private home'; 'everyone is friendly, the welcome is impeccable'. Myrtle Allen, who founded *Ballymaloe* in 1964, can still be found supervising the kitchen or dining room. Daughter-in-law Hazel is manager; another daughter-in-law, Darina, the cookery writer, runs the nearby cookery school. Afternoon tea, 'with delicious scones and home-made jam', is taken in a pretty conservatory. 'We love the series of dining rooms with green walls. The food is very good, totally unpretentious: our best dishes were turbot with herb hollandaise sauce; monkfish with scallops.' There are interesting murals, paintings, prints and sculptures in the public rooms. 'Our bedroom in a newish wing was filled with light; a door opened on to the garden.' The biggest rooms are in the main house. Breakfast has 'warm bread, always a fresh fish dish'.

Shanagarry

T: 00 353 21-465 2531
F: 00 353 21-465 2021
E: res@ballymaloe.ie
W: www.ballymaloe.ie

BEDROOMS: 30, 8 in adjacent building, 4 on ground floor, 5 self-catering cottages.
OPEN: all year except 24–26 Dec, 2 weeks mid-Jan.
FACILITIES: drawing room, 2 small sitting rooms, conservatory, 7 dining rooms, wedding and conference facilities, 6-acre gardens, 400-acre grounds (tennis, swimming pool, 10 by 4 metres), cookery school nearby.
BACKGROUND MUSIC: none.
LOCATION: 20 miles E of Cork.
CHILDREN: all ages welcomed.
DOGS: allowed in courtyard rooms, not in house.
CREDIT CARDS: all major cards.
PRICES: B&B €85–€130 per person, D,B&B €155–€200, set dinner €75, special breaks, New Year package.

**25% DISCOUNT VOUCHERS**

# STRAFFAN Co. Kildare

Map 6:C6

## BARBERSTOWN CASTLE

In a village 30 minutes' drive from Dublin, this 13th-century castle with an attached Elizabethan house was sold in 1987 by the rock musician, Eric Clapton, to Ken Healey. He has added a large extension to create a country hotel which he has furnished with antiques. Richard Millea is the manager, leading a 'friendly' international staff. In the restaurant in the castle keep, head chef Bertrand Malabat serves French/Irish dishes, perhaps Dublin Bay prawns, tomato and pepper compote; slow-cooked pork belly, black pudding, onion jam. Afternoon tea and lighter meals are served all day in the conservatory-style *Tea Room*, which has a terrace facing the landscaped gardens. Bedrooms are named after people who have lived in the castle (including Eric Clapton); a large room was 'nicely decorated and well equipped'. There is turn-down service during dinner. Country pursuits available in the grounds or nearby include horse riding, clay-pigeon shooting, archery and fishing; golf can be arranged at the nearby K Club, home of the 2006 Ryder Cup. Free Wi-Fi is available. More reports, please.

Straffan

T: 00 353 1-628 8157
F: 00 353 1-627 7027
E: info@barberstowncastle.ie
W: www.barberstowncastle.ie

BEDROOMS: 58, 21 on ground floor, 3 suitable for &.
OPEN: Feb–Dec, except Christmas.
FACILITIES: ramps, lift, bar, 2 lounges, restaurant, tea room, terrace, banqueting/conference/wedding facilities, business centre, 20-acre grounds (walking, archery, clay-pigeon shooting), fishing, golf, horse riding nearby.
BACKGROUND MUSIC: in public areas.
LOCATION: village 12 miles W of Dublin.
CHILDREN: all ages welcomed.
DOGS: only allowed in grounds.
CREDIT CARDS: Amex, MasterCard, Visa.
PRICES: [2010] B&B €97.50–€115 per person, D,B&B €129, set dinner €45–€55, special breaks, New Year package.

**25% DISCOUNT VOUCHERS**

# WATERFORD Co. Waterford

Map 6:D5

## FOXMOUNT COUNTRY HOUSE

**NEW**

On a working dairy farm, David and Margaret Kent's 'elegant' creeper-covered 17th-century country house is reached by a long tree-lined drive. It returns to the *Guide* after a period without reports. 'Wonderful hosts, well-decorated bedrooms, lovely breakfasts,' say the nominators. Guests are encouraged to take tea in the drawing room, perhaps after a walk on signposted routes in the surrounding countryside, and to bring their own pre-dinner drinks. The 'comfortable' bedrooms overlook the 'lovely' gardens. They are clean, 'homely', and have fresh fruit; good towels in the bathroom. Mrs Kent has won awards for her breakfasts, which use the farm's produce. They have fresh orange juice, stewed rhubarb and yogurt, home-made muesli; 'excellent' home-baked brown bread, hot scones and preserves; porridge with fresh cream and honey; a cheese plate, free-range eggs cooked to order; black pudding with the Irish fry-up. Recommendations are given for 'very good' local restaurants. The immaculately kept garden is a 'relaxed place'. (*Peter and Celia Gregory*)

Passage East Road
Waterford

T: 00 353 51-874308
F: 00 353 51-854906
E: info@foxmountcountryhouse.com
W: www.foxmountcountryhouse.com

BEDROOMS: 4.
OPEN: mid-Mar–mid-Oct.
FACILITIES: sitting room, dining room, 2-acre gardens in 200-acre grounds, unsuitable for &.
BACKGROUND MUSIC: none.
LOCATION: 3 miles SW of Waterford.
CHILDREN: all ages welcomed.
DOGS: not allowed.
CREDIT CARDS: none.
PRICES: B&B €65 per person.

# SHORTLIST

The Shortlist complements our main section by
including potential but untested new entries and
a selection of appropriate places in areas where we
have limited choice. It also has some hotels that
have previously had a full entry in the *Guide*,
but have not attracted sufficient feedback
from our readers.

## LONDON

Map 2:D4

**Apex City of London**, 1 Seething Lane, EC3N 4AX. Tel 0845-365 0000, www.apexhotel.co.uk. In a side street near the Tower of London, this large, contemporary, high-tech hotel (stainless steel, marble and grainy wood) is managed by Yousif Al-Wagga. All bedrooms are stylish and well equipped; some are internal without a view. *Addendum* restaurant and gastro bar (background music); business facilities; gym (sauna); garden. Wi-Fi. Free local telephone calls. Children welcomed. 179 bedrooms: £150–£266. Breakfast £15, dinner £19.50. (Underground: Tower Hill)

**B+B Belgravia**, 64–66 Ebury Street, SW1W 9QD. Tel 020-7259 8570, www.bb-belgravia.com. Penny Brown, Sue Bertram and Kate Green have given this elegant Grade II listed Georgian town house a clean-lined, contemporary interior. Their aim is to provide good design and comfort at an affordable price. Lounge (fireplace, complimentary tea/coffee/hot chocolate and biscuits, DVD/book library). Open-plan kitchen/breakfast room (organic breakfasts). Free Wi-Fi and bicycles. No background music. Small garden. 17 bedrooms (2 family; 1 suitable for &). Dogs welcomed. B&B £60–£99 per person. (Underground: Victoria)

**base2stay**, 25 Courtfield Gardens, SW5 0PG. Tel 020-7244 2255, www.base2stay.com. A well-designed, minimalist hotel, in a pillared, white stucco town house. The bedrooms are light and smart, each with a mini-kitchen. Reception, lobby (background music). Wi-Fi, music library, games. Children welcomed. 67 bedrooms (some with bunk beds; 2 suitable for &): £84–£207. (Underground: Earls Court, Gloucester Road)

**The Bingham**, 61–63 Petersham Road, Richmond, TW10 6UT. Tel 020-8940 0902, www.thebingham.co.uk. In two Georgian town houses, Ruth Trinder's elegant hotel has a riverside garden. The decor is contemporary: Art Deco-style bedrooms are 'sophisticated, yet comfortable'. Cocktail bar, *Michelin*-starred restaurant with river views (Shay Cooper is chef), terrace (alfresco dining). Background music. Function facilities. Civil wedding licence. Children welcomed. 15 bedrooms: £190–£285. Breakfast £11–£15, dinner £60. (Underground: Richmond, 10 mins' walk)
**25% DISCOUNT VOUCHERS**

**Charlotte Street Hotel**, 15 Charlotte Street, W1T 1RJ. Tel 020-7806 2000, www.charlottestreethotel.com. The decoration in Tim and Kit Kemp's Fitzrovia hotel is influenced by Bloomsbury artists Vanessa Bell, Duncan Grant and Roger Fry, whose original work hangs on the walls. Public rooms have wood panelling, logs burning in sandstone fireplaces, striking modern pieces. Drawing room, library, *Oscar* bar; restaurant (open plan, run by chef, Rachel Hitchcock). 3 private dining/meeting rooms, 74-seat screening room, gym. No background music. Children welcomed. 52 bedrooms: £230–£1,050. (Underground: Goodge Street, Tottenham Court Road)

**CITY INN WESTMINSTER**, 30 John Islip Street, SW1P 4DD. Tel 020-7630 1000, www.cityinn.com. There are fine river and city views from this 'admirable' large, contemporary hotel (City Inn group) near Tate Britain. Diners can take Alexis Guillemot's modern European dishes inside, or alfresco on Art Street (a covered boulevard, created by artist Susanna Heron, which runs alongside the hotel). Lounge (ruby-red decor; background music); *Millbank Lounge* bar, *City Café* restaurant; gym. Wi-Fi. Function facilities. 460 bedrooms: £59–£319. (Underground: Pimlico)

**COUNTY HALL PREMIER INN**, Belvedere Road, SE1 7PB. Tel 0871-527 8648, www.premierinn.com. Beside the London Eye, this budget hotel (owned by Whitbread) is in the old County Hall building across the river from the Houses of Parliament. Check-in is self-service, the manager is Nuno Sacramento. Lobby, bar, restaurant; lift. Background music. Children welcomed. 314 bedrooms (some suitable for &): from £69. Meal deal (dinner and breakfast) £20 per person. (Underground: Waterloo)

**COVENT GARDEN HOTEL**, 10 Monmouth Street, WC2H 9HB. Tel 020-7806 1000, www.coventgardenhotel.co.uk. In a cobbled street in theatreland, this Firmdale hotel has a suitably dramatic style; the manager is Helle Jensen. Drawing room, library, refurbished bar and restaurant, *Brasserie Max*; meeting rooms; screening room; gym; beauty treatments. No background music. Wi-Fi. 58 bedrooms (CD/DVD-player, flat-screen TV; 1 suite has 'largest four-poster bed in London'): £240–£1,195. Breakfast £19.50, dinner from £22.50. (Underground: Covent Garden)

**THE DRAYCOTT**, 26 Cadogan Gardens, SW3 2RP. Tel 020-7730 6466, www.draycotthotel.com. In three Edwardian houses on a quiet square, close to Knightsbridge and the King's Road, this small luxury hotel is owned by Adrian Gardiner and managed by John Hanna. Rooms are named after literary and theatrical figures. Guests are welcomed with complimentary afternoon tea at 4 pm, champagne at 6 pm, hot chocolate at bedtime. 2 drawing rooms (honesty bar), no restaurant (room-service meals), breakfast room. No background music. 1-acre communal garden. Wi-Fi. DVDs and CDs provided. Children welcomed. Dogs allowed in 3 bedrooms. 35 bedrooms (*excluding VAT*): £114.50–£155. (Underground: Sloane Square)

**DUKES HOTEL**, 35 St James's Place, SW1A 1NY. Tel 020-7491 4840, www.dukeshotel.com. Part of Campbell Gray Hotels (see *One Aldwych*, main entry), this town house hotel is 'central, convenient and quiet'. Debrah Dhugga is the manager. It has been given a contemporary look and up-to-date technology. Drawing room, bar, restaurant (classic British dishes); 24-hour room service; health club; courtyard garden. No background music. Wi-Fi. Children welcomed. 90 bedrooms: from £220. Breakfast £24.50. (Underground: Green Park)

**EGERTON HOUSE**, 17–19 Egerton Terrace, SW3 2BX. Tel 020-7589 2412, www.egertonhousehotel.com. Perfectly placed for Knightsbridge shopping, this welcoming, luxury town house hotel (Red Carnation group) is managed by Sandra Anido. Rooms are sumptuous and well equipped (iPod docking station, flat-screen TV, etc). Guests have use of a gym and pool at a local club. Drawing room, bar (background music), breakfast room. 24-hour butler service. Wi-Fi. Children welcomed. 28 bedrooms (*excluding VAT*): £235–£895. Breakfast £24.50, dinner £60. (Underground: Knightsbridge, South Kensington)

**FOX & ANCHOR**, 115 Charterhouse Street, EC1M 6AA. Tel 020-7250 1300, www.foxandanchor.com. By Smithfield, a renovated pub with a 'buzzy feel', that has retained its Victorian heritage, along with modern, 'chic, tasteful' rooms. An offshoot of Malmaison hotels (the London *Malmaison* is next door), it is managed by Scott Malaugh. Dining room, 3 snugs, 'cosy, evocative of times past'; oyster bar; real ales. Background music. Some late-night/early-morning street noise. 6 bedrooms (*excluding VAT*): £95–£250. Breakfast £8.95, dinner £25. (Underground: Barbican)

**THE HALKIN**, 5 Halkin Street, SW1X 7DJ. Tel 020-7333 1000, www.halkin.como.bz. Asian simplicity is blended with chic Italian design (tones of taupe, cream and beige) in Christina Ong's luxury hotel in a Belgravia side street. Australian chef David Thompson has a *Michelin* star for his Thai cooking in *nahm* restaurant; Thai cookery classes are run by Matthew Albert. Light meals, snacks and afternoon tea are served in the sleek bar area. Bar, restaurant.

Wi-Fi. 41 bedrooms: £450–£1,500. (Underground: Hyde Park Corner)

**HAYMARKET HOTEL**, 1 Suffolk Place, SW1Y 4BP. Tel 020-7470 4000, www.haymarkethotel.com. In three John Nash-designed buildings near the Theatre Royal, this Firmdale hotel has a bold and colourful style. It is managed by Lisa Brooklyn. Lift, drawing room, library, bar, *Brumus* restaurant; background music. Indoor swimming pool, gym. 50 bedrooms: £250–£2,500. (Underground: Green Park, Piccadilly)

**HIGH ROAD HOUSE**, 162 Chiswick High Road, W4Y 1PR. Tel 020-8742 1717, www.highroadhouse.co.uk. Part of the Soho House group, this hotel/private members' club has been decorated in retro-modern style. There is a lively brasserie (some outdoor seating) and bar. Bedrooms are bright white with vibrant touches. The Games Room has red leather sofas, TV, pool table, football table, board games; The Playground has low-level seating for watching TV and screenings, Wi-Fi. The Playpen has comfortable seating and a bar. Kristen Cronin is the new manager. Background music. 14 (small, minimalist) bedrooms: £145–£165. English breakfast £9.50. (Underground: Turnham Green)

**HOTEL 55**, 55 Hanger Lane, W5 3HL. Tel 020-8991 4450, www.hotel55-london.com. Converted into a 'luxury budget' hotel from a former hostel/brothel, this North Ealing hotel has a cool, contemporary interior with low seating and original art on the walls. The restaurant is Japanese, operated by Momo. The designer garden is minimalist in style, with decking and attractive outdoor furniture. Bar, restaurant (background music). Wi-Fi. Children welcomed. Limited parking. 30 mins from Heathrow; Piccadilly line to central London. 25 bedrooms (2 suitable for &). B&B (continental) £45–£99 per person. (Underground: North Ealing)

**THE HOXTON**, 81 Great Eastern Street, EC2A 3HU. Tel 020-7750 1000, www. hoxtonhotels.com. Sinclair Beecham, co-founder of Pret A Manger, introduced a radical early-booking system for his buzzy hotel: periodically, five rooms a night are sold at £1, and five at £29. The style is industrial-chic: exposed brickwork, leather sofas, open fires; bedrooms in chocolate brown and café au lait colours. Huge lobby, sitting area, bar, *Hoxton Grill* brasserie (background music); business facilities; lift; shop. Courtyard, garden. Children welcomed. Wi-Fi. 205 bedrooms. B&B (Pret Lite breakfast) from £69 per person. (Underground: Old Street)

**INDIGO**, 16 London Street, W2A 1HL. Tel 020-706 4444, www.hipaddington. com. Occupying nine adjoining Georgian houses this hip hotel (Intercontinental Hotel group) is three minutes' walk from Paddington station and the London–Heathrow Express. Inside are wood floors, striking colours and huge photographic murals of interesting local architecture. Lounge/lobby, *Phi* brasserie. Fitness studio; terrace. Wi-Fi. Background music. 64 bedrooms (some have private balcony or terrace): £149–£205. Breakfast £10.95. (Underground: Paddington)

**KNIGHTSBRIDGE HOTEL**, 10 Beaufort Gardens, SW3 1PT. Tel 020-7584 6300, www.knightsbridgehotel.com. Gisele Clark manages this white-pillared hotel (in a peaceful, tree-lined cul-de-sac near the shops) for the Firmdale group. Decorated in contemporary English style, it has an intimate feel, with several cosy sitting areas and open fires. Bathrooms are done in granite and oak. Drawing room, library, bar. Room service. No background music. Wi-Fi. 44 bedrooms: £170–£625. (Underground: Knightsbridge)

**THE MAIN HOUSE**, 6 Colville Road, Notting Hill, W11 2BP. Tel 020-7221 9691, www.themainhouse.co.uk. Caroline Main owns this stylish Victorian town house B&B, in a quiet location off Portobello Road. Each room/suite occupies an entire floor and has period features, antique furnishings and modern technology, and an airy, uncluttered look. No background music. Guests may borrow bicycles and DVDs. There are special day rates for Lambton Place health club, and a deli nearby. Roof terrace. Wi-Fi. Children welcomed. 4 bedrooms: from £55 per person (excluding breakfast; no single-night bookings). (Underground: Notting Hill Gate)

**MANDEVILLE HOTEL**, Mandeville Place, W1U 2BE. Tel 020-7935 5599, www. mandeville.co.uk. A large hotel with a glitzy interior in Marylebone (Summit Hotels & Resorts), managed by Alexander Watenphul. Bedrooms are more restrained. Afternoon teas can be 'Fashion' (on Zandra Rhodes china) or 'Men's' (hearty, with optional alcohol); cocktails in the colourful *de Vigne* bar;

organic produce in the *de Ville* restaurant (Matthew Edmond is chef); background music. Wi-Fi. Function facilities. 142 bedrooms (6 suitable for &): £289–£429. Breakfast £17.25–£22.50, dinner £75. (Underground: Bond Street)

**MONTAGU PLACE**, 2 Montagu Place, W1N 2ER. Tel 020-7467 2777, www. montagu-place.co.uk. In a quiet location near Baker Street, this intimate hotel, managed by Dimitrios Neofitidis, is a conversion of two Grade II listed Georgian town houses. Bedrooms are categorised as 'Comfy', 'Fancy' or 'Swanky', all decorated in cream and earth tones. Lounge, bar, breakfast room; meeting room. No background music. Wi-Fi. 16 bedrooms: £200–£250. Continental breakfast £10–£13.95. (Underground: Marylebone, Baker Street)

**THE PELHAM**, 15 Cromwell Place, SW7 2LA. Tel 020-7589 8288, www. pelhamhotel.co.uk. Stripy awnings give a festive air to this white Victorian terraced hotel with pillars and balconies. The interiors are chic, with a wood-panelled drawing room and library, and open fires. Bedrooms have a mix of modern and antique furniture, and interesting fabrics. 'Helpful staff; good food.' Managed by Ian Dick. Drawing room, library, bar, *15* bistro/bar, 3 private dining/meeting rooms; gym. No background music. Wi-Fi. 52 bedrooms: £187–£519. Breakfast £14.55–£17.50. (Underground: South Kensington)

**THE ROOKERY**, 12 Peter's Lane, Cowcross Street, EC1M 6DS. Tel 020-7336 0931, www.rookeryhotel.com. In an area once notorious for cutpurses,

Peter McKay and Douglas Blain (who also own *Hazlitt's*, see main entry) have restored three 18th-century houses, in a traffic-free lane in Smithfield, to form a discreet hotel with the atmosphere of a private club. Period plumbing fittings, antiques, old paintings on panelled walls and flagstone floors. Drawing room, library, conservatory; courtyard garden; meeting rooms. No restaurant, but a limited room-service menu is available. No background music. Children welcomed. 33 bedrooms: £216–£285. (Underground: Farringdon, Barbican)

**ST JAMES'S HOTEL AND CLUB**, 7–8 Park Place, SW1A 1LS. Tel 020-7316 1600, www.stjameshotelandclub.com. In a quiet cul-de-sac, this luxury hotel (part of Althoff Hotel Collection) has been renovated with contemporary opulence. It has chandeliers, fabrics of silk, velvet and cashmere, restful bedrooms and a dramatic dining room. Original artwork includes a collection of portraits from the 1920s to the 1940s. The penthouse has a roof terrace with views across the London skyline. Henrik Muehle is the manager. *William's* bar and bistro, *Seven Park Place* restaurant, headed by William Drabble; 4 meeting rooms. Wi-Fi. Children welcomed. 60 bedrooms: £229.50–£1,102.50. Breakfast £16–£22. (Underground: St James's Park)

**SAN DOMENICO HOUSE**, 29–31 Draycott Place, SW3 2SH. Tel 020-7581 5757, www.sandomenicohouse.com. In a Victorian red brick Chelsea house, Marisa Melpignano's hotel is sumptuously furnished with plush fabrics, paintings and antiques. There is no restaurant, but an extensive room-service menu; the staff are Italian. Lobby, lounge (background music), breakfast room; fitness/massage rooms; roof terrace; meeting facilities. Children welcomed. 15 bedrooms (*excluding VAT*): £210–£360. Breakfast £18–£21. (Underground: Sloane Square)

**THE SANCTUARY HOUSE**, 33 Tothill Street, SW1H 9LA. Tel 020-7799 4044, www.fullershotels.com. In a 'first-class' location near Westminster Abbey and the Houses of Parliament, this good-value B&B (Fuller's Hotels) has rooms (with 'real feather quilts; Fairtrade tea and coffee') above a traditional ale-and-pie house. Sol Yepes is the manager: the staff are 'terrific, friendly and thoughtful'. Bar, restaurant. Room service. Wi-Fi (free in public rooms). 34 bedrooms. B&B from £62.50 per person. (Underground: St James's Park)

**THE SOHO HOTEL**, 4 Richmond Mews, off Dean Street, W1D 3DH. Tel 020-7559 3000, www.sohohotel.com. In a quiet side street in Soho, a glamorous hotel with funky touches. It belongs to the Firmdale group and is managed by Carrie Wicks. Rooms are spacious, with luxurious bathroom. Lift. Drawing room, library. Popular bar. *Refuel* restaurant (Robin Read is chef); background music; 4 private dining rooms; gym; 2 screening rooms. 91 bedrooms (some suitable for &): £290–£2,750. (Underground: Leicester Square)

**SYDNEY HOUSE CHELSEA**, 9–11 Sydney Street, SW3 6PU. Tel 020-74376 7711, www.sydneyhousechelsea.com. The first in Abode Hotel group's 'Baby Abode' collection, a Georgian town house on

seven floors with a sleek interior and every modern comfort. The Room at the Top has its own 'romantic' private roof garden. Drawing room, bar, boardroom; room service. Background music in lobby. Children welcomed. 21 bedrooms: £145–£275. Breakfast (continental) £5.50. (Underground: South Kensington)

**TEN MANCHESTER STREET**, Marylebone, W1U 4DG. Tel 020-7378 2499, www.tenmanchesterstreethotel. com. Just off Marylebone High Street, a discreet, designer-furnished hotel (Bespoke Hotel Company) in an Edwardian building. A small all-day menu is available in *Ten Lounge Bar*, which also has beer and ale from a London microbrewery. For cigar smokers, there is a humidor and large cigar menu, and an all-weather smoking terrace. Managed by Stefano Lodi. Lounge/bar. Wi-Fi. 24-hour room service; chauffeur service on request. 45 bedrooms (9 suites): £129–£519. Breakfast £10. (Underground: Bond Street)

**THREADNEEDLES**, 5 Threadneedle Street, EC2R 8AY. Tel 020-7657 8080, www.theetoncollection.com. The marble floors, ornate pillars and impressive stained-glass dome over the reception lounge have been retained at this opulent conversion of a Victorian banking hall near the Bank of England. Bedrooms are modern, with contemporary art on the walls. It is managed for the Eton Collection by Julian Payne. Background music. Bar, *Bonds* restaurant (French cuisine and tapas; Barry Tonks is chef; closed at weekends); lift; 3 meeting rooms;

conference facilities. Wi-Fi. 69 bedrooms (some suitable for &): £145–£545. Breakfast £19. (Underground: Bank)

## ENGLAND

**BABBACOMBE Devon**
**Map 1:D5**
THE CARY ARMS, Beach Road, TQ1 3LX. Tel 01803-327110, www.caryarms.co.uk. Overlooking the beach near Torquay, this 'magical' pub has been revamped in sympathetic style by Lana de Savary. Jen Podmore is the manager. Downstairs are original stone walls and planked floors; bedrooms have been given a fresh, seaside look. The chef, Denise Tarriela, specialises in fish and seafood; there's an outdoor fireplace and pizza oven. Lounge, bar, restaurant; garden, terrace; spa, treatment room. No background music. Children and dogs welcomed. 8 bedrooms (2 on ground floor). B&B £75–£125 per person; D,B&B £100–£150. Also 3 self-catering cottages.
25% DISCOUNT VOUCHERS

**BAMPTON Devon**
**Map 1:C5**
THE BARK HOUSE, Oakfordbridge, EX16 9HZ. Tel 01398-351236, www. thebarkhouse.co.uk. Built to store bark for use in the tanning process, this old, wisteria-covered building is run by 'delightful' hosts, Melanie McKnight and Martin French. It is 'a place to get away from it all', with 'excellent', generous home-cooked meals ('not fancy, just well done'), good breakfasts and afternoon teas on arrival. By busy road, overlooking Exe valley; 9 miles N of Tiverton. Lounge, dining room (occasional background music). Garden.

Children and dogs welcomed. Parking. 6 bedrooms. B&B £40–£60 per person; D,B&B £65–£85.
25% DISCOUNT VOUCHERS

**BATH Somerset**
**Map 2:D1**
AQUAE SULIS, 174–176 Newbridge Road, BA1 3LE. Tel 01225-420061, www.aquaesulishotel.co.uk. Owners David and Jane Carnegie run their traditionally furnished Edwardian home as a guest house. The city centre can be reached by a pleasant 30-minute riverside stroll, or by bus. 2 lounges (1 with bar, 1 computer room); background music. Wi-Fi. Children welcomed. Small garden. Convenient parking. 14 bedrooms (a large one in annexe). B&B £33–£99 per person.

BROOKS GUESTHOUSE, 1 Crescent Gardens, BA1 2NA. Tel 01225-425543, www.brooksguesthouse.com. Period furnishings and modern facilities (radios with iPod docking) are combined at this Victorian town house a few minutes' walk from the Royal Crescent. Bathrooms have been stylishly renovated. The lounge has an honesty bar for drinks and snacks. The breakfast menu has locally sourced ingredients. Wi-Fi. Background music in the sitting room (jazz) and the breakfast room (classical); courtyard gardens (front and back). Children welcomed (cots, highchairs, toys). 21 bedrooms. B&B £37.50–£75 per person.

DORIAN HOUSE, 1 Upper Oldfield Park, BA2 3JX. Tel 01225-426336, www.dorianhouse.co.uk. A 'quirky' B&B in a characterful Victorian stone house with good views over the city. It is owned by Tim and Kathryn Hugh, and managed by Robert and Lize Briers. It is on a steep incline, a ten-minute downhill walk to the centre (plenty of buses come back up the hill). Original and unusual modern art. A wide choice at breakfast, served by 'incredibly attentive and pleasant uniformed waiting staff'. Lounge (open fire), breakfast room/music library; classical background music. Wi-Fi. 'Immaculately manicured, vertiginous' small garden. Parking. 13 bedrooms (1 on ground floor). B&B £69–£165 per person.

**DUKES HOTEL**, Great Pulteney Road, BA2 4DN. Tel 01225-787960, www. dukesbath.co.uk. Alan Brookes and Michael Bokenham's elegant sandstone town house in the city centre has period furniture, fine fabrics, prints and portraits. Tina Paradise is the manager. Lounge, bar, *Cavendish* restaurant in basement (chef Fran Snell uses local produce; background music). Patio garden with pond and fountain (alfresco dining). 17 bedrooms (1 on ground floor). B&B £69.50–£119.50 per person; D,B&B £104.50–£154.50.

**HARINGTON'S HOTEL**, 8–10 Queen Street, BA1 1HE. Tel 01225-461728, www.haringtonshotel.co.uk. In a quiet cobbled street near the abbey, Melissa and Peter O'Sullivan's contemporary hotel is formed from a group of 17th-century houses. Lounge, bar, restaurant (background music; Steph Box is chef). Patio. Reserved parking nearby. Wi-Fi. 13 bedrooms (free Sky movies and sports), 2 self-catering apartments. B&B £44–£150 per person. Dinner £33.

**THE KENNARD**, 11 Henrietta Street, BA2 6LL. Tel 01225-310472, www.kennard.co.uk. 'Perfect for walking everywhere', Giovanni and Mary Baiano's town house B&B (built in 1794) is just over Pulteney Bridge (drivers are given a free parking permit). The interior is ornate, with a touch of Italian flamboyance on the landings (there are 6 flights of stairs). The small Georgian-style garden is inspired by Jane Austen. No background music. 2 sitting areas, breakfast room; courtyard. Children over 8 allowed. 12 bedrooms (2 on ground floor). B&B £49–£70 per person.

**PARADISE HOUSE**, 86–88 Holloway, BA2 4PX. Tel 01225-317723, www.paradise-house.co.uk. In secluded grounds, this listed Georgian house with Victorian extension has panoramic views over the city, which is a ten-minute walk away (steep hill). Owners David and Annie Lanz have furnished it traditionally, and added modern entertainment systems; Nicci and Russell Clarke are the managers. Drawing room, breakfast room. Classical background music. Wi-Fi. Children welcomed. Parking for 6 cars. 11 bedrooms (4 on ground floor, 2 in annexe in ½-acre landscaped walled garden). B&B £32.50–£115 per person.

**BATHFORD Somerset**
**Map 2:D1**
**EAGLE HOUSE**, Church Street, BA1 7RS. Tel 01225-859946, www.eaglehouse.co.uk. There are frequent bus services to Bath from John and Rosamund Napier's B&B, in their peacefully situated Georgian mansion, three miles outside the city. Drawing room, breakfast room.

No background music. 2-acre grounds: croquet lawn, grass tennis court, tree house, sandpit. Wi-Fi. Children welcomed; dogs (by arrangement; resident dog and cat). 8 bedrooms (2 in garden cottage). B&B (continental) £36–£68 per person. Cooked breakfast £5.50.
**25% DISCOUNT VOUCHERS**

### BELFORD Northumberland
Map 4:A3
**WAREN HOUSE**, Waren Mill, NE70 7EE. Tel 01668-214581, www. warenhousehotel.co.uk. 'A delight in a lovely spot', this Georgian country house is owned by Anita and Peter Laverack. It overlooks the natural bird sanctuary of Budle Bay, with Holy Island in view. *Grays* restaurant, under head chef Steve Owens, has won awards. Drawing room, dining room. No background music. Wi-Fi. Formal garden in 6-acre grounds; secure parking. Dogs welcomed. 15 bedrooms (4 in courtyard; 3 suitable for &). B&B £70–£95 per person; D,B&B £95–£120.

### BELPER Derbyshire
Map 2:A2
**DANNAH FARM**, Bowmans Lane, Shottle, DE56 2DR. Tel 01773-550273, www.dannah.co.uk. On a large working farm in the Derbyshire Dales, Joan and Martin Slack's comfortable country house B&B has luxurious touches and sybaritic bathrooms (double spa bath, wet room). Farmhouse breakfasts; supper platters can be provided. Overlooking rolling countryside, the Leisure Cabin (hot tub, sauna, steam shower) can be booked for private use. Medieval moat. 2 sitting rooms, dining room. No background music. Wi-Fi. Meeting room; licensed

for weddings. Large walled garden; arbour. Parking. Children welcomed. 8 bedrooms (4 in courtyard; 3 suitable for &). B&B £75–£112.50 per person. Supper £15.95.
**25% DISCOUNT VOUCHERS**

### BILDESTON Suffolk
Map 2:C5
**THE BILDESTON CROWN**, High Street, IP7 7EB. Tel 01449-740510, www.thebildestoncrown.com. A warm, red dining room, with original beams and good artwork, is at the heart of this mellow, timber-framed 15th-century coaching inn (Grade II listed). It was restored by local farmer James Buckle, who supplies much of the local produce, and is managed by Chris (the chef) and Hayley Lee. 'This was a lovely place to spend my birthday weekend. I felt spoiled.' Bedrooms are glamorous, cottagey or plain; all have a modern bathroom and state-of-the-art gadgetry. Wi-Fi. Lounge with log fire, 2 bars, dining room. No background music. Courtyard (alfresco dining). 12 bedrooms. B&B £75–£150 per person. Dinner from £22.

### BIRKENHEAD Merseyside
Map 4:E2
**THE RIVERHILL HOTEL**, Talbot Road, Oxton, CH43 2HJ. Tel 0151-653 3773, www.theriverhill.co.uk. 'Good value for money', Nick and Michele Burn's small hotel is in a residential area on the Wirral peninsula. Set back from the road in landscaped gardens, it has a restaurant which is open to non-residents. 'Good menu selection' and 'a laden sweet trolley brought to the table'. Lounge, bar, *Bay Tree* restaurant (background music). Wedding/business

facilities. The Birkenhead tunnel and the Woodside ferry to Liverpool are five minutes' drive away. Children welcomed. 15 bedrooms: £69.50–£145. Breakfast £7.95–£9.95, dinner from £22.95.

## BIRMINGHAM West Midlands
### Map 2:B2
**SIMPSONS**, 20 Highfield Road, Edgbaston, B15 3DU. Tel 0121-454 3434, www.simpsonsrestaurant.co.uk. In a Grade II listed Georgian mansion in Edgbaston, this *Michelin*-starred restaurant with themed bedrooms (French, Oriental, Venetian, Colonial) is run by chef/patron Andreas Antona, with Luke Tipping and Adam Bennett. Dining areas; private dining room (no background music); terrace (alfresco dining); garden, summer house. Parking. Cookery school; boutique. 4 bedrooms. B&B (continental) £80–£112.50 per person. Dinner £40–£50 (3 courses).

## BLACKBURN Lancashire
### Map 4:D3
**THE MILLSTONE AT MELLOR**, Church Lane, Mellor, BB2 7JR. Tel 01254-813333, www.millstonehotel.co.uk. 'Excellent in every way.' Anson Bolton is the chef/patron of this restaurant-with-rooms in a quaint, stone-built former coaching inn (owned by Shire Hotels). It is in an attractive village in the Ribble valley, near Blackburn. Residents' lounge (log fire), bar, *Millers* restaurant (emphasis on regional specialities); background music. Children welcomed. Parking. 23 bedrooms (6 in courtyard; 1 suitable for &.). B&B £49.50–£84.50 per person; D,B&B from £76.

## BLACKPOOL Lancashire
### Map 4:D2
**NUMBER ONE ST LUKES**, 1 St Lukes Road, South Shore, FY4 2EL. Tel 01253-343901, www.numberoneblackpool.com. In a quiet area on the South Shore, this detached house is run as a small, contemporary B&B by proprietors Mark and Claire Smith, who also own *Number One South Beach* on the promenade (see below). State-of-the-art design and gadgetry. Dining room. No background music. Garden. Ample parking. 3 bedrooms. B&B £60–£70 per person.

**NUMBER ONE SOUTH BEACH**, 4 Harrowside West, FY4 1NW. Tel 01253-343900, www.numberonesouthbeach.com. A well-equipped, low-carbon-footprint boutique hotel, with sea views over South Beach Promenade. It is owned by Claire and Mark Smith with Janet and Graham Oxley. Lounge, bar, restaurant; background music; pool table; meeting/conference facilities. Lift. Garden with putting green. Parking. 14 bedrooms (some with balcony; some with four-poster; disabled facilities). B&B £60–£140 per person.

**RAFFLES HOTEL & TEA ROOM**, 73–77 Hornby Road, FY1 4QJ. Tel 01253-294713, www.raffleshotelblackpool.co.uk. Close to the shops, the Winter Gardens and the promenade, Ian Balmforth (chef) and Graham Poole's small hotel and tea room has a colourful array of flowers around the bay-fronted windows. The furnishing is traditional. Lounge, bar, English tea room (closed Mon); classical background music. Parking. Children welcomed. 17 bedrooms, plus 3 apartment suites. B&B £34–£39 per person.

## BONCHURCH Isle of Wight
Map 2:E2

**WINTERBOURNE COUNTRY HOUSE**,
Bonchurch Village Road, PO38 1RQ.
Tel 01983-852535, www.winterbourne
house.co.uk. Charles Dickens wrote
*David Copperfield* while staying at
this sea-facing country house with
subtropical gardens. Public rooms have
recently been renovated; Andrew Eccott
and Andy Harper are the managers.
2 lounges, breakfast room, snug;
classical background music. Garden:
swimming pool, terrace, stream, private
path to small beach. 7 bedrooms. B&B
£60–£160 per person.

## BOSCASTLE Cornwall
Map 1:C3

**THE BOTTREAUX**, PL35 0BG. Tel 01840-
250231, www.boscastlecornwall.co.uk.
Most bedrooms have sea views at this
old white building at the top of the
village. Privately owned, it is 'expertly'
managed by Heather Graham.
'Recommended: very comfortable beds,
a large modern bathroom.' 'Excellent'
breakfast. Lounge, bar, restaurant
(background music; closed Sun and
Wed). 8 bedrooms. B&B £35–£50 per
person; D,B&B £59.50–£74.50.

**TREROSEWILL FARMHOUSE**, Paradise,
PL35 0BL. Tel 01840-250545, www.
trerosewill.co.uk. A hot tub with
panoramic views: Lunday Island is
visible while you soak on the raised
terrace of Steve and Cheryl Nicholls's
environmentally friendly B&B. Breakfast
is home made, using seasonal, local
produce; packed lunches are available. 2
lounges, conservatory dining room;
DVD/video library. No background
music. 1-acre garden; summer house;

hot tub. 9 bedrooms (3 suites; self-
catering apartment in converted dairy).
B&B £35–£45 per person.

## BOURNEMOUTH Dorset
Map 2:E2

**URBAN BEACH**, 23 Argyll Road,
BH5 1EB. Tel 01202-301509, www.
urbanbeachhotel.co.uk. Run by 'laid-
back' owner Mark Cribb, with manager
James Fowler, this contemporary,
relaxed hotel is close to Boscombe beach.
Individually decorated rooms have
modern comforts. Bar (large cocktail
list), bistro (local produce, home-made
bread); background music; seating deck.
Hotel guests get priority booking at a
new beachfront restaurant, *Urban Reef*.
Wi-Fi; DVD library; wellies, umbrellas.
Complimentary use of local gym. 12
bedrooms. B&B £35–£85 per person.
Dinner from £25.

## BOWNESS-ON-WINDERMERE
Cumbria
Map 4: inset C2

**LINDETH HOWE**, Lindeth Drive,
Longtail Hill, LA23 3JF. Tel 015394-
45759, www.lindeth-howe.co.uk.
Overlooking the lake, this country
house near the town was the home of
the Potter family in the early 20th
century. Beatrix wrote *The Tale of
Timmy Tiptoes* and *The Tale of Pigling
Bland* here. There is an award-
winning restaurant under chef Marc
Guibert; Alison Magee Barker is the
manager. Lounge, library, bar,
restaurant. Background music. Sun
terrace; swimming pool, sauna, fitness
room. 6-acre grounds. 34 bedrooms
(some on ground floor). B&B £60–£175
per person; D,B&B £114–£204.
**25% DISCOUNT VOUCHERS**

## BRADFORD-ON-AVON Wiltshire
## Map 2:D1
SWAN HOTEL, 1 Church Street, BA15 1LN. Tel 01225-868686, www. theswanbradford.co.uk. Beside a 14th-century bridge, this old country inn, in a black-and-white Grade II listed building, has been slickly modernised (muted colours, wooden floors, leather furniture). David Evans is the 'welcoming, attentive and hard-working' proprietor; Kevin King the newly appointed chef (Mediterranean-influenced food). Lounge, cellar bar, restaurant; patio. Background music. Function facilities. Parking. 12 bedrooms. B&B £42.50–£85 per person. Dinner £35–£40.
25% DISCOUNT VOUCHERS

WOOLLEY GRANGE, Woolley Green, BA15 1TX. Tel 01225-864705, www. woolleygrangehotel.co.uk. On the edge of the town, this Jacobean stone manor house is part of the von Essen family hotels group. Clare Hammond is the manager. There is much for children to do: a nursery for the youngest; games room, outdoor heated pool (indoor pool planned), trampoline, play area. Children's meals are served; parents can enjoy more sophisticated evening meals by chef Mark Bradbury, who uses produce from the kitchen garden. 2 lounges, TV room, bar, restaurant, conservatory. No background music. Function facilities. 26 bedrooms (7 in *Stone Cottage*, 2 in *Coach House*, 3 in *Pavilion* in grounds; 1 suitable for &.). B&B £90–£260 per person; D,B&B £160–£510.

## BRIDPORT Dorset
## Map 1:C6
THE BULL HOTEL, 34 East Street, DT6 3LF. Tel 01308-422878, www. thebullhotel.co.uk. In the centre of the market town, this Grade II listed former coaching inn is run as an informal café, bar and gastropub-with-rooms by Richard and Nikki Cooper. Bedrooms are 'glitzy'. Food (from chef Marc Montgomery) is 'good, popular with locals'. 2 bars (background music), restaurant; ballroom; private dining room; courtyard. Function facilities. Children welcomed. 14 eclectically styled bedrooms. B&B £40–£170 per person. Dinner from £36.

## BRIGHTON East Sussex
## Map 2:E4
FIVEHOTEL, 5 New Steine, BN2 1PB. Tel 01273-686547, www.fivehotel.com. The sea is a minute away, and it is a short stroll to The Lanes from Caroline and Simon Heath's contemporary B&B in a period town house on a Kemp Town Regency square. 'Lovely room. We watched the sun sparkle on the water, the yachts race in the bay.' 2 public rooms; roof terrace. Communal 'Sussex' breakfasts (local, organic ingredients; no background music). Wi-Fi; DVD library. 10 bedrooms (some with sea views). B&B £40–£75 per person.

## BUCKFASTLEIGH Devon
## Map 1:D4
KILBURY MANOR, Colston Road, TQ11 0LN. Tel 01364-644079, www. kilburymanor.co.uk. 'Outstandingly kind and welcoming', Julia and Martin Blundell and their dogs, Dillon and Buster, receive visitors at their renovated

17th-century longhouse in the Dart valley. 'Rooms are tastefully furnished and offer guests all the comfort they need.' There are peaceful areas to sit in the garden and courtyard, and direct access to the river from a meadow. Breakfast room. No background music. Wi-Fi. Children over 8 allowed. 4 bedrooms (2 in the converted stone barn; plus one 1-bedroom cottage). B&B £42.50–£50 per person.

**BUCKHORN WESTON Dorset**
**Map 2:D1**
THE STAPLETON ARMS, Church Hill, SP8 5HS. Tel 01963-370396, www.thestapletonarms.com. In a village on the fringes of Blackmore Vale, this old coaching inn has been transformed by hospitable owner Kav Javvi into a stylishly modern pub with an unpretentious atmosphere. Walls are painted in vibrant colours; there are comfy sofas, old wooden tables and open fires; wellies for walkers. Bar, dining room (Mediterranean-influenced food). No background music. Terrace; garden. Children welcomed. 4 bedrooms. B&B £45–£96 per person. Dinner £30.

**BUDE Cornwall**
**Map 1:C3**
BANGORS ORGANIC, Poundstock, EX23 0DP. Tel 01288-361297, www.bangorsorganic.co.uk. Gill and Neil Faiers are passionate about organic food. Their B&B and restaurant (open to non-residents) is on a five-acre holding on the unspoiled north Cornish coast. They provide 'carbon-neutral' home-grown food, solar-heated water and green electricity. Background music 'when requested'. Rooms are plainly furnished, with stylish bathroom (roll-top bath; wet room). Wood fires. No smoking in grounds. Widemouth Bay beach nearby. Garden and farmland. Holistic treatments. 4 contemporary bedrooms (2 suites in coach house; 1 suitable for ♿). B&B £50–£120 per person. Dinner £25.

**BUNGAY Suffolk**
**Map 2:B6**
EARSHAM PARK FARM, Old Railway Road, Earsham, NR35 2AQ. Tel 01986-892180, www.earsham-parkfarm.co.uk. Bobbie and Simon Watchorn's homely Victorian farmhouse has sweeping views over Waveney valley. It stands on a 600-acre working farm (arable crops, free-range pig herd). Breakfast is taken at a communal table. Lounge, dining room. No background music. Garden. Children, dogs and horses welcomed. 3 bedrooms. B&B £37.50–£47.50 per person.
**25% DISCOUNT VOUCHERS**

**BURFORD Oxfordshire**
**Map 2:C2**
THE HIGHWAY INN, 117 High Street, OX18 4RG. Tel 01993-823661, www.thehighwayinn.co.uk. Friendly owners Scott and Tally Nelson have renovated this informal inn (dating back to 1480), retaining its carved stone entrance, low beams, stone walls, ancient flagging and creaky sloping floors. In the centre, it is a popular hub with locals for drinking, dining (home-cooked, modern British, Cotswold food) and for takeaway fish and chips (Sun to Wed nights). Bar, restaurant; private dining room; 'medieval' courtyard (alfresco dining). Children and dogs welcomed. 10 bedrooms. B&B £44.50–£79 per person. Dinner £30.

## BURY ST EDMUNDS Suffolk
## Map 2:B5

THE ANGEL HOTEL, Angel Hill, IP33
1LT. Tel 01284-714000, www.theangel.
co.uk. Overlooking the cathedral, this
historic ivy-covered coaching inn has
been run by the Gough family for more
than 20 years; Lynn Cowan is the
manager. The design is contemporary,
with modern art. A popular eating place
with locals. Lounge (log fire), bar,
restaurant (Simon Barker serves modern
'attractively presented' British food, and
'generous portions'); background music.
Function facilities. Child-friendly. Dogs
welcomed (£5 charge). 75 bedrooms
(some with views of Abbey gardens
and ruins). B&B £50–£150 per person.
Dinner £40.

OUNCE HOUSE, Northgate Street, IP33
1HP. Tel 01284-761779,
www.ouncehouse.co.uk. There is a
homely atmosphere at Simon and Jenny
Pott's spacious Victorian merchant's
house which they run as a B&B. It is
traditionally furnished with antiques
and period furniture, photographs and
knick-knacks. Drawing room (honesty
bar), snug/bar/library. Communal
breakfasts. No background music.
Wi-Fi. Parking. 5 bedrooms (quietest
2 face ¾-acre walled garden). B&B £60–
£95 per person.

## BUXTON Derbyshire
## Map 3:A6

GRENDON, Bishops Lane, SK17 6UN.
Tel 01298-78831, www.grendonguest
house.co.uk. Hilary and Colin Parker
run this welcoming B&B with spacious
rooms, on a quiet country lane near the
town. Lounge, breakfast room (home-
made bread and muesli); terrace. No

background music. 1-acre garden
overlooking golf course. Parking.
Wi-Fi. 5 bedrooms. B&B £30–£47
per person.

HARTINGTON HALL, Hall Bank,
SK17 0AT. Tel 0845-371 9740,
www.yha.org.uk/hartington. In
extensive grounds on the edge of
Dovedale, this youth hostel has a
distinguished setting: an old manor
house (1611) with mullioned
windows, oak panelling and log fires.
Accommodation is spread over three
buildings (main house, coach house,
barn). It is managed by William
Greenwood. Lounge, bar, restaurant
(traditional English, local ingredients);
background music; games room, self-
catering kitchen, drying room, meeting
rooms; beer garden; adventure
playground; pet area. Civil wedding
licence. 35 bedrooms (19 en suite; 10 in
barn annexe, 5 in coach house; 1 suitable
for &). B&B from £12–£35 per person.
Dinner £12.50.

## BYLAND North Yorkshire
## Map 4:D4

THE ABBEY INN, Byland Abbey, nr
Coxwold, YO61 4BD. Tel 01347-868204,
www.bylandabbeyinn.com. By the ruins
of Byland Abbey ('romantic and
majestic, and when floodlit at night,
quite breathtaking'), this 'very pretty'
12th-century inn was given an elaborate
make-over by English Heritage. It is
leased to Melanie and TJ Drew. There
are 'lots of extras' in the rooms
(bathrobes and slippers, Madeira, sweets
and biscuits, an honesty bar, luxury
toiletries), and 'immaculate' bathrooms.
Much of the furniture is 'Mouseman',
made in the nearby village of Kilburn.

Background music. 3 dining rooms *Abbey Cider*, *Brown Brothers* and *Louis Roederer* (named after favourite drinks). 1-acre garden; patio. Licensed for weddings. 3 bedrooms (accessed by outside stairs). B&B £50–£160 per person. Dinner from £28.

### CADNAM Hampshire
Map 2:E2

TWIN OAKS, Southampton Road, SO40 2NQ. Tel 02380-812305, www. twinoaks-guesthouse.co.uk. Guests can walk straight into the woods from the gardens surrounding Carol Gerrett and Chris Perry's homely New Forest house. Inside are flagstone floors, exposed oak beams, and an original bread oven in the inglenook fireplace; bedrooms are cosy. The owners are committed to good environmental management. Southampton is 10 minutes' drive away. Lounge, breakfast room. Classical background music. Wi-Fi. Children welcomed. 6 bedrooms (1 on ground floor; ramp). B&B £35–£50 per person.

### CAMBER East Sussex
Map 2:E5

THE PLACE AT THE BEACH, Camber Sands, New Lydd Road, TN31 7RB. Tel 01797-225057, www.theplaceatthebeach. co.uk. Opposite the dunes of a huge sandy beach near Rye, this white, single-storey building (owned by Harry Cragoe and Tudor Hopkins, the manager) has a 'driftwood' decor. Sitting room, brasserie (seasonal produce; background jazz/classical music); conference facilities. Terrace; decked area. Children welcomed. 18 bedrooms (all on ground floor). B&B £42.50–£62.50 per person. Dinner £30.

### CAMBRIDGE Cambridgeshire
Map 2:B4

HOTEL FELIX, Whitehouse Lane, Huntingdon Road, CB3 0LX. Tel 01223-277977, www.hotelfelix.co.uk. On the edge of the city, this extended late Victorian, yellow brick mansion with a contemporary interior stands in spacious grounds. Shara Ross is the manager. Small lounge, bar, *Graffiti* restaurant overlooking terrace and garden; Tom Stewart has taken over as chef, serving modern Mediterranean dishes; background music. Function facilities. Children welcomed. 4-acre garden, terrace, gazebo. Parking. 52 bedrooms (4 suitable for &). B&B (continental) £95–£152.50 per person; D,B&B £99. Cooked breakfast £7.50, dinner from £30. **25% DISCOUNT VOUCHERS**

### CAMPSEA ASHE Suffolk
Map 2:C6

THE OLD RECTORY, Station Road, IP13 0PU. Tel 01728-746524, www. theoldrectorysuffolk.com. 'A delightful find', Sally Ball's Georgian rectory in a rural setting has 'wonderful', tranquil gardens. A family home, it has a modern interior; log fires, traditional four-poster beds, cast iron baths. Organic produce is sourced for the meals. Sitting room, dining room, conservatory; terrace. No background music. 8 miles NE of Woodbridge. 7 bedrooms (1 on ground floor; dogs allowed in 2 garden rooms). B&B £42.50–£70; D,B&B £70–£97.50 (Mon–Fri).

### CANTERBURY Kent
Map 2:D5

EBURY HOTEL, 65–67 New Dover Road, CT1 3DX. Tel 01227-768433, www.ebury-hotel.co.uk. The owner of this 'splendid' Victorian house, Henry Mason, is from a family who have been hoteliers for 100 years. It is well located, one mile south of the centre and the cathedral. 'Spacious' bedrooms are traditionally furnished; the staff are friendly; 'very good food'. Lounge, restaurant (French cuisine from Jean-Pierre Cabrol using local produce). Background music. Wi-Fi. Indoor swimming pool. Large grounds. Parking. Children and dogs welcomed. Charlie, the labradoodle, has his own web page. 15 bedrooms; self-catering cottages. B&B £40–£85 per person; D,B&B £60–£105.

**MAGNOLIA HOUSE**, 36 St Dunstan's Terrace, CT2 8AX. Tel 01227-765121, www.magnoliahousecanterbury.co.uk. In a residential street close to the centre, Isobelle Leggett's Georgian guest house has been extensively renovated, with new bathrooms. She serves dinner by arrangement in winter; no licence, bring your own bottle. Sitting room, dining room (background music). Wi-Fi. Walled garden. Parking. No children under 12. 6 bedrooms (some four-poster beds). B&B £47.50–£65 per person.

**CASTLE COMBE** Wiltshire
**Map 2:D1**
**THE CASTLE INN**, nr Chippenham, SN14 3HN. Tel 01249-783030, www. castle-inn.info. In the market place of one of England's prettiest villages, this old inn, in several cobbled-together buildings, has been sympathetically renovated. It is owned by Ann and Bill Cross and managed by Joanne Worsley. Chef Jamie Gemmell's modern dishes are served in an elegant green candlelit dining room. 2 lounges, bar, dining room, conservatory breakfast room; small courtyard. Background music. Children welcomed. 11 bedrooms. B&B £55–£115 per person. Dinner £40.

**CHARMOUTH** Dorset
**Map 1:C6**
**THE ABBOTS HOUSE**, The Street, DT6 6QF. Tel 01297-560339, www. abbotshouse.co.uk. Many original features have been retained in the renovation of Sheila and Nick Gilbey's restaurant-with-rooms, in a house with medieval origins. They have created comfortable colour-coordinated bedrooms, equipped with state-of-the-art fittings. There is a flat-screen TV in bathrooms, a sophisticated sound system and up-to-date heating and plumbing. Close to the centre, it is a short walk to the beach. Lounge, restaurant (local produce, fusion cooking; supper picnics on Sun and Mon; open to non-residents on Fri and Sat evenings), garden room. Background music. 4 bedrooms. B&B from £80 per person. Dinner £24–£28.

**CHELTENHAM** Gloucestershire
**Map 3:D5**
**BEAUMONT HOUSE**, 56 Shurdington Road, GL53 0JE. Tel 01242-223311, www.bhhotel.co.uk. In large gardens, south of the city, Alan Bishop's B&B is in a cream-painted house built as a grand family home for a wealthy Victorian merchant. Bedrooms and bathrooms are modern and stylish; two (Out of Asia and Out of Africa) are themed and have a whirlpool bath. Complimentary tea, coffee and biscuits and an honesty bar are available in the lounge. Dinner can be served in the bedroom between Mon and Thurs. Breakfast is taken in

the dining room, which overlooks the flowery garden. Lounge (background music/local radio). Wi-Fi. Parking. 16 bedrooms. B&B £39–£99.50 per person.

**THE CHELTENHAM TOWNHOUSE**, 12–14 Pittville Lawn, GL52 2BD. Tel 01242-221922, www.cheltenhamtownhouse. com. Adam and Jayne Lillywhite's B&B in a grand Regency building has a 'good location', a short walk from Pittville Pump Rooms. It has been given an elegant contemporary interior; 'comfortable and quiet'. Lounge (honesty bar), breakfast room (background music); sun deck. Lift. Wi-Fi. Children welcomed. Parking. 22 bedrooms. B&B £32.50–£60 per person.

**HANOVER HOUSE**, 65 St. George's Road, GL50 3DU. Tel 01242-541297, www. hanoverhouse.org. 'Beautiful, and full of interesting objects', this elegant Italianate-style house (Wolsey Lodges) is the home of 'charming' Veronica Ritchie and her husband, James. It has a 'splendidly varied selection of books'. Bedrooms are comfortable; organic breakfasts are taken at a communal table. It is close to the centre; helpful advice is offered on local restaurants. Drawing room (open fire in winter), breakfast room. Classical background music. Wi-Fi. 3 bedrooms: B&B £45–£70 per person.

**HOTEL DU VIN CHELTENHAM**, Parabola Road, GL50 3AQ. Tel 01242-588450, www.hotelduvin.com. Within an imposing, white-painted facade, in the fashionable Montpellier district, this modern hotel is managed by Tom Ross. There are spacious public areas around a showpiece spiral staircase. *Champagne* and *Grain and Grape* bars, bistro; function facilities; alfresco dining. No background music. Wi-Fi. Spa, beauty treatment rooms. Children welcomed. 49 bedrooms: £145–£285. Breakfast £10.95–£13.95, dinner from £40.

**THIRTY TWO**, 32 Imperial Square, GL50 1QZ. Tel 01242-771110, www. thirtytwoltd.com. Designers Jonathan Sellwood and Jonathan Parkin have created a stunning contemporary interior at their town house on a beautiful Georgian square overlooking Imperial Gardens. They run it as a small, relaxed B&B, and a showcase for their design business and shop, where lighting, furniture, accessories, scents and fragrances can be purchased. Drawing room, breakfast room (soft background music). Parking. 4 bedrooms. B&B £77–£189 per person.

## CHESTER Cheshire
### Map 3:A4
**THE CHESTER GROSVENOR AND SPA**, Eastgate, CH1 1LT. Tel 01244-324024, www.chestergrosvenor.com. In the historic centre, near the Roman walls and the cathedral, this luxury hotel has a timbered facade (Grade II listed), and an elegant modern interior. It is owned by the Duke of Westminster; Ross Grieve is the manager. Lounge, *Arkle* bar, restaurant *Simon Radley at The Chester Grosvenor* (*Michelin* star, 'an experience not to be missed'), *La Brasserie*. Background music. Function facilities. Spa (crystal steam room, herb sauna, themed shower, ice fountain). 80 bedrooms and suites (*excluding VAT*): £205–£855. Breakfast £20, dinner £35–£80.

**GREEN BOUGH**, 60 Hoole Road, CH2 3NL. Tel 01244-326241, www.chestergreenboughhotel.com. One mile from the city centre, Janice and Philip Martin's 'well-run' conversion of two Victorian town houses has a rooftop garden and water feature. Lounge, bar, *Olive Tree* restaurant (Neil Griffiths is chef), function room, conference suite. Background music (classical, jazz). 15 bedrooms (8 in lodge, linked by feature bridge; some suitable for &). Off-street parking. B&B £87.50–£172.50 per person; D,B&B £97.50.

## CHICHESTER West Sussex
### Map 2:E3
**CROUCHERS**, Birdham Road, PO20 7EH. Tel 01243-784995, www.croucherscountryhotel.com. South African owners Lloyd van Rooyen and Gavin Wilson have given their hotel a 'sophisticated rustic' decor; there are wooden beams and soaring rafters in the dining room, brightly coloured furniture in the public areas, neutral shades in the bedrooms. Previously known as *Crouchers Bottom*, it is in separate buildings three miles south of the town centre. Patios and grassy areas overlook farmland, and give 'plenty of scope for relaxing'. 'Cooking and menus are varied and delectable.' Lounge, bar, restaurant (no background music); courtyard; 2-acre garden. Wi-Fi. Wedding, function facilities. 26 bedrooms (in coach house, barn and stables; back ones are quieter). B&B £55–£75 per person; D,B&B £80–£100.

**THE SHIP**, North Street, PO19 1NH. Tel 01243-778000, www.theshiphotel.net. Within the city's old Roman walls, and convenient for the theatre

(five minutes' walk), this Georgian building (Grade II listed) has a circular Adam staircase and striking black-and-white flooring. The bedrooms and brasserie (pale wood, leather and suede) have been revamped in modern style. It is privately owned; the manager is Patrick Burfield. Bar, brasserie (Mark Evans is chef; background music, piano) with conservatory (light oak floor, tub seating); conference facilities. Lift. Wi-Fi. Parking. 36 bedrooms (on 3 floors; some family). B&B £49.50–£75 per person; D,B&B £65–£77.50.
**25% DISCOUNT VOUCHERS**

## CHIDDINGFOLD Surrey
### Map 2:D3
**THE CROWN INN**, The Green, Petworth Road, GU8 4TX. Tel 01428-682255, www.thecrownchiddingfold.com. On the village green, this cream-painted 14th-century inn is 'everyone's idea of an English country pub'. Recently renovated, it has dark oak beams, sloping floors, 'passageways, a bit like a rabbit warren', wood-panelled walls and stained glass windows. 'Breakfast was excellent.' 2 bars, restaurant (background music/radio); courtyard. 8 bedrooms (front ones hear traffic). B&B £62.50–£100 per person. Dinner £35.
**25% DISCOUNT VOUCHERS**

## CHRISTCHURCH Dorset
### Map 2:E2
**CAPTAIN'S CLUB HOTEL**, Wick Ferry, Wick Lane, Mudeford, BH23 1HU. Tel 01202-475111, www.captainsclubhotel.com. On Christchurch Quay, this modern metal and glass spa hotel, has a style-conscious interior and panoramic

views over the harbour. It is owned by Robert Wilson and Timothy Lloyd. Lounge, bar, *Tides* restaurant; terrace (Andrew Gault is chef; alfresco dining); function facilities. Background music. Spa (pool, sauna; treatments). Lift. Wi-Fi. Children welcomed. 29 bedrooms (12 apartments; some suitable for &). B&B £114.50 per person; D,B&B £144.40.

## CLEARWELL Gloucestershire
Map 3:D5
**TUDOR FARMHOUSE**, GL16 8JS. Tel 01594-833046, www.tudorfarmhouse hotel.co.uk. 'Full of character', Hari and Colin Fell's converted farm, parts of which date back to the 13th century, has massive oak beams, an inglenook fireplace, original oak panelling and a spiral staircase. 'A warm atmosphere, with friendly, professional staff who looked after us well.' Bedrooms vary in size: some are in the attic, some in the cider house and the converted barn. In a quiet village in the Royal Forest of Dean, it is a short walk from Clearwell Castle. 2 lounges, restaurant (background music in evening). Wi-Fi. Parking. Children and dogs welcomed. 20 bedrooms (some with four-poster beds and spa bath). B&B £45–£65 per person; D,B&B £72.50–£92.50.
**25% DISCOUNT VOUCHERS**

## COLCHESTER Essex
Map 2:C5
**PRESTED HALL**, Feering, CO5 9EE. Tel 01376-573300, www.prested.co.uk. With 15th-century origins, this part-moated manor house has an Arts and Crafts interior and, unusually, two real tennis courts. It stands within extensive parkland with an orchard, as well as organic vegetable and fruit gardens. It is managed by Rachel Bones; Chris Jagger is the chef. Reception room, drawing room/library, restaurant, bistro, private dining. Background music. Leisure suite (indoor pool, sauna, steam room; flotation tank planned; beauty and holistic treatments). Wi-Fi. Function facilities in *The Orangery*. Children welcomed. 10 bedrooms (6 serviced 1- and 2-bedroom apartments in health club building; 1-bed luxury retreat The Dingle). B&B £40–£90 per person; D,B&B £60–£110.
**25% DISCOUNT VOUCHERS**

## CORFE CASTLE Dorset
Map 2:E1
**THE PURBECK VINEYARD**, Harmans Cross, BH20 5HU. Tel 01929-481525, www.vineyard.uk.com. On their working vineyard, which is open for tasting tours and wine sales, Rob and Theresa Steel offer B&B in striking bedrooms (some with balcony) overlooking lovely countryside. The Swanage Steam Railway runs at the bottom of the valley. Locally sourced ingredients are used for Laszlo Cselik's cooking. 2 lounges, restaurant (closed Mon). Patio. Background music. Garden; parkland. Civil wedding licence. Children welcomed. 9 bedrooms. B&B £55–£85 per person; D,B&B £75.

## CRANBROOK Kent
Map 2:E4
**CLOTH HALL OAST**, Coursehorn Lane, TN17 3NR. Tel 01580-712220, www.clothhalloast.co.uk. Katherine Morgan's 'impeccable' converted oast house stands in 'spectacular' grounds on a peaceful estate in the Weald of Kent. She is a 'helpful and knowledgeable'

hostess, advising on places to visit and things to do. The dining room has three galleried floors above, and an impressive wrought iron chandelier. Sitting room, dining room (no background music); decked terrace; heated outdoor pool, fishpond, pergola; croquet. 3 bedrooms. B&B £45–£65 per person. Dinner £25.
25% DISCOUNT VOUCHERS

**CRAYKE North Yorkshire**
**Map 4:D4**
THE DURHAM OX, Westway, YO61 4TE. Tel 01347-821506, www.thedurhamox. com. There are stunning views over the vale of York from Mike and Sasha Ibbotson's 300-year-old pub-with-rooms. The style is traditional, with exposed beams, carved wood panelling, inglenook fireplace and a fire in the wood-burning stove in winter. Food is unpretentious, specialising in Crayke game, local meats, fresh fish and seafood dishes. 2 bars (*Bottom* and *Top*), restaurant; private dining room; function facilities in separate marquee. Background music. Children and dogs welcomed. Convenient for Park and Ride into York. 5 bedrooms (1 suite, accessed from external stairs; others in converted farm cottages; 2 on ground floor). B&B £40–£80 per person. Dinner £26.50.

**CROMER Norfolk**
**Map 2:A5**
NORTHREPPS COTTAGE, Nut lane, Northrepps, NR27 0JN. Tel 01263-579202, www.northreppscottage.co.uk. Built in 1793, Deborah and Simon Gurney's peaceful country house, near Cromer on the north Norfolk coast, stands in gardens designed by Humphry Repton. The public rooms are contemporary in style; bedrooms have touches of luxury. Matt Galasky is the manager. Lounge bar (*Humphry's*), *Repton's* restaurant (the chef is Howard Bowen). Background music. Wi-Fi. 7 bedrooms (1 suitable for &). B&B £61–£75 per person; D,B&B £25 added.
25% DISCOUNT VOUCHERS

**DARLINGTON Co. Durham**
**Map 4:C4**
HEADLAM HALL, nr Gainford, DL2 3HA. Tel 01325-730238, www. headlamhall.co.uk. *The Orangery* restaurant is a recent addition to the Robinson family's handsome 17th-century country house in rolling countryside near Darlington. It has a Jacobean hall, stone walls, huge fireplaces, traditional furnishing. 3 lounges, drawing room, bar, restaurant (classical/jazz background music). Lift. Spa (pool, sauna, gym, treatment rooms). Terraces. 4-acre walled garden: lake, ornamental canal; tennis, 9-hole golf course, croquet. Children welcomed. 40 bedrooms (6 in mews, 9 in coach house, 7 in spa; 2 suitable for &). B&B £57.50–£95 per person; D,B&B £79–£82.

**DARTMOUTH Devon**
**Map 1:D4**
BROWNS, 27–29 Victoria Road, TQ6 9RT. Tel 01803-832572, www. brownshoteldartmouth.co.uk. Clare and James Brown's contemporary hotel (managed by Robin Tozer) is up a side street, within easy reach of the seafront. The bedrooms are decorated in 'fun' style; the atmosphere is informal. Lounge, bar (open fire, squashy sofas), restaurant (Mediterranean-inspired dishes). Modern/jazz background music.

Children welcomed. 10 bedrooms. B&B £45–£90 per person; D,B&B from £49.50.

**THE NEW ANGEL**, 51 Victoria Road, TQ6 9BH. Tel 01803-839425, www. thenewangel.co.uk. On the riverfront, Clive Jacobs's restaurant has six well-equipped bedrooms in a house nearby. Nathan Thomas, sous-chef at the *Ledbury* (two *Michelin* stars) in London, was appointed chef in 2010. The restaurant is on two floors, with an open kitchen, and a more intimate dining area above. Lounge, dining room. No background music. 6 bedrooms. B&B £42.50–£62.50 per person. Dinner £25–£33.50.

## DEDHAM Essex
### Map 2:C5
**MAISON TALBOOTH**, Stratford Road, CO7 6HN. Tel 01206-322367, www. milsomhotels.com. In Constable country, this Victorian mansion is run as a hotel by the Milsom family. Guests may eat at the family's restaurant, *Le Talbooth*, and hotel/brasserie, *milsom's*, both nearby. Daniel Courtney is the manager. Large drawing room, *Garden Room* (breakfasts, light lunches; no background music). Ramp. 2-acre grounds: heated outdoor pool; sun terrace; hot tub; tennis court; beauty treatment rooms. Available for private house parties. Children welcomed. 12 bedrooms (some on ground floor). B&B (continental) from £100 per person; D,B&B from £145.
**25% DISCOUNT VOUCHERS**

## DERBY Derbyshire
### Map 2:A2
**CATHEDRAL QUARTER**, 16 St Mary's Gate, DE1 3JR. Tel 01332-546080, www.cathedralquarterhotel.com. Near the cathedral, these Grade II

listed buildings (the former council offices, a bank vault and a police station) have been turned into a contemporary hotel. Interesting features (a Scaglioli marble staircase, ornate ceilings, stained-glass windows) have been retained. Part of the Finesse Collection, it is managed by Ben Orton. Lounge, *Sixteen* bar, *Opulence* restaurant (chef Dean Crews cooks modern British dishes); small conference facilities; spa. Background music. Wi-Fi. 38 bedrooms (some with cathedral views; 2 adapted for &). B&B from £55 per person. Dinner from £40.

## DITTISHAM Devon
### Map 1:D4
**FINGALS**, Coombe, Dartmouth, TQ6 0JA. Tel 01803-722398, www.fingals. co.uk. In countryside near Dartmouth, Richard and Sheila Johnston welcome families to their extended old farmhouse, a 'quirky, relaxed place'. The public rooms in the old house have inglenook fireplaces, oak beams, wood panelling. Dinner is generally served at one long table in the oak-panelled dining room, but can be taken at separate tables in a smaller room. Food is locally sourced with an emphasis on organic produce. Lounge, dining room, honesty bar, library. Indoor heated pool with partly removable roof, spa bath, sauna; orangery, summer house; grass tennis court, croquet lawn; games room. 11 bedrooms (2 family suites). B&B £50–£85 per person; D,B&B £80–£100.

## DODDISCOMBSLEIGH Devon
### Map 1:C4
**THE NOBODY INN**, nr Exeter, EX6 7PS. Tel 01647-252394, www.nobodyinn.co.uk. 'Although it takes a little bit of finding,

it was worthwhile as a stop-over.' Hidden amid hills and fields, in a village near Exeter, Susan Burdge's 16th-century inn has inglenook fireplaces, beams and memorabilia. 2 bars, restaurant. Small cottage garden, patio. Over 250 whiskies and wines are served. No background music. 5 bedrooms (all with DVD-player). B&B £45–£65 per person. Dinner £25.

**DORCHESTER Dorset**
Map 1:D6
**THE KING'S ARMS**, 30 High Street, DT1 1HF. Tel 01305-265353, www.kingsarmsdorchester.com. Chef/proprietor Simon Monsai's porticoed Georgian coaching inn (Best Western) in the town centre. 'The standard of accommodation (country house decoration with four-poster beds; smart, modern bathrooms) exceeded our expectations.' Bar, 'superb' restaurant ('easy listening' background music; 'fresh and local' food supplies). Function facilities. Civil wedding licence. Wi-Fi. Parking. 37 bedrooms. B&B from £47.50 per person. Dinner £45.

**DOVER Kent**
Map 2:D5
**LODDINGTON HOUSE**, 14 East Cliff, CT16 1LX. Tel 01304-201947, www.loddingtonhousehotel.co.uk. Kathy Cupper and her son, Robert, run this guest house in a Regency Grade II listed property overlooking the harbour. 'Dinner superb. High standard of cleanliness.' Some traffic noise. Lounge (balcony with sea view), dining room (evening meal by arrangement, £25). No background music. Small garden. 6 bedrooms (4 en suite; rear ones quietest). B&B £32.50–£55 per person.

**DULVERTON Somerset**
Map 1:B5
**THREE ACRES COUNTRY HOUSE**, Brushford, TA22 9AR. Tel 01398-323730, www.threeacrescountryhouse.co.uk. On the edge of Exmoor, Julie and Edward Christian's hillside hideaway is in mature grounds, overlooking a peaceful village. Bedrooms have a large bed, lovely views; a fridge. Sitting room with open fire, bar, dining/breakfast room (wholesome breakfasts, with home-grown fruit from berry garden; light meals by arrangement); sun terrace. No background music. Wi-Fi. Picnic hampers; 2 miles S of Dulverton. Country pursuits arranged. Children welcomed. The house is also available for exclusive use. 6 bedrooms (1 on ground floor). B&B £45–£75 per person.
**25% DISCOUNT VOUCHERS**

**DURHAM Co. Durham**
Map 4:B4
**CATHEDRAL VIEW**, 212 Gilesgate, DH1 1QN. Tel 0191-386 9566, www.cathedralview.co.uk. With 'great views across Durham', Jim and Karen Garfitt's B&B in a traditionally furnished Georgian merchant's house is well located for city sightseeing. 'Good' breakfasts. No background music. Lounge. Garden, with seating. Wi-Fi. Children over 12 allowed. 6 bedrooms. B&B £40–£90.
**25% DISCOUNT VOUCHERS**

**EAST GRINSTEAD West Sussex**
Map 2:D4
**GRAVETYE MANOR**, Vowels Lane, RH19 4LJ. Tel 01342-810567, www.gravetyemanor.co.uk. Now owned by Jeremy Hoskings, and managed by Amy Gleadow, this creeper-clad Elizabethan manor house stands amid

'magic' gardens (designed by William Robinson, pioneer of the English natural garden). It has oak-panelled rooms, highly polished furniture and rich fabrics. 2 sitting rooms, bar; private dining rooms, gazebo (for 8 people dining). No background music. 35-acre grounds. 18 bedrooms (1 on ground floor): £200–£355; D,B&B £170 per person (Oct–Apr). Breakfast £13.
**25% DISCOUNT VOUCHERS**

**EASTBOURNE East Sussex**
**Map 2:E4**
**THE BIG SLEEP**, King Edwards Parade, BN21 4EB. Tel 01323-722676, www.thebigsleephotel.com. On the seafront, this funky hotel has a brightly coloured retro-style interior. It is part owned by Cosmo Fry and John Malkovich. Breakfast is self-service in the canteen-like dining room. Lounge, bar (background music); ping-pong, pool, darts. Wi-Fi. Children and dogs welcomed. 50 bedrooms. B&B (continental) £29.50–£70 per person.

**GRAND HOTEL**, King Edwards Parade, BN21 4EQ. Tel 01323-412345, www.grandeastbourne.com. Around the corner from the cliffs of Beachy Head (Debussy completed *La Mer* here in 1905), this huge white edifice embodies the grandeur of the Victorian seaside hotel. 'The spaciousness takes one's breath away.' Traditions are maintained: monthly teatime Palm Court quartet; a live band at weekends. Children welcomed (playroom, carers, high teas). 3 lounges, bar, *Mirabelle* and *Garden* restaurants (both with background music); conference/function facilities; health spa; heated indoor and outdoor swimming pools; 2-acre garden: putting,

etc. Parking. 152 bedrooms (many with sea view). B&B £97.50–£270 per person; D,B&B £130–£302.50.
**25% DISCOUNT VOUCHERS**

**OCKLYNGE MANOR**, Mill Road, BN21 2PG. Tel 01323-734121, www.ocklyngemanor.co.uk. Wendy Dugdill's fairy-pink Georgian mansion (built on the site of a monastery of the Knights of the Order of St John of Jerusalem) stands amid gardens with sunny and shaded places to sit. It provides comfortable accommodation and organic breakfasts (home-made bread and marmalade). The seafront is one mile away. Sitting room. No background music. Walled garden. Parking. Wi-Fi. DVD-players. 3 bedrooms. B&B £40–£80 per person.

**FALMOUTH Cornwall**
**Map 1:E2**
**THE GREENBANK**, Harbourside, TR11 2SR. Tel 01326-312440, www.greenbank-hotel.co.uk. Many of the bedrooms and public rooms at this hotel, overlooking the Fal estuary, have sea or river views. Kearan McVey is the manager; chef Sanjay Kumar uses local ingredients (rock lobsters caught from the hotel pier) for his menus for the *Harbourside* restaurant. Wi-Fi. Lounge, bar, restaurant (background music), function suite. 1½-acre gardens. Children welcomed. 60 bedrooms (some suitable for &). B&B £64.50–£89 per person. Dinner £30–£35.

**THE ROSEMARY**, 22 Gyllyngvase Terrace, TR11 4DL. Tel 01326-314669, www.therosemary.co.uk. Niall and Nikki MacDougall have recently taken over and renovated this B&B in a white-walled Edwardian house, a short walk from the town centre and a two-minute stroll to the beach. There are displays of contemporary Cornish artists on the walls, and sea views from most rooms. Bar, lounge, dining room (no background music); south-facing garden, sun deck. Wi-Fi. Children welcomed. Closed end Dec until Feb. B&B £39–£45 per person.

**FOLKESTONE Kent**
Map 2:E5
THE RELISH, 4 Augusta Gardens, CT20 2RR. Tel 01303-850952, www.hotelrelish.co.uk. Close to the town centre, this grand 1850s merchant's house has been given a contemporary interior by Sarah and Chris van Dyke, who run it as a B&B. Complimentary coffee or tea with home-made cake, or a glass of wine or beer is offered on arrival. Lounge (with open fire), breakfast room (Radio 2 played). Wi-Fi. Small terrace. Families welcomed. Direct access to private 4-acre Augusta Gardens. Parking. 10 bedrooms. B&B £45–£70 per person.

**FROGGATT EDGE Derbyshire**
Map 3:A6
THE CHEQUERS INN, Hope Valley, S32 3ZJ. Tel 01433-630231, www.chequers-froggatt.com. Beneath Froggatt Edge in a 'lovely area for walks straight from the hotel', this Grade II listed 16th-century inn is owned by Jonathan and Joanne Tindall, and managed by Debbie Robinson. A new chef, Karim Maoui, serves local food in a pub-style dining room or alfresco in the elevated garden. 'Good service and a friendly, relaxed atmosphere.' Background music ('discreet classical'). Garden.

Children welcomed. Overlooks a busy road. 5 bedrooms. B&B £37.50–£50. Dinner from £35.

**GATWICK West Sussex**
Map 2:D4
LANGSHOTT MANOR, Ladbroke Road, Langshott, RH6 9LN. Tel 01293-786680, www.alexanderhotels.co.uk. In landscaped grounds close to Gatwick airport, this timber-framed Tudor house has original features (exposed beams and oak panelling), and modern luxuries. It is managed by Matthew Callard. Elegant public rooms; log fires. Some bedrooms have a four-poster and feature fireplace. 2 lounges, bar, *Mulberry* restaurant (Phil Dixon is chef; background music); conference facilities; civil wedding licence. Wi-Fi. Children welcomed. 22 bedrooms (7 in mews; 8 across garden). B&B £75–£160 per person. Dinner £42.
25% DISCOUNT VOUCHERS

**GRANGE-OVER-SANDS Cumbria**
Map 4: inset C2
CLARE HOUSE, Park Road, LA11 7HQ. Tel 015395-33026, www.clarehousehotel.co.uk. The Read family have owned and run this 'delightful', traditional Victorian hotel with wonderful views over Morecambe Bay for more than 40 years. Food is 'outstanding; excellent 4-course breakfast, including home-made croissants'; the welcome is 'very friendly'. 2 lounges, dining room. No background music. Parking. ½-acre grounds. Mile-long promenade at bottom of garden (bowling greens, tennis courts, putting green; easy access to Ornamental Gardens). 18 bedrooms (1 on ground floor suitable for ♿). B&B £61–£65 per person; D,B&B £81–£85.
25% DISCOUNT VOUCHERS

## GRASMERE Cumbria
Map 4: inset C2

**Moss Grove**, LA22 9SW. Tel 015394-35251, www.mossgrove.com. Susan Lowe has furnished her Victorian house with reclaimed-timber beds and other natural materials (glass, sheep's wool, clay paints). She runs it as an organic B&B ('without loss of style or luxury'). It stands in a 'very pretty' Lakeland village near Ambleside. Breakfast is a Mediterranean-style organic buffet. Lounge, kitchen. No background music. Wi-Fi. 11 bedrooms (2 on ground floor). B&B £62.50–£265 per person.

**Oak Bank Hotel**, Broadgate, LA22 9TA. Tel 015394-35217, www.lakedistricthotel.co.uk. Glynis and Simon Wood offer a 'warm, friendly welcome' to visitors at their hotel in the heart of Grasmere. Rooms have extra touches, food is 'exceptional'; good selection at breakfast; 'the dinner menu is outstanding', with an emphasis on locally sourced ingredients. 2 lounges (1 bar lounge), dining room, conservatory dining room. Background music ('easy listening'/classical in dining rooms and bar). Wi-Fi. ½-acre grounds. Children welcomed. 14 bedrooms. B&B £35–£71 per person; D,B&B £50–£86.50.
**25% DISCOUNT VOUCHERS**

## GREAT LANGDALE Cumbria
Map 4: inset C2

**Old Dungeon Ghyll**, LA22 9JY. Tel 015394-37272, www.odg.co.uk. Fell walkers and climbers have stayed at this remote, extended house in the Great Langdale valley for more than 300 years. It is run by Jane and Neil Walmsley ('welcoming, kind') for the National Trust. There are comfortable rooms, open fires; no television. Lounge, residents' bar, public *Hikers' Bar* (old cow stalls); live music on first Wed of every month; no background music; dining room, drying room. 1-acre garden. Children, walkers, cyclists and dogs welcomed. 13 bedrooms (5 with shared facilities). B&B £50–£55 per person. Dinner £22 (3 courses).

## HAMPTON POYLE Oxfordshire
Map 2:C2

**The Bell**, 11 Oxford Road, OX5 2QD. Tel 01865-376242, www.thebellathamptonpoyle.co.uk. In a village between Oxford and Bicester, this 18th-century roadside pub has flagstone floors, beams, leather furniture and a large log fire. Bedrooms have neutral tones and pale wood furniture. A wood-burning oven is used for grilling fish and shellfish, meat (from local suppliers), and for pizzas. Bar (background music), restaurant; terrace. Wedding facilities. Wi-Fi. Parking. 9 bedrooms (some on ground floor). B&B £42.50–£110 per person.

## HARROGATE North Yorkshire
Map 4:D4

**The Bijou**, 17 Ripon Road, HG1 2JL. Tel 01423-567974, www.thebijou.co.uk. 'Extremely convenient' for the town centre, Stephen and Gill Watson's B&B in a Victorian villa is sleekly decorated in mellow colours. 'We stayed in the *Coach House*, which was very good, with exceptional lighting and an open and airy feel.' Lounge (afternoon teas), breakfast room. Background music. Wi-Fi. Small front garden. Parking. Children welcomed. 10 bedrooms. (2 in coach house; 1 on ground floor). B&B £40–£55 per person.

## HASTINGS East Sussex
## Map 2:E5
**BLACK ROCK HOUSE**, 10 Stanley Road, TN34 1UE. Tel 01424-438448, www. black-rock-hastings.co.uk. 'Beautiful room, great hosts.' Tracey-Anne Cook and Lesley Russell-Dean have decorated their turreted Victorian villa with great attention to detail, in chic tones of sea and sky. The 'best B&B I have ever been in' has views of the sea and is within a few minutes' walk of the beach, the town centre and Hastings Old Town. Breakfast has a large choice. Lounge, breakfast room (background music); small terrace. Wi-Fi. Children over 5 allowed. 5 bedrooms (1 on ground floor). B&B £52.50–£80 per person.
**25% DISCOUNT VOUCHERS**

## HATCH BEAUCHAMP Somerset
## Map 1:C6
**FROG STREET FARMHOUSE**, nr Taunton, TA3 6AF. Tel 01823-481883, www. frogstreet.co.uk. Louise and David Farrance have taken over from her parents, the Coles, and rejuvenated this B&B in a listed 15th-century Somerset longhouse near Ilminster. Along with original Jacobean panelling, flagstone floors, exposed beams and stonework is a fresh, contemporary interior and modern technology. The rooms are 'clean, light, spacious'. Louise provides 'delicious', wholesome 3-course dinners. Large sitting room (wood-burning stove; flat-screen TV). No background music. 3 bedrooms. B&B £45 per person.

## HAWORTH West Yorkshire
## Map 4:D3
**ASHMOUNT COUNTRY HOUSE**, Mytholmes Lane, BD22 8EZ. Tel 01535-645726, www.ashmounthaworth.co.uk.

Near the Brontë Parsonage, this stone-built guest house is run 'with hotel standards' by Ray and Gill Capeling. It was once the home of Dr Amos Ingham, physician to the Brontë sisters. Now there are romantic rooms, private patios and hot tubs, sauna cabins and whirlpool baths, music and 'mood lighting'. Afternoon tea; light refreshments in the evenings. Lounge, 2 dining rooms. Soft background music. Mature garden; open views; ample private parking; Yorkshire breakfasts. Picnics available. Wi-Fi. Function facilities. 10 bedrooms (2 on ground floor). B&B £42.50–£117.50 per person.

## HAY-ON-WYE Herefordshire
## Map 3:D4
**TINTO HOUSE**, 13 Broad Street, HR3 5DB. Tel 01497-821556, www. tinto-house.co.uk. Away from the bustle, but within easy reach of the town, Karen and John Clare's handsomely decorated B&B is in a Georgian town house with a large secluded garden bounded by the River Wye. Karen Clare, who runs *Sage Femme* across the road, selling antique French textiles, and John, an artist, have filled the house and garden with original paintings, drawings and wooden sculptures. The converted stable block contains an art gallery. Dining room; library. No background music. 1-acre garden. Children welcomed. 4 bedrooms. B&B £40–£70 per person.

## HELMSLEY North Yorkshire
## Map 4:C4
**NO54**, 54 Bondgate, YO62 5EZ. Tel 01439-771533, www.no54.co.uk. In a Victorian town house near the market square, Lizzie Would's B&B has simple, well-equipped rooms around a peaceful,

sunny courtyard. Breakfast, at a communal table, includes muffins and kedgeree. The North Yorkshire Moors national park is nearby. Breakfast/sitting room. No background music. Garden. Picnics available. 3 bedrooms in courtyard. Dogs welcomed (£5 charge). B&B £45–£65 per person.

### HEREFORD Herefordshire
### Map 3:D4

CASTLE HOUSE, Castle Street, HR1 2NW. Tel 01432-356321, www.castlehse. co.uk. Terraced gardens lead down to the old castle moat at this 'delightful' luxury hotel in the centre, sensitively converted from two Grade II listed town houses. The owner, David Watkins, supplies the kitchen with produce and beef from the pedigree Herefordshire herd on his farm; Claire Nicholls is the chef. Michelle Marriott-Lodge manages. Lounge, *Bertie's* bar, restaurant; light jazz/classical background music. Lift. Garden, terrace. Parking. 16 bedrooms (1, on ground floor, suitable for &). B&B £92.50–£125 per person; D,B&B £117.50–£145.
**25% DISCOUNT VOUCHERS**

### HEXHAM Northumberland
### Map 4:B3

THE HERMITAGE, Swinburne, NE48 4DG. Tel 01434-681248, email katie. stewart@themeet.co.uk. Approached through a grand arch and up a long drive, Katie and Simon Stewart's rural family home has a 'true country house atmosphere'. 'A delight to stay there.' The solid, stone-built house is three miles from Hadrian's Wall. Drawing rooms, breakfast room; 4-acre grounds: terrace, tennis. No background music. Children over 7 allowed. 7 miles N of

Corbridge. 3 bedrooms. B&B £40–£50 per person. Open Mar to Oct.

### HOARWITHY Herefordshire
### Map 3:D4

ASPEN HOUSE, HR2 6QP. Tel 01432-840353, www.aspenhouse.net. Sally Dean and Rob Elliott are passionate about 'real' food at their environmentally friendly B&B. Breakfasts are organic, using scrupulously sourced eggs, rare-breed bacon and home-made bread and muesli. Their pink 18th-century farmhouse lies in a tranquil Wye valley village; good walking from the front door (maps and drying facilities provided). Lounge (opening onto a decked area overlooking the garden). No background music. ¾-acre garden. Real Food Discovery weekends. 3 bedrooms. B&B from £37 per person.

### HOLMFIRTH West Yorkshire
### Map 4:E3

SUNNYBANK, 78 Upperthong Lane, HD9 3BQ. Tel 01484-684857, www. sunnybankguesthouse.co.uk. 'Superb' hosts, Peter and Anne White, run their B&B with 'impressive attention to detail'. The Victorian gentleman's hillside residence has a large garden, and 'delightful' views over the Derwent valley. 'Delicious' breakfasts in the oak-panelled dining room (open fire in winter; no background music). Wi-Fi. 2-acre wooded garden. ¼ mile from centre. 5 bedrooms (2 on ground floor). B&B £40–£110 per person.

### HOPE Derbyshire
### Map 3:A6

LOSEHILL HOUSE, Edale Road, S33 6RF. Tel 01433-621219, www.losehillhouse. co.uk. On a hillside in the Peak District

national park, this secluded spa hotel has panoramic views over the Hope valley. The solid, white-painted house, owned by Paul and Kathryn Roden, is furnished in a comfortable modern style. Drawing room, bar, *Orangery* restaurant; lift. Background music (evenings). 1-acre garden; terrace. Indoor swimming pool; hot tub; treatment rooms. Function/conference facilities. Civil wedding licence. Footpath access to Peak District national park. 21 bedrooms (4 with external entrance). B&B £72.50–£175 per person; D,B&B £102.50–£155.
**25% DISCOUNT VOUCHERS**

## HUDDERSFIELD West Yorkshire
### Map 4:E3
**THE THREE ACRES INN & RESTAURANT**, Roydhouse, Shelley, HD8 8LR. Tel 01484-602606, www.3acres.com. In Pennine countryside, Neil Truelove and Brian Orme's characterful old roadside drovers' inn has a popular restaurant ('always packed'). Chef Jason Littlewood serves modern British regional food. It is five miles from the town centre (busy morning traffic). *Seafood Bar*, 2 dining rooms; background music. Small function/private dining facilities. Terraced garden; decked dining terrace. Children welcomed. 20 bedrooms (1 suitable for &; 6 in adjacent cottages). B&B £50–£125 per person. Dinner from £36.95.

## HULL East Yorkshire
### Map 4:D5
**WILLERBY MANOR**, Well Lane, Willerby, HU10 6ER. Tel 01482-652616, www.bw-willerbymanor.co.uk. In a rural setting west of Hull, Alexandra Townend's hotel (Best Western) is in an

Edwardian mansion in extensive grounds. The public rooms have a contemporary decor; bedrooms are more traditionally furnished. *Figs* bar/brasserie, *Icon* restaurant; terrace (alfresco dining). Background jazz. Health club (swimming pool, sauna, steam room, gym, beauty room); crèche; wedding/extensive business/function facilities. 3-acre garden. 4 miles W of centre. Dogs (by arrangement). Parking. 51 bedrooms (1 suitable for &). B&B £65–£98 per person; D,B&B £85–£118.

## HUNGERFORD Berkshire
### Map 2:D2
**THE BEAR**, 41 Charnham Street, RG17 0EL. Tel 01488-682512, www.thebearhotelhungerford.co.uk. 'Comfortable, attractive', this ancient roadside inn in the centre has a large courtyard for alfresco dining, and a peaceful riverside garden. It has been stylishly renovated in contemporary style, and is managed by Colin Heaney. 2 lounges, bar. Background music. Function facilities. Civil wedding licence. Large courtyard with umbrellas, tables, chairs. 41 bedrooms (some on ground floor). B&B £42.50–£95 per person; D,B&B £75–£115.
**25% DISCOUNT VOUCHERS**

## ILMINGTON Warwickshire
### Map 3:D6
**THE HOWARD ARMS**, Lower Green, nr Stratford-upon-Avon, CV36 4LT. Tel 01608-682226, www.howardarms.com. On the green of an attractive village, this busy country pub is managed by Tim Churchman. The flower-covered 400-year-old Cotswold stone building has antique furniture, flagstone floors and log fires; the latest technology in the

bedrooms. Chef Bob Stratta uses local suppliers for his modern menus. Snug, bar, dining room ('easy listening' background music); patio/garden. Wi-Fi. Parking. Children welcomed. 8 bedrooms (4 through separate door under covered walkway). B&B £67.50–£90 per person. Dinner £28.

**IRONBRIDGE Shropshire**
**Map 2:A1**
THE LIBRARY HOUSE, Severn Bank, TF8 7AN. Tel 01952-432299, www. libraryhouse.com. Some of the original shelving remains at what was formerly the village library (Grade II listed), now run as a guest house by Liz Steel. Only yards from the historic bridge, it has panoramic views over the River Severn. Original lithographs of Ironbridge by a local artist are displayed on the walls. Sitting room, dining room. No background music. Resident dog, Fizz the terrier. Wi-Fi. Courtyard garden. Parking (passes supplied). Restaurants nearby. 3 bedrooms (1 with private terrace). B&B £37.50–£75 per person.

**KINGHAM Oxfordshire**
**Map 3:D6**
THE KINGHAM PLOUGH, The Green, nr Chipping Norton, OX7 6YD. Tel 01608-658327, www.thekinghamplough.co.uk. Opposite the green in a 'charming' Cotswolds village, this old pub-with-rooms has been revamped by 'enthusiastic' owners Miles Lampson and his wife, Emily Watkins (chef, once sous-chef at *The Fat Duck*). The restaurant prides itself on 'making practically everything and wasting little', using local, seasonal produce. 4 miles SW of Chipping Norton. Bar,

restaurant (background music); terrace, garden. Wi-Fi. Children welcomed, dogs also (annexe only; £10). 7 bedrooms (3 in annexe). B&B £42.50–£100 per person. Dinner £40.

**KING'S LYNN Norfolk**
**Map 2:A4**
CONGHAM HALL, Lynn Road, Grimston, PE32 1AH. Tel 01485-600250, www.conghamhallhotel.co.uk. In an 'exceptionally peaceful' setting on a 30-acre estate near King's Lynn, this Georgian country house has been renovated and expanded by von Essen hotels. It is managed by Julie Woodhouse. Each of ten new bedrooms has a private garden. Lounge, brasserie, *Orangery* restaurant; terrace. Spa (treatment rooms, relaxation area, hydrotherapy pool, thermal suite, private outside hot tub, fitness suite). No background music. 25 bedrooms. B&B £110–£255 per person. Dinner £41–£48.

**KINGSBRIDGE Devon**
**Map 1:D4**
THURLESTONE HOTEL, Thurlestone, TQ7 3NN. Tel 01548-560382, www.thurlestone.co.uk. Owned by the Grose family since 1896 (managed by Julie Baugh), this large, white, 'almost Art Deco' hotel in subtropical gardens has stunning views over gardens and out to sea. There is plenty for families to do; coastal walks and sandy beaches are close by. 'Well equipped and decorated. Staff well trained and helpful.' Lounges, bar, *Margaret Amelia* restaurant (Hugh Miller cooks); outdoor *Rock Pool* eating area (teas, lunches, snacks, dinners), terrace (alfresco dining); *The Village Inn*

16th-century pub; leisure complex/
beauty spa (indoor and outdoor heated
swimming pools); tennis, squash,
badminton. No background music.
Function facilities. Civil wedding
licence. 19-acre gardens. 4 miles SW of
Kingsbridge. 64 bedrooms (2 suitable
for &; some with balcony, sea views).
B&B £66–£180 per person; D,B&B
£76–£200.

### KIRKBY LONSDALE Cumbria
**Map 4: inset C2**
**SUN INN**, 6 Market Street, LA6 2AU.
Tel 015242-71965, www.sun-inn.info.
In the centre of the market town, this
white-painted 17th-century inn is
festooned with flower baskets. Owners
Lucy and Mark Fuller have combined
traditional flagstone and wood floors,
panelling, exposed stonework, roaring
fires, with contemporary furnishing
in the bedrooms and restaurant. The
manager is Steven Turner; Sam Carter
is chef. Bar (background music),
restaurant. Children and dogs welcomed.
11 bedrooms. B&B £50–£75 per person.
Dinner £33.

### KIRTLINGTON Oxfordshire
**Map 2:C2**
**THE DASHWOOD**, South Green, Heyford
Road, OX5 3HJ. Tel 01869-352707,
www.thedashwood.co.uk. Owned by
Martin and Ros Lewis, and managed
by Michal Zgaimski, this contemporary
restaurant-with-rooms (Grade II listed)
is in a pretty village near Bicester.
Natural materials (brick, wood, stone)
and neutral tones are offset by splashes
of colour and artwork. New chef
Andrew Hart provides a 'Best of
British' menu. Bar, restaurant; patio.
Function facilities. Background music.

Wi-Fi. Children welcomed. 12 bedrooms
(7 in a converted barn; 1 suitable for &).
B&B £57.50–£82.50 per person; D,B&B
£82.50–£107.50.
**25% DISCOUNT VOUCHERS**

### KNUTSFORD Cheshire
**Map 4:E3**
**BELLE EPOQUE**, 60 King Street,
WA16 6DT. Tel 01565-633060, www.
thebelleepoque.com. Built in 1907, the
Mooney family's restaurant-with-rooms
has a wealth of original features (a
Venetian glass floor, marble pillars,
art nouveau fireplaces). The decor is
lavish; bedrooms either overlook the
Mediterranean roof garden or have their
own balcony. The restaurant, under
executive chef Phil Ashman, serves local
food (farmers and suppliers credited
on the menu). Wi-Fi. Bar, restaurant.
Background jazz. Function facilities.
Civil wedding licence. 7 bedrooms. B&B
£57.50–£95 per person. Dinner £40.
**25% DISCOUNT VOUCHERS**

### LANCASTER Lancashire
**Map 4:D2**
**THE ASHTON**, Wyresdale Road,
LA1 3JJ. Tel 01524-68460, www.
theashtonlancaster.com. Dark, dramatic,
candlelit rooms lend charisma to this
sandstone Georgian house which has been
renovated in dashing style by James Gray,
a former TV and film set designer. It
stands in large grounds near Williamson
Park, on the outskirts of the city. Lounge,
dining room (occasional background
music). Simple evening meals are served
by arrangement. Wi-Fi. Children
welcomed (no baby equipment provided).
5 bedrooms (1 on ground floor; some
overlook the garden and park). B&B
£59–£98 per person. Dinner £39.95.

**LANGHO** Lancashire
Map 4:D3
NORTHCOTE, Northcote Road, nr
Blackburn BB6 8BE. Tel 01254-240555,
www.northcote.com. Chef/patron
Nigel Haworth and his business
partner, Craig Bancroft, run their
restaurant-with-rooms (*Michelin* star;
Lisa Allen is head chef) in a renovated,
late Victorian house with original
features (beautiful wooden doors and
windows). With views of the Ribble
valley, it stands in wooded grounds,
close to the busy A59 (windows are
double glazed). Drawing room, bar,
restaurant (background music); meeting
room; civil wedding licence. 2-acre
organic garden. 14 bedrooms (4 on
ground floor; 1 suitable for &). B&B
£100–£210 per person; D,B&B
£142.50–£385.

**LAVENHAM** Suffolk
Map 2:C5
THE SWAN, High Street, CO10 9QA.
Tel 01787-247477, www.theswanat
lavenham.co.uk. Three timber-framed
medieval buildings form this hotel,
part of a small Suffolk group. The
snug bar is filled with air force
memorabilia, including a wall signed
by British and American airmen
stationed at Lavenham Airfield during
World War II. Bedrooms, each named
after a Suffolk village, are richly
furnished; some have a four-poster
bed. Lounge, 2 bars, galleried dining
room, garden lounge (chef Nick
Wilson cooks locally sourced seasonal
ingredients). Occasional background
music. Garden; business facilities.
Wi-Fi. Children welcomed. 45
bedrooms. B&B £85–£135 per person;
D,B&B £115–£165.

**LEEDS** West Yorkshire
Map 4:D4
42 THE CALLS, 42 The Calls, LS2 7EW.
Tel 0113-244 0099, www.42thecalls.co.uk.
Overlooking the River Aire (fishing rods
supplied), this 18th-century grain mill
has been converted into a contemporary
hotel (part of Eton Collection). Belinda
Dawson is the manager. There are
exposed girders and brickwork, beamed
ceilings and contemporary art. Lounge,
bar, breakfast room (radio at breakfast);
room service; lift; conference facilities.
*Brasserie 44* next door. Children and
dogs welcomed. Street noise at night. 41
bedrooms (1 suitable for &): £85–£395.

WOODLANDS, Gelderd Road,
Gildersome, LS27 7LY. Tel 0113-238
1488, www.tomahawkhotels.co.uk.
Once the Victorian residence of a local
textile mill owner, this contemporary
hotel (Tomahawk group) stands in
landscaped grounds, four miles west
of the city centre. It is owned by Rob
Foulston and Tom Horsforth; Simon
Grybas is the new manager. Robert
Corless is chef. 2 bars, 4 dining rooms.
Conservatory; patio. Background music
throughout (modern and classical). 4-
acre garden in 50-acre grounds. Function
facilities. Civil wedding licence; marquee.
Children welcomed. 23 bedrooms, each
named after an unusual fabric (some on
ground floor): £139–£249; D,B&B from
£99 per person. Breakfast £14.95.
25% **DISCOUNT VOUCHERS**

**LEWDOWN** Devon
Map 1:C3
LEWTRENCHARD MANOR, nr
Okehampton, EX20 4PN. Tel 01566-
783222, www.lewtrenchard.co.uk.
Extensive, peaceful grounds (a dovecote,

sunken garden and lake with swans) surround this 'atmospheric' Jacobean stone manor house run by chef/patron Jason Hornbuckle for the von Essen group. He has introduced a private viewing area, *Purple Carrot*, where diners can watch the kitchen on split-screen TVs. He is committed to a 'back to nature' policy: 80 per cent of the produce is grown in the walled garden. 'Breakfasts were imaginative.' Lounge, bar, 2 restaurants, ballroom. Children and dogs welcomed. 14 bedrooms (4 in courtyard annexe; bridal suite in 2-storey Folly; 1 suitable for &). B&B £62.50–£110 per person. Dinner £55.
**25% DISCOUNT VOUCHERS**

### LEWES East Sussex
### Map 2:E4
**BERKELEY HOUSE**, 2 Albion Street, BN7 2ND. Tel 01273-476057, www. berkeleyhouselewes.co.uk. 'Cordial' owners Roy Patten and Steve John have run their late Georgian town house as a B&B for more than 20 years. They are helpful with information for Glyndebourne (taxis ordered, etc). 'Cosy' residents' lounge, dining room; roof terrace with views over town to the South Downs. Wi-Fi. 3 bedrooms (1 might hear traffic). Off-street parking (£4 per day). B&B £37.50–£55 per person.
**25% DISCOUNT VOUCHERS**

**THE SHELLEYS**, 135 High Street, BN7 1XS. Tel 01273-472361, www. the-shelleys.co.uk. Once owned by a member of the poet's family, this 16th-century manor house in the town centre is now a family-owned hotel. It has a rabbit warren of corridors, steps and

doors. 'Our room was large, warm and comfortable.' Lounge, bar, *Apostrophe* restaurant (Nicholas Miles is chef); terrace, garden; function facilities; civil wedding licence. Background music. Parking adjacent. Children welcomed. 19 bedrooms. B&B £57.50–£190 per person; D,B&B from £100.

### LINCOLN Lincolnshire
### Map 4:E5
**THE CASTLE**, Westgate, LN1 3AS. Tel 01522-538801, www.castlehotel.net. 'Very good value, simple accommodation.' Close to the cathedral and castle, this Grade II listed house in the historic centre is owned and run as a traditional hotel by the Worrell family. 2 small lounges, bar (a popular local), *Knights* restaurant (evenings only; background radio/CDs). Parking. 19 bedrooms (some in attic, some in converted stables; 1 suitable for &). B&B £49.50–£89 per person; D,B&B £70–£111.

**THE OLD BAKERY**, 26–28 Burton Road, LN1 3LB. Tel 01522-576057, www.the old-bakery.co.uk. Well located behind the castle, and 'a short step from the cathedral', this 'no-frills' restaurant-with-rooms is owned by Alan Ritson and his daughter, Tracey. Many of the building's original Victorian bakehouse features are retained (brick walls, stone floors, bread ovens). The chef, Ivano de Serio (Mr Ritson's son-in-law), serves modern English food with a European twist in the glassed-in garden restaurant. 'Delicious and superbly cooked; we have never seen such a choice of cheeses; staff were very friendly and attentive.' Background music. Cookery courses. In quiet street, but some noise at night. 4 simple bedrooms (2 en suite; 2 with private bathroom). B&B £31.50–£50 per person; D,B&B £67.50.

## LIVERPOOL Merseyside
**Map 4:E2**

**HARD DAYS NIGHT**, Central Buildings, North John Street, L2 6RR. Tel 0151-2361964, www.harddaysnighthotel.com. Inspired by the Beatles, this large hotel in a Grade II listed building in the old merchant quarter (noisy at night) has artwork and photographs devoted to the Fab Four. The decor is contemporary, with panelled walls, leather armchairs and Italian marble; gadgetry is state of the art. Michael Dewey is the manager; Andrew Scott is the chef. Lounge, *Bar Four, Blake's* restaurant; art gallery. Background music. 110 bedrooms: £105–£295. Breakfast £10, dinner £40.

## LOOE Cornwall
**Map 1:D3**

**BARCLAY HOUSE**, St Martins Road, PL13 1LP. Tel 01503-262929, www.barclayhouse.co.uk. Managed by Graham and Gill Brooks, this white-painted Victorian villa has spectacular views over the East Looe river from its hillside position. The chef, Benjamin Palmer, has won awards for his modern coastal cooking. Sitting room, bar, restaurant (background jazz); terrace (alfresco dining); gym, sauna, outdoor heated swimming pool. Children welcomed. 10 bedrooms (1 on ground floor). Also 8 self-catering cottages. B&B £57.50–£170 per person; D,B&B £82–£194.

**FIELDHEAD HOTEL**, Portuan Road, Hannafore, PL13 2DR. Tel 01503-262689, www.fieldheadhotel.co.uk. With 'fantastic' elevated views across Looe

Bay, this traditional hotel (built in 1896 as a private residence) is owned by Julian Peck. It is 15 minutes' walk from the centre. Many rooms have been recently refurbished. Lounge, bar, *Horizons* restaurant (sea views). Background music (radio). Wi-Fi. 1½-acre award-winning tropical garden, veranda, terrace (views, parasols); outdoor heated swimming pool. Children and dogs welcomed. Parking. 16 bedrooms (most with sea view; 3 with balcony). B&B £44–£80 per person; D,B&B £68–£104. **25% DISCOUNT VOUCHERS**

**TRELASKE HOTEL & RESTAURANT**, Polperro Road, PL13 2JS. Tel 01503-262159, www.trelaske.co.uk. In four-acre grounds, Hazel Billington and Ross Lewin's white hotel has 'spacious', 'spotless' bedrooms with balcony or patio. She is 'a superb host'. He serves 'traditional British with a modern twist' dishes, with an emphasis on seasonal, local ingredients (fruit and vegetables from the hotel's own polytunnels). 2 miles from town. 2 lounges, bar/conservatory (background music); terrace (summer barbecues). Function facilities. Wi-Fi. Children welcomed. 7 bedrooms (4 in building adjacent to main house; dogs allowed in 2 rooms, £6.50 per night). B&B £49.50–£98 per person; D,B&B £74–£148.

## LOWER FROYLE Hampshire
**Map 2:D3**

**THE ANCHOR INN**, GU34 4NA. Tel 01420-23261, www.anchorinnatlowerfroyle.co.uk. This handsome old inn in a prosperous South Downs village is part of the small Miller's Collection. Public rooms have low beams, a clutter of imperial memorabilia. Bedrooms are named after First World War poets. The chef, Keith Chandler, serves simple British dishes. Bar, lounge, dining room (background music); courtyard garden. 5 bedrooms. B&B £45–£60 per person.

## LOWESTOFT Suffolk
### Map 2:B6

**IVY HOUSE**, Ivy Lane, off Beccles Road, Oulton Broad, NR33 8HY. Tel 01502-501353, www.ivyhousecountryhotel. co.uk. Caroline Coe's converted farm is in a 'lovely' location on the southern shores of Oulton Broad. It has a 'beautiful' large garden, with lily ponds and a summer house, within 60-acre meadows. The bedrooms (all in an annexe) are a mix of modern and traditional; spacious executive rooms have added extras (bathrobes and cafetière). Chef Martin Whitelock uses local ingredients in the *Crooked Barn* restaurant (an 18th-century thatched, beamed barn). Wi-Fi. 2 sitting rooms, conservatory; background music in restaurant and 1 sitting room. Function/conference facilities. 20 bedrooms (1 suite; 1 suitable for &). B&B £67.50–£135 per person. Dinner £27.50.

## LUDLOW Shropshire
### Map 3:C4

**DINHAM HALL**, by the castle, SY8 1EJ. Tel 01584-876464, www.dinhamhall. co.uk. In the market square, this 'very attractive' 18th-century mellow stone building formerly accommodated boarders of Ludlow grammar school. 'Lovely views from our bedroom over gardens and roofs of Ludlow and out to the hills beyond.' The staff are 'young and charming'. The cooking of chef Wayne Smith is admired. Sitting room, library, bar, restaurant (light background

jazz). 1-acre walled garden. Function facilities. Civil wedding licence. Parking. 13 bedrooms (2 in cottage). B&B £62.50–£195 per person.

**FISHMORE HALL**, Fishmore Road, SY8 3DP. Tel 01584-875148, www. fishmorehall.co.uk. Owner/manager Laura Penman runs this 'very comfortable' hotel in a symmetrical, white Regency house with panoramic views over countryside, outside the town. 'Delightful colours, efficient lighting, plenty of cupboard space, comfortable seating.' Chef David Jaram serves a Shropshire tasting menu. Lift; bar, sitting room, restaurant (background music). Wi-Fi. Garden; terrace. Function facilities. Civil wedding licence. Children and dogs (£30 charge) welcomed. 15 bedrooms (1 suitable for &). B&B £70–£125 per person. Dinner £46.50–£55.

## LYME REGIS Dorset
### Map 1:C6

**ALEXANDRA HOTEL**, Pound Street, DT7 3HZ. Tel 01297-442010, www. hotelalexandra.co.uk. 'In a super position' in private gardens above the Cobb and seafront, the *Alexandra* has been run for the last 25 years by one family. Kathryn Haskins, now in charge, has renovated 'beautifully' throughout (stripped wood floors, antique furniture, 'really pretty' upholstered chairs). Wi-Fi. 3 sitting rooms, cocktail bar, conservatory (light lunches: 'delicious'), restaurant (local seafood and market-influenced food under Ian Grant). Packed lunches available. Aromatherapy treatments. Background music (light jazz). 1½-acre garden with viewing deck; pathway to beach. Children welcomed. Parking. 24 bedrooms (these vary in size and noise insulation). B&B £60–£95 per person; D,B&B £90–£125.

## LYNMOUTH Devon
## Map 1:B4
SHELLEY'S, 8 Watersmeet Road, EX35 6EP. Tel 01598-753219, www. shelleyshotel.co.uk. Shelley honeymooned at this 18th-century house which overlooks the harbour, and has views over Lynmouth Bay. Jane Becker and Richard Briden now run it as a B&B. The airy bedrooms have sea views. Lounge, bar, conservatory breakfast room. No background music. 11 bedrooms (1 on ground floor). B&B £49–£139.75 per person.

## LYNTON Devon
## Map 1:B4
LYNTON COTTAGE HOTEL, North Walk, EX35 6ED. Tel 01598-752342, www.lynton-cottage.co.uk. David Mowlem and Heather Biancardi's small hotel stands on a clifftop on North Walk, part of the North Devon Coast Path. The beamed bedrooms are furnished traditionally; some have a four-poster bed and roll-top bath. Lounge, bar (background music); terrace; 3-acre gardens. Beauty treatment and holistic therapies. Parking. Children and dogs welcomed. Closed Dec to mid-Jan. 16 bedrooms (some with sea-view balcony). B&B £45–£82 per person. Dinner £40.
**25% DISCOUNT VOUCHERS**

## LYTHAM Lancashire
## Map 4:D2
CLIFTON ARMS, West Beach, FY58 5QJ. Tel 01253-739898, www.cliftonarms-lytham.com. 'A lovely, welcoming hotel'

(Fairhaven group), this historic beachfront town house overlooks Lytham green and seafront. It is managed by Victoria Tipper. Lift; *Churchills* bar/lounge (brasserie menu), library/TV room, *West Beach* restaurant (classical background music; chef, James Rodgers); conference/banqueting facilities. 'Splendid breakfasts.' Small garden. Parking. 48 bedrooms. B&B £62.50–£130 per person. Dinner £29.50.
**25% DISCOUNT VOUCHERS**

THE ROOMS, 35 Church Road, FY8 5LL. Tel 01253-736000, www.theroomslytham. co.uk. Near the memorial gardens, Andy and Jackie Baker run their sophisticated B&B with a personal touch. Bedrooms have king-size bed and state-of-the-art equipment. Breakfast has a wide choice, including champagne at weekends. Breakfast room (background radio). Walled garden. Wi-Fi. 5 bedrooms (plus a two-bedroomed serviced apartment). B&B £57.50–£125 per person.

## MANCHESTER
## Map 4:E3
CITY INN, 1 Piccadilly Place, 1 Auburn Street, M1 3DG. Tel 0161-242 1000, www.cityinn.com/manchester. Near the railway station, this contemporary, purpose-built chain hotel (City Inn group) is managed by Stewart Davies. Work by local artists is exhibited in the public areas. The bedrooms have state-of-the-art fittings; there are floor-to-ceiling opening windows, mist-free mirrors, walk-in power showers, etc. The modern European cuisine under Phil Green has won awards. *Piccadilly* lounge, *City* café; terrace. Background music. Wi-Fi. Fitness suite. Meeting

rooms. Children welcomed. 285
bedrooms (14 suitable for &). B&B £50–
£115 per person; D,B&B £64–£179.

**ELEVEN DIDSBURY PARK**, 11 Didsbury
Park, Didsbury Village, M20 5LH. Tel
0161-448 7711, www.elevendidsburypark.
com. In a peaceful suburb, Eamonn
and Sally O'Loughlin's small Victorian
villa is convenient for both the airport
(10 minutes' drive) and the centre.
Decoration is smart, with simple
furnishing and muted colour schemes.
Andrew Hughes is the manager. 2
lounge/bars (background music all day),
veranda. Gym; treatment room.
Conference facilities. Large walled
garden. Parking. 20 bedrooms (1, on
ground floor, suitable for &): £75–£240.
Breakfast £12.50–£14.50.

**MARGATE Kent**
Map 2:D5
**THE READING ROOMS**, 31 Hawley
Square, CT9 1PH. Tel 01843-225166,
www.thereadingroomsmargate.co.uk.
Each bedroom in this Grade II listed
town house spreads across an entire
floor ('it felt like a large Parisian
apartment') and has views across the
Georgian square. Louise Oldfield and
Liam Nabb have renovated it in 'shabby-
chic' style: distressed walls, unfinished
wood floors, antique French armoires
and chunky radiators. 'The bathroom
was stunning.' Breakfast is brought to
the room. 3 bedrooms: B&B from £62.50
per person.

**MARTINHOE Devon**
Map 1:B4
**THE OLD RECTORY**, Exmoor National
Park, EX31 4QT. Tel 01598-763368,
www.oldrectoryhotel.co.uk. In a

'magnificent' setting, this Georgian
rectory stands in large gardens
surrounded by National Trust land.
Owners Huw Rees and Sam Prosser
have upgraded the bedrooms. 'Excellent
food and wine' is served in the 'superb'
conservatory. 2 lounges, dining room
(classical/jazz background music).
Wi-Fi. 8 bedrooms (2 on ground floor
suitable for &). B&B £70–£90 per person;
D,B&B £95–£120.
25% DISCOUNT VOUCHERS

**MATLOCK Derbyshire**
Map 3:A6
**THE RED HOUSE COUNTRY HOTEL**,
Old Road, Darley Dale, DE4 2ER.
Tel 01629-734854, www.theredhouse
countryhotel.co.uk. 'Excellent in every
way': David and Kate Gardiner's
Victorian country retreat is in 'a very
quiet location', well placed for exploring
the Peak District. Service is 'personal
and friendly'. The bedrooms are
individually decorated. Alan Perkins
uses 'outstanding' ingredients for his
cooking; breakfasts are 'simply the best'.
Complimentary home-made tea and
cake. No background music. Wi-Fi.
¾-acre lawned garden. Parking. 9
bedrooms (2 four-poster; 2, on ground
floor in coach house, suitable for &).
B&B £52.50–£87.50 per person; D,B&B
£65–£115.

**MELTON MOWBRAY Leicestershire**
Map 2:A3
**SYSONBY KNOLL**, Asfordby Road, LE13
0HP. Tel 01664-563563, www.sysonby.
com. On the River Eye, this extended
and recently refurbished red brick
Edwardian house has a 'magical' garden
with a pond, manicured lawns, and
beehives which supply the hotel's honey.

Owned and personally managed by the same family since 1965, it is now run by Jenny and Gavin Howling. Most bedrooms overlook a quadrangle around a central courtyard. 'The four-poster room was large and comfortable.' Lounge, bar, restaurant (Susan Meakin's menu has English/European food). Garden and 3 acres of meadow; fishing. Wi-Fi. Children and dogs welcomed. 30 bedrooms (some on ground floor; ramp). B&B £45–£98 per person; D,B&B £57.50–£78.50.
**25% DISCOUNT VOUCHERS**

## MEVAGISSEY Cornwall
Map 1:D2
**KILBOL COUNTRY HOUSE HOTEL**, Polmassick, PL26 6HA. Tel 01726-842481, www.kilbol.co.uk. In a hidden valley, Captain and Mrs Woollam's small hotel is 'unpretentious', 'personal and charming'. The main house has 16th-century origins: there are beamed ceilings, cottage-style windows, an inglenook fireplace, and lots of paintings, plants and books. 'The food, on a sensibly short menu, is delicious.' Lounge, bar, dining room (background music), conservatory; small outdoor swimming pool; croquet. 2-acre garden. Dogs welcomed (3 resident springer spaniels). 7 bedrooms (all have garden views, some have patio or balcony); plus two 2-bedroom cottages. B&B £30–£52 per person; D,B&B £50–£70.
**25% DISCOUNT VOUCHERS**

## MIDHURST West Sussex
Map 2:E3
**PARK HOUSE**, Bepton, GU29 0JB. Tel 01730-819000, www.parkhousehotel.com. This family-owned country hotel, managed by James and Rebecca Coonan,

is located in a 'heaven-sent setting' at the foot of the South Downs. 'Excellent, friendly staff' encourage a relaxed atmosphere. Lounge, honesty bar, dining room, conservatory; terrace. No background music. Spa: indoor pool, sauna, treatment rooms. 10-acre grounds: heated swimming pool, tennis, croquet, pitch-and-putt golf. Conference/function facilities. 2½ miles SW of Midhurst. Children and dogs welcomed. 21 bedrooms (some in 2 luxuriously appointed cottages; 1 on ground floor). B&B £72.50–£147.50 per person; D,B&B £100–£172.50.

## MILLOM Cumbria
Map 4: inset C2
**BROADGATE HOUSE**, Broadgate, Thwaites, LA18 5JY. Tel 01229-716295, www.broadgate-house.co.uk. A good base for exploring the western Lake District, this Georgian home (which has been in Diana Lewthwaite's family for almost 200 years) overlooks the Dudden estuary and salt marshes. Immaculate grounds have a walled garden, terraces, croquet lawn and an 'oasis' with a palm tree. Drawing room, cosy sitting room (wood-burning stove), dining room (food is locally sourced), breakfast room. Country house decor. No background music. 4 bedrooms (bathroom not en suite but private; throne loo; freestanding bath). B&B £45–£55 per person; D,B&B £70–£80.
**25% DISCOUNT VOUCHERS**

## MORPETH Northumberland
Map 4:B4
**ESHOTT HALL**, NE65 9EP. Tel 01691-611015, www.eshott.co.uk. This symmetrical, wisteria-clad, 17th-century building stands on a 500-acre estate

(farm, walled garden, arboretum, formal gardens), 30 minutes' drive from Newcastle. It has been renovated by Robert and Gina Parker. Panelling, ornate plasterwork, stained glass and 'fine furnishing and fittings'. Drawing room, dining room, library, orangery. No background music. Tennis court. Weddings (civil licence), house parties, small conferences a speciality. 11 bedrooms. B&B £55–£180 per person. Dinner £45.

## MULLION Cornwall
Map 1:E2
MULLION COVE HOTEL, Mullion, Helston, TR12 7EP. Tel 01326-240328, www.mullion-cove.co.uk. The Grose family, who bought this cliff-top hotel in 2006, have been renovating throughout. On the Lizard peninsula, it is well positioned for walking holidays. The family is 'present in a very positive way'. Dinner was 'quite exceptional'. 3 lounges, bar, restaurant (background music at night); 2-acre garden. Outdoor heated pool. Wi-Fi (ground floor only). Gourmet weekends, painting, photography courses. 30 bedrooms (some ground-floor rooms; lift). Dogs welcomed. B&B £60–£140 per person; D,B&B £70–£150.
**25% DISCOUNT VOUCHERS**

## NEW MILTON Hampshire
Map 2:E2
CHEWTON GLEN, Christchurch Road, BH25 6QS. Tel 01425-275341, www.chewtonglen.com. 'A delight.' There are plenty of activities to enjoy at this 'truly wonderful' luxury country house hotel and spa (privately owned; Relais & Châteaux), in extensive gardens, parkland and woodland on the edge of

the New Forest, and a short walk to the sea. Staff provide 'excellent service whilst maintaining their own personality'. 3 lounges, *Marryat* restaurant. Spa; treatments; gym; dance studio. 130-acre grounds; 9-hole par 3 golf course; a practice range; 2 indoor and 2 outdoor tennis courts; indoor and outdoor swimming pools; croquet lawn; putting green. 58 bedrooms (23 suites). B&B £164.50–£329 per person; D,B&B from £249.

## NEWCASTLE UPON TYNE
Tyne and Wear
Map 4:B4
MALMAISON, The Quayside, NE1 3DX. Tel 0191-245 5000, www.malmaison.com. On the quay near the Millennium Bridge and the Baltic Art Gallery, this large contemporary hotel is a conversion of a grain and cotton warehouse. Lizzy Kelk is the manager. There are plush fabrics, bold patterns and colours, and quirky touches. 2 lounges, café, bar, brasserie (dimly lit); background music. Wi-Fi (first 30 mins is free). Lift. Spa (holistic/beauty treatments). Children welcomed. 122 bedrooms (most with river views; 4 suitable for &): £160–£350. Breakfast £11.95–£13.95, dinner from £25.

THE TOWNHOUSE, 1 West Avenue, Gosforth, NE3 4ES. Tel 0191-285 6812, www.thetownhousehotel.co.uk. In a leafy suburb, two miles N of the centre, Cathy Knox and Sheila Armstrong have turned this Victorian town house into an elegant hotel and café. Done in a mix of contemporary and classical styles, bedrooms have luxury touches; bathrooms are theatrical. The frequently changing blackboard menu features wholesome local produce. Breakfast room, café (open until 7 pm; room service). Background music. Wi-Fi; iPod docking station. Children welcomed. 10 bedrooms. B&B £42.50–£62.50 per person. Dinner £20.

### NEWQUAY Cornwall
**Map 1:D2**

THE HEADLAND HOTEL, Fistral Beach, TR7 1EW. Tel 01637-872211, www.headlandhotel.co.uk. By Fistral beach, this red brick Victorian hotel has been owned and managed by the Armstrong family for three decades. 'Wonderful communal areas' have a traditional yet contemporary feel. Twenty bedrooms have been refurbished this year. Lounges, bar, *Sand Brasserie*; *Terrace Restaurant* (alfresco dining; sea view); no background music; conference/event facilities; snooker; table tennis; 10-acre grounds. 2 heated swimming pools (indoor and outdoor); sauna; croquet; 3 tennis courts; 9-hole golf approach course and putting green; on-site surf school. Families welcomed (bunk beds, baby-listening, entertainment, etc). Dogs welcomed (£13 per night). Civil wedding licence. 97 bedrooms (hotel suitable for &). B&B £39.50–£194.50 per person; D,B&B £62–£217.

### NORWICH Norfolk
**Map 2:B5**

NORFOLK MEAD, Church Loke, Coltishall, NR12 7DN. Tel 01603-737531, www.norfolkmead.co.uk. 'Refreshingly quirky', this Georgian merchant's house has a 'near-perfect' location on the edge of the Norfolk Broads. Lawns run down to the River Bure. It is owned by Jill and Don Fleming, and managed by Sharon

Hardy. Lounge, bar, restaurant (chef Mark Sayers sources seasonal Norfolk fare; traditional Sunday lunches); background music; conference facilities. 7 miles NE of Norwich. 8-acre grounds: walled garden, unheated swimming pool; fishing lake; off-river mooring. Civil wedding licence. Private dining. Children welcomed. 13 bedrooms (2 beamed ones in cottage suite; some with four-poster). B&B £50–£95 per person. Dinner £35.

### NOTTINGHAM Nottinghamshire
**Map 2:A3**

LACE MARKET HOTEL, 29–31 High Pavement, NG1 1HE. Tel 0115-852 3232, www.lacemarkethotel.co.uk. Opposite the Galleries of Justice and next to the 14th-century church of St Mary the Virgin, four Georgian and Victorian town houses (one a former lace factory) have been elegantly converted into a contemporary hotel (Finesse Collection), managed by Jessica Macdonald. Rooms (five categories) vary: some have freestanding bath and twin basins; some have views over the churchyard. Lounge, *Saint* cocktail bar, *Merchants* restaurant, *Cock & Hoop* gastropub (Dean Crews is chef). Background music. Wi-Fi. Lift. Function facilities. Civil wedding licence. Complimentary access to nearby health club. Children and dogs welcomed. 42 bedrooms: £99–£289. Breakfast £9.95–£14.95, dinner £45.

### OTLEY West Yorkshire
**Map 4:D3**

CHEVIN COUNTRY PARK HOTEL, Yorkgate, LS21 3NU. Tel 01943-467818, www.crerarhotels.com. In extensive woodland with three fishing lakes, this spa hotel (Crerar Hotels) has recently been refurbished. Organic food is served in the lakeside restaurant, which has a terrace and roof balcony. 11 miles NW of Leeds. Conservatory lounge, bar, restaurant; background music. Indoor swimming pool, sauna; gym; tennis court. Wi-Fi. Civil wedding licence. 49 bedrooms (19 in main house; 30 in pine lodges; some on ground floor; 3 self-catering). B&B £55–£170 per person; D,B&B £19.95 added.

## OTTERBURN Northumberland
## Map 4:B3

THE OTTERBURN TOWER, NE19 1NS. Tel 01830-520620, www.otterburntower. com. The views are 'magnificent' at this fortified country house on an ancient site (founded in 1086 by a cousin of William the Conqueror). It stands within extensive woodland. Inside are stained-glass windows, a Florentine marble fireplace and oak-panelled rooms. John Goodfellow is the 'hands-on' manager; John Carlton is chef ('excellent cuisine and service'). Newcastle is 30 minutes' drive away. 2 drawing rooms, stable bar/bistro, breakfast room, *Oak Room* restaurant (farm produce; outdoor eating); classical background music; function facilities; lake; private stretch of River Rede (fishing). Civil wedding licence. Children welcomed. 18 bedrooms (1 suitable for &). B&B £65–£80 per person; D,B&B £85–£100.

## OXFORD Oxfordshire
## Map 2:C2

BURLINGTON HOUSE, 374 Banbury Road, OX2 7PP. Tel 01865-513513, www.burlington-house.co.uk. Recently renovated, this handsome Victorian

house in leafy Summertown has boldly patterned bedrooms and modern amenities. Home-made breakfasts are substantial. There is a frequent bus service into the centre. Sitting room, breakfast room. Wi-Fi. No background music. Small Japanese garden. Parking. 12 bedrooms (some in courtyard). B&B £42–£88 per person.

THE RANDOLPH, Beaumont Street, OX1 2LN. Tel 0844 8799132, www. macdonaldhotels.co.uk/randolph. An Oxford institution, this stately hotel in a Gothic Revival building is opposite the Ashmolean Museum. Michael Grange is the manager for the Macdonald group. Drawing room (pianist on Sat), *Morse* bar, restaurant (Tom Birks is chef; classical background music); lift; cellar spa (vaulted ceilings, Italian tiling, candlelight; thermal suite, hydrotherapy bath, relaxation room). Conference facilities. Civil wedding licence. Children and dogs welcomed. 151 bedrooms (1 suitable for &). B&B £73.50–£154 per person; D,B&B £93.50–£164.

## PENRITH Cumbria
## Map 4: inset C2

WESTMORLAND HOTEL, nr Orton, CA10 3SB. Tel 01539-624351, www. westmorlandhotel.com. 'Wow, just wonderful.' Surrounded by open fell, this secluded modern hotel ('so quiet and peaceful') is at the Tebay Motorway Services on the M6; Jeff Brimble is the manager. A farm shop nearby sells local and artisan produce, which can be sampled in the restaurant; Bryan Parsons is chef. 'Highly recommended as a stop-over, or as a base for touring that side of the Lakes.' Contemporary design is blended with traditional materials. Lounge, bar (log fires), split-level dining room; background music. Wi-Fi. Function facilities. Civil wedding licence. Children welcomed. 51 bedrooms (1 suitable for &). B&B £50–£84 per person; D,B&B £73–£106.

**25% DISCOUNT VOUCHERS**

**POOLE Dorset**
Map 2:E1
HOTEL DU VIN POOLE, Thames Street, BH15 1JN. Tel 01202-685666, www.hotelduvin.com. 'The rooms are very comfortable, the staff are efficient and charming; the food is excellent.' This branch of the Hotel du Vin chain is a converted Georgian town house in a quiet cul-de-sac near the harbour. It is managed by John Wilcock. Bedrooms, each named after a wine, have soft colour schemes; some have a bath, or even two, in the room. Library. Bar (traditional pub); bistro (European dishes); courtyard (alfresco dining); function facilities. No background music. Parking. 38 bedrooms: £180–£360. Dinner from £25.

**POSTBRIDGE Devon**
Map 1:D4
LYDGATE HOUSE, Dartmoor, PL20 6TJ. Tel 01822-880209, www.lydgatehouse.co.uk. The setting of this Victorian country house ('in the middle of nowhere', near a famous clapper bridge over the River Dart) is 'wonderful'. It is well placed for walkers, having immediate access to moorland. There are 'superb' views over the East Dart valley and river. The owners, Douglas and Anna Geikie, are friendly. Each of the comfortable bedrooms is named after a bird. Sitting room/bar, snug,

conservatory dining room; terrace. Dinner is not available on Sun and Mon evenings. Background music (jazz/classical). 7 bedrooms. B&B £45–£60 per person; D,B&B £75–£90.

**PRIORS MARSTON Warwickshire**
Map 2:B2
THE OLD VICARAGE, CV47 7RT. Tel 01327-282626, www.theoldvicarage.com. Judith and David Adams's 400-year-old house (with Georgian additions) has a 'delightful garden with a magnolia tree, pond, and chickens that provide the breakfast eggs'. It has been decorated with imagination. The owners share the cooking of the 'superlative' four-course dinners. Drawing room (log fires), dining room. No background music. Private annexe; wedding facilities in separate barn. 6 bedrooms. B&B £50–£135 per person.

**ROCK Cornwall**
Map 1:D2
ST ENODOC, nr Wadebridge, PL27 6LA. Tel 01208-863394, www.enodoc-hotel.co.uk. 'In a super position' overlooking the Camel estuary, this white-fronted hotel is family-friendly. It is decorated in a bright, colourful style. Kate Simms is the manager. Chef Nathan Outlaw oversees two restaurants: one offers fine dining, while the *Outlaw Seafood & Grill* is informal, with daily-changing simply cooked meals. 2 lounges, library, bar, 2 restaurants (classical background music); playroom (TV and video, table tennis, table football); billiard room; sauna, heated outdoor swimming pool. Terrace; ½-acre garden. Sandy beach nearby. 20 bedrooms (4 family suites). B&B £65–£185 per person. Dinner £45.

## ROSS-ON-WYE Herefordshire
## Map 3:D5

**THE HILL HOUSE**, Howle Hill, HR9 5ST. Tel 01989-562033, www. thehowlinghillhouse.com. Duncan and Alex Stayton run their 17th-century house in eco-friendly style. It stands in woodlands high above the Royal Forest of Dean. Guests can contribute to the 'Wisdom and Poetry wall', look for the ghost of the White Lady, or watch the shooting stars while soaking in the giant outdoor hot tub. Food is organic, from small local producers and the hotel's vegetable garden, and free-range hens. Aga-cooked breakfasts; packed lunch/evening meal by arrangement. Vegetarians are catered for. Morning room, lounge, bar (background music: morning Radio 4), restaurant; hot tub; sauna (charge); cinema (DVD film library). Garden. 5 bedrooms. B&B £25–£35 per person. Supper £15.

**PENCRAIG COURT**, Pencraig, HR9 6HR. Tel 01989-770306, www.pencraig-court. co.uk. 'No fuss or unnecessary frills at this hotel, which has a happy atmosphere.' Malcolm and Liz Dobson's yellow-painted Georgian country house overlooks the River Wye four miles from the town. The decoration and the cooking are traditional in style. 'Liz's dinners, using garden produce, are nicely presented and cooked; the menu changes daily. Breakfasts are equally pleasing.' 3½-acre garden (croquet) and woodlands; lovely views. 2 lounges, dining room (classical background music). Children and dogs (£5 per night) welcomed. 11 bedrooms (1 family). B&B £49.50–£75 per person. Dinner from £28.

## ROTHBURY Northumberland
## Map 4:A3

**ORCHARD HOUSE**, High Street, NE65 7TL. Tel 01669-620684, www. orchardhouserothbury.com. The atmosphere at Graham and Lisa Stobbart's Georgian town house is informal, with touches of luxury (a refreshing hot towel and drink on arrival; bathrobes and fresh fruit in the contemporary bedrooms). In a small village on the edge of Northumberland national park, it makes 'a good base for walking and outdoor pursuits'. Drawing room, breakfast room; garden. No background music. Wi-Fi. Complimentary daily newspaper. Children welcomed. 6 bedrooms. B&B £49.50–£185 per person.

## RYE East Sussex
## Map 2:E5

**THE SHIP INN**, The Strand, TN31 7DB. Tel 01797-222233, www.theshipinnrye. co.uk. Quaint and quirky, Karen Northcote's town-centre pub, with cosy rooms above, was built in 1592 as a warehouse to store contraband seized from smugglers. It has old beams, wooden floors and eclectic decoration. Breakfast has extensive choice, with bread from a local artisan baker. Dinner, based on British seasonal ingredients, has 'lots of Rye Bay fish, just what I want to eat at the seaside'. Bar, restaurant upstairs; terrace. Background music. Children and dogs welcomed. 10 bedrooms. B&B £45–£90 per person. Dinner £30.

**SIMMONS OF RYE**, 68–69 The Mint, TN31 7EW. Tel 01797-226032, www. simmonsofrye.co.uk. In the town centre, this 14th-century Grand Hall has been

renovated with style: flat-screen TVs and MP3-enabled digital radios alongside oak beams and period features. It is run as a small guest house by Mark Spreckley and Ray Weston, who provide a 'tailored service', helping with dinner reservations, special occasions and travel arrangements. Wi-Fi. *Club Room* (dining area/lounge). No background music. Small courtyard garden. 4 bedrooms (3 en suite, 1 with private bathroom). B&B £65–£80 per person.
**25% DISCOUNT VOUCHERS**

**ST AGNES Cornwall**
**Map 1:D2**
**ROSE IN VALE**, Mithian, TR5 0QD. Tel 01872-552202, www.rose-in-vale-hotel. co.uk. On the edge of a village on the north Cornish coast, this Georgian manor house is run as a country hotel by James and Sara Evans. It is in a peaceful wooded valley (home to badgers, buzzards, woodpeckers, herons, etc). The chef, Colin Hankins, uses Cornish produce for his modern dishes. Drawing room, lounge (traditionally furnished), bar, *Valley* restaurant (classical background music; resident pianist Sat night); function facilities. 10-acre grounds with outdoor pool, ponds. Dog-friendly. 20 bedrooms (2 in annexe; 2 suitable for &). B&B £50–£150 per person. Dinner £30.
**25% DISCOUNT VOUCHERS**

**ST IVES Cornwall**
**Map 1:D1**
**BLUE HAYES**, Trelyon Avenue, TR26 2AD. Tel 01736-797129, www.bluehayes. co.uk. High up on Porthminster Point, Malcolm Herring's immaculate small hotel in a 1920s house has stunning

views of the harbour and bay. A gate from the small garden leads directly to the beach (five minutes) or to the harbour (ten minutes). 2 lounges, bar, dining room (Mediterranean-style light suppers prepared by Nicola Martin); terrace (panoramic views). No background music. Small function facilities. Civil wedding licence. Parking. Open Mar to Oct. 6 bedrooms (some with balcony, roof terrace or patio). B&B £75–£105 per person. Supper £12–£16.

**THE PORTHMINSTER HOTEL**, The Terrace, TR26 2BN. Tel 01736-795221, www.porthminster-hotel.co.uk. In subtropical gardens overlooking the bay and Godrevy Lighthouse, this traditional hotel, in a Victorian building, is managed by Ben Young for Harbour Hotels. It has direct access to the beach. Lift. Lounge, bar, cocktail bar, restaurant (modern European fare; fish and seafood); background jazz; function/business facilities; civil wedding licence. Wi-Fi. Heated indoor swimming pool, tennis. 42 bedrooms (some family). B&B £40–£150 per person; D,B&B £65–£175.
**25% DISCOUNT VOUCHERS**

**PRIMROSE VALLEY HOTEL**, Primrose Valley, TR26 2ED. Tel 01736-794939, www.primroseonline.co.uk. In a terrace of Edwardian houses above Porthminster beach, this seaside villa has a striking modern interior. The owners, Sue and Andrew Biss and Rose Clegg, run it on eco-friendly lines; Anna Pascoe is the manager. Lounge, bar (gourmet snacks), breakfast room; small terrace overlooking sea. Background music. *The Ren Room* (treatments). Children

over 8 accepted. Closed Jan. 9 bedrooms (some with sea views, some with balcony). B&B £50–£117.50 per person.
**25% DISCOUNT VOUCHERS**

### SALCOMBE Devon
**Map 1:E4**
**SOUTH SANDS**, Bolt Head, TQ8 8LL. Tel 01548-859000, www.southsandshotel. co.uk. By South Sands beach, this hotel has been renovated in contemporary style. The well-equipped bedrooms have DVD-player, iPod station, etc. In the terrace restaurant, chef Brian Moore uses local seafood for his Mediterranean-inspired dishes. Bar, restaurant; terrace. Wi-Fi. Parking. Children and dogs welcomed. 22 bedrooms plus 5 beach apartments. B&B £90–£162.50 per person. Dinner from £22.

### SALISBURY Wiltshire
**Map 2:D2**
**LEENA'S**, 50 Castle Road, SP1 3RL. Tel 01722-335419, leenas@btinternet.com. Leena and Malcolm Street have run this good-value, welcoming B&B for many years. Their Edwardian house on busy Amesbury road (double glazing) is a short riverside walk from the centre. Lounge, breakfast room. No background music. Wi-Fi. Children welcomed. Garden. Parking. 6 bedrooms (1 on ground floor). B&B £34–£51 per person.

**SPIRE HOUSE**, 84 Exeter Street, SP1 2SE. Tel 01722-339213, www.salisbury-bedandbreakfast.com. Lois and John Faulkner run their B&B in an 18th-century Grade II listed town house near the cathedral. They give helpful advice on sights to visit and places to eat. Breakfast has healthy eating options

alongside traditional dishes. The house is near a main road: some traffic noise may be heard. No background music. Walled garden. Parking opposite. 4 bedrooms. B&B £37.50–£65 per person.

### SANDWICH Kent
**Map 2:D5**
**THE BELL HOTEL**, The Quay, CT13 9EF. Tel 01304-613388, www.bellhotelsandwich.co.uk. There is 'a general air of friendly welcome and helpfulness' at this tastefully refurbished 19th-century listed building by the River Stour. Manager Matt Collins co-owns it with Matthew Wolfman. Lounge, club room, *The Old Dining Room* restaurant (Stephen Piddock's cooking is 'very tasty'). Breakfast is 'impressive', too. Background music. Conservatory, sun terrace. Wi-Fi. Civil wedding licence. Limited parking. 37 bedrooms. B&B £55–£215 per person; D,B&B £85–£275.

### SCARBOROUGH North Yorkshire
**Map 4:C5**
**PHOENIX COURT**, 8/9 Rutland Terrace, YO12 7JB. Tel 01723-501150, www.hotel-phoenix.co.uk. Ten minutes' walk from the town centre, Alison and Bryan Edwards's refurbished guest house is created from two Victorian terrace houses on the headland overlooking North Bay. Lounge, bar area, dining room (background music). Packed lunches; drying facilities for walkers. Local and Fairtrade produce at breakfast. Children welcomed. Parking. 14 bedrooms (9 with sea views, 1 on ground floor). B&B £27–£40 per person.
**25% DISCOUNT VOUCHERS**

## SEAHOUSES Northumberland
Map 4:A4

ST CUTHBERT'S HOUSE, 192 Main Street,
North Sunderland, NE68 7UB. Tel
01665-720456, www.stcuthbertshouse.
com. Jeff and Jill Sutheran have restored
the dilapidated Presbyterian church
(built in 1810) that adjoined their home,
the manse. The original pulpit, a
balcony viewing area, a communion
table and original pillars have all been
preserved: the restoration is 'impressive,
in keeping with the character of the old
building'. 'Breakfasts were like the
house, rather stylish.' It is on a quiet
road, one mile inland from the village.
Lounge, breakfast room. Limited
parking. 6 bedrooms (1 suitable for &).
B&B £47.50–£105 per person.

## SHEFFIELD South Yorkshire
Map 4:E4

THE LEOPOLD, Leopold Street, S1 2JG.
Tel 0114-252 4000, www.leopoldhotel.
co.uk. In the revitalised Leopold Square
area, this large hotel has been quirkily
converted from a former boys' grammar
school, retaining the sombre colours
and memorabilia of its past. There are
panelled walls, arched doorways, old
school photos and ranks of coat pegs.
George Arizmendi is the manager for
the Irish PREM group. Bar, dining
room; terrace; afternoon teas, bar snacks;
24-hour room service. Background
music. Wi-Fi. Conference/function
facilities. Civil wedding licence. 90
bedrooms (6 suitable for &): £59–£75.
Breakfast £7.50–£10.95.

## SHREWSBURY Shropshire
Map 3:B4

CHATFORD HOUSE, Bayston Hill,
Chatford, SY3 0AY. Tel 01743-718301,

www.chatfordhouse.co.uk. In a peaceful
hamlet south of the city (with views of
The Wrekin), Christine and Rupert
Farmer take B&B visitors at their
Grade II listed farmhouse. Guests are
welcomed with tea or coffee, cake or
biscuits on arrival. The bedrooms are
decorated in a cottage style; breakfast
is cooked on the Aga, using local
ingredients. Sitting room, breakfast
room (background piano, CDs).
Country garden. Children welcomed.
No credit cards. 3 bedrooms. B&B £30–
£70 per person.

## SIDLESHAM West Sussex
Map 2:E3

THE CRAB & LOBSTER, Mill Lane,
PO20 7NB. Tel 01243-641233, www.
crab-lobster.co.uk. Structural engineer
turned hotelier Sam Bakose and his
wife, Janet, have renovated this 350-
year-old inn to give it a spare, modern
interior. It is on the banks of Pagham
Harbour nature reserve, an area of
outstanding natural beauty and special
scientific interest. The cooking is based
on local produce, with an emphasis on
seafood. Bar, restaurant (background
music); terrace; garden. 6 bedrooms
(2 in adjoining cottage; deluxe ones with
binoculars/telescope). B&B £65–£85 per
person. Dinner £40.

## SIDMOUTH Devon
Map 1:C5

HOTEL RIVIERA, The Esplanade, EX10
8AY. Tel 01395-515201, www.hotelriviera.
co.uk. The Wharton family have run
this 'very welcoming', traditional
seafront hotel overlooking Lyme Bay for
over three decades. The staff are 'long
serving and courteous'. The restaurant,
specialising in local seafood, is open to

non-residents. Lounge, bar (live pianist), restaurant; ballroom; terrace. Lift. Children welcomed. 26 bedrooms. B&B £109–£169 per person; D,B&B £125–£185.

**VICTORIA HOTEL**, The Esplanade, EX10 8RY. Tel 01395-512651, www. victoriahotel.co.uk. 'Our favourite bolt hole.' Matthew Raistrick manages this large hotel (at the western end of the esplanade) for the Brend group. 'Beautifully maintained and equipped public rooms.' David Gardener is the chef ('delicious food'). Sun lounge, bar, *Jubilee* restaurant; background music. Wi-Fi. Lift. Snooker; gym; outdoor swimming pool; spa (indoor pool, whirlpool, sauna, solarium, hot stone beds); tennis; putting. Parking. Families welcomed. 61 bedrooms (some with sea views and balcony; 3 suites around pool complex): £175–£350. Breakfast £18, dinner from £40.

**SKIPTON North Yorkshire**
**Map 4:D3**
**THE LISTER ARMS**, Malham, 22 The Lane, BD23 4DB. Tel 01729-830330, www.listerarms.co.uk. Chef/patron Terry Quinn serves traditonal Yorkshire fare at this popular pub in a stone-built 17th-century coaching inn (Shire Hotels) opposite the green of a 'charming' village in the southern Dales. Good walking on the Pennine Way which passes through the village. Bar, dining room. Background music. Wi-Fi. Garden. Children and dogs welcomed. 9 bedrooms. B&B £30–£65 per person. Dinner £26.

**SNETTERTON Norfolk**
**Map 2:B5**
**HOLLY HOUSE**, Snetterton South End, Diss, NR16 2LG. Tel 01953-498051,

www.hollyhouse-guesthouse.co.uk. 'Bedrooms and bathrooms are decorated and furnished to an extremely high standard, luxurious even.' This 300-year-old thatched cottage, painted pink, is the restored family home of Laurel ('an accomplished cook') and Jeff Stonell. 'We were made most welcome.' Drawing room (log fires), dining room. No background music. Parking. 18 miles W of Norwich. Resident dogs. 3 bedrooms. B&B £45–£55 per person. Dinner (by arrangement) £28–£32.

**SOMERTON Somerset**
**Map 1:C6**
**THE LYNCH COUNTRY HOUSE**, 4 Behind Berry, TA11 7PD. Tel 01458-272316, www.thelynchcountryhouse. co.uk. On the edge of a small town above the Cary valley, this 'peaceful' Grade II listed Regency house is run as a B&B by Roy Copeland, a former jazz musician. The manager is Dave Williamson. Breakfasts are served in the 'bright, attractive' orangery, whose tall windows overlook a lake in the grounds. No background music. Children and dogs welcomed. 9 bedrooms (4 in coach house, on ground floor). B&B £35–£70 per person.

**SOUTHAMPTON Hampshire**
**Map 2:E2**
**WHITE STAR TAVERN AND DINING ROOMS**, 28 Oxford Street, SO14 3DJ. Tel 02380-821990, www.whitestartavern. co.uk. In a former seafarers' hotel made stylishly shipshape, this friendly bar and restaurant (renamed after the famous shipping line) is managed by Oliver Weeks. The well-equipped bedrooms are decorated in contemporary style; bathrooms have mosaic tiles, large

shower. Jim Haywood is chef. Lounge, bar restaurant (background music); roof terrace. Wi-Fi. 13 bedrooms, plus one 3-bedroom serviced apartment: £99–£149. Breakfast £3.50–£8, dinner £30.

## SOUTHPORT Merseyside
Map 4:E2
THE VINCENT, 98 Lord Street, PR8 1JR. Tel 01704-883800, www.thevincenthotel. com. Developed from an old cinema by local restaurateur Paul Adams, this trendy hotel on a fashionable boulevard has a contemporary glass facade and state-of-the-art features. Rooms, called V-Residences, V-Suites, V-Corner Suites and V-Penthouse, are decorated in soothing colours. Bar, *V* café/sushi bar (outdoor seating); background music; spa; gym; beauty treatments. Wi-Fi. Function facilities. Civil wedding licence. Valet parking. 'Enthusiastic, helpful staff.' Children welcomed. 60 bedrooms (3 suitable for &) on 6 floors. B&B from £70 per person. Dinner from £12.95.

## SOUTHWOLD Suffolk
Map 2:B6
THE SWAN, Market Place, IP18 6EG. Tel 01502-722186, www.adnamshotels. co.uk. On the square of the market town, this 300-year-old building has been brought up to date with renovation of the bar, lounge and 20 bedrooms. It is managed for Adnams by Martin Edwards. Rory Whelan is the chef. 'The cooking is first rate; tasty and generous portions; great value.' Lift. Lounge, bar, reading room, restaurant; private dining room; function facilities. No background music. Garden. Parking. Beach 200 yds. Children and dogs (in 'lighthouse' rooms with own patio) welcomed. 42

bedrooms (1 suitable for &). B&B £95–£210 per person; D,B&B £125–£270.

## STANSTED Essex
Map 2:C4
OAK LODGE, Jacks Lane, Smiths Green, Takeley, CM22 6NT. Tel 01279-871667, www.oaklodgebb.com. In lovely two-acre gardens in a tranquil village, this 16th-century house is run as a B&B by 'welcoming' owners Jan and Ron Griffiths. Decorated in 'old English' style, it has beamed public rooms, cottagey bedrooms. 2 miles NW of Stansted airport. Lounge, breakfast room. Wi-Fi. No background music. Parking (moderate long-term rates). 4 bedrooms. B&B £50–£60 per person.

## STOKE FLEMING Devon
Map 1:D4
STOKE LODGE, Cinders Lane, TQ6 0RA. Tel 01803-770523, www.stokelodge.co.uk. Christine and Steven Mayer have created a cosy atmosphere, with plenty to occupy guests at their extended country hotel dating back to the 17th century. On the south Devon coast, 2 miles from Dartmouth. 2 lounges, bar, restaurant (Paul Howard is the chef; background music); terrace; games room, snooker room; indoor swimming pool (sauna, whirlpool); 3-acre garden (heated swimming pool); tennis; giant chess. Children welcomed. 26 bedrooms. B&B £47.50–£53.50 per person; D,B&B £75–£81.
25% DISCOUNT VOUCHERS

## SWAY Hampshire
Map 2:E2
THE NURSE'S COTTAGE, Station Road, nr Lymington, SO41 6BA. Tel 01590-683402, www.nursescottage.co.uk.

'Hands-on, almost omnipresent' chef/
proprietor Tony Barnfield runs his
restaurant-with-rooms in a small
house that was the home of Sway's
district nurses between 1913 and 1983.
Meticulously kept, it has well-equipped
bedrooms. 'Den' (computer, ironing,
books, CDs, DVDs, videos), conservatory
restaurant; shop selling local goods.
Background music ('nostalgic'). Wi-Fi.
Dogs welcomed. 5 bedrooms (all on
ground floor; good accessibility). D,B&B
£95–£115 per person.
**25% DISCOUNT VOUCHERS**

**SWINDON Wiltshire**
**Map 2:C2**
**CHISELDON HOUSE HOTEL**, New Road,
Chiseldon, SN4 0NE. Tel 01793-741010,
www.chiseldonhousehotel.co.uk. In a
'quiet, pleasant' location near the M4,
John Sweeney's Italianate Grade II
listed country hotel stands in large,
well-maintained grounds. 'Does the job
of providing a good night's lodging
unobtrusively and well.' 5 miles SE of
Swindon. Lounge, bar, *Orangery*
restaurant (Robert Harwood is chef);
'mellow' background jazz; terrace;
extensive gardens. Civil wedding
licence. Conference facilities. Children
welcomed (some restrictions in
restaurant). 21 bedrooms. B&B £55–£90
per person; D,B&B £58.25–£110.

**THE LANDMARK HOTEL**, Station Road,
Chiseldon, SN4 0PW. Tel 01793-740149,
www.landmarkhotel.com. Trevor
Mitchell, the owner, and Paul Heal (the
manager) run this good-value hotel
opposite a doctor's surgery, in the centre
of Chiseldon. Outside is a profusion of
flowers in hanging baskets and pots.
The spacious bedrooms are comfortable;

the food is freshly prepared. Lounge/bar
area, restaurant (background music);
courtyard; small function facilities.
Wi-Fi. 16 bedrooms (5 with balcony;
5 with courtyard garden access). B&B
£30–£40 per person; D,B&B £45.

**TETBURY Gloucestershire**
**Map 3:E5**
**OAK HOUSE NO.1**, The Chipping,
GL8 8EU. Tel 01666-505741, www.
oakhouseno1.com. Gary Kennedy, an
interior designer and art collector, has
filled his Georgian town house in the
centre of the town with an eclectic mix
of antiques and artefacts gathered
during his travels. The bedrooms
are classical in style, the bathrooms
contemporary. Dinner (for groups
of four to eight people) is taken
communally. Sitting room, dining
room. Walled garden. Picnic hampers.
Beauty treatments. Children over 11
accepted. 4 bedrooms. B&B £77.50–
£127.50 perperson. Dinner £35 (4-course
set menu).
**25% DISCOUNT VOUCHERS**

**THIRSK North Yorkshire**
**Map 4:C4**
**OSWALDS**, Front Street, Sowerby, YO7
1JF. Tel 01845-523655, www.oswalds
restaurantwithrooms.co.uk. 'An
enjoyable visit.' This restaurant-with-
rooms was converted from old farm
buildings on a tree-lined street
('blissfully quiet'), a short walk from
the racecourse. It is owned by David
Hawkins's IDH group, and has a new
manager this year, Peter Syzmanski.
John Paul is chef. Lounge, bar,
restaurant; background music; function
facilities. Wi-Fi. Parking. Children
welcomed. 16 bedrooms (3 in stable

block, 5 in old farmhouse; 1 suitable for &. B&B £35–£100 per person; D,B&B £47.50–£115.

## THORPE ST ANDREW Norfolk
Map 2:B5
THE OLD RECTORY, 103 Yarmouth Road, NR7 0HF. Tel 01603-700772, www.oldrectorynorwich.com. Overlooking the River Yare, this creeper-clad Georgian rectory (Grade II listed) is home to Sally and Chris Entwistle, son James, and Birman cats Rolo and Milli. 'A comfortable and friendly place to stay; lives up to its reputation as "the best-kept secret in Norwich".' Drawing room, dining room (background music: classical/light jazz), conservatory; terrace. Wi-Fi. Meeting/function facilities. 1-acre garden: unheated outdoor swimming pool. 2½ miles from Norwich. Children welcomed. 8 bedrooms (3 in coach house; all have bathrobes, LCD TV, CD-player). B&B £65–£95 per person; D,B&B from £80.

## THURNHAM Kent
Map 2:D4
THURNHAM KEEP, Castle Hill, ME14 3LE. Tel 01622-734149, www.thurnhamkeep.co.uk. Approached up a long drive, Amanda Lane's graceful Edwardian house stands in terraced gardens with views over the Weald of Kent. Bedrooms are lavishly furnished. A copious breakfast is served at a communal table, with home-made jams, and honey from the garden hives. A kitchen supper can be arranged; plenty of pubs and restaurants are nearby. Oak-panelled sitting room (wood-burning stove), conservatory, dining room; snooker room. Background music (evenings only; 'easy listening'/classical/

jazz). 7-acre garden: heated outdoor swimming pool (June to early Sept), pond, kitchen garden, dovecote, summer house; tennis, croquet. 3 bedrooms. B&B £60–£70 per person. Supper £35.

## TISBURY Wiltshire
Map 2:D1
BECKFORD ARMS, Fonthill Gifford, SP3 6PX. Tel 01747-870385, www.beckfordarms.com. By the rolling parkland of the Fonthill Estate, this traditional stone-built country pub was updated in modern style in 2009 by Dan Brod, Charlie Luxton and Mark Blatchford (the chef). Local ingredients are used for the seasonal menus; tea and snacks are available all day. Bedrooms have hi-tech entertainment systems, paintings by local artists on the walls. Sitting room, bar, restaurant, private dining room; terrace (alfresco dining). Background music. Private dining room; function facilities. Wi-Fi. 1-acre garden: hammocks, boules piste. Children welcomed. 9 bedrooms (1 family suite). B&B £35–£90 per person.

THE COMPASSES INN, Lower Chicksgrove, SP3 6NB. Tel 01722-714318, www.thecompassesinn.com. There is good walking in an area of outstanding natural beauty from the door of Alan and Susie Stoneham's thatched, 14th-century pub. It has a separate entrance to the plain, light bedrooms. 'Pub grub' is cooked by Dave Cousin. Bar, dining room. Garden. No background music. Small function facilities. Children and dogs welcomed. 4 bedrooms (plus 2-bedroom cottage). B&B £42.50–£65 per person. Dinner from £24.
**25% DISCOUNT VOUCHERS**

## TOTNES Devon
## Map 1:D4

**ROYAL SEVEN STARS**, The Plains, TQ9 5DD. Tel 01803-862125, www. royalsevenstars.co.uk. Owners Nigel and Anne Way are committed to environmentally friendly initiatives at their imposing, white 17th-century coaching inn with a modern interior. Margaret Stone is the manager. It is a popular local watering hole; light bar meals are available all day; brasserie food is served in the evening. Lounge, 2 bars (background music; log fires in winter); *TQ9* restaurant; alfresco dining; terrace; balcony. Wi-Fi. Business facilities. Civil wedding licence. Children welcomed. Parking. 21 bedrooms (quietest at back). B&B £59.50–£115 per person; D,B&B £80–£135.

## TRESCO Isles of Scilly
## Map 1: inset C1

**THE NEW INN**, TR24 0QE. Tel 01720-422844, www.tresco.co.uk. Near the harbour of Robert Dorrien-Smith's private car-free island, this informal inn stays open all year round. It is a real ale pub, decorated with nautical memorabilia. The bars and restaurant are popular with visitors to the timeshare cottages on the island. Lounge, 2 bars (background music), pavilion, restaurant, patio. Outdoor heated swimming pool. Children welcomed. Music, beer and cider festivals. 16 bedrooms (some with terrace, some with sea views). B&B £70–£115 per person. Dinner from £30.

## TRURO Cornwall
## Map 1:D2

**MANNINGS HOTEL**, Lemon Street, TR1 2QB. Tel 01872-270345, www.mannings hotels.co.uk. Close to the cathedral, this Grade II listed stone building has been refurbished in contemporary style, with much glass, wood, and leather seating. Convivial atmosphere in the bar. Lounge, brasserie. Background music. Children welcomed. Parking. 43 bedrooms, 9 apartments in stable block (1 suitable for &). B&B £79–£129 per person. Dinner £35.

## TUNBRIDGE WELLS Kent
## Map 2:D4

**HOTEL DU VIN TUNBRIDGE WELLS**, 13 Crescent Road, TN1 2LY. Tel 01892-526455, www.hotelduvin.com. 'Excellent, attentive service.' In an 'outstanding position', this branch of the Hotel du Vin chain, an 18th-century Grade II listed sandstone mansion, is managed by Mike Auld. Bars ('fun, but can get crowded'), lively bistro; function facilities. No background music. Wi-Fi (free for 30 mins). 1-acre garden: terrace; boules. Limited parking. Children and dogs welcomed. 34 bedrooms: £140–£230. Breakfast £10.95–£13.95, dinner from £25.

**SMART AND SIMPLE**, 54–57 London Road, TN1 1DS. Tel 0845-402 5744, www.smartandsimple.co.uk. Five minutes from the centre, William Inglis's hotel in an Edwardian terrace is recommended for its good value. The modern bedrooms, plainly furnished, have views over a 'secret' garden (lots of steps down) or the town common. Lounge, bar, conservatory; snacks and tapas dishes, conservatory; 3 meeting rooms; small gym (£5 fee). Wi-Fi. Background music. Small car park. 40 bedrooms (2 family rooms; some suitable for &). B&B (continental) £32.50–£85 per person.

## TWO BRIDGES Devon
### Map 1:D4
**PRINCE HALL HOTEL**, Dartmoor, PL20 6SA. Tel 01822-890403, www.princehall. co.uk. On Dartmoor, with panoramic views over West Dart valley, this cream-painted country house (built 1787) is reached by an avenue of ancient beech trees. 'Welcoming', hands-on proprietors Fi and Chris Daly have renovated the dining room, making it light and airy. Chef Raoul Ketelaas's 'memorable' seasonal menus use produce from listed local suppliers. 2 sitting rooms, bar, dining room; classical background music in early evening. Dogs welcomed. 8 bedrooms. B&B £70–£90 per person; D,B&B £95–£110.

## UPPINGHAM Rutland
### Map 2:B3
**THE LAKE ISLE**, 16 High Street East, LE15 9PZ. Tel 01572-822951, www. lakeisle.co.uk. On the High Street, this Grade II-listed building is run as a restaurant-with-rooms by Richard and Janine Burton; Stuart Mead is the chef. 'Dinner was very good; the coffee with home-made chocolates also got top marks.' Lounge, bar, restaurant; occasional background music. Wi-Fi. Courtyard. Small wedding/business facilities. Limited parking. Children welcomed. 12 bedrooms (recently renovated). B&B £37.50–£75 per person; D,B&B £65–£92.50.

## VENTNOR Isle of Wight
### Map 2:E2
**THE ROYAL HOTEL**, Belgrave Road, PO38 1JJ. Tel 01983-852186, www. royalhoteliow.co.uk. 'High-quality food and personal, friendly service in a building of comfortable character.' In subtropical grounds close to the seafront (five minutes' walk), this large seaside hotel is run on unashamedly traditional lines by the owner, William Bailey, and manager, Lindsay Perkins. 2 lounges, bar with terrace, restaurant; conservatory; resident pianist during peak season weekends; function rooms; civil wedding licence. 2-acre gardens: heated outdoor swimming pool, children's play area. Sandy beach nearby (hilly walk). Parking. 54 bedrooms (some suitable for &). B&B £90–£145 per person; D,B&B £130–£185.
**25% DISCOUNT VOUCHERS**

## WADEBRIDGE Cornwall
### Map 1:D2
**ST MORITZ HOTEL**, Trebetherick, PL27 6SD. Tel 01208-862242, www. stmoritzhotel.co.uk. The atmosphere is informal at this white, Art Deco-influenced purpose-built hotel with sweeping views of the Camel estuary. It is owned by Steve Ridgeway (CEO of Virgin Atlantic) and his brother, Hugh; William Pound is the manager. Sitting areas, bar, restaurant (Cornish fish dishes a speciality of chef James O'Connor), *Cowshed* spa; leisure suite (indoor pool, steam room, sauna, treatments); gym, fitness classes. 3-acre grounds: heated outdoor pool, tennis. Children welcomed. 45 bedrooms (also 15 apartments; and villas in grounds). B&B £49.50–£154.50 per person. Dinner £35.

## WELLS Somerset
### Map 2:D1
**STOBERRY HOUSE**, Stoberry Park, BA5 3LD. Tel 01749-672906, www. stoberry-park.co.uk. In parkland on the edge of the city, Frances Young's elegant

stone house has 'lovely' views over the Vale of Avalon. She runs it as a 'good-value' B&B. Sitting room, breakfast room. 'Superb' historic 6-acre grounds (wildlife ponds, water features, sculpture, 1½-acre walled garden, sunken garden, gazebo, potager, lime walk). 5 bedrooms (1 studio cottage). Function facilities. B&B (continental) £47.50–£62.50 per person (cooked breakfast £5–£10).
**25% DISCOUNT VOUCHERS**

**WEM Shropshire**
**Map 3:B5**
**OLD RECTORY HOTEL**, Lowe Hill Road, SY4 5UA. Tel 01939-233233, www.oldrectorywem.co.uk. Keith and Kathy Hanmer spent ten years lovingly restoring their handsome Georgian house in walled gardens on the edge of the market town; their daughter, Selina Cuss, is the manager. The house has been furnished in keeping with its origins. Drawing room, bar, *Orangery* (light snacks), restaurant (arched ceiling; background music); terrace; small function facilities; civil wedding licence. Wi-Fi. 3½-acre grounds. 14 bedrooms. B&B £45–£99.50 per person; D,B&B £64.50–£99.50.

**WESTON-SUPER-MARE Somerset**
**Map 1:B6**
**BEACHLANDS**, 17 Uphill Road North, BS23 4NG. Tel 01934-621401, www.beachlandshotel.com. Charles and Beverly Porter's 'excellent', traditional hotel overlooks sand dunes and an 18-hole golf course. 'The staff were all cheerful and helpful.' 2 lounges, bar, restaurant; background music. 10-metre indoor swimming pool, sauna; function/business facilities. Wi-Fi. Garden. Parking. Children welcomed.

21 bedrooms (some on ground floor). B&B £62–£100 per person. Dinner £21.50.

**CHURCH HOUSE**, 27 Kewstoke Road, BS22 9YD. Tel 01934-633185, www.churchhousekewstoke.co.uk. By the village church, this Georgian house was the residence of Kewstoke vicars. It is now run as a B&B (with a contemporary interior) by Jane and Tony Chapman. Breakfast includes eggs from their own hens, and free-range Gloucester Old Spot sausages. 2½ miles from Weston-super-Mare. Lounge, conservatory, breakfast room. Wi-Fi. Small garden. 5 bedrooms. B&B £40–£60 per person.
**25% DISCOUNT VOUCHERS**

**WHITBY North Yorkshire**
**Map 4:C5**
**DUNSLEY HALL**, Dunsley, YO21 3TL. Tel 01947-893437, www.dunsleyhall.com. Bill and Carol Ward run their traditional hotel, in a hamlet near Whitby, in a mansion built for a Victorian shipping family; the seafaring connections can be seen in an unusual stained-glass window. It is full of original features: oak panelling, inglenook fireplace; four-poster beds. Lounge, *Pyman's* bar (background music), restaurant (Graham Hughes is chef; at breakfast 'the most delicious kipper I've ever tasted'). Function facilities; civil wedding licence. 4-acre gardens: putting, croquet, tennis. Hotel's working farm nearby; sea 1 mile. Parking. 26 bedrooms (8 in new wing; 1 suitable for &). B&B £77–£100 per person; D,B&B £90–£115.
**25% DISCOUNT VOUCHERS**

## WIGMORE Herefordshire
Map 3:C4

**PEAR TREE FARM**, HR6 9UR. Tel 01568-770140, www.peartree-farm.co.uk. On the edge of a small village with castle ruins near Ludlow, Jill Fieldhouse and Steve Dawson run their traditional 17th-century stone-built farmhouse as an upmarket B&B. Bedrooms have much character; touches of luxury in the bathrooms (candles, oils, fluffy bathrobes). Dinner is served by arrangement at weekends only (free-range Herefordshire dishes). Sitting room with log fire, dining room. 2-acre garden. 2 resident dogs, 1 cat. 3 bedrooms (1 on ground floor). B&B (2-night min. stay) £52.50–£105 per person; D,B&B £82.50. Closed Jan to Mar, except for house parties.

## WINDERMERE Cumbria
Map 4: inset C2

**CEDAR MANOR**, Ambleside Road, LA23 1AX. Tel 015394-43192, www.cedarmanor.co.uk. Visitors are 'well satisfied with the hospitality' at Caroline and Jonathan Kaye's hotel in a 'very convenient location for Lake Windermere'. Built in 1854 as a private country retreat, the house stands in a walled garden, dominated by a 200-year-old cedar tree. The comfortable, traditional rooms are well equipped. Lounge, dining room (light background music during meals). Children welcomed. 11 bedrooms (2, noisier, in coach house). B&B £50–£100 per person; D,B&B £80–£160.

**HOLBECK GHYLL**, Holbeck Lane, LA23 1LU. Tel 015394-32375, www.holbeckghyll.com. In January 2010, Lisa and Stephen Leahy bought this luxurious Lakeland hotel in extensive grounds which run down to the lake. They have appointed Andrew McPherson (formerly at *Swinton Park*, Masham) as manager. 'We liked the relaxed ambience, good service and country house feel.' Chef David McLaughlin has a *Michelin* star for his modern cooking. 2 lounges (background music in 1), bar, restaurant. Function facilities; civil wedding licence. Small spa. 14-acre grounds: tennis, croquet. 25 bedrooms (1 suitable for ⅃). D,B&B £139–£245 per person.

**1 PARK ROAD**, 1 Park Road, LA23 2AW. Tel 015394-42107, www.1parkroad.com. In a former gentleman's residence in a quiet area close to the centre, this small guest house is run by considerate hosts Mary and Philip Burton. 'A great base for exploring the lakes.' Lounge (grand piano), dining room (locally sourced food; dinner Fri and Sat only). Background music ('a key point of life here') at dinner, sometimes at breakfast. Picnic hamper/rucksack available. Wi-Fi. Children welcomed. Parking. 6 bedrooms. B&B £42–£52 per person. Dinner £20.50–£22.50.
**25% DISCOUNT VOUCHERS**

## WOODSTOCK Oxfordshire
Map 2:C2

**THE FEATHERS**, 16–20 Market Street, OX20 1SX. Tel 01993-812291, www.feathers.co.uk. In the centre of the attractive village, near Blenheim Palace, this former 17th-century coaching inn was recently renovated. Traditional furnishing, antiques, paintings and log fires are retained; bedrooms have been smartened; some bathrooms have walk-in shower and freestanding bath. Luc

Morel is the manager; chef Marc Hardiman serves modern dishes in the wood-panelled dining room. 'Terrific, friendly service.' Study, bar/bistro (jazz/classical background music), restaurant; courtyard (alfresco dining); function facilities; beauty treatments. Children welcomed. 21 individual bedrooms (5 in adjacent town house; 1 suitable for &; 1 suite has private steam room). B&B £50–£187.50 per person; D,B&B £94.50–£231.50.

## WROXTON Oxfordshire
### Map 2:C2
**WROXTON HOUSE HOTEL**, Silver Street, OX15 6QB. Tel 01295-730777, www. wroxtonhousehotel.com. Dating back to 1649, this 'exquisite' thatched-roof manor house in a village near Banbury is run as a hotel (Best Western) by the Smith family. It has many original features (inglenook fireplace, original oak beams). Bedrooms are 'spotless' (much renovation in 2010). Chef Steve Mason-Tocker's cooking is of an 'extremely high standard'. Wi-Fi. 2 lounges (piped music in main one), bar, *1649* restaurant; 2 private function rooms. Parking. Civil wedding licence. Children welcomed. 32 bedrooms (3 in adjoining cottage). B&B £44.50–£110 per person; D,B&B £66.50–£132.
**25% DISCOUNT VOUCHERS**

## WYE Kent
### Map 2:D5
**THE WIFE OF BATH**, 4 Upper Bridge Street, TN25 5AF. Tel 01233-812232, www.thewifeofbath.com. 'The welcome from the staff was outstanding' at this informal restaurant-with-rooms in a smartly renovated Victorian bay-fronted house on the edge of the village. 'Our

bedroom was well appointed, immaculately clean, and delightful.' Robert Hymers is the chef: 'Excellent cooking, in a pleasant dining room.' Breakfasts have local Kentish apple juice, home-made granola, Greek yogurt and fresh berries. Lounge, restaurant (closed Mon). 5 bedrooms (2 in garden annexe). Parking. Children welcomed. B&B £47.50–£75 per person. Dinner £35.

## YORK North Yorkshire
### Map 4:D4
**BAR CONVENT**, 17 Blossom Street, YO24 1AQ. Tel 01904-643238, www. bar-convent.org.uk. 'Unlike any hotel in which I have stayed.' This centrally located Grade I listed Georgian building (built 1760) is England's oldest active convent (the guest house is run by nuns and housekeeping staff). Rooms are simple; beds are 'wickedly' comfortable. Notable are the 'magnificent' glass-roofed entrance hall, and a library full of antique Catholic texts. Wi-Fi. Communal self-catering facilities. Lounges (on each floor, each with TV); games room; licensed café; meeting rooms; museum, shop; 18th-century domed chapel (Catholic weddings); function facilities. Lift. No background music. ½-acre garden. 18 bedrooms (some suitable for &). B&B (continental) £33–£67 per person (cooked breakfast £4.50); D,B&B £45–£77.

**THE BLOOMSBURY**, 127 Clifton, YO30 6BL. Tel 01904-634031, www. bloomsburyhotel.co.uk. 'Enthusiastic' new owners Stephen and Tricia Townsley have taken over this B&B in a Victorian house and given it a make-over. In a leafy area, it is less than a mile from the centre, which can be reached

via a scenic river walk. Sitting room, dining room (background music); terrace. Wi-Fi. Flowery courtyard. Parking. Children welcomed. 6 bedrooms. B&B £35–£55 per person.
**25% DISCOUNT VOUCHERS**

**HOTEL DU VIN YORK**, 89 The Mount, YO24 1AX. Tel 01904-557350, www. hotelduvin.com. 'Terrific, friendly service.' This branch of the du Vin chain is a converted 19th-century Grade II listed building (once an orphanage) in a tranquil area just outside the city walls. It is managed by Rohan Slabbert. 'Huge, comfy bed; excellent, efficient bathroom.' Bar, bistro (Nico Cecchella is chef); courtyard (alfresco dining); background music; function facilities; 3-acre grounds. Limited parking. 44 bedrooms (some suitable for ♿): £140–£350. Breakfast £10.95–£13.50.

## SCOTLAND

### ABERDEEN
**Map 5:C3**
**THE MARCLIFFE HOTEL AND SPA**, North Deeside Road, Pitfodels, AB15 9YA. Tel 01224-861000, www.marcliffe.com. In wooded grounds in the lower Dee valley, this large, luxury country house is owned by Stewart Spence, and managed by Tom Ward. Game and fish are specialities on the menus of chef Mike Stoddard. It is 20 minutes' drive from the centre and airport. Drawing room, lounge, snooker room, bar, conservatory restaurant; terrace (alfresco dining); lift. 24-hour room service. No background music. Spa (treatments); gym. Wedding/function facilities. 11-acre grounds: putting. 42 bedrooms (1 suitable for ♿; complimentary soft drinks and snacks).

B&B £75–£225 per person; D,B&B £122.50–£142.50.

### ACHILTIBUIE Highland
**Map 5:B1**
**SUMMER ISLES HOTEL**, IV26 2YG. Tel 01854-622282, www.summerisleshotel. com. Chef Chris Firth-Bernard has a *Michelin* star for his five-course menus (everything home produced or locally caught) at this hotel/restaurant in a 'beautiful, remote location' overlooking the Summer Isles. It is managed by Duncan Evans for the owners, Terry and Irina Mackay. The original crofters' bar, dating back to the mid-19th century, is open all day for coffee and snacks, lunch and less formal evening meals. Lounge, bar (background music), garden. Children over 8 allowed; dogs welcomed. Ullapool is 30 mins' drive. 3 bedrooms in main house; log cabin sleeps 4; stone croft sleeps 2; cottage sleeps 4. B&B £72.50–£175 per person. Dinner £56.

### ALYTH Perth and Kinross
**Map 5:D2**
**LANDS OF LOYAL**, Blairgowrie, PH11 8JQ. Tel 01828-633151, www. landsofloyal.com. In extensive grounds overlooking the vale of Strathmore, Verity Webster's country house hotel has an impressive Grand Hall, modelled on a saloon on the *Mauritania* (chandelier and light fittings from the liner). Hall/sitting area (background music: jazz, swing), bar, 4 dining rooms (food locally sourced where possible, some is grown on site). 4½-acre garden. Children and dogs welcomed. Wedding facilities. 16 bedrooms (3 in adjacent coach house). B&B £70–£110 per person; D,B&B £105–£145.
**25% DISCOUNT VOUCHERS**

**ARDUAINE Argyll and Bute**
Map 5:D1

LOCH MELFORT HOTEL, by Oban, PA34 4XG. Tel 01852-200233, www. lochmelfort.co.uk. 'A perfect place to relax.' Run by 'hands-on' owners Calum and Rachel Ross, this Victorian country hotel has a 'wonderful' setting on Asknish Bay overlooking Jura. Sitting room, library, bar, *Arduaine* restaurant ('great food'; locally caught fish and shellfish), bistro. No background music. 17-acre gardens (part-owned by National Trust). 25 bedrooms (with balcony or terrace, and sea views; 20 in annexe; 10 have wheelchair access). B&B £69–£134 per person; D,B&B £95–£149.

**ARISAIG Highland**
Map 5:C1

CNOC-NA-FAÍRE, Back of Keppoch, PH39 4NS. Tel 01687-450249, www. cnoc-na-faire.co.uk. Before they retire to bed, a complimentary dram is offered to guests at Jenny and David Sharpe's small hotel with 'gorgeous views', on the Road to the Isles. The original croft house (with Art Deco extension) has plaid-furnished bedrooms. Light lunches and suppers are served in the lounge bar; dinner in the restaurant (food with a Scottish twist; background music). Wedding facilities (marquee); house parties. Substantial breakfast. Wi-Fi. Children welcomed; dogs by arrangement (£5 charge for charity). Parking; bicycle storage. 6 bedrooms (no telephone). B&B £45–£125 per person. Dinner £25–£30.

**AUCHENCAIRN Dumfries and Galloway**
Map 5:E2

BALCARY BAY, Shore Road, Castle Douglas, DG7 1QZ. Tel 01556-640217, www.balcary-bay-hotel.co.uk. Once the hideout of 17th-century smugglers, this remote hotel has 'great views' across to Heston Island. The manager, Graeme Lamb, and his staff provide 'attentive and polite service'. Chef Grant Walker uses Scottish ingredients for dishes with a classic French influence. 'Good value for money.' 2 lounges, bar, restaurant, conservatory. 3½-acre garden. Children welcomed. Closed early Dec to late Jan. 20 bedrooms (3 on ground floor, with patio). B&B £63–£78 per person; D,B&B £85–£91.
**25% DISCOUNT VOUCHERS**

**BALLYGRANT Argyll and Bute**
Map 5:D1

KILMENY COUNTRY HOUSE, Isle of Islay, PA45 7QW. Tel 01496-840668, www.kilmeny.co.uk. On a working farm in an elevated position on the edge of a village, Margaret Rozga's white-painted 19th-century house has 'spectacular views' over the surrounding countryside. She provides a 'really nice' welcome, with complimentary tea and cakes; whisky and home-made biscuits in the bedrooms. Dinners (Tues and Thurs only; BYO wine) are 'wonderful', and include drinks and canapés before, and petits fours afterwards, in the sitting room. No background music. Sitting room, sun room. Garden. 5 bedrooms (1 with separate entrance). B&B £57.50–£72.50 per person. Dinner £36.

**BOWMORE Argyll and Bute**
Map 5:D1

HARBOUR INN AND RESTAURANT, The Square, Isle of Islay, PA43 7JR. Tel 01496-810330, www.harbour-inn.com. This whitewashed old inn is by the shore in a village on the east side of

Loch Indaal; there are views of the Paps of Jura across the loch. Owners Neil and Carol Scott have given it a light, fresh decor. Sandra Stevenson cooks seasonal specialities (eg, 'fabulous' crowdie terrine with home-made pear chutney). Conservatory lounge, *Schooner* bar, restaurant ('mellow Celtic' background music). Wi-Fi. Small garden. Children over 10 allowed. 7 bedrooms (some in neighbouring *Inn Over-by*). B&B £60–£75 per person. Dinner £35–£40.

## BRAE Shetland
## Map 5:A2
BUSTA HOUSE, ZE2 9QN. Tel 01806-522506, www.bustahouse.com. 'The setting is idyllic, the welcome warm; super breakfasts.' This grand, white-painted country house, on the shores of Busta Voe, was built in 1588 by the Gifford family. It is now owned and run as a small hotel by Joe and Veronica Rocks. Bedrooms (slightly old-fashioned) are named after islands around the coast of mainland Shetland. 2 lounges, bar/dining area, restaurant (Daniel Okroj is chef). Garden. Wi-Fi. Children welcomed. Wedding facilities. 22 bedrooms. B&B £55–£95 per person; D,B&B £75–£100.

## CASTLEBAY Western Isles
## Map 5: inset A1
CASTLEBAY HOTEL, Isle of Barra, HS9 5XD. Tel 01871-810223, www.castlebayhotel.com. On the southernmost of the Western Isles, this 'excellent' small hotel overlooks Kisimul Castle and the harbour. It is owned by Terry MacKay, and managed by John Campbell. 'Good food and a spacious, well-equipped room with sea views.' Easy to reach by ferry from Oban. Lounge, bar,

restaurant (Slawomir Pilarski specialises in seafood); conservatory/sun porch; background music. ¼-acre garden. Children welcomed. 15 bedrooms (1 suitable for &). B&B £38.50–£71 per person; D,B&B £15 added.

THE CRAIGARD HOTEL, Isle of Barra, HS9 5XD. Tel 01871-810200, www.craigardhotel.co.uk. Helpful owner Julian Capewell runs this small, white hotel on a hillside above the town ('breathtaking views' of the bay and southern islands). The restaurant is popular with locals for lunch and dinner. Lounge, 2 bars (pool table), restaurant; terrace (panoramic views). Beach airport 6 miles; town and ferry terminal close by. Parking. Children welcomed (not in public bar). 7 bedrooms. B&B from £40 per person.

## CONNEL Argyll and Bute
## Map 5:D1
ARDS HOUSE, by Oban, PA37 1PT. Tel 01631-710255, www.ardshouse.com. On the rocky shoreline, Margaret Kennedy's white Victorian villa has views across the Firth of Lorn to the Morvern hills beyond. The comfortable bedrooms are colourfully decorated. Scottish breakfasts cater for vegetarian and special diets. Lounge (grand piano), dining room. Pets welcomed. Parking. 5 bedrooms (3 face the firth). B&B £35–£60 per person.

## CRIANLARICH Perth and Kinross
## Map 5:D2
WEST HIGHLAND LODGE, FK20 8RU. Tel 01838-300283, www.westhighland lodge.com. In an elevated position with views east to Ben More, this B&B, a low-

built, white Victorian lodge, is within Loch Lomond and Trossachs national park. 'We were made most welcome' by hosts Paul and Jen Lilly. Lounge (background music). Wi-Fi. 6-acre garden. Free pickup service from Crianlarich and Tyndrum. B&B from £32 per person. Dinner £15.

### DALKEITH Midlothian
**Map 5:D2**
THE SUN INN, Lothianbridge, EH22 4TR. Tel 0131-6632456, www.thesun innedinburgh.co.uk. On the outskirts of Edinburgh, this country inn has been renovated in traditional style as a gastropub-with-rooms. It has log fires, oak beams and panelling, exposed stone. Upstairs, modern bedrooms are equipped with plasma TV, luxury bedding, monsoon shower. The busy bistro follows a policy of 'supporting Scotland's farmers and fishermen'. Bar, bistro; courtyard (alfresco dining); secret garden. Background music. 5 bedrooms (1 suite with copper bath). B&B from £40 per person.

### DERVAIG Highland
**Map 5:D1**
KILLORAN HOUSE, Isle of Mull, PA75 6QR. Tel 01688-400362, www. killoranmull.co.uk. Janette and Ian McKilligan are the 'helpful, friendly' owners of this small hotel in a 'gorgeous setting' on a hillside near Calgary Bay. He cooks a daily-changing four-course set dinner. 'The food was imaginative and well presented.' Packed lunches are provided. Sitting room, study (books, DVDs and CDs), conservatory dining room. No background music. 6 bedrooms. B&B £50–£93.75 per person. Dinner £35.

### DORNOCH Highland
**Map 5:B2**
DORNOCH CASTLE HOTEL, Castle Street, IV25 3SD. Tel 01862-810216, www.dornochcastlehotel.com. 'Worth a detour.' Opposite the cathedral, this 15th-century castle (with a modern extension) is run by the Thompson family and their long-serving staff. 'The old bedrooms are fantastic: a huge antique bed, high ceiling, open fireplace; an ultra-modern spa bath. We were delighted with this stylish mixture.' Bar, *Garden* restaurant (Mikael Helies is the new chef; background music); walled garden. 21 bedrooms (some in garden wing). B&B £46–£111.50 per person. Dinner £23–£29.

### DUNDEE
**Map 5:D3**
APEX CITY QUAY HOTEL & SPA, 1 West Victoria Dock Road, DD1 3JP. Tel 01382-202404, www.apexhotels.co.uk. In the city quay development, this five-storey modern hotel has 'stunning' views over the River Tay. It looks unprepossessing from outside, but the sleekly contemporary rooms are 'good for sitting in'. Marcus Kenyon is the manager. *Metro* bar/brasserie, *Alchemy* restaurant (Bruce Price is chef); *Yu* spa: gym, sauna, hot tubs, treatments; conference/events centre; background music throughout. Wi-Fi; complimentary newspaper. Function/wedding facilities. Parking. Children welcomed. 152 bedrooms: from £64. Breakfast £12.50.

DUNTRUNE HOUSE, Duntrune, DD4 0PJ. Tel 01382-350239, www. duntrunehouse.co.uk. Family history enthusiasts, and supporters of the Green

Business Tourism Scheme, Barrie and Olwyn Jack take delight in sharing their lovingly restored manor house (1826) with B&B guests. It stands in large grounds and woodland with 'all-year interest'. 5 miles NE of city. Sitting room, breakfast room. Dinner by arrangement. No background music. Wi-Fi. Parking. Children welcomed. Closed Nov to Mar. 4 bedrooms (1 on ground floor; all with garden view). B&B £35–£50 per person; D,B&B £55–£70.

## DUNOON Argyll and Bute
## Map 5:D1
**HUNTERS QUAY HOTEL**, Marine Parade, PA23 8HJ. Tel 01369-707070, www.huntersquayhotel.co.uk. 'Excellent dinner; massive breakfast.' Graham and Christine Togwell's white seafront Victorian villa on the Cowal Peninsula overlooks the Firth of Clyde. 'Huge' lounge, restaurant (Scottish cooking). No background music. Garden, mature woodland. Wi-Fi. Wedding/conference facilities. 10 bedrooms (some with panoramic views of River Clyde). B&B £35–£130 per person. Dinner £25.

## EDINBURGH
## Map 5:D2
**ACER LODGE**, 425 Queensferry Road, EH4 7NB. Tel 0131-336 2554, www.acerlodge.co.uk. A frequent bus service provides easy access to the city centre from Gillian and Terry Poore's traditional guest house in the western suburbs. The simply furnished rooms are spacious, well equipped; 'good value for money'. No background music. Wi-Fi. Children welcomed. Parking. 5 bedrooms (some on ground floor). B&B £27.50–£45 per person.

**GLENORA GUEST HOUSE**, 14 Rosebery Crescent, EH12 5JY. Tel 0845-180 0045, www.glenorahotel.co.uk. In the quiet Haymarket district, this Victorian town house has been renovated in understated modern style. Wendy Phillips, the manager, follows eco-friendly policies. Reception, breakfast room (organic produce served). No background music. Wi-Fi. Nintendo Wii available for hire. Limited parking. Children welcomed. 11 bedrooms. B&B £42.50–£75 per person.

**THE HOWARD**, 34 Great King Street, EH3 6QH. Tel 0131-557 3500, www.thehoward.com. This discreet luxury hotel (managed by Fiona McIlroy for the Town House Collection) is formed from three Georgian houses in a central New Town street. Guests can opt for a dedicated butler service, which provides services from ironing to organising evenings out. William Poncelot is the chef for the *Atholl* restaurant (background music). Drawing room. Wi-Fi. Parking. 18 bedrooms (5 suites). B&B £92.50–£350 per person. Dinner £32.

**LE MONDE**, 16 George Street, EH2 2PF. Tel 0131-270 3900, www.lemondehotel.co.uk. For the young at heart, this centrally located Georgian town house has been transformed into a themed, hip hotel. There are three bars, *Milan*, *Vienna*, *Paris* (food is served in all three; a complimentary cocktail token is given at check-in). Guests have a VIP pass to the *Shanghai* nightclub. The decor and lighting are funky. A rose petal turn-down and bath butler service is available. Wi-Fi. 18 bedrooms. B&B £72.50–£205 per person.

**MILLERS64**, 64 Pilrig Street, EH6 5AS. Tel 0131-454 3666, www.millers64.com. 'Warmly welcoming' sisters Shona and Louise Clelland provide B&B accommodation 'of enormous comfort' at their renovated Victorian house in the centre. 'Breakfast was excellent, the price exceptional value.' Muffins, banana bread, jams and marmalades are home made. Dining room; garden, patio (alfresco breakfasts). No background music. Children welcomed. 3 bedrooms. B&B £40–£80 per person.

**94DR**, 94 Dalkeith Road, EH16 5AF. Tel 0131-662 9265, www.94dr.com. Owner Paul Lightfoot seeks to create 'a small, friendly place with a big personality' at his Victorian town house B&B, ten minutes by bus from the centre. He has merged traditional features with contemporary design, using muted greys and luxury fabrics. Lounge, *Orangery* breakfast room. Background music (classical/jazz/'easy listening'). Wi-Fi. Children welcomed. 6 bedrooms. B&B £40–£150 per person.
25% **DISCOUNT VOUCHERS**

**PRESTONFIELD**, Priestfield Road, EH16 5UT. Tel 0131-225 7800, www.prestonfield.com. In Royal Holyrood Park by Arthur's Seat, James Thomson's opulent hotel is a riot of rich furnishings and textures. Service is by black-kilted staff. The bedrooms have state-of-the-art technology; complimentary bottle of champagne on arrival. The manager is Alan McGuiggan. Mr Thomson also owns *The Witchery by the Castle* (see next page). 2 drawing rooms, 2 bars, *Rhubarb* restaurant; 3 private dining rooms; background music; Wi-Fi. Lift. Function facilities. Terraces; 'Gothic' tea house;

20-acre garden/parkland. Children and dogs welcomed. Parking. 23 bedrooms (1 suitable for &). B&B £142.50–£235 per person; D,B&B £172.50–£250.

**THE SCOTSMAN**, 20 North Bridge, EH1 1YT. Tel 0131-556 5565, www.thescotsmanhotel.co.uk. Staff are 'well trained and friendly' at this luxury hotel (part of the Eton Collection), a conversion of the former offices of the *Scotsman* newspaper. Baroque features retained include a black-and-white marble staircase, intricate stained-glass windows, turrets, ornate ceilings. 'Downright sumptuous; the food was delicious.' Background music. Drawing room, breakfast room, bar/brasserie; lift, ramps; cinema; health spa (16-metre swimming pool, sauna, gym, treatment rooms; juice bar, café); wedding facilities. Wi-Fi. Children welcomed. 69 bedrooms (2 suitable for &). B&B £72.50–£400 per person.

**SIX MARY'S PLACE**, Raeburn Place, EH4 1JH. Tel 0131-332 8965, www.sixmarysplace.co.uk. 'Rooms of enormous comfort and quietness; reasonably priced; convenient location.' This Georgian building in the Stockbridge area, ten minutes' walk from the centre, has been tastefully modernised. It is run in eco-friendly style by the manager, Muriel Campbell. Lounge, conservatory, meeting room. Garden. No background music. Wi-Fi. Children welcomed. 8 bedrooms (1 family). B&B £47–£94 per person.

**SOUTHSIDE GUEST HOUSE**, 8 Newington Road, EH9 1QS. Tel 0131-668 4422, www.southsideguesthouse.co.uk. Near the Meadows and Holyrood Park, the

Victorian terraced home of Franco and Lynne Galgani is a 'friendly' B&B. The comfortable bedrooms are colourful; there are wrought iron and four-poster beds. Quietest rooms are at the back (the house is on a main road). Breakfast room (Scottish breakfasts with a daily speciality; vegetarians catered for); background music (light classical). Wi-Fi. Parking limited. Children over 8 allowed. 8 bedrooms. B&B £40–£85 per person.

**TIGERLILY**, 125 George St, EH2 4JN. Tel 0131-225 5005, www.tigerlilyedinburgh. co.uk. David Hall manages this ultra-modern hotel in a Georgian house in a 'fantastic location', with shops and restaurants nearby. The chic bedrooms are well equipped. 2 bars (opulent *Lulu* bar with booths, revolving glitter balls, beaded curtains; and a club below, crowded at weekends); lively restaurant (background music). Wi-Fi. Children welcomed. 33 bedrooms. B&B £60–£185 per person; D,B&B from £82.50.

**THE WITCHERY BY THE CASTLE**, Castlehill, EH1 2NF. Tel 0131-225 5613, www.thewitchery.com. At the top of the Royal Mile, this idiosyncratic restaurant-with-suites is in adjacent 16th- and 17th-century buildings. It is owned by restaurateur James Thomson (see *Prestonfield*, previous page); Steve Hall and Jacqui Sutherland are the managers. Decorated in Gothic style, it has ornate red and gold paintwork, decadent drapery, sybaritic bathrooms. 2 restaurants (Douglas Roberts uses Scottish produce; background music); terrace. 8 suites (in 2 buildings): £295 (includes continental breakfast, bottle of champagne). Dinner from £30.

**ELGIN Moray**
**Map 5:C2**
**MANSION HOUSE HOTEL & COUNTRY CLUB**, The Haugh, IV30 1AW. Tel 01343-548811, www.mansionhousehotel. co.uk. In large grounds on the banks of the River Lossie, a short walk from the centre, this 19th-century baronial mansion has a sumptuous country house interior. Owned by David Baker, it is managed by Lynn Macdonald. Piano lounge, bar, restaurant, bistro. Background music. Leisure club (indoor swimming pool, sauna, steam room; treatments; gym; snooker room); function/business facilities. Parking. 23 bedrooms (some interconnecting). B&B £77–£101 per person; D,B&B £100.50–£113.50.

**FORT WILLIAM Highland**
**Map 5:C1**
**HUNTINGTOWER LODGE**, Druimarbin, PH33 6RP. Tel 01397-700079, www. huntingtowerlodge.com. Chris and Jackie Clifford's low-built, eco-friendly lodge has panoramic views of Loch Linnhe where sea birds, porpoise, otter and seal can be sighted. The interior is light and modern; some low, sloping walls in the 'well-appointed' bedrooms. Lounge (CD/DVD library); drying facilities; garaging for bicycles. No background music. Wi-Fi. Home-baked biscuits, cakes and bread. 4-acre woodland: wild-flower garden, waterfall, roe deer, red squirrels, pine martens. 2 miles SW of Fort William. 4 bedrooms. B&B £35–£50 per person.

**INVERLOCHY CASTLE**, Torlundy, PH33 6SN. Tel 01397-702177, www.inverlochycastlehotel.com. In the foothills of Ben Nevis, this grand baronial pile has a lavishly embellished interior; there are Venetian chandeliers and a frescoed ceiling in the Great Hall. Jane Watson is the manager; Philip Carnegie is executive chef. 4 miles N of Fort William. Drawing room, dining rooms (live classical piano some evenings), billiard room; terrace; wedding/conference facilities. 50-acre grounds: walled garden, tennis, loch, fishing. Children welcomed; dogs by arrangement. 17 bedrooms. B&B £75–£205 per person; D,B&B £107.50–£270.

## FORTROSE Highland
## Map 5:C2

THE ANDERSON, Union Street, by Inverness, IV10 8TD. Tel 01381-620236, www.theanderson.co.uk. On the cathedral square, this 1840s building is run as a restaurant-with-rooms by American owners Jim and Anne Anderson. She cooks a daily-changing menu of international dishes, using local ingredients. The *Whisky Bar* (240 single malts) has a 'pleasant, lively ambience'. Public bar (real ales), dining room. Cosy atmosphere; oak floors; wood-burning stoves. Background music. Wi-Fi. Beer garden. Children welcomed. 9 bedrooms. B&B £45–£50 per person. Dinner £27.

## GATEHOUSE OF FLEET Dumfries and Galloway
## Map 5:E2

THE BANK OF FLEET, 47 High Street, DG7 2HR. Tel 01557-814302, www.bankoffleet.co.uk. On the edge of Galloway Forest Park, this small budget hotel with a simple decor is run by chef/manager Ian Hogg. He serves an extensive choice of dishes, from traditional Scottish recipes to Indian, Chinese and Italian. Bar/restaurant

(inglenook fireplace) overlooking the walled garden (alfresco eating); wedding/small function facilities; background music. 6 bedrooms. B&B £32.50–£65 per person. Dinner £20.

## GIGHA Argyll and Bute
## Map 5:D1

GIGHA HOTEL, Isle of Gigha, PA41 7AA. Tel 01583-505254, www.gigha.org.uk. By the ferry terminal of a community-owned island off the Mull of Kintyre, this small hotel is managed by Colin Johnston for the island trust. He is overseeing renovation, which has started with work on the dining room. There are log fires in the public rooms. Lounge, bar (occasional background music), restaurant (Scottish dishes: prawns, clams, lobsters, lamb, beef, Gigha cheese). Garden (alfresco eating). Wedding/function facilities. 13 simple, spacious bedrooms. B&B £49.50–£58 per person. Dinner £33.

## GLASGOW
## Map 5:D2

THE BELHAVEN, 15 Belhaven Terrace, G12 0TG. Tel 0141-339 3222, www.belhavenhotel.com. In the West End, near the Botanic Gardens, David Kerr's restored town house hotel has high ceilings, spacious, red-themed bedrooms. One has a spa bath big enough for two. The Great Western Road is close by; some traffic noise may be heard. Lounge bar (light meals; background music). Parking. 16 bedrooms: B&B £36–£52 per person.

MALMAISON, 278 West George Street, G2 4LL. Tel 0141-572 1000, www.malmaison.com. Lovers of architecture will exult in this hotel, a converted

Greek Orthodox church in the financial district. It has an Art Nouveau iron sculpted central staircase, huge vaulted ceilings; the decoration is fittingly bold and plush. Stephen Williams is the manager. Lift. Lounge, bar, brasserie (Graham Digweed is chef); background music. Children and dogs welcomed. 72 bedrooms: £160–£210. Breakfast £13.95, dinner £23–£30.

## GLENFINNAN Highland
**Map 5:C1**

**THE PRINCE'S HOUSE**, by Fort William, PH37 4LT. Tel 01397-722246, www.glenfinnan.co.uk. In a rural village famed for its railway viaduct and monument to the Jacobite rebellion, this traditional, white-painted coaching inn (1658) is run by chef/proprietor Kieron Kelly and his 'welcoming' wife, Ina. It makes a useful stop-over for the Mallaig ferry. 17 miles W of Fort William. Lounge, bar (*The Stage House*, for informal dining), restaurant (an 'exciting menu'), conservatory; classical background music; log fire. 'Breakfast excellent, very generous.' Closed Jan to Mar. 9 bedrooms. B&B £45–£70 per person; D,B&B £75–£100.
**25% DISCOUNT VOUCHERS**

## GRANTOWN-ON-SPEY Highland
**Map 5:C2**

**THE PINES**, Woodside Avenue, PH26 3JR. Tel 01479-872092, www.thepines grantown.co.uk. A hotel since the 1930s, this Victorian house is owned and run by Michael and Gwen Stewart, who have filled it with family portraits and objets d'art. The small library is well stocked with books about the area. Mrs Stewart discusses her dinner menu at breakfast. Landscaped gardens lead into woodland. 2 lounges, library, dining room; 1-acre garden. 5 bedrooms. B&B £63–£83 per person; D,B&B £96–£116.

**RAVENSCOURT HOUSE**, Seafield Avenue, PH26 3JG. Tel 01479-872286, www.ravenscourthouse.co.uk. Owners Andrew and Sheena Williamson, and their son, Mark, run their small traditional hotel in a stone-built former Church of Scotland manse near the centre. The chef, Dmitri Sobczak, cooks 'unpretentious' dishes using local produce. 2 lounges, conservatory restaurant (classical background music). Wi-Fi. Small garden. Children welcomed. 8 bedrooms. B&B £27.50–£90 per person; D,B&B from £52.50.

## INVERNESS Highland
**Map 5:C2**

**CULLODEN HOUSE**, IV2 7BZ. Tel 01463-790461, www.cullodenhouse.co.uk. In 40 acres of parkland on the edge of Culloden Forest, this creeper-covered Palladian country house is run by mother and son Pat and Steven Davies, 'warm' hosts. Some bedrooms have chandelier and marble fireplace. There is a dungeon sauna (treatments are also available in the bedrooms). Chef Michael Simpson's cuisine is modern Scottish, using local ingredients. Lounge, dining room (classical background music); croquet, tennis, golf practice nets; wedding/corporate facilities. Wi-Fi. Children welcomed. 25 bedrooms. B&B £125–£187.50 per person.

**GLENMORISTON HOTEL**, 20 Ness Bank, IV2 4SF. Tel 01463-223777, www.glenmoristontownhouse.com. Barry Larsen's town house hotel on the banks of the River Ness is well situated for walking in to the centre. 'Rooms are well equipped and comfortable.' Lounge, piano bar (live music on Fri and Sat). *Contrast* brasserie (river views; alfresco dining in summer), *Abstract* French restaurant (William Hay is chef); wedding/function facilities. Wi-Fi. Garden. 30 bedrooms (in 2 separate buildings; 1 suitable for &.). B&B £50–£95 per person.

**MOYNESS HOUSE**, 6 Bruce Gardens, IV3 5EN. Tel 01463-233836, www.moyness. co.uk. 'A good guest house with residents' lounge; neat and clean.' Richard and Jenny Jones have imaginatively decorated their white-painted Victorian villa near the centre. Sitting room, dining room. Wi-Fi. Garden. Children over 4 accepted. Parking. 6 bedrooms. B&B £35–£50 per person.

**ROCPOOL RESERVE**, Culduthel Road, IV2 4AG. Tel 01463-240089, www. rocpoolreserve.com. There is an Albert Roux restaurant with views over the River Ness at this luxurious hotel in the city centre (sister to *Inverlochy Castle*, Fort William, see previous page). The manager is Aileen Mackinnon. The bedrooms range from 'hip' to 'extra decadent'; some have hot tub and balcony. Cocktail bar (*R Bar*), *Chez Roux* restaurant. Children welcomed (Xboxes, children's DVDs, board games). Wedding/conference facilities. Parking. 11 bedrooms. B&B £85–£182.50 per person; D,B&B £115–£212.

## KELSO Borders
## Map 5:E3
**THE CROSS KEYS**, 36–37 The Square, TD5 7HL. Tel 01573-223303, www. ckhkelso.co.uk. On a cobbled square,

this former coaching inn is run by the Becattelli family. 'Delightful owners and staff.' Lounge, *No. 36* bar, restaurant (modern Scottish and continental dishes produced by David Whyte); contemporary background music. Ballroom. Lift. Conference facilities. Children and dogs welcomed. 26 bedrooms. B&B £37.50–£54 per person; D,B&B £53.75–£70.50.

**25% DISCOUNT VOUCHERS**

## KILDRUMMY Aberdeenshire
## Map 5:C3
**KILDRUMMY CASTLE HOTEL**, by Alford, AB33 8RA. Tel 01975-571288, www.kildrummycastlehotel.co.uk. Overlooking the ruins of a 13th-century castle, this gabled, castellated house is owned by Jayne Faber and her Dutch husband, Frans (the chef). The fine interior has ornately panelled walls and ceilings, a carved oak staircase. Drawing room, library, bar, restaurant. Small wedding/function facilities. Children and dogs welcomed. 35 miles W of Aberdeen. Private trout/salmon fishing on River Don nearby. 16 bedrooms. B&B £69.50–£90 per person. Dinner £33.50.

## KIRKBEAN Dumfries and Galloway
## Map 5:E2
**CAVENS**, by Dumfries, DG2 8AA. Tel 01387-880234, www.cavens.com. 'Tops: good service, beautiful room, great food.' Angus and Jane Fordyce's manor house stands in extensive grounds in a 'glorious position' on the edge of a village. He cooks French-influenced 'slow' food using ingredients from the kitchen garden. No background music. Wi-Fi. Open fires. 12 miles S of Dumfries. Children welcomed (high tea in kitchen at 6 pm for young ones). Dogs

welcomed. 8 bedrooms (1 suitable for &; plus self-catering lodge in grounds). B&B £40–£90 per person; D,B&B £65–£110.
25% DISCOUNT VOUCHERS

## KIRKCUDBRIGHT Dumfries and Galloway
**Map 5:E2**
THE MARKS, DG6 4XR. Tel 01557-330854, www.marksfarm.co.uk. Sheila Watson and Chris Caygill's 16th-century dower house is on a working upland farm with a dairy herd and sheep (it specialises in farming worms for organic waste management), 4 miles E of Kirkcudbright. Drawing room, study, breakfast room. No background music. Rambling gardens (woods, loch, walks, stabling; on national cycle route 7), fishing. 3 bedrooms. B&B £30–£35 per person; D,B&B £45.

## LARGOWARD Fife
**Map 5:D3**
THE INN AT LATHONES, KY9 1JE. Tel 01334-840494, www.theinn.co.uk. Nick White's 400-year-old coaching inn is in a hamlet near St Andrews. The bedrooms are in a cluster of modern single-storey buildings around the inn. Morag Peattie is the manager. Lounge, bar, restaurant; function room; background music; live gigs; music memorabilia on walls. Chef Richard Brackenberry serves modern European dishes. Function facilities. Children and dogs welcomed. 21 bedrooms. B&B £45–£122.50 per person. Dinner £30.
25% DISCOUNT VOUCHERS

## LOCHINVER Highland
**Map 5:B1**
INVER LODGE, Iolaire Road, IV27 4LU. Tel 01571-844496, www.inverlodge.com.

Nicholas Gorton is the 'hands-on' manager of this purpose-built hotel in a 'stunning' setting on a hill above the harbour. 'Perhaps the best hotel experience either of us has ever enjoyed.' There has been extensive renovation this year. Albert Roux has taken over the kitchen, promising 'hearty country cooking using all the wonderful products from the sea, which is at the doorstep'. Lounge, bar, restaurant; snooker, sauna; fishing. No background music. 1-acre garden. Children and dogs welcomed. 21 bedrooms. B&B £105 per person; D,B&B £140.
25% DISCOUNT VOUCHERS

## LOCKERBIE Dumfries and Galloway
**Map 5:E2**
THE DRYFESDALE, Dryfebridge, DG11 2SF. Tel 01576-202427, www.dryfesdalehotel.co.uk. In elevated parkland, this former manse (1762) is run as a hotel (Best Western) by Glenn Wright. The restaurant, which has fine country views, has been extended to include a terrace area. The menu, based on locally sourced produce, changes with the seasons. 1 mile from town centre (near M74 exit 17). Lounge, *Malt* bar (around 130 malts), *Glenlouis* restaurant; conference/function facilities; background music. 5-acre grounds. Child-friendly; pets welcomed. 28 bedrooms (some in garden suites with patio; some suitable for &). B&B £55–£89 per person; D,B&B £85–£99.

## MELROSE Borders
**Map 5:E3**
BURT'S, Market Square, TD6 9PL. Tel 01896-822285, www.burtshotel.co.uk. The Henderson family have run their homely hotel in this listed 18th-century

building on the square (black-and-white facade; window boxes) for over 40 years. In the restaurant (with classical background music), head chef Trevor Williams serves modern British dishes. 2 lounges, bar/bistro (over 90 malt whiskies). ½-acre garden. Parking. 20 bedrooms. B&B from £70 per person; D,B&B from £95.

THE TOWNHOUSE, Market Square, TD6 9PQ. Tel 01896-822645, www. thetownhousemelrose.co.uk. Popular with locals, across the square from the Henderson family's other hotel, *Burt's*, this white-painted building has comfortable rooms and an informal atmosphere. Bar, brasserie, restaurant (Scottish fusion food from Iain Chapman); conservatory; background music; patio. Wi-Fi. Wedding/function facilities. Children welcomed. 11 bedrooms. B&B £86–£95 per person. Dinner £32.50.

**MONTROSE Angus**
**Map 5:D3**
LINKS HOTEL, Mid Links, DD10 8RL. Tel 01674-671000, www.linkshotel.com. On the historic Mid Links, within walking distance of a sandy beach, this grand Edwardian town house (Best Western) is managed by Kasper Ninteman. It has a fine entrance hall; an imposing staircase; an interesting stained-glass window. Bar, *Koffiehuis* bistro, restaurant (Frank Rivault cooks Scottish and French dishes in an open-view kitchen; background music); folk, jazz and classical evenings; function facilities. Children, and small pets (£15 per night) welcomed. Wi-Fi. 25 bedrooms. B&B from £39–£98 per person. Dinner £22–£27.

**NORTH BERWICK East Lothian**
**Map 5:D3**
THE GLEBE HOUSE, 4 Law Road, EH39 4PL. Tel 01620-892608/Mobile 07973 965814, www.glebehouse-nb.co.uk. In a secluded garden, this well-proportioned Georgian manse overlooks the seaside town. The beach is a two-minute walk away. Gwen Scott has decorated her home in period style with antiques, and a large collection of Staffordshire china. Bedrooms are comfortable; Scottish breakfasts are hearty. Sitting room, dining room. Children welcomed. 2-acre garden. Parking. 3 bedrooms. B&B £50–£75 per person.

**OBAN Argyll and Bute**
**Map 5:D1**
DUN NA MARA, Benderloch, PA37 1RT. Tel 01631-720233, www.dunnamara. com. This white-painted Edwardian guest house, in a village north of Oban, is a 'gorgeous retreat' by the sea. Owners Mark and Suzanne McPhillips have given the elegant bedrooms a chic, contemporary look. Sitting room, dining room ('delicious breakfast'). No background music. Wi-Fi. Informal gardens lead to a private beach. 7 bedrooms (1st floor, no lift). B&B £49–£60 per person.

**PEEBLES Borders**
**Map 5:E2**
CRINGLETIE HOUSE, off Edinburgh Road, EH45 8PL. Tel 01721-725750, www.cringletie.com. Owned by Jacob and Johanna van Houdt, this luxury hotel is a turreted, pink stone Victorian baronial mansion on a wooded estate outside the town. Jeremy Osborne is the manager. Lift. Lounge, library, bar, *Sutherland* restaurant (spectacular

painted ceiling; Craig Gibb cooks Scottish produce); background music. Wi-Fi. Walled garden; outdoor chess; pétanque. Children and dogs welcomed. 12 bedrooms (1 suitable for &). B&B £80–£395 per person. Dinner £42.50.

## PERTH Perth and Kinross
## Map 5:D2
THE PARKLANDS, 2 St Leonard's Banks, PH2 8EB. Tel 01738-622451, www.theparklandshotel.com. Owners Scott and Penny Edwards 'put in that bit extra to ensure complete satisfaction' at their 'excellent' hotel overlooking South Inch Park, near the centre. The public rooms of the Victorian stone-built house are traditionally furnished; bedrooms are modern, well equipped. Lounge, bar, *Acanthus* restaurant, *Number 1 The Bank* bistro; light background music; private dining room; function facilities. Wi-Fi. Terrace. Garden leading to park. Parking. Dogs welcomed. 15 bedrooms. B&B £49–£87.50 per person; D,B&B £57.50–£94.50.
25% DISCOUNT VOUCHERS

SUNBANK HOUSE, 50 Dundee Road, PH2 7BA. Tel 01738-624882, www.sunbankhouse.com. There are pleasant walks in a hill park behind this late Victorian house in landscaped gardens near the River Tay. Georgina and Remigio Zane have furnished it traditionally. An Italian, he cooks snacks and light dishes with a flavour of his homeland, by arrangement. Lounge/bar, restaurant (light background music). Wi-Fi. Parking. 2 miles E of centre. Children welcomed. 9 bedrooms (some on ground floor; 1 suitable for &). B&B £40–£70 per person.
25% DISCOUNT VOUCHERS

## PITLOCHRY Perth and Kinross
## Map 5:D2
EAST HAUGH HOUSE, by Pitlochry, PH16 5JS. Tel 01796-473121, www.easthaugh.co.uk. 'Fantastic food, location and people.' Chef/proprietor Neil McGown, his wife, Lesley, and their daughter, Sophie (the manager), run this 350-year-old turreted stone house on the Atholl estate as a small hotel/restaurant. The decor has a home-spun feel, with tweedy fabrics and tartan carpets. Bar (fresh local produce; alfresco dining), *Two Sisters* restaurant; garden, patio; river beat. 13 bedrooms (5 in a converted 'Bothy' beside the hotel). Wedding/business facilities. B&B £75–£129 per person; D,B&B £99–£149.

GREEN PARK, Clunie Bridge Road, PH16 5JY. Tel 01796-473248, www.thegreenpark.co.uk. The McMenemie family's Highlands hotel has a 'superb position' on Loch Faskally, on the edge of the town. It is popular with older visitors: 'We go twice a year, and have done for over 15 years.' 3 lounges, library, bar, restaurant; 2 new lifts. No background music. Children and dogs welcomed. 3-acre garden. Activity breaks (putting, fishing, boat hire on loch): bridge, art, Scrabble and crosswords; Pitlochry theatre. 51 bedrooms. B&B £62–£74 per person; D,B&B £65–£98.
25% DISCOUNT VOUCHERS

PINE TREES, Strathview Terrace, PH16 5QR. Tel 01796-472121, www.pinetreeshotel.co.uk. In a quiet, wooded location on a hillside above the town, the Kerr family's majestic Victorian mansion is classically furnished. There are cosy seating areas in rooms with half-panelled walls. Lounge (Wi-Fi), bar, *Garden* restaurant (Scottish fare with a cosmopolitan twist). 'Good food; speedy, efficient service; sensible wine list.' Background music. 'Well-kept' 20-acre grounds. 20 bedrooms. Dogs welcomed. B&B £49–£65 per person; D,B&B £69–£85.

## PORT CHARLOTTE Argyll and Bute
### Map 5:D1

PORT CHARLOTTE HOTEL, Main Street, Isle of Islay, PA48 7TU. Tel 01496-850360, www.portcharlottehotel.co.uk. 'The views are magnificent' from Grahame and Isabelle Allison's small waterfront hotel on a sandy beach, in a pretty conservation village. Lounge (polished floors, oriental rugs), live traditional music in bar, restaurant (chef Rangasamy Dhamodharan uses local fish, seafood and lamb for his specialities; booking advisable). 10 bedrooms (9 with sea view). B&B £80–£95 per person. Dinner £45.

## PORTREE Highland
### Map 5:C1

CUILLIN HILLS HOTEL, Isle of Skye, IV51 9QU. Tel 01478-612003, www.cuillinhills-hotel-skye.co.uk. In wooded grounds overlooking Portree Bay, this gabled, white-walled former Victorian hunting lodge is managed by Peter Sim. The interior has been rejuvenated; the lounge has been strikingly decorated in copper wall covering with scarlet motifs; there is a new brasserie; *The View* restaurant is set within a gallery displaying work by Skye artists. Lounge, bar, brasserie, restaurant (Chris Donaldson's cooking is 'very good'); background music. Wi-Fi. 26 bedrooms (some on ground floor; 7 in annexe). B&B £100–£150 per person; D,B&B £135–£185.

## ST ANDREWS Fife
### Map 5:D3

RUFFLETS, Strathkinness Low Road, KY16 9TX. Tel 01334-472594, www.rufflets.co.uk. In award-winning gardens just outside 'the home of golf', this white, turreted, creeper-clad baronial-style mansion is owned by Ann Murray-Smith and managed by Stephen Owen. It was built in the 1920s for a Dundee jute baron. Rooms, some of which have been recently refurbished, are a mix of traditional or chic contemporary. Drawing room, music room, bar, *Terrace* restaurant (chef Mark Nixon cooks modern Scottish dishes using local, seasonal produce); background music ('easy listening'); wedding/function facilities. 10-acre grounds. Children welcomed. 24 bedrooms (3 in *Gatehouse*; 2 in *Lodge*; 1 suitable for &). B&B £80–£125 per person; D,B&B £115–£160.

## SCARISTA Western Isles
### Map 5:B1

SCARISTA HOUSE, Isle of Harris, HS3 3HX. Tel 01859-550238, www.scaristahouse.com. On the remote west coast of Harris, this handsome white Georgian manse overlooks a sandy beach. Tim and Patricia Martin (co-owners with Neil King) run it, serving daily-changing set-menu dinners. Everything is home made (including pasta and ice cream), grown in the garden or locally sourced. 15 miles SW of Tarbert. Drawing room, library (books, CDs; open fires), dining room. No background music; no television. 1-acre garden: trampoline. Open Mar to Dec. Children welcomed. Pets by arrangement (resident cat and dog).

5 bedrooms (2 self-catering units in
*The Glebe House* across the garden).
B&B £95–£100 per person. Dinner £40–
£49.50.

## SCOURIE Highland
## Map 5:B2

EDDRACHILLES HOTEL, Badcall Bay,
IV27 4TH. Tel 01971-502080, www.
eddrachilles.com. At the head of Badcall
Bay (Scotland's first 'Global Geopark'),
this white-painted 200-year-old manse
stands in grounds that run down to
the shore. 'Helpful' owners Isabelle
and Richard Flannery provide 'a
gastronomic delight in a wild area'.
Public rooms have stone walls,
flagstone floors; bedrooms are simply
furnished. Reception, conservatory, bar
(125 single malt whiskies), restaurant
(French/Scottish cooking: local produce
where possible, seafood; extensive
wine list); classical background music.
Children welcomed (high tea for
under-6s). Wi-Fi. 4-acre garden. 2 miles
S of village. 11 bedrooms. B&B £47–£50
per person; D,B&B £65–£68. Closed
Oct to Apr.

SCOURIE HOTEL, IV27 4SX. Tel 01971-
502396, www.scourie-hotel.co.uk.
Patrick and Judy Price run their old
coaching inn above Scourie Bay as a
fishing hotel. Guests have exclusive
access to 36 fishing beats; there are also
beats on lochs Stack and More (sea
trout and salmon). 2 lounges, 2 bars,
table d'hôte restaurant. No background
music; no TV; radios on request. 7-acre
grounds leading to sea (5 mins' walk
to sandy beach). 20 bedrooms (bay or
mountain views; 2 family rooms in
garden). B&B £38–£51 per person;
D,B&B £59–£75.

## SLEAT Highland
## Map 5:C1

DUISDALE HOUSE, Isle of Skye, IV43
8QW. Tel 01471-833 202, www.duisdale.
com. Anne Gracie and Ken Gunn, who
own nearby *Toravaig House* (see main
entry), have upgraded this small
'friendly' hotel in a forest overlooking
the Sound of Sleat. They have given the
Victorian building a striking decor (foil
wallpaper; fabrics in stripes and spots).
Refurbished bedrooms have a rich
colour scheme; a new bathroom. The
restaurant has two dining areas (one a
conservatory facing the garden). 'Our
meal was outstandingly good.' Lounge,
restaurant, conservatory. 17 bedrooms.
B&B £84.50–£134.50 per person; D,B&B
£119–£167.

## STRACHUR Argyll and Bute
## Map 5:D1

THE CREGGANS INN, PA27 8BX. Tel
01369-860279, www.creggans-inn.co.uk.
Archie and Gill MacLellan are the
welcoming owners of this informal inn
in a 'fantastic location' on the shores of
Loch Fyne. 'Very, very good. The
residents' lounge on the first floor, with
view of the loch, is perfect for after-
dinner coffee.' Hector is the resident
dog. 2 lounges, *MacPhunn's* bar/restaurant
('easy listening' background music),
*Loch Fyne* restaurant: Gordon Smillie
is chef). 2-acre garden. Children
welcomed. 14 bedrooms. B&B £50–£90
per person; D,B&B £75–£120.

## STRATHYRE Perth and Kinross
## Map 5:D2

CREAGAN HOUSE, FK18 8ND. Tel
01877-384638, www.creaganhouse.co.uk.
'A most delightful and memorable stay
in the Scottish Highlands.' The pace is

'relaxed and leisurely' at Gordon and Cherry Gunn's restaurant with 'finely furnished, comfortable' rooms in a renovated 17th-century farmhouse. He is the award-winning chef ('magnificent menu of locally selected ingredients'); she is the 'caring' front-of-house. The dining hall is baronial with a grand fireplace and antiques. Lounge, restaurant; private dining room. No background music. Landscaped gardens. ¼ mile N of village. 5 bedrooms (1 on ground floor). B&B £60–£90 per person; D,B&B £89.50–£99.50.

## SWINTON Borders
## Map 5:E3
THE WHEATSHEAF AT SWINTON, Main Street, TD11 3JJ. Tel 01890-860257, www.wheatsheaf-swinton.co.uk. Opposite the village green, Chris and Jan Winson's old stone-built country roadside inn has spruce, simply furnished rooms and a popular restaurant serving contemporary Scottish food cooked by Tim Holmes. Paintings by local artists are on display. 2 lounges, bar, 2 dining rooms (1 in the conservatory with vaulted pine ceiling and stone walls); background music; conservatory; small garden. Wi-Fi. 10 miles SW of Berwick-upon-Tweed. Children welcomed. 10 bedrooms (1 suitable for &). B&B £56–£95 per person; D,B&B £86–£125.

## TARBERT Western Isles
## Map 5:B1
HOTEL HEBRIDES, Pier Road, Isle of Harris, HS3 3DG. Tel 01859-502364, www.hotelhebrides.com. By the pier, Angus and Chirsty Macleod's small, contemporary hotel with loch and harbour views is popular with locals and visitors. The *Mote* lounge bar, which has a wood-burning stove and comfortable sofas, hosts traditional Scottish music nights. Well-equipped bedrooms are decorated in soft moorland colours. Bar, *Pierhouse* restaurant (Richard Agnew uses seasonal, local ingredients). Wi-Fi. Conference facilities. Children welcomed. 21 bedrooms. B&B £65–£70 per person. Dinner £60.

## TAYNUILT Argyll and Bute
## Map 5:D1
ROINEABHAL COUNTRY HOUSE, Kilchrenan, PA35 1HD. Tel 01866-833207, www.roineabhal.com. This smart, small country guest house near Loch Awe is the family home of Roger and Maria Soep. Booking is advisable for her four-course dinners, featuring Scottish game and seafood; bread is home baked. Lounge, dining room (background music at night); covered veranda. 2-acre garden. Afternoon teas. Children and pets welcomed. 18 miles E of Oban. 3 bedrooms (1 on ground floor). B&B £50–£70 per person. Dinner £45.

## THORNHILL Dumfries and Galloway
## Map 5:E2
TRIGONY HOUSE, Closeburn, DG3 5EZ. Tel 01848-331211, www.countryhousehotelscotland.com. This former shooting lodge for Closeburn Castle is run as a country hotel with a 'friendly, relaxed atmosphere' by chef/patron Adam Moore. Lounge, bar (background music), dining room (organic rustic cuisine). 'Excellent food; welcoming staff.' Wood-burning stoves. 4-acre grounds: walled garden. Wi-Fi. Children and dogs welcomed

(resident Labrador). Country activities organised. 1 mile S of Thornhill. 10 bedrooms (1 on ground floor with conservatory and private garden). B&B £50–£75 per person; D,B&B £80–£105.

## THURSO Highland
**Map 5:B2**
**FORSS HOUSE HOTEL**, Forss, by Thurso, KW14 7XY. Tel 01847-861 201, www. forsshousehotel.co.uk. In woodland below a waterfall on the River Forss, this grand old Georgian mansion is managed by Anne Mackenzie. Chef Darren Sivenright serves seasonal dishes in the restaurant ('the finest rice pudding in the land'). Lounge/ conservatory (log fire), dining room; background music (jazz/swing); fishing, local golf and shooting; wedding/ function facilities. Children and dogs welcomed. 14 bedrooms (2 in *Fishing Lodge*, 4 in *River House*). B&B £62.50–£110 per person. Dinner £35.
**25% DISCOUNT VOUCHERS**

## TOBERMORY Argyll and Bute
**Map 5:D1**
**THE TOBERMORY HOTEL**, Main Street, PA75 6NT. Tel 01688-302091, www. thetobermoryhotel.com. On the Isle of Mull, this popular harbour-front hotel is managed by owners Ian and Andi Stevens. The simple bedrooms are in a row of colourful converted fishermen's cottages. Helen Swinbanks cooks modern Scottish dishes. 'Food and service good.' 2 lounges, bar, *Water's Edge* restaurant. Background music. Packed lunches available. Drying facilities. Landscape photography workshops. Children and dogs welcomed. 16 bedrooms (most with sea

view; 1 suitable for ♿). B&B £38–£61 per person; D,B&B £60.50–£92.50.
**25% DISCOUNT VOUCHERS**

## ULLAPOOL Highland
**Map 5:B2**
**RIVERVIEW**, 2 Castle Terrace, IV26 2XD. Tel 01854-612019, www. riverviewullapool.co.uk. 'Friendly' owner Nadine Farquhar has decorated the bedrooms in her 'excellent, modern' village B&B in calming tones of cream, chocolate brown and white. 'Superb' breakfasts (Achiltibuie kippers are on the menu) in the open-plan lounge/dining room are served at flexible times; evening meals are by arrangement. 'Nadine makes you feel at home.' No background music. Wi-Fi; DVD library. Complimentary use of leisure centre. Closed Oct to Feb. 3 bedrooms. B&B £30 per person.

**THE SHEILING**, Garve Road, IV26 2SX. Tel 01854-612947, www.thesheiling ullapool.co.uk. With gardens leading directly to the shore of Loch Broom, Iain and Lesley MacDonald's modern, white, low-roofed home has bright, pine-furnished interiors. The town centre is a ten-minute walk away. Lounge (log fire), breakfast room (Scottish fare; occasional background music). Sauna. Drying room. Wi-Fi. Parking. 1-acre garden; patio; fishing permits. Children welcomed. 6 bedrooms (2 on ground floor). B&B £33–£42 per person.

### WALES

## BARMOUTH Gwynedd
**Map 3:B3**
**LLWYNDU FARMHOUSE HOTEL**, Llanaber, LL42 1RR. Tel 01341-280144, www.llwyndu-farmhouse.co.uk. Peter

and Paula Thompson run their 'sympathetically restored' 16th-century farmhouse (Grade II listed) as a small hotel/restaurant. It has many quirky features: a stone spiral staircase; a sink fitted to a door; a walk-in wardrobe in an old latrine. Some bedrooms are in the converted granary. He uses Welsh produce for his 'excellent' Mediterranean-influenced cooking, served in the candlelit dining room. Lounge, restaurant (occasional soft classical background music); 3-acre garden. 2 miles N of town. Children and dogs welcomed. 7 bedrooms (4 in adjacent building). B&B £47–£53 per person; D,B&B £74–£82.

## BRECON Powys
Map 3:D3
**CANTRE SELYF**, 5 Lion Street, LD3 7AU. Tel 01874-622904, www.cantreselyf.co.uk. 'A delightful place to stay.' Welcoming hosts, Helen and Nigel Roberts, offer B&B in their 17th-century sandstone town house (Grade II* listed). In a 'lovely' garden near St Mary's church, it is within easy distance of the town. Lounge, dining room ('delicious' traditional Welsh/continental breakfast; local organic produce). 1-acre walled garden. No background music. Parking. Children welcomed. 3 bedrooms (with beamed ceilings, Georgian fireplaces, cast iron beds). B&B £36–£41 per person.

## CAERNARFON Gwynedd
Map 3:A2
**PLAS DINAS COUNTRY HOUSE**, Bontnewydd, LL54 7YF. Tel 01286-830214, www.plasdinas.co.uk. Andy and Julian Banner-Price, the 'amiable, witty' owners, have handsomely refurbished their Grade II listed gentleman's

residence (with extensive Victorian additions). It was the country home of the Armstrong-Jones family: the Gun Room is festooned with royal memorabilia. Drawing room, dining room (closed Sun/Mon; background music). Wi-Fi. Small function facilities; civil wedding licence. 'Outstanding views.' 15-acre wooded grounds. No children under 12. Dogs welcomed (£10 charge). 10 bedrooms (1 suitable for ♿). B&B £44.50–£112.50 per person; D,B&B £69.50–£137.50.
**25% DISCOUNT VOUCHERS**

## CRICKHOWELL Powys
Map 3:D4
**THE MANOR**, Brecon Road, NP8 1SE. Tel 01873-810212, www.manorhotel. co.uk. In the Brecon Beacons national park, this white-painted 18th-century manor house is owned by Glyn and Jess Bridgeman and Sean Gerrard; Roger Francis is the manager. Locally reared organic meat and poultry, mainly from the family farm, supply the kitchen. Lounge, bar, bistro (background music); leisure suite (indoor swimming pool, sauna, steam room, whirlpool, gym); conference facilities; civil wedding licence. ¼ mile from town. 22 bedrooms. B&B £37.50–£90 per person; D,B&B £67.50–£120.

## DOLGELLAU Gwynedd
Map 3:B3
**FFYNNON**, Brynffynnon, Love Lane, L40 1RR. Tel 01341-421774, www. ffynnontownhouse.com. Stephen L Holt and Debra Harris have renovated their former Victorian parsonage with flair. It is a short walk to the town centre. Guests are offered afternoon tea on arrival; breakfasts come with a selection of daily

newspapers. Lounge, library, dining room, butler's pantry (honesty bar, light meals and snacks; picnic lunches). Background music. ½-acre garden: patio, hot tub, outdoor play area. Small function facilities. Wi-Fi. Parking. Children welcomed (high tea, baby-listening). Steps and level changes. 5 bedrooms. B&B £67.50–£120 per person.
**25% DISCOUNT VOUCHERS**

## HAVERFORDWEST Pembrokeshire
### Map 3:D1
COLLEGE GUEST HOUSE, 93 Hill Street, St Thomas Green, SA61 1QL. Tel 01437-763710, www.collegeguesthouse.com. Once a college for Baptist ministers, this centrally located Georgian town house (Grade II listed) is run as a B&B by Colin Larby and Pauline Good. Lounge (tea/coffee available all day), dining room (Welsh breakfast); background music. Wi-Fi. Parking. Small garden. Public swimming pool 100 yds; beach 6 miles. 8 bedrooms (some family). B&B £35–£50 per person.

## LAMPETER Ceredigion
### Map 3:D3
TŶ MAWR MANSION, Cilcennin, SA48 8DB. Tel 01570-470033, www.tymawrmansion.co.uk. Catherine and Martin McAlpine have restored their Grade II listed country house, giving it hi-tech gadgetry and a 30-seat cinema. Ramps; 3 lounges, restaurant (chef Jeremy Jones uses Welsh produce, mainly from the garden or within a 10-mile radius; 'easy-listening' background music). Wi-Fi. 12-acre mature grounds. 4 miles E of Aberaeron. 9 bedrooms (1 suite on ground floor in annexe). B&B £90–£140 per person; D,B&B £120–£170.

## LAUGHARNE Carmarthenshire
### Map 3:D2
HURST HOUSE ON THE MARSH, East Marsh, SA33 4RS. Tel 01994-427417, www.hurst-house.co.uk. Overlooking wild marshland, this 16th-century dairy farm has been converted by Professor Jeremy Stone into a 'lovely, relaxed' luxury hotel and spa. It has eclectic contemporary and antique decoration. Organic produce from the kitchen garden is used in Dave Watts's seasonal cooking, served in the glass-fronted dining room. Cookery demonstrations and tours of the garden are hosted by award-winning chef Martin Blunos. Bar lounge, dining room; terrace; courtyard. Background music. Spa: pool, treatment rooms, gym. Garden. Civil wedding licence; business facilities. Children welcomed. 17 bedrooms (4 in main house; the rest in courtyard; plus 1 cottage). B&B £132.50–£175 per person. Dinner £31.

## LLANDEILO Carmarthenshire
### Map 3:D3
FRONLAS, 7 Thomas Street, SA19 6LB. Tel 01558-824733, www.fronlas.com. Guests arriving by train receive a complimentary box of chocolates at this ecologically run B&B. 'Without skimping on luxury', Eva and Owain Huw have modernised their Edwardian town house with a 'striking' decor, using designer wallpaper and colourful fabrics. Green initiatives include solar panels, organic mattresses and bedding; composting and recycling. The house is on a hillside in a peaceful location, 5 minutes' walk from the centre. Lounge (honesty bar), breakfast room (organic breakfasts: 'scrambled eggs were excellent'; background music). Garden.

Children welcomed. 3 bedrooms (all look over Tywi valley to the Brecon Beacons). B&B £42.50–£95 per person.

## LLANDUDNO Conwy
### Map 3:A3
OSBORNE HOUSE, The Promenade, 17 North Parade, LL30 2LP. Tel 01492-860330, www.osbornehouse.co.uk. On the promenade, this sumptuously decorated hotel is owned by Elyse Waddy with Len and Elizabeth Maddocks. Bedroom suites have a canopied bed, a marble bathroom and a sitting room with a Victorian fireplace. Lounge, bar, café/bistro (opulent with chandeliers, candles, swags and drapes; brasserie-style cooking from Tim McCall); background music. Wi-Fi. 6 suites (sea views; gas fire). Parking. Use of pool and spa at *Empire Hotel* (100 yards). B&B £65–£100 per person; D,B&B £80–£105.
25% DISCOUNT VOUCHERS

## LLANDYRNOG Denbighshire
### Map 3:A4
PENTRE MAWR, LL16 4LA. Tel 01824-790732, www.pentremawrcountryhouse. co.uk. At his family's home since more than 400 years, Graham and Bre Carrington-Sykes give guests the choice of a country house-style bedroom or a luxury 'canvas lodge' in the grounds (oak floor, bathroom with freestanding bath and shower, super-king-size leather bed, hot tub). They also run *Sychnant Pass House*, Conwy (see main entry). Drawing room, study, restaurant (piano/classical background music). Children over 12 allowed. 1-acre walled garden; solar-heated swimming pool; 200 acres of meadow, park, woodland. 10 bedrooms (named after TS Eliot's

'Practical Cats'; 2 suites in cottage; 3 in lodges). B&B £50–£90 per person; D,B&B £82–£122.50.

## LLANGOLLEN Denbighshire
### Map 3:B4
GALES, 18 Bridge Street, LL20 8PF. Tel 01978-860089, www.galesofllangollen. co.uk. The Gale family run their 18th-century town house as a wine bar with accommodation. Characterful bedrooms have chunky wood furniture, carved bedhead, and beams. Wine bar/restaurant (Sarah Davis cooks rustic food; background music); conference facilities. Wi-Fi. Small patio area; car park. Children welcomed. 15 bedrooms (8 above wine bar, 7 in older building; 1 suitable for &). B&B (continental) £35 per person; D,B&B £60. Cooked breakfast £5, dinner £30.

## LLANWRTYD WELLS Powys
### Map 3:D3
LASSWADE COUNTRY HOUSE, Station Road, LD5 4RW. Tel 01591-610515, www.lasswadehotel.co.uk. On the outskirts of the UK's smallest town, amid the foothills of the Cambrian mountains, Roger and Emma Stevens show 'excellent attention to detail' at their traditional Edwardian house. They follow a green agenda; ingredients for the 'outstanding' organic dishes from local farms. Drawing room, library, restaurant; conservatory; function room. No background music. Garden: kennels. Children welcomed. Parking. 8 bedrooms. B&B £40–£55 per person; D,B&B £72–£87.

## MUMBLES Swansea
### Map 3:E3
PATRICKS WITH ROOMS, 638 Mumbles Road, SA3 4EA. Tel 01792-360199,

www.patrickswithrooms.com. On the bay, this contemporary restaurant-with-rooms is owned and managed by Catherine and Patrick Walsh (the chef), and Sally (Catherine's sister) and Dean Fuller. All the spacious bedrooms have sea views. Breakfasts are imaginative (eg, kedgeree of prawns, smoked fish and boiled egg with a tangy eastern sauce). 5 miles SW of Swansea. Lounge/bar; restaurant; background music; gym; greenhouse for herbs. Children welcomed. 16 sea-facing bedrooms. B&B £57.50–£175 per person. Dinner from £33 (3 courses).

### NARBERTH Pembrokeshire
### Map 3:D2

THE GROVE, Molleston, SA67 8BX. Tel 01834-860915, www.thegrove-narberth. co.uk. In rolling countryside, this white 18th-century country house, remodelled in Arts and Crafts style, is in a small hollow on a hill, with views of the Preseli mountains. Since 2007, the owners, Neil Kedward and Zoe Agar, have transformed it into a luxury hotel, keeping the quirkiness intact. Original art is displayed on the walls and is for sale. Dinner, and lunch (Thurs to Sun), is taken in the panelled restaurant or in the *Garden Room* restaurant and terrace. Nigel Marriage serves modern country food. Lounge, library (log fires); 10-acre garden. 12 bedrooms (plus 4 cottages). B&B £50–£70 per person.

### NEWTOWN Powys
### Map 3:C4

THE FOREST COUNTRY GUEST HOUSE, Gilfach Lane, Kerry, SY16 4DW. Tel 01686-621821, www.bedandbreakfast newtown.co.uk. This white-painted Victorian house in the Vale of Kerry is the home of Paul and Michelle Martin, their two children and assorted pets. Bedrooms, each named after a Welsh forest, are decorated in country house style. Drawing room, dining room; kitchenette; games room; DVDs; toy box. No background music. Wi-Fi. 4-acre garden; play area; tennis. Children and dogs welcomed (kennels £5 per night); stabling available. 3 miles SE of Newtown (train and bus stations). 5 bedrooms (plus 4 holiday cottages in outbuildings). B&B £37.50–£75 per person.

### PENARTH Vale of Glamorgan
### Map 3:E4

HOLM HOUSE, Marine Parade, CF64 3BG. Tel 029-2070 1572, www. holmhouse.com. Behind the esplanade, this 1920s mansion has been given a glitzy decor by owners Susan Sessions (also the manager) and Margaret Hewlett. They have introduced foil wallpaper, freestanding copper baths, opulent bed covers. The chef, Matt Powell, cooks modern British food, using local ingredients. Cardiff is 15 minutes' drive away. Lounge/bar, large restaurant (background jazz); spa: indoor 7½-metre hydrotherapy pool. ¾-acre garden. 12 bedrooms (2 on courtyard; 1 suitable for &). B&B £77.50–£135 per person; D,B&B £105–£170.

### PONTDOLGOCH Powys
### Map 3:C3

THE TALKHOUSE, Caersws, SY17 5JE. Tel 01686-688919, www.talkhouse.co.uk. Jacqueline and Stephen Garratt (the chef) are the welcoming owners of this low, whitewashed roadside coaching inn. He cooks classic, 'superlative' dinners;

lighter lunchtime meals are served from Wednesday to Saturday. Lounge, bar (beams, log fires), 2 dining rooms: one opens on to the garden (alfresco dining; 'easy listening' background music). Garden. 5 miles W of Newtown. 3 'cosy' bedrooms. B&B £62.50–£80 per person. Dinner from £27.

### RUTHIN Denbighshire
### Map 3:A4

MANORHAUS, Well Street, LL15 1AH. Tel 01824-704830, www.manorhaus.com. A most interesting and unusual place to stay.' Christopher Frost and Gavin Harris's boutique hotel/art gallery is housed within a Grade II listed Georgian building off the main square. Each 'visually stylish' bedroom is a mini gallery displaying the work of contemporary Welsh artists. Gavin Porter serves 'good' locally sourced and sustainable menus in the restaurant. Lounge, bar, dining area, library; 'easy listening' background music; cinema; fitness room, sauna, steam room; seminar/meeting facilities. Wi-Fi. Children welcomed. Parking nearby. 8 bedrooms. B&B £45–£110 per person; D,B&B £70–£135.

### ST DAVID'S Pembrokeshire
### Map 3:D1

OLD CROSS HOTEL, Cross Square, SA62 6SP. Tel 01437-720387, www. oldcrosshotel.co.uk. In the centre of this small city, within walking distance of the Coast Path, Alex and Julie Babis's traditional stone-built hotel is managed by Janet Davies. 2 lounges, bar (popular with locals; TV for sports events; background radio), restaurant; garden: alfresco meals in summer. Small function facilities. Wi-Fi (£5 per day).

Children, and dogs (£6.50 per night) welcomed. Parking. 16 bedrooms. B&B £35–£65 per person; D,B&B £57.50–£87.50.

## CHANNEL ISLANDS

### KINGS MILLS Guernsey
### Map 1: inset D5

FLEUR DU JARDIN, Grand Moulins, Castel, GY5 7JT. Tel 01481-257996, www.fleurdujardin.com. Ian and Amanda Walker (owners of *Bella Luce Hotel*, St Martin, see next page) have given a fresh seaside look to this pub/restaurant-with-rooms. There are bleached wood walls, simple furnishing and sandstone bathrooms. 'Very warm welcome; immaculate bedroom.' It is a 20 minutes' bus ride into town; also 20 minutes' walk to the beach. Bar, restaurant (David Hayden is chef; 'excellent evening meals'); background music; health suite (beauty treatments, relaxation rooms). 2-acre garden: heated swimming pool, sunny terrace. Children welcomed. 17 bedrooms (2 garden suites). B&B £44–£68 per person. Dinner from £20.
**25% DISCOUNT VOUCHERS**

### ST BRELADE Jersey
### Map 1: inset E6

ST BRELADE'S BAY, JE3 8EF. Tel 01534-746141, www.stbreladesbayhotel.com. The Colley family has run this 'large, glamorous' hotel facing Jersey's loveliest bay for five generations. The white, modern building has elegant public rooms and spacious bedrooms, some with a balcony and 'fantastic' views. Chef Franz Hacker is commended for his 'amazing', 'never repetitive' dinners. The English breakfast is 'superb'.

Lounge, bar, restaurant (pianist 3 nights a week); games room, snooker room; sun veranda. 7-acre grounds: outdoor restaurant, 2 heated swimming pools, sauna, mini-gym; croquet, tennis, putting. No background music. Children welcomed (playroom, TV room, 2 small pools and slides, etc, in small garden area; high teas, babysitting, baby-listening provided). 82 bedrooms. B&B £70–£172 per person. Dinner £49.50.

### ST HELIER Jersey
**Map 1: inset E6**
**THE CLUB HOTEL & SPA**, Green Street, JE2 4UH. Tel 01534-876500, www. theclubjersey.com. Tim Phillips manages this contemporary spa hotel of understated luxury, in a convenient location in town. Library (honesty bar), *Club* café, adjacent *Bohemia* bar (light meals) and restaurant (Shaun Rankin has a *Michelin* star); roof terrace; background music ('fairly muted'). Wi-Fi. Spa: saltwater pool, sauna, hydrotherapy bench, treatments. Beaches nearby. Parking. 46 bedrooms (suites have sitting room and balustrade). B&B (continental) £107.50–£245 per person. Dinner £49.50.

### ST MARTIN Guernsey
**Map 1: inset E5**
**BELLA LUCE HOTEL**, La Fosse, GY4 6EB. Tel 01481-238764, www.bellaluce hotel.com. In the south of the island, this charming manor house with 12th-century origins has been given a chic makeover by owners Ian and Amanda Walker – they also own *Fleur du Jardin*, Kings Mills (see previous page). The bedrooms are modern, clean-lined. Menus based on Guernsey produce are

served in the *Hemmingway Room* and the *Garden Room*. Bar; background music; wedding/function facilities. Wi-Fi. Garden (alfresco dining); swimming pool (heated in summer). Rock beach 5 mins' walk. It is 2 miles to St Peter Port. 24 bedrooms (some family; 1 suitable for &). B&B £65–£144 per person. Dinner £22.50.

### ST PETER PORT Guernsey
**Map 1: inset E5**
**THE CLUBHOUSE @ LA COLLINETTE**, St Jacques, GU1 1UT. Tel 01481-710331, www.lacollinette.com. Near the seafront and centre, this white hotel with colourful window boxes has been run for nearly 50 years by the Chambers family. Rooms are bright and modern; lounges open on to the lawns, pool terrace or balcony. A former German naval signals bunker has been turned into a museum. Bar; restaurant (seafood and local produce); background music; DVD library; conference facilities. Garden: heated swimming pool. Children welcomed: children's pool; play area. 30 bedrooms (plus self-catering cottages and apartments). B&B £50–£95 per person. Dinner from £20.

**LA FRÉGATE**, Les Cotils, GY1 1UT. Tel 01481-724624, www.lafregatehotel. com. The interiors are contemporary at this 18th-century manor house high above the town, with views over the harbour. Chris Sharp is the manager. The chef, Neil Maginnis, uses locally caught lobster and sole; home-grown vegetables. Lounge, bar, restaurant; terrace; *Orangery* (function facilities). No background music. Small, secluded garden. 2 mins' walk from centre.

Children welcomed. 22 bedrooms (all with sea views; some with balcony). B&B £74–£195 per person. Dinner £30.

### ST SAVIOUR Guernsey
Map 1: inset E5

**THE FARMHOUSE**, Bas Courtils, GY7 9YF. Tel 01481-264181, www. thefarmhouse.gg. David and Julia Nussbaumer 'personally oversee' their luxurious hotel, a conversion of an old farmhouse; Alan Sillett is the manager. It has a sophisticated modern interior; bedrooms are spacious; bathrooms luxurious. The well-regarded chef, Ankur Biswas, is committed to using fresh, organic and Fairtrade produce. Bar, restaurant ('easy listening' background music; live music at weekends); courtyard. Wedding/ conference facilities. Wi-Fi. Large garden: heated swimming pool. Children welcomed. 14 bedrooms. B&B £60–£105 per person. Dinner £38.

### SARK Guernsey
Map 1: inset E6

**HOTEL PETIT CHAMP**, via Guernsey, GY9 0SF. Tel 01481-832046, www.hotel petitchamp.co.uk. Spectacular sunsets can be seen from this low, late Victorian granite building on the west coast. There is a new manager, Zena Chaplin, and a new chef, Liam Foster. His five-course menus are served in the formal dining room, with local lobster and crab dishes a speciality. 3 sun lounges, library, TV room, bar, restaurant (background music). 15 mins' walk from village. 1-acre garden: solar-heated swimming pool, putting, croquet. Children over 10 allowed. 10 bedrooms. B&B £53–£75 per person; D,B&B £73–£95.

## IRELAND

### BALLINROBE Co. Mayo
Map 6:C5

**JJ GANNONS HOTEL**, Main Street. Tel 00 353 094-954 1008, www.jjgannons. com. Jay and Niki are the third generation of the Gannon family to run this central bar/restaurant-with-accommodation. The traditional building has a stylishly refurbished interior: leather seating, wood floors, colourful decor. Lounge, bar, *Red Room* restaurant (herbs, vegetables and fruit from the kitchen garden; Paul Moran is chef). 'Food straightforward, fresh and interesting.' Background music. Lift. Business facilities. Golf nearby. 10 bedrooms (some suitable for &.). B&B €52.50–€120 per person. Dinner €40.

### BALLINTOY Co. Antrim
Map 6:A6

**WHITEPARK HOUSE**, 150 Whitepark Road, BT54 6NH. Tel 028-2073 1482, www.whiteparkhouse.com. Near the Giant's Causeway, Bob and Siobhan Isles run their B&B in a crenellated 18th-century house. They have furnished it with artefacts from their travels. There are peat fires, spacious rooms, Irish breakfasts (vegetarians catered for), and a folly in the garden. Sitting room, conservatory. No background music. Wi-Fi. 3 bedrooms. B&B £50–£75 per person.

### BELFAST
Map 6:B6

**MALMAISON**, 34–38 Victoria Street, BT1 3GH. Tel 028-9022 0200, www. malmaison-belfast.com. The stone gargoyles, iron pillars and beams are still in place at this 'stylish', contemporary conversion of two red brick seed warehouses in the cathedral quarter, near the River Lagan. Helen Caters is the manager. Red and gold velvet, stripy lampshades and sombre lighting lend the bedrooms a 'bordello' air. Public areas are funky. Lounge, bar, brasserie; background music; gymtonic; small business centre. Wi-Fi. Children welcomed. 64 bedrooms: £52.50–£145. Breakfast £11.95–£13.95.

**THE OLD RECTORY**, 148 Malone Road, BT9 5LH. Tel 028-9066 7882, www. anoldrectory.co.uk. In a leafy suburb, Mary Callan's guest house is in a former Church of Ireland rectory. Many original features are in evidence: stained-glass windows, high ceilings, tiled floors, fireplaces. Breakfast choices include 'Ulster' and vegetarian; home-made raspberry jam, whiskey marmalade and wheaten bread. A small supper menu is available from Mon to Fri. Drawing room. Wi-Fi. Parking. 4 bedrooms. B&B £41–£52 per person.

**BLARNEY Co. Cork**
**Map 6:D5**
**THE MUSKERRY ARMS**, Tel 00 353 21-438 5200, www.muskerryarms.com. Nell O'Connor and sons run this characterful, yellow-painted, timber-panelled public house-with-rooms in the village centre. There is lively craic in the bar (music sessions every weekend; sporting events on eight plasma TV screens). Spacious bedrooms have wood flooring and a soothing colour scheme. Lounge, bar, *Tavern* restaurant. Wi-Fi. Parking. 11 bedrooms (some in *Lodge*, reached by walkway). B&B from €39–€49 per person. Dinner from €32.

**BUSHMILLS Co. Antrim**
**Map 6:A6**
**BUSHMILLS INN**, 9 Dunluce Road, BT57 8QG. Tel 028-2073 3000, www. bushmillsinn.com. Alan Dunlop has enlarged this historic coaching inn and mill house (sections date back to 1608 when Bushmills distillery was granted the world's first licence to distil whiskey). It has a web of interconnecting public rooms; there are turf fires, ancient wooden booths. Drawing room, 'secret' library, gallery, loft, 2 bars, restaurant in 4 sections; Garden Room; 'New Irish' cooking; classical background music, live music Sat night; courtyard; conference facilities. Wi-Fi. 3-acre garden. Children welcomed (family rooms). Parking. 41 bedrooms (some on ground floor; spacious ones in *Mill House*, smaller ones in inn). B&B £74–£159 per person. Dinner £30–£35.

**CALLAN Co. Kilkenny**
**Map 6:D5**
**BALLAGHTOBIN COUNTRY HOUSE**. Tel 00 353 56-772 5227, www.ballaghtobin. com. Fourteen generations of the Gabbett family have lived on the site of Ballaghtobin. The building, in parkland on a working farm, was recently refurbished in country house style. It is run by Catherine Gabbett in an 'easy-going' way. Drawing room, dining room, sun room. No background music. Tennis, croquet, clock golf. Children and dogs welcomed. 3 bedrooms. B&B €50–€60 per person. Closed Nov to Mar.

**CASTLEBALDWIN Co. Sligo**
**Map 6:B5**
**CROMLEACH LODGE**, Lough Arrow. Tel 00 353 71-916 5155, www.cromleach.com.

The Ciúnas Spa, built on three levels, has been added to Moira and Christy Tighe's purpose-built hotel on a low hillside above Lough Arrow. It is managed by Nicholas Ryan. The views over the lake to the Bricklieve Mountains and beyond are 'fantastic'. Lounge, *Nuada's* bar, *Moira's* restaurant (Lanka Fernando cooks modern Irish food); background music; spa (sauna, steam room, outdoor whirlpool, treatment rooms); wedding/function facilities. 30-acre grounds: forest walks; private access to Lough Arrow (fishing, boating, surfing); walking, hill climbing. Dogs welcomed (dog-grooming parlour). 57 bedrooms. B&B €75–€130 per person; D,B&B €125–€180. Closed Nov.

## CLONAKILTY Co. Cork
### Map 6:D4
AN GARRÁN CÓIR, Tel 00 353 23-884 8236, www.angarrancoir.com. The name of Michael and Jo Calnan's eco-aware guest house translates as 'a plentiful grove'. All the vegetables, fruit and herbs used in Jo Calnan's cooking are grown in the garden. The white-painted house has panoramic views of rolling countryside. Lounge, Irish coffee bar; patio (barbecues); tennis. Background music. Wi-Fi. 5 bedrooms. B&B €55–€80 per person. Dinner €20–€30.

## CONG Co. Mayo
### Map 6:C4
LISLOUGHREY LODGE, The Quay. Tel 00 353 94-9545 400, www.lisloughrey.ie. 'There are few more scenic places to be' than at this imposing, white country house overlooking Lough Corrib. Once the home of the former head gamekeeper of the Ashford Estate, it has been given a modern look, which 'works well'. The public rooms 'offer space, and fine nooks and crannies to hide away'. Bedrooms and suites are in the courtyard, linked to the main house. *Malt* bar and brasserie, *Salt* restaurant (local ingredients; modern Irish dishes by chef Wade Murphy; cookery courses); background music. Vault with pool table; games room; private screening room. Spa suite; beauty treatments; gym. Wi-Fi. Wedding/function facilities. Children welcomed (playroom). 50 bedrooms. B&B from €125 per person. Dinner €65.

## CORK Co. Cork
### Map 6:D5
CAFÉ PARADISO, 16 Lancaster Quay. Tel 00 353 21-427 7939, www.cafeparadiso. ie. Dennis Cotter (author of three cookery books, with a fourth in the pipeline) serves mouth-watering vegetarian dishes at his intimate restaurant-with-rooms. Seasonal, organic produce comes from Gortnanain Farm nearby (visits are arranged). Background music. No television. Wi-Fi. Restricted parking. Children welcomed. 2 bedrooms (1 faces the river). D,B&B €100 per person. Restaurant open Tues to Sat.

## DERRY Co. Londonderry
### Map 6:B6
SERENDIPITY HOUSE, 26 Marlborough Street, Bogside, BT48 9AY. Tel 028-7126 4229, www.serendipityrooms.co.uk. On a hill overlooking the city walls (the room at the top has great views), this cosy B&B is run by father and son, Paul and Stephen Lyttle. They are

friendly hosts. The bedrooms have original modern art. Lounge, dining room (background music at breakfast); panoramic sun deck. The city centre is five mins' walk away. Wi-Fi. Children welcomed. Dogs by arrangement. 5 bedrooms. B&B £20–£60 per person.

## DINGLE Co. Kerry
### Map 6:D4
**MILLTOWN HOUSE**. Tel 00 353 66-915 1372, www.milltownhousedingle.com. Mark and Anne Kerry, and their daughter, Tara, run this B&B, a white, 19th-century gabled house on a peninsula looking back towards the harbour. Lounge, conservatory/breakfast room (light meals available). No background music. 1½-acre garden. Golf driving range, pitch and putt behind house. 2 miles W of town. Parking. 10 bedrooms (some with views of garden or sea). B&B €65–€85 per person.

## DONEGAL Co. Donegal
### Map 6:B5
**HARVEY'S POINT**. Tel 00 353 74-972 2208, www.harveyspoint.com. The Gysling family (from Switzerland) have run this luxury hotel on Lough Eske with Deirdre McGlone for over 20 years. Bedrooms are elegantly furnished. The chef, Paul Montgomery, serves gourmet dishes in a dining room with views of the lake. Lounge, bar, restaurant; ballroom; resident pianist; Irish/classical background music; wedding/conference facilities; beauty treatments. Lift. Wi-Fi. 2-acre garden. 4 miles from town. Children (early supper) and dogs welcomed. 70 bedrooms (some in courtyard). B&B €99–€160 per person. Dinner €59.

## DUBLIN
### Map 6:C6
**BLAKES HOTEL & SPA**, 50 Merrion Road, Dublin 4. Tel 00 353 1-668 8324, www.blakeshotelandspa.com. The ultra-modern design of this new hotel, which opened in June 2010, contrasts with its more sedate sister hotel, *Merrion Hall*, next door, with which it shares facilities (see below). Lounge, bar, dining room. Background music (classical). Austrian-themed spa and wellness centre. Wi-Fi. Children welcomed. 34 bedrooms. B&B €74.50–€129 per person.

**MERRION HALL**, 54–56 Merrion Road, Dublin 4. Tel 00 353 1-668 1426, www.halpinsprivatehotels.com. Pat Halpin's smart, creeper-covered Edwardian hotel is opposite the RDS exhibition centre in the south of the city. He also owns *Aberdeen Lodge* (main entry). 2 drawing rooms, dining room/conservatory ('delicious' local and international dishes); background music; function facilities. Wi-Fi. Courtyard, small garden. Parking. 28 bedrooms (2 suitable for &). B&B €74.50–€129 per person.

**WATERLOO HOUSE**, 8–10 Waterloo Road, Dublin 4. Tel 00 353 1-660 1888, www.waterloohouse.ie. Bright red doors proclaim Evelyn Corcoran's 'inviting' B&B, which is in two Georgian buildings in a peaceful Ballsbridge avenue. The colourful decoration continues inside. Lounge (classical background music), dining room, conservatory. Wi-Fi. Garden. Parking. Lift, ramp. Irish breakfast includes 'catch of the day'. Children welcomed. 17 bedrooms (some suitable for &). B&B €54.50–€89 per person.

**DUNGARVAN Co. Waterford**
Map 6:D5
**POWERSFIELD HOUSE**, Ballinamuck
West. Tel 00 353 58-45594, www.
powersfield.com. Eunice Power runs a
catering business and cookery school at
her symmetrical, white neo-Georgian
house on a little peninsula 1 mile outside
Dungarvan. It is homely, and simply
decorated, with an 'eclectic collection of
artwork'. The atmosphere is relaxed.
Breakfast ('above the average fare') is
served until 10 am 'or later', and may
be taken in bed. Background CDs/radio
if wanted. Wi-Fi. Garden. Children
welcomed. Jams, marmalades, chutneys
are for sale. Fly fishing on Blackwater
River nearby; Clonea Strand beach is
nearby. Children welcomed. 6 bedrooms
(1 suitable for &). B&B €50–€100 per
person. Dinner (by arrangement)
€27.50–€35.

**DUNLAVIN Co. Wicklow**
Map 6:C6
**RATHSALLAGH HOUSE**. Tel 00 353 45-
403112, www.rathsallagh.com. In
converted stables (the original Queen
Anne house burned down in the
rebellion of 1798), the O'Flynn family's
gracious country hotel stands in
extensive grounds with an 18-hole golf
course and driving range. 'Food is A1;
superb breakfasts.' Drawing room
(turf and log fires), dining room
(background music); snooker room;
tennis, croquet; clay-pigeon shooting,
archery; sauna with spa bath and steam
room; massage and spa treatments.
Less than an hour's drive from Dublin.
Wi-Fi. Wedding/conference facilities.
Dogs welcomed (heated kennels). 31
rooms. B&B €95–€150 per person.
Dinner €76.50.

**GALWAY Co. Galway**
Map 6:C5
**THE g**, Wellpark. Tel 00 353 91-865200,
www.theg.ie. 'A most enjoyable stay.'
This large, glamorous hotel overlooking
Lough Atalia has been designed with a
'wow' factor by milliner Philip Treacy.
The dining area is vibrant, with plush
jewel-coloured fabrics (pink, cerise,
purple) and mirrors. There are swirling
carpets in the 'ladies' lounge', and an
arresting black marble lobby. German
chef Stefan Matz creates contemporary
Irish menus with a European influence.
Damien O'Riordan is the manager. 4
lounges, champagne-drinking area,
*Matz* restaurant; 'funky' background
music; lift; spa (indoor swimming pool,
treatments); wedding/function facilities;
'secret' bamboo garden. Children
welcomed. 101 rooms. B&B €80–€240
per person. Dinner from €29.50.

**KENMARE Co. Kerry**
Map 6:D4
**SHEEN FALLS LODGE**. Tel 00 353 64-664
1600, www.sheenfallslodge.ie. Once the
country retreat of the Marquis of
Lansdowne, this manor house
overlooks a waterfall in mature
woodlands. Owner Bent Hoyer has
extended it as a luxury hotel (Relais &
Châteaux), with a choice of restaurants.
Chef Heiko Reibandt specialises in
seafood, with organic vegetables and
cheeses from local suppliers in the more
formal *La Cascade* (panoramic views of
the falls). Alan Campbell is manager.
Lift. Lounge, sun lounge, library, 2
bars, *Oscar's* bistro, *La Cascade*
restaurant; background music; billiard
room; terrace; health club (swimming
pool, whirlpool, sauna, treatments);
tennis. 2 miles SE of town. 66

bedrooms. B&B €102.50–€300 per person; D,B&B from €135.

## KILLARNEY Co. Kerry
Map 6:D4

**DUNLOE CASTLE**, Beaufort. Tel 00 353 64-664 4111, www.thedunloe.com. Owned by Killarney Hotels and managed by Jason Clifford, this large country hotel stands in rolling countryside with views of the Gap of Dunloe. Lounge, bar; background music/live pianist in bar and *The Park* restaurant, snacks at the *Garden Café* (Franz Josef Osterloh is the chef, using local ingredients and herbs from the kitchen garden); wedding/function facilities. 20-acre subtropical garden; indoor swimming pool, sauna, steam room, fitness room, treatment rooms; 2 indoor tennis courts; putting; pony trekking on Haflinger ponies; salmon fishing. Children welcomed: playground, indoor play centre, evening movie show. 102 bedrooms. B&B €85–€145 per person; D,B&B from €135. Closed Nov to Apr.

## KINSALE Co. Cork
Map 6:D5

**THE OLD PRESBYTERY**, 43 Cork Street. Tel 00 353 21-477 2027, www.oldpres. com. A 'rabbit-warren' of ups and downs, and full of character, this central Georgian town house was built 200 years ago as the home of priests attached to St John the Baptist Church across the street. Now Philip and Noreen McEvoy offer traditionally furnished B&B accommodation. Lounge, dining room; classical/Irish background music; sun patio. Parking. Children welcomed. 9 bedrooms (3 suites – 2 self-catering). B&B €45–€90 per person.

## LAHINCH Co. Clare
Map 6:C4

**MOY HOUSE**. Tel 00 353 65-708 2800, www.moyhouse.com. Overlooking the bay, this mid-18th-century building, with a central tower, has been converted 'with panache' by owner Antoin O'Looney. Brid O'Meara is the manager. Drawing room (honesty bar), library, dining room (Daniel O'Brien produces 'modern Irish with French and world-influenced dishes'; background music). Popular with golfers (Lahinch has a championship course). Children welcomed. 15-acre grounds; access to beach. Closed Dec to mid-Feb, except New Year. 9 bedrooms. B&B €92.50–€180 per person. Dinner €55.

## LIMERICK Co. Limerick
Map 6:D5

**NO. 1 PERY SQUARE**, Pery Square. Tel 00 353 61-402402, www.oneperysquare. com. In a terrace (regarded as one of the finest examples of late Georgian architecture in the city), opposite the People's Park, this elegant boutique hotel is owned by Patricia Roberts. Authentic period decoration and furnishings combine with modern luxuries. The 'Irish Organic' spa in the vaulted basement offers sound-wave therapy among a variety of treatments. Lounge, drawing room, *Park Room* bar, *Brasserie One* restaurant (chef Alan Burns uses locally sourced ingredients). Background music. Lift. Private dining available. Wine shop; small gym. Parking. Children welcomed (babysitting). 20 bedrooms (2 suitable for &). B&B €82.50–€165 per person; D,B&B €132.50.
**25% DISCOUNT VOUCHERS**

## LONGFORD Co. Longford
### Map 6:C5
**VIEWMOUNT HOUSE**, Dublin Road. Tel 00 353 43-334 1919, www.viewmount house.com. Beryl and James Kearney have painstakingly restored their large Georgian house next to the golf course, adding bedrooms and the *VM* restaurant in converted stables and an extension. The main building has rich colour schemes, many original features. Chef Gary O'Hanlon cooks modern Irish/European dishes. Sitting room, reception room, library. Background music in restaurant. Wedding facilities. Children welcomed. 3¾-acre gardens (Japanese garden, knot garden, orchard). 12 bedrooms (7 in modern extension; some on ground floor; garden views). B&B €50–€120 per person; D,B&B €100.
**25% DISCOUNT VOUCHERS**

## MAGHERAFELT Co. Derry
### Map 6:B6
**LAUREL VILLA TOWNHOUSE**, 60 Church Street, BT45 6AW. Tel 028-7930 1459, www.laurel-villa.com. Eugene and Geraldine Kielt pay tribute to Irish poets at their Victorian house in the centre of this small town. They showcase paintings, photographs, first editions in glass cases; there is a Seamus Heaney exhibition. The host (a Blue Badge guide) arranges tours of 'Heaney country', and poetry readings. No background music. 2 lounges, dining room. Children welcomed. 4 bedrooms. B&B £45–£50 per person.

## NEWTOWNARDS Co. Down
### Map 6:B6
**BEECH HILL COUNTRY HOUSE**, 23 Ballymoney Road, Craigantlet, BT23 4TG. Tel 028-9042 5892, www. beech-hill.net. In the Holywood hills, close to Belfast, Victoria Brann's Georgian-style house is decorated in period fashion. 'Lots of places to sit and read. Fresh flowers around the house, including a vase of garden flowers in my room.' Drawing room, dining room, conservatory. No background music. Wi-Fi. 3 bedrooms (on ground floor; also *The Colonel's Lodge*). B&B £45–£60 per person.

## PORTSTEWART Co. Londonderry
### Map 6:A6
**THE YORK**, 2 Station Road, BT55 7DA. Tel 028-7083 3594, www.theyork portstewart.co.uk. By the sea, this comfortable, modern guest house is owned by Jonathan Davis. There is a choice of dining options. A courtesy bus is available (by arrangement) for airport pickups, and for visiting local attractions. Bar, terrace/conservatory, *Inn* (fine dining) and *York* restaurants (piano; jukebox). Wi-Fi. 8 bedrooms (1 suitable for &). B&B £55–£89 per person.

## RATHMULLAN Co. Donegal
### Map 6:B5
**FORT ROYAL**. Tel 00 353 74-915 8100, www.fortroyalhotel.ie. This large, white 19th-century building, overlooking sandy Rathmullan Beach, has been in 'affable' Tim Fletcher's family for three generations. It stands in large grounds (one lawn leads down to the beach). Most of the fruit, vegetables and herbs served at meals are grown in the grounds. Breakfasts are 'good'. 2 lounges, bar, dining room. No background music. Tennis, pitch-and-putt golf. 11 bedrooms (plus 3 self-catering cottages). Closed Nov to Easter. B&B €65–€110 per person; D,B&B €110–€155.

THE WATER'S EDGE, Balliboe. Tel 00 353 74-915 8182, www.thewatersedge.ie. In a 'superb setting' on Lough Swilley, Neil and Mandy Blaney run their restaurant-with-rooms in this extended inn by the sea. The modern bar is busy with locals and holidaymakers alike (live music at weekends). All the light and airy bedrooms and the barn-like dining room (with soaring rafters) have sea views. 'We had a magnificently huge room just feet away from the water; a spectacularly huge white bathroom.' Children welcomed. 10 bedrooms. B&B €40–€60 per person. Dinner from €30.

### RECESS Co. Galway
Map 6:C4

LOUGH INAGH LODGE, Connemara. Tel 00 353 95-34706, www.loughinagh lodgehotel.ie. 'Enjoyed it no end.' Máire O'Connor's refurbished hotel in a former fishing lodge is on the shores of a freshwater lough beneath the Twelve Bens mountain range. It is decorated in modern country house style. There are open log fires in the library and oak-panelled bar. Seafood and game dishes feature on Julie Flaherty's 'Irish with European' menus. Outdoor activities include fishing, shooting, hill walking, pony trekking and golf. Closed mid-Dec to Mar. Bar, drawing room, library, dining room; 5-acre grounds. No background music. Wedding facilities. Children welcomed. 13 bedrooms (4 on ground floor). B&B €55–€90 per person; D,B&B €90–€135.

### STRANGFORD Co. Down
Map 6:B6

THE CUAN, 6–10 The Square, BT30 7ND. Tel 028-4488 1222, www.thecuan. com. Run as a licensed guest house by owners Peter and Caroline McErlean, this green-painted, flower-decorated building is on a square in a conservation village on the southern tip of Strangford Lough. Bedrooms are modern and comfortable. The restaurant specialises in fish and seafood. 2 lounges, bar, restaurant (open May to Oct; traditional background music); function/conference facilities. Children welcomed. 9 bedrooms (1 suitable for &). B&B £37.50–£55 per person; D,B&B £53–£70.

### UPPERLANDS Co. Londonderry
Map 6:B6

ARDTARA COUNTRY HOUSE, 8 Gorteade Road, BT46 5SA. Tel 028-7964 4490, www.ardtara.com. Built by the linen magnate Harry Jackson Clark, this handsome Victorian house is run as a country hotel. It has high ceilings, bow-fronted windows and original fireplaces, and is furnished with antiques. The comfortable bedrooms, decorated in period style, have modern bathroom and amenities. Chef Julian Davidson serves contemporary dishes in an elegant room with a large skylight. 2 lounges, sun room, bar, dining room (background music); 8-acre wooded grounds (lawns, exotic plantings and woodland); tennis. Wedding/conference facilities. Wi-Fi. 9 bedrooms (1 on ground floor). Children welcomed. Dogs by arrangement. B&B from £65 per person. Dinner £32.

### WESTPORT Co. Mayo
Map 6:C4

CLEW BAY HOTEL, James Street. Tel 00 353 98-28088, www.clewbayhotel.com. Darren Madden and Maria Ruddy's cream-painted hotel has a stylish, contemporary interior. They hold exhibitions of art and sculpture by

Westport artists in the airy, glass-roofed reception area. The house backs on to the Carrowbeg River in the town centre. Lounge, bar (live music), *Madden's* bistro, *Riverside* restaurant ('easy listening' background music; Bart Chicack is chef). Beauty treatments. Lift. Wi-Fi. There is complimentary access to Westport Leisure Park next door (25-metre swimming pool, sauna, steam room, plunge pool, fitness suite). Children welcomed (playroom). 54 bedrooms. B&B €50–€120 per person. Dinner €35.

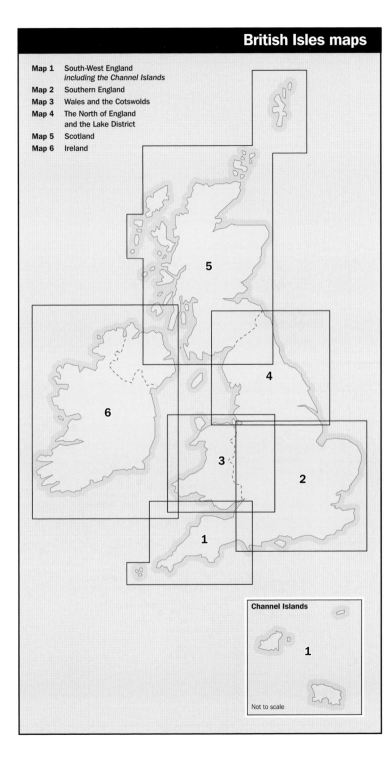

# British Isles maps

**Map 1**  South-West England
*including the Channel Islands*

**Map 2**  Southern England

**Map 3**  Wales and the Cotswolds

**Map 4**  The North of England
and the Lake District

**Map 5**  Scotland

**Map 6**  Ireland

5

4

6

3

2

1

**Channel Islands**

1

Not to scale

# 1 South-West England

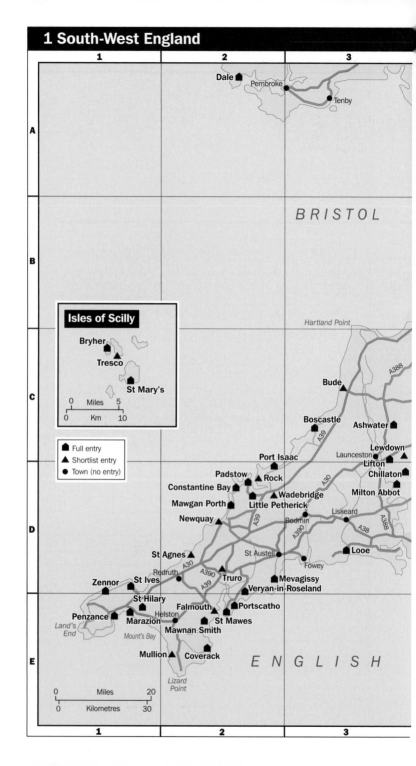

**Isles of Scilly**

Bryher

Tresco

St Mary's

0  Miles  5

0  Km  10

- ■ Full entry
- ▲ Shortlist entry
- ● Town (no entry)

BRISTOL

Hartland Point

Dale

Pembroke

Tenby

Bude

Boscastle

Ashwater

Lewdown

Launceston

Lifton

Chillaton

Milton Abbot

Port Isaac

Padstow  Rock

Constantine Bay

Wadebridge

Mawgan Porth

Little Petherick

Liskeard

Newquay

Bodmin

St Austell

Fowey

Looe

St Agnes

Redruth

Truro

Mevagissy

Zennor  St Ives

Veryan-in-Roseland

St Hilary

Falmouth

Portscatho

Penzance

Marazion

St Mawes

Land's
End

Helston

Mawnan Smith

Mount's Bay

Mullion

Coverack

ENGLISH

Lizard
Point

0  Miles  20

0  Kilometres  30

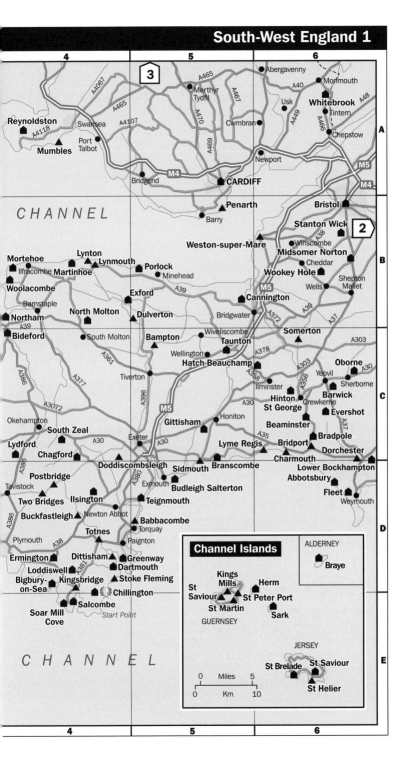

**3**

Abergavenny
Monmouth
Merthyr Tydfil
A465
A467
A470
A40
Usk
A449
**Whitebrook**
Tintern
A466
A48
Cwmbran
Chepstow

**A**

Reynoldston
A4118
Swansea
A4107
A465
Port Talbot
**Mumbles**
Bridgend
A469
M4
**CARDIFF**
Newport
M5
M4

CHANNEL

**Penarth**
Barry

**Bristol**

**2**

**Stanton Wick**
Winscombe
A38
**Weston-super-Mare**
**Midsomer Norton**
Cheddar
**Wookey Hole**
Wells
Shepton Mallet

**B**

Mortehoe
**Lynton**
**Lynmouth**
Ilfracombe
**Martinhoe**
**Porlock**
Minehead
**Woolacombe**
Barnstaple
**Exford**
A39
M5
**Cannington**
**Northam**
**North Molton**
**Dulverton**
Bridgwater
A372
A39
A37
**Bideford**
South Molton
**Bampton**
Wiveliscombe
**Somerton**
A303
A39

**C**

A386
A377
A361
**Taunton**
Wellington
A378
A303
**Oborne**
A30
Yeovil
Sherborne
Tiverton
A396
**Hatch-Beauchamp**
A358
Ilminster
A356
**Barwick**
A30
Crewkerne
**Evershot**
A37
Okehampton
A3072
M5
**Hinton St George**
**Beaminster**
**Bradpole**
**South Zeal**
**Gittisham**
Honiton
A35
**Lydford**
Exeter
A30
**Lyme Regis**
**Bridport**
**Dorchester**
**Chagford**
**Charmouth**
**Lower Bockhampton**

**D**

**Postbridge**
**Doddiscombsleigh**
**Sidmouth**
**Branscombe**
**Abbotsbury**
Tavistock
Exmouth
**Fleet**
**Two Bridges**
**Ilsington**
**Budleigh Salterton**
Weymouth
**Buckfastleigh**
Newton Abbot
**Teignmouth**
**Babbacombe**
Plymouth
A38
Torquay
**Totnes**
Paignton
**Ermington**
**Dittisham**
**Greenway**
**Loddiswell**
**Dartmouth**
**Bigbury-on-Sea**
**Kingsbridge**
**Stoke Fleming**
**Chillington**
**Salcombe**
**Soar Mill Cove**
Start Point

**Channel Islands**

ALDERNEY
**Braye**

**Kings Mills**
**Herm**
**St Saviour**
**St Peter Port**
**St Martin**
**Sark**
GUERNSEY

JERSEY
**St Brelade**
**St Saviour**
**St Helier**

0 Miles 5
0 Km 10

CHANNEL

**E**

4 5 6

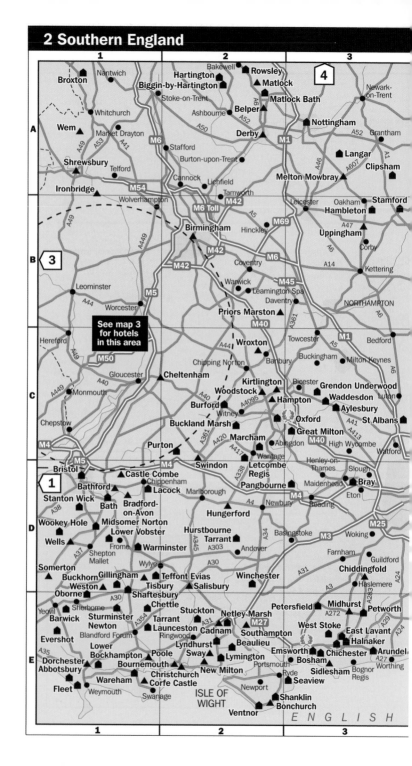

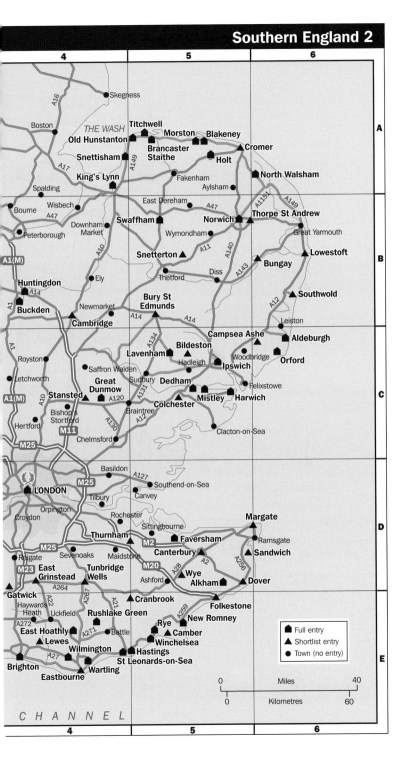

**4** **5** **6**

Skegness

Boston

THE WASH  Titchwell  Morston  Blakeney
Old Hunstanton  Cromer
Brancaster
Snettisham  Staithe  Holt

A16
A149

King's Lynn  Fakenham  North Walsham
Spalding  Aylsham  A1151  A149

Bourne  Wisbech  East Dereham  A47
A47  Thorpe St Andrew
Downham  Swaffham  Norwich
Peterborough  Market  Great Yarmouth
Wymondham

A1(M)  Snetterton  Lowestoft
A11  A140
A10  Thetford  Diss  Bungay
Huntingdon  Ely  A143
A14  Southwold
Buckden  Newmarket  Bury St  A12
Cambridge  Edmunds
A14  A14  Leiston

Royston  A134  Campsea Ashe  Aldeburgh
Bildeston
Lavenham  Orford
Letchworth  Saffron Walden  Hadleigh  Woodbridge
Great  Sudbury  Ipswich
A1(M)  Stansted  Dunmow  Dedham  Felixstowe
A10  A120  A131  Mistley  Harwich
Bishop's  Colchester
Hertford  Stortford  Braintree
M11  A130  Clacton-on-Sea
Chelmsford

Basildon  A127
M25  Southend-on-Sea
LONDON  Tilbury  Canvey
Orpington
Croydon  Rochester  Margate
Thurnham  Sittingbourne  Ramsgate
M25  Faversham
Reigate  Sevenoaks  Maidstone  Canterbury  Sandwich
M23  East  Tunbridge  M20  A2  A256
Grinstead  Wells  Ashford  Wye  Dover
A264  Alkham
Gatwick  Cranbrook
Haywards  A22  A267  A21  Folkestone
Heath  Uckfield  Rushlake Green  A259  New Romney
A272  Battle  Rye
East Hoathly  Camber
Lewes  Winchelsea
Wilmington  Hastings
A27  St Leonards-on-Sea
Brighton  Wartling
Eastbourne

**A**
**B**
**C**
**D**
**E**

CHANNEL

■ Full entry
▲ Shortlist entry
● Town (no entry)

0        Miles        40
0        Kilometres        60

**4** **5** **6**

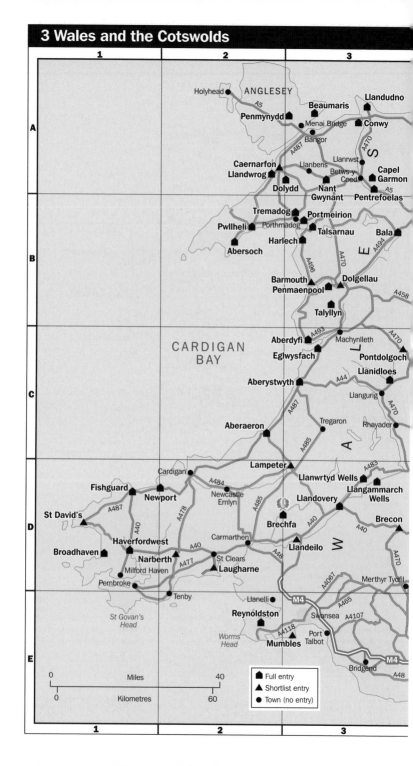

ANGLESEY

Holyhead

A5

Beaumaris
Penmynydd
Menai Bridge
Llandudno
Bangor
Conwy

A487

A470

S

Caernarfon
Llandwrog
Llanberis
Betws-y-Coed
Llanrwst
Capel
Garmon

Dolydd
Nant
Gwynant
Pentrefoelas

A5

Tremadog
Portmeirion
Pwllheli
Porthmadog
Talsarnau
Bala

Harlech
E

Abersoch

A496

A470

A494

Barmouth
Dolgellau
Penmaenpool

A458

Talyllyn

CARDIGAN
BAY

Aberdyfi
A493
Machynlleth
L
A470

Eglwysfach
Pontdolgoch

Llanidloes

Aberystwyth
A44

Llangurig

A487

A470

Aberaeron
Tregaron
Rhayader

A485

A

Lampeter
A483

Cardigan
A484
Llanwrtyd Wells

Fishguard
Newcastle
Emlyn
Llangammarch
Wells

Newport
A485
Llandovery

St David's
A487
A40
A478
Brechfa
A40
Brecon

Haverfordwest
Carmarthen
A40
A470

Broadhaven
Narberth
St Clears
Llandeilo
W

Milford Haven
A477
Laugharne
A48

Pembroke
A4067
Merthyr Tydfil

Tenby
Llanelli
M4

St Govan's
Head
Reynoldston
Swansea
A4107

A465

Worms
Head
A4118
Port
Talbot

Mumbles

Bridgend
M4

A48

0 Miles 40

0 Kilometres 60

■ Full entry
▲ Shortlist entry
● Town (no entry)

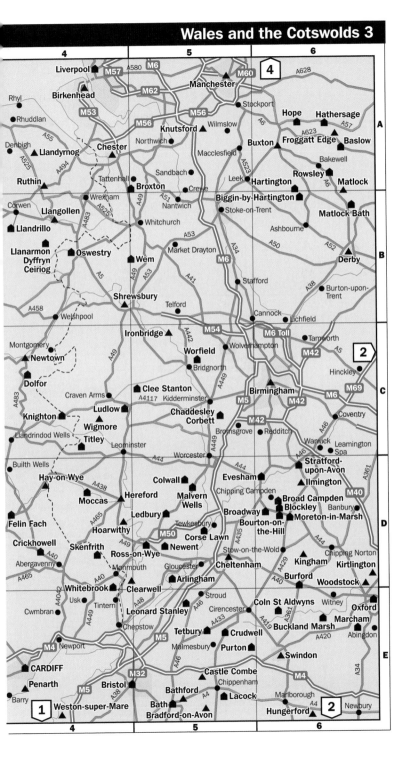

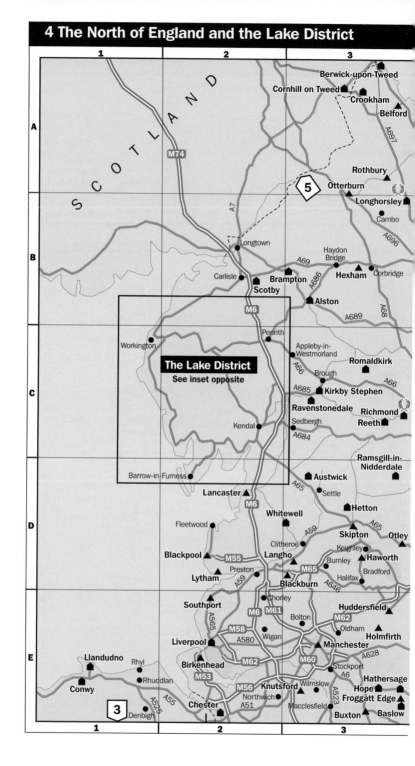

SCOTLAND

**Berwick-upon-Tweed**
**Cornhill on Tweed**
**Crookham**
**Belford**

M74

A7

**Rothbury**
5
**Otterburn**
**Longhorsley**
Cambo

A696

Haydon
Bridge
A69
**Hexham**
Corbridge
A686

Longtown

B

Carlisle
**Brampton**
**Scotby**
**Alston**

A689
A68

M6

**Workington**
Penrith

**The Lake District**
See inset opposite

Appleby-in-
Westmorland
**Romaldkirk**
A66
Brough
A66

C

**Kirkby Stephen**
A685
**Ravenstonedale**
**Richmond**
Sedbergh
**Reeth**
**Kendal**
A684

**Ramsgill-in-
Nidderdale**

**Barrow-in-Furness**
**Austwick**
A65
Settle

**Lancaster**
M6
**Hetton**

D

Fleetwood
**Whitewell**
A59
**Skipton**
**Otley**

Clitheroe
Keighley
**Blackpool**
M55
**Langho**
Burnley
**Haworth**
Bradford
**Lytham**
Preston
M65
Halifax
A59
**Blackburn**
A646

Chorley
**Southport**
**Huddersfield**
M6
M61
A565
M62
**Liverpool**
M58
A580
Wigan
Bolton
Oldham
**Holmfirth**
A628
**Manchester**
**Llandudno**
Rhyl
M60
A6
**Hathersage**
**Birkenhead**
M62
M56
Stockport
A523
**Hope**
**Conwy**
Rhuddlan
M53
Wilmslow
**Froggatt Edge**
A55
**Knutsford**
A525
Northwich
Macclesfield
**Baslow**
3
Denbigh
**Chester**
A51
**Buxton**

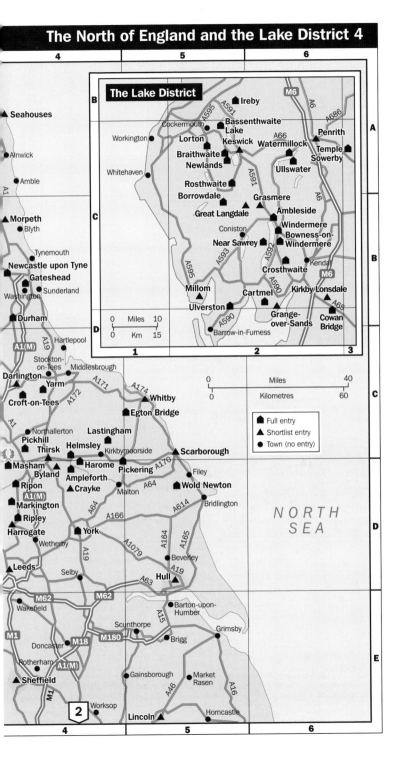

## The Lake District

Ireby
Cockermouth
Workington
Lorton
Bassenthwaite Lake
Keswick
Watermillock
Penrith
Braithwaite
Newlands
Temple Sowerby
Whitehaven
Ullswater
Rosthwaite
Borrowdale
Grasmere
Great Langdale
Ambleside
Coniston
Windermere
Near Sawrey
Bowness-on-Windermere
Kendal
Crosthwaite
Millom
Cartmel
Kirkby Lonsdale
Ulverston
Grange-over-Sands
Cowan Bridge
Barrow-in-Furness

Miles 10
Km 15

Seahouses
Alnwick
Amble
Morpeth
Blyth
Tynemouth
Newcastle upon Tyne
Gateshead
Washington
Sunderland
Durham
Hartlepool
Stockton-on-Tees
Middlesbrough
Darlington
Yarm
Croft-on-Tees
Whitby
Egton Bridge
Northallerton
Lastingham
Pickhill
Helmsley
Thirsk
Kirkbymoorside
Scarborough
Masham
Harome
Byland
Ampleforth
Pickering
Filey
Ripon
Crayke
Malton
Wold Newton
Markington
Ripley
Bridlington
Harrogate
York
Wetherby
Beverley
Leeds
Selby
Hull
Wakefield
Barton-upon-Humber
Scunthorpe
Grimsby
Doncaster
Brigg
Rotherham
Sheffield
Gainsborough
Market Rasen
Worksop
Lincoln
Horncastle

Miles 40
Kilometres 60

Full entry
Shortlist entry
Town (no entry)

NORTH SEA

# 5 Scotland

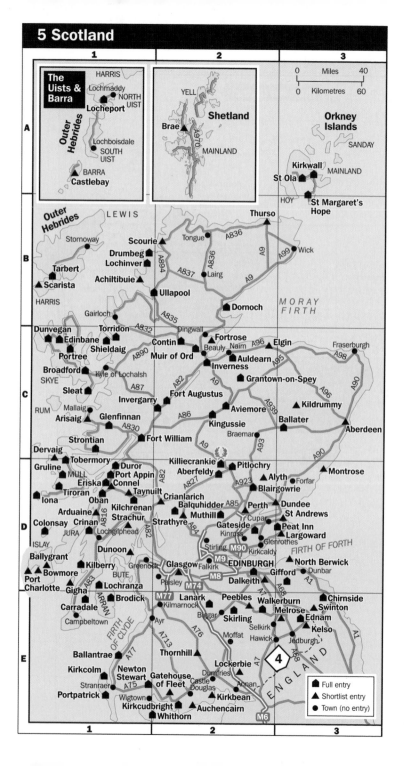

**The Uists & Barra**

HARRIS
Lochmaddy
NORTH UIST
Locheport
Outer Hebrides
Lochboisdale
SOUTH UIST
BARRA
Castlebay

**Shetland**

YELL
Brae
A970
MAINLAND

**Orkney Islands**

SANDAY
Kirkwall
St Ola
MAINLAND
HOY
St Margaret's Hope

0 Miles 40
0 Kilometres 60

## A

## B

Outer Hebrides
LEWIS
Stornoway
Scourie
Tongue A836
Thurso
Drumbeg
Lochinver
A894
A837
A836
A9
Wick
Tarbert
Achiltibuie
Lairg
A9
Scarista
Ullapool
HARRIS
Gairloch
A835
Dornoch
MORAY FIRTH

## C

Dunvegan
Torridon
A832
Dingwall
Fortrose
Elgin
Fraserburgh
Edinbane
Contin
Beauly
Nairn
A96
Shieldaig
A890
Muir of Ord
Auldearn
A98
Portree
Inverness
A95
Broadford
Kyle of Lochalsh
Grantown-on-Spey
SKYE
A87
A96
A90
Sleat
A82
Invergarry
Fort Augustus
RUM
Mallaig
A9
Aviemore
A939
Kildrummy
Arisaig
Glenfinnan
A86
Kingussie
Ballater
A830
Fort William
Braemar
Aberdeen
Strontian
A9
A93
A90
Dervaig

## D

Tobermory
Killiecrankie
Pitlochry
Montrose
Gruline
Aberfeldy
Alyth
MULL
Duror
Forfar
Port Appin
A827
Blairgowrie
Eriska
Connel
A923
Iona
Tiroran
Taynuilt
Crianlarich
Perth
Dundee
Oban
Balquhidder
A85
St Andrews
Kilchrenan
Muthill
Cupar
Peat Inn
Arduaine
Strachur
Strathyre
Gateside
Largoward
Colonsay
Crinan
Lochgilphead
A84
Kinross
JURA
A82
Stirling
M90
Glenrothes
FIRTH OF FORTH
ISLAY
Dunoon
Kirkcaldy
Ballygrant
Glasgow
M9
EDINBURGH
North Berwick
Bowmore
Kilberry
Greenock
Falkirk
M8
Gifford
Dunbar
Port Charlotte
BUTE
Paisley
Dalkeith
A1
Gigha
Lochranza
M74
A68
ARRAN
Brodick
M77
Lanark
Peebles
Walkerburn
Chirnside
Carradale
Kilmarnock
Biggar
Swinton
Campbeltown
Ayr
Skirling
Melrose
Ednam
FIRTH OF CLYDE
A76
Selkirk
Kelso
Moffat
Hawick
Jedburgh
A1

## E

Ballantrae
A77
Thornhill
Lockerbie
A7
A68
Kirkcolm
Newton Stewart
Gatehouse of Fleet
Dumfries
Castle Douglas
Annan
ENGLAND
Stranraer
A75
Wigtown
Kirkbean
Portpatrick
Kirkcudbright
Auchencairn
Whithorn
M6

■ Full entry
▲ Shortlist entry
● Town (no entry)

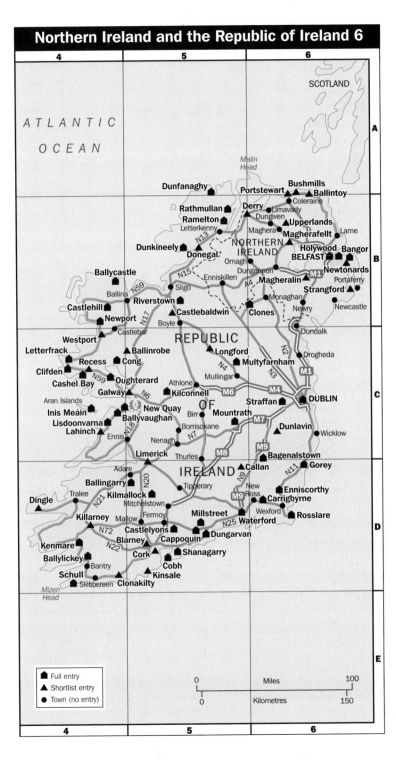

| | 4 | 5 | 6 |
|---|---|---|---|

SCOTLAND

ATLANTIC

OCEAN

**A**

Malin
Head

Dunfanaghy
Portstewart
Bushmills
Ballintoy
Coleraine
Rathmullan
Derry
Limavady
Ramelton
Dungiven
Upperlands
Letterkenny
Maghera
Magherafellt
Larne
Dunkineely
N13
Holywood
Bangor
Donegal
BELFAST
Newtonards
Omagh
NORTHERN
IRELAND
Portaferry

**B**

Ballycastle
N15
Enniskillen
Dungannon
Magheralin
Ballina
N59
Sligo
AA
Strangford
Castlehill
Riverstown
Castlebaldwin
Clones
Monaghan
Newcastle
Newport
Castlebar
Boyle
Newry

Westport
REPUBLIC
Longford
Dundalk
Letterfrack
Ballinrobe
Multyfarnham
Drogheda
Recess
Cong
N4
Clifden
N59
Oughterard
Athlone
Mullingar
M6
M4
M1
Cashel Bay
Galway
N6
Kilconnell
OF
DUBLIN
Aran Islands
New Quay
Birr
Straffan
Inis Meáin
Ballyvaughan
Mountrath
M7
Lisdoonvarna
Borrisokane
Dunlavin
Lahinch
Ennis
N7
Wicklow
Nenagh
M8
M9
Limerick
Thurles
Bagenalstown

**C**

Adare
IRELAND
Callan
Gorey
Ballingarry
N20
N9
N11
Kilmallock
Tipperary
New
Enniscorthy
Dingle
Tralee
Mitchelstown
Ross
Carrigbyrne
Killarney
Mallow
Fermoy
Millstreet
Wexford
Rosslare
N72
Castlelyons
Dungarvan
N25
Waterford
Kenmare
N22
Blarney
Cappoquin
Ballylickey
Cork
Shanagarry
Bantry
Cobh
Schull
Kinsale
Skibbereen
Clonakilty
Mizen
Head

**D**

**E**

Full entry
Shortlist entry
Town (no entry)

| 0 | Miles | 100 |
|---|---|---|
| 0 | Kilometres | 150 |

# THE TRULY INDEPENDENT GUIDE

**THIS IS** the leading independent guide to hotels in Great Britain and Ireland. Hotels cannot buy their entry as they do in most rival guides. No money changes hands, and the editors and inspectors do not accept free hospitality on their anonymous visits to hotels. The only vested interest is that of the reader seeking impartial advice to find a good hotel.

**OUR HOTELS** are as independent as we are. Most are small, family owned and family run. They are places of character where the owners and their staff spend time looking after their guests, rather than reporting to an area manager. We look for a warm welcome, with flexible service.

**DIVERSITY** is the key to our selection. Grand country houses are listed alongside simple B&Bs. Some of our favourite places may not have the full range of hotel-type facilities. We include a few chain hotels, especially in the larger cities: each one will have met our criteria of high standards of service.

**OUR WEBSITE** works in tandem with the printed *Guide*. It carries the entries for many, but not all, of our selected hotels (unlike the printed *Guide*, hotels pay a small fee for inclusion on the website). It has pictures for each entry, and a comprehensive search engine.

**OUR READERS** play a crucial role by reporting on existing entries as well as recommending new discoveries. The editors make a balanced judgment based on these reports, backed where necessary by an anonymous inspection. Reader reports, written on the forms at the back of the book or sent by email, bring our entries to life, and give the Guide a unique 'word-of-mouth' quality. Many correspondents join our Readers' Club (see page 16).

**ANNUAL UPDATES** give the *Guide* an added edge. A significant number of hotels are omitted every year and many new ones are added. We drop a hotel or demote it to the Shortlist if there has been a change of owner (unless reports after the change are positive), if this year's reports are negative, or in rare cases where there has been no feedback.

**Please send your reports to:**

The *Good Hotel Guide*, Freepost PAM 2931, London W11 4BR

NOTE: No stamps needed in the UK.

**Letters/report forms posted outside the UK should be addressed to:**

The *Good Hotel Guide*, 50 Addison Avenue, London W11 4QP, England, and stamped normally.

Unless asked not to, we assume that we may publish your name. If you would like more report forms please tick ☐

NAME OF HOTEL:  _____

ADDRESS:  _____

_____

Date of most recent visit: _____ Duration of stay: _____

☐ New recommendation                ☐ Comment on existing entry

REPORT:

*Please continue overleaf*

*I am not connected directly or indirectly with the management or proprietors*

Signed: _____

Name: <small>(CAPITALS PLEASE)</small>_____

Address: _____

_____

Email address: _____

**Please send your reports to:**

The *Good Hotel Guide*, Freepost PAM 2931, London W11 4BR

NOTE: No stamps needed in the UK.

**Letters/report forms posted outside the UK should be addressed to:**

The *Good Hotel Guide*, 50 Addison Avenue, London W11 4QP, England, and stamped normally.

Unless asked not to, we assume that we may publish your name. If you would like more report forms please tick ☐

NAME OF HOTEL: _____

ADDRESS: _____

_____

Date of most recent visit: _____ Duration of stay: _____

☐ New recommendation          ☐ Comment on existing entry

REPORT:

*Please continue overleaf*

*I am not connected directly or indirectly with the management or proprietors*

Signed: _____

Name: (CAPITALS PLEASE) _____

Address: _____

_____

Email address: _____

**Please send your reports to:**

The *Good Hotel Guide*, Freepost PAM 2931, London W11 4BR

NOTE: No stamps needed in the UK.

**Letters/report forms posted outside the UK should be addressed to:**

The *Good Hotel Guide*, 50 Addison Avenue, London W11 4QP, England, and stamped normally.

Unless asked not to, we assume that we may publish your name. If you would like more report forms please tick ☐

NAME OF HOTEL:   _____

ADDRESS:   _____

_____

Date of most recent visit: _____ Duration of stay: _____

☐ New recommendation   ☐ Comment on existing entry

REPORT:

*Please continue overleaf*

*I am not connected directly or indirectly with the management or proprietors*

Signed: _____

Name: (CAPITALS PLEASE) _____

Address: _____

_____

Email address: _____

# INDEX OF HOTELS BY COUNTY
(S) indicates a Shortlist entry

# ALPHABETICAL LIST OF HOTELS
(S) indicates a Shortlist entry

*Fort Royal* Rathmullan (S) 593
*Fortingall* Aberfeldy 342
*42 The Calls* Leeds (S) 540
*Foveran* St Ola 397
*Fox & Anchor* London (S) 512
*Foxmount Country House* Waterford 507
*La Frégate* St Peter Port (S) 586
*Frewin* Ramelton 500
*Frog Street Farmhouse* Hatch Beauchamp (S) 535
*Frogg Manor* Broxton 125
*Fronlas* Llandeilo (S) 582

**G**

*g* Galway (S) 591
*Gales* Llangollen (S) 583
*George* Buckden 127
*George* Hathersage 184
*George* Stamford 301
*George in Rye* Rye 283
*Gidleigh Park* Chagford 134
*Gigha* Gigha (S) 571
*Gilpin Hotel and Lake House* Windermere 331
*Gladstone House* Kirkcudbright 380
*Glangrwyney Court* Crickhowell 421
*Glebe House* North Berwick (S) 575
*Glenapp Castle* Ballantrae 346
*Glenfinnan House* Glenfinnan 370
*Glenmoriston* Inverness (S) 572
*Glenora Guest House* Edinburgh (S) 568
*Gliffaes* Crickhowell 422
*Goring* London 59
*Grand* Eastbourne (S) 532
*Grange* Fort William 367
*Grange at Oborne* Oborne 253
*Gravetye Manor* East Grinstead (S) 531
*Great House* Lavenham 202
*Green Bough* Chester (S) 527
*Green Park* Pitlochry (S) 576

*Greenbank* Falmouth (S) 532
*Gregans Castle* Ballyvaughan 466
*Grendon* Buxton (S) 523
*Greshornish House* Edinbane 361
*Grey Cottage* Leonard Stanley 206
*Grosvenor* Shaftesbury 296
*Grove* Narberth (S) 584
*Gruline Home Farm* Gruline 372
*Gurnard's Head* Zennor 339
*Gwesty Cymru* Aberystwyth 413

**H**

*Hafod Elwy Hall* Pentrefoelas 445
*Halkin* London (S) 512
*Hambleton Hall* Hambleton 177
*Hambrough* Ventnor 318
*Hand at Llanarmon* Llanarmon Dyffryn Ceiriog 431
*Hanover House* Cheltenham (S) 526
*Harbour* Bowmore (S) 565
*Harbourmaster* Aberaeron 410
*Hard Days Night* Liverpool (S) 542
*Harington's* Bath (S) 517
*Hartington Hall* Buxton (S) 523
*Hart's* Nottingham 252
*Hartwell House* Aylesbury 85
*Harvey's Point* Donegal (S) 590
*Hastings House* St Leonards-on-Sea 288
*Haymarket* London (S) 512
*Hazel Bank* Rosthwaite 280
*Hazelwood House* Loddiswell 211
*Hazlitt's* London 60
*Headlam Hall* Darlington (S) 529
*Headland* Newquay (S) 548
*Heasley House* North Molton 247
*Hebrides* Tarbert (S) 579
*Heddon's Gate* Martinhoe 225
*Hell Bay* Bryher 126
*Henley* Bigbury-on-Sea 101
*Hermitage* Hexham (S) 536
*High Road House* London (S) 512